Psychological and Educational Perspectives on Learning Disabilities

Psychological and Educational Perspectives on Learning Disabilities

EDITED BY

JOSEPH K. TORGESEN

Department of Psychology
Florida State University
Tallahassee, Florida

BERNICE Y. L. WONG

Faculty of Education
Simon Fraser University
Burnaby, British Columbia
Canada

1986

ACADEMIC PRESS, INC.

Harcourt Brace Jovanovich, Publishers

Orlando   San Diego   New York   Austin
London   Montreal   Sydney   Tokyo   Toronto

ACADEMIC PRESS, INC.
Orlando, Florida 32887

United Kingdom Edition published by
ACADEMIC PRESS INC. (LONDON) LTD.
24–28 Oval Road, London NW1 7DX

LIBRARY OF CONGRESS CATALOGING-IN-PUBLICATION DATA

Main entry under title:

Psychological and educational perspectives on learning
    disabilities.

    Includes bibliographies and indexes.
    1. Learning disabilities—Addresses, essays,
lectures.   I. Torgesen, Joseph K.   II. Wong, Bernice
Y. L.
LC4704.L395   1985   371.9   85-7337
ISBN 0-12-695490-9 (alk. paper)
ISBN 0-12-695491-7 (paperback)

PRINTED IN THE UNITED STATES OF AMERICA

86 87 88 89   9 8 7 6 5 4 3 2 1

Contents

3. Approaches to Assessment

Gerald Tindal and Doug Marston

Part II. Psychological Characteristics of Learning-Disabled Children   85

4. Cognitive Processes and the Reading Problems of Learning-Disabled Children: Evaluating the Assumption of Specificity

Keith E. Stanovich

Contributors

Numbers in parentheses indicate the pages on which the authors' contributions begin.

Bryan, Tanis (193), College of Education, University of Illinois at Chicago, Chicago, Illinois 60680

Deshler, Donald D. (329), Institute for Research in Learning Disabilities, The University of Kansas, Lawrence, Kansas 66045

Donahue, Mavis (193), Educational Psychology and Special Education, University of Illinois at Chicago, Chicago, Illinois 60680

Ellis, Edwin S. (329), Program for Exceptional Children, Department of Educational Psychology, University of South Carolina, Columbia, South Carolina 29208

Kistner, Janet A. (225), Department of Psychology, Florida State University, Tallahassee, Florida 32306

Koorland, Mark A. (297), Department of Childhood, Reading, and Special Education, Florida State University, Tallahassee, Florida 32306

Krupski, Antoinette (161), Graduate School of Education, University of California at Los Angeles, Los Angeles, California 90024

Licht, Barbara G. (225), Department of Psychology, Florida State University, Tallahassee, Florida 32306

Mann, Virginia A. (133), Department of Psychology, Bryn Mawr College, Bryn Mawr, Pennsylvania 19010

Marston, Doug (55), Experimental Teaching Project, University of Minnesota, Minneapolis, Minnesota 55455

Pearl, Ruth (193), Educational Psychology and Special Education, University of Illinois at Chicago, Chicago, Illinois 60680

Pelham, William E., Jr. (259), Department of Psychology, Florida State University, Tallahassee, Florida 32306

Ryan, Ellen Bouchard (367), Department of Psychiatry, Faculty of Health Sciences, McMaster University, Hamilton, Ontario L8N 3Z5, Canada

Schumaker, Jean B. (329), Institute for Research in Learning Disabilities, The University of Kansas, Lawrence, Kansas 66045

Senf, Gerald M. (27), Editor-in-Chief, Journal of Learning Disabilities, Tucson, Arizona 85718

Short, Elizabeth J. (367), Department of Psychology, Case Western Reserve University, Cleveland, Ohio 44106

Stanovich, Keith E. (87), Department of Psychology, Oakland University, Rochester, Michigan 48063

Tindal, Gerald (55), Department of Special Education, University of Oregon, Eugene, Oregon 97403

Torgesen, Joseph K. (417), Department of Psychology, Florida State University, Tallahassee, Florida 32306

Weed, Keri A. (367), Department of Psychology, State University of New York, Binghamton, Binghamton, New York 13901

Williams, Joanna P. (399), Department of Human Development, Cognition, and Learning, Teachers College, Columbia University, New York, New York 10027

Wong, Bernice Y. L. (3), Faculty of Education, Simon Fraser University, Burnaby, British Columbia V5A 1S6, Canada

Preface

The past 10 years have been an exciting time for those interested in understanding and helping children with learning disabilities. This last decade has seen enormous growth of the area, both as an educational specialty and as a focus of research activity. In the recent past, many older beliefs about learning disabilities have been abandoned and new ideas have emerged to take their place. Significant change has occurred both in the theories that are used to explain learning disabilities and in the methods that are employed to treat them.

The purpose of this book is to present a synthesis of some of the most interesting and exciting work on learning disabilities that has taken place within the past decade. Some of this work is revolutionary in that it represents a fundamental departure from traditional ideas about learning disabilities; other research reported here provides a refinement and update on ideas that have been in existence for some time. This book is intended for use by graduate students, researchers, and experienced practitioners as a source of timely and authoritative treatments of recent developments in our field. In keeping with balance between basic and applied research in learning disabilities, the book gives roughly equal consideration to issues of theory and treatment.

The chapters in the volume can be divided into three broad categories. In Part I, issues concerning definition, research methodology, and assessment are considered. Although we know much more about learning disabilities than we did 10 years ago, some fundamental problems with regard to definition and assessment remain unresolved. This part elaborates some of the remaining conceptual questions in the field and also provides an important new perspective on the assessment and identification of learning-disabled children.

·The second part of the book focuses on recent advances in our understanding of the psychological characteristics of learning-disabled children. This work draws heavily on concepts and methods from developmental and experimental psychology. For example, newer conceptualizations of the cognitive deficits of learning-disabled children are thoroughly grounded in the information-processing metaphor, which has been the dominant theoretical framework in cognitive psychology for at least the past 15 years. The work on motivation and social behavior reported in this section also draws heavily on work from developmental psychology. Rather than providing broad coverage of research on the characteristics of children with learning disabilities, the chapters in Part II concentrate on areas in which recent research has produced a consensus that represents solid new perspectives on learning disabilities.

Part III presents discussions of new intervention techniques. The major change that has occurred in this area over the past 10 years is the sheer number of new treatment approaches that are now available. Whereas treatment of learning disabilities was dominated by one or two major approaches up until 10 or 15 years ago, many new and innovative methods are now being evaluated. We expect that the techniques covered in this section will be those in common use 5 or 10 years from now, although their use is not necessarily widespread at present.

We would like to thank all those who have been involved in the production of this volume, particularly the contributors who worked so diligently to provide us with the kind of manuscripts we desired. Our thanks are also to dedicated teachers such as Kay Young, Sylvia Walford, Heather Fortier, and Audrey Roadhouse, who provide us with examples of personal qualities in teaching that are not easily measured but are at least as important in helping learning-disabled children as is the information contained in this volume.

Joseph K. Torgesen
Bernice Y. L. Wong

PART I

Definition, Identification, and Assessment

The three chapters in this section are devoted to a consideration of issues involved in the definition, identification, and assessment of learning disabilities. Although there are many interesting problems to focus on in the study of children with learning disabilities, the problem of defining the population is arguably one of the most important. In the first chapter in this section, Bernice Wong discusses four factors that have contributed to current definitional confusion in the field. Her chapter is a broad overview of problems in this area, and it lays the groundwork for the more focused discussions that follow.

In the second chapter, Gerald Senf provides an analysis of sociological factors that contribute to continued ambiguity of the definition and potential bias in samples of learning-disabled children identified by the schools. He also suggests that most attempts to refine our understanding of learning disabilities are hampered because they start with biased, or school-identified, samples. He argues that researchers should adopt a much broader frame of reference in selecting their samples as they attempt to understand variability among children in academic success at school. The last chapter in this section is distinguished from the first two in that it offers an extensive description of a functioning program designed to solve many of the problems present in current assessment practices. Although the assessment program offered by Gerald Tindal and Doug Marston may not solve all the problems identified in

1

this section, it does provide a practical solution to some of the most important problems and represents a refreshing alternative to traditional approaches.

Two broad themes are present in all the chapters of this section. First, they all express dissatisfaction with current approaches to the identification and assessment of learning-disabled children. Second, they all suggest that continued effort toward development of better ideas and procedures in this area is a worthwhile goal for both basic and applied research. The last two chapters, in particular, offer specific suggestions that, if followed, could have a profound impact on the way we define, identify, and assess learning-disabled children in years to come.

1

Problems and Issues in the Definition of Learning Disabilities

BERNICE Y. L. WONG

Why is it so difficult to define a learning-disabled (LD) child or adolescent? Why is it that 20 years after its inception, the learning disabilities field is still grappling with definitional problems? The answer to these questions lies, at least in part, in the difficulty of resolving issues in four areas: (1) problems in operationalizing the definition of learning disabilities (LD), (2) the role of processing disabilities, (3) the different demands of administrators, teachers, and researchers on the LD definition, and (4) problems in research. Clearly, these issues are very diverse, ranging from procedural to conceptual problems, to others that appear indigenous to the LD field. The purpose of this essay is to analyze the definitional problems stemming from these four sources, and to consider some ways of resolving them.

PROBLEMS IN OPERATIONALIZING THE DEFINITION OF LEARNING DISABILITIES

When one thinks of mentally retarded children, one immediately comes up with some definite notions about them, such as restrictive intellectual capacities and social immaturity. One also thinks of genetic or physiological links, for example, in cases of familial retardation and the Downs-syndrome child. In short, both the layman and professional possess some clear-cut and definite notions of what a mentally retarded child is like. They also encounter relatively little difficulty in ascertaining

3

Psychological and Educational
Perspectives on Learning Disabilities

presence of mental retardation in any child, because assessment instruments of intelligence and social maturity are both available and provide relatively clear profiles of this condition. When one thinks of children with learning disabilities, one may come up with equally definite notions about them, such as a discrepancy between ability and achievement, processing problems, and academic underachievement. But in contrast with the definitive notions one has about mentally retarded children, except for academic underachievement, one's notions about LD children run into serious problems because they are difficult to assess.

The assessment problems in learning disabilities arise from three issues: (1) the use of different diagnostic criteria and instruments, (2) the issue of the validity and reliability of assessment tools, and (3) human biases operating in the various phases of assessment.

The use of different diagnostic criteria in arriving at a diagnosis of LD is clearly indicated in the survey of Child Service Demonstration Centers (CSDCs) by Mann, Davis, Boyer, Metz, and Wolford (1983). Although the CSDCs unanimously used the criterion of academic underachievement, only two-thirds of them (42/61) abided by two of the remaining three federal criteria for LD: (1) average mental ability, defined as no more than one standard deviation below I.Q. 100, (2) evidence of some form of psychological process disorder. The one most likely to be left out was (3) lack of other handicapping conditions or cultural deprivation. Only 3 CSDCs used all the diagnostic criteria. Moreover, 36 CSDCs did not distinctly state discernable diagnostic criteria.

On a more microscopic level, Perlmutter and Parus's (1983) study illustrates nicely the use of different diagnostic criteria and tests. This research found significant variations within one state in applying the criterion of discrepancy between ability and performance in diagnosing LD. Some school districts required a discrepancy of one standard deviation between ability and performance, while others required two standard deviations, or relied on clinical judgment. Concerning diagnostic test administration, Perlmutter and Parus reported that the number of tests used varied from 2 in one district to 13 in another! Moreover, examiners' personal preferences in choice of tests and use of different I.Q. cutoff points in diagnosing LD were found.

Such inconsistencies in application of diagnostic criteria and tests produce situations in which one individual may be diagnosed as LD by one examiner or team and not so by another. Repetitions of such situations ultimately undermine the credibility of the concept and definition of LD. Similar detriments to the credibility of a diagnosis of LD occur in the use of assessment tests of dubious validity and reliability (Arter & Jenkins,

1979; Smith & Marx, 1971; Torgesen & Dice, 1980), and in the presence of assessment biases (Ysseldyke & Algozzine, 1979).

How does one explain the diagnostic chaos regarding diagnostic criteria and instruments? I submit the reason for this state of affairs lies in the fundamental problem of operationalizing the key components of learning disabilities, namely, the discrepancy between ability and performance, and processing problems. Further, on the issue of bias undermining the validity of the diagnosis and placement of the child/adolescent, I submit the problem reflects our failure to recognize the role of value judgment in the diagnosis of LD. I shall elaborate on these two issues.

THE CHOICE OF A FORMULA TO QUANTIFY THE
ABILITY–ACHIEVEMENT DISCREPANCY IN STUDENTS

The key components in the definition of learning disabilities are basic psychological process problems and the discrepancy between ability and achievement. Because of measurement problems in diagnosing process problems, the focus in operationally identifying learning-disabled students has shifted to the discrepancy component. This shift is clear in the Federal Register's (1977) definition. However, attempts at measuring the discrepancy between ability and achievement in students encounter the serious problem of choosing an appropriate quantitative formula.

Formulas for quantifying the ability–achievement discrepancy in students fall into four categories: The Expectancy Formula; Deviation from Grade Level; Standard-Score Comparison; and Regression Analysis (Algozzine, Forgnone, Mercer, & Trifiletti, 1979; Harris, 1970; Johnson & Myklebust, 1967; Kaluger & Kolson, 1969). Cone and Wilson (1981) used seven critical variables as a general framework to evaluate the various methods in quantifying the ability-achievement discrepancy in students. These critical variables included: (1) ease of administration, (2) number of years a student has been enrolled in school, (3) consideration of the gradual increase in range and heterogeneity of obtained achievement scores as students progress to upper grades, (4) interrelationship between a student's mental ability and his/her achievement at all ability levels, (5) error of measurement, (6) regression toward the mean, and (7) a priori examination of incidence and comparability of norms (Cone & Wilson, 1981).

Cone and Wilson's evaluation indicated that the Deviation from Grade Level method addresses the fewest of the seven critical variables, whereas Standard-Score Comparison and Regression Analysis procedures address the most. The Standard-Score comparison does not account for the major effects of regression nor does it give a basis for a prior estimation of approximate incidence. Cone and Wilson (1981) themselves favor the Regression Analysis procedure. However, they realized the practical limitations in using the Regression Analysis procedure in that many of the assessment instruments currently used in identifying learning disabilities do not satisfy psychometric standards (Thurlow & Ysseldyke, 1979) or have available the necessary correlations between the measures being examined (McLeod, 1983). To overcome these practical limitations, Cone and Wilson (1981) suggest combining the Regression Analysis with the Standard-Score Comparison procedure. However, implementing this combined procedure of Standard-score Comparison and Regression Analysis depends on availability of specific tables of values. Although these materials are available at the Iowa State Department of Public Instruction (cf. Cone & Wilson, 1981, p. 370), it remains a question whether other states and Canadian provinces will decide to follow suit in adopting the combined Standard-Score Comparison and Regression Analysis approach in quantifying discrepancy.

Ultimately, all methods in determining academic discrepancy need empirical validation (Cone & Wilson, 1981). Meanwhile, the lack of widely accepted and adequate procedures in determining discrepancy erodes the effectiveness of this definitional component of learning disabilities.

THE ISSUE OF VALUE JUDGMENT

The role of value judgments in the whole process of identifying learning-disabled students needs to be thoroughly assessed because of the confusion they introduce into the diagnostic process. For example, how significant must a student's difficulties be in acquiring academic skills, or how severely discrepant must his/her academic performance be, before one can classify him/her as learning-disabled and provide necessary remediation (cf. Sulzbacher & Kenowitz, 1977)? If numerous students are identified on the basis of deficient spelling alone, how critical is it to provide them with learning disabilities services (Danielson & Bauer, 1978)?

These confusions highlight our preoccupation with operationalizing the definition of learning disabilities in the most objective manner. Such preoccupation obscures the fact that, in all classification decisions, value judgments do come into play, whether we (openly) acknowledge them or not. Blanton (1975, p. 174) deals with the issue under discussion most clearly:

Scientific and technical information is used by persons who have been given responsibility for making practical decisions. Especially where such decisions concern other persons, they are made in a context of *recognized* and *unrecognized* values, precedents, persuasive communications, and public policies to a domain, in short, of *social value* and *attitude*. A practical decision, therefore, is never exclusively scientific, no matter what the information on which it is based; and scientific information, no matter how accurate or erroneous, is always applied in the interest of practical human goals. (emphasis added)

RESOLUTION OF OPERATIONAL PROBLEMS IN THE LD DEFINITION

Obviously, research on quantitative formulas for computing the ability-achievement discrepancy must continue. However, other alternatives in assessment of LD should also be considered and tried. One alternative that addresses the problems of relevance and efficiency in service delivery is the curriculum-based assessment proposed by Tindal and Marston in this volume (Chapter 3). Specifically, their proposed assessment approach focuses on timed samples of student behavior in various academic areas; for example, oral reading, math computations, writing. To illustrate, a student may be asked to read aloud for 5 minutes and his/her oral reading be examined for decoding accuracy and reading rate in words per minute (wpm). The advantages of this assessment mode lie in the simplicity of implementation, proximity of test materials to instructional materials (both coming from the same source, namely, the student's school curriculum), and ease of translating test results into instructional programming. Clearly, here is a possibility of an ecologically valid, fast, and efficient assessment method, which can be implemented by either the classroom teacher or the Learning Assistance teacher. Of course, within this curriculum-based assessment method, further fine tuning in evaluating the quality of writing is required. Ways of evaluating reading comprehension need also to be developed. Moreover, modifications of Tindal and Marston's suggested categorization of LD and mentally retarded students appear to be necessary, as their proposed categorization puts severely LD students (those who show academic retardation of 3 or more years below grade level) into the same category as the mentally retarded.

Although the curriculum-based assessment presents an *alternative* assessment method, it does not contribute to clarifying the existent definitional problems in LD. Essentially, it avoids *all* the traditional aspects of LD definition.

Incidentally, implementing a curriculum-based assessment of students' academic achievements is not a new endeavor. Dale Gentry

(1977) at the University of Washington Experimental Education Unit described such an approach for use in classrooms by classroom teachers. He called it "probes." Using the same kinds of curriculum-based assessments for LD students, however, involves some reconceptualization of the role of school psychologists. Hitherto, school psychologists have been instrumental in psychoeducational assessments of LD. If we adopt a curriculum-based assessment approach towards identifying LD students, then the classroom teachers and Learning Assistance teachers would assume a major role, rather than the school psychologists. The latter's role may shift to one of ascertaining the existence of ability-achievement discrepancy and the reliability of the classroom/Learning Assistance teachers' findings.

PSYCHOLOGICAL PROCESS PROBLEMS

The use of psychological process problems to help define learning disabilities is difficult because of two thorny issues. The first concerns the role of process problems in assessments of learning disabilities. The second concerns the role of process problems in a definition of learning disabilities.

THE ROLE OF PROCESS PROBLEMS IN AN ASSESSMENT OF LEARNING DISABILITIES

Process problems are a core concept in most learning disabilities definitions. However, because of lack of valid assessment tools, the concept has remained inoperative in diagnostic procedures for learning disabilities. The ensuing question is whether or not we should remove process problems in diagnostic procedures altogether. One argument for removing process problems in assessments of learning disabilities comes from those who think a functional definition does not require a statement on etiology. "To remove a wart, to clear up a sore throat, to alleviate a deprived social environment, or to eliminate a child's emotional disturbance may or may not depend upon understanding the etiology. It does depend on some kind of observation which can predict some kind of outcome" (Cromwell, Blashfield, & Strauss, 1975, p. 10).

Such an argument appears to be myopic in the case of learning disabilities. If processing problems are a core concept differentiating learning-disabled students from other underachieving students, eventually, we will demonstrate them and devise treatments to go with them. Indeed, structural problems in short-term memory and rule-learning in specific homogeneous groups of learning-disabled children have been demonstrated (Manis & Morrison, 1985; Torgesen & Houck, 1980). Follow-up research should address how these process problems affect learning-disabled students' academic learning and what treatments may be indicated. Moreover, as researchers begin to identify processing skills required by complex academic tasks such as reading (Mason, in press; Resnick & Weaver, 1979), we will have the necessary knowledge to design diagnostic tasks to tap students' competency in those component skills. A case in point is the research on metalinguistic awareness. Various researchers (Liberman, Shankweiler, Fischer, & Carter, 1974; Mason, in press; Ryan, 1980; Williams, 1980) have indicated the importance of phonemic awareness in children's learning to read. This important research information has been incorporated in the design of an experimental reading readiness test (Mason, in press) and a formal test of early reading abilities (Reid & Hresko, 1981). Through the use of such assessment devices, we can discover deficiencies in metalinguistic awareness in children and devise appropriate instructional remediation. Hence, it is myopic to think that because of current assessment difficulties, we should forget process problems in assessment of learning disabilities.

THE ROLE OF PROCESS PROBLEMS IN THE DEFINITION OF
LEARNING DISABILITIES

There are two objections to having process problems in the definition of learning disabilities. The first is that process problems have yet to be shown to affect learning-disabled children's academic retardation. The second is the negative history of process training which left a substantial number of learning-disabilities professionals with the view that the construct of psychological process problems ill-served the field and is superfluous.

ESTABLISHING A CAUSAL LINK BETWEEN PROCESSING
PROBLEMS AND LEARNING-DISABLED INDIVIDUALS'
ACADEMIC RETARDATION

It is true that currently we have little empirical information on a causal link between learning-disabled children's processing problems and their academic failures (Kirk & Gallagher, 1979; Torgesen, 1979). However, this state of knowledge deficiency reflects our lack of knowledge concerning cognitive processes crucial for learning—and academic learning in particular—and our lack of programmatic, analytical research on putative processing problems of learning-disabled students. When research information cumulates from these two areas, we should be in a position to investigate causal links between processing problems in learning-disabled students and their academic failures. Some headway on processes required for learning to read has been reported (Lesgold, Resnick, & Beck, 1978; Resnick & Weaver, 1979), as has research on memory processes in learning-disabled children (Torgesen, 1981). Consequently, eliminating the concept of process problems appears to be premature.

THE NEGATIVE HISTORY OF REMEDIATION BASED ON PSYCHOLOGICAL PROCESS PROBLEMS

Historically, when the concept of psychological process problems was first used in the National Advisory Committee on Handicapped Children (NACHC, 1968) definition of learning disabilities, the meaning and nature of the concept were ambiguous (Hammill 1972). Despite the lack of conceptual clarity here, process-training studies were launched by various investigators, (cf. Lerner, 1981). These studies were unsuccessful for three reasons: (1) the theoretical model of these process-training studies was wrong in that cognitive processes were conceptualized to operate in isolation rather than in an interrelated and interactive way (Adams & Collins, 1979; Reid & Hresko, 1981); (2) the training studies were done without prior research establishing a causal link between a particular processing deficiency and the learning-disabled children's academic retardation. The researchers assumed de facto such causal links; and (3) process training was found consistently to have no transfer to learning-disabled children's reading improvement (Hammill & Larsen, 1974a, 1974b). Instead of leading to improved research, the problems and failures of process training resulted in an unnecessary and heated controversy between those who staunchly defended it and those who questioned its efficacy. The controversy created a partisan split in the learning-disabilities field (Wong, 1979). One of the unfortunate aftermaths appears to be the conviction among some that so long as we recognize the *intrinsic* nature of learning disabilities, the concept of psychological process problems is superfluous in the learning-disabilities definition. Having that concept in a definition of learning disabilities only invokes ambiguity and negative associations of process training (Hammill, Leigh, McNutt, & Larsen, 1981).

The points made by Hammill *et al.* (1981) are understandable. Nevertheless, there are some counterpoints for consideration. First, as Wozniak (1979) has pointed out, the failure of process-oriented remedial techniques to prove their effectiveness is not necessarily evidence against the basic concepts involved, but may be more related to the lack of adequate descriptions of the processing skills that are important for effective academic learning, and the lack of adequate technology for measuring processing deficiencies (Torgesen, 1979).

Second, we cannot bypass psychological processes if we want to understand learning-disabled students' difficulties in listening, speaking, reading, and writing because all these are information-processing activities *mediated* by mental operations. Since mental operations are inaccessible to direct observations and have to be *inferred*, we must use hypothetical constructs to represent them. If this premise is accepted by LD researchers and teachers, our next logical step is to actively select an appropriate theoretical framework to elucidate, study, and analyze deficient information processing in learning-disabled individuals. For that purpose, I submit that cognitive psychology presents one viable framework because information processing is a dominant viewpoint in cognitive psychology (Anderson, 1975), and because "cognitive psychology is a theory-rich psychology concerned to a large extent with problems of representation and process" (Mandler, 1981, p. 12). Indeed, a cognitive or information-processing approach to studying learning disabilities has been persuasively advocated by Bauer (1982) and Reid and Hresko, (1981).

The particular relevance of cognitive psychology to the issue of processing problems in LD children lies in clarifying and rectifying goals that were conceptually flawed in previous process training. Within the framework of cognitive psychology, training (instructional research) assumes a very different goal and meaning from psycholinguistic or perceptual training. Specifically, unlike the psycholinguistic or perceptual training approach, cognitive skills (cognitive strategies) training is *not* designed for, *nor* does it claim to increase basic capacities. What is trained are thinking skills, self-questioning skills, strategies or procedural routes to enhance learning such as various modes of elaboration, and *learning how to learn* (Bransford, 1979; Brown, 1980). To illustrate the essence of cognitive skills training, the following descriptions of specific research activities are given.

THINKING SKILLS TRAINING

There is a group of researchers working on how to teach and/or improve students' thinking and problem-solving skills in physics (Larkin, 1979), engineering (Greenfield, 1979), and analytical reasoning (Whimbey & Lochhead, 1979). The group focuses on understanding the processes of analytical thinking and problem solving that students must engage in to perform successfully a variety of tasks. Moreover, the thinking and problem-solving processes in experts are contrasted with those of novices in order to better understand where the novices fumble and err, and to gain insight for debugging the novices' thinking. Knowledge gained through such research should enable instructors to devise optimal ways of teaching students useful thinking and problem-solving skills. The teaching of these skills is called "cognitive process instruction" (Lochhead, 1979; Lochhead & Clement, 1979).

The researchers described have backgrounds in physics, mathematics, engineering, and computing science. They advocate cognitive process instruction, which is based on the premise that cognitive processes can be studied and that students can profit from the knowledge gained through such studies. They claim that it is becoming possible to "isolate specific cognitive skills and to design instructional materials appropriate for each skill" (Lochhead, 1979, p. 2). Although they emphasize that we should teach students *how* rather than *what* to think, advocates of cognitive process instruction do not claim that their particular approach can solve all the problems in education. Rather, they believe their approach will provide a framework for systematic research on students' thought processes in realistic educational settings. Moreover, they believe their approach promises highly important, though gradual, improvements in our instructional methods (Lochhead, 1979). Indeed, cognitive process instruction has ushered in new instructional courses in schools of engineering (e.g., at the University of West Virginia and at McMaster in Canada). In these courses, students are taught to engage in detailed analyses of their own problem-solving strategies, and students' awareness of their own cognitive processes is emphasized. There is, at present, a continuous cooperative program of course development in problem solving, supported by research on human cognitive processing at M.I.T., Carnegie-Mellon, University of California, Berkeley, and the University of Massachusetts (Lochhead, 1979).

SELF-QUESTIONING SKILLS TRAINING

Bransford, Stein, Shelton, & Owings (1981) taught fifth-grade poor readers to appreciate the importance of generating self-questions to activate relevant schema or to clarify seemingly arbitrary information, and to learn to generate such questions in aid of reading comprehension.

Bransford *et al.* (1981) showed that new information may appear arbitrary to novices until they activate prior knowledge by asking themselves the significance of the new information. Bransford *et al.* used examples from biology. To a novice in biology, facts such as the properties of arteries being thick, muscular, and elastic, and those of veins being thin, having valves, and so on may appear very arbitrary despite his/her knowledge of elasticity. The apparent arbitrariness of the new facts disappears when beginners in biology are trained to ask themselves the question of why these structural properties are important to arteries/veins. Asking questions about the functional significance of the structural properties of arteries and veins enables the novice in biology to master what *initially* appears as a series of arbitrary statements. Through repeating the process of asking relevant, clarifying self-questions, the student ultimately gains a substantial body of new knowledge in a new domain.

Using modeling, Palincsar (1982) taught seven learning-disabled students in the seventh grade four specific strategies to enhance their reading comprehension. These students had adequate decoding skills but deficient reading-comprehension skills. The strategies taught included: (1) prediction of what authors might discuss next in the passages, (2) construction of questions teachers might ask in testing their knowledge of the text, (3) summarizing, and (4) detecting textual anomalies. In 18 daily successive sessions, Palincsar used modeling and corrective feedback to teach the learning-disabled students these four questioning strategies.

A multiple baseline design was used. The criterion measure for reading comprehension was a 10-item test given every day during intervention, and tests for maintenance which occurred after an 8-week delay. The test contained four text-explicit, four text-implicit, and two script-implicit questions. Additionally, generalization probes were given in class by the regular classroom teachers, using social studies and science curricula. The results clearly indicated that the students' reading comprehension scores improved substantially during intervention and were well maintained during follow-up. Moderate gains were observed in transfer measured by the classroom probes, but training did improve the quality of students' questioning. Initially during intervention, their questions were unclear, and their statements incomplete or incorrect. As training progressed, their questions became clearer and more focused, and targeted more main ideas. Moreover, near-transfer was observed in students' ability to implement summarization rules, question prediction, and detection of textual anomalies. The far-transfer measure of rating thematic importance indicated little improvement in the students. It seems that Palincsar (1982) had chosen a very difficult task to measure far-transfer. Thus, the lack of generalization here does not necessarily detract from the strength of her training procedure.

The descriptions given of cognitive skills training indicate a new, vibrant trend in research on cognitive processes with important implications for LD. Clearly, lucid conceptualization and proper goal setting within a cognitive psychology framework should result in fruitful use of the process-problem concept as a theoretical construct in LD in identifying LD individuals, in research, and in remedial instruction.

DEFINITIONAL PROBLEMS ARISING FROM DIFFERENT DEMANDS ON THE LD DEFINITION BY DIFFERENT INTEREST GROUPS

Administrators, teachers, and researchers all have different demands on the LD definition. More importantly, they have *conflicting* demands on the same definition, basically reflecting different purposes for classifying students as learning disabled. In the following sections, the different and conflicting demands of administrators, teachers, and researchers are described.

THE ADMINISTRATOR'S PERSPECTIVE OF THE LD DEFINITION

The administrator wants a LD definition that enables him/her to channel funding into a particular category of special educational services. For this purpose, the definition has to be very clear-cut and non-arbitrary in differentiating between those who deserve LD special services from those who do not. In 1977, the Federal Register (USOE) issued the definition of LD mandated by Congress. This definition was necessary because earlier, Congress had passed PL 94–142, the Education for All Handicapped Children Act (1975), which means that learning-disabled students are legally entitled to special educational services in schools. This 1977 LD definition was the same as that issued by the NACHC in 1968. The reason for the retention of the NACHC (1968) definition was the view that, in 1977, there were no data available to effect any change in that definition. Until such data exist, the 1968 definition will remain.

However, the second part of the Federal Register's (1977) definition shows a general concern with provision of criteria that can be implemented. Specifically, evaluation of process problems is de-emphasized whereas evaluation of discrepancy (between ability and achievement) is considered the primary focus of LD identification (Algozzine *et al.*, 1979). This emphasis on the discrepancy criterion has been challenged by Campbell (1979) and McLeod (1975) who argue that LD are far more complex than is conveyed by the notion of ability-achievement discrepancy. Because of the specification of the operational criteria in the second part of the Federal Register's (1977) definition, administrators may assume there is now a straightforward and economic diagnostic procedure in LD identification and educational placement. Such assumption, as will be shown, conflicts with what teachers expect from the definition.

THE TEACHERS' PERSPECTIVE OF THE LD DEFINITION

Teachers actively engaged in diagnosis and remedial instruction of LD students want a definition of LD that leads to diagnostic procedures that will enable them to develop readily Individualized Educational Programs (IEP's). To extract instructional pointers from the diagnostic process entails thorough and comprehensive testing by the teachers. In implementing comprehensive assessment procedures, teachers run into problems such as heavy caseloads, time-consuming evaluations of test data, and write-ups of IEP's. Thus, their need for instructional guidance from comprehensive assessment data conflicts with the administrator's desire for a fast and economic diagnostic procedure.

THE RESEARCHER'S PERSPECTIVE ON THE LD DEFINITION

The purposes of LD research are to investigate the characteristics of LD, to test the appropriateness of particular conceptual frameworks, and to examine the effectiveness of particular interventions. Such purposes require researchers to have homogeneous subject samples. In turn, achieving homogeneity of subjects means researchers must use very specific and exclusive selection criteria. For example, in studying memory deficits in LD children, Torgesen and Houck (1980) used subjects characterized by a severely limited, auditory short-term memory.

Why should researchers carefully select subjects with *target* characteristics rather than just using captive LD students in schools? Because schools use very inconsistent procedures in identifying LD students. Analogous to what occurs in the mental retardation field, procedural variabilities in LD identification arise from (1) variations in referrals, (2) variations in screening for referrals, and (3) variations in placement/nonplacement in special educational programs. These procedural inconsistencies occur because the decision-making process in school identification of LD are notoriously influenced by local contexts, political, financial, and practical considerations (Keogh, 1983). When researchers use school-identified LD students as subjects in their studies, they *assume* that, because schools must abide by state regulations in LD identification, all their subjects are LD. Such an assumption reflects a confusion of the purpose of school (system)-identification versus the purpose in sampling for research (Keogh, 1983; MacMillan, Myers, & Morrison, 1980).

The purpose in school (system)-identification is service delivery. Because system-selection decisions are biased by political, budgetary, and practical considerations, students netted into learning assistance programs are by no means all LD (cf. Mann *et al.*, 1983), and, therefore, not necessarily representative of the LD population. Researchers who use school-identified subject pools will end up drawing conclusions about LD from a mixed sample, only some of whom are LD. The conclusions are, in essence, based on one subset of LD (Keogh, 1983). The usefulness of such data in enhancing our understanding of the complex nature of LD is obviously questionable.

Clearly, to obtain useful information, researchers need homogenous samples of LD subjects in their studies. To achieve the desired homogeneity, they resort to very specific and exclusive selection criteria in an operational definition of LD. Whereas such definitional specificity and exclusivity meet the purpose of the researcher, they go counter to the teacher's perception of the purpose of a LD definition. As mentioned previously, teachers want a straightforward, operationalized LD definition to identify all the LD students for remedial purposes. To meet their goal, they cannot use the identification criteria in the researcher's operational definition of LD.

To illustrate the unsuitability of researchers' identification criteria for teachers, four of Pavlidis's (1983) subject-selection criteria are briefly described: (1) verbal or performance IQ is to be equal or greater than the normal range, with a minimum of one standard deviation below the mean plus two standard errors (i.e., WISC–R verbal 92, performance 94); (2) if the child is over 10 years old, reading retardation is to be at least 2 years behind chronological age; if the child is under 10, reading retardation is to be $1\frac{1}{2}$ years behind chronological age; (3) the subject should come from middle-class socioeconomic strata; and (4) the child should have no more than two school changes in the first 3 years of schooling, barring transfer from nursery to primary school. Obviously, these criteria in subject selection recommended for use by researchers are utterly unsuitable for use by teachers. From the teachers' perspective, the nature of LD is heterogeneous regarding academic underachievement, IQ level, and socioeconomic strata. They would argue, and rightly so, that LD students typically range from being 1 to more than 3 years below grade in academic underachievement; they range from dull–normal to superior in intelligence, and from working class to lower middle class to upper middle-class socioeconomic strata.

To summarize, administrators, teachers, and researchers all want a LD definition to fulfill certain functions. Because they differ from one another on the perceived purpose of the LD definition, confusion results, creating a very difficult definitional problem.

How do we resolve the problem? An initial step is to make administrators, teachers, and researchers realize the difference in their goals for the LD definition. Understanding the different and conflicting demands each group exerts on the LD definition should lead researchers to attach specific criteria in subject selection additional to those stated in the Federal Register (1977). In this way, researchers could obtain samples of subjects who are homogeneous regarding specific target characteristics for their intended study. On the other hand, teachers would realize the researchers' identification criteria have no place in their identification of LD students in schools. They should adopt a broad, easily operationalized definition. As for administrators, they can confer with local school boards to thrash out some mutually agreeable definitional guidelines for funding purposes.

RESEARCH PROBLEMS IN LD

LACK OF SOLID EMPIRICAL BASE

What does it mean to say that the LD field lacks a solid empirical base when there has been much research since 1968? Undeniably, there has been a great deal of research on learning disabilities. However, much of it is poor—for four reasons: (1) sampling problems, (2) poor methodology, (3) atheoretical nature of the research, and (4) type of research questions asked.

Sampling problems stem from researchers' use of school-identified LD populations in their research. As mentioned previously, school-identified LD populations cannot be assumed to contain only LD students. In studies which purport to investigate the nature of LD, the consequence of using samples that include subjects other than LD students is drastic. Such studies gather data that: (1) lead to invalid inferences concerning the nature of LD, (2) impede comparisons between studies, and (3) provide ungeneralizable data.

Concerning poor methodology, Torgesen and Dice (1980) found that tests used in research conducted from the period 1976–1978 were usually not properly validated. Again, when these unvalidated tests are used to differentiate between non-LD and LD students with the purpose of enlightening us as to the nature of LD, the data can easily lead to invalid conclusions. Moreover, much of the research is atheoretical (Senf, 1976; 1978; Wong, 1979). Consequently, the cumulative research on the characteristics of LD children becomes a huge catalogue of specific, disparate deficits. Comparative research of LD and non-LD children becomes almost redundant since the former children invariably give inferior performances, compared to non-LD children. Additionally, the overwhelming majority of researchers have not asked the right questions such as "Under what conditions do LD and non-LD students differ? Under what conditions do they not differ in their performance?" Put differently, researchers have not conceptualized their questions within an interactional framework which will yield more useful information for the beneficiaries of our research, namely, LD students. Casting research questions in an interactional framework and conducting programmatic research would bring us a clearer understanding of the nature of LD, with important implications for the definition of learning disabilities.

The cited research problems in LD explain why we lack a solid empirical base despite much research activity. Although we have a mass of data, much of it is uninterpretable and ungeneralizable. However, the pertinent question is: How does the lack of an empirical base contribute to the definitional problems in LD?

To define a complex phenomenon, the more we know about its characteristics, the more precise information we have on its parameters and the manipulations which affect its functions, the clearer we understand its nature; therefore, the better we can define it. Because of much wasted research effort, we have not progressed substantially in understanding the nature of this complex phenomenon of LD. Hence, our research efforts have not helped our task of defining LD. In fact, the catalogue of specific and disparate deficits serves only to confuse the issue of the nature of LD. Thus, the research problem contributes to the definitional problems in LD.

The solution, obviously, is to address each of these problems. First and foremost is improving sampling procedures. Several methods have been suggested: rational definition of subgroups (Torgesen, 1982), cluster analysis (Satz & Morris, 1981), and marker variables (Keogh & MacMillan, 1983). Second, among researchers, there should be *more* theory-based research (Cohen, 1976; Keogh, 1976; Senf, 1976; Wong, 1979), and more attention paid to experimental design and methodology to ensure internal and external validity (Torgesen & Dice, 1980; Harber, 1982).

WAYS OF IMPROVING SAMPLING PROCEDURES

Using rationally defined subgroups in sampling requires the researcher to decide on which particular target characteristics of LD students to focus for study. Formation of the LD subgroup proceeds from researchers using an operational definition to carefully select subjects that possess the target characteristic. For example, in studying *one* type of LD problem, namely, memory deficits, Torgesen selected LD children who demonstrated severe auditory short-term memory deficits on the Digit Span subtest of the WISC–R (Torgesen & Houck, 1980). Additionally, the researchers used two comparison groups: LD and normally achieving children with adequate auditory short-term memory on the same test. Torgesen & Houck's (1980) use of a second control group of LD children with adequate auditory short-term memory demonstrates good experimental methodology in that manipulated parameters that affect one group but not the other LD group gives us highly pertinent information on the role of severe auditory short-term memory in the subjects' task performance. Torgesen (1982) makes three recommendations for those who wish to use rationally defined subgroups of LD children in research: (1) one should use experimentation to identify essential processing disabilities; (2) one should establish the relationship between failure on the criterion task and failure in school; and (3) one should develop remedial programs that are responsive to the processing deficits of LD children.

The logic of the use of rationally defined subgroups in LD research is sound, and the procedure (cf. Torgesen, 1982) straightforward. We should, however, realize that the decision on target characteristics of LD students follows from our individual conceptualization of the nature of the LD problem. For example, Torgesen (1982) conceptualizes LD within an information-processing framework in which memory processes assume a vital role. Thus, in choosing particular target characteristics in LD students as focus of our studies, we must attend to the conceptual framework to which we can clearly relate the targeted characteristics (Keogh & MacMillan, 1983).

Cluster analysis is another method of forming homogeneous subgroups of LD students. Basically, the subjects are given a battery of tests, and the data subsequently analyzed statistically. Subjects are matched or clustered into various groups according to similarity of performance patterns on selected variables. Consequently, relatively homogeneous subgroups are created within a total sample (Keogh & MacMillan, 1983). The researchers examine the nature of each group thus clustered and label the groups according to the variables that predominate in each group. For example, one group may show poor performance on visual-motor tests, but good performance on verbal tests, whereas another group may show the reverse performance pattern. The researchers may label the first as the visual group and the second the verbal group. Paul Satz is one researcher noted for using this statistical procedure of cluster analysis to obtain homogeneous LD subgroups (Satz & Morris, 1981). Another researcher using the cluster analysis for the same purpose is James McKinney (1984) who is currently using it in a large-scale longitudinal study.

The tests and the theoretical frameworks used in this approach depend entirely on the researchers. The drawback of this approach concerns the cost and need, initially, for large subject pools, and the fact that factors churned out through cluster analysis of the data depend on the nature of tests used. Thus, the subgroups and variables obtained by one researcher may not be replicated by another.

The marker variables approach to forming homogeneous LD subgroups focuses on researchers' using consensual reference points (benchmarks) or *markers* in describing characteristics of the sample in one's study (Keogh, Major-Kingsley, Omori-Gordon & Reid, 1982). Specifically, Keogh *et al.* (1982) suggest four types of operational markers for use in LD research, as follows: (1) descriptive markers which refer to size of sample, age (in months), grade level(s), location, ethnicity, sources of sample, socioeconomic strata, language, educational history, educational placement, and status of physical health; (2) substantive markers which refer to general intelligence, academic achievements (reading, mathematics), and behavioral and emotional adjustment; (3) topical markers which refer to level of activity, attention, auditory perception, fine motor coordination, gross motor coordination, memory, oral language, and visual perception; and (4) background markers which refer to years of study, geographical location, exclusionary criteria used to select subjects into the sample, and control group data.

Keogh *et al.'s* (1982) proposed use of marker variables is an attempt to get LD researchers to systematize sample selection and description. Sloppiness in sample selection and description has resulted in much ungeneralizable data in the field of learning disabilities. When LD researchers use a common set of subject-selection criteria (markers), they will gather data that are generalizable. Moreover, when they report on full-sample characteristics, they allow comparisons between and across studies. The implementation of marker variables is basically very straightforward, and should be used by responsible researchers. Recently, the research committee of the Council of LD (CLD) issued guidelines for reporting sample characteristics for those who intend to submit papers to the journal, *LD Quarterly*, published by CLD. Interestingly, these guidelines appear to be very similar to the types of marker variables suggested for use among researchers by Keogh *et al.* (1982). Thus, CLD implicitly endorses the underlying principles of the use of marker variables.

CONCEPTUALIZING LD RESEARCH

The need for more theory-based research in LD has long been pointed out (Cohen, 1976; Keogh, 1976; Senf, 1972). As Senf (1972) aptly stated, we need theoretical frameworks to direct systematic research and to integrate and interpret meaningfully the obtained data. However, the use of theoretical frameworks alone does not suffice to produce good research in LD. Of equal importance is the formulation of research questions in interactive terms. Specifically, we can draw from Jenkins' (1979) tetrahedral model of memory research to understand why couching research questions in interactive terms would provide us with more useful knowledge. Jenkins (1979) described four sources that contribute to a subject's performance in a given task. They include: (1) the subject's cognitive repertoire or background knowledge, skills, and aptitudes; (2) the learning activities the subject engages in, for example, rehearsal in a memory task; (3) the nature of the stimuli used, that is, the organization of the stimuli, the presentation mode of the stimuli; and (4) the criterion task—free recall or recognition test. Each one of these four sources affects the student's learning outcome. But their interactions weigh far more in the ultimate effects on the subject's learning outcome. For example, memory-processing problems impair the recall performance of LD children (Torgesen, 1981). However, inducing appropriate rehearsal strategies in LD children dramatically improves their recall (Bauer, 1977, 1979, 1982; Torgesen & Goldman, 1977; Wong, 1979). Even more specific information was obtained from Torgesen and Houck (1980) in which the use of incentives improved the recall performance of LD children with mild memory-processing problems but not that of LD children with severe memory-processing problems. Clearly, formulating research questions in interactive terms would yield more specific, hence, more useful, information on LD students, and should be encouraged among LD researchers.

EPILOGUE

The need to develop a practical, flexible, and empirically based definition is not a problem unique to the LD field. The same problem plagues fields such as mental retardation and mental disorders, both of which have a far longer history of development and research than LD (Blanton, 1975; Clausen, 1968, 1972; Spitzer, Williams, & Skodol, 1980). Yet, the intransigent problems of definition, valid application and reliability of diagnostic tools, and determination of appropriate cases continue to be issues of debate and remonstrance (Blanton, 1975; Garmezy, 1978; Spitzer et al., 1980).

Realization of similar definitional and classificatory problems in other fields gives us a *needed* perspective on our own difficulties in LD. Consequently, to persist in criticism of the LD definition without concurrent constructive action to improve on it, is to court and, ultimately, beget cynicism. To persist in preserving the present definitional status quo is to retard the growth of our field. I submit that the only sound and constructive alternative is to persist with single-mindedness toward the development of different definitions, each with a clearly defined— though limited—sphere of application. One would be a *functional*, serviceable definition for practical users of the LD definition, such as teachers and administrators; another would be for use by researchers. The use of different LD definitions may solve some of the definitional problems, namely, those arising from conflicting expectations of it. The resolution of other definitional problems entails well-designed programmatic research on the complex nature of LD. Finally, we need to remember, as other more seasoned and wise colleagues in related fields have observed, definitions must be reviewed at regular intervals to see if they are still justified by use, and to see in light of new data, what modifications may be necessary (Blanton, 1975; Cromwell et al., 1975; Kramer, 1975; Phillips, Draguns, & Bartlett, 1975).

REFERENCES

Adams, M. J., & Collins, A. C. (1979). A schema-theoretic view of reading. In R. Freedle (Ed.), *New Directions in Discourse Processing* (pp. 1–22). Norwood, NJ: Ablex.

Algozzine, B., Forgnone, C., Mercer, C. D., & Trifiletti, J. J. (1979). Toward defining discrepancies for specific learning disabilities: An analysis and alternatives. *Learning Disability Quarterly, 2*, 25–31.

Anderson, J. R. (1975). *Cognitive psychology and its implications*. San Francisco: W. H. Freeman and Company.

Arter, J. A., & Jenkins, J. R. (1979). Differential diagnosis-prescriptive teaching: A critical appraisal. *Review of Educational Research, 49*(4), 517–555.

Bauer, R. H. (1977). Short-term memory in learning disabled and nondisabled children. *Bulletin of the Psychonomic Society, 10*, 128–130.

Bauer, R. H. (1979). Recall after a short delay and acquisition in learning-disabled and nondisabled children. *Journal of Learning Disabilities, 12*, 596–608.

Bauer, R. H. (1982). Information processing as a way of understanding and diagnosing learning disabilities. *Topics in Learning and Learning Disabilities, 2*(2), 33–45.

Blanton, R. L. (1975). Historical perspectives on classification of mental retardation. In N. Hobbs (Ed.), *Issudes in the Classification of Children*, Vol. I (pp. 164–193). San Francisco: Jossey-Bass Publishers.

Bransford, J. D. (1979). *Human cognition: Learning, understanding and remembering.* Belmont, CA: Wadsworth Publishing Co.

Bransford, J. D., Stein, B. S., Shelton, T. S., & Owings, R. A. (1981). Cognition and adaptation: The importance of learning to learn. In J. Harvey (Ed.), *Cognition, Social Behavior and the Environment* (pp. 93–110). Hillsdale, NJ: Lawrence Erlbaum Associates.

Brown, A. L. (1980). Metacognitive development and reading. In R. J. Spiro, B. B. Bruce, & W. F. Brewer (Eds.), *Theoretical Issues in Reading Comprehension* (pp. 453–481). Hillsdale, NJ: Lawrence Erlbaum Associates.

Campbell, S. B. G. (1979). Problems for clinical diagnosis. *Journal of Learning Disabilities,* 12(8), 511–513.

Clausen, J. A. (1968). A comment on Halpern's note. *American Journal of Mental Deficiency,* 72, 950.

Clausen, J. A. (1972). Quo Vadis, AAMD? *Journal of Special Education,* 6, 51–60.

Cohen, S. A. (1976). The fuzziness and the flab: Some solutions to research problems in learning disabilities. *Journal of Special Education,* 10(2), 129–139.

Cone, T. E., & Wilson, L. R. (1981). Quantifying a severe discrepancy: A critical analysis. *Learning Disability Quarterly,* 4, 359–371.

Cromwell, R. L., Blashfield, R. K., & Strauss, J. S. (1975). Criteria for classification systems. In N. Hobbs (Ed.), *Issues in the Classification of Children,* Vol. I (pp. 4–25). San Francisco: Jossey-Bass Publishers.

Danielson, L. C., & Bauer, J. N. (1978). A formula-based classification of learning-disabled children: An examination of the issues. *Journal of Learning Disabilities,* 11(3), 163–176.

Federal Register (1977). *Education of Handicapped Children: Implementation of Part B of the Education of the Handicapped Act.* Federal Register, Part II. Washington, DC: U.S. Office of Education; U.S. Department of Health, Education, and Welfare. August 23, 1977.

Garmezy, N. (1978). DSMI–III: Never mind the psychologists: Is it good for the children? *The Clinical Psychologist,* 31, 1–6.

Gentry, M. D. (1977). *Using probes and daily measurement to insure pupil progress.* Unpublished paper. Seattle: Experimental Education Unit, University of Washington.

Greenfield, L. B. (1979). Engineering student problem solving. In J. Lochhead & J. Clement (Eds.), *Cognitive Process Instruction: Research on teaching thinking skills* (pp. 229–238). Philadelphia, PA.: The Franklin Institute Press.

Grossman, R. P. (1978). LD and the problem of scientific definitions. *Journal of Learning Disabilities,* 11(3), 120–123.

Hammill, D. D., Leigh, J. E., McNutt, G., & Larsen, S. C. (1981). A new definition of learning disabilities. *Learning Disability Quarterly,* 4, 336–342.

Hammill, D. D., & Larsen, S. C. (1974a). The relationship of selected auditory perceptual skills and reading ability. *Journal of Learning Disabilities,* 7(7), 429–435.

Hammill, D. D., & Larsen, S. C. (1974b, September). The effectiveness of psycholinguistic training. *Exceptional Children,* 5–15.

Harber, J. R. (1981). Learning disability research: How far have we progressed? *Learning Disability Quarterly,* 4(4), 372–381.

Harris, A. (1970). *How to increase reading abilities* (5th ed.). New York: Appleton-Century-Crofts.

Jenkins, J. J. (1979). Four points to remember: A tetrahedral model and memory experiments. In L. S. Cermak & F. I. M. Craik (Eds.), *Levels and Processing in Human Memory* (pp. 429–446). Hillsdale, NJ: Lawrence Erlbaum Associates.

Johnson, D., & Myklebust, H. (1967). *Learning disabilities: Educational principles and practices* New York: Grune & Stratton, 1967.

Kaluger, G., & Kolson, C. (1969). *Reading and learning disabilities*. Columbus, OH: Charles E. Merrill.

Keogh, B. K. (1976). Another way to drown in the name of science: A response to S. A. Cohen's proposed solution to research problems in learning disabilities. *Journal of Special Education, 10*(2), 137–139.

Keogh, B. K. (1983). Classification, compliance, and confusion. *Journal of Learning Disabilities, 16*, 25.

Keogh, B. K., & MacMillan, D. L. (1983). The logic of sample selection: Who represents what? *Exceptional Education Quarterly, 4*(3), 84–96.

Keogh, B. K., Major-Kingsley, S., Omori-Gordon, H., & Reid, H. P. (1982). *A system of marker variables for the field of learning disabilities*. Syracuse, NJ: Syracuse University Press.

Kirk, S. A., & Gallagher, J. J. (1979). *Educating exceptional children* (3rd ed.). Boston: Houghton-Mifflin Co.

Kramer, N. (1975). Diagnosis and classification in epidemiological and health-services research. In N. Hobbs (Ed.), *Issues in the Classification of Children*, Vol. I (pp. 56–87). San Francisco: Jossey-Bass Publishers.

Larkin, J. H. (1979). Information-processing models and science instruction. In J. Lochhead & J. Clement (Eds.), *Cognitive Process Instruction: Research on Teaching Thinking Skills* (pp. 109–118). Philadelphia, PA.: The Franklin Institute Press.

Lerner, J. (1981). *Learning disabilities: Theories, diagnosis and teaching strategies* (3rd ed.). Boston: Houghton-Mifflin Co.

Lesgold, A. M., Resnick, L. B., & Beck, J. L. (1978). *Preliminary results of a longitudinal study of reading acquisition*. Paper presented at the Psychonomic Society Meeting, 11th November, San Antonio, TX.

Liberman, J. Y., Shankweiler, D., Fischer, F. W., & Carter, B. (1974). Explicit syllable and phoneme segmentation in the young child. *Journal of Experimental Child Psychology, 18*, 201–212.

Lochhead, J. (1979). On learning to balance perceptions by conceptions: A dialogue between two science students. In J. Lochhead & J. Clement (Eds.), *Cognitive Process Instruction: Research on Teaching Thinking Skills* (pp. 147–180). Philadelphia, PA.: The Franklin Institute Press.

Lochhead, J., & Clement, J. (Eds.) (1979). *Cognitive process instruction: Research on teaching thinking skills*. Philadelphia, PA.: The Franklin Institute Press.

McKinney, J. D. (1984). The search for subtypes of specific learning disability. *Journal of Learning Disabilities, 17*, 43–50.

McLeod, J. (1975). Comment on D. Divoky's article. *Journal of Learning Disabilities, 8*, 68–69.

McLeod, J. (1983). Learning disability is for educators. *Journal of Learning Disabilities, 16*, 23–24.

MacMillan, D. L., Meyers, C. E., & Morrison, G. M. (1980). System identification of mildly retarded children: Implications for integrating and conducting research. *American Journal of Mental Deficiency, 85*(2), 108–115.

Mandler, G. (1981). *What is cognitive psychology? What isn't?* Invited address. Division of Philosophical Psychology, American Psychological Association convention (August), Los Angeles.

Manis, F. R., & Morrison, F. J. (1985). Reading disability: A deficit in rule learning? In L. S. Siegel & F. J. Morrison (Eds.), *Progress in Cognitive Development Research* (Vol. VI, pp. 1–26). *Cognitive development in atypical children*. New York: Springer-Verlag.

Mann, L., Davis, C. H., Boyer, C. W., Jr., Metz, C. M., & Wolford, B. (1983). LD or not LD, that was the question: A retrospective analysis of child service demonstration centers' compliance with the federal definition of learning disabilities. *Journal of Learning Disabilities, 1,* 14–17.

Mason, J. M. (1984). Prereading: A developmental perspective. In P. D. Pearson (Ed.), *Handbook of Research in Reading* (pp. 505–543). New York: Longman.

National Advisory Committee on Handicapped Children (1968). *Special Education for Handicapped Children.* First Annual Report. Washington, DC: U.S. Department of Health, Education, and Welfare. January 31, 1968.

Palincsar, A. S. (1982). *Improving the reading comprehension of junior high students through reciprocal teaching of comprehension-monitoring strategies.* Unpublished doctoral dissertation, University of Illinois, Champaign–Urbana.

Pavlidis, G. (1983). *Research diagnostic criteria for dyslexia.* Unpublished paper, Rutgers Medical School, New Brunswick, NJ.

Perlmutter, B. F., & Parus, M. V. (1983). Identifying children with learning disabilities: A comparison of diagnostic procedures across school districts. *Learning Disability Quarterly, 6,* 321–328.

Phillips, L., Draguns, J. G., & Bartlett, D. P. (1975). Classification of behavior disorders. In N. Hobbs (Ed.), *Issues in the Classification of Children,* Vol. I (pp. 26–55). San Francisco: Jossey-Bass Publishers.

Reid, D. K., & Hresko, W. P. (1981). *A cognitive approach to learning disabilities.* New York: McGraw-Hill Book Co.

Resnick, L. B., & Weaver, P. A. (Eds.). (1979). *Theory and practice of early reading,* Vol. 1. Hillsdale, NJ: Lawrence Erlbaum Associates.

Ryan, E. B. (1980). *Metalinguistic development and reading acquisition.* Final Report (July) to the National Science Foundation Grant BNS76–09559.

Satz, P., & Morris, R. (1981). Learning disability subtypes: A review. In F. J. Pirozzolo & M. C. Wittrock (Eds.), *Neuropsychological and Cognitive Processes in Reading* (pp. 109–141). New York: Academic Press.

Senf, G. M. (1972). An information-integration theory and its application to normal reading acquisition and reading disability. In N. D. Bryant and C. E. Kass (Eds.), *Leadership Training Institute in Learning Disabilities: Final Report,* Vol. 2 (pp. 305–391). Tucson: University of Arizona.

Senf, G. M. (1976). Future research needs in learning disabilities. In R. P. Anderson and C. G. Halcomb (Eds.), *Learning Disabilities/Minimal Brain Dysfunction Syndrome: Research Perspectives and Application* (pp. 249–267). Springfield: Charles C. Thomas.

Senf, G. M. (1978). Some methodological considerations in the study of abnormal conditions. In R. N. Walsh and W. T. Greenough (Eds.), *Environments as Therapy for Brain Dysfunction* (pp. 343–360). New York: Plenum Press.

Smith, P. A., & Marx, R. W. (1971). The factor structure of the Illinois Test of Psycholinguistic Abilities. *Journal of Learning Disabilities, 8,* 349–356.

Spitzer, R. L., Williams, J. B. W., & Skodol, A. E. (1980). DSM–III: The major achievements and an overview. *American Journal of Psychiatry, 137,* 151–155.

Sulzbacher, S., & Kenowitz, L. A. (1977). At last, a definition of learning disabilities we can live with. *Journal of Learning Disabilities, 10,* 67–69.

Thurlow, M., & Ysseldyke, J. (1979). Current assessment and decision-making practices in model LD program. *Learning Disability Quarterly, 2,* 15–24.

Torgesen, J. K. (1979). What shall we do with psychological processes? *Journal of Learning Disabilities, 12,* 514–522.

Torgesen, J. K. (1981). The story of short-term memory in learning-disabled children: Goals, methods, and conclusions. In K. Gadow & I. Bailer (Eds.), *Advances in Learning and Behavioral Disabilities* (pp. 117–149). Greenwich, CT: JAI Press.

Torgesen, J. K. (1982). The use of rationally defined subgroups in research on learning disabilities. In J. P. Das, R. J. Mulcahy, & T. E. Wall (Eds.), *Theory and Research in Learning Disabilities* (pp. 111–131). New York: Plenum Press.

Torgesen, J. K., & Dice, C. (1980). Characteristics of research on learning disabilities. *Journal of Learning Disabilities, 13,* 531–535.

Torgesen, J. K., & Goldman, T. (1977). Rehearsal and short-term memory in reading disabled children. *Child Development, 48,* 56–60.

Torgesen, J. K., & Houck, G. (1980). Processing deficiencies in learning-disabled children who perform poorly on the digit span task. *Journal of Educational Psychology, 72,* 141–160.

Whimbey, A., & Lochhead, J. (1979). *Problem solving and comprehension: A short course in analytical reasoning.* Philadelphia, PA: The Franklin Institute Press.

Williams, J. P. (1980). Teaching decoding with emphasis on phoneme analysis and phoneme blending. *Journal of Educational Psychology, 72,* 1–15.

Wong, B. Y. L. (1979). The role of theory in learning-disabilities research. *Journal of Learning Disabilities, 12*(9), 585–595.

Wozniak, R. H. (1979). *Soviet psycho-educational research on learning disabilities: Implications for American research and practice.* Reston, VA: Council for Exceptional Children, ERIC Clearinghouse for Handicapped and Gifted Children.

Ysseldyke, J. E., & Algozzine, B. (1979). Perspectives on assessment of learning-disabled students. *Learning Disability Quarterly, 2,* 3–14.

2

LD Research in Sociological and Scientific Perspective

GERALD M. SENF

INTRODUCTION

The initial years I was concerned with what we now call "learning disabilities" (LD) were relatively uncomplicated. Existing, as I did, outside of the social system of special education and that of medicine as well, I was able to use terms such as "learning disabled," "learning disordered," "dyslexic," "reading retarded," and similar broad descriptors with relative indiscretion. The journals in which I published were then equally oblivious to the distinctions which derived from sociological and scientific concerns. My habit of using these terms interchangeably derived not from any disdain for the differences in conception held by others, but more basically from a lack of appreciation for the perspectives from which these different conceptualizations arose. It would be simple to say that I now know the distinctions among these terms, use them as the rest of those knowledgeable do, and have essentially put definitional confusions behind me. However, no such clarity has eventuated.

Initially, I was impatient with definitional concerns, feeling that definitions represented precursors upon which data sets could be built rather than the basis for heated debate. I grew impatient with the incessant definitional obsession of my "special education" colleagues. Some odd "necessity of agreement" pervaded their consciousness, a necessity which required that everyone mean the same thing by the same labels,

27

Psychological and Educational
Perspectives on Learning Disabilities

even if they did not believe all of the same things about the persons so named. The push for agreement seemed motivated by concerns related to application—not science—and hence, appeared misguided. Within a scientific framework, concern for agreement was appropriate in that it is useless to debate the characteristics of anything, be it a phenomenon or a group of people, if there is no agreement about how to identify the phenomenon or group for further study. More than 20 years ago, Zigler and Phillips (1961) referred to this principle of scientific endeavor as distinguishing between classification principles and class correlates.

Class principles concern consensus by observers regarding the presense or absence of an object or an event. It is, in essence, reliability of observation. Once reliability of observation has been obtained, one might seek to identify phenomena which relate to the various classes. The simplicity of this thinking is not to be demeaned, as it represents the basic structure upon which scientific observation and discovery rest. The basic point is that the value of a classification system rests not on the events designated but upon the knowledge subsequently assembled about these events. Such study involves first observing in a reliable fashion instances of the class principles to determine whether there are valid class correlates of interest. Failing to find class correlates of use, interest, or utility, one could readily abandon the whole classificatory system in favor of some other. In a word, the whole classification system can be altered or discarded if it fails to produce new knowledge (cf., Zigler & Phillips, 1961; Senf, 1976a for a more thorough discussion).

MORE THAN IGNORANCE AT WORK

Then, as today, there existed considerable disagreement among professionals and concerned parents as to what percentage of the population could legitimately be called "learning disabled" (cf., Tucker, Stevens, & Ysseldyke, 1983). The epidemiological disparity stemmed from the lack of specificity of the definitions in use, both then and now. The definitions in question are conceptual in nature rather than operational and provide for tremendous latitude in interpretation. The field quickly fell into a position where those who were alleged moderates claimed that 2–3% of the children had a significant specific learning disability; some claimed the condition to be a mere hoax, whereas others saw the prevalence to be well above 50%. Such lack of reliability among professionals should cause skeptics to ask, "What's up?" In fact, there was a lot at stake in this definitional issue, more than either the government apparently had forecast or many of the field's initiators had reckoned on (but see Cruickshank, 1977, 1978; Kirk, 1963).

Some time later, I discovered there were more variables at play in determining the class principles of learning disabilities than would be admitted into a scientific nomenclature. Not that too many existed, but some existed that were not only ill-defined but unstated. The whole host of sociological variables that come into play when public monies are made available for services to the populace necessarily were at work, controlling the flow of funds and, by implication, the definition of the term as it evolved in practice.

Of first importance was the rapid development of social institutions supporting the broad construct of learning disabilities. Teacher-training institutions, state and local governmental agencies, parent groups, and private schools, among others, were involved in this "new" handicap. Clearly, there was an incentive to make the condition appear to be as prevalent as possible, for government incidence figures are typically linked to dollars: The more learning-disabled people there are, the more dollars there are available for services.

The sociological development of the field certainly did not stop with these initial funds. Instead, these funds (Senf 1976b) acted as "seed" money to initiate new programs for teacher training within colleges of education and to operate model demonstration programs for learning-disability children nationwide (Kirk & Elkins, 1975; Mann, Davis, Boyer, Metz, & Wolford, 1983; Norman & Zigmond, 1980). There is nothing really new in this type of sociological phenomenon: All we were witnessing was the inevitable consequence of money being made available for learning-disabled children through their incorporation into the Education for All Handicapped Children Act of 1974 (PL 94–142). As a group of children, they were no longer simply those who needed the teacher's additional concern. They now brought with them a coupon which was redeemable by many segments of the educational/psychological/medical and allied communities for services to be rendered, either directly in schools and clinics, indirectly in research activities, or in preparation programs for future remedial specialists.

THE CASUALTIES

To illustrate that this line of thinking is not simply historical speculation or of no practical importance, note the casualties in the creation of the category of handicap called "learning disabilities." The importance of recognizing these casualties is that subtle changes in the thinking of those intimately involved attend the formal changes. The major sociological casualties attest to subtle changes in the way certain groups of children began to be considered and points to the more general principle that how we conceive of something inextricably alters how we deal with it. In the field of mental health, those who were once viewed as witches were eventually viewed as mentally ill and, more recently, as having problems in living. These different conceptions dealt those labeled very different fates! In the case of the learning disabled, one of the most crucial issues is the problem the conceptualization of LD posed the educational community (Weener & Senf, 1982).

When one considers that three-quarters of learning-disabled youngsters have problems in the area of reading (Kirk & Elkins, 1975; Norman & Zigmond, 1980), it becomes apparent that what might have been seen earlier as corrective or remedial reading cases had been reclassified as learning disabled. The implications for hiring new personnel and distributing funds within school districts and state facilities were direct. So, too, was the question of who should teach the child with a reading disability, a question which I posed within this sociological context a decade ago (Senf, 1975). Given that learning disabilities know no academic content boundaries—the areas of mathematics, reading, spelling, expressive writing, communication skills, and even the interpersonal domain being legitimate fare for the LD profession—resources both tangible and intangible were removed from traditional areas and channeled instead into a new institution that was viewed as an enlightened solution to many of education's problems.

Certainly, I have not painted an exhaustive picture of the sociological implications of the emergence of learning disabilities on the educational scene, but I do not think that I have rendered a distorted vision. The crucial point is that lacking a specific definition of its mission, the field was free to accept challenges, enlarging its domain of concern into territory previously occupied by other professions. In so doing, it claimed both a right to be present and a superiority in dealing with the problems encountered (cf., Sarason 1970, 1982, for a thorough treatment of the sociological impact of such abrupt change). What then were the implications for research of such a new field?

SCIENCE MEETS SOCIAL REALITY

If this analysis is correct to the present point, then my puzzlement of years ago disappears. More importantly, the inability of the field to develop an operational definition of learning disabilities need not be seen as inadequacy, delinquency, or scientific indecision. Instead, there is motive in our failure to define who is and who is not learning disabled. That is to say, various persons and institutions involved in the educational/health delivery system benefit by the ambiguity of the LD diagnosis, more specifically, by the ambiguity of the definition and its regulations in federal and state law. Because I wish to spend more of this chapter on the research strategies that have evolved than on the intellectual context spawned by this social history, I shall be brief here.

First, it should be recognized that service under the LD rubric is most easily rendered to those whose families possess social competence (Senf, 1981). To be able to approach a school principal, present one's case, and gain the ear of the psychometrist or other school personnel makes access to extra services much more likely. Such are the features of parents from the upper socioecomomic range who often have a sole (usually male) breadwinner, leaving the mother time to interact gainfully with the school on behalf of the child. Such factors may help explain why learning disabilities—as a field—has gained the reputation of being a white, middle-class disorder. In the present context, what is most important is that numerous research studies rely upon the diagnostic judgments of those in the public school to provide research samples. This subset is, as noted, heavily influenced in many unknown ways by a host of sociological factors, many economically based. Surely, one must question whether a valid information base can be built on samples of such diverse and unknown make-up. I shall return to this issue when considering alternative research strategies.

OTHER SAMPLE BIAS

Other biasing factors are readily evident as well. For example, LD programs are not solely supported by the federal government. They also attain state and often district-level support. More local-level support tends often to derive from the reallocation or diversion of discretionary funds into such programs "when the need is present." Such funding is more likely when the constituency is vocal, immediately concerned with their children's schooling, and capable of spending the time necessary to gain the ear of the educational establishment.

Still another factor tends to bias the samples utilized in research. There exists an elaborate sociological system of diagnosis and certification which identifies learning-disabled children. Universities typically are not located in impoverished areas and typically cultivate contacts primarily with neighboring areas where learning-disability programs flourish. This *folie à deux* between the university personnel—who do the research—and the school systems—which provide the LD programs—creates a distorted reality of what might otherwise be the learning-disabilities field. Although it is not as "white" as it might historically have been, nor as "highly intelligent" as some believe it should be, nor as confined to the suburbs as it used to be, these factors still substantially bias our research through subject selection in unknown ways.

Equally confounding for research, though diametrically opposed in effect to the previously mentioned bias, is the extension of learning-disability research into the urban neighborhoods where lower SES and, often, lower IQ subjects are identified as learning disabled. As I have argued—that the definition is open to judgment—I would be the last to say that the studies of high SES, average IQ, white children are any more appropriately representative of learning disabilities than are the studies of lower SES and (correlatively) lower-IQ minority children. The point is not which is more correct but rather that neither have unique legitimacy. The researcher, lacking any benchmark, does well to describe subject samples in great detail, comparing research results only with those studies that have used subjects reasonably equated on basic demographic, personality, and programmatic variables (see Keogh, Major-Kingsley, Omori-Gordon, & Reid, 1982).

Whereas the sociological underpinnings of LD often go unrecognized, the single most striking aspect of this type of sociological analysis is that it is intuitive, conjured up from one's own experience. Despite the 20-year history of the field, there has been no systematic sociological analysis of those factors influencing how the field is studied. Individuals selected as research subjects and who, as a result, contribute to our knowledge of the learning-disabled person are left to vary widely. This same fact holds true for essays regarding the learning-disabled adult. These individuals are often studied within a college context and are described without reference to any socioeconomic, racial, educational, or developmental/medical background. These oversights form a backdrop against which the material discussed further in this chapter needs to be viewed.

The importance of introducing the field of learning disabilities within the realm of social concern and policy is that these dimensions directly affect research thinking and the nature of the research accomplished. In the next section, I shall illustrate some of these points, referring often to prior papers which discuss the points in greater detail.

PROBLEMS IN DEFINING THE LD SAMPLE

One of the most pressing problems involved in defining LD samples involves the growing consensus that learning disabilities are represented by severe discrepancies between IQ and school skills (Federal Register, December 29, 1977; Kirk, Senf & Larsen, 1981). I have argued against this simplistic conceptualization of what is, clearly, a more encompassing psychosocial, emotional, and often, a measurable neuropsychologically based educational problem (Senf, 1978). The federal government's view (Federal Register, December 29, 1977) has been widely adopted by the states, primarily because of its simplicity. The issue of the number of children served, more specifically, the cost of the service, once again comes into play. When governmental agencies are required to play a role both in the identification and consequent service of any condition, there is an understandable tendency to estimate the number of those involved so that budgetary constraints are not overrun. One can question the scientific integrity of a community which will permit manipulation of prevalence figures based on political whim. Instead, scientific sensibility requires that the incidence of a condition be established once a reliable operational definition of the condition is drafted. Given that operational definition, one could determine the number of those who fit the definition. The issue really is one of integrity, both scientific and ethical. If one seeks solely to concoct a formula by which a certain percentage of the populace is served, say 2–3%, then such can easily be done. To do so by manipulating the specific choices of psychometric or other tests and to term the resultant group "learning disabled" is, essentially, to be dishonest and unethical (Weener & Senf, 1982). Conversely, a scientific process would allow free and unencumbered results: No one would specify ahead of time the answer to the empirical question, "How many fit the LD definition?" Federal and state governments cannot be so open-minded and, hence, prejudice the process by specifying ahead of time the number to be served.

This process certainly is not science, nor is it good social policy (Luick & Senf, 1979). As I have argued in the initial section of this chapter, the funds go to those who are most adept at petitioning or are willing to have their children accept the label of handicap for the extra services they might receive. Although one can praise the social competence of some families, one must call into question a system which places in jeopardy those who do not wish their child or their culture to be branded as deficient in order to receive adequate schooling (cf., Dunn, 1968; Senf, 1981).

ISSUES HAVING RESEARCH IMPLICATIONS

I have already outlined a number of reasons why the learning-disability group as we know it does not suit us well for research purposes. I have asserted that persons are labeled LD for a host of reasons, many of which have sociopolitical foundations which bias in two ways the identification process. First, there is the inclusion of persons who, without the petition of someone in a position of power, might not have been included. Second, when limited funds are utilized to serve persons not technically eligible, others are omitted from the potential sample.

So many papers of an experimental nature claim to have studied learning-disability pupils who conform to the dictates of a particular state's regulations, typically via individual education plan (IEP) team consensus, but this claim in no way obviates the sample bias, nor does a careful delineation of as many marker variables (Keogh et al., 1982) as one could imagine. The marker variables do help one assess sample distinctiveness and are to be encouraged in reporting, but the sample remains biased in unknown ways.

Another problem for researchers is that learning disabilities is a label that was originally adopted for administrative convenience. There are few today, I would hope, who fail to realize that the term "learning disabilities" was never meant to describe a homogeneous group of children who suffered from some common deficiency. Rather, it was meant to be an umbrella term subsuming—for administrative purposes—those children who have difficulty in school despite otherwise adequate intellectual resources. Other conceptualizations—often based on intraskill discrepancies which denounce the importance of IQ—are equally valid. These conceptualizations derived from the history of special educators' concern for what were then termed the "minimally brain damaged" (Clements, 1966; Cruickshank, 1977; Orton, 1937; Strauss & Kephart, 1955; Strauss & Lehtinen, 1947; cf. Senf, 1973; Weiderholt, 1974, for a brief history of the field). However, the emphasis on IQ achievement discrepancy in school narrowed and reshaped the field (Senf, 1978). Learning disabilities, as a field, was no longer organized around disease entities nor a particular educational handicap, but encompassed instead a group of handicapping problems, all of which prejudiced the otherwise capable child from performing in school. As Lieberman has pointed out, the LD term was legislatively recognized within the context of other handicapping conditions: "When this mandate was given, a handicapped child was not handicapped because he was failing in school; he was failing in school because he was handicapped" (1980, p. 66). The reader may need to examine this distinction a number of times before it becomes clear that the pivotal term is "handicapped." Failure at school is relatively easy to determine, whereas being handicapped (as the presumed cause of that failure) is anything but obvious. In fact, the definitional issues which persist until today (see the special feature regarding definition in the *Journal of Learning Disabilities*, January 1983) illustrate the difficulty in establishing the construct of handicap independent of school failure. Some have asserted that there is essentially no difference between the alleged handicapped learning-disabled youngster and the underachiever (McLeod, 1983). Others (Ysseldyke & Algozzine, 1983) have called for a new conceptualization, based on the fact that it is difficult to discriminate LD youngsters from other children (both those with other handicaps and those considered normal) with an acceptable degree of reliability (Ysseldyke, 1983).

The concept of the LD child as handicapped is closely associated with the problem of hetrogeneity in research samples. There have been many suggestions during the 20-year history of the LD field that the difficulty in learning more about the children so termed stemmed from the inherent heterogeneity of the population. That is, any particular subject sample contains children with such diversity that correlates are hard to establish. When relationships are found, they are deemed to be insufficiently powerful to make practical decisions and, hence, are erroneously termed "educationally meaningless" (Hammill & Larsen, 1974).

In understanding the effects of sample heterogeneity on experimental outcomes, it is important to take into account the purpose for which the experiment was conducted. This distinction is important because, if the purpose of an experiment is simply to advance knowledge about learning disabilities, the amount of variance accounted for in the experiment is unimportant relative to the basic demonstration that a variable or variables have been isolated, which reliably account for stable prediction of the dependent variable. Under such conditions, what is of primary theoretical importance is the isolation of the relationship, not whether the relationship is strong or weak. It is possible that the relationship might be very strong among some subjects and weak among others; may be strong throughout, but masked by other variables in the experiment; or may even be weak throughout but may interact with other variables (in all or some subjects) to yield very marked effects. The relevance of some research is that a relationship was established, not that the relationship was very strong. This point is, typically, overlooked by those who criticize research findings as lacking "educational relevance."

Alternatively, there are situations, such as the development of useful screening measures, where the degree of variance accounted for is most important. It is often in these cases that the low level of relationships between variables is said to be due to the "heterogeneity" of the LD sample. Such argument is misguided.

Heterogeneity speaks to variability among the subjects in a group. Typically, it is utilized as an excuse for finding low-level relationships between one's independent and dependent variable. Within a predictive model, heterogeneity has no place: It is a word substituting for either unreliability or invalidity (Zigler & Phillips, 1961). Simply, the inability to agree upon which entities should belong in the LD group is an occasion of unreliability of diagnosis. If people cannot agree upon who is to be studied as a representative of LD, then there is no possible way that knowledge can be accumulated scientifically (Senf, 1976c).

The other occasion for heterogenity to be used as an excuse for less than sterling findings occurs when the predicted correlate lacks sufficient relationship to be statistically significant. Here, the experimentor claims that had these subjects been more homogeneous, the effect would have shown itself as statistically reliable. But such an argument is simply sour grapes. What has happened is that the sample chosen according to principles under the control of the experimentor did not distinguish itself sufficiently from the contrast group. That is all one can say. To blame unknown characteristics among the experimental group is to flaunt one's own ignorance, although this ignorance may actually be a reflection of the inadequacy of the basic class principles by which we form groups of LD children for study, especially the failure to recognize the sociopolitical machinations the selection process undergoes.

BAND-AID APPROACHES TO HETEROGENEITY

One way of making sense of near-statistically significant data, or even data which are highly reliable, is an examination of the distribution of scores of the subjects in crucial cells of the experiment. Looking at the simplest case—one LD and one control group—one can posit that the distribution of scores is significant at the .05 level or greater, but that there still exists overlap between the two groups (see Weener, 1981, for a discussion of this issue of sample overlap). Assuming that one is trying to determine the importance of an independent variable as a distinguishing characteristic of the learning-disabled group and one finds that the variable, in fact, distinguishes the LD from the normal group at the .05 level or greater, one is tempted to—in fact, one often does—impute to all subjects in the learning-disability category a psychology predicated upon the differences found. For example, when one finds that the learning-disabled group shows significantly different scores on a measure of Locus of Control (LOC) relative to some control group, one is prone to suggest that learning-disabled children have differential beliefs about their ability to control their environment.

The basic error here is twofold. First, it is erroneous to impute to a whole sample psychological characteristics that differentiate them from the control group. A more careful examination of the data would show that the group's scores heavily overlapped, that only a few of the LD subjects had Locus of Control scores outside the range of those shown by the normal sample, and that the mean difference between the two samples on the LOC measure was likely less than a single standard deviation (Weener, 1981).

Although the first problem is one of commission, the second is one of omission: failure to investigate the variability in one's data. Very often, there is greater variability among the learning-disability sample's scores than among those of their normal peers. This phenomenon has typically led some experimentors to cry "heterogeneity," as though they had been victimized by not having selected only those subjects who score discrepantly relative to the controls. A more balanced interpretation of the data simply is that the hypothesis may be true for some of the subjects. Though the work is likely not publishable without replication, one can learn a great deal by examining all data available about those subjects who occupy the extremes of the distribution. With supporting data, one might be able to learn why those who fit the hypothesis among the experimental group differed from those who appeared to perform similarly to the controls. In any event, the process one is undertaking is necessarily exploratory for the formation of furthur research. First, one should not blame the predicament on heterogeneity; second, one should not overlook the knowledge potentially available in the data collected.

There is another approach to one's data when group differences are significant and one believes they ought to be shared with colleagues. When the findings appear unique or otherwise of value, the experimentor may wish to ask questions about both the control and LD group's distribution of scores. For example, one could ask: "What percentage of the LD sample lies outside of one standard deviation (or some other cutting score) of the normal sample?" Such a question gives one a feel of the dispersion of the phenomena among the LD sample. Also, by examining the distribution of the scores of the LD sample, one may discover that part of the distribution resembles that of the normal group whereas some subset of the LD sample—often a minority—carries the weight of the variance producing the statistically significant effect. Such observations can add immeasurably to the interpretation of one's data. Important, too, it provides the writer an avenue for escaping the obvious error of imputing to all subjects in the LD group a common characteristic which the data, themselves, deny. Instead, one can alert other researchers and practitioners to the likely existence of some subset of LD youngsters who are distinctive in some respect.

THE CONTEXT OF CLASSIFICATION

At first blush, it would appear that the solution to the problem of heterogeneity in the LD population is simply to select some subset of the population for closer scrutiny. By selecting a more homogeneous group of LD youngsters, a greater probability of finding valid correlates of a subgroup should result. But if these groups are to have meaning within the broader context, one would seem obliged to specify the population from which any subgroup derives. Failure to do so will result in research characterized as a patchwork of studies on various subsamples of children who are failing at school or who have abnormal behavioral, psychological, or neurological characteristics thought related to academic achievement. A recent review of such work confirms this concern (McKinney, 1984). The resulting collection of studies will lack a common empirical foundation. Consequently, it will be most difficult to integrate the findings across studies if each investigator has selected idiosyncratic subgroups from an undefined population.

What is really at issue here is the relationship of the subgroup to the broader classification schema or taxonomy. Subgroups should have as members those with at least some feature or features common to each supraordinate group in the system. For example, the animal taxonomic categories share with members of a species some of the characteristics of the genus to which they belong, and some of the characteristics of the family to which the genus belongs, and so forth up the taxonomic scale.

In this context, we can ask what the broadest classification principle for learning disabilities should be. The universe of persons with whom we are concerned is potentially all humans: those of our particular concern are ones who have difficulty in the educational process. Some might argue that our particular concern is for those who manifest clear, organic brain dysfunction whereas others may qualify for both or either group with exclusory requirements, that is, not blind, deaf, and so forth, such as those in the Federal Law (Federal Register, December 29, 1977). It remains the researcher's task to specify the population, for the popula-

˙tion represents: (1) the broadest class to which findings can be generalized; and, (2) the group from which subgroups will derive. To examine a subgroup from an unknown population is to learn only about that specific subgroup—an undertaking of dubious value.

There are many persons who have embraced the IQ achievement-discrepancy definition of learning disabilities (Kirk *et al.*, 1981). One could argue for this type of class principle for defining the broad group of learning disabilities for research purposes. Although apparent numerical precision may be its best asset, this procedure really needs to be examined in terms of the standard error of measurement of the difference score between the achievement and the IQ test in question. Further, such an approach would cut the research endeavor loose from the historical underpinnings of neuropsychological and related theoretical formulations (Senf, 1978).

As problematic for me in accepting such an entry point for the broad group to be studied is the logic involved in the discrepancy score itself. Stripped of the excess meaning in the terms intelligence and achievement, all we are doing is subtracting from a global measure designed to predict school achievement (IQ), another score indicative of some aspect of school achievement. Among the total population, these two scores correlate highly. What we are doing is selecting for our major group those children for whom the prediction of achievement by the IQ score is very low and for whom the IQ score is the greater. Logically, we are imputing more validity to the predictor (IQ) than we are to the resulting behavior (achievement). We are postulating that the IQ score is correct and are saying that the child should be performing better in the given academic area were not something wrong with the child! In a science where prediction seldom approaches perfection, it strikes me as inelegant and, indeed, presumptuous to choose as one's population for study those for whom prediction has failed.

CLASSIFICATION AS PRAGMATIC

An obvious first question is to ask what one wants a classification system to do. If one cannot answer this question, there is no sense in classifying and doing subsequent research. After all, when one classifies events into a group, one loses specific information about the individual. One hopes this loss of information about individuality is compensated for by some new knowledge gained by finding valid group correlates, features that the members hold in common, and are not included in the class principles used to assign the people to the group in the first place.

This is the essential trade-off in medical diagnosis where the person's individuality is sacrificed to diagnostic classification based on a few symptoms which may suggest a disease process, an etiology, a treatment plan, and a prognosis.

In asking what one wishes the classification system to do, one is reiterating the prior argument that classification systems are mutable though the class principles within any given one are not. Said colloquially, there are many ways to carve up the pie. So, when we ask what it is we want a classification system to do, we are, essentially, specifying what we desire to predict by assigning individuals to different groups within the system.

CLASSIFICATION AS THEORY

Given the task of segmenting a large group of individuals into subgroups so as to learn more about them, one must be guided by some notion about what one wishes to accomplish or, as said previously, what one wishes the system to do. Certainly, one could accept into the system all children with a IQ achievement discrepancy of a certain specific magnitude and then proceed to divide them into subgroups based on hair color, height, and (heaven and the federal government forbid) skin color. The mindlessness of such action simply illustrates that the process of selecting a group and deriving subgroups must be guided by some theoretical notions about the set of problems to be distinguished in the supraordinate group. Because one wishes to forge subgroups, which have potentially demonstrable high-level correlates of use, one needs some theory as a guide.

This thinking is in direct contrast to the prevailing procedures of sample selection. Although it is typical for a researcher to apply a set of theoretical principles when studying some subset of individuals, the role of theory in designating the individuals under study is typically ignored or at least totally deemphasized. Selection of the appropriate deviant sample (one which well represents the population of deviant individuals similarly labeled by other researchers) is conceived in an operational rather than a theoretical context. The researcher typically views the designation of the sample as necessary but theoretically unimportant step in assessing the hypothesis. Once a sample has been selected, then the theoretical proposition to be tested is framed through the use of an appropriate design and an applicable research paradigm.

I think this tendency to ignore the theoretical relevance of the sample selection process stems from our willingness to reify deviance labels such as "learning disabilities." Consequently, one accepts the prevailing methods of designation when forming samples for study. In the LD area, a prominent method involves referral for, and inclusion in, some special education program, often bolstered by a measured IQ achievement discrepancy. There is little concern about how the particular type of deviant behavior fits into a broader classification scheme and how the broader group could be subdivided by applying some of the same theoretical notions to be utilized subsequently in the experiment.

Another tendency besides our proclivity for reification is a prevailing view that deviant persons function in such a totally different manner than do "normals" that we consider them a different "kind" of organism. As a consequence, we tend to conjur up theoretical notions peculiar to the deviant, for example, minimal brain dysfunction, biochemical imbalance, allergic reactions, and so forth. A striking and really obvious alternative, seen frequently in the application of psychological models, is to view one's deviant group within the context of normal behavior. Such an approach accepts as a premise that the deviant individual is not one different in kind but rather in some way or ways to be understood within theory relating to all humans, these differences being of sufficient magnitude or being mutually dependent so as to produce deviant outcome behavior.

Some examples might clarify the difference this way of thinking reflects, for instance, consider a generic information-processing model (Senf, 1972). For simplicity, let us assume that the model only has five constructs: channel capacity, input modality, short-term memory buffers, long-term storage, and information type (semantic versus nonsemantic). Assume that one could understand the functioning and the development of children with these five constructs (though such an assumption is clearly invalid). The point is that one can pose the questions, "Do the children under consideration have equivalent channel capacity relative to their peers?" "Are differences in information-extraction capability of the various modalities more discrepant within the target individual relative to the distribution of such discrepancies in their normal peers?" "If a discrepancy in modality strength is found, does it interact with information type, that is, is it more pronounced when semantic information is being processed as opposed to nonsemantic information?" "If the visual modality among some of these children of concern is disproportionately deficient at extracting information relative to their own ability in other modalities, is the visual short-term memory buffer also deficient or does the problem lie subsequent to the short-term visual information buffer and perhaps relate to a long-term storage and/or a retrieval problem?"

Note that all these questions derive from a simple five-construct model applicable to any human organism. A marked intraindividual deficiency in the ability of one of the modalities to extract information from the environment could, reasonably, be the cause for reliance on the person's stronger, more reliable modalities. Utilizing one's "strong suit" can reasonably be postulated to be more reinforcing than attempting to utilize the weak modality, implying that the individual's channel capacity more likely will be devoted to information striking the receptors of the strong modality. This process likely will be developmental so that a positive feedback loop will result causing the individual to become increasingly less capable at the weak modality. Consequent instruction aimed at that weak modality will be relatively unsuccessful and cause frustration and other negative affect.

While this brief vignette may strike some as familiar and a bit seductive, others may rightfully note that the example is oversimplified. My point is not linked to the specifics of the example but to the illustration of the ability of a theory applying to all humans to understand deviance through the postulation of deviant scores or deviant patterns of scores on the parameters of a theory applicable to all humans.

NORMAL THEORY AND DEVIANT SUBGROUPS

Returning now to the question of what constitutes the broadest population of concern, one can see that within the framework described here, all humans can be included. More practically, though, the concerns of those interested in learning disabilities need some finer group for the selection of a subject sample upon which to conduct research. However, it would be antithetical to the reasoning described here to select willy-nilly those persons identified as learning disabled by a local school system. One could adopt a psychometric operational definition or any other reliable set of operationally defined class principles suggestive of what many might think of as learning disabilities. Such a tactic would be consistent with the strategy described. However, one must be cognizant of the risk prejudgment at this stage represents. If one is too restrictive, subjects will go undesignated as LD but will later be found to be undistinguishable from other conditions—one of LD research's present problems (Ysseldyke, 1983). Admitting that more than pure operationism is involved, one needs to ask what the category and its subgroups hope to reveal. I would like to know why some children find the challenge of school so difficult. Being partial to the early years, I would choose 5–12-year-olders. Application of measurements—theoretically selected—to this group in conjunction with statistical algorithms could produce subgroups. Most subgroups would not be of particular interest as their school behavior will be uneventful. Interested in deviance, I would hope to find subgroupings whose empirically derived class principles suggest correlates for empirical test. Although one or more subgroups—or subsubgroups derived subsequently—may resemble what you or I would term "true LD," such an outcome is of consequence only insofar as preexisting literature suggests new experiments—an important event!

One's theory would be a guide as to the selection of variables in constituting subgroups. A recent book edited by Rourke (1985) well illustrates the use of various neuropsychological models to form subgroups from patterns of theoretically relevant variables. One need not be enamored of neuropsychological theories: Others can (and should) be used in the formation of subgroups. The general point here is that any theoretical orientation can be utilized to carve out subgroups which can be postulated to behave differently on measures of relevance to educators and the broader society. If behavior of relevance is not found, then one should reexamine one's theory. For, if such a statistically coherent subgrouping procedure as this does not yield high-level correlates of the subgroups constructed, applying the same research paradigm to an unselected group of learning-disabled children served by the school system will surely not yield the correlates of interest!

ALTERNATIVE GROUPING STRATEGIES

Without dismissing the important role of theory in delineating subgroups, one may wish to be more exacting in one's major group selection, what we might term one's "generic population." Some researchers, for example, are interested in reading failure and not in the myriad of other skill, social, and personal problems people encounter. One reasonably could start with a sample of subjects who are deficient on some aspect of reading, of interest to the researcher, again with the caveat that one's measurements be sufficiently developed to ensure construct validity. From this atheoretical population, one could then employ a theoretical model to create subgroups for further analysis, each subgroup containing those subjects whose reading deficit is thought to be linked to a particular constellation of scores derived from constructs in the theory. According to the theory selected, there might be one, two, or more reasons why subjects would have problems. Given the nature of the problem postulated for each of the subgroups' deficit, the dependent variable(s) under study should characterize some of the subgroups more than others, whereas it may be the case that one or more of the subgroups might be predicted to perform on the dependent variable similarly to those without any such deficit.

What this strategy of subgrouping based on theory allows one to do is to compare subjects sharing a similar deficit against each other rather than simply against a control group lacking the problem. The increased power here is that all the variables associated with failure to perform such as aversion to the task, low self-esteem, and so forth are roughly equated and, hence, do not confound the dependent variable–as is the case with comparing disability groups with nondisabled controls.

The strategy of limiting one's population to those possessing a particular skill deficit eliminates the potential of learning about other skill deficits and of how different school skills relate to each other, that is, are mediated by similar processes. Whether one approaches the definition of the broader population which is to be divided into subgroups from the perspective of one's theory versus the perspective of a particular skill deficit reveals one's research focus. Some investigators are more concerned with theory construction and validation and, hence, prefer to derive their subgroups on the basis of theoretical concerns and then conduct research to determine what the particular correlates (e.g., academic skills, ease of remediation, etc.) are for each subgroup. Conversely, other investigators may be particularly interested in a certain behavioral domain such as social skill, reading, expressive language, and so on. Selecting subjects with those problems as the initial population, such researchers might use constructs from one or more theories to derive groups which should, in theory, perform differently on the behavior(s) of interest.

The latter tactic would seem to have more promise in yielding information concerning a particular deficiency. Conceived as a final common path, the deficient behavior can be viewed as a task to be analyzed into its component parts. Those who involve themselves with task analysis sometimes do not seem fully aware that the subtasks they posit as necessary to accomplish the criterion behavior represent the application of but one of a myriad of theoretical models. The apparent simplicity of task analysis disappears when one recognizes that the behavioral linearity suggested by such analyses (where one subtask follows another in an inevitable progression) is likely false.

Problems encountered at any of the subtasks along the way to the criterion behavior can distort the whole process as the organism uses compensory strengths to solve subproblems when their particular deficiencies disrupt their progress. Were those interested in task analysis also to be interested in research, one could readily ask, "What if?" questions regarding each subtask posited and thus generate different subgroups of persons who accomplish the task more or less well using different strategies. Then, these subgroups' various psychological characteristics, as seen in their utilization of different task solutions, could be validated by doing the necessary research.

EMPIRICALLY DEFINED GROUPS

Cluster analysis (Anderberg, 1973; Tryon & Bailey, 1970), known in biological circles as "numerical taxonomy" (Sokal & Sneath, 1963), represents a collection of algorithms useful in isolating coherent patterns in a data set. Typically, the algorithms attempt to minimize the discrepany between all scores in the data set, segmenting into groups those subjects whose scores show the least discrepancy from other members of the subgroup. This tool has but recently been utilized in the LD field (cf. McKinney, 1984; Satz & Morris, 1981; Senf, Luick, & Larsen, 1976).

Like other statistical procedures such as factor analysis, the utility of the data derived from the analysis is directly linked to the meaningfulness of the data utilized for the analysis. The expression "GIGO" (garbage in—garbage out) holds for cluster analysis as for other statistical procedures. In both procedures, irrespective of the data input, one will obtain factors or clusters, respectively. Whether they have any meaning in the sense that the researcher can use them to learn more about the phenomenon or group of interest remains an empirical question. As such, both procedures are hypothesis-generating and should be seen in that context. More specifically, once one cluster analyzes a group of scores obtained by a sample of subjects and finds that the group divides itself reasonably well into, say, seven subgroups, one is obliged to demonstrate that the subgroups relate differentially to other variables of interest. Otherwise, one has simply segmented a data set and nothing more.

Again, the failure to understand that the groups obtained will be more understandable and, hence, generate more fruitful hypotheses—if the variables entered into the cluster analysis derive from some theory—should be recognized. Selecting whatever data happen to be in the files is a near-useless endeavor. But with a theory guiding the selection of the variables entered into the cluster analysis, the meaning of a subgroup, say, deficient on variables 1 and 3, but average to above average on variables 2 and 4–8, could reasonably be interpreted and hypotheses developed which would contrast this group from a second and third group characterized by a different pattern of deficiencies and strengths. One must do more than simply describe each subgroup in terms of demographic (e.g., age, SES, sex, etc.) and other variables such as achievement scores (cf. Satz & Morris, 1981). One should use one's theory to predict behavior of interest distinctive to each subgroup.

My own attitude is that a working theory, in combination with factor analysis and cluster analysis, selecting subjects without regard to their particular academic difficulty, represents the best single strategy available for the construction of subgroups. One of the problems with it is expense, as these statistical procedures, particularly cluster analysis, require data sets in the hundreds for statistical stability. Preferably, one should have approximately 500 subjects so that the cluster analysis could be accomplished twice on random halves of the sample. Such research may appear prohibitive, but once clusters (subgroups) are discovered and deemed stable, experiments with small, homogeneous subgroups can be fruitful. Single-subject designs would also be expected to be more powerful as a subject's subgroup membership being known adds theoretical leverage to the selection of variables for study.

RATIONALLY DEFINED, CLINICAL/INTUITIVE, AND BEHAVIORAL GROUPING

I think it useful to put into the present context other terms used to describe grouping techniques. Rational grouping procedures can be a means by which the investigator selects subjects having more or less of a given behavior or trait. For example, one may wish to study children with hyperactive tendencies and thus utilize a scale such as that derived by Conners (1969) into subgroups of hyperactive, normal reactive, and hypoactive respondents. Such a strategy produces reliable groupings (known through the reliability coefficient of the scale utilized). However, this strategy seems often to result in a simple design in which subjects' other characteristics are contrasted, based on subgroup membership. Such studies simply represent the group-design equivalent of a correlational study: One could have chosen not to segment the distribution and have treated the relationship between the independent variable and others of interest with correlational statistical techniques.

Rational groups based on a single variable need not necessarily limit one to a correlational design. Torgesen's research (1982; Torgesen & Houck, 1980), for example, distinguished school-designated LD students on short-term memory (STM) ability (WISC–R Digit Span). Weak and average STM LD groups and a normal control were then studied on a variety of manipulated variables theoretially relevant to STM performance. The goal of this research, guided by a broad STM literature, has been to discover the nature of the processing deficits accounting for the deficient STM, to link these deficient processes to academic failure, and eventually, to examine remedial strategies.

Torgesen notes that "it will probably not be sufficient to define subgroups by only one or two variables" (1982, p. 115). There are many reasons: (1) symptoms—such as poor Digit Span performance—likely are diversely caused (e.g., attention, anxiety) and would be seen as such were additional variables used in conjunction; (2) other variables will interact with the one selected to affect outcome measures; for example, compensatory skills may distort the relationship between poor STM and academic achievement; (3) the importance of any single variable is likely to change across age with respect to different academic tasks; (4) variables such as IQ and cognitive style may be strong mitigating factors (recognizing this problem, Torgesen [1982] required the LDs to have a minimum IQ of 85; had IQ been used as a variable in creating subgroups, low-IQ, poor-STM LDs might have been found to have different underlying process problems); and, (5) basically, single-variable subgroups are a misnomer as one has already selected school-certified LD students. As discussed, this heterogeneous group has enormous diversity of characteristics among its members. Accepting them as one's parent group is analogous to selecting general hospital ward patients for medical research. Certainly, homogeneity is increased by the preselection of school-referred students, just as it would be using hospitalized patients instead of the general public. The problem remains, however, that the parent population is unknown as the school-referred group's defining variables are obscure.

McKinney (1984) describes inferential classification as the use of "a priori decision rules" and uses as examples Boder's (1973) three types of language-disability groupings of dysphonetic, dyseidetic, and mixed. Another example he gives is that of the well-known Bannatyne WISC groupings (1974). It is certainly quite possible that groups formed by decision rules forged from clinical analysis of behaviors of interest will prove to have more valid and useful class correlates than will empirically derived groupings. As the two procedures are in no way mutually exclusive, an interesting comparison would be to determine whether certain outcomes are more predictable from subgroups derived by the clinically

based decision rules, whereas other outcomes may prove more predictable from subgroups derived by a cluster algorithm which seeks statistical
coherence between members of a group.

McKinney also describes behavioral LD subtypes, implying a distinction between subgroups derived through cluster analysis of behavioral
ratings as opposed to those derived from cluster analysis of psychoeducational, psychoneurological, or other psychometric test scores. This
distinction is really gratuitous in that, logically, there is no difference
between such data sets. Reliability of each and their theoretical relevance remain the two key issues which will influence their validity as
predictors of correlates of interest.

In all these cases, the same overarching concern applies: Has one
preselected the population from which one subsequently seeks subgroups? For example, McKinney describes subgroups based on a cluster
analysis of "59 school defined first and second grade LD children on
measures of intellectual ability (WISC–R), achievement (PIAT), and
classroom behavior (Classroom Behavior Inventory) taken when these
children were placed in special education classes." (1984, p. 47). Although clusters necessarily resulted—four in this case—one must be
careful not to assume that these subgroups are either unique to school-
defined LD children or, conversely, are generalizable to so-called LD
persons in other contexts, such as those referred to hospital diagnostic
clinics. It may well be the case that a group of unselected children from
the school's resource room would have yielded similar subgroups or, at
the very least, that subjects diagnosed as behaviorally disordered, or
emotionally disturbed, or educably mentally handicapped might have
been indistinguishable from so-called LD children and, hence, have
been placed in some of the subgroups had they been included in the
study. Such an expectation derives from knowledge of our inability to
distinguish substantially these diagnostic entities (Ysseldyke, 1983). Furthermore, there is no guarantee that an unselected group of children
from the same school might not have yielded the same or similar clusters
suggesting that the clusters may have little to do with the problem
surrounding what some may view as learning disability but may be the
grouping characteristics which result from normal statistical variability
of the scores in the given population.

The important issue is that one consciously understands the domain
of one's supraordinate population. By allowing a broader range of subjects into one's search for subgroups, and by treating the formation of
subgroups as part of one's experimental procedures rather than accepting a sample already constituted, knowledge otherwise excluded may be
uncovered. For example, one may find a continuum of subgroups show-

ing similar profiles but of different degrees of severity, those less severe perhaps being schooled in regular classrooms without any benefit of special assistance. They may differ only in degree but not in kind from students served by special education. One may find similar subgroups with minor variations as age increases, leading to new developmental hypotheses. One may also find subgroups which, by the researcher's theoretical orientation and definitional preference, embody the true meaning of specific learning disabilities.

Such subgroups may then be used as the focus for subsequent research in a manner described previously. But among the subjects in the subgroups thought to be true LD subjects, one may be most surprised to find children who have not been referred or diagnosed LD but who remain without special assistance in regular education. Their absence from special education services would likely be explained by the sociological variables (discussed earlier in this chapter), or behavioral docility, or compensory strengths, or other personality characteristics acceptable in the regular education context. The implication of this suggestion is enormous: It is that one can choose one's own subgroups—those of interest—for study without prejudicing one's findings by the omission of subjects from the sample due to the host of sociological and personality variables that intervene in the diagnostic referral and placement process. Bias added by the inclusion of subjects labeled "LD" by virtue of this same set of confounding variables is also avoided. The problem for the researcher, though, is that thought must be given to the subject-selection process and questions of pragmatic and theoretical nature answered well prior to what is now typically conceived of as the initiation of one's actual experiment.

THE SOCIOLOGICAL CONTEXT OF EDUCATIONAL FAILURE

Up to these closing remarks, I have treated personality, social, pedagogical, and sociological variables as though they all were variables confounding our search for the true LD sample. Certainly, with the procedures described, one could select subgroups defined by a set of scores reasonably free of the influence of such confounding variables. Such scores, though, would likely have to be carefully assessed in a laboratory context and represent measures of traits or behaviors uninfluenced by these allegedly confounding variables. One might even employ the additional tactic of establishing normative tables with which to regress out the effects of sociological variables such as race, personality variables such as locus of control, and so forth. In the interest of isolating more "pure" LD groups—ones in which the problem clearly lies within the individual rather than in the school or home context—one could attempt to eliminate all these influences from the measures. But here one must be most careful to assure that one's research in its sample selection does not become a slave to social fiction: the existence of a sole LD group whose disorders stem exclusively from intrinsic deficits. One may be discarding some of the most predictive and interesting variables involved in understanding children's learning problems.

Certainly, researchers have every right to choose their sample as they wish, and I have argued throughout this chapter that it is their abdication of this responsibility, not their abuse of it, that has resulted in the plethora of studies which defy integration. One may seek pure LD subjects with missionary zeal, but one should do so only after asking whether such is one's real concern. If one is interested in literal comprehension deficits, should one reasonably omit from one's sample bilingual children not labeled LD? Or perhaps, one should include them and find empirically that some represent a particular subgroup whose deficit is due to their bilingualism, whereas others resemble the single-language child on all measures and had best be understood within that context. An open mind on such issues may generate more knowledge than one which falls prey to definitional prejudgment. Similarly, should a subject's disproportionately weak visual skills (to the point of being legally blind) cause the researcher to omit the child from the sample when it may be the case that this child on all other scores excluding visual acuity resembles that of a subgroup of what otherwise is seen as learning disabled? In essence, by prejudging a child's group membership for research purposes, adopting instead those groupings simplistically rendered by tradition and present practice based upon administrative concerns, researchers abdicate their role of finding new knowledge about those who struggle with deficits. In doing so, they perpetuate the administrative structure by being dependent upon it—and bias their research in the process.

If research is ever to have an impact on children whose deficits, either alone or in combination with educational and other sociological variables, cause them to fail in school, researchers must free themselves of preconceived notions about children's school failure. Instead, researchers must be willing to plot their own course, to suspend judgment, and to employ their best guesses in the form of theoretical models to the broadest population of relevance. By allowing the data to speak for themselves without the biases brought to research by present social policy, we may uncover knowledge about the nature and the remediation of deficient performance. Such new knowledge may cause us to rethink our whole educational delivery system, let alone the specific remedial strategies appropriate for any given child.

REFERENCES

Anderberg, M. R. (1973). *Cluster analysis for application*. New York: Academic Press.

Bannatyne, A. (1974). Diagnosis: A note on recategorization of the WISC Scaled scores. *Journal of Learning Disabilities, 7,* 272–274.

Boder, E. (1973). Developmental dyslexia: A diagnostic approach based on three atypical reading-spelling patterns. *Developmental Medicine and Child Neurology, 15,* 663–687.

Clements, S. (1966). *Minimal brain dysfunction in children*. Public Health Service Publications, No. 415. Washington, D.C.: Department of Health, Education, and Welfare.

Connors, C. K. (1969). A teacher rating scale for use in drug studies with children. *American Journal of Psychiatry, 126,* 152–156.

Cruickshank, W. M. (1977). Myths and realities in learning disabilities. *Journal of Learning Disabilities, 10,* 51–58.

Cruickshank, W. M. (1978). Response to Elkins. *Journal of Learning Disabilities, 11,* 69–70.

Dunn, L. (1968). Special education for the mildly retarded: Is much of it justified? *Exceptional Children, 35,* 5–24.

Federal Register. (1977). Procedures for evaluating specific learning disabilities. 42(250) (December 29): Section 121a.541. Washington, D.C.: Department of Health, Education and Welfare, Office of Education.

Hammill, D. D., & Larsen, S. (1974). The relationship of selected auditory perceptual skills and reading ability. *Journal of Learning Disabilities, 7,* 429–435.

Keogh, B., & Major-Kingsley, S., Omori-Gordon, & Reid, H. P. (1982). *A system of marker variables for the field of learning disabilities*. Syracuse, NY: Syracuse University Press.

Kirk, S. A. (1963). Behavioral diagnosis and remediation of learning disabilities. In O. M. Chute (Ed.). *Conference on Exploration into the Problems of the Perceptually Handicapped Child*. Evanston, IL., Fund for Perceptually Handicapped Children, Inc.

Kirk, S. A., & Elkins, J. (1975). Characteristics of children enrolled in the child service demonstration centers. *Journal of Learning Disabilities, 8,* 630–637.

Kirk, S. A., & McCarthy, J. M. (1975). *Learning Disabilities: Selected ACLD papers*. Boston: Houghton Mifflin.

Kirk, S. A., Senf, G. M., & Larsen, R. P. (1981). In W. M. Cruickshank & A. A. Silver (Eds.). *Bridges to Tomorrow*. Vol. 2 (pp. 1–16). Syracuse, Syracuse University Press.

Lieberman, L. M. (1980). The implications of noncategorical special education. *Journal of Learning Disabilities, 13,* 65–68.

Luick, A. H., & Senf, G. M. (1979). Where have all the children gone? *Journal of Learning Disabilities, 12,* 285–287.

Mann, L., Davis, C. H., Boyer, C. W., Metz, C. M., & Wolford, B. (1983). LD or not LD, that was the question: A retrospective analysis of child service demonstration centers compliance with the federal definition of learning disabilities. *Journal of Learning Disabilities, 16,* 14–17.

McKinney, J. D. (1984). The search for subtypes of learning disability. *Journal of Learning Disabilities, 17,* 43–50.

McLeod, J. (1983). Learning disability is for educators. *Journal of Learning Disabilities, 16,* 23–24.

Norman, C. A., & Zigmond, N. (1980). Characteristics of children labeled and served as learning disabled in school systems affiliated with child service demonstration centers. *Journal of Learning Disabilities, 13,* 542–547.

Orton, S. T. (1937). *Reading, writing and speech problems in children.* New York: Norton.

Rourke, B. P. (1985). *Neuropsychology of learning disabilities.* New York: The Guilford Press.

Sarason, S. B. (1970). *The creation of settings and the future of societies.* San Francisco: Jossey-Bass Publishers.

Sarason, S. B. (1982). *The culture of the school and the problem of change.* 2nd ed. Boston: Allyn & Bacon.

Satz, P., & Morris, R. (1981). Learning disability subtypes: A review. In F. J. Pirozzolo & M. C. Wittrock (Eds.). *Neuropsychological and Cognitive Processes in Reading.* New York: Academic Press.

Senf, G. M. (1972). An information integration theory and its application to normal reading acquisition and reading disability. In N. D. Bryant & C. E. Kass (Eds.). *Leadership Training Institute in Learning Disabilities,* Vol. II, pp. 303–391. Tucson: University of Arizona.

Senf, G. M. (1973). Learning Disabilities. In H. J. Grossman (Ed.). Symposium on learning disorders. *Pediatric Clinics of North America, 20:*3 (pp. 607–640). Philadelphia: W. B. Saunders.

Senf, G. M. (1975). Now whom would you hire to teach a failing reader? *Journal of Special Education, 9,* 151–154.

Senf, G. M. (1976a). Future research needs in learning disabilities. In R. P. Anderson & C. G. Halcomb (Eds.). *Learning Disability/Minimal Brain Dysfunction Syndrome: Research Perspectives and Applications* (pp. 249–267) Springfield, IL: Thomas.

Senf, G. M. (1976b). Model centers program for learning disabled children: Historical perspective. In R. P. Anderson & C. G. Halcomb (Eds.). *Learning Disability/Minimal Brain Dysfunction Syndrome: Research Perspectives and Applications* (pp. 10–26). Springfield, IL: Thomas.

Senf, G. M. (1976c). Some methodological considerations in the study of abnormal conditions. In R. Walsh & W. Greenough (Eds.). *Environment As Therapy for Brain Dysfunction.* New York: Plenum Press.

Senf, G. M. (1977). A perspective on the definition of LD. *Journal of Learning Disabilities, 10,* 537–539.

Senf, G. M. (1978). Implications of the final procedures for evaluating specific learning disabilities. *Journal of Learning Disabilities, 11,* 124–126.

Senf, G. M. (1981). Issues surrounding the diagnosis of learning disabilities: Child handicap versus failure of the child-school interaction. In T. R. Kratochwill (Ed.). *Advances in School Psychology,* Vol 1 (pp. 83–131). Hillsdale: Lawrence Erlbaum Associates.

Senf, G. M., Luick, A. H., & Larsen, R. P. (1976). Consistent screen performance profiles isolated among first graders with school problems by using cluster analysis. Paper presented at Association for Children with Learning Disabilities International Conference, Seattle (March).

Sokal, R. R., & Sneath, P. H. A. (1963). *Principles of numerical taxonomy.* San Francisco: W. H. Freeman.

Strauss, A., & Kephart, N. C. (1955). *Psychopathology and education of the brain-injured child,* Vol II. New York: Grune and Stratton.

Strauss, A., & Lehtinen, L. (1947). *Psychopathology and education of the brain-injured child,* Vol I. New York: Grune and Stratton, 1947.

Torgesen, J. K. (1982). The use of rationally defined subgroups in research on learning disabilities. In J. D. Das, R. F., Mulcahy, A. F. Wall (Eds.). *Theory and Research in Learning Disabilities.* New York: Plenum Press.

Torgesen, J. K., & Houck, G. (1980). Processing deficiencies in learning disabled children who perform poorly on the digit span task. *Journal of Educational Psychology, 72,* 141–160.

Tryon, R. C., & Bailey, D. E. (1970). Cluster analysis. New York: McGraw-Hill Book Co.

Tucker, J., Stevens, L. J., & Ysseldyke, J. E. (1983). Learning disabilities: The experts speak out. *Journal of Learning Disabilities, 16,* 6–14.

Weener, P. (1981). On comparing learning disabled and regular classroom children. *Journal of Learning Disabilities, 14,* 227–232.

Weener, P., & Senf, G. M. (1982). Learning Disabilities. In H. E. Mitzel (Ed.). *Encyclopedia of Educational Research.* New York: Macmillan.

Wiederholt, J. L. (1974). Historical perspectives on the education of the learning disabled. In L. Mann & D. A. Sabatino (Eds.). *The Second Review of Special Education.* Philadelphia: JSE Press.

Ysseldyke, J. E. (1983). Current practices in making psychoeducational decisions about learning disabled students. *Journal of Learning Disabilities, 16,* 226–233.

Ysseldyke, J. E., & Algozzine, B. (1983). LD or not LD: That's not the question! *Journal of Learning Disabilities, 16,* 29–31.

Zigler, E., & Phillips, L. (1961). Psychiatric diagnosis, a critique. *Journal of Abnormal and Social Psychology, 63,* 607–617.

3

Approaches to Assessment

GERALD TINDAL
DOUG MARSTON

INTRODUCTION

One of the greatest problems facing educators today is that of developing appropriate assessment procedures, ones that contribute to establishing meaningful educational programs. The extent of this problem is reflected readily in many of the practices currently found in schools. As Ysseldyke, Thurlow, Graden, Wesson, Algozzine, and Deno (1983) state, current psychoeducational decision making is characterized by many serious deficiencies. In their summary of generalizations from 5 years of research, nine conclusions have direct implications for the current practice of assessment.

1. The special-education team decision-making process, as currently employed in public school settings, is, at best, inconsistent. The process operated to verify problems first cited by teachers.
2. Placement decisions made by teams of individuals have very little to do with the data collected on students.
3. Many nonhandicapped students are being declared eligible for special-education services.
4. There currently is no defensible system for declaring students eligible for LD services.
5. The identification of a student as learning disabled depends on what criteria are used.
6. There are no reliable psychometric differences between students labeled learning disabled and those simply considered to be low achievers.

55

Psychological and Educational
Perspectives on Learning Disabilities

7. The most important decision made in the entire assessment process is the decision by a regular classroom teacher to refer a student for assessment. There is a high probability that the (referred) student will be assessed and placed in special education.
8. There *are* technically adequate norm-referenced tests that can be used to make decisions about students. Most tests currently *used* in the psychoeducational decision-making process are technically inadequate.
9. Psychologists and special-education teachers were able to differentiate between low-achieving students and students labeled learning disabled with only 50% accuracy. Naive judges . . . evidenced 75% accuracy.

The problems that characterize the assessment of learning disabilities are not minor. Few issues related to the education of exceptional children are surrounded by as much controversy as that of assessing learning disabilities. Furthermore, the critical nature of this problem increases when it is recognized that in the 1981–1982 school year, over 1.74 million students were assessed and classified as learning disabled (*Education of the Handicapped*, 1983). Against this backdrop, scores of books and journal articles attempt to define the problems and propose solutions, whereas both state and federal legislation and the process of litigation define policy and implementation procedures.

Despite the increased attention given to the assessment of learning disabilities, problems continue to undermine the development of an empirically based and effective system for identifying and serving learning-disabled children. It is the purpose of the first part of this chapter to review the issues surrounding traditional assessment and to clearly define the major problems. In the second half, a viable alternative will be proposed, including both the theoretical framework and the empirical support upon which it is based.

ISSUES IN CURRENT MODELS OF ASSESSMENT

Generally, assessment is recognized to include a broad band of information-gathering activities. For example, Ysseldyke defines it as "the process of collecting data for the purposes of making educational decisions for and about children. Assessment is not synonymous with testing; testing is one part of assessment" (1977, p.4). In like manner, Smith and Niesworth refer to assessment as "distinctly different from . . . testing. Assessment involves obtaining a view of the individual as an organism interacting with its environment . . . and [leading] directly to the formulation of a diagnosis and appropriate remediation "(1969, pp.12–13).

It is generally accepted within the field that assessment must include a wide array of procedures. In the area of testing alone, a diverse battery of instruments may be administered, including intelligence tests, achievement tests, perceptual motor tests, diagnostic or criteria-referenced tests (both formal and informal), and personality tests. Further data may be collected through interviews (of parents, teachers, and students themselves), checklists, direct observation, and review of student records (Heron & Heward, 1982).

Not only are many procedures used in assessment, but assessment data also are collected for many purposes. There are at least five major psychoeducational decisions for which assessment data are collected (Salvia & Ysseldyke, 1981).

1. Screening/Identification includes the initial process of collecting assessment data and determines those students who may need special services. Often, further evaluation is warranted.
2. Classification/Placement involves the actual diagnosis of the child's specific learning disability, based upon an intensive assessment.
3. Instructional planning is often the result of further diagnostic assessment of the child's skills, knowledge, and achievement. Intervention programs or curricula then are chosen and introduced to the pupil.
4. Pupil evaluation encompasses the monitoring of the student's response to the prescribed intervention. Decisions regarding continuation or termination of the intervention are a function of the assessment data.
5. Program evaluation is similar to pupil evaluation except that data collection and analysis is aggregated across individuals. In this way, decisions concerning the effectiveness of programs such as Title I, remedial, compensatory, or special education can be evaluated at the administrative level.

Given the current technology of measurement and the model of psychoeducational decision making, "each of the five kinds of decisions requires that we use different assessment procedures and devices" (Ysseldyke, 1977, p. 6). Ysseldyke notes that decision makers generally have failed to differentiate their assessment strategies and procedures in light of the decision to be made. For example, intelligence tests are used to plan specific educational interventions, though they initially were developed to provide a normative reference for making indentification/classification decisions.

Although the practice of failing to select assessment procedures for the decision to be made is recognized as the source of many problems in

current psychoeducational decision making, another questionable practice has not received much attention. When different data are collected
at each juncture of the decision-making process, it is not possible to
validate consistently any of the decisions made, and the potential for
developing an effective evaluation methodology is lost. That is, the data
base is incohesive when different measurement systems are used for
each decision, thus precluding the assessment of change over time or
the aggregation of data within and across decisions.

A major premise of this chapter is that the need for a complete assessment, to provide a diverse and well-rounded picture of the student,
should not preclude the use of a consistent measurement system. And,
although different decisions may well confront educators throughout
the development and delivery of an educational program, again, there is
no inherent need to change the measurement system. In essence, it is
suggested that rather than obtaining a view of student functioning at
one point in time (and in one environment) through the use of a diverse
array of procedures and instruments, the focus of assessment should be
on documenting student functioning in several diverse environments
over time, utilizing a consistent measurement procedure.

A second major premise underlying this chapter is that assessment is
an ongoing activity throughout the delivery of special education services
and is not confined to a routine procedure conducted at the initiation of
such services. Although the focus of the decisions to be made may well
change during a student's educational program, the need for current
and relevant assessment data does not change. To date, the major focus
of assessment has been on identification and classification. In this regard, assessment has become an end in its own right, with little concern
for its role in providing appropriate educational programs. Nevertheless, "the primary purpose of evaluating children with learning problems should be to gather information that can be used in planning instructional programs" (Wallace & Larsen, 1978, p. 6). To accomplish
this, assessment procedures must be developed which, in addition to
having a consistent measurement base, also have relevance for all of the
different educational decisions—from identification and classification
through pupil and program evaluation.

A third major premise of this chapter is that efforts to broaden the role
of assessment throughout the decision-making process are limited by
both the philosophy upon which current practice is based and the measurement technology that is employed in most schools at present. The
remainder of this part presents a review of the major problems involved
in traditional assessment. The five decisions outlined earlier have been
reduced to two essential purposes for conducting assessment: (1) identi-

fication and classification (decisions 1 and 2), and (2) instructional planning and evaluation (decisions 3,4, and 5) (Wallace & Larsen, 1978)

ISSUES AND PROBLEMS IN IDENTIFICATION AND CLASSIFICATION

Without question, educators involved in assessment most commonly engage in gathering data for purposes of identifying and classifying pupils. The results of a recent survey indicate that school psychologists spend approximately 70% of their testing time for these purposes (Goldwasser, Meyers, Christenson, & Graden, 1983). It is not surprising then, that most of the literature in assessment revolves around issues in the identification and classification of students as learning disabled.

DEFINITIONAL AMBIGUITY

Lack of agreement in defining learning disabilities has hindered the development of effective assessment procedures. This definitional ambiguity is clearly outlined in a recent issue of *Journal of Learning Disabilities* (January 1983), and is also evident in the ever-changing definitions supplied by the Department of Education. In the past 2 decades, definitions have ranged from emphasis upon perceptual process, to "empirical" formulas, to evidence of significant aptitude-achievement discrepancies.

The question becomes, if we are unable to define LD, how can we adequately assess learning disabilities? Recent evidence suggests we cannot. Ysseldyke, Algozzine, Shinn, and McGue (1982) compared LD and non-LD (low-achieving) students on a wide range of intelligence, achievement, perceptual, and behavioral measures. On 49 psychometric test scores, there was a high degree of overlap between the two groups, thus suggesting little difference between members of each group. Further research by Ysseldyke, Algozzine, and Epps (1983) demonstrated that the diagnosis of LD was a function of the criteria used in assessment. When these researchers applied several popular LD definitions to the test scores of "normal" students, they found that 85% of the students were identified as LD by at least one definition. When the same criteria were applied to LD students, 4% were not labeled LD by any definition. Finally, when educators were provided normal test data in a simulated decision-making task, more than half of the participants identified an average student as eligible for special education (Algozzine & Ysseldyke, 1981).

OVERGENERALIZATION AND REIFICATION OF THE LABEL

Goldstein, Arkell, Ashcroft, Hurley, and Lilly (1975) argue that assessment and classification schemes encourage overgeneralizations about individual children. In essence, there is a tendency for educators to perceive similarly labeled children as alike in strengths and weaknesses, when, in fact, they usually are quite different. These researchers claim that such categorization does nothing to enhance the educational opportunities of handicapped children and lessens their chances for individuation of instruction.

Classification systems based upon test scores also can be faulted for their propensity to reify the resultant label (Goldstein et al., 1975). The phenomenon begins with a label being a descriptive term and culminates with the same label being used as an explanatory construct. For example, the poor performance of an LD child on the Visual Sequential Memory (VSM) subtest of the Illinois Test of Psycholinguistic Abilities (ITPA) often is attributed to a deficiency in the pupil's "visual sequential memory." This circular explanation serves only to reify the VSM subtest and encourages use of a fictional psychological process.

NATURE OF INSTRUCTION

A major deficiency of traditional assessment and classification systems is the tendency to ignore the interactive nature of instruction and to place sole responsibility upon the child (White & Haring, 1980). The view that we must attend to instructional interactions is shared by many who urge that poor performance should not be perceived solely as a child-based deficit (Coles, 1978; Lovitt, 1967). Adelman (1971) expresses this perspective in the following way:

> There is a viable alternative to this "disordered child" model. This alternative view emphasizes the dynamic nature of the process by which school skills are acquired. Thus, the model stresses that a given youngster's success or failure in school is a function of the interaction between his strengths, weaknesses, and limitations and the specific classroom situation factors he encounters, including individual differences among teachers and differing approaches to instruction. Stated differently, learning problems result not only from the characteristics of the youngster but also from the characteristics of the classroom situation to which he is assigned. (p.529)

Most measures used in the assessment of learning disabilities simply are not designed to focus on anything other than within-child characteristics.

TECHNICAL ADEQUACY

Any review of assessment procedures must include the test standards set forth by the American Psychological Association, the American Educational Research Association, and the National Council on Measurement in Evaluation (1974). Specifically, the validity, reliability, and norms of assessment instruments are vital to any discussion of technical adequacy.

Validity refers to how well a test measures the subject it was designed to assess (Nunnally, 1967). In the assessment of learning disabilities, we are beset with a number of tests that have questionable validity. Coles' (1978) review of perceptual tests such as the (Kirk, McCarthy, & Kirk, 1968), the Bender Visual-Motor Gestalt Test (Bender, 1938), the Developmental Test of Visual Perception (DTVP) (Frostig, Lefever, & Whittlesey, 1964), the Wepman Auditory Discrimination Test (Wepman, 1958), the Lincoln-Oseretsky Test of Motor Development (Sloan, 1955), the Graham-Kendall Memory for Designs Test (Graham & Kendall, 1960), and the Purdue Perceptual-Motor Survey (Roach & Kephart, 1966) reveals that these common LD assessment procedures possess uncertain validity. Reports of dubious validity are not specific to the perceptual tests; in addition, Coles (1978) suggests that the use of intelligence tests, for example, Wechsler Intelligence Scale for Children (Wechsler, 1949), and neurological tests are suspect as valid indicators of learning disability. Similar conclusions are reached by Arter and Jenkins (1979), Newcomer and Hammill (1975), and Hammill and Larsen (1974).

The extent to which a test provides consistent or repeatable data is an index of its reliability. Cronbach (1970) suggests that reliability coefficients approaching .90 are necessary for educational decision making. However, a review of tests commonly used in the diagnosis of learning disabilities, including the ITPA, DTVP, the Bender, and the Wepman, reveals that these devices have not established sufficient evidence of reliability (Arter & Jenkins, 1979). For example, Salvia and Ysseldyke (1981) report that the subtest reliabilities for the ITPA range from .45 to.93 for internal consistency, and .12 to .86 for test-retest reliability.

Finally, the standardization of norm-referenced tests plays an important role in determining the appropriateness of an assessment instrument. Ysseldyke (1979) warns that the pupil assessed must match the characteristics of the test's standardization sample. Thus, tests with small, restricted, or undefined standardization samples are of limited diagnostic value. Salvia and Ysseldyke (1981) list 27 tests commonly used in LD assessment, all having norms that are inadequately constructed or described.

BIAS AND DISCRIMINATION

The existence of bias and discrimination in assessment is an issue of great concern. Goldstein *et al.* (1975) report that discrimination against minority groups and the poor, due to culturally biased assessment, results in questionable educational practice. Litigation in our nation's courts has increased dramatically because of biased assessment. Goldstein *et al.* (1975) delineate three issues of primary concern to child advocates.

First is the issue of overrepresentation in special education of children from minority cultures. In *Larry P. v. Riles* (1979), the court agreed that wrongful placement in special education produced irreparable harm. As a result, the use of standardized intelligence tests for the purpose of placing Black students in educable mentally retarded (EMR) classes was suspended in the state of California. Additionally, the defendants were ordered to correct the imbalance in the proportion of Black students placed in special education. In this case, it had been determined that there was "less than one chance in a million" that a color-blind system of placement would have resulted in the overenrollment of Black children and underenrollment of non-Black children in the classes for EMR that actually had occurred in 1976-1977 (p.24).

A second issue concerns the administration of assessment procedures to children for whom English is not the primary language. In *Diana v. State Board of Education* (1970), the court ruled that such children must be assessed in both their primary language and English; clear guidelines were set to remedy the disproportionate numbers of students placed in special education.

Protection of parent and child rights in placement proceedings is viewed as the third significant issue before the courts. The case *Mills v. D.C. Board of Education* (1972) established the need for informed parent involvement during placement and the right to a hearing if there is disagreement with the school's placement decision.

Federal legislation (P.L. 94–142) seeks to rectify many of these problems by requiring non-discriminatory assessment procedures, placement in the least restrictive environment, and right to due process. Whereas the latter two safeguards can be promoted sufficiently in special-education delivery systems, the development of non-discriminatory assessment remains an elusive goal. Several researchers comment that there is little agreement on what constitutes non-discriminatory assessment (Hunter & Schmidt, 1976; McNemar, 1975; Peterson & Novick, 1976).

MISUSE OF TESTS AND TEST SCORES

When a child is referred for learning-disability services, it is essential that appropriate assessment procedures be employed by the diagnostician. This practice would seem to be easy enough to follow. To the contrary, Ysseldyke and Shinn (1981) were alarmed that "in many instances students are assessed with little clear consideration of the reasons for assessment as evidenced when those who assess children use the same assessment battery with all, independent of the reason for referral" (p. 420). These same authors suggest that tests often are not used for the purposes for which they were designed. As mentioned earlier, the Wechsler Intelligence Scale for Children—Revised (Wechsler, 1974) was specifically developed for identification purposes, yet many advocate its use in educational program planning. Research does not support such practice.

The misuse of test scores is also common in LD assessment. Percentile and grade-equivalent (GE) scores are highly susceptible to overinterpretation. As Thorndike and Hagen (1969) point out, they are not equal interval units. Subsequently, the aggregation or averaging of these scores must be viewed as highly suspect. Jenkins, Deno, and Mirkin (1979) argue that GE scores do not actually represent scores achieved by students performing above or below grade level. These scores are only estimates. For example, we cannot say that a fifth grader with a GE of 3.0 is performing at the third grade level. The use of normal curve equivalent (NCE) scores is a viable alternative; however its use is limited to those times that coincide with the test's norming periods.

APTITUDE-ACHIEVEMENT DISCREPANCIES AND
SUBTEST SCATTER

Recent federal definitions of learning disabilities specify that a significant discrepancy between a child's ability and his/her actual achievement must be demonstrated. Thus, how a child performs on standardized tests of intelligence (ability) and achievement has great impact on whether he/she is pronounced learning disabled. Similarly, discrepancy or variability among subtests of intelligence measures, commonly referred to as "subtest scatter," is viewed as indicative of learning difficulties (Sattler, 1974).

Neither practice is without severe limitations. First, the reliability-of-difference scores is notoriously low (Cronbach & Furby, 1970; Salvia & Clark, 1973). Thorndike and Hagen (1969) cite an example where two tests with high reliabilities—(.90) and substantial intercorrelation (.80)—produce a reliability-of-difference score of only .50. This situation is not uncommon in LD assessment, where intelligence and achievement measures with high reliabilities and intercorrelations are used to make probable unreliable decisions. The unreliability-of-difference scores also may explain the results of a study by Algozzine, Ysseldyke, and Shinn (1982) that compared two test batteries used in determining aptitude-achievement differences. LD pupils were administered the Woodcock-Johnson Psycho-Educational Battery (Woodcock & Johnson, 1977) and the WISC–R and Peabody Individual Achievement Tests (Dunn & Markwardt, 1970). These researchers found little agreement between the two discrepancy models for determining which students were learning disabled.

Second, the evidence refuting the use of subtest scatter as indicative of learning disabilities is just as compelling. In several studies, no significant differences between LD and non-LD children were found on WISC–R Verbal Performance discrepancy scores (Black, 1973; Kallos, Grabow & Guarino, 1961; Rudel & Denckla, 1976). In addition, examination of subtest scatter on the WISC–R in normal populations suggests that considerable variability is present (Kaufman, 1976); similar variability has been found for the Woodcock-Johnson Battery (Marston & Ysseldyke, in press). In all, the practice of interpreting discrepancy scores as diagnostic indicators of learning disabilities raises many concerns. Certainly, as Hallahan and Bryan (1981) conclude, "it is inadvisable to use discrepancy scores as the sole criterion for designating a child as learning disabled" (p.143).

ISSUES AND PROBLEMS IN INSTRUCTIONAL PLANNING AND EVALUATION

Although some standardized intelligence and achievement measures may possess the technical adequacy to aid in the identification and classification of LD students, they often are irrelevant for instructional purposes. Evidence for this statement is taken from two surveys of teachers. Ysseldyke and Shinn (1981) cite a 1961 study of over 5000 teachers where 71% reported that psychological assessments were not helpful. A more recent survey by Thurlow and Ysseldyke (1982) indicated that although a majority of psychologists believe the information they provided teachers for planning instruction was useful, far from a majority of the teachers believed it would be useful for such purposes. The following sections attempt to delineate the reasons for the failure of standardized assessment to satisfy teachers' needs for data relating to instructional planning and evaluation.

INADEQUATE SAMPLING OF CURRICULUM

After examining the vocabularies of several popular reading curricula, Jenkins and Pany (1978) did a content analysis of frequently used standardized achievement tests of decoding and reading skills. Their research established that there was little overlap among the tests and curricula. More specifically, any given standardized achievement test differentially sampled the vocabularies of the various reading series. Thus, a pupil's reading score on a given test is likely to be a function of the curriculum he/she is placed in or the test administered. This situation renders test scores almost meaningless, and certainly not useful for instructional planning.

In a more recent analysis by Floden, Porter, Schmidt, and Freeman (1980), the content coverage of four test series in fourth-grade mathematics was analyzed. They noted that "although . . . the tests are quite similar in some respects, striking differences are also evident" (p.111). In general, they found considerable variation in the content of the tests and concluded that the tests do not necessarily measure the same achievement, creating the potential for incongruity between the content of instruction and the measurement of outcome.

The essential point to be recognized here is that standardized achievement tests are samples of behavior. As such, they should be considered limited samples, for they are administered infrequently and do not adequately sample curricular content. The result is a general dissatisfaction among educators who need effective assessment strategies for educational planning.

APTITUDE-TREATMENT INTERACTION

Throughout the 1960s and early 1970s, learning-disabilities assessment was dominated by the Ability Training Model. The theories of Cruickshank (Hallahan and Cruickshank, 1973), Frostig (Frostig and Horne, 1964), Kirk (Kirk and McCarthy, 1961), and Kephart (1964) persuaded educators to assess students' strengths and weaknesses with a variety of tests that were designed to measure perceptual-motor, psycholinguistic, and psychological processing abilities. Once this diagnosis of the LD child was complete, pupil strengths were matched to corresponding instructional strategies. For example, visual learners were taught with teaching techniques that emphasized visual activities.

This matching of pupils' learning modalities with instructional modalities is known as the "aptitude-treatment interaction approach"; it has generated considerable research and comment. Clearly, the data are unfavorable to the Ability Training Model (Arter & Jenkins, 1977; Hammill & Larsen, 1974; Ysseldyke & Mirkin, 1982), demonstrating the ineffectiveness of prescribing teaching strategies based upon assessment of perceptual strengths. It would appear that instructional planning is not guided appropriately by this type of traditional LD assessment.

SENSITIVITY TO PUPIL PROGRESS

Standardized achievement and aptitude tests are not the answer to the question of how to best measure the progress of LD children. First, these tests usually are administered in a pre-post fashion, a questionable methodology given the acknowledged unreliability of change scores (Cronbach & Furby, 1970). Second, such tests, which are usually norm-referenced, are designed to measure individual differences, not student learning (Carver, 1974; Hively & Reynolds, 1975). Attempts to monitor pupil progress on IEP goals and objectives are subject to failure because percentile ranks, grade-equivalent scores, and standard-scale scores do not adequately reflect within-individual change.

Given these limitations of standardized tests, it is not surprising that entry into special education is a one-way street (Goldstein *et al.*, 1975). Once a student is placed in special classes, on the basis of test scores that are not designed to measure change, reentry into regular education will be problematic. The use of these types of standardized tests in measuring pupil progress, then, actually is not in compliance with the requirements of the least restrictive environment section of P. L. 94–142 (Jenkins, Deno, & Mirkin, 1979).

CONTINUITY OF DATA ACROSS EDUCATIONAL DECISIONS

An issue that involves both identification and instructional-planning decisions is the need for continuity in assessment data for each child across all decisions. Currently, it is probable that different tests will be used at each decision-making point during a child's special education placement. With respect to measuring pupil progress and instructional effectiveness, this type of educational practice evokes the familiar analogy of comparing apples and oranges. Without a common metric across educational decisions, assessment data may become ambiguous, inconsistent, and contribute dissonance rather than resolution to decision-making. For example, when given an LD child who has been identified with a WISC–R and PIAT, but whose progress is monitered with the Brigance, Key Math, and Stanford Diagnostic Reading Test, which information is most critical in making decisions concerning evaluation and possible termination of special education services? Recognizing this dilemma, Jenkins, Deno and Mirkin (1979) insist that consistent measurement across these domains must be developed.

AN ALTERNATIVE MODEL OF ASSESSMENT USING DIRECT AND FREQUENT MEASUREMENT

Although the litany of problems characterizing assessment practices currently used in schools could be expanded, there is little utility in such an endeavor. Rather, it is important to note that the problems are sufficient in depth and scope to preclude, not only the continuation of such practices, but probably any efforts at their improvement or modification. The measurement system appears to be the source of many problems; however, there also are problems inherent in the basic philosophy and assumptions upon which the current assessment system is based. Indeed, what is needed is a basic paradigm shift (Kuhn, 1970). Instead of retaining the current assumptions and models of assessment and evaluation, effort needs to be directed toward developing new models and extending them into school practice. Whereas there have been many critics of current practice and/or advocates of alternative procedures, there has been very little policy change as a consequence, and the educational system as a whole has not incorporated alternative procedures into practice. Before describing such alternative procedures, however, it is important to establish the principles upon which they are founded.

FOCUS OF ASSESSMENT

As noted by Ysseldyke and Algozzine (1983), current practice appears to be derived from a "search for pathology" premise (Sarason & Doris, 1979). The initial assumption made in the assessment process is that the problem resides within the student. All subsequent testing and measurement is aimed at documenting the specific nature and degree of disturbance. In fact, as noted earlier, the entire system of classification is based on this model.

An equally plausible assumption, however, is that the problem does not reside in the student, but rather in the environment and the interaction between the environment and the student. The recommendations to the Project on the Classification of Exceptional Children (Hobbs, 1975) by Goldstein *et al.* (1975) also hint at these directions. Specifically, their recommendation:

> is based on the premise that labels for children are less relevant in the classroom than appropriate pedagogy and evaluation. We therefore recommend that labels and systems of classification be abandoned in favor of more precise descriptions of the characteristics of individual children as they have implications for classroom interactions. (p. 55)

Essentially, these authors state that assessement should be directed at those functional skills and behaviors essential to the academic and social lives of LD children. In addition to an analysis of functional skills, the recommendation calls for an assessment of instruction, and indeed, the entire environment of the child. Lilly (1970) refers to this as examining exceptional situations rather than exceptional children.

> An exceptional school situation is one in which interaction between a student and his teacher has been limited to such an extent that external intervention is deemed necessary by the teacher to cope with the problem. . . . [Such a definition] does not specify the child (or the teacher) as the causative agent in any given situation. In essence, it demands a complete analysis of the classroom situation before statements are made concerning the nature of the problem and steps necessary to bring about a solution. (p. 48)

Engelmann, Granzin, and Severson (1979), arguing from the same perspective, propose a basic methodology for conducting this type of assessment. According to them, the diagnostic dilemma involves determining whether (and to what extent) the learner's behavior is a function of predisposition ("all factors that remain unaffected by instruction," p. 357) or instruction ("the effects of teaching," p. 357). The only way to extricate ourselves from this position is to rule out one of these two variables. However, since there is no obvious way to control predisposition, the focus of assessment must be on instruction. If as Engelmann *et al.* (1979) posit, instruction "is basically faultless and incapable of contributing to the learner's problems, we can draw conclusions about both predisposition and instruction. . . . The diagnosis perforce must be of instruction, not of the learner" (p. 357). The difference between this methodology and that in current practice reveals itself not only in the focus of measurement and assessment, but more importantly, in how measurement and assessment is conducted.

To date, most assessment practices are based on extremely limited samples of behavior. Generally, the techniques that are employed— whether tests, interviews, checklists, or observations—are administered only once. The emphasis is on documenting performance at that point in time only. As White and Liberty (1976) note, "the assessment of change has never been given as much attention as the procedures to obtain a single measure of performance" (p. 55). However, as they further state, "It matters not where a child is, it only matters how fast she/he is growing. . . . The big product should be change" (p. 55). The same approach is suggested by Carver (1974), in his statement that schools must go beyond traditional *psychometric* assessment where individual differences are the primary concern of evaluation. He prescribes an *edumetric* approach in which assessment is designed to measure change within individuals. The criterion-referenced test movement would appear to be a step in this direction (Hively & Reynolds, 1975; Popham, 1971).

Incorporating this into practice, however, necessitates a very fundamental change in the measurement system: A dependent variable must be developed that can be used on a continuous basis. As noted by Deno, Mirkin, and Shinn (1979), this measurement system must incorporate the following characteristics if it is to be usable on a frequent basis: (1) short duration (1–5 minutes), (2) easy to administer and score, (3) capable of generating many (unlimited) alternate forms, and (4) sensitive to changes in performance.

TECHNICAL ADEQUACY

A series of recent studies by Deno, Mirkin, and Chiang (1982), Deno, Mirkin, Lowry, and Kuehnle (1980), and Deno, Marston, and Mirkin (1982) investigated the technical adequacy—reliability and validity—of an alternative measurement system in the areas of reading, spelling, and written expression. The conceptual theme underlying these investigations was to develop an evaluation system based on the use of direct and frequent measurement of student performance in a curriculum. The strategy for conducting the research included the identification of various potential procedures within each of the content areas, procedures that appeared to exhibit the four characteristics previously noted. These measurement procedures then were validated with respect to several technically adequate published achievement tests.

In the area of reading, five measures were investigated: (1) having the student read aloud words from a list of words randomly sampled from the basal reader; (2) having the student read aloud passages taken out of the basal reader; (3) having the student orally define the meaning of words appearing in the basal reader; (4) having the student provide the word(s) that had been deleted in a passage sampled from the basal reader; and (5) having the student read words that were underlined in a passage taken from the basal reader (Deno, Mirkin, & Chiang, 1982). For all five measurement procedures, the number of words read correctly and incorrectly served as the dependent measures. The same students also were administered the following achievement tests: Subtest Five, Part A (Reading Comprehension) of Form B from the Stanford Diagnostic Reading Test (Karlsen, Madden, & Gardner, 1975), the Reading Comprehension subtest from the Peabody Individual Achievement Test (Dunn & Markwardt, 1970), the Word Identification and Word Comprehension subtests of Form A from the Woodcock Reading Mastery Test (Woodcock, 1973), and the Phonetic Analysis and Reading Comprehension subtests from the Stanford Achievement Test (Madden, Gardner, Rudman, Karlsen, & Merwin, 1973). After the issue of what to measure was investigated, research began on logistical considerations, such as where to measure from (the domain of sampling), how long to measure (length of administration), and how to score (dependent measure). From this research, it was determined that counting the number of words read aloud in 1 minute from either a word list or a passage in the basal reader would serve as a valid measure of a student's reading proficiency. The correlations between the reading rate measures of performance and the criterion measures ranged from .73 to .91, with most coefficients in the .80s. Further research by Fuchs and Deno (1981) in the area of reading established that this measurement system was also valid in monitoring progress through the curriculum.

In the area of spelling, the same procedures were used to identify a system for measuring student performance (Deno et al., 1980). The parameters of this measurement system again included the domain for sampling words, the length of test administration, and various scoring procedures (words spelled correctly and incorrectly, correct and incorrect letter sequences (White & Haring, 1980). The published achievement tests of spelling that were administered included the Test of Written Spelling (Larsen & Hammill, 1976), the spelling subtest from the Peabody Individual Achievement Test (Dunn & Markwardt, 1980), and the spelling section of the Stanford Achievement Test Primary III (Madden et al., 1973). The findings from this research indicated that the number of words spelled correctly or the number of correct letter sequences spelled in response to a dictated word list (sampled from either spelling or reading curricula) would serve as an appropriate measure of spelling. The correlations between the spelling rate measures of performance and the criterion measures were high, ranging from .80 to .96. Further, tests of 1-,2-, and 3-minute durations provided indices of spelling achievement consistent with the longer-duration published tests of spelling achievement.

In the area of written expression, the research focused on five procedures for measuring performance; (1) the total number of words written; (2) the number of words spelled correct; (3) the number of large words written (words with seven or more letters); (4) the number of uncommon words (those not appearing in a list of common words compiled by Finn, 1977); and (5) the average number of words per T-unit (Hunt, 1965). The parameters of the measurement system that were investigated included the use of different stimuli for generating writing (pictures, story starters, and topic sentences) and various time limits. The criterion measures used to establish the validity of the measures included the Test of Written Language (Hammill & Larsen, 1978), the Stanford Achievement Test, Intermediate I, Word Usage subtest (Madden *et al.*, 1973) and the Developmental Sentence Scoring System (Lee & Canter, 1971). The results from this research indicated that counting the total number of words written or the total number of correctly spelled words, in response to either a story starter or a topic sentence, provided an appropriate index of writing proficiency and correlated well (.70 or higher) with the criterion measures (Deno, Marston, & Mirkin, 1982).

The measurement system developed in math includes random sampling of computation problems for each operation (addition, subtraction, multiplication, and division), providing four separate measures, each 2 minutes in duration. Student performance is scored for the number of digits correct and incorrect. At this time, research has not yet been conducted on the criterion validity of measures of mathematics. In two field settings where this measurement system has been implemented, there is some preliminary evidence establishing the discriminant validity of these procedures.

The work of Marston (1982) corroborated the findings of the criterion validity of the alternate measures of reading, spelling, and written expression. In addition, he examined their reliability (both test-retest and alternate form) and found high coefficients (.80 to .90) for rate correct in reading and spelling, and moderate coefficients (.60) for written expression. Two other investigations of the reliability of these measures have been conducted, with similar conclusions. Using a standard measurement task, Tindal, Marston, and Deno (1983) determined the reliability of the measures in reading, spelling, and most areas of math to be high or moderately high (.70 to .95). In written expression and two areas of math, the coefficients were moderate (.55). Another study, conducted specifically on grade-level measures, used in one special education cooperative in Minnesota (Pine County), reached the same conclusions regarding reliability (Tindal, Germann, & Deno, 1983).

Throughout all of this research, analyses were conducted on changes in performance levels over time. In the original validation research, it was determined that there was consistent growth over grades. In the research by Marston (1982) and Tindal, Germann, and Deno (1983), consistent growth occurred both over grades and within each grade, over periods of 10 weeks and 8 months, respectively.

In conclusion, much of this research has established that: (1) these alternative measures of reading, spelling, and writing are highly related to more accepted and commonly used measures of achievement in each of the respective areas; (2) the measures are reliable; and (3) the measures are sensitive to growth and show developmental changes within and across grades.

IDENTIFICATION / ELIGIBILITY

Although the alternative measures initially were developed for use by the classroom teacher in the evaluation of his/her instructional programs, recent research focused on using this same data base for assessment to determine eligibility. In a study by Shinn, Ysseldyke, Deno, and Tindal (1982), the direct measures in reading, spelling, and writing were administered to 49 students. These students were a subset of students who had been tested during the previous year on a wide range of commonly used psychometric tests (Ysseldyke *et al.*, 1982). Although the results from the published psychometric instruments revealed an extreme amount of overlap in the scores of learning-disabled students and low-achieving students, the results from the direct measures of students' reading, writing, and spelling skills indicated considerably less overlap, with the performance of learning-disabled students significantly lower than their low-achieving counterparts.

In studies by Deno, Marston, Shinn, and Tindal (1983) and Marston (1982), it was determined that students receiving learning-disability services read significantly fewer words correctly than did students receiving Title I services. It is interesting to note that in all of the above studies, slope of improvement was investigated as a potential discriminator between the learning-disabled students and their regular education counterparts, and no differences were found.

Finally, Marston, Tindal, and Deno (1982) using a post-hoc classification based on a discriminant function analysis, found that the direct measures of reading and written expression correctly identified 83% and 73%, respectively, of the students already deemed eligible for special education, using more traditional criteria involving ability and achievement discrepancies. In contrast, the use of published achievement tests—the PIAT (Dunn & Markwardt, 1970) and the SAT (Karlsen, Madden & Gardner, 1975) or the TOWL (Hammill & Larsen, 1978)—resulted in the correct placement of 86% and 80% in the areas of reading and written expression, respectively. They concluded that not only do the measures of fluency predict correct membership into special education about as accurately as the commercial measures of achievement, but both do quite well compared to more complicated procedures incorporating measures of ability. That is, most of the variance accounted for in the classification of students into special education appears to be from achievement.

To use the direct measures in the assessment of student eligibility for learning disabilities, however, it is necessary to have a criterion or standard upon which to base decisions. In the initial work of Deno and Mirkin (1977), an eligibility criterion was established by comparing referred students' performances to the median performance of a random sample of students from regular education. This index, called a "discrepancy ratio," is calculated by dividing the lower performance level (typically from the referred student) into the higher performance level (typically the median performance of regular education students). The result is a value that describes how many times less proficient referred students are compared to the normative performance of their regular education peers. For instance, if a student referred for special education reads 35 words per minute from a grade-appropriate basal passage and his/her peers read median of 105 words per minute, the resulting fraction is 105/35, which reduces to a 3.0 discrepancy. That is, the referred student is three times less proficient ($-3.0\times$) in reading than his/her peers. Deno and Mirkin (1977) initially suggested a cutoff for placement into special education at a discrepancy ratio of 2.0. Although further investigation needs to be conducted on this issue, recent research from three studies corroborates this criterion for placement into special education.

In a study conducted by Marston, Tindal, and Deno (1984), an analysis was conducted on the percentages of students identified, using various discrepancy criteria (ranging from $-1.5\times$ to $-3.0\times$). Using national incidence rates as an informal criterion, it appeared that a discrepancy ratio of $2.0\times$ results in percentages comparable to national rates. For 1981–1982, approximately 6.3% of the school-age population in the United States was identified as either LD or MR (*Education of the Handicapped*, 1983). In contrast, using rate of performance in identifying exceptionality (LD/MR) in grades 3–6, and in the areas of reading, spelling, and written expression, the approximate percentage of students identified as $2.0\times$ less proficient was around 5.5–9%; with $2.5\times$ and $3.0\times$ as the criteria, the percentages were approximately 3–6%. In the first and second grades, the percentages identified were much higher, suggesting a need to reconsider either the criteria used in eligibility or the domain from which the measurement items are sampled. That is, a more stringent criterion could be adopted (i.e., 5.0 × discrepant) or the measurement procedures could sample items which generate more responses at grades 1 and 2.

> Of the two solutions suggested, only the second is satisfactory. . . . Given the standard error of measurement for the procedures used with any of the academic tasks, the use of a more stringent criterion on a narrow range of scores could result in an unstable identified population. The task at hand should be to develop more and diverse items for each of the academic areas for the early grades. (Marston *et al.*, 1984)

Two studies have been conducted in which the measurement system was implemented in school settings, and comparisons were made to screening and identification procedures, using more typical procedures of teacher referral and ability-achievement measurement. In a study by Marston, Mirkin, and Deno (1984), a comparison was made between two groups on the rate of referral, differences in ability, achievement, and social behavior of the students referred, and differential rates of referral according to sex. They found that, overall, the same numbers of students were referred by the two procedures. However, teacher referrals consisted of significantly more males (80%) whereas the weekly measurement system showed no significant difference in rates of referral according to sex of the student. Academic achievement appeared to be the most important consideration in teacher referrals, although students referred by teachers were somewhat more likely to be rated as behavior problems. Finally, "students referred (and assessed) through weekly achievement measurement were as likely to have an aptitude-achievement discrepancy as students referred by teachers" (Marston *et al.*, 1984 p. i). That is, the level of ability or the discrepancies of ability and achievement did not differentiate the two groups.

In an analysis of eligibility criteria used in the Pine County Special Education Cooperative, which are based on the direct measures, comparisons were made of the percentages of students identified for various categories of disability services by the direct measures and by state and national incidence levels of the same categories (Tindal *et al.*, 1983). In the classification of learning disabilities, the percentages were similar, with 4.10% identified in Pine County, compared to 4.05% nationally, and 4.80% for the state of Minnesota. For the EMR category, approximately 1% more students were identified in Pine County than at the state or national levels. It should be noted, however, that the classification system used in Pine County is still in an experimental phase. During the year of this research, the criteria used for differential classification of LD and EMR included both level of discrepancy and the number of areas in which discrepancies occurred. Students discrepant in one area at a level of approximately $-2.0\times$ (2 times less proficient than peers) were identified as LD, whereas students discrepant in two or more areas at levels of $-3.0\times$ or more (3 times or more less proficient than peers) were identified as EMR. This classification system is not inflexible and is currently under further investigation. Indeed, when the procedure of classification is viewed as essentially a sociopolitical process based on very little scientific rigor (Tucker, Stevens, & Ysseldyke, 1983), adjustments can be made in the system to attain a level of identification in keeping with both the problems exhibited by the student population and the resources available to the school system.

Although the initial assessment is very critical in classifying students (i.e., as either LD or EMR), the use of a continuous measurement system throughout the educational program also becomes very important in corroborating the initial classification. As mentioned previously, the model of assessment proposed by Engelmann *et al.* (1979) is an attempt to delineate the degree to which the learners' problems are a function of "predisposition" and/or the environment. In this effort, assessment consists of the systematic arrangement and manipulation of the environment for purposes of weighing the importance of these two dimensions. Rather than relying on the construct validity of various measurement devices, there is a low-inference process of data collection to empirically document the scope and level of skills, given a particular environmental structure.

An adaptation of this perspective involves determining the degree to which the environment must be structured to accommodate the learners' problems. With students for whom the environment can be minimally modified and result in behavioral change, it can be inferred that predisposition is of less influence than the environment. In contrast, if major environmental changes must be made to accommodate individual students and create change in behavior, it can be inferred that predisposition is a more influential factor in influencing the outcome.

In this effort, there is very little concern with determining etiology or classifying students in any kind of explanatory fashion. The purpose of assessment and classification is to provide an administrative organization for allocating an appropriate type and level of service. Classification is not considered a definitive statement without further recourse to change. Rather, in determining whether a student is "learning disabled" or "educable mentally retarded," the emphasis is on providing an environment which is appropriate to the individual student, has the potential for changing the student's performance, and is a reasonable allocation of resources within the school. If this outcome is not achieved in the initial classification process, as indicated by progress monitoring, changes are made and the process is continued.

Because students are measured frequently and change of performance calculated as the critical index, it is possible to make this evaluation. For example, if, during the first year a student receives special education, there is improvement in response to minimal program changes, the inference can be made that the environment is quite influential and the student's disability quite specific. In this case, a classification of LD would be corroborated. However, if the data from this first year of special education indicate there is little improvement in performance in response to major program changes, the inference can be made that the environment is less influential and that the problem is more a function of the student's disability or his/her own unique characteristics. In this case, a classification of EMR would be corroborated. Again, it is important to note that, in this system, classification is viewed primarily as a process for obtaining the appropriate type and level of service for each individual student, not as a rigid statement concerning the etiology of the student's problems. In those cases where the initial classification is inappropriate and not corroborated, a reclassification would take place and special education services adjusted accordingly. In this system, analysis of classification is primarily dependent upon student performance outcomes during the delivery of special education, now in a process of corroboration.

In summary, there is ample empirical support for using a direct measurement system to determine eligibility for special education. The students identified as mildly handicapped (LD/EMR) are quite similar in many characteristics to those identified using more traditional procedures involving assessment of ability and achievement. Furthermore, the measurement system appears to be sensitive in discriminating current categories of exceptionality (EMR, LD, and Title I) from low achievers. Although measurement in this sytem is oriented toward documentation of achievement, with no formal assessment of ability, most of the variance is accounted for in the classification of students. Perhaps the distinction between ability and achievement is less than typically assumed. Indeed, this distinction recently has become blurred. As the Kaufmanns state in an interview, "we see existing intelligence tests as measuring what children have *learned* rather than their real mental-processing abilities" (Morris, 1983, p. 5). Similarly, in discussing the construct validity of standardized achievement tests, Airasian and Madaus (1983) state that "evidence suggests that they measure a general factor that is not much different from the general factor measured by many ability tests" (p. 106).

A measurement system based on achievement makes it possible to extend the range of decisions that can be addressed. That is, the same data base will prove useful in developing Individual Educational Plans (IEPs) and in evaluating the effects of instruction at both the individual and systems levels. In several school districts of the Midwest, the alternative measurement and evaluation procedures outlined in this essay have been implemented. In one system in particular, there has been systems-level implementation. Here, all psychoeducational decisions utilize curriculum-based measurement data, including the initial assessment, planning and evaluating IEPs, and summative evaluation at the individual and system level. The following is a very brief description of this system.

For purposes of assessment and eligibility determination, a local normative sample was established. Using a series of measures in all academic areas, some of which sampled from the local curriculum and some from across several curricula, approximately 30% of the regular education population was tested. During the course of 4 years, students were tested three times each year—in the fall (mid-September), winter (mid-January), and spring (mid-May)—for 2 consecutive years. This testing was conducted for 2 years at the elementary schools and for 2 years at the high schools. At the end of this norms-development project, approximately 8000 independently sampled students had been assessed in all three periods for both years. The actual norms calculated were the median scores for each grade and each academic year as well as the combined average for the 2 years.

These normative data were used for two primary purposes: determination of eligibility and outcome effectiveness. An eligibility criterion was established for allocating special-education services to those students falling out of the normal range on the curriculum-based measures. When students were referred, they were administered the same measures used in the development of the norms. The performance of these students was then compared to the average performance for the appropriate grade level and time of year, and a discrepancy quantified for determining the degree of deviance. In this school system, the discrepancy utilized a procedure from Deno and Mirkin (1977) referred to as the "discrepancy index." Computation of this index was accomplished by simply dividing the lower performance level (usually obtained by special education referrals) into the higher performance levels (usually obtained from the normative sample). Recent analyses on this index has revealed that it generally correlates with z scores. In the latest report from this school system, it was determined that the average performance of students found eligible for special education was over 2 standard deviations below the mean in spelling, and $1\frac{1}{2}$ standard deviations below the mean in reading and written expression. The discrepancy index for these areas ranged from four times below in spelling, to three times below and two times below in reading and written expression, respectively. In all three academic areas, the outcome of special education showed positive growth throughout the year. Using both z-scores and the discrepancy index, students served in special education performed at a higher level in the spring than the fall.

Whereas assessment data traditionally are used solely for purposes of screening and eligibility determination, a more efficient approach is to incorporate the results directly into an IEP. Considering the great cost in time and money spent on assessment, the data should serve more than classification purposes. As mentioned previously, the measurement procedures of data-based program modification, initially proposed by Deno and Mirkin (1977), are used for evaluating individual educational programs and developing appropriate modification. A major premise upon which that work was based involved the assumption that "at the present time we are unable to prescribe specific and effective changes in instruction for individual pupils with certainty" (p. 11). This assumption is just as valid today as it was 7 years ago. With the passage of P. L. 94–142, the principles and procedures of data-based program modification provide a very appropriate methodology for developing and monitoring progress on IEP goals. In this school system, it is important to note that the IEPs (both goals and objectives) provide a working document for the formative evaluation of instructional programs. Unlike what probably occurs with most IEPs (put away in the student's folder for future use only), this document is written in a manner that allows for frequent measurement and evaluation. All the information supplied on the IEP is transcribed onto a graph, which is referred to regularly in the evaluation process.

By incorporating the initial-assessment data into the monitoring of progress on IEP goals, both pupil and program evaluation can be established. The same data base is used for both and incorporates 2 measures of student achievement: (1) outcome on the IEP, and (2) performance relative to peers. These measures provide both a criterion-referenced and norm-referenced approach to evaluation, with the former providing greater emphasis on formative evaluation throughout the delivery of services and the latter providing greater emphasis on summative evaluation following the delivery of services. As alluded to earlier, the most recent outcome data from this school system indicate that special education services are indeed effective, a finding in stark contrast to the data reported by Carlberg and Kavale (1980). These latest data are in concert with the previous findings reported by Tindal et al., (1983).

In the final analysis, the adoption and implementation of a curriculum-based assessment/measurement/evaluation model must be data-based. This system should not be viewed as a singular procedure for educational decision making, but rather as a process for conducting such decisions. The alternative system described in this chapter clearly has capacity for expanding the role of assessment beyond simple classification. By obtaining the same data at the initial assessment and throughout program development and implementation, the potential exists not only for validating IEPs, but also for conducting both individual- and systems-level analyses of program effectiveness. And, a methodology is provided for evaluating potential solutions for addressing the many problems encountered by educators. As Kavale and Glass (1982) state, "special educators have too long been in the mildly embarrassing position of knowing less than has been proven" (p. 5). What is necessary is not simply an alternative measurement system, but one which provides an empirical basis for developing and evaluating educational programs.

REFERENCES

Adelman, H. S. (1971). The not-so-specific learning disability population. *Exceptional Children, 37,* 528–533.
Airasian, P., & Madaus, G. (1983). Linking testing and instruction: Policy issues. *Journal of Educational Measurement, 20*(2), 103–118.
Algozzine, B., & Ysseldyke, J. E. (1981). Special education services for normal children: Better safe than sorry. *Exceptional Children, 48,* 238–243.
Algozzine, B., Ysseldyke, J., & Shinn, M. (1982). Identifying children with learning disabilities: When is a discrepancy severe? *Journal of School Psychology, 20,* 299–305.
American Psychological Association, American Educational Research Association, and National Council on Measurement in Education (1974). *Standards for educational and psychological tests.* Washington, DC: American Psychological Association.
Arter, J., & Jenkins, J. (1977). Examining the benefits and prevalence of modality considerations in special education. *Journal of Special Education, 11,* 281–298.
Arter, J. A., & Jenkins, J. R. (1979). Differential diagnosis-prescriptive teaching: A critical appraisal. *Review of Educational Research, 49,* 517–555.
Bender, L. (1938). A visual-motor gestalt test and its clinical use. *American Orthopsychiatric Association Research Monograph, 3.*
Black, F. W. (1973). Neurological dysfunction and reading disorders. *Journal of Learning Disabilities, 6,* 313–316.
Blatt, B., & Garfunkel, F. Teaching the mentally retarded (1973). In R. Travers (Ed.). *Second Handbook of Research on Teaching* (pp. 632–656) Chicago: Rand-McNally, 1973.
Carlberg, C., & Kavale, K. (1980) The efficacy of special versus regular class placement for exceptional children: A meta-analysis. *Journal of Special Education, 14*(3), 295–309.

Carver, R. P. (1974). Two dimensions of tests: (1974). Psychometric and edumetric. *American Psychologist, 29*, 512–518.

Coles, G. S. (1978). The learning disabilities test battery: Empirical and social issues. *Harvard Educational Review, 48*, 313–340.

Cronbach, L. J. (1970). *Essentials of psychological testing.* New York: Harper & Row.

Cronbach, L. J., & Furby, L. (1970). How we should measure "change"—or should we? *Psychological Bulletin, 1*, 68–80.

Deno, S., Marston, D., & Mirkin, P. K. (1982). Valid measurement procedures for continuous evaluation of written expression. *Exceptional Children, 48*, 368–371.

Deno, S., Marston, D., Shinn, M., & Tindal, G. (1983). Oral reading fluency: A simple datum for scaling reading disability. *Topics in Learning and Learning Disabilities, 2*(4), 53–59.

Deno, S., & Mirkin, P. K. (1977). *Data-based program modification: A manual.* Reston, VA: The Council for Exceptional Children.

Deno, S., Mirkin, P. K., & Chiang, B. (1982). Identifying valid measures of reading. *Exceptional Children, 49*, 36–45.

Deno, S., Mirkin, P. K., Lowry, L., & Kuehnle, K. (1980). *Relationships among simple measures of spelling and performance on standardized achievement tests* (Research Report No. 21). Minneapolis: University of Minnesota, Institute for Research on Learning Disabilities (ERIC Document Reproduction Service No. ED 197 508).

Deno, S., Mirkin, P., & Shinn, M. (1979) *Behavioral perspectives on the assessment of learning disabled children* (Monograph No. 12). Minneapolis: University of Minnesota, Institute for Research on Learning Disabilities (ERIC Document Reproduction Service No. ED 185 769).

Diana v. State Board of Education (Jan 7, 1970; June 18, 1973). Civ. Act. No. 70–37 RFP (N. D. Cal.).

Dunn, L. M., & Markwardt, F. C. (1970). *Peabody individual achievement test.* Circle Pines, MN: American Guidance Service.

Education of the Handicapped. (1983). Arlington, VA: Capitol Publications, *9*, 13.

Engelmann, S., Grazin, A., & Severson, H. (1979). Diagnosing instruction. *Journal of Special Education, 13*, 355–363.

Finn, P. (1977). Computer-aided description of mature word choices in writing. In C. R. Cooper & L. Odell (Eds.). *Evaluating Writing: Describing, Measuring, Judging.* Urbana, IL: National Council of Teachers of English.

Floden, R., Porter, A., Schmidt, W., & Freeman, D. (1980) Don't they all measure the same thing? In E. Baker & E. Quellnalz (Eds.). *Educational Testing and Evaluation.* (Beverly Hills, CA: Sage.

Frostig, M., Lefever, W., & Whittlesey, J. (1964). *Developmental test of visual perception.* Palo Alto, CA: Consulting Psychologist Press.

Frostig, M., & Horne, D. (1964) *The Frostig program for development of visual perception.* Chicago: Follett.

Fuchs, L., & Deno, S. L. (1981). *The relationship between curriculum-based mastery measures and standardized achievement tests in reading* (Research Report No. 57). Minneapolis: University of Minnesota, Institute for Research on Learning Disabilities (ERIC Document Reproduction Service No. 212–662).

Fuchs, L., Fuchs, D., & Warren, L. (1982). *Special education practice in evaluating student progress toward goals* (Research Report No. 81). Minneapolis: University of Minnesota, Institute for Research on Learning Disabilities (ERIC Document Reproduction Service No. ED 224 197).

Glass, G. Integrating findings: (1977). The meta-analysis of research. *Review of Research in Education, 5*, 351–379.

Goldstein, H., Arkell, C., Ashcroft, S. C., Hurley, O. L., & Lilly, S. M. (1975). Schools. In N. Hobbs (Ed.). *Issues in the Classification of Children.* (pp. 4–61) San Francisco: Jossey-Bass Publishers.

Goldwasser, E., Meyers, J., Christenson, S., & Graden, J. (1983). The impact of P. L. 94–142 on the practice of school psychology: A national survey. *Psychology in the Schools, 20*, 153–164.

Graham, F. K., & Kendall, B. S. (1960) *Memory for designs test.* Missoula, MT: Psychological Test Specialist.

Hallahan, D. P., & Bryan, T. H. (1981). Learning disabilities. In J. M. Kauffman & D. P. Hallahan (Eds.). *Handbook of Special Education.* Englewood Cliffs, NJ: Prentice-Hall.

Hallahan, D., & Cruikshank, W. (1973). *Psychoeducational foundations of learning disabilities.* Englewood Cliffs, NJ: Prentice-Hall.

Hammill, D. D., & Larsen, S. C. (1974). The effectiveness of psycholinguistic training. *Exceptional Children, 41*, 5–14.

Hammill, D. D., & Larsen, S. C. (1978). *The test of written language.* Austin, TX: Pro-Ed.

Heron, T., & Heward, S. (1982). Ecological assessment: Implications for teachers of learning disabled students. *Learning Disability Quarterly, 5*(2), 117–125.

Hively, W., & Reynolds, M. C. (Eds.) (1975) *Domain-referenced testing in special education.* Reston, VA: The Council for Exceptional Children.

Hobbs, N. (Ed.) (1975). *Issues in the classification of children* (vols. 1 & 2). San Francisco: Jossey-Bass Publishers.

Hunt, K. W. (1965). *Grammatical structures written at three grade levels* (Research Report No. 3). Champaign, IL: National Council of Teachers of English.

Hunter, J. E., & Schmidt, F. L. (1976) Critical analysis of the statistical and ethical implications of various definitions of test bias. *Psychological Bulletin, 83*, 1053–1071.

Jenkins, J. R., Deno, S. L., & Mirkin, P. K. (1979). Measuring pupil progress toward the least restrictive alternative. *Learning Disability Quarterly, 2*, 81–92.

Jenkins, J., & Pany, D. (1978). Standardized achievement tests: How useful for special education? *Exceptional Children, 44* (6), 448–453.

Kallos, G. L., Grabow, J. M., & Guarino, E. A. (1961). The WISC profile of disabled readers. *Personnel and Guidance Journal, 39*, 476–478.

Karlsen, B., Madden, R., & Gardner, E. F. (1975). *Stanford diagnostic reading test* (Green level, Form B). New York: Harcourt Brace Jovanovich.

Kaufman, A. (1976). A new approach to the interpretation of test scatter on the WISC–R. *Journal of Learning Disabilities, 9*(3), 33–41.

Kavale, K., & Glass, G. (1982). The efficacy of special education interventions and practices: A compendium of meta-analysis findings. *Focus on Exceptional Children, 15*(4), 1–16.

Kephart, N. (1964). Perceptual motor aspects of learning disabilities. *Exceptional Children, 31*(4), 201–206.

Kirk, S., & McCarthy, J. (1961). *The ITPA: An approach to differential diagnosis.* Urbana, IL: University of Illinois Press.

Kirk, S. A., McCarthy, J. J., & Kirk, W. D. (1968). *Illinois test of psycholinguistic abilities.* Urbana: University of Illinois Press.

Kuhn, T. S. (1970). *The structure of scientific revolutions.* Chicago: University of Chicago Press.

Larry P. v. Riles (Oct. 16, 1979). No. C–71–2770 RFP (N. D. Cal.)

Larsen, S. C., & Hammill, D. D., (1976). *Test of written spelling.* Austin, TX: Empiric Press.

Lee, L., & Canter, S. M. (1971). Developmental sentence scoring. *Journal of Speech and Hearing Disorders, 36,* 335–340.

Liberty, K. A. (1975). *Decide for progress: Dynamic aims and data decisions.* Seattle: Experimental Education Unit, Child Development and Mental Retardation Center, University of Washington.

Lilly, M. S. (1970). Special education: A teapot in a tempest. *Exceptional Children, 37,* 43–49.

Lovitt, T. C. (1967). Assessment of children with learning disabilities. *Exceptional Children, 34,* 233–239.

Madden, R., Gardner, E., Rudman, H., Karlsen, B., & Merwin, J. (1973). *Stanford achievement test, primary level III.* New York: Harcourt Brace Jovanovich.

Marston, D. (1982). *The technical adequacy of direct, repeated measurement of academic skills in low achieving elementary students.* Unpublished Doctoral Dissertation. Minneapolis: University of Minnesota.

Marston, D., Mirkin, P. K., & Deno, S. (1984). Curriculum-based measurement: An alternative to traditional screening, referral and identification of learning disabled students. *Journal of Special Education, 18*(2), 109–118.

Marston, D., Tindal, G., & Deno, S. L. (1982). *Predictive efficiency of direct, repeated measurement: An analysis of cost and accuracy in classification* (Research Report No. 104). Minneapolis: University of Minnesota, Institute for Research on Learning Disabilities (ERIC Document Reproduction Service No. ED 226–052).

Marston, D., Tindal, G., & Deno, S. L. (1984). Eligibility for learning disability services: A direct and repeated measurement approach. *Exceptional Children, 50*(6), 554–556.

Marston, D., & Ysseldyke, J. (1984). Concerns in interpreting subtest scatter on the Woodcock-Johnson Psycho-Educational Battery. *Journal of Learning Disabilities, 17*(10), 588–591.

McNemar, Q. (1975). On so-called test bias. *American Psychologist, 30,* 848–851.

Mills v. Board of Education of D.C. (1972). 348 F. Supp 866 (D.D.C.).

Mirkin, P. K., & Deno, S. L. (1980). *Formative evaluation in the classroom: An approach to improving instruction* (Research Report No. 10). Minneapolis: University of Minnesota, Institute for Research on Learning Disabilities (ERIC Document Reproduction Service No. ED 185 754.

Mirkin, P., Deno, S., Tindal, G., & Kuehnle, K. (1983). Frequency of measurement and data utilization strategies as factors in standardized behavioral assessment of academic skill. *Journal of Behavioral Assessment, 4*(4), 361–370.

Morris, J. (June, 1983). An interview with Alan and Nadeen Kauffman. *Communique, 11*(8).

Newcomer, P. L., & Hammill, D. D. (1975). ITPA and academic achievement: A survey. *Reading Teacher, 28,* 731–741.

Nunnally, J. (1967). *Psychometric theory.* New York: McGraw–Hill Book Co.

Peterson, N. S., & Novick, M. R. (1976). An evaluation of some models for culture-fair selection. *Journal of Educational Measurement, 13,* 3–29.

Popham, W. J. (1971). *Criterion referenced measurement: An introduction.* Englewood Cliffs, NJ: Educational Technology Publications.

Roach, E. G., & Kephart, N. C. (1966). *The Purdue perceptual-motor survey.* Columbus, OH: Merrill.

Rudel, R. G., & Denckla, M. B. (1976). Relationship of IQ and reading score to visual, spatial, and temporal matching tasks. *Journal of Learning Disabilities, 9,* 169–178.

Salvia, J., & Clark, J. (1973). Use of deficits to identify the learning disabled. *Exceptional Children, 39,* 305–308.

Salvia J., & Ysseldyke, J. E. (1981). *Assessment in special and remedial education* (2nd ed.). Boston: Houghton-Mifflin.

Sarason, S. B., & Doris, J. (1979). *Educational handicap, public policy, and social history.* New York: Free Press.

Sattler, J. M. (1974). *Assessment of children's intelligence.* Philadelphia: W. B. Saunders.

Shinn, M., Ysseldyke, J., Deno, S. L., & Tindal, G. (1982). *A comparison of psychometric and functional differences between students labeled learning disabled and low achieving* (Research Report No. 71). Minneapolis: University of Minnesota, Institute for Research on Learning Disabilities (ERIC Document Reproduction Service No. ED 218–853).

Sloan, W. (1955). *Lincoln-Oseretsky test of motor development.* Chicago: Stoelting.

Smith, R., & Niesworth, J. (1969). Fundamentals of informal educational assessment. In R. M. Smith (Ed.). *Teacher Diagnosis of Educational Difficulties.* Columbus, OH: Charles E. Merrill.

Thorndike, R. L., & Hagen, E. (1969) *Measurement and evaluation in psychology and education.* New York: John Wiley.

Thurlow, M. L., & Ysseldyke, J. E. (1982). Instructional planning: Information collected by school psychologists vs. information considered useful by teachers. *Journal of School Psychology, 20,* 3–10.

Tindal, G., Germann, G., & Deno, S. (1983). *Descriptive research on the Pine County norms: A compilation of findings* (Research Report No. 132). Minneapolis: University of Minnesota, Institute for Research on Learning Disabilities.

Tindal, G., Germann, G., Marston, D., & Deno, S. (1983). *The effectiveness of special education: A direct measurement approach* (Research Report No. 123). Minneapolis: University of Minnesota, Institute for Research on Learning Disabilities.

Tindal, G., Marston, D., & Deno, S. (1983). *The reliability of direct and repeated measures* (Research report No. 109). Minneapolis: University of Minnesota, Institute for Research on Learning Disabilities.

Tucker, J., Stevens, L., & Ysseldyke, J. (1983). Learning disabilities: The experts speak out. *Journal of Learning Disabilities, 16,* 6–14.

Wallace, G., & Larsen, S. (1978). *Educational assessment of learning problems: Testing for teaching.* Boston: Allyn and Bacon.

Wechsler, D. I. (1949). *The Wechsler intelligence scale for children.* New York: Psychological Corporation.

Wechsler, D. I. (1974). *Manual for the Wechsler Intelligence Scale for Children—Revised.* New York: Psychological Corporation.

Wepman, J. (1958). *Wepman, auditory discrimination test.* Chicago: Chicago Language Research Associates.

White, O. R., & Haring, N. G. (1980) *Exceptional teaching* (2nd ed.). Columbus, OH: Charles E. Merrill.

White, O., & Liberty, K. (1976). Behavioral assessment and precise educational measurement. In N. G. Haring & R. L. Schiefelbusch (Eds.). *Teaching Special Children* (pp. 31–71). New York: McGraw-Hill Book Co.

Woodcock, R. W. (1973). *Woodcock reading mastery test (Form A).* Circle Pines, MN: American Guidance Service.

Woodcock, R. W. (1978). *Development and standardization of the Woodcock-Johnson Psycho-Educational Battery.* Boston: Teaching Resources.

Woodcock, R., & Johnson, M. (1977). *Woodcock-Johnson psycho-educational battery.* Boston: Teaching Resources.

Ysseldyke, J. (1977). *Assessing the learning disabled youngster; The state of the art* (Research

Report No. 1). Minneapolis: University of Minnesota, Institute for Research on Learning Disabilities (ERIC Document Reproduction Service No. ED 185 746).

Ysseldyke, J. E. (1979). Issues in psychoeducational assessment. In G. D. Phye & D. J. Reschly (Eds.). *School Psychology: Perspectives and Issues.* New York: Academic Press.

Ysseldyke, J., & Algozzine, B. (1983). On making psychoeducational decisions. *Journal of Psychoeducational Assessment, 1,* 187–195.

Ysseldyke, J., Algozzine, B., & Epps, S. (1983). A logical and empirical analysis of current practices in classifying students as handicapped. *Exceptional Children, 50*(2), 160–166.

Ysseldyke, J. E., Algozzine, B., Shinn, M., & McGue, M. (1982). Similarities and differences between underachievers and students labeled learning disabled. *Journal of Special Education, 16,* 73–85.

Ysseldyke, J. E., & Mirkin, P. K. (1982). The use of assessment information to plan instructional interventions: A review of the research. In C. Reynolds & T. Gutkin (Eds.). *A Handbook for School Psychology* (pp. 395–409). New York: John Wiley.

Ysseldyke, J. E., & Shinn, M. R. (1981). Psychoeducational evaluation. In J. M. Kauffman & D. P. Hallahan (Eds.), *Handbook of special education* (pp. 410–440). Englewood Cliffs, NJ: Prentice-Hall.

Ysseldyke, J. E., Thurlow, M. L., ˙Graden, J. L., Wesson, C., Algozzine, B., & Deno, S. (1983). Generalizations from five years of research on assessment and decision making: The University of Minnesota Institute. *Exceptional Education Quarterly, 4*(1), 75–93.

PART II

Psychological Characteristics of Learning-Disabled Children

In spite of the difficulties defining and selecting samples of learning-disabled children as outlined in the previous section, the past 10 years have seen a substantial increase in our knowledge of the psychological characteristics of children who have special learning problems in school. Although sample selection problems continue to make it difficult to compare results across studies, enough research is being done in many areas that substantial and reliable findings are beginning to emerge. The chapters by Keith Stanovich and Virginia Mann, for example, report on an extensive body of research, indicating that many learning-disabled children have serious language-processing problems. Both chapters outline a particularly important role for phonological processing ability in the acquisition of early reading skills.

The role of attention deficits in accounting for learning disabilities has been a focus of study since the early, ground-breaking work of Heinz Werner and Alfred Strauss with "brain damaged" children at the Wayne County Boy's Training School. The chapter by Antoinette Krupski adds to the extensive literature in this area by analyzing the role of vigilance and selective attention in accounting for learning problems. Krupski's careful analysis of the concept of selective attention suggests that it may no longer be helpful in understanding the cognitive difficulties of learning-disabled children.

The final two chapters in this section deal with areas of less traditional concern in the study of learning disabilities. However, both topics have emerged recently as important areas of study because of their potential impact on the long-term adjustment and success of learning-disabled children. The chapter by Ruth Pearl, Mavis Donahue, and Tanis Bryan documents the extensive problems that these children have in their relationships with others. The authors make the point that the social difficulties of learning-disabled children are as much in need of remediation as their more well-known academic difficulties. Barbara Licht and Janet Kistner, in their chapter on the motivational and attributional characteristics of learning-disabled children, also make a case for interventions with these children that go beyond simple academic instruction. This chapter carefully interweaves data and theory from developmental psychology with work on learning disabilities to present a complex picture of the way that academic failure can affect the motivation and attitudes of children at different ages. Although the work presented here is very new, it represents the beginnings of a highly detailed account of the effects of chronic failure that is of potentially great importance to our understanding of learning-disabled children.

4

Cognitive Processes and the Reading Problems of Learning-Disabled Children: Evaluating the Assumption of Specificity

KEITH E. STANOVICH

INTRODUCTION

To integrate the concept of learning disability with ideas in the psychology of reading, it is necessary to become involved in some of the most difficult and perplexing issues in educational psychology. However, reconciling ideas in these two fields is a task of great importance because the vast majority of children who are labeled "learning disabled" receive the designation because of failures in learning to read (Bateman, 1979; Gaskins, 1982; Kirk & Elkins, 1975; Lerner, 1975). The task is a difficult one, however, because conceptual problems arise that are a great challenge to both fields (see Shepard, 1980). For example, it is well known that performance on intelligence tests (IQ) correlates with reading achievement. This correlation is usually in the range of .3–.5 in the early elementary grades, but rises to the range of .6–.75 in adult samples (see Stanovich, Cunningham, & Feeman, 1984a). To put the problem in its simplest form, an individual with a reading disability is a person for whom this performance linkage does not hold (or for whom it is, at least, severely attenuated). Such an individual has severely depressed performance on one variable (reading) but virtually normal performance on the other (IQ test score).

87

Psychological and Educational
Perspectives on Learning Disabilities

How should we conceptualize such a statistical outlier? One alternative would be to call such an individual just that, a statistical outlier, the inevitable result of the imperfect correlation between two variables. We could attribute some proportion of the outlier status of these individuals to measurement error, the latter ensuring (via statistical regression) that, on a retesting, this group of individuals would score somewhat lower on the IQ test and somewhat higher on the reading test (see Calfee, 1976; Hall & Humphreys, 1982) and simply leave it at that. This particular group of individuals could become the subject of remediation efforts, but these would not necessarily be any different from those received by other problem readers performing at a similar level.

It will be obvious to the readers of this volume that the course outlined above has not been the one chosen by the field of learning disabilities, since clearly it would have precluded the very development of the field. Instead, a special status has been attributed to individuals violating the IQ-reading correlation; a status other than that of a statistical anomaly. A large number of causal hypotheses involving brain and behavior relationships have been posited to *explain* the IQ-reading disassociation in this group. Without discussing in detail each of these hypotheses it is sufficient to point out that they all have a certain logical similarity. The learning disabled are posited to have a brain/cognitive deficit that is reasonably specific to the cognitive requirements of the reading task. This general point will be termed the "assumption of specificity." We will see below that the assumption is challenged by a large body of research on the cognitive characteristics of school-labeled reading-disabled children, and can only be maintained if learning disabilities researchers adopt a stricter psychometric criterion for labeling a child "reading disabled."

WHAT COGNITIVE PROBLEMS ARE ASSOCIATED WITH DELAYED READING ACQUISITION?

The literature on the relation between various cognitive processes and reading ability is large and continues to grow. An attempt has been made to link virtually every cognitive process that has ever been studied to reading ability and, indeed, a plethora of such linkages have been uncovered. However, research has demonstrated that some linkages are much stronger than others. In this section, we will review the major classes of cognitive processes that have dominated research on the psychological underpinnings of reading disability.

BASIC VISUAL PROCESSES

The hypothesis that a deficit in a basic visual process is a critical cause of reading failure has garnered enormous attention in the learning-dis-abilities literature. In explaining the initial popularity of the hypothesis, it is probably difficult to underestimate Orton's influence. His theory that reading disability was due to faulty visual sequencing that resulted from delayed lateral dominance had face validity and logical appeal. Unfortunately, the initial promise of the theory has not been fulfilled. The evidence for the delayed development of lateral dominance in dis-abled readers is equivocal at best (Aman & Singh, 1983; Harris, 1979; Hiscock & Kinsbourne, 1982; Leong, 1980; Naylor, 1980; Young & Ellis, 1981).

The sequencing and reversal errors (b/d, was/saw) that loomed so large in importance in Orton's theory have proven to be a dead end (and indeed, a useful lesson in how case study evidence can be misleading; see Stanovich, 1982a). Much recent evidence has indicated that such errors do not have the unique diagnosticity that has been attributed to them and that verbal/linguistic factors rather than visual factors are im-plicated in their occurrence (Calfee, 1977; Cohn & Stricker, 1979; Fischer, Liberman, & Shankweiler, 1978; Harman, 1982; Holmes & Peper, 1977; Park, 1978–1979; Shankweiler & Liberman, 1972, 1978; Valtin, 1978–1979; Vellutino, 1979). Systematic studies of the distribution of error types across reading ability have indicated that poor readers make more errors of *all* types, but that their number of reversal errors as a *proportion* of the total number of errors is no higher than that displayed by good readers.

Of course, Orton's visuospatial-sequencing hypothesis is not the only theory that has implicated basic visual processes in reading failure, and there is, obviously, more involved in visual perception that just the processes revealed by reversal errors. Many different kinds of visual tasks (e.g., masking tasks, fusion paradigms, detection tasks, partial-report paradigms, and reaction-time tasks) have been used to study various aspects of visual perception (e.g., feature extraction, visual seg-mentation, encoding, and visual persistence). Whereas some studies have demonstrated a relationship between reading ability and visual processing efficiency (e.g., Badcock & Lovegrove, 1981; Gross & Rothen-berg, 1979), a very large number of well-controlled studies have failed to uncover a relationship (e.g., Arnett & DiLollo, 1979; Bouma & Legein, 1980; Ellis, 1981; Fisher & Frankfurter, 1977; Gupta, Ceci, & Slater, 1978; Hulme, 1981; Liberman & Shankweiler, 1979; Mason, 1975; Morrison, Giordani, & Nagy, 1977; Stanley, 1976; Stanovich, 1981; Swanson, 1978, 1983; Valtin, 1978–1979; Vellutino, 1979).

Although the bulk of the evidence supports a minimal or nonexistent relationship between basic visual processing operations and reading ability, the issue should not be decided by merely adding up the number of studies on either side. Instead, we should invoke Calfee's (1977) concept of a "clean" psychological test, the idea being that before a deficit in a *specific* processing operation is hypothesized, investigators should ensure that the tasks employed isolate (as much as is feasible) that particular process without heavily involving other cognitive processes that could contaminate the inference of a specific processing deficit (see Stanovich, 1978; Torgesen, 1975, 1979; Vellutino, 1979). Unless many precautions are taken, such apparently visual tasks as masking paradigms, perceptual integration judgments, visual persistence judgments, post-stimulus forced-choice reports, and serial item naming easily can become confounded by many nonspecific and nonvisual factors. Alternative explanations involving short-term memory strategies, verbal labeling, criterion shifts, differential familiarity with the stimuli, changing mechanisms of masking, differential attentiveness and motivation, and differences in understanding the task instructions, particularly regarding the use of partial information, are just a few of those that have been considered (Elliot, 1970; Ericksen, 1980; Lawrence, Kee, & Hellige, 1980; Libkuman, Velliky, & Friedrich, 1980; Ross & Ward, 1978; Ryan & Jones, 1975; Stanovich, 1978; Stanovich & Purcell, 1981a, 1981b; Vellutino, 1979). When this point is emphasized, the research literature appears to support Vellutino's (1979) conclusion: The more an experiment specifically isolates a visual process, the smaller the difference between good and poor readers. As a result of applying the clean test criterion, the general conclusions of several recent reviews of the research in this area all have converged on the conclusion that visual processing abilities are, at best, weakly related to reading acquisition (Aman & Singh, 1983; Carr, 1981; Mitchell, 1982; Rutter, 1978; Vellutino, 1979).

The results of training studies in this area agree with the findings from correlational studies in questioning a strong linkage between visual processing deficits and poor reading. Generally, it is accepted that visual perception training programs have been ineffective in promoting reading acquisition (Bateman, 1979; Coles, 1978; Hammill & Larsen, 1974, 1978; Kavale & Mattson, 1983; Larsen & Hammill, 1975; Larsen, Parker, & Hammill, 1982; Mann, 1970; Seaton, 1977; Vellutino, 1979). The literature on perceptual training thus is consistent with the correlational research in casting doubt on a large causal role for visual perception in reading disabilities. Of course, the existing empirical evidence does not rule out the possibility that basic visual processes do account for some proportion of reading variance, or that a small group of poor readers may be characterized by visual deficits. However, the literature suggests that the numerical upper bounds on these two possibilities must be very low.

Finally, when discussing the role of visual processes in reading failure, mention should be made of that perennial red herring in reading disability research—eye movements. The idea that deficient eye movements cause reading problems is apparently difficult to resist, because it continually reappears despite the fact that its fallaciousness was exposed long ago by Tinker (1958), whose conclusions have been documented amply by others (Aman & Singh, 1983; Lahey, Kupfer, Beggs, & Landon, 1982; Rayner, 1978; Taylor, 1965). Its latest reincarnation is in the work of Pavlidis (1981) who claims to have shown that dyslexic children are inferior at tracking nonverbal stimuli. Although Pavlidis (1981) is careful to point out that the deficit could be due to a general sequencing problem rather than to visual/oculomotor difficulties, the point appears to be moot as his results have already failed to replicate in three different laboratories (Brown, Haegerstrom-Portnoy, Adams, Yingling, Galin, Herron, & Marcus, 1983; Olson, Kliegl, & Davidson, 1983; Stanley, Smith, & Howell, 1983). Thus, there appears to be no reason to alter Tinker's (1958) original conclusions. The consensus of researchers in the field remains that erratic eye-movement patterns are the result, not the cause, of poor reading.

There is a more general lesson for the field of learning disabilities (and for other scientific fields that interface with pressing social problems) in the history of research on eye movements as a cause of dyslexia. The popularity of the hypothesis (like Orton's) undoubtedly is due to its great face validity and general plausibility. Add to this a few case reports (it is, of course, not difficult to garner case reports supporting *anything*, including the existence of leprechauns) and you have the momentum for a completely unsupported hypothesis to enter textbooks and clinical practice as "fact." Most school districts, if they carefully searched their storage basements, would find the dusty eye-movement trainers that were purchased (often at the expense of books—one "device" we *know* that works) during the last eye-movement fad. The lesson here is: There is no substitute for careful, controlled scientific scrutiny of a hypothesis. General plausibility and a few case reports *are not enough*. As the history of this problem clearly shows, it is not only the scientific process that is damaged by premature action on an unproven hypothesis; our long-term ability to develop effective treatment techniques is also impaired.

PHONOLOGICAL PROCESSES

The conclusion of the previous section, that basic visual processes do not account for a large proportion of reading variance, should not be interpreted as indicating that psychological processes operating at the word and subword level in reading are not implicated in reading acquisition. Quite the contrary. It is well established that the speed and accuracy of word recognition is related to reading comprehension ability. Although the relationship is found even in samples of fluent adult readers (e.g., Briggs & Underwood, 1982; Frederiksen, 1978; Mason, 1978), it is particularly strong in the early grades. Correlations for the latter are often in the range of .50–.80 (e.g., Biemiller, 1977–1978; Curtis, 1980; Deno, Mirkin, & Chiang, 1982; Groff, 1978; Lesgold & Curtis, 1981; McCormick & Samuels, 1979; Perfetti, Finger, & Hogaboam, 1978; Shankweiler & Liberman, 1972; Stanovich, 1981; Stanovich, Cunningham, & Feeman, 1984b; Stanovich, Cunningham, & West, 1981; Stevenson, Parker, Wilkinson, Hegion, & Fish, 1976; Weaver & Rosner, 1979). Finally, there is increasing evidence that word-recognition skill is causally related to reading comprehension (Biemiller, 1970; Groff, 1978; Guthrie & Tyler, 1976; Lesgold & Resnick, 1982; Lomax, 1982). However, the psychological processes that are linked to individual differences in decoding ability appear to be primarily in the phonological rather than the visual realm.

From the very earliest stages of skill acquisition, phonological processes are strongly linked to reading ability. Children must, at some point, acquire skill at breaking the spelling-to-sound code (for excellent discussions, see Gough & Hillinger, 1980; Liberman, 1982). This is necessary if the child is to gain the reading independence that eventually leads to the levels of practice that are a prerequisite to fluent reading (see LaBerge & Samuels, 1974). However, several prerequisite and facilitating subskills are critical to success at spelling-to-sound code-breaking. One, clearly, is the ability to discriminate letters, the visual segments of words. This, as we saw in the previous section, appears not to be a source of difficulty for problem readers. Letters, however, must be mapped onto phonemic segments, and here appears a critical point of difficulty for the disabled reader. First, the reader must become aware of the phoneme as the basic unit of the spoken word. There is much evidence that phonological segmentation skills that are based on linguistic awareness at the phoneme level are strongly linked to the speed of initial reading acquisition and to reading disability (Bradley & Bryant, 1978, 1983; Fox & Routh, 1976, 1980, 1983; Golinkoff, 1978; Helfgott, 1976; Lewkowicz, 1980; Liberman, 1973, 1982; Liberman & Shankweiler, 1979; Mann, 1981; Perfetti, Beck, & Hughes, 1981; Rozin & Gleitman, 1977; Savin, 1972; Treiman & Baron, 1981; Williams, 1980). Although the linkage is probably one characterized by reciprocal causation (see Ehri, 1979; Perfetti *et al.*, 1981), there is mounting evidence that phonological awareness ability is causally related to later reading skill (Bradley & Bryant, 1983; Fox & Routh, 1976; Goldstein, 1976; Litcher & Roberge, 1979; Mann, 1981; Perfetti et al., 1981; Treiman & Baron, 1983; Williams, 1980).

The work of Fox and Routh (1980, 1983) provides a good example of the importance of phonological awareness skills in determining the ease of initial reading acquisition and their usefulness as a marker for children at risk for reading disabilities. Originally, they tested a group of first-graders on a relatively simple phoneme-segmentation task. The experimenter simply asked the child to "say a little piece of" a one-syllable word. The performance of the first-graders who were average readers was at ceiling on the task, whereas a group of poor readers could segment almost none of the words. Fox and Routh followed up these children 3 years later and found that, although all children could now segment phonemes, those who failed the task in the first grade suffered from relatively severe reading disabilities. They were over 2 years behind the IQ-matched control group in reading achievement and displayed a tendency to produce bizarre dysphonetic spelling errors.

Early difficulty in becoming aware of phonemes as the segments of spoken words quite naturally leads to a delay in developing the spelling-to-sound linkages that are necessary for word decoding on a phonological basis. It should not be surprising, therefore, that the ability to accurately and rapidly access the lexicon via phonological coding is strongly related to reading skill and is negatively associated with reading disability (Barron, 1978a, 1978b, 1980, 1981; Hogaboam & Perfetti, 1978; Jorm & Share, 1983; Kochnower, Richardson, & DiBenedetto, 1983; Mason, 1978; Pace & Golinkoff, 1976; Perfetti & Hogaboam, 1975; Seymour & Porpodas, 1980; Steinheiser & Guthrie, 1978). The linkage has been demonstrated in a wide variety of tasks that tap facility at grapheme-to-phoneme conversion. For example, in the large literature on individual differences in reading ability, one of the tasks that most clearly differentiates good and poor readers is the speed and accuracy with which they name pseudowords (Jorm & Share, 1983).

Snowling (1980) compared the performance of a group of children who had been diagnosed as dyslexic after extensive psychometric testing with that of a younger group of nondyslexic children who were matched on reading ability. Despite some performance similarities on some of the tasks administered, the two groups responded differently on a nonsense-word, visual–auditory matching task that mimicked the grapheme–phoneme conversion process in reading. The dyslexic subjects were markedly inferior in this condition. Furthermore, within the dyslexic group of children, there was no correlation between reading level and performance on the visual–auditory matching task, unlike the case in the nondyslexic sample where a significant correlation was obtained. In a follow-up study, Snowling (1981) observed that dyslexic subjects were poorer at naming nonsense words than younger nondyslexic subjects who were matched on reading level. Snowling (1980) has suggested that normal development in reading is characterized by an increase in grapheme–phoneme decoding ability and in the size of sight vocabulary, whereas the development of reading skill in dyslexic subjects is due primarily to increases in sight vocabulary because the development of grapheme–phoneme decoding skills in this group is severely delayed.

Skill at grapheme–phoneme conversion might confer another processing advantage in addition to providing a more efficient mode of word recognition. During reading, sequences of words must be held in short-term memory, while comprehension processes operate on the words to integrate them into a meaningful conceptual structure that can be stored in long-term memory. There is evidence (e.g., Baddeley, 1966; Conrad, 1964) that, for this purpose, the most stable short-term memory code is a phonetic code. Thus, it has been suggested that the ability to rapidly form a stable phonological code in short-term memory may be related to reading comprehension ability (Perfetti & Lesgold, 1977; see Perfetti & McCutchen, 1982, for an important discussion of this issue). This conjecture has received considerable support. Research on phonological confusability effects in memory tasks has indicated that the inferior performance of less skilled and more severely disabled readers may be due to inefficient phonological coding of stimuli and/or an inability to maintain a phonological code in working memory (Brady, Shankweiler, & Mann, 1983; Byrne, 1981; Byrne & Shea, 1979; Mann, Liberman, & Shankweiler, 1980; Olson, Davidson, Kliegl, & Davies, 1984; Perfetti & Lesgold, 1977, 1979; Perfetti & McCutchen, 1982; Shankweiler, Liberman, Mark, Fowler, & Fischer, 1979; but see Hall, Wilson, Humphreys, Tinzmann, & Bowyer, 1983).

The conclusion also is supported by the results of several studies that show that poor readers display memory deficits on tasks where the stimuli are easily labeled, but that the same poor readers do not show performance deficits when the stimuli are not verbally codable (Holmes & McKeever, 1979; Hulme, 1981; Katz, Shankweiler, & Liberman, 1981; Mann, 1981; Swanson, 1978, 1983). Cohen and Netley (1981) provided further converging evidence by designing a memory task that precluded strategy usage and observing a performance difference between reading-disabled children and control subjects. They argued by process of elimination that the only remaining viable explanation was a difference in phonological coding abilities (see also Cohen, 1982).

Finally, although it was previously thought that the phonological analysis deficits revealed in the studies reviewed were due to problems in becoming consciously *aware* of phoneme units rather than in basic speech discrimination processes (see Groff, 1975; Vellutino, 1979; Wallach, Wallach, Dozier, & Kaplan, 1977), recent evidence may lead to a qualification of this conclusion. In fact, the speech problems of the disabled reader may be broader than was first thought. For example, Godfrey, Syrdal-Laskey, Millay, and Knox (1981) have reported differences between disabled and nondisabled readers in the categorical perception of certain speech contrasts. Brady, *et al.* (1983) found that poor readers made more preceptual errors when listening to speech in noise. Tallal (1980) has an even broader conception of the auditory perception deficits that underlie the reading problems of disabled readers. She argues that a basic deficit in processing rapidly presented nonverbal auditory information may be the key mechanism that mediates the difficulties that disabled readers experience in analyzing phonetic codes. Clearly, more research is needed on the issue of how broadly to conceptualize the auditory and speech problems of the disabled reader. This question is definitely worth pursuing, however, as it is clear is that the area of phonological and auditory processing is a critical locus of individual differences in readers of varying skill.

NAME RETRIEVAL SPEED

There is some research in the reading literature that suggests that disabled subjects are characterized by deficits in accessing the name code of a symbolic stimulus (Denckla & Rudel, 1976; Spring & Capps, 1974; Spring & Farmer, 1975; Wigg, Semel, & Nystrom, 1982). For example, Denckla and Rudel (1976) have shown that severely disabled readers are slower at naming lists of various stimulus types (letters, numbers, pictures, etc.). However, there appear to be several reasons for exercising caution in generalizing these results. First, it seems that the relationship is only strong when subjects at the extremes of reading ability are included in the sample. When poor readers from regular classrooms are employed as subjects, a relationship between naming speed and reading ability is obtained, but it is usually much weaker (Curtis, 1980; Ehri & Wilce, 1983; Perfetti *et al.*, 1978; Stanovich, 1981; Stanovich *et al.*, 1981; Stanovich, Feeman, & Cunningham, 1983), particularly in the early grades. A second caveat concerns the type of tasks that have been used in research of this type. It appears that the magnitude of the relationship may depend also on the discrete or continuous nature of the naming task (Stanovich *et al.*, 1983). Continuous tasks (that involve the serial naming of a list of items) tend to yield higher correlations than discrete tasks (that involve taking a reaction time to a single stimulus), probably because the former implicate many other reading-related processing operations in addition to name access (see Eakin & Douglas, 1971; Staller & Sekuler, 1975; Stanovich *et al.*, 1983; Torgesen & Houck, 1980).

To study individual differences in name-retrieval speed, Jackson and McClelland (1979) and Hunt (1978) have made extensive use of the letter-matching paradigm of Posner and Mitchell (1967). These investigators used the reaction-time difference between a physical match (AA) and a name match (Aa) as an index of name-retrieval time. Both Jackson and McClelland (1979) and Hunt (1978) found significant correlations between this index and reading ability in a group of adult subjects. Employing the same methodology, Ellis (1981) found that a group of reading disabled children displayed slower name-retrieval times than a group of matched controls. Thus, there appears to be a relationship between this index of retrieval speed and reading ability at all levels of reading skill.

The main problem surrounding the interpretation of the results from the letter-matching paradigm is one of correlation/causation. There is, presently, no strong evidence (see Jackson, 1980, for one of the few relevant studies) that addresses the question: Is name-retrieval speed a causal determinant of reading ability, or does the greater amount of practice received by the better reader (see Biemiller, 1977–1978) develop the ability to more efficiently code symbolic stimuli? Nevertheless, the speed of symbolic name retrieval does seem, in some way, linked with reading ability, and the nature and magnitude of the relationship deserves further study.

CONTEXTUAL PROCESSES THAT FACILITATE WORD RECOGNITION

Of course, word recognition may involve more than just grapho-phonemic information. Various contextual cues also are available to aid word processing. In this part, we will review the evidence on whether the tendency to use contextual cues to facilitate word recognition is associated with individual differences in reading skill and with reading disability. Before beginning the discussion, a very important note of clarification and caution is in order.

There are probably few research issues in reading so fraught with confusion as the subtopic we might generically label "studies of context use." One reason for this state of affairs is that this research area had already become a reasonably hot topic before the field of reading had fully inculcated some of the most important lessons from the rapidly developing allied field of cognitive psychology. One of the most important implications from work in the latter is that one gains great theoretical power by viewing performance in complex tasks in terms of "isolable" processing operations (see Fodor, 1983; Posner, 1978). These isolable subsystems may be arranged in a variety of different ways, but the more general point is that theoretical advance occurs through a more detailed knowledge of how sets of variables *selectively* influence specific isolable subsystems. The lesson for reading researchers is that, if theoretical progress is to be made, investigators must be careful to distinguish (or at least be aware that a distinction is possible) the specific subsystems that are being affected by a particular experimental manipulation. However, reading researchers generally have not been careful in specifying what level in the processing system was being tapped by the particular contextual manipulation employed in a given experiment. This is why there is still considerable looseness and confusion surrounding the term "context effect." One never knows what to expect of a reading article that contains the term in the title. The point is that there can be many different *types* of context effects. For example, context can act to speed ongoing word recognition during reading. This process is the topic of this part. Alternatively, context can be used to facilitate the memory and comprehension of text (e.g., Bransford & Johnson, 1973). This is a very *different* type of context effect that we will take up later.

One of the most influential theories of the relationship between reading development and the use of context to facilitate word recognition has been developed in the work of Goodman (1965, 1976) and Smith (1971). Their hypothesis is that, due to sensitivity to the semantic and syntactic cues (i.e., to the redundancy) afforded by previous text, the reader develops hypotheses about upcoming words and is then able to confirm their identities by sampling only a few features from their visual representations. They further hypothesize that the fluent reading of good readers partially is due to their superior ability to utilize contextual redundancy to facilitate word recognition. The poor reader is thought to be deficient at utilizing context to speed recognition. Although this view has enjoyed considerable popularity, there is actually little empirical evidence favoring it and, indeed, a considerable body of evidence that contradicts it.

The mismatch between the popularity of the hypothesis-testing view of individual differences in contextual facilitation and the data supporting it is due partially to the failure to distinguish the different types of contextual effects discussed previously. Although there is considerable evidence that better readers are more facile at using contextual information to aid *comprehension* (see below), the evidence on the hypothesis-testing theory is very different when the question concerns individual differences in word recognition. Indeed, studies supporting the former hypothesis often are cited inappropriately as if they confirmed the latter (see Stanovich, 1980, 1984). Studies employing a wide variety of paradigms have failed to find that good readers rely more on context for word recognition than poorer readers. This research includes studies of oral reading errors (Allington & Fleming, 1978; Batey & Sonnenschein, 1981; Biemiller, 1970, 1979; Cohen, 1974–1975; Coomber, 1972; Juel, 1980; Lesgold & Resnick, 1982; Perfetti & Roth, 1981; Richardson, Di-Benedetto, & Adler, 1982; Weber, 1970; Whaley & Kibby, 1981), timed text reading (Allington, 1978; Biemiller, 1977–1978; Doehring, 1976; Stanovich et al., 1984b), text disruption manipulations (Allington & Strange, 1977; Ehrlich, 1981; Schwartz & Stanovich, 1981; Siler, 1973–1974; Strange, 1979), single-word priming (Becker, 1982; Schvaneveldt, Ackerman, & Semlear, 1977; Simpson, Lorsbach, & Whitehouse, 1983), sentence priming (Perfetti & Roth, 1981; Schwantes, Boesl, & Ritz, 1980; Stanovich, West, & Feeman, 1981; West & Stanovich, 1978; West, Stanovich, Feeman, & Cunningham, 1983), and paragraph priming (Perfetti, Goldman, & Hogaboam, 1979; Schwantes, 1981, 1982).

A series of studies conducted by Perfetti, Goldman, & Hogaboam (1979) illustrate the importance of distinguishing hypotheses about contextual effects that are operative at the word-recognition level and those that are implicated in text-level comprehension procedures. They found that the same skilled readers who displayed smaller context effects than less-skilled readers on a word-recognition task were superior on a cloze-like prediction task. These results suggest that, although the more highly skilled readers may possess superior text-level prediction abilities than poorer readers, they are less likely actually to use those abilities to aid in recognizing words. This is because the skilled reader's processes of word recognition are largely automatic (and thus not in need of contextual facilitation), allowing attention to be allocated to text-level comprehension processes (see Stanovich, 1980, 1982a, 1982b, 1984). The results of Perfetti et al. (1979) also point to the importance of distinguishing between the degree to which a reader can display a particular subskill in an experimental situation designed to tap the subskill and the degree to which the subskill is implicated in performance when the real-time processing constraints of reading are imposed.

Whereas most of the studies cited have not employed severely disabled readers as a contrast group, it is very likely that the conclusions would generalize to school-labeled, learning-disabled children and probable that the conclusions also would apply to more severely disabled readers. Deno *et al.*, (1982) found very high correlations between reading comprehension and the ability to read words in isolation. The correlations were very similar for the learning-disabled subjects and the nondisabled control group. Batey and Sonnenschein (1981) studied the oral reading errors of a group of learning-disabled children and a younger control group who were matched on reading ability. The children read a normally structured paragraph and a paragraph with the words scrambled. The oral reading errors of the two groups of children were not differentially affected by scrambling the paragraph.

Finally, how should we explain the frequently reported description of disabled readers as plodding through the text, not using context, and understanding little? For years, in many educational writings (e.g., Goodman's work) it has been assumed that such readers have learned certain inefficient strategies (over reliance on phonic strategies in Goodman's case) and have failed to learn contextual strategies. The best available evidence now contradicts this view (see Liberman, 1982; Mitchell, 1982; Perfetti & Roth, 1981; Richardson *et al.*, 1982; Stanovich, 1982b, 1984; Stanovich *et al.*, 1984b).

Less-skilled readers reliably display context effects on word recognition *when they understand the context*, and here, perhaps, is the key to the apparent conflict between case reports and controlled experimental studies. In many texts, the slow and inaccurate word-decoding processes of the poor reader may, in fact, degrade the contextual information that they receive, rendering it unusable. The observation that, under such conditions, poor readers do not rely on context, should not be interpreted as indicating that they *cannot* use context to facilitate word recognition. Rather, the finding may merely be an epiphenomenon of their poor decoding skills.

Using a longitudinal research design, Stanovich *et al.*, (1984b) recently demonstrated that when poorer readers reach the particular reading stage where they can decode a particular passage with the same speed and accuracy as a group of skilled readers, the poor readers display just as much contextual facilitation. However, when readers are compared on the same passage at the same point in time (in a cross-sectional comparison), the better readers display larger contextual effects, because they are more completely and accurately *decoding* the passage. These results support a decoding epiphenomenon rather than a strategy-use explanation of the contextual failures that poorer readers display in some reading materials. They also converge with much recent evidence that indicates that failure at the "psycholinguistic guessing game" has been vastly overrated as an explanation of reading disability, and that, in contrast, the ability to rapidly and automatically access individual word meanings on a graphophonemic basis is much more critically implicated in reading failure. Indeed, there is now a strong consensus in the reading literature on this point (Barron, 1981; Bateman, 1979; Biemiller, 1977–1978; Carr, 1981; Carroll & Walton, 1979; Chall, 1979; Crowder, 1982; Gough, 1981; Gough, Alford, & Holley-Wilcox, 1981; Gough & Hillinger, 1980; Juel, 1983; Lesgold & Perfetti, 1978; Liberman, 1982; Mitchell, 1982; Perfetti & Roth, 1981; Samuels, 1979; Shankweiler & Liberman, 1972; Stanovich, 1980, 1982a, 1982b; Vellutino, 1979).

SHORT-TERM MEMORY

There is considerable evidence indicating that performance on a wide variety of short-term memory tasks is related to reading ability (Bauer, 1977, 1979, 1982; Cohen, 1982; Cohen & Netley, 1981; Cummings & Faw, 1976; Dallago & Moely, 1980; Daneman & Carpenter, 1980; Goldman, Hogaboam, Bell, & Perfetti, 1980; Manis & Morrison, 1982; Masson & Miller, 1983; Newman & Hagen, 1981; Payne & Holzman, 1983; Tarver, Hallahan, Kauffman & Ball, 1976; Torgesen, 1977a, 1977b, 1978–1979; Torgesen & Goldman, 1977; Wong, Wong, & Foth, 1977). Of course, the finding that poor readers display short-term-memory deficits has the status of correlational evidence. However, since comprehension processes depend on the ability of short-term memory to hold recently accessed information, short-term memory deficits could directly impair the ability to comprehend text. Thus, there is some reason to assume a causal connection between short-term memory deficits and reading ability.

Two general explanations have been advanced to account for the memory deficits displayed by poor readers. One, the hypothesis of a deficit in the formation and maintenance of phonological codes in short-term memory, was discussed in a previous section. Such a deficit would impair comprehension processes that make use of a verbal code. This hypothesis has considerable support. The other explanation hypothesizes that poor readers are less prone to employ the active, planful, memorization strategies (e.g., verbal rehearsal, imagery, and elaboration) that have been shown to facilitate memory performance. Untangling the proportion of variance that is associated with each of these hypotheses may be difficult (for example, strategies such as verbal rehearsal may be difficult to separate from phonological coding processes) because they are not mutually exclusive (see Cohen, 1982; Torgesen, 1978–1979; Torgesen & Houck, 1980). Indeed, the research evidence suggests that poor readers may display inferior short-term-memory performance due to deficits in *both* phonological processing and strategic planning. In this section we briefly review some of the evidence on the latter.

Research has shown that poor readers are less likely to employ a variety of cognitive strategies that facilitate memory performance (Bauer, 1977, 1979, 1982; Newman & Hagen, 1981; Tarver et al., 1976; Torgesen, 1977a, 1977b, 1978–1979, 1980; Torgesen & Goldman, 1977; Wong, 1978; Wong et al., 1977). For example, findings such as depressed primacy effects in the serial-position curves of poor readers indicate that they are less likely to use a verbal rehearsal strategy. However, Torgesen (1977a) and Torgesen and Goldman (1977) have shown that instruction in the use of memory strategies can attenuate the performance deficits displayed by poor readers (see also Newman & Hagen, 1981). Thus, poor readers appear less prone actually to employ cognitive strategies even when the strategies are within their capabilities, a conclusion supported by other research (see below). Also implicating strategy usage in the memory problems of the poor reader is the finding that performance deficits are somewhat reduced (although usually not entirely eliminated; see Cohen, 1982; Torgesen & Houck, 1980) in tasks that are designed to preclude the use of strategies (Cermak, Goldberg, Cermak, & Drake, 1980).

Learning-disabled subjects display particularly marked performance deficits on memory tasks that require several different strategies and control processes for successful completion. Foster and Gavelek (1983) reported some research with a directed forgetting task that indicated substantially inefficient memory functioning on the part of the learning-disabled children. Such a task minimally requires maintenance rehearsal while the cue is processed, differential encoding of to-be-remembered and to-be-forgotten items, and elaborative rehearsal of the to-be-remembered items. In the Foster and Gavelek (1983) study, the control group of nondisabled children displayed stronger indications of strategic functioning on virtually all of the measures, including item differentiation and category clustering. These investigators came to the familiar conclusion of inefficient strategy usage on the part of disabled readers, and reiterated Torgesen's (1977a, 1977b) arguments about the importance of the concept of executive control over existing strategies in understanding learning disabilities. Clearly, the research on short-term memory functioning in learning-disabled individuals has extended the theoretical locus of the disability beyond merely the "holding" operations of memory into more general areas of cognitive planning and study strategies. Thus, the nature of the deficits that have been hypothesized to explain depressed performance on short-term memory tasks are such that they could encompass more complex text-level processing operations. The empirical evidence currently available indeed indicates such a linkage.

ASPECTS OF LANGUAGE AND COMPREHENSION COMMON
TO READING AND LISTENING

The question of whether deficits in more general compehension strategies are associated with reading disability interfaces with a closely related issue in the reading research literature—whether processes beyond decoding are responsible for individual differences in reading skill.
This question is usually answered in the affirmative. Although there is
no question that a considerable amount of reading variance is explained
by individual differences in decoding skill (see above), it has been demonstrated that processes independent of decoding ability are also linked
to reading ability (Oakhill, 1982; Wilkinson, 1980). This is particularly
true at the more advanced levels of reading acquisition. For example,
almost all studies of subjects beyond the early elementary grades report
significant correlations between listening-comprehension ability and
reading skill. The relationship is particularly strong in adults (Daneman
& Carpenter, 1980; Jackson, 1980; Jackson & McClelland, 1979; Jenkins &
Pany, 1981), moderately strong in the middle grades, and weak, but still
significant, in the early elementary grades (Berger, 1978; Chall, 1983;
Curtis, 1980; Duker, 1965; Stanovich *et al.*, 1984a). These findings are
consistent with the data indicating that, as the absolute reading level of
the sample under study increases, the proportion of reading variance
accounted for by listening comprehension ability also increases (Carver
& Hoffman, 1981; Chall, 1979, 1983; Curtis, 1980; Fletcher, Satz, &
Scholes, 1981; Jenkins & Pany, 1981; Kintsch, 1979; Stanovich *et al.*,
1984a; Sticht, 1979).

Several studies have demonstrated that reading-disabled children display large deficits in listening comprehension. Berger (1978) studied a
group of reading-disabled, fifth-grade children and found that, when
compared to an IQ-matched control group, their listening comprehension performance was just as depressed as their reading performance.
Similarly, Smiley, Oakley, Worthen, Campione, and Brown (1977) observed strikingly inferior listening comprehension in a group of seventh-
grade poor readers. Kotsonis and Patterson (1980) found that two different age groups of learning-disabled children had greater difficulty in
monitoring their listening comprehension than did two age- and IQ-
matched nondisabled control groups. These comprehension problems
are probably implicated in the well-known fact that poor readers, including those labeled "reading disabled," display inferior performance on
cloze tasks (Bickley, Ellington, & Bickley, 1970; DiVesta, Hayward, &
Orlando, 1979; Perfetti *et al.*, 1979; Perfetti & Roth, 1981; Ruddell, 1965;
Siegel & Ryan, 1984).

The pervasive comprehension deficits could result from a very generalized lack of linguistic awareness that is characteristic of learning-disabled children (Downing, 1980; Menyuk & Flood, 1981). In addition, the general comprehension problems undoubtedly are related to the finding that reading-disabled children have difficulty dealing with complex syntactic structures in spoken language. For example, Vogel (1974) found that the performance of a group of reading-disabled second-graders was inferior to that of a control group of nondisabled children on seven of nine measures of oral language syntactic ability. Her findings converged with the results of Wiig, Semel, and Crouse (1973), which indicated a lack of morphological knowledge on the part of poor readers. Newcomer and Magee (1977) found that learning-disabled children were inferior to control children on spoken language tests of grammatical understanding, sentence imitation, and grammatical completion (see also Byrne, 1981; Hallahan & Bryan, 1981; Menyuk & Flood, 1981).

The language problems experienced by disabled readers are not confined to syntax (see Blalock, 1982; Donahue, Pearl, & Bryan, 1983; Hallahan & Bryan, 1981; Vellutino, 1979). Newcomer and Magee (1977) examined seven different aspects of spoken language and found a statistically significant difference between reading-disabled and control children on six tests, all seven revealing inferior performance on the part of the disabled children. Siegel and Ryan (1984) also administered a series of language tasks to reading-disabled and nondisabled children and found the latter to be superior on measures of sentence repetition accuracy, oral cloze, oral sentence-error location, and grammatical closure. In short, the results indicated a pervasive language deficit on the part of the reading-disabled subjects. Finally, Rutter and Yule (1975) found that their specific reading-retardation group was characterized by delays in language acquisition and articulation problems that were twice as prevalent as those observed in a control group.

As regards the cognitive underpinnings of successful reading acquisition, the general language comprehension problems of the learning-disabled child interact in a particularly unfortunate way with the deficiencies in metacognitive strategy monitoring that were demonstrated in the memory research reviewed above. The result is a child who is exceedingly unequipped to deal with the task requirements of reading at the more advanced levels. Poor readers have difficulty with a wide variety of the cognitive interactions with text that are necessary for fluent reading. For example, they are less adept at comprehension monitoring (Bos & Filip, 1982; but see Baker, 1982), approach text in a more passive manner (Bransford, Stein, & Vye, 1982; Brown, 1981; Paris & Myers, 1981), display less efficient text-scanning strategies (DiVesta *et al.*, 1979; Garner & Reis, 1981), less sensitivity to text structure (Meyer, Brandt, & Bluth, 1980; Pearson & Camperell, 1981; Smiley *et al.*, 1977), and are less likely to elaborate the encoding of text (Levin, 1973; Merrill, Sperber, & McCauley, 1981; Pearson & Camperell, 1981). There is evidence that the training of text-level comprehension strategies and linguistic awareness can partially reduce the performance lag shown by reading-disabled children (Bransford *et al.*, 1982; Brown, 1981; Hansen, 1981; Hansen & Pearson, 1983; Levin, 1973; Ryan, 1981; White, Pascarella, & Pflaum, 1981).

SUMMARY INDICES OF COGNITION; INTELLIGENCE

A great deal of ink has been spilled in the learning-disabilities literature on definitional issues. Despite continuing controversy over many subissues, most researchers probably would agree on a prototypical definition that grossly defines a reading disability as marked difficulty in acquiring reading skills despite essentially normal intelligence and the absence of extreme environmental or physiological handicaps. One of the sticky points, of course, has always been the idea of "essentially normal intelligence." Reports of learning disabilities in the general print and electronic media have considerably exaggerated this particular aspect. The typical media learning-disabled youngster is, if anything, a somewhat brighter-than-average and creative child who, due to an unexplained (but usually implied physiological) quirk, cannot read. This is a demonstrably inaccurate portrayal (see below), yet, for a variety of reasons, parents and professional groups have been noticeably unenthusiastic about taking steps to correct it.

Learning-disabilities researchers have had their own problems with just what is meant by "essentially normal intelligence." Most have taken this to mean more than just "not retarded." The latter definition obviously opens the door for the creation of research or classroom groupings of "learning-disabled" children with mean IQs of, say, 82. Anyone remotely familiar with the logic of measurement error, the normal curve, and the study of behavioral phenomena would immediately recognize that it would be highly unlikely that such a group would show behavioral and cognitive patterns qualitatively different from a group of children who were labeled educably mentally retarded (EMR) and had a mean IQ of 68. A solution to this problem has been to operationally define "essentially normal intelligence" as "far enough from the IQs of EMRs so that they won't be confused with them"; hence, the often-imposed research criterion of not including in the learning-disabled group any child with an IQ less than 90. A problem occurs when we let this imposed criterion subtly affect our thinking about learning disabilities in a manner that turns the phrase "essentially normal intelligence" into "intelligence equal to that of a randomly sampled control population." The latter is an empirically verifiable statement that has been falsified by much research.

It has been pointed out in numerous research reports that a substantial number of children whom schools label learning disabled would be equally good candidates for the EMR or borderline retardation categories (Ames, 1968; Bryan, 1974; Kirk & Elkins, 1975; Miller & Davis, 1982; Norman & Zigmond, 1980). Even on nonverbal and performance IQ tests, the mean IQ of children labeled learning disabled does not approximate 100, but is usually closer to 90 (Anderson, Kaufman, & Kaufman, 1976; Camp & Dolcourt, 1977; Gajar, 1979; Hallahan & Kauffman, 1977; Klinge, Rennick, Lennox, & Hart, 1977; Leinhardt, Seewald, & Zigmond, 1982; McLeskey & Rieth, 1982; Norman & Zigmond, 1980; Satz & Friel, 1974; Shepard, Smith, & Vojir, 1983; Smith, Coleman, Dokecki, & Davis, 1977; Tarver, 1982; Valtin, 1978–1979). For example, a school- and medically defined, learning-disabled sample studied by Anderson et al. (1976) had a mean performance IQ of 89; a sample studied by Gajar (1979) had a performance IQ of 92; the sample reported in Hallahan & Kauffman (1977) obtained an IQ of 91; a sample studied by Klinge et al. (1977) had a performance IQ of 94; and the sample of Smith et al. (1977) had an IQ of 93. The large sample of children from the Child Service Demonstration Centers that were surveyed by Kirk and Elkins (1975) had a median IQ of 93.

These findings are not confined to survey studies of learning-disabled children. Similar trends are apparent even in research where an attempt has been made to match (or range restrict) the learning disabled and control groups on environmental variables and cognitive variables not directly tied to reading (Fletcher et al., 1981; Hallahan & Kauffman, 1977; Klinge et al., 1977). From a group of 108 learning-disabled children, Klinge et al. (1977) selected 30 children to match 30 controls on sex, race, age, and socioeconomic and geographic community. Despite the matching, the performance IQ of the learning-disabled group (94) was 9 points lower than that of the control group (103). Surveys of research reports repeatedly have found that, although matching procedures may have ensured that the IQs of the learning-disabled sample approximate 100 and are not significantly different from those of the control group, the IQs of the LD group are invariably lower than those of the control group (see McLeskey & Rieth, 1982). In a formal survey of the research literature, Torgesen & Dice (1980) found the mean IQ of the learning-disabled group to 6 points lower than that of the control group. Wolford (1981) informally confirmed this observation by noting that of the 23 studies in his reprint file where IQs were reported, 22 reported lower IQs for the LD group. The mean difference between the groups was 5.4 points. Vellutino's (1979) studies show the same pattern.

It is thus clear that "essentially normal intelligence" should not be interpreted to mean "intelligence equal to that of a randomly sampled control population". A more accurate interpretation would be "intelligence not in the retarded range but somewhat below normal." The latter, more accurate, interpretation of what the intelligence phrase in the LD definition means has the advantage of emphasizing aspects of the learning-disabilities concept that have impeded understanding, particularly in the area of reading failure.

Intelligence is, of course, a controversial construct within psychology. However, much of the controversy is tangential to the concerns of the present review. If we leave aside questions of heredity versus environment, how much intelligence can be increased by training, what does culture-fair mean, and so on, and propose that a score on a well-standardized IQ test is a rough index of the current level of a person's overall cognitive functioning (see Detterman, 1982), we will have a statement that will draw at least minimal agreement from the vast majority of psychologists. Viewed in this way, the concept of intelligence provides a problem for the assumption of specifity in learning-disabilities research. As reviewed, the population of school-labeled, learning-disabled children and the samples of learning-disabled children who are selected for most research studies score approximately one-half of a standard deviation below appropriate control groups on IQ tests. This finding indicates that learning-disabled children are characterized by a mild but generalized cognitive deficit, rather than a specific, highly localized problem in reading. One implication is that the assumption of specificity must be considerably weakened, perhaps to something like "a reading deficit that is somewhat greater than the deficits displayed in other facets of cognitive functioning." This rephrasing is consistent with recent suggestions that learning disability be viewed as a "fuzzy set" concept, in the technical sense (Hagen, Barclay, & Schwethelm, 1982; Horvath, Kass, & Ferrell, 1980).

There are, however, several possible objections to this conceptualization. First, note that the assumption that an IQ score is a rough index of current, overall cognitive functioning does not entail that such a score reflect a unitary trait, or a reified g. To the contrary, the present author would endorse the view that a full-scale score reflects the operation of many isolable component processes. Higher-order concepts like g or executive capacity are rough indices of the overall functioning of a system with many interrelated parts (see Detterman, 1982). It is thus possible that the one-half standard-deviation-IQ deficit displayed by learning-disabled children might result not from uniformly depressed performance, but instead, from severely subpar performance on one or two subtests that tap the particular cognitive process implicated in their reading problem. Although this remains a logical possibility, the author knows of no strong evidence favoring it. Most studies do not report the necessary information, but the data from the few that have has not been supportive of the idea that the overall IQ deficit results from depressed performance on one or two scales. For example, Klinge *et al.* (1977) reported the scaled subtest scores from the 11 subscales of the Wechsler for both the learning-disabled group and the matched control. The learning-disabled children scored lower on every single subtest, displaying deficits of 2.0, 1.1, 1.6, 1.2, 2.2, 0.6, 0.6, 1.3, 2.0, 1.4, and 1.3 points, respectively. Feagans and McKinney (1981) report essentially similar results. The performance of their learning-disabled sample was significantly inferior on 9 of the 11 Wechsler subtests. Finally, efforts to find a Wechsler profile that was distinctive of learning-disabled children have not been notable for their success (Feagans, 1983; Feagans & McKinney, 1981; Huelsman, 1970; Kender, 1972). Of course, such findings could be the result of combining in one sample learning-disabled subjects who are characterized by specific, but different, deficits (see below). Thus, it is clearly premature to reject the possibility that there may exist a subpopulation of poor readers who *are* characterized by a lack of any generalized cognitive deficit. Present research only suggests that the performance of the vast majority of school-labeled disabled readers and a good number of disabled children in research samples seem not to be characterized by such specifity.

It follows from the conclusion that learning disability be viewed as a fuzzy set concept that it may be difficult to differentiate the reading failure of learning-disabled children from that of other poor readers not labeled learning-disabled. In short, are the nature of the cognitive processes that mediate inferior reading performance in learning-disabled children fundamentally different from those implicated in the reading problems of non-LD children? The research literature on this issue is embarrassingly meager—given its importance—and the results from the studies conducted are equivocal. The theoretical rationale and diagnostic utility of the concept of learning disability continue to be questioned (Arter & Jenkins, 1979; Cohen, 1976; Coles, 1978; Gross & Gottlieb, 1982; Miller & Davis, 1982; Ysseldyke & Algozzine, 1979), partially due to the failure of research consistently to demonstrate that the performance profiles of learning-disabled and/or dyslexic subjects differ reliably from those of other poor readers (see Algozzine & Ysseldyke, 1983; Coles, 1978; Gottesman, Croen, & Rotkin, 1982; Taylor, Satz, & Friel, 1979).

Studies by Bloom, Wagner, Reskin, and Bergman (1980) and by Taylor *et al.*, (1979) provide good illustrations of the problem. Bloom *et al.* (1980) tested two groups of 9-year-old subjects: one termed "intellectually delayed" (mean IQ = 75.3) and one termed "reading disabled" (mean IQ = 97.1). The reading achievement of the two groups (as measured by the total reading score on the Woodcock Reading Mastery Tests) was nearly equal, and significantly below the expected achievement for their chronological age. The performance of the two groups did not differ greatly across the various subtests of the Woodcock (letter identification, word identification, word attack, word comprehension, and passage comprehension) and their verbal IQ/performance IQ discrepancies were not different. Taylor *et al.* (1979) compared the performance of a group of children who met the World Federation of Neurology's definition of dyslexia with the performance of another group of poor readers who did not meet the definition. The two groups did not differ on any of the characteristics examined, including future progress in reading acquisition, frequency of reversal errors, familial reading attainment, math skills, neurobehavioral performance, and personality variables.

The best existing evidence in favor of demarcating reading disability as a qualitatively distinguishable behavioral concept comes from the epidemiological Isle of Wight study (Rutter & Yule, 1975; Rutter, 1978; Yule, 1973). From a total sample of 2300 9–11-year-old children, two groups were created. One, termed the "reading backwardness group," was more than 2 years, and 4 months below their chronological age in reading achievement. The reading achievement of the other group, termed the "specific reading retardation group," was more than 2 years and 4 months below the level predicted from their chronological age and Wechsler IQ. Both groups were equal in reading achievement (each approximately 33 months below the general population control group), but the mean IQ of the specific reading-retardation group (102.5) was significantly higher than that of the reading backwardness group (80). Rutter and Yule (1975) reported several similarities between their two groups, but also several significant differences. The specific reading retardation group was less likely to have organic brain damage and to display various neurological abnormalities. The backward group was more likely to display a variety of motor abnormalities and to show left/ right confusion. The groups had similar proportions of family members with histories of reading difficulties and similar histories of delays in language development, although the specific group was superior on a test of current complexity of language usage. A follow-up assessment conducted 5 years later indicated that the specific group had made significantly less progress in reading.

How should we reconcile the results of Rutter and Yule (1975) with the many previous failures to differentiate reading disabled (or dyslexic) children from other poor readers (e.g., Bloom *et al.*, 1980; Coles, 1978; Taylor *et al.*, 1979)? It is suggested here that the seeming inconsistancy, rather than being a cause for despair, can actually contribute to alleviating the conceptual confusion that plagues the concept of reading disability. It is extremely important to note that Rutter and Yule (1975) carefully and conservatively formed their specific reading retardation sample in such a way that this group comprised just 3.7% of their total sample. Thus, they were careful to ensure that their specific group was comprised of extreme outliers. It must be recognized that this presents a very different situation from that obtained in natural populations of school-labeled, learning-disabled children, where the magnitude of specific reading retardation is typically much more moderate—averaging one grade below mental age and one-half grade below arithmetic achievement—(see Hallahan & Bryan, 1981; Kirk & Elkins, 1975; Norman & Zigmond, 1980; Tarver, 1982). Such school-labeled LD children will encompass much more of the naturally occurring continuous variation in reading and cognitive skills than will the group of Rutter and Yule (1975). This point reinforces Eisenberg's (1966, 1979) caution to practitioners and researchers: that the vast majority of poor readers in our schools do not have a medically or behaviorally distinct syndrome. The lesson for reading-disabilities researchers and practioners is: Only by exercising some restraint and specificity in our application of the label will be arrive at a concept that has some scientific and educational utility. This is one of the most important implications of the work of Rutter and Yule, (1975). (Note, however, that they are careful to point to the fact that many aspects of the classic "dyslexic syndrome" are, in fact, *not* disproportionately found in their specific reading retardation group, e.g., left/right confusion, neurological signs, directional confusion, and familial linkage.)

The regression approach with conservative criterion (i.e., a criterion designed to isolate true outliers, rather than the "noise" inevitably resulting from measurement error) used by Rutter and Yule (1975; see Horn & O'Donnell, 1984) seems to hold promise as a technique for overcoming some of the conceptual and empirical confusion in the area of reading disabilities. Likely, it would be easier to find support for the assumption of specificity if all studies of reading disability defined subjects according to the criteria adopted by Rutter and Yule (1975). Empirical support for the assumption is weak because of lack of restraint in applying the reading-disability label and the fact that many researchers define their samples on the basis of school labeling rather than by a strict psychometric criterion.

CONCLUSIONS: THE ASSUMPTION OF SPECIFICITY REVISITED

What picture of the cognitive characteristics of the poor reader have we arrived at by way of this review? First, a number of popular hypotheses about reading failure seem to lack empirical support. The idea that a deficit in basic visual-processing operations would underlie the problems of reading-disabled children has fared poorly under scrutiny. Variants of this hypothesis dominated the learning-disabilities literature for years, and it is only recently that the weight of evidence is beginning to become more widely appreciated, with the result that the scientific consensus on this issue is beginning to filter down to practitioners. Similarly, the long-held view that eye movements hold the key to understanding reading disability has not survived careful empirical tests; however, no amount of conflicting evidence appears to diminish the popularity of this hypothesis. Finally, research has indicated that failure at the "psycholinguistic guessing game" is not characteristic of poor readers. An inability to use contextual information to aid word recognition is not associated with poor reading. Poor readers do display contextual failures, but these appear to be due to inadequate decoding skills rather than to a strategic inability to guess at words.

However, there do appear to be a variety of cognitive functions that are associated with reading failure. A careful consideration of this variety leads naturally back to the assumption of specificity: the idea— almost always implicit if not explicitly stated—that the concept of a specific reading disability requires that the deficits displayed by the disabled reader not extend too far into other domains of cognitive functioning. Were this the case, there already would exist research and educational designations for such children (low intelligence, "slow learner," etc.). The research reviewed presents severe problems for the assumption of specificity and, in questioning the assumption, presents a challenge for future scholarship in the field of learning disabilities. A brief survey of the major conclusions will highlight the seriousness of this challenge.

Reading-disabled individuals are characterized by pervasive language problems. At the lowest level, these include the ability to render the phonemic structure of speech transparent. This underdeveloped processing skill probably directly impairs the ability to break the spelling-to-sound code, a necessary prerequisite to early reading success. A phonological processing impairment that probably is closely related interferes with the poor reader's ability to form long-lasting, short-term memory codes. Briggs and Underwood (1982) argue for a deficit in the speech code that is closer to articulatory in level and Tallal (1980) even has uncovered processing deficits with nonspeech auditory stimuli. Naming deficits have also been associated with reading failure. Indications are, then, that the speech and auditory processing problems of the poor reader are multiple and pervasive in nature.

It has also not been difficult to uncover language-processing differences at other levels. An increasing number of recent studies have focused on the fact that syntactic knowledge and awareness seems to be a particular area of difficulty for the poor reader. They display comprehension problems that are independent of (that is, in addition to) decoding problems. Different studies have indicated that disabled readers are also poor listeners. Comprehension strategies that are very general seem to be deficient. Given the pervasiveness of these language problems, it is difficult to describe them as representing any type of specific disability.

The relationship of language to intelligence and cognition is an important, but complex, topic in the fields of cognitive and developmental psychology. However, most discussions trace at least part of the complexity to the multitude of interacting relationships that are present. In short, language is an important underlying aspect of intelligence that facilitates cognitive functioning in many areas. Language deficits as pervasive as those displayed by reading-disabled individuals only can be seen as undermining the assumption of specificity.

Work on short-term memory as a psychological locus of the processing difficulties of problem readers originally was motivated by the desire to uncover a specific site of the problem. It is almost certainly true that some proportion of the performance difference between good and poor readers on short-term memory tasks is due to the specific phonological coding problems experienced by the latter. However, research on individual differences in memory performance soon pushed the possible mediating cognitive mechanisms far beyond an explanation purely in terms of phonological coding. As discussed, cognitive and developmental psychologists have linked a plethora of processing strategies to memory performance, and research has shown learning-disabled children to be deficient in their use of, and willingness to employ, virtually every one of these strategies. This finding has led to characterizations of the underlying cognitive deficit of learning-disabled children that are notable for their generality. For example, Torgesen's (1977a, 1977b) early work on memory functioning led to his positing the idea of the learning-disabled child as an inactive learner, one who fails to apply to tasks even cognitive strategies that are within their capabilities.

Torgesen's (1977a, 1977b) notion is, of course, similar to the currently popular ideas regarding the importance of metacognitive or executive functioning. Indeed, recent work on the performance of learning-disabled children has reinforced his earlier position and explicitly tied in the idea with recent views on metacognitive functioning (Baker, 1982; Bos & Filip, 1982; Foster & Gavelek, 1983; Hagen, Barclay, & Newman, 1982; Hallahan & Bryan, 1981; Wiens, 1983; Wong, 1984). However, the tendency to link deficiencies in metacognitive functioning with reading disability is actually embarrassing to the assumption of specificity. Recent conceptualizations often point to metacognitive awareness of available strategies as a sine qua non of *intelligence* (Baron, 1978; Campione & Brown, 1978; Sternberg, 1980, 1982a, 1982b)! Further developments along these lines will thus end up telling us, essentially, that reading-disabled individuals are deficient in intelligence (i.e., metacognitive awareness), a generalized ability to deal with cognitive tasks of all types. This would, of course, be consistent with the IQ evidence discussed, but similarly, would be inconsistent with the assumption of specificity.

The idea that the cognitive problems characteristic of reading-disabled individuals may be generalized rather than specific has been alluded to by several different investigators. Valtin (1978–1979) was so impressed with the generalized performance deficits displayed by her subjects that she commented, "these data suggest the conclusion that in the case of many of these children, dyslexia is only one aspect of a broader learning disability, which is frequently coupled with auditory and speech-motor deficiencies" (p. 207). Cohen (1982), in his comparative review of the short-term memory functioning of dyslexic and retarded children, pointed to the fact that research has shown that the former group is also characterized by pervasive cognitive deficits. Morrison (1984) and Morrison and Manis (1982) have argued that reading-disabled children have a fundamental deficiency in their ability to learn complex or irregular rule systems, a problem that is manifest in learning even nonalphabetic symbol systems. Although Morrison's (1984) conceptualization remains controversial (see Vellutino & Scanlon, 1984) to the extent that it contains a grain of truth, it adds to the evidence indicating a more generalized cognitive deficit than is commonly assumed.

It should be emphasized, however, that most of the theoretical conceptualizations of learning disabilities that have pointed to pervasive deficits are moot on the underlying cause of the generalized performance problem. It does not follow that the conclusions drawn here support only genetic or constitutional explanations of learning disabilities. For example, the possibility that many school-achievement problems are due to nonoptimal instruction has been inadequately considered (see Calfee, 1983). It is also important to note that Rutter and Yule (1975), using regression procedures that controlled for intelligence, found that the incidence of specific reading retardation in an inner borough of London was twice that observed on the Isle of Wight. In a further report (Rutter, Yule, Quinton, Rowlands, Yule, & Berger, 1974) they identified several environmental factors such as large families and teacher turnover in schools that were associated with specific reading retardation and that differentiated the London and Isle of Wight samples. Finally Torgesen (1980) has wisely pointed out that one thing that all learning-disabled children have in common is the experience of school failure. Thus, some of the performance deficits that are observed, rather than being a cause of achievement lags, could be the *result* of failure-induced motivational problems that would negatively affect scores on all school-like tasks. Recent research (e.g., Butkowsky & Willows, 1980; Torgesen & Licht, 1983) has suggested that an academic "learned helplessness" is characteristic of learning-disabled children. If further research supports this notion, it will go a long way toward explaining the generalized deficits that learning-disabled children display on many academic tasks.

In short, the possibility of reciprocal causation must be considered seriously. This possibility has implications for evaluating the assumption of specificity. For example, it is possible that the performance of learning-disabled children is characterized by a highly specific deficit upon entering school. The subsequent failure in a critical and highly valued task such as reading may cause motivation problems and trigger inefficient metacognitive strategies that interfere with performance on a wide variety of cognitive tasks. Thus, a specific processing deficiency could develop into a more generalized intellectual/motivational problem. There is some suggestive evidence supporting this conjecture. Studies of individual differences in the cognitive subskills underlying reading have indicated that these subskills are initially (i.e., in the first grade or earlier) only weakly related to each other. With development and/or increases in reading proficiency, the interrelationships among the subskills increase in number and strength (compare the data of Curtis, 1980; Guthrie, 1973; Jackson & McClelland, 1979; Stanovich *et al.*, 1984a; and Stevenson *et al.*, 1976). Guthrie (1973) and Stanovich *et al.*, (1984a) speculated that, at the more advanced levels, reading itself may foster mutual facilitation among cognitive subskills (or, conversely, reading failure may inhibit such facilitation). This conjecture suggests that any evaluation of the assumption of specificity must take developmental factors into account. Specificity may characterize *early* reading failure. This specificity, however, may gradually break down and turn into a more generalized cognitive deficit, not necessarily because of purely intrinsic factors, but due to the behavioral/cognitive/motivational spinoffs from failure at a crucial educational task like reading.

There is another objection to the characterization of the research evidence on reading disabilities as questioning the assumption of specificity that is both important and valid, and, therefore, it needs to be discussed as a potential caveat. The point is that there may be different subtypes of dyslexia, and that by combining several subtypes (each with a distinct, but different, single-factor deficit) in a research sample, the overall results from the sample are made to artifactually portray reading-disabled children as suffering from multiple deficits. There is no doubt that this is a logical possibility that should be kept in mind when evaluating the state of the research evidence. To the extent that it is true, it would attenuate the view of the reading-disabled population as suffering from pervasive processing deficits, and it would serve to bolster the assumption of specificity against some of the weakening empirical evidence that has been presented in this review. This particular caveat has not been more strongly emphasized because the evidence that is available in the subtyping literature is equivocal (see Vellutino, 1979, pp.354–358; Olson *et al.*, 1985). An assessment of the earlier literature (see Boder, 1973; Denckla, 1972; Harris, 1982; Mattis, French, & Rappin, 1975; Petrauskas & Rourke, 1979; Vellutino, 1979) inevitably leads to Jorm's (1983) conclusion that "there is no agreed-upon taxonomy of subtypes" (p. 312). However, statistically and empirically, sound work on subtypes is just in its infancy. Newer, sounder research methodologies (see Doehring, Trites, Patel, & Fiedorowicz, 1981; Torgesen, 1982) are just beginning to be evaluated. At present, many investigators probably would agree with McKinney's (1984) point, that subtyping work is in an embryonic stage, but promises to have great impact on the field.

Another possible objection to the conclusions drawn is that they have been partially based on research studies where the poor readers were not extremely disabled, but just significantly below the control group and/or population norms. This criticism raises two important points. First, it should be noted that the objection actually serves to reinforce a conclusion that has been made repeatedly in this review. Reading ability forms a continuum, and the farther up on it the poor reader resides, the less likely it is that he/she will be characterized by a qualitatively different syndrome. Logically, the wider the net that is cast by the term "reading disability," the vaguer the term will become, and the difficulties in distinguishing poor-reading children with the label from those who do not carry it (e.g., slow learners, borderline retardation, EMR) will increase. The evidence reviewed provides empirical support for this logical hypothesis. Large numbers of school-labeled, learning-disabled children are simply not cognitively differentiable from other nonlabeled poor readers (a warning that has repeatedly reappeared in the literature, see Kirk & Elkins, 1975). Second, this potential objection leads one to reiterate an important conclusion (Carr 1981; see also Jorm, 1983): that a thorough review of the reading literature indicates that the cognitive differences displayed by good and poor readers have been remarkably consistent regardless of the exact points on the reading continuum from which the two groups of readers have been drawn. It does not seem that the variables accounting for individual differences in reading ability are markedly different at the very extremes of reading skill. Most available evidence suggests the opposite in indicating a great degree of similarity. The variables that differentiate slightly below-average readers from those slightly above average appear to be the same variables that distinguish the severely disabled reader from a normal control group, a trend that is indirectly threatening to the assumption of specificity via an appeal to parsimony.

The critique of the assumption of specificity presented here flowed from a review of the state of the current evidence on the cognitive correlates of reading disability. Although the outcome of the review is critical of the assumption, it should not necessarily be concluded that the entire concept of a reading disability is misconceived; rather, that the current development of the concept is in need of considerable refinement. Such a conceptual refinement, based on the best available research evidence, rather than undermining the concept, could lead to a theoretical view that is more likely to withstand the critical scrutiny that is the wellspring of scientific advance.

This review has provided some direction for future attempts at refining the learning-disabilities concept. First, the identification procedures used by Rutter and Yule, 1975, and Yule, Rutter, Berger, and Thompson, 1974, were suggested. The essential features were (1) use of a nonverbal intelligence test as an initial screening device; (2) regression-equation procedures to identify outliers; and (3) a conservative criterion for classifying a case as an outlier, resulting in approximately 3.7% of their cases being classified as "specifics." Another general strategy for refinement of the learning-disability concept might be for researchers to try to falsify the general conclusion of pervasive processing deficits. Two tactics for attempting such a falsification have been suggested. One is to continue to refine research on subtypes to the point where it can be demonstrated that the results of the individual difference research (which seems to indicate that learning disabled children have a plethora of deficits) are artifactual, resulting from the combination of many different subject samples, each having a single (or a very few) specific deficit. Another strategy would be to attempt to garner support for the hypothesis of reciprocal causation: the idea that the plethora of deficits might be real, but that they *result* from a reading failure that might have been due initially to a specific processing deficit. Such a strategy, regardless of its outcome, would have the beneficial effect of building a developmental component into models of learning disabilities, a research strategy championed by some investigators (e.g., Satz, Taylor, Friel, & Fletcher, 1978), but still all too rare in the learning-disabilities field.

REFERENCES

Algozzine, B., & Ysseldyke, J. (1983). Learning disabilities as a subset of school failure: The over-sophistication of a concept. *Exceptional Children, 50*, 242–246.

Allington, R. (1978). Effects of contextual constraints upon rate and accuracy. *Perceptual and Motor Skills, 46*, 1318.

Allington, R., & Fleming, J. (1978). The misreading of high-frequency words. *Journal of Special Education, 12*, 417–421.

Allington, R., & Strange, M. (1977). Effects of grapheme substitutions in connected text upon reading behaviors. *Visible Language, 11*, 285–297.

Aman, M., & Singh, N. (1983). Specific reading disorders: Concepts of etiology reconsidered. In K. Gadow & I. Bialer (Eds.) *Advances in Learning and Behavioral Disabilities, Vol. 2.* (pp. 90–130). Greenwich, CT: JAI Press.

Ames, L. (1968). A low intelligence quotient often not recognized as the chief cause of many learning difficulties. *Journal of Learning Disabilities, 1*, 45–48.

Anderson, M., Kaufman, A., & Kaufman, N. (1976). Use of the WISC–R with a learning disabled population: Some diagnostic implications. *Psychology in the Schools, 13*, 381–386.

Arnett, M., & DiLollo, V. (1979). Visual information processing in relation to age and to reading ability. *Journal of Experimental Child Psychology, 27*, 143–152.

Arter, J., & Jenkins, J. (1979). Differential diagnosis-prescriptive teaching: A critical appraisal. *Review of Educational Research, 49*, 517–555.

Badcock, D., & Lovegrove, W. (1981). The effects of contrast, stimulus duration, and spatial frequency on visible persistence in normal and specifically disabled readers. *Journal of Experimental Psychology: Human Perception and Performance, 7*, 495–505.

Baddeley, A. (1966). Short-term memory for word sequences as a function of acoustic, semantic, and formal similarity. *Quarterly Journal of Experimental Psychology, 18*, 362–365.

Baker, L. (1982). An evaluation of the role of metacognitive deficits in learning disabilities. *Topics in Learning and Learning Disabilities, 2*, 27–35.

Baron, J. (1978). Intelligence and general strategies. In G. Underwood (Ed.). *Strategies in Information Processing* (pp 403–450). London: Academic Press.

Barron, R. (1978a). Access to the meanings of printed words: Some implications for reading and learning to read. In F. Murray (Ed.). *The recognition of words: IRA series on the development of the reading process* (pp. 34–56). Newark, DE: International Reading Association.

Barron, R. (1978b). Reading skill and phonological coding in lexical access. In M. Gruneberg, P. Morris & R. Sykes (Eds.). *Practical aspects of memory* (pp. 468–475). London: Academic Press.

Barron, R. (1980). Visual-orthographic and phonological strategies in reading and spelling. In U. Frith (Ed.). *Cognitive Processes in Spelling* (pp. 195–213). London: Academic Press.

Barron, R. (1981). Reading skill and reading strategies. In A. Lesgold & C. Perfetti (Eds.). *Interactive Processes in Reading* (pp. 299–327). Hillsdale, NJ: Erlbaum Associates.

Bateman, B. (1979). Teaching reading to learning disabled and other hard-to-teach children. In L. Resnick & P. Weaver (Eds.). *Theory and Practice of Early Reading. Vol. 1* (pp. 227–259). Hillsdale, NJ: Lawrence Erlbaum Associates.

Batey, O., & Sonnenschein, S. (1981). Reading deficits in learning disabled children. *Journal of Applied Developmental Psychology, 2,* 237–246.

Bauer, R. (1977). Memory processes in children with learning disabilities: Evidence for deficient rehearsal. *Journal of Experimental Child Psychology, 24,* 415–430.

Bauer, R. (1979). Memory, acquisition, and category clustering in learning-disabled children. *Journal of Experimental Child Psychology, 27,* 365–383.

Bauer, R. (1982). Information processing as a way of understanding and diagnosing learning disabilities. *Topics in Learning & Learning Disabilities, 2,* 33–45.

Becker, C. (1982). The development of semantic context effects: Two processes or two strategies?. *Reading Research Quarterly, 17,* 482–502.

Berger, N. (1978). Why can't John read? Perhaps he's not a good listener. *Journal of Learning Disabilities, 11,* 633–638.

Bickley, A., Ellington, B., & Bickley, R. (1970). The cloze procedure: A conspectus. *Journal of Reading Behavior, 2,* 232–249.

Biemiller, A. (1970). The development of the use of graphic and contextual information as children learn to read. *Reading Research Quarterly, 6,* 75–96.

Biemiller, A. (1977–1978). Relationships between oral reading rates for letters, words, and simple text in the development of reading achievement. *Reading Research Quarterly, 13,* 223–252.

Biemiller, A. (1979). Changes in the use of graphic and contextual information as functions of passage difficulty and reading achievement level. *Journal of Reading Behavior, 11,* 307–319.

Blalock, J. (1982). Persistent auditory language deficits in adults with learning disabilities. *Journal of Learning Disabilities, 15,* 604–609.

Bloom, A., Wagner, M., Reskin, L. & Bergman, A. (1980). A comparison of intellectually delayed and primary reading disabled children on measures of intelligence and achievement. *Journal of Clinical Psychology, 36,* 788–790.

Boder, M. (1973). Developmental dyslexia; A diagnostic approach based on three atypical reading-spelling patterns. *Developmental Medicine and Child Neurology, 15,* 663–687.

Bos, C., & Filip, D. (1982). Comprehension monitoring skills in learning disabled and average students. *Topics in Learning and Learning Disabilities, 2,* 79–85.

Bouma, H., & Legein, C. (1980). Dyslexia: A specific recoding deficit? An analysis of response latencies for letters and words in dyslectics and in average readers. *Neuropsychologia, 18,* 285–298.

Bradley, L., & Bryant, P. (1978). Difficulties in auditory organization as a possible cause of reading backwardness. *Nature, 271,* 746–747.

Bradley, L., & Bryant, P. (1983). Categorizing sounds and learning to read: A causal connection. *Nature, 301*, 419–421.

Brady, S. Shankweiler, D. & Mann, V. (1983). Speech perception and memory coding in relation to reading ability. *Journal of Experimental Child Psychology, 35*, 345–367.

Bransford, J., & Johnson, M. (1973). Consideration of some problems in comprehension. In W. G. Chase (Ed.). *Visual Information Processing* (pp. 383–438). New York: Academic Press.

Bransford, J., Stein, B., & Vye, N. (1982). Helping students learn how to learn from written texts. In M. Singer (Ed.). *Competent Reader, Disabled reader: Research and Application* (pp. 141–150). Hillsdale, NJ: Lawrence Erlbaum Associates.

Briggs, P., & Underwood, G. (1982). Phonological coding in good and poor readers. *Journal of Experimental Child Psychology, 34*, 93–112.

Brown, A. (1981). Metacognition: The development of selective attention strategies for learning from texts. In M. Kamil (Ed.), *30th Yearbook of the National Reading Conference*, (pp. 21–43). Clemson, SC: National Reading Conference.

Brown, B., Haegerstrom-Portnoy, G., Adams, A., Yingling, C., Galin, D., Herron, J., & Marcus, M. (1983). Predictive eye movements do not discriminate between dyslexic and control children. *Neuropsychologia, 21*, 121–128.

Bryan, T. (1974). Learning disabilities: A new stereotype. *Journal of Learning Disabilities, 7*, 46–31.

Butkowsky, S., & Willows, D. (1980). Cognitive-motivational characteristics of children varying in reading ability: Evidence for learned helplessness in poor readers. *Journal of Educational Psychology, 72*, 408–422.

Byrne, B., (1981). Deficient syntactic control in poor readers: Is a weak phonetic memory code responsible? *Applied Psycholinguistics, 2*, 201–212.

Byrne, B., & Shea, P. (1979). Semantic and phonetic memory codes in beginning readers. *Memory & Cognition, 7*, 333–338.

Calfee, R. (1976). Book review of "The Psychology of Reading" by E. Gibson & H. Levin. *Proceedings of the National Academy of Education, 3*, 1–80.

Calfee, R. (1977). Assessment of independent reading skills: Basic research and practical applications. In A. S. Reber & D. L. Scarborough (Eds.). *Toward a Psychology of Reading* (pp. 289–323). Hillsdale, NJ: Lawrence Erlbaum Associates.

Calfee, R. (1983). Review of "Dyslexia: Theory and Research." *Applied Psycholinguistics, 4*, 69–79.

Camp, B., & Dolcourt, J. (1977). Reading and spelling in good and poor readers. *Journal of Learning Disabilities, 10*, 300–307.

Campione, J., & Brown, A. (1978). Toward a theory of intelligence: Contributions from research with retarded children. *Intelligence, 2*, 279–304.

Carr, T. (1981). Building theories of reading ability: On the relation between individual differences in cognitive skills and reading comprehension. *Cognition, 9*, 73–113.

Carroll, J., & Walton, M. (1979). Has the reel reeding prablum bin lade bear? In L. Resnick & P. Weaver (Eds.). *Theory and Practice of Early Reading.* Vol. 3 (pp. 603–640). Hillsdale, NJ: Lawrence Erlbaum Associates.

Carver, R., & Hoffman, J. (1981). The effect of practice through repeated reading on gain in reading ability using a computer-based instructional system. *Reading Research Quarterly, 16*, 374–390.

Cermak, L., Goldberg, J., Cermak, S. & Drake, C. (1980). The short-term memory ability of children with learning disabilities. *Journal of Learning Disabilities, 13*, 25–29.

Chall, J. (1979). The great debate: Ten years later, with a modest proposal for reading stages. In L. Resnick & P. Weaver (Eds.). *Theory and Practice of Early Reading.* Vol. 1., (pp. 29– 55). Hillsdale, NJ: Lawrence Erlbaum Associates.

Chall, S. (1983). *Stages of reading development.* New York: McGraw-Hill Book Co.

Cohen, A. (1974–1975). Oral reading errors of first grade children taught by a code emphasis approach. *Reading Research Quarterly, 10,* 615–650.

Cohen, R. (1982). Individual differences in short-term memory. In N. Ellis (Ed.). *International Review of Research in Mental Retardation.* Vol. 11 (pp. 43–77). New York: Academic Press.

Cohen, R., & Netley, C. (1981). Short–term memory deficits in reading disabled children, in the absence of opportunity for rehearsal strategies. *Intelligence, 5,* 69–76.

Cohen, S. (1976). The fuzziness and the flab; Some solutions to research problems in learning disabilities. *Journal of Special Education, 10,* 129–136.

Cohn, M., & Stricker, G. (1979). Reversal errors in strong, average, and weak letter namers. *Journal of Learning Disabilities, 12,* 533–537.

Coles, G. (1978). The learning disabilities test battery: Empirical and social issues. *Harvard Educational Review, 48,* 313–340.

Conrad, R. (1964). Acoustic confusions in immediate memory. *British Journal of Psychology, 55,* 75–84.

Coomber, J. (1972). *A psycholinguistic analysis of oral reading errors made by good, average, and poor readers* (Technical Report No. 232). Madison: University of Wisconsin, Wisconsin Research and Development Center.

Crowder, R. (1982). *The psychology of reading.* New York: Oxford University Press.

Cummings, E., & Faw, T. (1976). Short-term memory and equivalence judgments in normal and retarded readers. *Child Development, 47,* 286–289.

Curtis, M. (1980). Development of components of reading skill. *Journal of Educational Psychology, 72,* 656–669.

Dallago, M., & Moely, B. (1980). Free recall in boys of normal and poor reading levels as a function of task manipulations. *Journal of Experimental Child Psychology, 30,* 62–78.

Daneman, M., & Carpenter, P. (1980). Individual differences in working memory and reading. *Journal of Verbal Learning and Verbal Behavior, 19,* 450–466.

Denckla, M. (1972). Clinical syndromes in learning disabilities: The case for "splitting" vs "lumping." *Journal of Learning Disabilities, 5,* 401–406.

Denckla, M. & Rudel, R. (1976). Rapid automatized naming (RAN): Dyslexia differentiated from other learning disabilities. *Neuropsychologia, 14,* 471–478.

Deno, S., Mirkin, P., & Chiang, B. (1982). Identifying valid measures of reading. *Exceptional Children, 49,* 36–47.

Detterman, D. (1982). Does "g" exist? *Intelligence, 6,* 99–108.

DiVesta, F., Hayward, K., & Orlando, V. (1979). Developmental trends in monitoring text for comprehension. *Child Development, 50,* 97–105.

Doehring, D. (1976). Acquisition of rapid reading responses. *Monographs of the Society for Research in Child Development, 41* (2, Serial No. 165). Chicago: University of Chicago Press.

Doehring, D., Trites, R., Patel, P., & Fiedorowicz, C. (1981) *Reading disabilities: The interaction of reading, language, and neuropsychological deficits.* New York: Academic Press.

Donahue, M., Pearl, R., & Bryan, T. (1983). Communicative competence in learning disabled children. In K. Gadow & I. Bialer (Eds.). *Advances in learning and behavioral disabilities.* Vol. 2 (pp. 49–84). Greenwich, CT: JAI Press.

Downing, J. (1980). Learning to read with understanding. In M. McCullough (Ed.). *Persistent Problems in Reading Education* (pp. 163–178). Newark. DE: International Reading Association.

Duker, S. (1965). Listening and reading. *Elementary School Journal, 65,* 321–329.

Eakin, S., & Douglas, V. (1971). Automatization and oral reading problems in children. *Journal of Learning Disabilities, 4,* 26–33.

Ehri, L. (1979). Linguistic insight: Threshold of reading acquisition. In T. Walker & G. Mackinnon (Eds.). *Reading Research: Advances in Research and Theory*. Vol. 1 (pp. 63–114). New York: Academic Press.

Ehri, L., & Wilce, L. (1983). Development of word identification speed in skilled and less skilled beginning readers. *Journal of Educational Psychology, 75*, 3–18.

Ehrlich, S. (1981). Children's word recognition in prose context. *Visible Language, 15*, 219–244.

Eisenberg, L. (1966). Neuropsychiatric aspects of reading disability. *Pediatrics, 37*, 17–33.

Eisenberg, L. (1979). Reading disorders: Strategies for recognition and management. *Bulletin of the Orton Society, 29*, 39–55.

Elliot, R. (1970). Simple reaction time; Effects associated with age, preparatory interval, incentive shift, and mode of presentation. *Journal of Experimental Child Psychology, 9*, 86–104.

Ellis, N. (1981). Visual and name coding in dyslexic children. *Psychological Research, 43*, 201–218.

Ericksen, C. (1980). The use of a visual mask may seriously confound your experiment. *Perception & Psychophysics, 28*, 89–92.

Feagans, L. (1983). A current view of learning disabilities. *Journal of Pediatrics, 102*, 487–493.

Feagans, L., & McKinney, J. (1981). The pattern of exceptionality across domains in learning disabled children. *Journal of Applied Developmental Psychology, 1*, 313–323.

Fischer, F., Liberman, I., & Shankweiler, D. (1978). Reading reversals and developmental dyslexia; A further study. *Cortex, 14*, 496–510.

Fisher, D., & Frankfurter, A. (1977). Normal and disabled readers can locate and identify letters: Where's the perceptual deficit? *Journal of Reading Behavior, 9*, 31–43.

Fletcher, J., Satz, P., & Scholes, R. (1981). Developmental changes in the linguistic performance correlates of reading achievement. *Brain and Language, 13*, 78–90.

Fodor, J. (1983). *Modularity of mind*. Cambridge, MA: MIT Press.

Foster, R., & Gavelek, J. (1983). Development of intentional forgetting in normal and reading-delayed children. *Journal of Educational Psychology, 75*, 431–440.

Fox, B., & Routh, D. (1976). Phonemic analysis and synthesis as word attack skills. *Journal of Educational Psychology, 68*, 70–74.

Fox, B., & Routh, D. (1980). Phonemic analysis and severe reading disability. *Journal of psycholinguistic Research, 9*, 115–119.

Fox, B., & Routh, D. (1983). Reading disability, phonemic analysis, and dysphonic spelling: A follow-up study. *Journal of Clinical Child Psychology, 12*, 28–32.

Frederiksen, J. (1978). Assessment of perceptual, decoding, and lexical skills and their relation to reading proficiency. In A. Lesgold, J. Pellegrino, S. Fokkema, & R. Glaser (Eds.). *Cognitive Psychology and Instruction* (pp. 153–169). New York: Plenum Press.

Gajar, A. (1979). Educable mentally retarded, learning disabled, emotionally disturbed: Similarities and differences. *Exceptional Children, 45*, 470–472.

Garner, R., & Reis, R. (1981). Monitoring and resolving comprehension obstacles: An investigation of spontaneous text lookbacks among upper-grade good and poor comprehenders. *Reading Research Quarterly, 16*, 569–582.

Gaskins, I. (1982). Let's end the reading disabilities/learning disabilities debate. *Journal of Learning Disabilities, 15*, 81–83.

Godfrey, J., Syrdal-Lasky, A., Millay, K., & Knox, C. (1981). Performance of dyslexic children on speech perception tests. *Journal of Experimental Child Psychology, 32*, 401–424.

Goldman, S., Hogaboam, T., Bell, L., & Perfetti, C. (1980). Short-term retention of discourse during reading. *Journal of Educational Psychology, 72*, 647–655.

Goldstein, D. (1976). Cognitive-linguistic functioning and learning to read in preschoolers. *Journal of Educational Psychology, 63,* 680–688.

Golinkoff, R. (1978). Phonemic awareness skills and reading achievement. In F. Murray & J. Pikulski (Eds.). *The acquisition of reading* (pp. 23–41). Baltimore, MD: University Park Press.

Goodman, K. (1965). A linguistic study of cues and miscues in reading. *Elementary English, 42,* 639–643.

Goodman, K. (1976). Reading: A psycholinguistic guessing game. In H. Singer & R. Ruddell (Eds.). *Theoretical Models and Processes of Reading* (pp. 497–508). Newark, DE: International Reading Association.

Gottesman, R., Croen, L., & Rotkin, L. (1982). Urban second-grade children: A profile of good and poor readers. *Journal of Learning Disabilities, 15,* 268–272.

Gough, P. (1981). A comment on Kenneth Goodman. In M. Kamil (Ed.). *Directions in Reading: Research and Instruction* (pp. 20–25). Clemson, SC: National Reading Conference.

Gough, P., Alford, J., & Holley-Wilcox, P. (1981). Words and contexts. In O. Tzeng & H. Singer (Eds.). *Perception of print; Reading Research in Experimental Psychology* (pp. 100–120). Hillsdale, NJ: Lawrence Erlbaum Associates.

Gough, P., & Hillinger, M. (1980). Learning to read: An unnatural act. *Bulletin of the Orton society, 30,* 171–196.

Groff, P. (1975). Reading ability and auditory discrimination: Are they related? *The Reading Teacher, 28,* 742–747.

Groff, P. (1978). Should children learn to read words? *Reading World, 17,* 256–264.

Gross, J., & Gottlieb, J. (1982). The mildly handicapped: A service distinction for the future? In T. Miller & E. Davis (Eds.). *The Mildly Handicapped Student* (pp. 497–511). New York: Grune & Stratton.

Gross, K., & Rothenberg, S. (1979). An examination of methods used to test the visual perceptual deficit hypothesis of dyslexia. *Journal of Learning Disabilities, 12,* 670–677.

Gupta, R., Ceci, S., & Slater, A. (1978). Visual discrimination in good and poor readers. *Journal of Special Education, 12,* 409–416.

Guthrie, J. (1973). Models of reading and reading disability. *Journal of Educational Psychology, 65* 9–18.

Guthrie, J., & Tyler, S. (1976). Psycholinguistic processing in reading and listening among good and poor readers. *Journal of Reading Behavior, 8,* 415–426.

Hagen, J., Barclay, C., & Newman, R. (1982). Metacognition, self-knowledge, and learning disabilities: Some thoughts on knowing and doing. *Topics in Learning and Learning Disabilities, 2,* 19–26.

Hagen, J., Barclay, C., & Schwethelm, B. (1982). Cognitive development of the learning disabled child. In N. Ellis (Ed.). *International review of research in mental retardation.* Vol. 11 (pp. 1–41). New York: Academic Press.

Hall, J. W., & Humphreys, M. (1982). Research on specific learning disabilities: Deficits and remediation. *Topics in Learning and Learning Disabilities, 2,* 68–78.

Hall, J., Wilson, K., Humphreys, M., Tinzmann, M., & Bowyer, P. (1983). Phonemic-similarity effects in good vs. poor readers. *Memory & Cognition, 11,* 520–527.

Hallahan, D., & Bryan, T. (1981). Learning disabilities. In J. Kauffman & D. Hallahan (Eds.), *Handbook of Special Education* (pp. 141–164) Englewood Cliffs, NJ: Prentice-Hall.

Hallahan, D., & Kauffman, J. (1977). Labels, categories, behaviors: ED, LD, and EMR reconsidered. *Journal of Special Education, 11,* 139–149.

Hammill, D., & Larsen, S. (1974). The effectiveness of psycholinguistic training. *Exceptional Children, 41,* 5–15.

Hammill, D., & Larsen, S. (1978). The effectiveness of psycholinguistic training: A reaffirmation of position. *Exceptional Children, 44,* 402–417.

Hansen, J. (1981). The effects of inference training and practice on young children's reading comprehension. *Reading Research Quarterly, 16,* 391–417.

Hansen, J., & Pearson, P. (1983). An instructional study: Improving the inferential comprehension of good and poor fourth-grade readers. *Journal of Educational Psychology, 75,* 821–829.

Harman, S. (1982). Are reversals a symptom of dyslexia? *The Reading Teacher, 35,* 424–428.

Harris, A. (1979). Lateral dominance and reading disability. *Journal of Learning Disabilites, 12,* 337–343.

Harris, A. J. (1982). How many kinds of reading disability are there? *Journal of Learning Disabilities, 15,* 456–460.

Helfgott, J. (1976). Phonemic segmentation and blending skills of kindergarten children: Implication for beginning reading acquisition. *Contemporary Educational Psychology, 1,* 157–169.

Hiscock, M., & Kinsbourne, M. (1982). Laterality and dyslexia: A critical view. *Annals of Dyslexia, 32,* 177–228.

Hogaboam, T., & Perfetti, C. (1978). Reading skill and the role of verbal experience in decoding. *Journal of Educational Psychology, 70,* 717–729.

Holmes, D. & McKeever, W. (1979). Material specific serial memory deficit in adolescent dyslexics. *Cortex, 15,* 51–62.

Holmes, D., & Peper, R. (1977). An evaluation of the use of spelling error analysis in the diagnosis of reading disabilities. *Child Development, 48,* 1708–1711.

Horn, W. F., & O'Donnell, J. P. (1984). Early identification of learning disabilities: A comparison of two methods. *Journal of Educational Psychology, 76,* 1106–1118.

Horvath, M., Kass, C., & Ferrell, W. (1980). An example of the use of fuzzy set concepts in modeling learning disability. *American Educational Research Journal, 17,* 309–324.

Huelsman, C. (1970). The WISC subtest syndrome for disabled readers. *Perceptual and Motor Skills, 30,* 535–545.

Hulme, C. (1981). The effects of manual training on memory in normal and retarded readers: Some implications for multi-sensory teaching. *Psychological Research, 43,* 179–191.

Hunt, E. (1978). Mechanics of verbal ability. *Psychological Review, 85,* 109–130.

Jackson, M. (1980). Further evidence for a relationship between memory access and reading ability. *Journal of Verbal Learning and Verbal Behavior, 19,* 683–694.

Jackson, M., & McClelland, J. (1979). Processing determinants of reading speed. *Journal of Experimental Psychology: General, 108,* 151–181.

Jenkins, J., & Pany, D. (1981). Instructional variables in reading comprehension. In J. T. Guthrie (Ed.). *Comprehension and teaching* (pp. 163–202). Newark, DE: International Reading Association.

Jorm, A. F. (1983). Specific reading retardation and working memory: A review. *British Journal of Psychology, 74,* 311–342.

Jorm, A., & Share, D. (1983). Phonological recoding and reading acquisition. *Applied Psycholinguistics, 4,* 103–147.

Juel, C. (1980). Comparison of word identification strategies with varying context, word type, and reader skill. *Reading Research Quarterly, 15,* 358–376.

Juel, C. (1983). The development and use of mediated word identification. *Reading Research Quarterly, 18,* 306–327.

Katz, R., Shankweiler, D., & Liberman, I. (1981). Memory for item order and phonetic recoding in the beginning reader. *Journal of Experimental Child Psychology, 32,* 474–484.

Kavale, K., & Mattson, P. (1983). "One jumped off the balance beam": Meta-analysis of perceptual-motor training. *Journal of Learning Disabilities, 16,* 165–173.

Kender, J. (1972). Is there really a WISC profile for poor readers? *Journal of Learning Disabilities, 5,* 397–400.

Kintsch, W. (1979). Concerning the marriage of research and practice in beginning reading instruction. In L. B. Resnick & P. Weaver (Eds.). *Theory and Practice of Early Reading.* (pp. 319–330). Hillsdale, NJ: Lawrence Erlbaum Associates.

Kirk, S., & Elkins, J. (1975). Characteristics of children enrolled in the child service demonstration centers. *Journal of Learning Disabilities, 8,* 630–637.

Klinge, V., Rennick, P., Lennox, K., & Hart, Z. (1977). A matched subject comparison of underachievers with normals on intellectual, behavioral, and emotional variables. *Journal of Abnormal Child Psychology, 5,* 61–68.

Kochnower, J., Richardson, E., & DiBenedetto, B. (1983). A comparison of the phonic decoding ability of normal and learning disabled children. *Journal of Learning Disabilities, 16,* 348–351.

Kotsonis, M., & Patterson, C. (1980). Comprehension monitoring skills in learning-disabled children. *Developmental Psychology, 16,* 541–542.

LaBerge, D., & Samuels, S. (1974). Toward a theory of automatic information processing in reading. *Cognitive Psychology, 6,* 293–323.

Lahey, B., Kupfer, D., Beggs, V., & Landon, D. (1982). Do learning-disabled children exhibit deficits in selective attention? *Journal of Abnormal Child Psychology, 10,* 1–10.

Larsen, S., & Hammill, D. (1975). Relationship of selected visual perception abilities to school learning. *Journal of Special Education, 9,* 281–291.

Larsen, S., Parker, R., & Hammill, D. (1982). Effectiveness of psycholinguistic training: a response to Kavale. *Exceptional Children, 49,* 60–67.

Lawrence, Y., Kee, D., & Hellige, J. (1980). Developmental differences in visual backward masking. *Child Development, 51,* 1081–1089.

Leinhardt, G., Seewald, A., & Zigmond, N. (1982). Sex and race differences in learning disabilities classrooms. *Journal of Educational Psychology, 74,* 835–843.

Leong, C. (1980). Laterality and reading proficiency in children. *Reading Research Quarterly, 15,* 185–202.

Lerner, J. (1975). Remedial reading and learning disabilities: Are they the same or different? *Journal of Special Education, 9,* 119–131.

Lesgold, A., & Curtis, M. (1981). Learning to read efficiently. In A. Lesgold & C. Perfetti (Eds.). *Interactive Processes in Reading* (pp. 329–360). Hillsdale, NJ: Lawrence Erlbaum Associates.

Lesgold, A. & Perfetti, C. (1978). Interactive processes in reading comprehension. *Discourse Processes, 1,* 323–336.

Lesgold, A., & Resnick, L. (1982). How reading difficulties develop: Perspectives from a longitudinal study. In J. Das, R. Mulcahey, & A. Wall (Eds.). *Theory and research in learning disabilities* (pp. 155–187). New York: Plenum Press.

Levin, J. (1973). Inducing comprehension in poor readers: A test of a recent model. *Journal of Educational Psychology, 65,* 19–24.

Lewkowicz, N. (1980). Phonemic awareness training: What to teach and how to teach it. *Journal of Educational Psychology, 72,* 686–700.

Liberman, I. (1973). Segmentation of the spoken word and reading acquisition. *Bulletin of the Orton Society, 23,* 65–77.

Liberman, I. (1982). A language-oriented view of reading and its disabilities. In H. Myklebust (Ed.). *Progress in learning disabilities.* Vol. 5 (pp. 81–101) New York: Grune & Stratton.

Liberman, I., & Shankweiler, D. (1979). Speech, the alphabet, and teaching to read. In L. Resnick & P. Weaver (Eds.). *Theory and Practice of Early Reading.* Vol. 2 (pp. 109–132). Hillsdale, NJ: Lawrence Erlbaum Associates.

Libkuman, T., Velliky, R., & Friedrich, D. (1980). Nonselective read-out from iconic memory in normal, borderline, and retarded adolescents. *Intelligence, 4,* 363–369.

Litcher, J., & Roberge, L. (1979). First-grade intervention for reading achievement of high-risk children. *Bulletin of the Orton Society, 29,* 238–244.

Lomax, R. (1982). Causal modeling of reading acquisition. *Journal of Reading Behavior, 14,* 341–345.

McCormick, C. & Samuels, S. (1979). Word recognition by second graders: The unit of perception and interrelationships among accuracy, latency, and comprehension. *Journal of Reading Behavior, 11,* 107–118.

McKinney, J. (1984). The search for subtypes of specific learning disability. *Journal of Learning Disabilities, 17,* 43–50.

McLesky, J., & Rieth, H. (1982). Controlling IQ differences between reading disabled and normal children: An empirical example. *Journal of Learning Disabilities, 15,* 481–483.

Manis, F., & Morrison, F. (1982). Processing of identity and position information in normal and disabled readers. *Journal of Experimental Child Psychology, 33,* 74–86.

Mann, L. (1970). Perceptual training: Misdirections and redirections. *American Journal of Orthopsychiatry, 40,* 30–38.

Mann, V. (March 1981). *Reading and language skill.* Paper presented at The Meeting of the Society for Research in Child Development. Boston: Society for Research in Child Development.

Mann, V., Liberman, I., & Shankweiler, D. (1980). Children's memory for sentences and word strings in relation to reading ability. *Memory & Cognition, 8,* 329–335.

Mason, M. (1975). Reading ability and letter search time: Effects of orthographic structure defined by single-letter positional frequency. *Journal of Experimental Psychology: General, 104,* 146–166.

Mason, M. (1978). From print to sound in mature readers as a function of reader ability and two forms of orthographic regularity. *Memory & Cognition, 6,* 568–581.

Masson, M., & Miller, J. (1983). Working memory and individual differences in comprehension and memory of text. *Journal of Educational Psychology, 75,* 314–318.

Mattis, S., French, J., & Rapin, I. (1975). Dyslexia in children and adults: Three independent neurological syndromes. *Developmental Medicine and Child Neurology, 17,* 150–163.

Menyuk, P., & Flood, J. (1981). Linguistic competence, reading, writing problems and remediation. *Bulletin of the Orton Society, 31,* 13–28.

Merrill, E., Sperber, R., & McCauley, C. (1981). Differences in semantic encoding as a function of reading comprehension skill. *Memory & Cognition, 9,* 618–624.

Meyer, B., Brandt, D., & Bluth, G. (1980). Use of top-level structure in text: Key for reading comprehension of ninth-grade students. *Reading Research Quarterly, 16,* 72–103.

Miller, T., & Davis, E. (1982). *The mildly handicapped student.* New York: Grune & Stratton.

Mitchell, D. (1982). *The process of reading: A cognitive analysis of fluent reading and learning to read.* New York: John Wiley.

Morrison, F. (1984). Word decoding and rule learning in normal and disabled readers. *Remedial and Special Education, 5,* 20–27.

Morrison, F., Giordani, B., & Nagy, J. (1977). Reading disability: An information-processing analysis. *Science, 196,* 77–79.

Morrison, F., & Manis, F. (1982). Cognitive processes and reading disability: A critique and proposal. In C. Brainard & M. Pressley (Eds.). *Verbal Processes in Children* (pp. 59–93). New York: Springer-Verlag.

Naylor, H. (1980). Reading disability and lateral asymmetry: An information-processing analysis. *Psychological Bulletin, 87,* 531–545.

Newcomer, P., & Magee, P. (1977). The performance of learning (reading) disabled children on a test of spoken language. *The Reading Teacher, 30,* 896–900.

Newman, D., & Hagen, J. (1981). Memory strategies in children with learning disabilities. *Journal of Applied Developmental Psychology, 1,* 297–312.

Norman, C., & Zigmond N. (1980). Characteristics of children labeled and served as learning disabled in school systems affiliated with child service demonstration centers. *Journal of Learning Disabilities, 13,* 16–21.

Oakhill, J. (1982). Constructive processes in skilled and less skilled comprehenders' memory for sentences. *British Journal of Psychology, 73,* 13–20.

Olson, R., Davidson, B., Kliegl, R., & Davies, S. (1984). Development of phonetic memory in disabled and normal readers. *Journal of Experimental Child Psychology, 37,* 187–206.

Olson, R., Kliegl, R. & Davidson, B. (1983). Dyslexia and normal readers' eye movements. *Journal of Experimental Psychology: Human Perception and Performance, 9,* 816–825).

Olson, R., Kliegl, R., Davidson, B. & Foltz, G. (1984). Individual and developmental differences in reading disability. In T. Waller (Ed.). *Reading Research: Advances in Theory and Practice* (pp. 20–40). New York: Academic Press.

Pace, A., & Golinkoff, R. (1976). Relationship between word difficulty and access of single-word meaning by skilled and less skilled readers. *Journal of Educational Psychology, 68,* 760–767.

Paris, S., & Myers, M. (1981). Comprehension monitoring, memory, and study strategies of good and poor readers. *Journal of Reading Behavior, 13,* 5–22.

Park, R. (1978–1979). Performance on geometric figure-copying tests as predictors of types of errors in decoding. *Reading Research Quarterly, 14,* 100–118.

Pavlidis, G. (1981). Sequencing, eye movements and the early objective diagnosis of dyslexia. In G. Pavlidis & T. Miles (Eds.). *Dyslexia Research and Its Applications to Education* (pp. 99–163). Chichester, England: John Wiley.

Payne, M., & Holzman, T. (1983). Auditory short-term memory and digit span; Normal versus poor readers. *Journal of Educational Psychology, 75,* 424–430.

Pearson, P., & Camperell, K. (1981). Comprehension of text structures. In J. T. Guthrie (Ed.). *Comprehension and Teaching,* Newark, DE: International Reading Association.

Perfetti, C., Beck, I., & Hughes, C. (March 1981). *Phonemic knowledge and learning to read.* Paper presented at The Meeting of the Society for Research in Child Development. Boston: Society for Research in Child Development.

Perfetti, C., Finger, E., & Hogaboam, T. (1978). Sources of vocalization latency differences between skilled and less skilled young readers. *Journal of Educational Psychology, 70,* 730–739.

Perfetti, C., Goldman, S., & Hogaboam, T. (1979). Reading skill and the identification of words in discourse context. *Memory & Cognition, 7,* 273–282.

Perfetti, C., & Hogaboam, T. (1975). Relationship between single word decoding and reading comprehension skill. *Journal of Educational Psychology, 56,* 461–469.

Perfetti, C., & Lesgold, A. (1977). Discourse comprehension and sources of individual differences. In M. Just & P. Carpenter (Eds.). *Cognitive Processes in Comprehension* (pp. 141–183). Hillsdale, NJ: Lawrence Erlbaum Associates.

Perfetti, C., & Lesgold, A. (1979). Coding and comprehension in skilled reading and implications for reading instruction. In L. B. Resnick & P. Weaver (Eds.). *Theory and Practice of Early Reading* (pp. 57–84). Hillsdale, NJ: Lawrence Erlbaum Associates.

Perfetti, C., & McCutchen, D. (1982). Speech processes in reading. In N. Lass (Ed.). *Speech and language: Advances in Basic Research and Practice.* Vol. 7 (pp. 237–269). New York: Academic Press.

Perfetti, C., & Roth, S. (1981). Some of the interactive processes in reading and their role in reading skill. In A. Lesgold & C. Perfetti, (Eds.). *Interactive Processes in Reading* (pp. 269–297). Hillsdale, NJ: Erlbaum Associates.

Petrauskas, R., & Rourke, B. (1979). Identification of subtypes of retarded readers; A neuropsychological, multivariate approach. *Journal of Clinical Neuropsychology, 1,* 17–37.

Posner, M. (1978). *Chronometric explorations of mind.* Hillsdale, NJ: Lawrence Erlbaum Associates.

Posner, M., & Mitchell, R. (1967). Chronometric analysis of classification. *Psychological review, 74,* 392–409.

Rayner, K. (1973). Eye movements in reading and information processing. *Psychological Bulletin, 85,* 618–660.

Richardson, E., Dibenedetto, B., & Adler, S. (1982). Use of the decoding skills test to study differences between good and poor readers. In K. Gadow & I Bialer (Eds.). *Advances in learning and behavioral disabilities.* Vol. 1 (pp. 25–74). Greenwich, CT: JAI Press.

Ross, L., & Ward, T. (1978). The processing of information from short-term visual store; Developmental and intellectual level differences. In N. Ellis (ED.). *International Review of Research in Mental Retardation.* Vol. 9 (pp. 1–28). New York: Academic Press.

Rozin, P., & Gleitman, L. (1977). The structure and acquisition of reading II: The reading process and the acquisition of the alphabetic principle. In A. Reber & D. Scarborough (Eds.). *Toward a Psychology of Reading* (pp, 55–141). Hillsdale, NJ: Lawrence Erlbaum Associates.

Ruddell, R. (1965). The effect of similarity of oral and written patterns of language structure on reading comprehension. *Elementary English, 42,* 403–410.

Rutter, M. (1978). Prevalence and types of dyslexia. In A. Benton & D. Pearl (Eds.), *Dyslexia: An appraisal of current knowledge* (pp. 5–28). New York: Oxford University Press.

Rutter, M., & Yule, W. (1975). The concept of specific reading retardation. *Journal of Child Psychology and Psychiatry, 16,* 181–197.

Rutter, M., Yule, B., Quinton D., Rolands, O., Yule, W., & Berger, M. (1974). Attainment and adjustment in two geographical areas: III. Some factors accounting for area differences. *British Journal of Psychiatry, 125,* 520–533.

Ryan, E. (1981). Identifying and remediating failures in reading comprehension: Toward an instructional approach for poor comprehenders. In T. Waller & G. Mackinnon (Eds.). *Reading Research: Advances in Theory and Practice.* Vol. 3) (pp. 223–261). New York: Academic Press.

Ryan, M. & Jones, B. (1975). Stimulus persistence in retarded and nonretarded children: A signal detection analysis. *American Journal of Mental Deficiency, 80,* 298–305.

Samuels, S. (1979). How the mind works when reading: Describing elephants no one has ever seen. In L. Resnick & P. Weaver (Eds.). *Theory and Practice of Early Reading.* Vol. 1) (pp. 343–368). Hillsdale, NJ: Lawrence Erlbaum Associates.

Satz, P., & Friel, J. (1974). Some predictive antecedents of specific reading disability: A preliminary 2-year follow-up. *Journal of Learning Disabilities, 7,* 437–444.

Satz, P., Taylor, H., Friel, J., & Fletcher, J. (1978). Some developmental and predictive precursors of reading disabilities: A 6-year follow-up. In A. Benton & D. Pearl (Eds.). *Dyslexia: An Appraisal of Current Knowledge* (pp. 315–347). New York: Oxford University Press.

Savin, H. (1972). What the child knows about speech when he starts to learn to read. In J. F. Kavanagh & I. Mattingly (Eds.). *Language by Ear and by Eye* (pp. 319–326). Cambridge: MIT Press.

Schvaneveldt, R., Ackerman, B., & Semlear, T. (1977). The effect of semantic context on children's word recognition. *Child Development, 48,* 612–616.

Schwantes, F. (1981). Effect of story context on children's ongoing word recognition. *Journal of Reading Behavior, 13,* 305–311.

Schwantes, F. (1982). Text readability level and developmental differences in context effects. *Journal of Reading Behavior, 14,* 4–12.

Schwantes, F., Boesl, S., & Ritz, E. (1980). Children's use of context in word recognition: A psycholinguistic guessing game. *Child Development, 51,* 730–736.

Schwartz, R., & Stanovich, K. (1981). Flexibility in the use of graphic and contextual information by good and poor readers. *Journal of Reading Behavior, 13,* 263–269.

Seaton, H. (1977). The effects of a visual perception training program on reading achievement. *Journal of Reading Behavior, 9,* 188–192.

Seymour, P., & Porpodas, C. (1980). Lexical and non-lexical processing of spelling in developmental dyslexia. In U. Frith (Ed.). *Cognitive Processes in Spelling* (pp. 443–473). London; Academic Press.

Shankweiler, D., & Liberman, I. (1972). Misreading: A search for causes. In J. Kavanagh & I. Mattingly (Eds.). *Language by Ear and Eye.* (pp. 293–317). Cambridge: MIT Press.

Shankweiler, D. & Liberman, I. (1978). Reading behavior in dyslexia: Is there a distinctive pattern?. *Bulletin of the Orton Society, 28,* 114–123.

Shankweiler, D., Liberman, I., Mark, L., Fowler, C., & Fischer, F. (1979). The speech code and learning to read. *Journal of Experimental Psychology: Human Learning and Memory, 5,* 531–545.

Shepard, L. (1980). An evaluation of the regression discrepancy method for identifying children with learning disabilities. *Journal of Special Education, 14,* 79–91.

Shepard, L., Smith, M., & Vojir, C. (1983). Characteristics of pupils identified as learning disabled. *American Educational Research Journal, 20,* 309–332.

Siegel, L. & Ryan, E. (1984). Reading disability as a language disorder. *Remedial and Special Education, 5,* 28–33.

Siler, E. (1973–1974). The effects of syntactic and semantic constraints on the oral reading performance of second and fourth graders. *Reading Research Quarterly, 9,* 603–621.

Simpson, G., Lorsbach, T., & Whitehouse, D. (1983). Encoding and contextual components of word recognition in good and poor readers. *Journal of Experimental Child Psychology, 35,* 161–171.

Singer, M. (1982). *Competent reader, disabled reader: Research and application.* Hillsdale, NJ: Lawrence Erlbaum Associates.

Smiley, S., Oakley, D., Worthen, D., Campione, J., & Brown, A. (1977). Recall of thematically relevant material by adolescent good and poor readers as a function of written versus oral presentation. *Journal of Educational Psychology, 69,* 381–387.

Smith, F. (1971). *Understanding reading.* New York: Holt, Rinehart and Winston.

Smith, M., Coleman, J., Dokecki, P., & Davis, E. (1977). Intellectual characteristics of school labeled learning disabled children. *Exceptional Children, 43,* 352–357.

Snowling, M. (1980). The development of grapheme-phoneme correspondence in normal and dyslexia readers. *Journal of Experimental Child Psychology, 29,* 294–305.

Snowling, M. (1981). Phonemic deficits in developmental dyslexia. *Psychological Research, 43,* 219–234.

Spring, C., & Capps, C. (1974). Encoding speed, rehearsal, and probed recall of dyslexic boys. *Journal of Educational Psychology, 66,* 780–786.

Spring, C., & Farmer, R. (1975). Perceptual span of poor readers. *Journal of Reading Behavior, 7,* 297–305.

Staller, J., & Sekuler, R. (1975). Children read normal and reversed letters: a simple test of reading skill. *Quarterly Journal of Experimental Psychology, 27,* 539–550.

Stanley, G. (1976). The processing of digits by children with specific reading disability. *British Journal of Educational Psychology, 46,* 81–84.

Stanley, G., Smith, G., & Howell, E. (1983). Eye movements and sequential tracking in dyslexic and control children. *British Journal of Psychology, 74,* 181–187.

Stanovich, K. (1978). Information processing in mentally retarded individuals. In N. R. Ellis (Ed.). *International Review of Research in Mental Retardation.* Vol. 9 (pp. 29–60). New York: Academic Press.

Stanovich,K. (1980). Toward an interactive-compensatory model of individual differences in the development of reading fluency. *Reading Research Quarterly, 16,* 32–71.

Stanovich, K. (1981). Relationships between word-decoding speed, general name-retrieval ability, and reading progress in first-grade children. *Journal of Educational Psychology, 73,* 809–815.

Stanovich, K. (1982a). Individual differences in the cognitive processes of reading I: Word decoding. *Journal of Learning Disabilities, 15,* 485–493.

Stanovich, K. (1982b). Individual differences in the cognitive processes of reading II: Text-level processes. *Journal of Learning Disabilities, 15,* 549–554.

Stanovich, K. (1984). The interactive-compensatory model of reading: A confluence of developmental, experimental, and educational psychology. *Remedial and Special Education, 5,* 11–19.

Stanovich, K., Cunningham, A., & Feeman, D. (1984a). Intelligence, cognitive skills, and early reading progress. *Reading Research Quarterly, 19,* 278–303.

Stanovich, K., Cunningham, A., & Feeman, D. (1984b). The relationship between early reading acquisition and word decoding with and without context: A longitudinal study of first-grade children. *Journal of Educational Psychology, 76,* 668–677.

Stanovich, K., Cunningham, A. , & West, R. (1981). A longitudinal study of the development of automatic recognition skills in first graders. *Journal of Reading Behavior, 13,* 57–74.

Stanovich, K., Feeman, D., & Cunningham, A. (1983). The development of the relation between letter naming speed and reading ability. *Bulletin of the Psychonomic Society, 21,* 199–202.

Stanovich, K., & Purcell, D. (1981a). Comment on "Input Capability and Speed of Processing in Mental Retardation." *Journal of Abnormal Psychology, 90,* 168–171.

Stanovich, K., & Purcell, D. (1981b). On Saccuzzo's reply. *Journal of Abnormal Psychology, 90,* 261–262.

Stanovich, K., West, R., & Feeman, D. (1981). A longitudinal study of sentence context effects in second-grade children: Tests of an interactive-compensatory model. *Journal of Experimental Child Psychology, 32,* 185–199.

Steinheiser, F., & Guthrie, J. (1978). Reading ability and efficiency of graphic-phonemic encoding. *Journal of General Psychology, 99,* 281–291.

Sternberg, R. (1980). Sketch of a componential subtheory of human intelligence. *Behavioral and Brain Sciences, 3,* 573–584.

Sternberg, R. (1982a). A componential approach to intellectual development. In R. Sternberg (Ed.) *Advances in the Psychology of Human Intelligence.* Vol. 1 (pp. 413–463). Hillsdale, NJ: Lawrence Erlbaum Associates.

Sternberg, R. (1982b). Introduction: Some common themes in contemporary approaches to the training of intelligent performances. In D. Detterman & R. Sternberg (Eds.). *How and How Much Can Intelligence Be Increased?* (pp. 141–146). Norwood, NJ: Ablex Publishing.

Stevenson, H., Parker, T., Wilkinson, A., Hegion, A., & Fish, E. (1976). Longitudinal study of individual differences in cognitive development and scholastic achievement. *Journal of Educational Psychology, 68,* 377–400.

Sticht, T. (1979). Applications of the audread model to reading evaluation and instruction. In L. B. Resnick & P. Weaver (Eds.). *Theory and Practice of Early Reading.* (pp. 209–226). Hillsdale, NJ: Lawrence Erlbaum Associates.

Strange, M. (1979). The effect of orthographic anomalies upon reading behavior. *Journal of Reading Behavior, 11,* 153–161.

Swanson, L. (1978). Verbal encoding effects on the visual short-term memory of learning-disabled and normal readers. *Journal of Educational Psychology, 70,* 539–544.

Swanson, L. (1983). A study of nonstrategic linguistic coding on visual recall of learning-disabled readers. *Journal of Learning Disabilities, 16,* 209–216.

Tallal, P. (1980). Auditory temporal perception, phonics, and reading disabilities in children. *Brain and Language, 9,* 182–198.

Tarver, S. (1982). Characteristics of learning disabilities. In T. Miller & E. Davis (Eds.). *The Mildly Handicapped Student,* (pp. 17–36). New York: Grune & Stratton.

Tarver, S., Hallahan, D., Kauffman, J., & Ball, D. (1976). Verbal rehearsal and selective attention in children with learning disabilities: A developmental lag. *Journal of Experimental Child Psychology, 22,* 375–385.

Taylor, H., Satz, P., & Friel, J. (1979). Developmental dyslexia in relation to other childhood reading disorders: Significance and clinical utility. *Reading Research Quarterly, 15,* 84–101.

Taylor, S. (1965). Eye movements while reading: Facts and fallacies. *American Educational Research Journal, 2,* 187–202.

Tinker, M. (1958). Recent studies of eye movements in reading. *Psychological Bulletin, 55,* 215–231.

Torgesen, J. (1975). Problems and prospects in the study of learning disabilities. In M. Hetherington & J. Hagen (Eds.). *Review of child development research.* Vol. 5 (pp. 1–25) New York: Russell Sage Foundation.

Torgesen, J. (1977a). Memorization processes in reading-disabled children. *Journal of Educational Psychology, 69,* 571–578.

Torgesen, J. (1977b). The role of nonspecific factors in the task performance of learning disabled children: A theoretical assessment. *Journal of Learning Disabilities, 10,* 27–34.

Torgesen, J. (1978–1979). Performance of reading disabled children on serial memory tasks. *Reading Research Quarterly, 14,* 57–87.

Torgesen, J. (1979). What shall we do with psychological processes? *Journal of Learning Disabilities, 12,* 514–521.

Torgesen, J. (1980). Conceptual and educational implications of the use of efficient task strategies by learning-disabled children. *Journal of Learning Disabilities, 13,* 364–371.

Torgesen, J. (1982). The use of rationally defined subgroups in research on learning disabilities. In J. Das, R. Mulcahey, & A. Wall (Eds.). *Theory and Research in Learning Disabilities* (pp. 111–131). New York: Plenum Press.

Torgesen, J., & Dice, C. (1980). Characteristics of research in learning disabilities. *Journal of Learning Disabilities, 13,* 531–535.

Torgesen, J., & Goldman, T. (1977). Verbal rehearsal and short-term memory in reading-disabled children. *Child Development, 48,* 56–60.

Torgesen, J., & Houck, D. (1980). Processing deficiencies of learning-disabled children who perform poorly on the digit span test. *Journal of Educational Psychology, 72,* 141–160.

Torgesen, J., & Licht, B. (1983). The learning disabled child as an inactive learner: Retrospect and prospects. In J. McKinney & L. Feagans (Eds.). *Topics in learning disabilities.* Vol. 1 (pp. 100–130). Norwood, NJ: Ablex Press.

Treiman, R., & Baron, J. (1981). Segmental analysis ability: Development and relation to reading ability. In T. Waller & G. Mackinnon (Eds.). *Reading research: Advances in theory and practice.* Vol. 3 (pp. 100–120). New York: Academic Press.

Treiman, R., & Baron, J. (1983). Phonemic-analysis training helps children benefit from spelling-sound rules. *Memory & Cognition, 11,* 382–389.

Valtin, R. (1978–1979). Dyslexia: Deficit in reading or deficit in research? *Reading Research Quarterly, 14,* 201–221.

Vellutino, F. (1979). *Dyslexia: Theory and research.* Cambridge, Mass: MIT Press.

Vellutino, F., Pruzek, R., Steger, J., & Meshouiam, V. (1973). Immediate visual recall in poor and normal readers as a function of orthographic-linguistic familiarity. *Cortex, 9,* 368–384.

Vellutino, F., & Scanlon, D. (1984). Converging perspectives in the study of the reading process: Reactions to the papers presented by Morrison, Siegel, and Stanovich. *Remedial and Special Education, 5,* 39–44.

Vogel, S. (1974). Syntactic abilities in normal and dyslexic children. *Journal of Learning Disabilities, 7,* 103–109.

Wallach, L., Wallach, M., Dozier, M., & Kaplan, N. (1977). Poor children learning to read do not have trouble with auditory discrimination but do have trouble with phoneme recognition. *Journal of Educational Psychology, 69,* 36–39.

Weaver, P., & Rosner, J. (1979). Relationships between visual and auditory perceptual skills and comprehension in students with learning disabilities. *Journal of Learning Disabilities, 12,* 51–55.

Weber, R. (1970). A linguistic analysis of first grade reading errors. *Reading Research Quarterly, 5,* 427–451.

West, R., & Stanovich, K. (1978). Automatic contextual facilitation in readers of three ages. *Child Development, 49,* 717–727.

West, R., Stanovich, K., Feeman, D., & Cunningham, A. (1983). The effect of sentence context on word recognition in second- and sixth-grade children. *Reading Research Quarterly, 19,* 6–15.

Whaley, J., & Kibby, M. (1981). The relative importance of reliance on intraword characteristics and interword constraints for beginning reading achievement. *Journal of Educational Research, 74,* 315–320.

White, C., Pascarella, E., & Pflaum, S. (1981). Effects of training in sentence construction on the comprehension of learning-disabled children. *Journal of Educational Psychology, 73,* 697–704.

Wiens, J. (1983). Metacognition and the adolescent passive learner. *Journal of Learning Disabilities, 16,* 144–149.

Wiig, E., Semel, E., & Crouse, M. (1973). The use of English morphology by high-risk and learning-disabled children. *Journal of Learning Disabilities, 6,* 457–465.

Wiig, E., Semel, E., & Nystrom, L. (1982). Comparison of rapid naming in language-learning-disabled and academically achieving 8-year-olds. *Language, Speech, and Hearing Services in Schools, 13,* 11–23.

Wilkinson, A. (1980). Children's understanding in reading and listening. *Journal of Educational Psychology, 72,* 561–574.

Williams, J. (1980). Teaching decoding with an emphasis on phoneme analysis and phoneme blending. *Journal of Educational Psychology, 72,* 1–15.

Wolford, G. (April 1981). *Reading deficits: Are they specific to reading?* Paper presented at The Meeting of the Society for Research in Child Development. Boston: Society for Research in Child Development.

Wong, B. (1978). The effects of directive cues on the organization of memory and recall in good and poor readers. *Journal of Educational Research, 72,* 32–38.

Wong, B. (1984). Metacognition and learning disabilities. In T. Waller, D. Forrest, & E. MacKinnon (Eds.). *Metacognition, Cognition, and Human Performance* (pp. 137–180). New York: Academic Press.

Wong, B., Wong, R., & Foth, D. (1977). Recall and clustering of verbal materials among normal and poor readers. *Bulletin of the Psychonomic Society, 10*, 375–378.

Young, A., & Ellis, A. (1981). Asymmetry of cerebral hemispheric functions in normal and poor readers. *Psychological Bulletin, 89*, 183–190.

Ysseldyke, J., & Algozzine, B. (1979). Perspectives on assessment of learning-disabled students. *Learning Disability Quarterly, 2*, 3–13.

Yule, W. (1973). Differential prognosis of reading backwardness and specific reading retardation. *British Journal of Educational Psychology, 43*, 244–248.

Yule, W., Rutter, M., Berger, M., & Thompson, J. (1974). Over-and underachievement in reading: Distribution in the general population. *British Journal of Educational Psychology, 44*, 1–12.

5

Why Some Children Encounter Reading Problems: The Contribution of Difficulties with Language Processing and Phonological Sophistication to Early Reading Disability

VIRGINIA A. MANN

INTRODUCTORY COMMENTS

Learning to read involves learning to decode a written representation of one's spoken language. Although it is a task which most children accomplish quite readily, it poses a specific difficulty for some 4–10% of children whom we refer to as dyslexic or reading-disabled. Such children tend not to be distinguished from their more successful cohorts by general intelligence, motivation, or prior experience. Yet, something limits their success in learning to read.

Many studies have been directed toward identifying the basis of early reading difficulty, and always they have been implicitly, if not explicitly, guided by certain assumptions as to what skilled reading is "all about." One such assumption, traditionally held by psychologists and educators alike, is that reading is primarily a complex visual skill which places certain demands on differentiation and recognition of visual stimuli. Owing to this assumption, models of skilled reading often have been biased toward clarification of the visual stages of the reading process, and many investigators have sought to blame early reading difficulty on some malfunction in the visual domain. Recently however, visual theo-

Psychological and Educational
Perspectives on Learning Disabilities

ries of reading disability have reached something of a cul-de-sac, for it seems that, at best, only a few of the children who encounter early reading difficulty suffer from perceptual malfunctions, which somehow prevent recognition, differentiation, or memory of the various orthographic forms (c.f. Rutter, 1978; Stanovich, 1982a; Vellutino, 1979; for recent reviews of these findings).

At present, a more fruitful approach to the problem of early reading disability is being guided by the assumption that reading is, first and foremost, predicated on language skills. In particular, recent research has shown that effectiveness of processes underlying spoken language as well as one's degree of sophistication about phonological structure are critical parameters in successfully learning to read. My goal in what follows will be to elucidate and discuss the consequences of this research and to see how it informs our understanding of specific reading difficulty. I will begin with a review of the requirements of skilled reading, as a way of introducing the role of language skills. From there I will consider some language skills that are essential to beginning reading, and then review findings that link many instances of early reading difficulty to linguistic difficulties. This will be followed by a consideration of the origins of the language deficiencies found among poor beginning readers, and finally, by some concluding remarks about their implications.

DECODING A WRITTEN REPRESENTATION OF SPOKEN LANGUAGE: WHAT SKILLED READING IS "ALL ABOUT"

HOW ORTHOGRAPHIES REPRESENT LANGUAGE

In justifying the assumption that reading is a language skill, the first point to be made concerns the manner in which writing systems, or orthographies, function as symbol systems transcribing spoken language. All orthographies must, somehow, appeal to the reader's intuitive appreciation of the structure of spoken language, as their function is to represent certain units of that language. Yet, individual orthographies may differ in the level of appreciation required, because they can differ in the precise level at which they map onto spoken utterances (Hung & Tzeng, 1981; Liberman, Liberman, Mattingly, & Shankweiler, 1980). Ideographies, for example, represent language at the level of "ideas" (i.e., American Indian petroglyphs), logographies represent words (i.e., Chinese and the Japanese Kanji), and syllabaries represent syllables (i.e.,

Classical Hebrew and the Japanese Kana), whereas alphabets, more or less, represent phonemes (i.e. Spanish, and English).

THE ENGLISH ALPHABET: ITS VIRTUES AND HINDRANCES

The English alphabet does not provide the broad phonetic transcription that Spanish or Serbo-Croatian does. Rather, it provides a morphophonological transcription which represents the word as a sequence of systematic phonemes, although preserving (on the whole) its constituent morphemes (i.e., units of meaning) and underlying phonology. It is distinct from a purely phonetic transcription in that it maps onto a deeper, more abstract level of language. This level corresponds, not so much to the consonants and vowels that speakers and hearers think they pronounce and perceive, as to the way generative phonologists assume that words are abstractly represented in the ideal speaker/hearer's mental dictionary, or lexicon (Chomsky, 1964).

The morphophonological representations of words in the lexicon are systematically related to the phonetic representations underlying pronunciation and perception by an ordered series of phonological rules that alter, insert, or delete segments. As discussed in Liberman et al. (1980), an example of the morphophonological nature of transcription by the English alphabet can be found in the way we use ea to transcribe the vowels in *heal* and *health*, preserving their abstract morphological and phonological similarity, although blurring certain phonetic distinctions. Insofar as letter sequences stand for morphophonological representations, they can provide a means of access to lexical information, including relevant syntactic and semantic properties. To derive the phonetic representation appropriate to a given letter sequence, the reader need only derive the appropriate morphophonological representation and apply the phonological rules of his language. That is, readers need only apply the very rules that are responsible for the phonetic realization of *heal* and *health* as [hiyl] and [helθ] in normal speech.

This account of the English orthography is, of course, somewhat idealized. Sometimes words are transcribed at a shallower, more phonetic, level than the morphophonological ideal, hence, the different spelling of the vowels in "well" and "wealth." Sometimes, too, the spelling of a word seems neither phonetically nor phonologically principled, such as the spelling of "sword." Certain of these exceptions have the advantage of disambiguating homophones; others are historically based, but their existence does not seriously undermine Chomsky's (1964) claim about the basic operating principle of the English orthography (Liberman et al., 1980).

There are certain virtues to the way in which the English alphabet represents the English language, and they are worth pointing out. These follow from the rule-governed nature of the relation between letter sequences, morphophonological representations, and phonetic representations. Knowledge of these rules allows the reader to access not only the linguistic representations of highly familiar words, but also those of less familiar ones, and even those of words never before seen in print. Whereas a skilled reader of a logography must have memorized thousands of distinct characters, and even then may encounter difficulty in reading a new word, a skilled reader of English need know only a limited set of phoneme-to-grapheme correspondences and the phonological rules of his spoken language to read any word (or phonologically plausible nonword) on the page. Armed with this basic knowledge, English readers can gain access to extant lexical information through recovery of the morphophonological representation which a string of letters transcribes. They can also derive the phonetic representation needed to read the word aloud (and to temporarily remember the word, as will be discussed later). Finally, they can even build their vocabulary by forming lexical representations for words they have never seen or heard before—a feat which is not possible in logographies, for example, where no systematic analytic code binds orthographic forms to the morphophonological representations which are stored in the mental lexicon.

But all of this comes at a certain cost, which brings me to the hindrances of the English alphabet and alphabets in general. Obviously, successful use of the English orthography demands phonological maturity in the form of tacit knowledge both of the representation of words in the lexicon, and of the phonological rules which relate morphophonological representations to phonetic ones. A comparable level of phonological maturity would not be so critical to the would-be reader of a logography, for example, since decoding logographies does not require application of phonological rules. In addition, alphabetic transcription requires that skilled readers of English go one step further than merely possessing tacit knowledge of phonology: they must achieve a degree of "liguistic awareness" (Mattingly, 1972). That is, would-be readers of English must access their tacit knowledge of phonemes, morphemes, and phonological rules and apply that knowledge in a fashion not required for spoken language. Unless such phonological sophistication is achieved, an alphabet will make no sense as a transcription of utterances and its virtues will remain unrealized (Mattingly, 1972; Liberman *et al.*, 1980). This is not the case for syllabaries, which have the virtue over alphabets in requiring a less fine-grained level of sophistication, and this is even more true of logographies. Thus, the former demand only an awareness of words, syllables, and certain phonological rules (such as the rules that determine vowel identity in Hebrew, and the rule in Japanese which makes "suki" sound like "ski"), whereas the latter demand only an awareness of words.

WHAT CHARACTERIZES A SKILLED READER?

Let me now put aside these theoretical assertions about the pertinence of phonological sophistication to the reading of words in alphabetically represented languages like English, to consider briefly some experimental evidence about the role of linguistic processes in the skilled reading of words, sentences, and paragraphs.

THE PERTINENCE OF LANGUAGE SKILLS TO LEXICAL ACCESS

The question of whether speech recoding mediates lexical access from print has preoccupied much research on the psychology of skilled reading (see Crowder, 1982; McCusker, Bias, & Hillinger, 1981; Perfetti & McCutchen, 1982, for recent reviews of the role of speech coding in the process of word perception). Some researchers offer a negative answer, based on findings that some high-frequency words may be perceived as visual units, instead of being analyzed into their separate phonetic constituents prior to lexical access. Other evidence has been interpreted as implicating some phonetic mediation in lexical access, and many psychologists now favor "dual access" models in which both phonetic and visual access occur in parallel. In any event, regardless of how the lexicon is accessed, it is, at base, the morphophonological representation of a word in the lexicon that is being accessed, and with it, the word's semantic extensions and syntactic properties. Phonetic recoding of orthographic material may not be necessary to gain lexical access from print, nor even be feasible if we accept Chomsky's (1964) contention, but morphophonological recoding clearly must occur, else lexical access is a vacuous concept.

THE PERTINENCE OF LANGUAGE SKILLS TO READING
SENTENCES AND PARAGRAPHS

From the point of lexical access onward, the involvement of speech processes in reading is clear (Perfetti & McCutchen, 1982). First, much evidence attests that temporary memory for such orthographic material as isolated letters, printed nonsense syllables, and printed words involves recoding the material into some kind of "silent speech," or phonetic representation. Both the nature of the errors that subjects make in recalling such material and the experimental manipulations that penalize their memory performance lend support to this conclusion (c.f. Baddeley, 1978; Conrad, 1964, 1972; Drenowski, 1980; Levy, 1977). More importantly, subjects also appear to rely on phonetic representation when they are required to comprehend sentences written in either alphabetic (Kleiman, 1975; Levy, 1977; Slowiaczek & Clifton, 1980) or logographic orthographies (Tzeng, Hung, and Wang, 1977). This is because, regardless of the way in which the orthography allows lexical access, the post-lexical processes involved in reading sentences and paragraphs place certain obvious demands on temporary memory, and temporary memory for language appears to capitalize on phonetic representation. Furthermore, it appears that reading shares not only the temporary-memory system, but also the parsing system that supports recovery of the syntactic structure of spoken language and allows comprehension of spoken discourse. This is obviated by the significantly high correlations found between reading and listening comprehension across a variety of languages and orthographies, including English (c.f. Curtis, 1980; Daneman & Carpenter, 1980; Jackson & McClelland, 1979), and Japanese and Chinese as well (Stevenson, Stiegler, Lucker, Hsu, & Kitamura, 1982).

In summary, then, skilled reading of the English orthography is supported by two linguistic skills: sophistication about phonological structure, and the adequacy of certain processes which are integral to spoken-language comprehension. That is, skilled reading is a derived language skill, of sorts. Recognition of this fact can now set the stage for the subsequent sections of this essay, which comprise a consideration of the role of language-processing skills and phonological knowledge in beginning reading, and a review of experimental findings which suggest that certain such skills tend to be deficient among many children who encounter difficulty in learning to read.

THE IMPORTANCE OF LANGUAGE SKILLS FOR BEGINNING READING

Obviously, beginning readers need to possess the visual skills which allow them to differentiate and remember the various letter shapes. Yet, they also need to be able to perceive and recognize spoken words and to combine them into phrases, sentences, and paragraphs. Without spoken English, there would be nothing for the English orthography to transcribe; the well-known difficulties of deaf readers attest to the importance of spoken-language skills for successful reading.

LANGUAGE PROCESSING SKILLS ESSENTIAL TO WOULD-BE READERS

Beginning readers should possess language-processing skills at five different levels. First of all, they should be capable of distinguishing the phonemes of their language, so that they can hear the difference between "cat" and "hat," for example. They also need to have a mental lexicon, although they need not necessarily possess mature morphophonological representations in their lexicons, given some evidence that the experience of reading, in and of itself, serves to stimulate and further phonological development (Moskowitz, 1973; Read, 1975). Beginning readers also should have an adequate means of storing language in temporary (short-term) memory, as this both supports retention of sufficient words to understand sentences and paragraphs, and may have a significant impact on the learning of syntax (Daneman & Case, 1981). Further, they should be able to recover the syntactic structure of phrases and sentences, although their mastery of syntax, like their mastery of phonology, may be facilitated by the experience of reading, in and of itself (Goldman, 1976). Finally, it goes without saying that beginning readers need to have a grasp of the semantics of language, so that they can understand what words and sentences mean.

PHONOLOGICAL SOPHISTICATION SKILLS ESSENTIAL TO WOULD-BE READERS

Such language-processing skills, however, are not sufficient. The nature of the English orthography, as explained above, necessitates that successful readers not only be able to process spoken language, but also be conscious of certain abstract units of that language—words, syllables, and especially, phonemes. Otherwise, the alphabet will make no sense as a transcription of their spoken language. But there is the special catch to learning to read an alphabetic orthography that was noted above: Whereas sophistication about words is sufficient for learning a logography, and sophistication about words and syllables is sufficient for syllabaries, children must know about these units and also about phonemes if the alphabet is to make sense and if they are to derive its full advantages.

Phonemes, however, are more abstract units than either words or syllables. Reflexively and unconsciously, we perceive them when we listen to the speech stream, because we have a neurophysiology uniquely and elegantly adapted to that purpose (cf. A. M. Liberman, 1982, Mann & Liberman, 1984). Yet, phonemes cannot be mechanically isolated from each other, or produced in isolation (Liberman, Cooper,

Shankweiler, & Studdert-Kennedy, 1967) as can syllables and words. In a tacit sense, of course, infants may distinguish phonemes (see Miller & Eimas, 1983, for a recent review of the speech-perception capabilities of infant listeners) and preschool-aged children may employ phonetic representation when holding linguistic material in short-term memory (Alegria & Pignot, 1979; Eimas 1975). But successful beginning readers must not only distinguish words such as "cat" and "hat," and be capable of holding them in memory, they must further possess the linguistic sophistication which allows them to cognize that, among other things, these words differ in one phoneme, namely the first, and share a final phoneme which is the initial one in "top." Otherwise, the alphabet will remain a mystery to them, and its virtues unrealized.

This is not to imply that there is anything inherently undesirable about reading a syllabary or logography. Ultimately, the utility of a given orthography rests upon the nature of the spoken language it transcribes. For example, a logography is appropriate for Chinese because it is independent of profound dialect differences and allows people who cannot understand each other's speech to read the same text. Likewise, for Japanese, the Kana syllabaries are quite utilitarian, given that there are only 100 or so syllables in the Japanese language. English, however, has less profound dialectical variation than Chinese, and employs more than 10 times as many syllables as Japanese. Hence, an alphabet is appropriate, and it would be a disservice to present the English writing system otherwise. Yet, to present it in its true light requires that the would-be reader possess both language-processing skills and phonological sophistication.

THE PROBLEM OF SPECIFIC READING DIFFICULTY

It has been suggested that the use of alphabetic transcriptions for Indo-European languages is particularly adaptive to man's cognitive and linguistic abilities, and that it is responsible for making the skills of reading and writing more widely available in Western civilization (Russell, 1982a). Nonetheless, for a minority of children (the 4–10% alluded to previously) learning to read the English alphabet presents something of an obstacle. What limits these children's success in learning to read, what factors distinguish them from those children who readily become skilled readers? Let me now turn to these issues.

As noted by Rutter (1978), learning to read is a specific example of a complex learning task which correlates about 0.6 with IQ. Yet, a low IQ cannot be the sole basis of reading problems, as there are children who are backward in reading ability but average in intelligence (Rutter & Yule, 1973). Such children are said to have a specific reading difficulty, as their actual reading ability lags between 1–2 years behind that predicted on the basis of their age, IQ, and social standing. They will be the focus of this review.

SOME FACTORS WHICH DO NOT OFTEN CAUSE SPECIFIC READING DIFFICULTY

As noted above, there is good evidence that deficient visuospatial skills are not very important determinants of specific reading difficulty. Let me briefly mention two pieces of supporting evidence. First, 5–6-year-old children identified as having deficient visual perception and/or visuomotor coordination skills show no more instances of reading difficulty at age 8–9 than do matched controls who possess no such deficits (Robinson & Schwartz, 1973). Second, although it is true that all young children tend to confuse spatially reversible letters such as b, d, p, g until they are 7 or 8 years old (Gibson, Gibson, Pick, & Osser, 1962), letter and sequence reversals actually account for only a small proportion of the reading errors made by children in this age range (Shankweiler & Liberman, 1972). Even children who have been formally diagnosed as dyslexic make relatively few letter- and sequence-reversal errors (Fisher, Liberman, & Shankweiler, 1977).

It is also unlikely that a problem with cross-modal integration of visual and auditory information is a basis of reading failure. Difficulties with cross-modal integration were once thought to cause reading difficulty because of findings that poor readers do less well than controls on tasks that required the matching of a temporal sequence of auditory taps to a spatial sequence of visual dots (Birch & Belmont, 1964; see reviews by Benton, 1975; Rutter & Yule, 1973). However, others have since then shown that poor readers have difficulty with perceptual discrimination and temporal/spatial integration of sequences within a given sensory modality (c.f. Blank, Weider, & Bridger, 1968; Bryden, 1972) which calls for a more general explanation. To account for these additional findings, several psychologists (c.f. Rutter, 1978; Vellutino, 1979) have suggested that the problem is not so much with cross-modal integration as with perceptual linking, perhaps owing to a difficulty in verbal coding. This possibility, that verbal coding is problematic for poor readers, is well supported in the literature, and will be discussed in a later section.

An inadequate short-term memory for all types of material, both linguistic and nonlinguistic, also has been cited as the cause of early reading problems (Morrison, Giordani, & Nagy, 1977), as has inadequate short-term retention of the order of items in a series (Corkin, 1974). Hypotheses of this variety are, perhaps, too general, for they cannot account for some other findings that good and poor readers do not differ on all tasks which require temporary memory of items or their order. Good and poor beginning readers are equivalent, for example, in ability to remember faces (Liberman, Mann, Shankweiler, & Werfelman, 1982) or visual stimuli which cannot readily be assigned verbal labels (Katz, Shankweiler, & Liberman, 1981; Liberman et al., 1982; Swanson, 1978). Only when the to-be-remembered stimuli can be linguistically coded do children who are poor readers consistently fail to do as well as good readers (Liberman et al., 1982; Katz et al., 1981; Swanson, 1978).

Various other general accounts of reading disability have been offered in the literature (see, for example, Carr, 1981, for a review), but they also fail to explain why poor readers often do as well as good readers on nonliguistic tasks, but consistently lag behind good readers in performance on many linguistic tasks. (For recent reviews, see Mann, 1984a; Stanovich, 1982a; Vellutino, 1979.) For the sake of brevity, such general accounts will not be discussed here.

INADEQUATE LANGUAGE SKILLS ARE OFTEN ASSOCIATED WITH READING DIFFICULTY

The importance of deficient language skills to early reading difficulty is evident when one considers the variety of studies which demonstrate the ability of certain linguistic tasks, as opposed to the failure of comparable nonlinguistic ones, to distinguish good and poor beginning readers (see, for example, Brady, Shankweiler, & Mann, 1983; Katz et al., 1981; Liberman et al., 1982; Mann & Liberman, 1984; Swanson, 1978). It is further evident when one considers, as did Rutter (1978), the frequency of reading difficulties in children with various sorts of handicaps. Whereas children deficient in visual-perceptual and/or visual-motor skills do not encounter reading difficulty any more frequently than matched controls (Money, 1973; Robinson & Schwartz, 1973), speech and language-retarded children encounter reading problems at least six times more often than do controls (Ingram, Mason, & Blackburn, 1970, 1976).

Considered broadly, the language disabilities that tend to be found among children who are poor readers fall within the two categories introduced in previous sections: language processing and phonological sophistication. Before considering each category, however, it is important to mention the issue of whether reading disability involves a single common deficit, or a family of subsyndromes. Certainly, this issue is a real one which many investigators have considered in some detail (see, for example, Carr, 1981; Ellis, 1985; Jorm, 1979; Vernon, 1979). Nonetheless, as Stanovitch (1982a) has noted, progress in science must first come through the search for unity in the face of diversity. At this time, we are still making progress towards discovering that, as a population, poor readers tend to be deficient in a variety of language skills. The question of whether the population of children with specific reading difficulty is homogeneous or heterogeneous in its profile of language difficulties cannot yet be resolved.

THE RELATION BETWEEN READING DIFFICULTY AND DIFFICULTIES WITH LANGUAGE PROCESSING

The past decade has witnessed considerable interest in the psychology of early reading problems. In it, study after study has uncovered some link between early difficulties in learning to read and difficulties with some aspect of spoken-language processing. Such a link is clearly established beyond question, not only in English (cf. Mann, 1984a), but in Swedish (Lundberg, Oloffson, & Wall, 1980), and in Japanese and Chinese as well (Stevenson et al., 1982). In the case of English, there also have been considerable attempts to more precisely specify the nature of the language problems that typify poor-beginning readers. For example, it has been asked whether the nature of the language problem is a general one, encompassing all levels of language processing, as opposed to being specifically confined to certain levels of processing. Let me address this issue after considering, in turn, each of the five levels of language processing that were identified in an earlier section as being important to beginning reading: phonetic perception, the mental lexicon, phonetic short-term memory, syntax, and semantics.

PHONETIC PERCEPTION

With regard to this initial level of processing, some of my colleagues and I (Brady et al., 1983) recently discovered that a group of poor readers in the third grade who did not differ from the good readers of their classrooms in age, IQ, audiometry scores, or ability to identify either clearly recorded or noise-masked environmental sounds were nonetheless deficient in the ability to identify noise-masked, spoken words. As long as the words were not masked by noise, the good and poor readers performed equivalently, implying that, as other research has suggested (Goetzinger, Dirks, & Baer, 1960), the speech perception difficulties of poor readers are most evident when speech perception is stressed. One potential explanation of these results is that the problem for the poor readers lies not in the initial encoding of phonetic information so much as in stages of lexical access. For example, poor readers might have a less extensive vocabulary, and hence, be less successful at identifying less familiar words. We may discard such an explanation, however, because the perceptual difficulties of those subjects studies by Brady *et al.* (1983) occurred for frequent and infrequent words alike. Thus, a more likely explanation is that poor readers possess some subtle, quite specific, difficulty with speech perception (Brady *et al.*, 1983).

Another suggestion to this effect comes from studies which compare the categorical perception of synthetic speech stimuli by good- and poor-beginning readers. In such studies, categorical perception was evident in both groups of subjects, yet the poor readers differed from the good readers either in failing to meet the level of intercategory discrimination predicted on the basis of their identification responses (Brandt & Rosen, 1980) or in failing to give as consistent identification responses (Godfrey, Syrdal-Lasky, Millay, & Knox, 1981). These findings have been interpreted as the reflection of deficient speech-perception processes on the part of poor readers. However, it is important to note that they, and the results obtained by Brady *et al.* (1983), could also reflect deficient phonetic-memory processes, as memory plays an obvious role in discrimination, and in many identification tasks.

THE MENTAL LEXICON

As noted, the findings of Brady *et al.* (1983) do not suggest an inferior vocabulary on the part of poor readers. Indeed, recognition vocabulary, in and of itself, is not a very significant associate of early reading ability (Mann & Liberman, in press). Certain findings, however, involving production vocabulary do suggest that aspects of the mental lexicon may, nonetheless, be deficient among poor readers. Specifically, the speed of object-naming is slower among poor readers, and poor readers tend to make more naming errors than good readers do (see, for example, Denckla & Rudel, 1976; Katz, 1982).

In a very interesting study, Katz (1982) recently reported that poor readers are particularly prone to difficulties in producing low-frequency and polysyllabic names, and suggested that, for such words, these children may possess less phonologically complete lexical representations than good readers do. On the basis of his research, he further suggests that, because poor readers often have access to aspects of the correct phonological representation of a word even though they are unable to produce that word correctly, their problem may be attributable to phonological deficiencies in the structure of the lexicon rather than to the process of lexical access, per se.

PHONETIC SHORT-TERM MEMORY

Questions concerning deficiencies in linguistic short-term memory have given rise to one of the more fruitful lines of research in the field. It often has been noted that poor readers tend to be deficient in ordered recall of strings of nameable objects, letters, digits, nonsense syllables, or words, whether the stimuli are presented by ear or by eye. They also fail to recall the words of spoken sentences as accurately as good readers (see Jorm, 1979; Mann, 1984a; Mann, Liberman, & Shankweiler, 1980; Torgesen & Houck, 1980, for references to these effects). Normally, such linguistic materials as these are held in short-term memory through use of phonetic representation. Hence, it was suggested by Shankweiler, Liberman, Mark, Fowler, & Fisher (1979) that the linguistic short-term memory difficulties of poor readers might reflect a problem with using phonetic representation.

Several experiments have supported this hypothesis by showing that in recall of letter strings (Shankweiler et al., 1979), word strings (Mann et al., 1980; Mann & Liberman, 1984), and sentences (Mann et al., 1980), poor readers are less affected than good readers by a manipulation of phonetic confusability (i.e., rhyme), which hinders use of phonetic representation. Indeed, good readers can be made to appear as poor readers in the face of this penalizing manipulation, which has led to the postulation that poor readers are, for some reason, less effective in their use of phonetic representation under normal circumstances (Mann et al., 1980; Shankweiler et al., 1979). Further evidence that phonetic representation in short-term memory is a specific problem for poor readers accrues from studies of the errors that poor readers make when attempting to recall or recognize spoken words (Byrne & Shea, 1979; Brady et al., 1983.) Support also comes from the finding that differences between good and poor readers in the use of phonetic representation can precede the attainment of reading ability, and may actually serve to presage future reading problems (Mann, 1984b; Mann & Liberman, 1984).

SYNTAX

One possible outcome of a difficulty with phonetic representation in short-term memory is a difficulty with comprehension of sentences whose processing somehow stresses short-term memory. This recently has been shown to be the case in a study (Mann, Shankweiler, & Smith, 1984) which finds that good and poor readers differ in both the ability to repeat and to comprehend spoken sentences which contain relative clauses. Other indications that poor readers have a deficit grasp of the easy/eager distinction (Byrne, 1981), the promise/tell distinction (Goldman, 1976), and the double-object construction (Fletcher, Satz, & Scholes, 1981) raise the possibility that poor readers might also be deficient in syntactic processes, above and beyond their problems with short-term memory. Research by my colleagues and myself does not suggest that poor readers have any difficulty with syntactic structure above and beyond the difficulties brought about by their memory constraint (Mann, 1984b; Mann et al., 1984). Byrne (1981), however, has interpreted his research as suggesting otherwise, although Goldman (1976) is correct in noting that such syntactic differences as have been reported among good and poor readers could be either the cause of reading difficulty or a consequence of different amounts of reading experience. At present, the issue of whether poor readers are deficient in syntactic skills is far from resolved, and will have to await further research. Such deficits as do exist are relatively subtle, with poor readers merely performing like somewhat younger children than the good readers.

SEMANTICS

As for the question of semantic impairments among poor readers, here, at least, there is no reason to presume any real deviance exists. If anything, poor readers place greater reliance on semantic context and semantic representation than do good readers, perhaps in compensation for their other language difficulties (see Stanovitch, 1982b, for a recent review, and also see Byrne & Shea, 1979; Simpson, Lorsbach, & Whitehouse, 1983, but see Vellutino & Scanlon, 1985, for an opposing view.)

A GENERAL IMPAIRMENT?

To summarize, then, phonetic perception, phonological aspects of lexical structure, and phonetic representation in short-term memory all tend to be deficient among many reading-disabled children. Correlations among such behaviors as speed of naming and digit span (Spring,

1976; Torgesen & Houck, 1980) also have been noted, and these, together with the logical interrelation between phonetic perception, morphophonological representation in the mental lexicon, and post-lexical phonetic representation in short-term memory, could suggest that poor readers have a pervasive difficulty with phonological processes. One could even entertain the possibility that all of the phonological difficulties of poor readers derive from an initial problem with phonetic perception (Brady *et al.*, 1983).

Aside from their difficulties in the domain of phonological processing, poor readers may also possess a specific difficulty with syntactic structure—although the data are equivocal in this regard—and it could well be the case that what appear to be syntactic deficiencies are really second-order consequences of either phonological difficulties or a lack of reading experience. In any event, however, semantic processes do not appear to be deficient among disabled beginning readers; it is, therefore, unlikely that reading disability is associated with a generalized language impairment. At most, the impairment would seem to involve the more formal phonological and syntactic aspects of language processing.

THE RELATION BETWEEN READING DIFFICULTY AND DEFICIENT PHONOLOGICAL SOPHISTICATION

Let me put aside the issue of deficient language processing to consider some of the evidence which suggests that deficient linguistic sophistication is also a factor in reading difficulty. Possessing adequate phonetic perception and short-term memory skills, an adequate mental lexicon, and the ability to recover the syntactic and semantic structure of utterances is only part of the requirement of reading success. Successful readers of the alphabet must go beyond these tacit language-processing abilities to achieve a degree of phonological sophistication; they must become explicitly aware of the phonological units of their language and of the phonological rules that relate lexical representations to phonetic representations. Thus, this section turns to studies concerned with the pertinence of phonological sophistication to success in learning to read an alphabetic orthography.

EVIDENCE FROM THE ANALYSIS OF READING ERRORS

Considerable evidence that deficient phonological sophistication is responsible for making beginning reading difficult can be found in the nature of the oral reading errors made by all young children (Shankweiler & Liberman, 1972), including dyslexics (Fisher et al., 1977). As noted earlier, these errors do not tend to involve visual confusions such as letter or sequence reversals to any appreciable degree. What they do appear to reflect is a problem with integrating the phonological information that letter sequences convey. Hence, children often tend to be correct as to the pronunciation of the first letter in a word, but have more and more difficulty with subsequent letters, and a particular problem with vowels as opposed to consonants. For more detailed presentation of these findings and their implications, the reader is referred to papers by Shankweiler and Liberman (1972) and Fisher et al. (1977), and also to a paper by Russell (1982b) that suggests that deficient phonological sophistication may account for the reading difficulties of adult dyslexics.

EVIDENCE FROM TASKS WHICH MEASURE PHONOLOGICAL
SOPHISTICATION DIRECTLY

There is also considerable evidence that early reading skill is related to performance on tasks that measure phonological awareness directly. Phonological sophistication develops later than phonetic perception and the use of phonetic representation. For example, in a sample of 4-, 5-, and 6-year-olds studied by Liberman, Shankweiler, Fisher, and Carter (1974, none of the nursery school children could identify the number of phonemes in a spoken word, whereas half of them managed to identify the number of syllables. Only 17% of the kindergartners could count phonemes, whereas, again, about half could count syllables. At 6, 90% of the children could segment by syllable, and 70% were able to segment by phoneme. From such findings, it is clear that linguistic sophistication develops considerably between the ages of 4 and 6. It is also clear that awareness of phonemes is slower to develop than awareness of syllables. Finally, both types of awareness markedly improve at just the age when children are learning to read (Liberman et al., 1974).

Numerous experiments involving widely diverse subjects, school systems, and measurement devices have shown a strong, positive correlation between a lack of awareness about phonemes, and current problems in reading (see, for example, Alegria, Pignot, & Morais, 1982; Fox & Routh, 1976; Lundberg et al., 1980; Liberman et al., 1980; Perfetti, Beck, & Hughes, 1981). There is also evidence that lack of awareness about syllables is associated with reading disability (Katz, 1982). Finally, studies of kindergarten children provide evidence that problems with phoneme segmentation (see, for example, Blachman, 1980; Helfgott, 1976;

Mann, 1984b; Stanovich, Cunningham & Cramer, 1984) and syllable segmentation (Mann & Liberman, 1984) can presage future reading difficulty. For example, 85% of a population of kindergarten children who went on to become good readers in the first grade correctly counted the number of syllables in spoken words, whereas only 17% of the future poor readers could do so (Liberman *et al.*, 1974).

SOME POSSIBLE ORIGINS OF DEFICIENT LANGUAGE SKILLS

Having reviewed some, though certainly not all, of the many findings which link reading difficulty to problems with language skills, let me turn to consideration of a related line of research which concerns the basis of these problems. There are both theoretical and practical matters at stake in such research, for it may provide insight into the psychology of written and spoken language development, while pointing to effective remedies for reading difficulty.

ORIGINS OF PROBLEMS WITH LINGUISTIC PROCESSING

As Rutter and Madge (1976) have noted, low socioeconomic status and large family size tend to be associated with low verbal intelligence and poor reading. In discussing their findings about "cycles of disadvantage," these investigators note that both genetic and environmental influences are to be held responsible. However, for the most part, those formal explanations of the language-processing problems found among poor-beginning readers that have appeared in the literature have been concerned with genetic antecedents.

That reading problems and language problems do tend to run in certain families was first noted by Thomas (1905), and has received considerable attention in recent literature (see, for example, Owen, 1978; Owen Adams, Forrest, Stolz, & Fischer, 1971; Rutter, 1978; Smith and Pennington, 1983). This, of course, suggests the possibility of a biological basis. Perhaps, the first such explanation was offered by Orton (1937) in his now-famous theory of strephosymbolia. In that theory, mirror reversals, which Orton erroneously thought to be the predominant symptom of reading disability, were attributed to insufficiently developed cerebral dominance. This insufficiency further manifested itself, according to Orton, in such abnormalities of lateral preference as mixed dominance.

Orton's (1937) theory has given rise to considerable research. On the one hand, it has been falsified by findings that reading difficulty is not associated with any particular pattern of handedness, eyedness, or foot-edness (see Rutter, 1978, for a review). It also has motivated a number of studies of cerebral lateralization for language processing among good and poor readers, with mixed results. Some studies have provided evidence that poor readers show a reversal of the normal anatomical as-symmetries between the left and right hemispheres, in conjunction with a lower verbal IQ (Hier, LeMay, Rosenberger, & Perlo, 1978). Others have reported that poor readers may show a lack of cerebral dominance for language processing (Keefe & Swinney, 1979; Zurif & Carson, 1970). But there can, at best, be only a weak association between abnormal lateralization and poor reading, as not all of the individuals who display abnormal cerebral lateralization are poor readers (Hier *et al.*, 1978). It must also be recognized that several other studies have failed to find that good and poor readers differ in the extent or direction of the laterali-zation for language processing (Fennel, Satz, & Morris, 1983; McKeever & van Deventer, 1975; Witelson, 1977). Recently, it has been suggested that most differences between the performance of normal and disabled readers on dichotic listening tasks, which are the most-often-used tests of cerebral lateralization, may reflect the known memory difficulties of disabled readers (Watson & Engle, 1982). Only those dichotic listening tasks which stress short-term memory tend to reveal differences be-tween good and poor readers, perhaps, because they cause the poor readers to perform at a floor level of accuracy which does not permit the expected left hemisphere advantage to emerge.

All in all, the data are not particularly supportive of Orton's (1937) thesis about incomplete cerebral dominance as the explanation of read-ing difficulty. Yet, Orton may still have been correct in the spirit, if not the letter, of his explanation. If we accept the left hemisphere to be the mediator of language processing (in the majority of individuals), and if we accept that language processes are deficient among poor readers, then certainly, we may suppose that some anatomical or neurochemical abnormality of the left hemisphere is implicated in early reading diffi-culty. But thus far, we have no reason to view this difference as the result of incomplete dominance.

A more adequate biological theory of poor readers' language difficul-ties involves the concept of a maturational lag (see, for example, Fletcher *et al.*, 1981; Satz & Sparrow, 1970) which may be specific to language development (Byrne, 1981; Mann & Liberman, in press). Maturational lag has been offered to explain the speech-perception difficulties of poor readers (Brandt & Rosen, 1980), their problems with phonetic representation in temporary memory (Mann & Liberman, 1984; Watson and Engle, 1982), and their sentence comprehension problems (Byrne, 1981; Mann *et al.*, in press). It has the virtue of providing a ready explanation for one of the more common findings in the field, namely, that the performance of poor readers never really deviates from that of good readers, but merely involves more of the kinds of errors typical of slightly younger children (Mann *et al.*, 1984).

Maturational-lag theories also are consistent with some other observations about the population of poor readers. First, there is the observation that boys encounter reading problems more often than girls (Liberman & Mann, 1980; Rutter & Yule, 1973). It is well known that boys mature less rapidly than girls do. It also has been shown that a slower rate of physical maturation tends to be associated with a pattern of mental abilities in which spatial processing skills are superior to language (Waber, 1977). Given these observations, one should, indeed, expect to find that, among children at a given age, there should be disproportionately many boys with lesser language skills, and therefore, disproportionately many boys who encounter reading difficulty. A second observation which may be explained by maturational lag is that children with low birth weight are at risk for reading problems (Rutter & Yule, 1973). Low birth weight often reflects a premature birth, and prematurely born infants may reach the first milestones of language development relatively later in postgestational life than do those infants born at full term (Gleitman, 1981). Hence, they show a lag in language development and might be expected to encounter reading problems.

The primary difficulty with the concept of maturational lag is that it cannot, as yet, explain why only certain language difficulties tend to be found among poor readers. Perhaps, we might want to conceive of a maturational lag in phonological processes, given the findings summarized earlier. Another problem with maturational-lag theories is that the language-processing difficulties of poor readers can persist past early childhood to adolescence (McKeever & van Deventer, 1975) and beyond (Jackson & McClelland, 1979). That is, the language-processing skills of poor readers may never really "catch up" to those of good readers. Perhaps, the concept of a lag in development will need to be refined to allow for the possibility that language development in poor readers reaches a premature plateau. In any event, such problems are not insurmountable, and the possibility that reading difficulty involves a specific maturational lag in the development of language-processing skills is a most intriguing one which should spark considerable research in the coming decade.

ORIGINS OF DEFICIENT PHONOLOGICAL SOPHISTICATION

In discussing the origins of deficient linguistic sophistication, it should be noted that such deficiencies tend to correlate, somewhat, with deficient language-processing skills (Mann & Liberman, 1984). Thus, to the extent that a maturational lag may explain deficient processing skills, it may help to explain deficient linguistic sophistication as well. However, the correlation is less than perfect, leaving room for the possibility that the two syndromes are independent. Certainly, it is logical to think that children who are deficient in processing skills might also lack linguistic sophistication, as the latter probably presumes the former. However, there may be some children who possess normal processing skills, but lack linguistic sophistication.

In considering the basis of deficient phonological awareness, let me begin by noting the spurt in phonological awareness that occurs at age 6 (Liberman et al., 1974). Phonological awareness is a cognitive skill of sorts, and, as such, must surely demand the attainment of a certain degree of intellectual maturity. Yet, 6 is the age at which most children in America begin to receive instruction in reading and writing, and there is reason to suspect that not only may phonological awareness be important for the acquisition of reading, but being taught to read may, at the same time, help to develop phonological awareness (see, for example, Alegria et al., 1982; Liberman et al., 1980; Morais, Carey, Alegria, & Bertelson, 1979).

The strongest evidence that phonological awareness is facilitated by reading instruction concerns awareness about phonemes. For example, it has been reported that illiterate adults are unable to manipulate the phonetic structure of spoken words (Morais et al., 1979). Another study, conducted in Belgium, reveals that first-graders taught largely by a phonics method did spectacularly better on a task requiring phoneme segmentation than did other children taught largely by a whole-word method (Alegria et al., 1982). Another longitudinal study of first-graders in America reveals that there is a reciprocal causal relationship between phoneme awareness and reading skill (Perfetti et al., 1981). All in all, it seems that awareness of phonemes is enhanced by methods of reading instruction that direct the child's attention to the phonetic structure of words, and even may depend on such instruction.

However, experience alone cannot be the only factor behind some childrens' failure to achieve phoneme awareness. This is aptly shown by a finding that among a group of 6-year-old skilled readers and 10-year-old disabled readers who were matched for reading ability, the disabled readers performed significantly worse on a phoneme awareness task, even though they would be expected to have had more reading instruction than the younger children (Bradley & Bryant, 1978). Here, it could be argued that some constitutional factor limited the disabled readers' ability to profit from instruction, and thus limited their attainment of phonological sophistication.

The possibility that a constitutional factor underlies the development of phonological awareness also is consistent with findings about the development of syllable segmentation. Both our work (Liberman *et al.*, 1974; Mann, 1984b; Mann & Liberman, 1984), and that of others (Alegria *et al.*, 1982) suggests that awareness of syllable-sized units can be expected to precede awareness of phoneme-sized units, and is probably a natural cognitive achievement that does not necessarily depend on reading instruction for its development. Most children can manipulate the syllables of an utterance by the time they are 6 years old; moreover, their ability to do so apparently is less influenced by the particular method of reading instruction (Alegria *et al.*, 1982). We might, therefore, return to the possibility of a maturational lag in language development as a constitutional factor responsible for some children's failure to develop phonological awareness despite favorable experience.

CONCLUDING REMARKS

This chapter has proceeded from a consideration of the importance of language skills to both skilled and beginning reading, to a review of evidence that deficient language-processing skills and deficient linguistic awareness are important factors in early reading disability, to a discussion of the possible origins of these deficiencies. One of the practical benefits of the research described herein is that it can suggest ways of presaging and remediating early reading difficulty. By way of a conclusion, let me make some of those benefits explicit.

One obvious benefit concerns screening devices for identifying children at risk for early reading problems. Such phonological processing skills as the ability to rapidly access the names of objects and the ability to make effective use of phonetic representation in short-term memory have already been shown to be effective kindergarten predictors of first-grade reading success (see, for example, Blachman, 1980; Mann, 1984b; Mann & Liberman, 1984). The time to refine such tests for larger-scale use is now upon us. Likewise, tests of phoneme and syllable awareness can presage reading success (Liberman *et al.*, 1974; Mann, 1984b; Mann & Liberman, 1984; Stanovich *et al.*, 1984), and they, too, should be refined for practical application.

Another benefit: Identifying the linguistic problems associated with specific reading difficulty may help to point the way to effective procedures for remediation. For example, if a maturational lag in language development is the cause of reading difficulty, then, perhaps, we should attempt to identify children at risk for such a lag, and consider the delay of beginning reading instruction until a time when language skills will be more optimal. We might also want to take seriously the possibility that environmental enrichment can mitigate the extent of these children's language difficulties, and pursue research to that effect. In any event, if it is accepted that reading difficulty can involve a specific lag in language development, as opposed to slower development in general, then, it is by no means desirable to withhold all forms of beginning instruction from the child who is considered at risk for specific reading difficulty. For example, instruction in mathematics, geography, and science should not be withheld.

Certainly, the brightest prospects for remediation are offered by findings that reading instruction can facilitate phoneme awareness. Some very interesting and practical advice on how to facilitate linguistic sophistication is currently available (Liberman, 1982; Mann, 1984b; Mann & Liberman, 1984; Liberman, Shankweiler, Blachman, Camp, & Werfelman, 1980). Perhaps, the best favor we can do for all children is to let them in on the secrets of the alphabetic principle as early as possible (Liberman, 1982; Liberman & Mann, 1980). This, of course, means phonics, phonics, and more phonics, but phonics integral to beginning reading instruction.

ACKNOWLEDGMENTS

This essay was completed while the author was a Fulbright Fellow at the Research Institute for Logopedics of Phoniatrics, University of Tokyo, Tokyo, Japan. Earlier stages of preparation, and much of the research herein described, were funded by NICHD Grant HD–01994 and BRS Grant 05596 to Haskins Laboratories, Inc.

REFERENCES

Alegria, J., & Pignot, E. (1979). Genetic aspects of verbal mediation in memory. *Child Development, 50,* 235–238.

Alegria, J., Pignot, E., & Morais, J. (1982). Phonetic analysis of speech and memory codes in beginning readers. *Memory & Cognition, 10,* 451–456.

Baddeley, A. D. (1978). The trouble with levels: A Reexamination of Craik and Lockhardt's framework for memory research. *Psychological Review, 85,* 139–152.

Benton, A. (1975). Developmental dyslexia: Neurological aspects. In W. J. Freelander (Ed.). *Advances in Neurology*. Vol. 7 (pp. 1–47). New York: Raven Press.

Birch, H. G., & Belmont, L. (1964). Auditory-visual integration in normal and retarded readers. *American Journal of Orthopsychiatry, 34*, 852–861.

Blachman, B. (1980). The role of selected reading-related measures in the prediction of reading achievement. Unpublished doctoral dissertation. Storrs, CT: University of Connecticut.

Blank, M., & Bridger, W. (1966). Deficiencies in verbal labeling in retarded readers. *American Journal of Orthopsychiatry, 36*, 840–847.

Blank, M., Weider, S., & Bridger, W. (1968). Verbal deficiencies in abstract thinking in early reading retardation. *American Journal of Orthopsychiatry, 38*, 823–834.

Brady, S., Shankweiler, D., & Mann, V. (1983). Speech perception and memory coding in relation to reading ability. *Journal of Experimental Child Psychology, 35*, 345–367.

Bradley, L., & Bryant, P. E. (1978). Difficulties in auditory organization as a possible cause of reading backwards. *Nature, 271*, 746–747.

Brandt, J., & Rosen, J. J. (1980). Auditory phonemic perception in dyslexia: Categorical identification and discrimination of stop consonants. *Brain and Language, 9*, 324–337.

Bryden, M. P. (1972). Auditory-visual and sequential-spatial imaging in relation to reading ability. *Child Development, 43*, 824–832.

Byrne, B. (1981). Deficient syntactic control in poor readers: Is a weak phonetic memory code responsible? *Applied Psycholinguistics, 2*, 201–212.

Byrne, B., & Shea, P. (1979). Semantic and phonetic memory in beginning readers. *Memory & Cognition, 7*, 333–338.

Carr, T. H. (1981). Building theories of reading ability: On the relation between individual differences in cognitive skills and reading comprehension. *Cognition, 9*, 73–114.

Chomsky, N. (1964). Comments for project literacy meeting. Project Literacy Report No. 2. Reprinted in M. Lester (Ed.). *Reading in Applied Transformational Grammar* (pp. 1–8). New York: Holt Rinehart and Winston.

Conrad, R. (1964). Acoustic confusions in immediate memory. *British Journal of Psychology, 55*, 75–84.

Conrad, R. (1972). Speech and reading. In J. F. Kavanaugh & I. G. Mattingly (Eds.). *Language by Ear and by Eye: The Relationships between Speech and Reading* (pp. 205–240). Cambridge, MA: MIT Press.

Crowder, R. (1982). The Psychology of reading. New York: Academic Press.

Curtis, M. E. (1980). Development of components of reading skill. *Journal of Educational Psychology, 72*, 656–669.

Corkin, S. (1974). Serial-order deficits in inferior readers. *Neuropsychologia, 12*, 347–354.

Daneman, M., & Carpenter, P. A. (1980). Individual differences in working memory and reading. *Journal of Verbal Learning and Verbal Behavior, 19*, 450–466.

Daneman, M., & Case, R. (1981). Syntactic form, semantic complexity and short-term memory: Influences on children's acquisition of new linguistic structures. *Developmental Psychology, 17*, 367–378.

Denckla, M. B., & Rudel, R. G. (1976). Naming of object drawings by dyslexic and other learning-disabled children. *Brain and Language, 3*, 1–15.

Drenowski, A. (1980). Memory functions for vowels and consonants: Are interpretation of acoustic similarity effects. *Journal of Verbal Learning and Verbal Behavior, 19*, 176–193.

Eimas, P. D. (1975). Distinctive feature codes in the short-term memory of children. *Journal of Experimental Child Psychology, 19*, 241–251.

Ellis, A. W. (1985). The Cognitive Neuropsychology of developmental (and acquired) dyslexia: A critical survey. *Cognitive Neuropsychology, 2*, 169–205.

Fennell, E. B., Satz, P., & Morris, R. (1983). The development of handedness and dichotic ear assymetries in relation to school achievement: A longitudinal study. *Journal of Experimental Child Psychology, 35,* 248–262.

Fisher, F. W., Liberman, I. Y., & Shankweiler, D. (1977). Reading reversals and developmental dyslexia: A further study. *Cortex, 14,* 496–510.

Fletcher, J. M., Satz, P., & Scholes, R. (1981). Developmental changes in the linguistic performance correlates of reading achievements. *Brain and Language, 13,* 78–90.

Fox, B., & Routh, D. K. (1976). Phonemic analysis and synthesis as word-attack skills. *Journal of Educational Psychology, 69,* 70–74.

Gibson, E. J., Gibson, J. J., Pick, A. D., & Osser, R. (1962). A developmental study of the discrimination of letter-like forms. *Journal of Comparative and Physiological Psychology, 55,* 897–906.

Gleitman, L. R. (1981). Maturational determinants of language growth. *Cognition, 10,* 103–114.

Godfrey, J. L., Syrdal-Lasky, A. K., Millay, K. K., & Knox, C. M. (1981). Performance of dyslexic children on speech perception tasks. *Journal of Experimental Child Psychology, 32,* 401–424.

Goetzinger, C., Dirks, D., & Baer, C. J. (1960). Auditory discrimination and visual perception in good and poor readers. *Annals of Otology, Rhinology and Laryngology, 69,* 121–136.

Goldman, S. R. (1976). Reading skill and the Minimum Distance Principle: A comparison of listening and reading comprehension. *Journal of Experimental Child Psychology, 22,* 123–142.

Helfgott, J. (1976). Phonemic segmentation and blending skills of kindergarten children: Implications for beginning reading acquisition. *Contemporary Educational Psychology, 1,* 157–169.

Hicks, C. (1980). The ITPA Visual Sequential Memory Test: An alternative interpretation of the implications for good and poor readers. *British Journal of Educational Psychology, 50,* 16–25.

Hier, D., LeMay, M., Rosenberger, P., & Perlo, V. (1978). Developmental dyslexia. *Archives of Neurology, 35,* 90–92.

Hung, D. L., & Tzeng, O. J. L. (1981). Orthographic variations and visual information processing. *Psychological Bulletin, 90,* 377–414.

Ingram, T. T. S., Mason, A. W., & Blackburn, I. (1970). A retrospective study of 82 children with reading disability. *Developmental Medicine and Child Neurology, 12,* 271–281.

Jackson, M. & McClelland, J. L. (1979). Processing determinants of reading speed. *Journal of Experimental Psychology: General, 108,* 151–181.

Jorm, A. F. (1979). The cognitive and neurological basis of developmental dyslexia: A theoretical framework and review. *Cognition, 7,* 19–33.

Jorm, A. F. (1979). The nature of the reading deficit in developmental dyslexia: A reply to Ellis. *Cognition, 7,* 421–433.

Katz, R. B., (1982). Phonological deficiencies in children with reading disability: Evidence from an object naming task. Unpublished Ph.D. thesis. Storrs, CT: University of Connecticut.

Katz, R. B., Shankweiler, D., & Liberman, I. Y. (1981). Memory for item order and phonetic recoding in the beginning reader. *Journal of Experimental Child Psychology, 32,* 474–484.

Keefe, B., & Swinney, D. (1979). On the role of hemispheric specialization in developmental dyslexia. *Cortex, 15,* 471–481.

Kleiman, G. (1975). Speech recoding in reading. *Journal of Verbal Learning and Verbal Behavior, 14*, 323–339.

Levy, B. A. (1977). Reading: Speech and meaning processes. *Journal of Verbal Learning and Verbal Behavior, 16*, 623–638.

Liberman, A. M. (1982). On finding that speech is special. *American Psychologist, 37*, 148–167.

Liberman, A. M., Cooper, F. S., Shankweiler, D., & Studdert-Kennedy, M. (1967). Perception of the speech code. *Psychological Review, 74*, 431–461.

Liberman, I. Y. (1982). A Language-oriented view of reading and its disabilities. In H. Mykelburst (Ed.). *Progress in Learning Disabilities*. Vol. 5. New York: Grune and Stratton.

Liberman, I. Y., Liberman, A. M., Mattingly, I. G., & Shankweiler, D. (1980). Orthography and the beginning reader. In J. Kavanaugh & R. Venezky (Eds.). *Orthography, Reading and Dyslexia*. (pp. 137–154). Baltimore: University Park Press.

Liberman, I. Y., & Mann, V. A. (1980). Should reading remediation vary with the sex of the child? In A. Ansara, N. Geschwind, A. Galaburda, N. Albert, & N. Gartrell (Eds.). *Sex Differences in Dyslexia* (pp. 151–168). Towson, MD: The Orton Society.

Liberman, I. Y., Mann, V. A., Shankweiler, D., & Werfelman, M. (1982). Children's memory for recurring linguistic and non-linguistic material in relation to reading ability. *Cortex, 18*, 367–375.

Liberman, I. Y., Shankweiler, D., Blachman, B., Camp, L., & Werfelman, M. (1980). Steps towards Literacy. Report prepared for Working Group on Learning Failure and Unused Learning Potential. President's Commission on Mental Health, Nov. 1, 1977. In P. Levinson & C. H. Sloan (Eds.). *Auditory Processing and Language: Clinical and Research Perspectives* (pp. 1–30). New York: Grune & Stratton.

Liberman, I. Y., Shankweiler, D., Fisher, F. W., & Carter, B. (1974). Explicit syllable and phoneme segmentation in the young child. *Journal of Experimental Child Psychology, 18*, 201–212.

Liberman, I. Y., Shankweiler, D., Liberman, A. M., Fowler, C., & Fischer, F. W. (1977). Phonetic segmentation and recoding in the beginning reader. In A. S. Reber & D. Scarborough (Eds.). *Towards a Psychology of Reading: The Proceedings of the CUNY Conference* (pp. 207–225). Hillsdale, NJ: Lawrence Erlbaum Associates.

Lundberg, I., Oloffson, A., & Wall, S. (1980). Reading and spelling skills in the first school years predicated from phoneme awareness skills in kindergarten. *Scandinavian Journal of Psychology, 21*, 159–173.

McCusker, L. X., Bias, R. G., & Hillinger, N. H., (1981). Phonological Recoding in Reading. *British Journal of Psychology, 89*, 217–245.

McKeever, W. F., & van Deventer, A. D. (1975). Dyslexic adolescents: Evidence of impaired visual and auditory language processing associated with normal lateralization and visual responsivity, *Cortex, 11*, 361–378.

Mann, V. A. (1984a). Reading skill and language skill. *Developmental Review, 4*, 1–15.

Mann, V. A. (1984b). Longitudinal prediction and prevention of early reading difficulty. *Annals of Dyslexia, 34*, 117–136.

Mann, V. A., & Liberman, A. M. (1983). Some differences between phonetic and auditory modes of perception. *Cognition, 14*, 211–235.

Mann, V. A., & Liberman, I. Y. (1984). Phonological awareness and verbal short-term memory: Can they presage early reading success? *Journal of Learning Disabilities, 17*, 592–599.

Mann, V. A., Liberman, I. Y., & Shankweiler, D. (1980). Children's memory for sentences and word strings in relation to reading ability. *Memory & Cognition, 8*, 329–335.

Mann, V. A., Shankweiler, D., & Smith, S. T. (1984). The association between comprehension of spoken sentences and early reading ability: The role of phonetic representation. *Journal of Child Language, 11,* 627–643.

Mason, W. (1976). Specific (developmental) dyslexia. *Developmental Medicine and Child Neurology, 9,* 183–190.

Mattingly, I. G. (1972). Reading, the linguistic process, and linguistic awareness. In J. F. Kavanaugh and I. G. Mattingly (Eds.). *Language by Ear and by Eye: The Relationship between Speech and Reading* (pp. 133–148). Cambridge, MA: MIT Press.

Miller, J. L., & Eimas, P. D. (1983). Studies on the categorization of speech by infants. *Cognition. 13,* 135–166.

Money, J. (1973). Turner's syndrome and parietal lobe functions. *Cortex, 9,* 387–393.

Morais, J., Cary, L., Alegria, J., & Bertelson, P. (1979). Does awareness of speech as a sequence of phonemes arise spontaneously? *Cognition, 7,* 323–331.

Morrison, F. J., Giordani, B., & Nagy, J. (1977). Reading disability: An information processing analysis. *Science, 196,* 77–79.

Moskowitz, B. A. (1973). On the status of vowel shift in English. In T. Moore (Ed.). *Cognitive Development and Acquisition of Language* (pp. 223–260). New York: Academic Press.

Noelker, R. W., & Schumsky, D. A. (1973). Memory for sequence, form and position in relation to the identification of reading retardation. *Journal of Educational Psychology, 64,* 22–25.

Orton, S. T. (1937). *Reading, writing and speech problems in children.* New York: Norton.

Owen, F. W. (1978). Dyslexia: Genetic aspects. In A. L. Benton & D. Pearl (Eds.). *Dyslexia: An Appraisal of Current Knowledge* (pp. 265–284). New York: Oxford University Press.

Owen, F. W., Adams, P. A., Forrest, T., Stolz, L. M., & Fischer, S. (1971). Learning disorders in children: Sibling studies. *Monographs of the Society for Research in Child Development, 36,* Chicago: University of Illinois Press.

Perfetti, C. A., Beck, I. L., and Hughes, C. (April 1981). Phonemic knowledge and learning to read. Paper presented at the meeting of the Society for Research in Child Development, Boston: Society for Research in Child Development.

Perfetti, C. A., & McCutchen, D. (1982). Speech processes in reading. *Speech and Language: Advances in Basic Research and Practice, 7,* 237–269.

Read, C. (1975). Children's categorization of speech sounds in English. *NCTE Research Report,* ERIC.

Robinson, M. E., & Schwartz, L. B. (1973). Visuo-motor skills and reading ability: A longitudinal study. *Developmental Medicine and Child Neurology, 15,* 280–286.

Russell, G. F. M. (1982a). Writing and dyslexia: An historical analysis. *Journal of Child Psychology and Psychiatry, 23,* 383–400.

Russell, G. F. M. (1982b). Impairment of phonetic reading in dyslexia and its persistence beyond childhood: Research note. *Journal of Child Psychology and Child Psychiatry, 23,* 459–475.

Rutter, M. (1978). Prevalence and types of dyslexia. In A. L. Benton and D. Pearl (Eds.). *Dyslexia: An Appraisal of Current Knowledge* (pp. 3–28). New York: Oxford Press.

Rutter, M., & Madge, N. (1976). *Cycles of disadvantage: A review of research.* London: Heinemann Educational.

Rutter, M., & Yule, W. (1973). The concept of specific reading retardation. *Journal of Child Psychiatry, 16,* 181–198.

Satz, P., & Sparrow, S. (1970). Specific developmental dyslexia: A theoretical framework. In D. J. Bakker & P. Satz (Eds.). *Specific Reading Disability: Advances in Theory and Method.* Rotterdam: Rotterdam University Press.

Shankweiler, D., & Liberman, I. Y. (1972). Misreading: A search for the causes. In J. F. Kavanaugh & I. G. Mattingly (Eds.). *Language by Ear and by Eye: The Relationships between Speech and Reading* (pp. 293–318). Cambridge, Mass: MIT Press.

Shankweiler, D., Liberman, I. Y., Mark, L. S., Fowler, C. A., & Fisher, F. W. (1979). The speech code and learning to read. *Journal of Experimental Psychology: Human Perception and Performance, 5,* 531–545.

Simpson, G. B., Lorsbach, T. C., & Whitehouse, D. (1983). Encoding and contextual components of word recognition in good and pooor readers. *Journal of Experimental Child Psychology, 35,* 161–171.

Slowiaczek, M. L., & Clifton, C. (1980). Subvocalization and reading for meaning. *Journal of Verbal Learning and Verbal Behavior, 19,* 573–582.

Smith, S. D., & Pennington, B. F. (1983). Genetic influences on learning disabilities II: Behavior genetics and clinical implications. *Learning Disabilities, 2,* 43–55.

Spring, C. (1976). Encoding speech and memory span in dyslexia children. *Journal of Special Education, 10,* 35–40.

Stevenson, H. W., Stiegler, J. W., Lucker, G. W., Hsu, C.-C., & Kitamura, S. (1982). Reading disabilities: The case of Chinese, Japanese and English. *Child Development, 53,* 1164–1181.

Stanovich, K. (1982a). Individual differences in the cognitive processes of reading: I. Word deciding. *Journal of Learning Disabilities, 15,* 485–493.

Stanovich, K. (1982b). Individual differences in the cognitive processes of reading: II. Text-level processes. *Journal of Learning Disabilities, 15,* 549–554.

Stanovich, K. E., Cunningham, A. E. & Cramer, B. B. (1984). Assessing phonological awareness in kindergarten children: Issues of task comparability. *Journal of Experimental Child Psychology, 38,* 175–190.

Swanson, L. (1978). Verbal encoding effects on the visual short-term memory of learning-disabled and normal children. *Journal of Educational Psychology, 70,* 539–544.

Thomas, C. C. (1905). Cogenital "word blindness" and its treatment. *Opthalmoscope, 3,* 380–385.

Torgesen, J. K. (1977). Memorization processes in reading-disabled children. *Journal of Educational Psychology, 69,* 551–578.

Torgesen, J. K., & Hoack, D. J. (1980). Processing deficiencies of learning-disabled children who perform poorly on the digit-span test. *Journal of Educational Psychology, 72,* 141–160.

Tzeng, O. J. L., Hung, D. L., & Wang, W. S.-Y. (1977). Speech recoding in reading Chinese characters. *Journal of Experimental Psychology: Human Learning and Memory, 3,* 621–630.

Vellutino, F. R. (1979). *Dyslexia: Theory and research.* Cambridge, MA: MIT Press.

Vellutino, F. R. & Scanlon, D. M. (1985). Free recall of concrete and abstract words in poor and normal readers. *Journal of Experimental Child Psychology, 39,* 363–380.

Vernon, M. D. (1979). Variability in reading retardation. *British Journal of Psychology, 70,* 7–16.

Waber, D. P. (1977). Sex differences in mental abilities, hemispheric lateralization, and rate of physical growth at adolescence. *Developmental Psychology, 13,* 29–38.

Watson, E. S., & Engle, R. W. (1982). Is it lateralization, processing strategies, or both that distinguish good and poor readers? *Journal of Experimental Child Psychology, 34,* 1–19.

Witelson, S. F. (1977). Developmental dyslexia: Two right hemispheres and none left. *Science, 195,* 309–311.

Zurif, E. B., & Carson, G. (1970). Dyslexia in relation to cerebral dominance and temporal analysis. *Neuropsychologia, 8,* 351–361.

Attention Problems in Youngsters with Learning Handicaps

ANTOINETTE KRUPSKI

INTRODUCTION

There is general agreement that children with a variety of learning problems are often likely to exhibit attention problems as well. In spite of this agreement, however, much confusion exists regarding the specific nature of attention problems, especially as they relate to various diagnostic classifications. Problems in the definition of diagnostic classifications as well as problems in definitions of attention appear to be two major sources contributing to the current confusion. For this reason, it is relevant to examine each of these areas in turn.

DEFINITIONS OF DIAGNOSTIC CLASSIFICATIONS

There is significant variability in the way learning-disabled youngsters have been operationally defined in the research literature (Keogh & MacMillan, 1983; Keogh, Major-Kingsley, Omori-Gordon, & Reid, 1982; Torgesen, 1982). In addition, the term *learning disability* often has been used vaguely and interchangeably with terms such as *underachievement*, *minimal brain dysfunction*, and *hyperactivity* (Douglas & Peters, 1979; Lambert & Sandoval, 1980). *Reading disabilities* and *attention-deficit disorder* are other terms that are often employed to describe youngsters with learning disabilities.

This diversity in definition and terminology probably reflects the diversity of conceptual perspectives regarding the nature of learning dis-

161

Psychological and Educational
Perspectives on Learning Disabilities

abilities. It probably also reflects the diversity of learning-disabled youngsters themselves. Children are labeled learning disabled for many different reasons. As Torgesen (1975) points out, the category of learning disabilities was never meant to represent a diagnostic category as such, but was merely to serve the purpose of loosely organizing a disparate group of problems under one heading. Thus, although problematic for comparing and generalizing research findings, this diversity appears to be a natural consequence of the category's origins.

Given the heterogeneity that characterizes samples of learning-disabled children, one would expect little order in the data regarding attention problems. Yet, to the contrary, consistent patterns appear in the data which suggest that many children with a variety of learning handicaps share particular types of attention problems to some degree. The approach taken in the present chapter is to review studies that employ youngsters described as learning disabled, hyperactive, and low-achieving, as well as those described as having minimal brain dysfunction, reading disabilities, and attention-deficit disorder. The collective term, *learning handicapped* is used in reference to children who have been designated as fitting into one or more of these classifications.

Whenever possible, distinctions between hyperactive and learning-disabled youngsters are made. Although attention problems are reported for both these groups, Douglas and Peters (1979) argue that these problems arise in each group for different reasons. This view stems from a broader argument in which it is suggested that hyperactivity has a different etiological basis and course of development than does learning disability. Hyperactive youngsters, for example, are characterized by Douglas and Peters (1979) as having "a constitutional predisposition involving poor impulse control, an inability to sustain attention, and poorly modulated arousal levels, which result in a tendency to seek stimulation and salience" (p. 233). A consequence of this cluster of deficits is that hyperactive children miss out on important learning experiences which can snowball and ultimately lead to potential backwardness in academic achievement. However, low academic achievement is hypothesized to be a secondary consequence of the more fundamental impulsivity, attention, and arousal deficits.

Learning-disabled youngsters, on the other hand, are hypothesized by these authors (Douglas & Peters, 1979) to have specific learning disorders as their basic deficit (e.g., a receptive language problem or inability to process visual symbols). These specific learning disorders are thought likely to lead to failure experiences. As a reaction to an inevitable succession of failure experiences, a learning-disabled child may develop avoidance behaviors which can resemble the behaviors of hyperactive youngsters (e.g., poor impulse control, poor sustained attention, etc.). However, in the case of the learning-disabled child, these hyperactive-like behaviors are considered to be secondary consequences to a more fundamental learning disorder.

Thus, although Douglas and Peters (1979) agree that both hyperactive and learning-disabled youngsters are characterized by attention problems, they argue that such problems arise in these subgroups for different reasons. This proposed distinction has many important implications for both theory and practice. Thus, whenever possible, evidence regarding this argument will be presented.

DEFINITIONS OF ATTENTION

The study of attention processes has a long and rich history (Lovie, 1983). Over the years, many definitions of attention have emerged and are still with us today. An example of this point is provided by Moray (1969) who argued that attention consisted of at least seven subdivisions including mental concentration, vigilance, selective attention, search, activation, set, and analysis by synthesis. The diversity among these components led Moray (1969) to conclude that there may be a need for as many different theories as there are subdivisions.

It is generally agreed that most research on attention problems in learning-handicapped youngsters has focused on either sustained or selective aspects of attention (Douglas & Peters, 1979; Krupski, 1980). These are the two types of attention that will be reviewed in this chapter. It is important to note, however, that even within these restricted categories, there are many variants.

For example, the operations used to define both sustained and selective attention have been many and diverse, suggesting that even restricted aspects of attention are probably best viewed as multidimensional in nature. In his discussion of selective attention, Kahneman (1973) provides a taxonomy of selective operations borrowed from Treisman (1969). He argues that the varieties of selective attention are "governed by different rules and are to be explained by different mechanisms" (p. 3).

In addition to problems arising from diverse definitions, measures of attention are often confounded with memory or other types of cognitive demands. Although all tasks require some degree of attention, few can be considered to be pure measures of attention. This, of course, makes it impossible to interpret performance on most tasks as being due to attention alone. Thus, any given task that is purported to measure some aspect of attention must be examined carefully to determine if processes

other than attention may be influencing performance and interpreta-
tions must be adjusted accordingly.

Up to this point, the discussion has rested on the assumption that
attention is, in fact, a process that can be studied with some degree of
independence from other processes. It is instructive to note that there
are theorists who do not hold this assumption. Neisser (1976), for example, argues that no separate mechanisms of attention exist. He states,
"Attention is nothing but perception: we choose what we will see by
anticipating the structured information it will provide" (p. 87). Thus, in
the eyes of some, the study of attention is viewed as a superfluous
effort.

In the remaining pages of this chapter, studies in which sustained
and selective aspects of attention have been examined in learning-handicapped youngsters will be reviewed. In the section on sustained attention, it will be demonstrated that youngsters with a variety of learning
handicaps frequently exhibit problems in this area. In the subsequent
section on selective attention, in contrast, it will be argued that selective
attention is a superfluous construct which should be discarded.

SUSTAINED ATTENTION

A number of measures have been developed for inferring the degree
to which attention is sustained among various learning handicapped
groups. The typical approach has been to compare performance on one
or more attention-demanding tasks between groups of learning-handicapped and nonhandicapped youngsters. Because much of this research
recently has been reviewed (Douglas & Peters, 1979; Krupski, 1980), it
will be briefly summarized here.Emphasis will be given to the most
recent studies which are characterized by attention to performance of
subgroups within the learning-handicapped samples tested.

A summary of findings with some of the more commonly used measures of sustained attention will be presented. These measures include
vigilance, reaction time, and physiological correlates of reaction time
performance.

VIGILANCE

Vigilance tasks have a long history of use as one measure of sustained
attention. In this task, the individual is required to monitor a continuous
stream of stimuli for an extended time period. Interspersed among the
background stimuli are infrequent and unpredictable signals which the

participant must detect. To perform this task, the individual must continuously monitor ongoing stimuli, for even a brief lapse in attention could result in a missed signal. Such demands for continuous monitoring give the vigilance task high face validity as a measure from which sustained attention can be inferred.

A variety of vigilance tasks have been developed over the years. Some require the individual to detect changes in, say, the brightness of a light flash or the loudness of a tone. Others have greater cognitive demands, such as the Continuous Performance Task (CPT) (Rosvold, Mirsky, Sarason, Bransome, & Beck, 1956). The CPT has been adapted for use with children and handicapped individuals and frequently is used as a measure of sustained attention in the developmental literature. The stimuli for this test are 12 letters which appear on a screen, one at a time. Each remains on the screen for 1–2 seconds, and there is a 1- to 2-second interval between letters where the screen is blank. The participant's task is to press a button each time an X appears; in a more difficult version of the task, the participant is required to respond to the X only after it has been preceded by an A. An auditory version of the CPT is also used (e.g., Swanson, 1980, 1983; Sykes, Douglas, & Morgenstern, 1973). In this case, the letters are presented auditorily at a rate of about one per second, with detection requirements remaining the same as in the visual CPT task.

Vigilance performance usually is reported as omissions, or number of signals missed. A decrement score often is reported; this refers to the decline in detections that occur over time. A third score, commission errors or false alarms, frequently is reported also. Total omissions and decrement scores usually are interpreted as measures of sustained attention whereas commission errors usually are interpreted as a measure of impulsivity.

Given the task demands inherent in the vigilance situation, it is not surprising that children with learning handicaps almost always perform more poorly on vigilance than their nonhandicapped peers. For example, hyperactive (Goldberg & Konstantareas, 1981; Kirchner, 1976; Klorman, Salzman, Pass, Borgstedt, & Danier, 1979; Kupietz, 1976; Loiselle, Stamm, Maitinsky, & Whipple, 1980; Michael, Klorman, Salzman, Borgstedt, & Dainer, 1981; Nuechterlein, 1983; Sykes, Douglas, Weiss, & Minde, 1971; and Sykes et al., 1973), learning disabled (Anderson, Halcomb, & Doyle, 1973; Danier, Klorman, Salzman, Hess, Davidson, & Michael, 1981; Doyle, Anderson, & Halcomb, 1976; Rugel, Cheatam, & Mitchell, 1978, and Swanson, 1980, 1983), low-achieving/reading retarded (Aman, 1979; Brackup & Knopf, 1978; Kirchner & Knopf, 1974; Noland & Schuldt, 1971), and educationally handicapped (Keogh &

Margolis, 1976) youngsters have all been reported to make more errors of omission than matched groups of nonhandicapped youngsters. Hyperactive (Kupietz, 1976; Nuechterlein, 1983; Sykes *et al.*, 1973), low-achieving (Brackup & Knopf, 1978), and educationally handicapped (Keogh & Margolis, 1976) youngsters also have been reported to exhibit greater decrement in vigilance performance over time than their respective matched control groups, suggesting a relatively greater deterioration in sustained attention over time.

It is important to note that children in all above reported experiments had IQs in the normal range and that vigilance tasks employed had minimal cognitive demands. The most demanding in this respect is the CPT, which required youngsters to recognize letters of the alphabet and, in some cases, retain a single letter in memory for several seconds. Since it is conventional to screen all youngsters on their knowledge of letters before enlisting them in such experiments, it is likely that recognition of letters was well within their ability range. In the case where retention of a letter was required, it is known that even moderately retarded youngsters can retain one to two items in memory for several seconds without problem (Krupski, 1984). Thus, it seems reasonable to conclude that cognitive processing demands in the vigilance experiments reported above were minimal and within the ability range of youngsters employed in these experiments.

If one accepts this argument and assumes that cognitive demands of the task can be eliminated as an explanation for group differences, then learning-handicapped youngsters' poor performance is explained, with few exceptions (e.g., Swanson, 1981, 1983), as a problem in sustained attention. This explanation is, of course, consistent with clinical observations and other characterizations of learning-handicapped youngsters.

The data indicate that problems of sustained attention which are reflected in vigilance performance appear consistently for different groups of children with learning problems—hyperactive, learning disabled, low achievers, reading retarded, and educationally handicapped. Douglas and Peters (1979) have argued that such results may be misleading. They suggest that poor vigilance performance (in the form of frequent omissions and decrement scores) may be attributed to hyperactive youngsters and not necessarily to youngsters with learning disabilities. Given this argument, it is important to examine whether there is evidence to support a distinction between learning-disabled and hyperactive groups on vigilance performance.

One problem in evaluating the available evidence on this point is that samples in many vigilance experiments are poorly described—a problem that extends throughout the field of learning disabilities (Keogh & MacMillan, 1983; Keogh et al., 1982). Thus, it is likely that children with hyperactivity are included in many samples described as consisting of learning-disabled youngsters and vice versa. Despite these definitional problems, however, there are eight studies in which deliberate attempts were made to carefully identify subgroups within the learning-handi-capped population. These studies provide a preliminary basis for evalu-ating Douglas and Peters' (1979) argument regarding possible distinc-tions between learning-disabled and hyperactive youngsters in the area of vigilance. Let us examine omission and decrement data first.

Overall, these studies provide little evidence for a distinction between these subgroups. For example, Keogh & Margolis (1976) subdivided an educationally handicapped group into hyperactive and nonhyperactive subgroups on the basis of a 15-item questionnaire administered to teach-ers; they found no significant differences between subgroups on either omission errors or decrement. In a similar vein, Doyle et al. (1976) subdi-vided their learning-disabled sample into hyperactive, normoactive, and hypoactive subgroups; they found no significant subgroup differences on correct detections. Although Doyle et al. (1976) included graphs de-picting decrement over time for each of the three subgroups, they pro-vided no statistical tests of these data. This, of course, makes any poten-tial subgroup differences in decrement impossible to evaluate. Taken together, then, the Doyle et al. (1976) data, like the Keogh and Margolis (1976) data, lead to the conclusion that the conventional measure of sustained attention typically inferred from vigilance performance (i.e., omissions and decrement) do not distinguish among learning-disabled subgroups which differ in level of hyperactivity. Although a third study (Anderson et al., 1973) did report differences in errors of omission among groups of hyperactive, normoactive, and hypoactive learning-disabled children, serious methodological problems in the study (such as non-replicable subgroup assignment procedures) make its use as evi-dence in the present argument unsuitable.

Four studies (Dainer et al., 1981; Swanson, 1980, 1981, 1983) examined vigilance performance in a group of learning-disabled children who were not hyperactive. The Conners Behavioral Rating Scale (Conners 1969) was one of several measures used in the above studies to screen out children who had problems in the area of hyperactivity. Given the careful selection procedures followed in these studies, one would expect few performance differences between the learning-disabled sample and its control group if, in fact, sustained attention is not a primary problem in learning disabilities. Contrary to this expectation, however, all papers contained reports of significant differences between learning-disabled and control groups with the learning-disabled samples making significantly more errors of omission. Decrement data were not reported.

In contrast to the reports reviewed thus far, there is one recent study that employed carefully selected groups of hyperactive and reading-disabled youngsters and found differences between them (Brown & Wynne, 1984). Although both clinical groups committed more omission errors than a nonhandicapped control group, hyperactive youngsters were found to miss more signals than their reading-disabled counterparts. Thus, this study stands alone in support of the Douglas and Peters (1979) argument.

Taking the available evidence together, there is little reason to believe that problems in sustained attention are confined only to youngsters with hyperactivity. In terms of performance on traditional vigilance measures from which sustained attention is usually inferred (omissions and decrement), both hyperactive and nonhyperactive learning-disabled youngsters appear to have serious problems.

Another measure obtained in vigilance procedures which may be more sensitive to the learning disabled/hyperactive distinction than omissions or decrement may be commission errors, typically interpreted as an index of impulsivity. Here, one would expect hyperactive youngsters to be more likely to make errors of commission than learning-disabled youngsters, since impulsivity is one of the characteristics more exclusively associated with hyperactivity. In general, more frequent errors of commission have been reported for both hyperactive (Brown & Wynne, 1984; Goldberg & Konstantareas, 1981; Hoy, Weiss, Minde, & Cohen, 1978; Kirchner, 1976; Klorman et al., 1979, Loiselle et al., 1980; Michael et al., 1981; Sykes et al., 1971; Sykes et al., 1973) and learning-disabled youngsters (Brown & Wynne, 1984; Dainer et al., 1981; Doyle et al., 1976; Keogh & Margolis, 1976; Swanson, 1980) when each group is compared with a control group.

When one examines only those studies that used replicable procedures for assigning youngsters to hyperactive or learning-disabled subgroups, one finds mixed results. Keogh and Margolis (1976) found no differences in commission errors between educationally handicapped children rated hyperactive and those not. Nor did Brown and Wynne (1984), who studied hyperactive and reading-disabled groups. Doyle et al. (1976), on the other hand, did find differences between groups of learning-disabled youngsters divided into hyperactive, normoactive, and hypoactive; hyperactives committed the greatest proportion of commission errors relative to the other subgroups. Swanson (1980, 1983) and Dainer et al. (1981), on the other hand, who only studied nonhyperactive learning-disabled children, found greater numbers of commission errors among their learning-disabled samples relative to non-learning, disabled control groups. In Swanson (1983), this effect occurred for 10- and 15-years-olds, but not for 8-year-olds.

Thus, one can conclude only that commission error data, like other vigilance measures, do not distinguish among hyperactive and nonhyperactive subgroups of learning-disabled youngsters. Of course, this conclusion is based on only six studies, so that it must be regarded as preliminary.

REACTION TIME

The reaction time task is another measure used to study sustained attention in children with learning problems. In this task, a warning signal is given, followed, usually, in a few seconds by a reaction signal. The participant's job is to press a button (or, in some cases, release a key) as quickly as possible when the reaction signal occurs. The time between reaction-signal onset and the participant's response is the primary measure of reaction-time performance, typically reported in milliseconds. "Preparatory interval" (PI) is the term generally used to designate the time between warning and reaction signals, as this is the time that the participant must prepare if he/she is to make a fast response. Even a brief lapse in attention during the PI could result in a slower reaction-time score. This demand for sustained attention during the PI is similar to the demands of vigilance. Unlike vigilance, however, reaction time consists of discrete trials which allows a relaxation of attentional demands between trials.

Despite this difference between reaction-time and vigilance procedures, results from the two types of studies are similar. Slower and/or more variable reaction-time performance has been reported for hyperactive (Cohen & Douglas, 1972; Firestone & Douglas, 1975), behaviorally deviant (Kupietz, Camp, & Weissman, 1976), and learning-disabled youngsters (Rugel & Rosenthal, 1974; Sroufe, Sonies, West, & Wright, 1973) as well as for youngsters with minimal brain dysfunction (Zahn, Abate, Little, & Wender, 1975; Zahn, Little, & Wender, 1978), relative to nonhandicapped control groups. As in vigilance, slower and/or more variable reaction times among atypical children have been interpreted as a reflection of these children's problems with sustained attention.

During reaction-time tasks, measures of physiological activity often are recorded simultaneously. One such measure that has been linked to attention processes is the degree of heart-rate deceleration which occurs at the reaction signal. The magnitude of this deceleration is correlated with performance such that greater magnitude decelerations are associated with faster reaction-time scores. As such, degree of deceleration is often interpreted as an index of preparedness or attention (Krupski, 1975).

Two studies report on such heart-rate deceleration responses of learning-handicapped youngsters. In one study, learning-disabled youngsters were studied (Sroufe *et al.*, 1973), whereas in the other, children with minimal brain dysfunction were studied (Zahn *et al.*, 1978). Results of both studies indicated that handicapped groups exhibited significantly smaller heart-rate decelerations than nonhandicapped control groups. Thus, the heart-rate deceleration results are consistent with performance data in providing evidence for problems in sustained attention among learning-handicapped youngsters.

Another measure of physiological activity that has been examined in reaction-time studies has been skin conductance, or its reciprocal, skin resistance (GSR). Such electrodermal responses often are reported to occur as part of the orienting reflex; as such, the occurrence of these responses has been linked to heightened states of arousal and, by inference, to attention (Firestone & Douglas, 1975; Krupski, Raskin, & Bakan, 1971). Four studies have as their focus the investigation of such responses (Cohen & Douglas, 1972; Firestone & Douglas, 1975; Rugel & Rosenthal, 1974; Zahn *et al.*, 1975). Although results of these studies are not as clear-cut as those employing heart-rate deceleration as the dependent variable, they appear consistent.

Zahn *et al.* (1975), for example, reported that youngsters with minimal brain dysfunction exhibited significantly lower-amplitude, skin-conductance responses during a reaction-time task relative to a nonhandicapped control group. Firestone and Douglas (1975), on the other hand, did not find differences between hyperactive and nonhyperactive control groups in skin conductance magnitude, but did find differences in frequency. Nonhyperactive control youngsters were found to produce more frequent skin conductance responses at the warning or reaction signals relative to hyperactive youngsters.

In a third study, Rugel and Rosenthal (1974) reported that groups of learning-disabled and nondisabled youngsters did not differ in GSR magnitude during reaction time. However, they did find a decrease in response magnitude over trials that was significantly greater for the learning-disabled youngsters.

Cohen and Douglas (1972) found hyperactive and nonhyperactive youngsters exhibited similar amplitude skin conductance responses to a series of tones to which they were simply required to listen. However, when task demands increased such that youngsters were required to make an active response in a reaction-time task, nonhyperactive control youngsters exhibited an increase in skin conductance amplitude, whereas hyperactives did not. Thus, groups responded similarly under passive task demands, differing only when the task acquired active demands. The authors interpret these findings as suggesting that the warning at the onset of each reaction-time trial did not have the intended effect of alerting the hyperactive child and preparing him or her to respond to the reaction signal.

Although these studies, taken together, suggest similar electrodermal responses in hyperactive and learning-disabled youngsters, it could be aruged that potential diagnostic group differences may have been obscured by the inclusion of, for example, a number of hyperactive youngsters in a learning-disabled sample. In an attempt to systematically investigate this point, Delamater, Lahey, and Drake (1981) studied carefully defined subgroups of hyperactive and nonhyperactive learning disabled youngsters. All children participated in a reaction-time task where skin conductance responses were recorded simultaneously. Although reaction-time performance data were not reported, skin conductance data indicated that subgroups did not differ. The authors (Delamater, *et al.*, 1981) interpret this finding as suggesting that previously identified physiological differences between learning-disabled and nondisabled samples is not an artifact of accidentally including a number of hyperactive children in the learning-disabled sample.

Thus, it appears reasonable to conclude that learning-disabled as well as hyperactive youngsters can be characterized as performing more poorly in reaction time relative to their nonhandicapped peers as well as exhibiting skin conductance responses thought to be incompatible with high states of attention and arousal. At this point, evidence from reaction-time performance and concurrent physiological responses do not support a distinction between these diagnostic categories.

SELECTIVE ATTENTION

It is generally acknowledged that, under normal circumstances, we do not "take in" or even notice most of the stimuli that impinge upon us at any given point in time. The sheer amount of available information would inundate us. Thus, we select only a sample of what we can hear, see, taste, or feel. This selection process usually is referred to as *selective attention*. Understanding the principles that guide such selection has been the focus of most research in this area.

Two of the most popular experimental paradigms which have been used to study selective attention in learning-disabled and hyperactive children are incidental learning and distractibility. Although the incidental-learning paradigm (Hagen, 1967) originally was introduced as a measure of selective attention, recent discussions of the task suggest that it more closely measures memory than attention processes (Copeland & Wisniewski, 1981; Douglas & Peters, 1979). Presently, it appears that incidental learning has little to contribute to an understanding of selective attention processes in children with learning problems (Fleisher, Soodak, & Jelin, 1984). Thus, this review will concentrate on problems of distractibility in learning-disabled and hyperactive youngsters.

From early statements of Strauss and Lehtinen (1947) to current clinical descriptions (e.g., Hallahan & Reeve, 1980), distractibility is often mentioned as a characteristic of children with a variety of learning handicaps. The implications of this description is that such youngsters are unusually sensitive to the multitude of stimuli in any given situation and, as a consequence, tend to respond to task-irrelevant stimuli to a greater extent than do their nonhandicapped peers. Poor performance on a variety of tasks often is attributed to the presumed disruptive influence of this alleged, indiscriminate response pattern.

Given the widespread acceptance of this characterization, it is surprising that the corresponding experimental evidence on this point is equivocal: In some studies, the performance of learning-handicapped youngsters is found to be significantly more impaired than their nonhandicapped counterparts when task-irrelevant stimuli are introduced, whereas in other studies, it is not.

These inconsistencies have been attributed, at least in part, to the diverse ways in which distraction has been studied. A diverse assortment of experimental designs characterize the distractibility literature. In addition, investigators have used varying definitions of distractibility and, as a result, have used the term "distractibility" as an explanation for a variety of behaviors. Finally, "distractor" is a term that has been applied to a variety of stimuli. This diversity in design, definitions, and measures makes generalization of findings across studies difficult and may account for the contradictory research findings.

The purpose of the section that follows will be to review this diverse set of studies. Although this literature has been summarized by others (e.g., Douglas & Peters, 1979; Hallahan & Reeve, 1980), the approach taken here differs from previous attempts. The tack will be to identify and examine the circumstances under which learning-handicapped youngsters are reported to be more distractible. These will be contrasted with circumstances under which such youngsters are reported to be unaffected by distraction. This approach allows the preliminary extraction of common features that characterize both situations which then can be used to formulate hypotheses regarding specific deficits and strengths in underlying processes.

To do this, it appeared necessary to establish a set of criteria to guide the selection of studies to be included in the review. These criteria were based on the assumption that distractibility is defined by differential deterioration in task performance of experimental and control groups in a distraction as opposed to a no-distraction condition. This definition is consistent with that employed in the literature (Douglas & Peters, 1979).

Following from this definition, studies were included in the subsequent review only if they met the following criteria: (1) inclusion of a control group; (2) inclusion of both distraction and no-distraction conditions, with order of presentation systematically controlled; and (3) inclusion of an independent measure of task performance other than off-task glances or activity level. These latter measures are problematic because they do not always correlate with actual task performance (Douglas & Peters, 1979; Rosenthal & Allen, 1978).

As a preliminary organizational device, all studies which met these criteria were classified into three categories based on the nature of the distractor. Several authors have pointed out that the distance between distractor and task may determine, at least in part, the potency of the distractor's disruptive influence (Hallahan & Reeve, 1980; Zentall, Zentall, & Barack, 1978a). For this reason, studies that employed distal, proximal, and embedded distrators are discussed in separate subsections.

DISTAL DISTRACTORS

One variety of distractor that has been found consistently to have no differential adverse effect on the performance of learning-handicapped youngsters are those that are some distance from the task at hand and are easily distinguishable from the task. These are often called distal distractors. Examples of such distractors are the playing of white noise (Sykes *et al.*, 1971), recordings of background classroom noise (Carter & Diaz, 1971; Nober & Nober, 1975), the introduction of intermittent chimes (Kirchner, 1976), as well as the intermittent flashing of lights on the ceiling and walls (Browning, 1967). Such distractors are presented while a youngster is engaged in a task such as vigilance (Kirchner, 1976; Sykes *et al.*, 1971), auditory discrimination (Nober & Nober, 1975), visual discrimination learning (Browning, 1967), or reading comprehension (Carter & Diaz, 1971).

Results of experiments employing distal distractors are consistent: Neither learning-disabled children (Nober & Nober, 1975), hyperactive children (Kirchner, 1976; Sykes *et al.*, 1971), nor children with minimal brain dysfunction (Browning, 1967; Carter & Diaz, 1971) are reported to be adversely affected by this type of distractor, relative to a group of nonhandicapped control children. Thus, although learning-handicapped youngsters are characterized as distractible, results of studies reviewed here demonstrate that such children are not more distractible under all conditions. They appear to ignore and/or inhibit responses to irrelevant stimuli that are distant and easily distinguishable from the task as well as their nonhandicapped peers.

PROXIMAL DISTRACTORS

A second class of distractor that has been used in various experiments are those that, like distal distractors, are easily distinguishable from the task at hand, but, unlike distal distractors, are in close proximity to the task. There is evidence that, at least under some conditions, proximal distractors do differentially influence the performance of learning-handicapped groups (Radosh & Gittelman, 1981; Samuels, 1967).

Radosh and Gittelman (1981), for example, had groups of hyperactive and normal boys perform 300 arithmetic problems on a teaching machine. A single problem appeared on the screen for a maximum of 3 seconds. In response, the child was required to press one of four buttons, only one of which displayed the correct answer. During one-third of the problems (i.e., 100 problems), the border around the problem was blank; this was called the "no appeal" condition. During another third of the problems, the border was filled with cutouts of colorful magazine pictures of toys, comical animals, and so forth; this was called the "high appeal" condition. The final third of the task included a border that contained colorful pictures free of meaningful content, such as fragments of abstract paintings; this was the "low appeal" condition. Number of errors was examined in relation to the three types of distraction conditions.

Results indicated that although groups of hyperactive and nonhyperactive boys did not differ significantly in total number of errors made during the task, they did differ in when they made the errors. Nonhyperactive youngsters performed consistently in the no-appeal and low-appeal conditions, making fewest errors in these conditions. They made significantly more errors in the high-appeal conditions. Thus, the control group appeared most affected by the high-appeal distractor but not the low- or no-appeal.

Hyperactive youngsters, on the other hand, showed a progressive deterioration of performance as a function of distractor appeal: They made fewest errors under the no-appeal condition, significantly more errors under the low-appeal condition, and the greatest number of errors when confronted with high-appeal distractors. Thus, although both groups' performance deteriorated when confronted with high-appeal distractors, only the hyperactives demonstrated marked deterioration under a moderate distractor condition as well.

In another study, Samuels (1967) had good and poor readers read a story which contained 50 different words. Half of the children in each group read the story from a book that contained pictures illustrating the text, whereas the other half read the same story from a book without pictures. After receiving group reading instruction, all children were given a post-test in which they were asked to name each of the 50 words that had appeared in the story. The post-test contained no pictures.

Results indicated that good readers recognized over 40 of the 50 words regardless of whether they read the story in the illustrated or non-illustrated books. Thus, for good readers, inclusion of pictures had very little influence on word recognition. Poor readers, on the other hand, learned to read significantly more words in the non-picture condition, relative to the condition which contained pictures. Samuels (1967) interprets these findings as indicating that pictures served as a distracting stimulus for the poor, or less capable reader, but not for the more capable readers.

Thus, in both studies where proximal distractors were used, there is evidence that learning-handicapped youngsters' performance suffered to a greater extent than did that of their nonhandicapped peers under distraction. This was found to be the case for both hyperactive youngsters (Radosh & Gittelman, 1981) as well as for poor readers (Samuels, 1967).

Even though the task-irrelevant stimuli in the proximal distractor studies could be considered easily distinguishable from the task (i.e., border surrounding arithmetic problems and illustrations of reading text), it is possible that they interfered with performance by virtue of their sheer proximity. A similar pattern of results is evident in some studies that employ distractors of even more pronounced proximity, that is, embedded distractors.

EMBEDDED DISTRACTORS

A total of 14 studies were found that employed distractors embedded in the task. Three of these studies used some form of color as the distractor, whereas 11 used other types of competing stimuli. As results of these two types of studies are different, they will be reviewed in separate sections.

Embedded Color Distractors

Results of the three studies that employed some form of color as the task-irrelevant stimuli generally suggest that this type of distractor does not disrupt the performance of hyperactive youngsters any more than it does nonhyperactive youngsters. For example, Sykes *et al.* (1973) examined choice reaction-time scores under conditions of distraction and nondistraction among hyperactive and control youngsters. Essentially, children were required to press a button corresponding to a particular stimulus appearing on a screen. In the nondistracting condition, both the figures on the screen and the figures on the buttons were white with black background. On the other hand, in the distracting condition, each of the figures on the screen had a colored background which was discrepant with the colored background of the corresponding figure on the button. Results indicated that all children took longer to respond under the distractor condition, with hyperactive youngsters not differentially affected.

Zentall and colleagues (Zentall, Zentall, & Barack, 1978; Zentall, Zentall, & Booth, 1978) performed one study that used color distractors on a set of perceptual tasks and a second study using a task that involved the learning of new spelling words. Results of these studies also showed minimal effects of color as a distractor for hyperactive children. Thus, it is reasonably safe to conclude that color alone is not a potent distractor for such children.

Studies Employing Other Types of Embedded Distractors

There are 11 studies meeting criteria imposed in this review that employed other types of embedded distractors. It will be noted that these studies also employed tasks that appear to have greater cognitive demands than those reviewed in the preceding section. In this sense, they may be judged as more difficult and, in some cases, the addition of a distractor may have served to increase the task difficulty even further. For the most part, results of these studies demonstrate differential effects of task-irrelevant stimuli on the performance of learning-handicapped youngsters.

Take, for example, the study conducted by Copeland and Wisniewski (1981), who administered a speeded classification test to a group of

learning-disabled youngsters and to a group of nonhandicapped youngsters. The task required children to sort decks of 24 cards on the basis of
a single attribute. That is, each deck was sorted into two piles, those
cards with the critical attribute (for example, containing a picture of a
square) and those without. A sample of the critical attribute was always
available to the child, thereby minimizing memory requirements of this
task.

Each deck was marked with one to three of the following stimuli: form
(circle or square), line (horizontal or vertical), and/or star (placed above
or below a central point). Thus, each deck could have zero, one, or two
irrelevant features or dimensions. When more than one stimulus was
included on a card, children were instructed to ignore all but the critical
one. Each child sorted 12 different decks in this experiment.

Although both sorting errors and time taken to sort each deck were
analyzed, the number of features factor and its interactions were examined only in relation to sort time. Overall, learning-disabled youngsters
made more errors and took longer to sort their decks, relative to control
youngsters. Further, learning-disabled youngsters as a group seemed
particularly affected by irrelevant features: They were found to sort
decks with two irrelevant features more slowly than the non-learning-
disabled children under all conditions. Younger learning-disabled children (mean age = 9 years) appeared particularly impaired in all aspects
of this task relative to both older learning-disabled (mean age = 11.35
years) and nonhandicapped youngsters. Copeland and Wisniewski
(1981) interpret the learning-disabled youngsters' impaired performance
on this task as being due to a deficiency in their use of selective attention.

It should be noted that the learning-disabled youngsters studied by
Copeland and Wisniewski (1981) had significantly higher hyperactivity
ratings on the Conners (1969) Teacher Questionnaire than the control
group. Thus, in this study, hyperactivity was confounded with learning
disabilities. Correlations between Conners (1969) scores and measures
of speeded classification indicated that more hyperactivelike children
took a longer time to sort, made more errors, and had to re-sort decks
more often to reach criterion, relative to less hyperactivelike children.

Studies of normal young children report findings similar to those
reported by Copeland and Wisniewski (1981) for learning-disabled/hy-
peractive youngsters. That is, the presence of irrelevant stimuli has been
found to interfere with the card-sorting performance of young normal
children to a greater extent than that of older children and adults (Strutt,
Anderson, & Well, 1975). Given the apparent parallels between perfor-

mance of these groups, it may be useful to consider explanations offered for the developmental findings as being of potential applicability in the case of learning-handicapped youngsters as well.

One explanation is based on the premise that young children perceive some stimuli in a different manner from older children and adults. Specifically, it is argued that adults and older children perceive stimuli such as those used in the speeded classification task in terms of separate dimensions. Young children (i.e., under 8 years of age), on the other hand, are thought to apprehend these dimensions as integral (Shepp & Swartz, 1976; Smith, 1981). There is evidence that young children are capable of perceiving separable dimensions but fail to use this information when performing on speeded classification tasks that employ simple stimuli which differ only by limited amounts on a few dimensions. Under these circumstances, dimensional information is thought to be much less salient to young children than to adults or older youngsters (Smith, 1981; Smith & Kemler, 1977).

As stated previously, this line of reasoning has not been applied directly to the study of youngsters with learning handicaps although it appears to have potential in this respect. As an illustration of this point, note the speeded classification results reported by Copeland and Wisniewski (1981). It is possible that the learning-disabled/hyperactive youngsters employed in this study may have responded to compound stimuli as integral whereas their nondisabled peers may have been responding to the same stimuli as separable. If this were the case, then such perceptual tendencies would be expected to influence performance on other types of tasks that contained similar demands. Although appealing, the utility of this notion only can be assessed with future research.

Another line of reasoning regarding selective attention in young, normal children that has a more direct link to the study of learning-handicapped youngsters is related to stimulus salience. Odom and his colleagues (Odom, 1972; Odom, Cunningham, & Astor-Stetson, 1977; Odom & Guzman, 1972; Odom & Lemond, 1975) have demonstrated that various dimensions present in a stimulus array can be rank-ordered in terms of their salience for a child. Odom (1972) suggests that the higher the salience value of a dimension, "the higher the probability of its being cognitively evaluated or stored, regardless of its appropriateness for problem solution" (p. 286). Along these lines, Odom (1972) presents evidence suggesting that normal children's problem-solving behavior is facilitated when the relevant dimension is highly salient.

In addition to Odom and his colleagues, (Odom, 1972; Odom *et al.*,

1977; Odom & Guzman, 1972; Odom & Lemond, 1975), salience has also been discussed by Wright and Vliestra (1975) in a somewhat different context. These latter authors argue that systematic search skills evolve progressively as a result of experience and maturation, with exploration being a necessary precursor to systematic search. Exploration, these authors argue, is spontaneous, is motivated by curiosity, and is guided by stimulus salience. Search behavior, on the other hand, is described as goal-directed, systematic, planned, and is based on relevance or informativeness of cues rather than salience.

Wright and Vliestra (1975) argue that salience is most likely to interfere with logical information processing if the child is in an exploratory mode. As the child moves more toward a search mode, the effects of salience are thought to weaken, but may still exert an influence under particular circumstances. It is only with full development of the systematic search mode that salience ceases to be a significant influence in tasks involving selective attention.

Thus, Wright and Vliestra's (1975) work suggests that salience may exert greatest influence on the performance of youngsters who have not developed full-fledged search skills. This category clearly includes the developmentally young. It might also include youngsters who, because of cognitive limitations, have not developed search skills commensurate with their chronological age. How this latter point may relate to learning-handicapped populations is suggested in a study conducted by Rosenthal and Allen (1980).

Rosenthal and Allen (1980) borrowed the principles stemming from Odom and Guzman's (1972) stimulus salience work to design a speeded classification experiment with hyperkinetic youngsters. They reasoned that hyperkinetic youngsters' performance may be particularly impaired in cases where the salience of the relevant dimension is low and also when the salience of the irrelevant dimension(s) is high.

To examine these predictions, Rosenthal and Allen (1980) tested groups of hyperkinetic and nonhyperkinetic youngsters on a version of the speeded classification task. Three dimensions were used: form (circle, square, triangle, or pentagon), color (red, yellow, green, or blue), and position (star located on top, bottom, right, or left of array). Prior to administering the speeded classification task, these investigators assessed salience of the three dimensions for each child.

Results indicated that hyperkinetic and nonhyperkinetic groups performed similarly when no irrelevant dimensions were present. This similarity disappeared, however, when irrelevant dimensions were present: Under these conditions, hyperkinetic youngsters made significantly more errors than their nonhyperkinetic counterparts. This result is consistent with that reported for learning-disabled youngsters by Copeland and Wisniewski (1981).

In addition, Rosenthal and Allen (1980) examined the effect of dimensional salience on performance. The main finding here was that groups did not differ when the irrelevant dimension was low in salience. They did differ, however, when the irrelevant dimension was of high salience. In this case, hyperkinetic youngsters made more errors than their nonhyperkinetic counterparts. Thus, it appears as though the deleterious effects of embedded distractors was most pronounced for hyperkinetic youngsters when these distractors were high in salience. The performance of nonhyperkinetic youngsters, in contrast, appear to have minimally affected by these embedded distractors even when they were of high salience. It was also predicted that hyperkinetic youngsters would perform more poorly relative to the control group when the salience of the relevant dimension was low; however, this prediction was not supported by the data.

Although not suggested by Rosenthal and Allen (1980), one might speculate on the basis of Wright and Vliestra's (1975) work that the reason high-salience distractors had differential effects may be related to differential development of search skills in the two groups. For example, more highly developed systematic-search skills in the control group may have served to prevent interference when high-salience distractors were present, whereas less highly developed search skills in the hyperkinetic sample could have predisposed these youngsters to greater interference effects. Clearly, such speculation requires systematic evaluation before its utility can be assessed, but it does suggest another way in which conceptualizations stemming from the normal developmental literature can be employed to potentially expand our knowledge of learning-handicapped youngsters.

In summary, results of two experiments employing a speeded classification task demonstrated that performance of neither learning-disabled/hyperactive nor hyperactive youngsters differed from their nonhandicapped counterparts when no irrelevant stimuli were present. These groups did differ, however, when the task included irrelevant stimuli, with the handicapped groups exibiting significantly greater performance decrements than their nonhandicapped peers.

Two other experiments, one employing poor readers and the other learning-disabled youngsters, resulted in findings inconsistent with these. Pelham (1979), for example, studied speeded classification performance among poor readers under two conditions: a no-distraction condition which contained no irrelevant stimuli and a distraction condition which contained two irrelevant stimuli. Results indicated that poor readers performed more poorly than a nonhandicapped control group under both conditions. Unlike results of the first two studies reviewed, poor readers in the Pelham (1979) study were not found to be differentially impaired under the distraction condition.

Unfortunately, Pelham's (1979) dependent variable differed from that used in the other experiments. He employed a single measure that combined error and latency data, whereas separate analyses of error and latency data were reported in the other experiments. Since it is not known how these two types of dependent variables may influence results, it is not possible to assess the importance of this methodological difference. Clearly, it would be useful if investigators conducting speeded classification studies would, in the future, report both types of measures so as to facilitate comparisons of results.

The other experiment which reported few differences between learning-disabled and nondisabled samples was conducted by Copeland and Reiner (1984). Although learning-disabled youngsters took longer to sort decks than their nonhandicapped controls, groups did not differ is number of errors, nor was there a significant interaction between diagnosis and number of critical features for either sort times or errors. This indicates that learning-disabled youngsters were not impaired differentially by the embedded distractor in this task.

Thus, the two studies that employed learning-disabled samples—presumably free of hyperactivity (Copeland & Reiner, 1984; Pelham, 1979)—found no evidence for differential distractor effects, whereas the two studies that examined hyperactive samples (Copeland & Wisniewski, 1981; Rosenthal & Allen, 1980) did. This pattern of findings suggests that speeded classification tasks may be differentially sensitive to the hyperactivity/learning-disability distinction. Unfortunately, no studies exist in which relatively "pure" hyperactive and learning-disabled samples are systematically and directly compared. Until such a comparison is made, it can be concluded that evidence for impaired speeded classification performance under conditions of distraction appears suggestive for hyperactive youngsters and not as likely for youngsters suffering from learning disabilities.

Seven other studies, all using procedures that differed from that used in speeded classification, also employed some form of embedded distractor. Although employing different tasks, all revealed significant distraction effects for learning-handicapped samples. Take, for example, an experiment conducted by Atkinson and Seunath (1973), who studied learning-disordered boys. In this study, youngsters watched successive arrays of 12 squares (5 colored and 7 white), which appeared on a screen for 5 seconds each. Their task was to press a button whenever a small, dark spot appeared on the red square. Two conditions were employed. In one condition, all the colored squares remained in the same position on every trial. In the second condition, the position of the colored squares was changed from trial to trial, randomly appearing in 1 of the 12 possible positions.

Results indicated that the performance of learning-disordered boys did not differ significantly from control boys when the squares remained in the same position. When, however, the position of squares was changed from trial to trial, learning-disordered youngsters made significantly more errors of omission than control youngsters. Thus, the performance of learning-disordered youngsters was impaired to a greater extent than that of control youngsters under the position-change condition.

Although this task differs in many respects from speeded classification, it appears possible to draw some parallels. For example, in the no-change condition, it could be argued that the combination of color and position served as the relevant dimension. In the position-change condition, it could be argued that color was relevant with position irrelevant and varied. Thus the addition of this embedded but irrelevant dimension affected the learning-disabled youngsters to a greater extent than it did the nonhandicapped control group. Although it is impossible to identify the reason for this effect with any degree of certainty, one could speculate that position may have been a salient dimension for these youngsters and, as a consequence, served as a source of interference when it was irrelevant to the task. Alternatively, perhaps learning-disabled youngsters perceived the dimensions of position and color as integral. If this were the case, the changing position of the relevant dimension from trial to trial would naturally be a potential source of interference.

Although Atkinson and Seunath (1973) did not make reference to either the integrality or salience work in their paper, their interpretation is consistent with those ideas. They state, "A possible explanation for this finding is that the change was associated more with the irrelevant stimuli than with the relevant stimulus. That is, because there were more irrelevant stimuli and therefore more changes within these stimuli, the children with learning problems were more likely to attend to irrelevant stimulation" (p. 573).

Other studies in which the influence of embedded distractors have been investigated have used tasks measuring span of apprehension (Blackwell, McIntyre, & Murray, 1983; Denton & McIntyre, 1978; McIntyre, Murray, Cronin, & Blackwell, 1978), ability to respond to auditory and written directions (Lasky & Tobin, 1973), number of math problems completed (Zentall & Shaw, 1980), and dichotic listening skills (Hebben, Whitman, Milberg, Andresko, & Galpin, 1981). In general, these studies can be summarized as demonstrating that a variety of visual and auditory embedded distractors had a greater effect on the performance of hyperactive and learning-disabled youngsters than on normal control groups. Further, in two of the studies employing auditory distractors, learning-handicapped children were found to be particularly impaired when the distractor was linguistic in nature (Lasky & Tobin, 1973; Zentall & Shaw, 1980). Thus, of the 11 studies that used embedded distractors, only two involving speeded classification tasks failed to report that learning-handicapped groups were adversely affected by distractors relative to nonhandicapped control groups. These findings represent a striking contrast to results of studies that employed embedded color distractors where no differential group effects were found.

It is relevant to note that of the nine studies reporting group differences, five employed learning-disabled samples (Atkinson & Seunath, 1973; Blackwell et al., 1983; Hebben et al., 1981; Lasky & Tobin 1973; McIntyre et al., 1981) whereas three employed hyperactive samples (Denton & McIntyre, 1978; Rosenthal & Allen, 1980; Zentall & Shaw, 1980). As noted previously, Copeland and Wisniewski's (1981) learning-disabled sample also was found to have higher hyperactivity ratings than the control group, suggesting that children in this study represented a combination of the two. With the exception of the speeded classification task results, the evidence suggests that both hyperactive and learning-disabled samples were differentially vulnerable to distractions presented in these studies.

CONCLUSIONS

The studies reviewed in this section lead to several conclusions regarding the nature of distractibility among learning-handicapped youngsters. First, they are no more distracted than their nonhandicapped peers when distal distractors are used. Nor do they appear seriously affected by embedded distractors that involve some form of color as the task-irrelevant stimuli. With two exceptions (Copeland & Reiner, 1984; Pelham, 1979), however, they do appear differentially impaired when task-irrelevant stimuli involve a dimension other than color that is embedded within the task.

This pattern of results clearly demonstrates that youngsters with mild learning handicaps are not distractible under all conditions, but that episodes of distractibility, when they occur, are task- or situation-specific. Such findings contrast sharply with the traitlike characterization of distractibility as it is often used in describing and, sometimes defining, learning-disabled, hyperactive, minimally brain damaged, and reading-disabled youngsters. Cruickshank (1975), for example, identifies distractibility and the inability to focus attention selectively as fundamental characteristics of the learning-disabled child. These characteristics, Cruickshank (1975) argues, stem from the learning-disabled child's inability to refrain from reaction to extraneous external or internal stimuli (p. 258–263). Clearly, empirical data demonstrate that this is not the case for the majority of youngsters classified as learning handicapped.

The relevant question that still remains, however, is why learning-handicapped youngsters' performance is impaired under some conditions and not others. To attribute those instances of impaired performance to greater distractibility on the part of learning-handicapped youngsters is not terribly informative, nor does it provide a basis for understanding why performance should suffer in certain tasks or situations and not others. In this sense, the construct of distractibility is not a very useful one.

One point that has been repeatedly stressed throughout this section is that the distractibility literature is extremely diverse. This may be due to the fact that much of the distractibility research has followed an atheoretical course. Few theoretically based principles have guided the selection of stimuli to serve as distractors. Likewise, few such principles have been used to predict the types of behavior that might be used as indices of distractibility. In fact, explicit statements of rationale for the choice of distractors or particular behaviors later interpreted as distractible are almost always absent. Instead, investigators have provided ad hoc operational definitions of distractors and distractible behaviors but have failed to provide a clear conceptualization of distractibility itself. This situation has been noted by others (e.g., Rosenthal & Allen, 1978).

Perhaps, this deficit in theory simply reflects the fact that distractibility is not a useful construct. It may be more parsimonious to conceptualize disruptions in processing particular types of information as a cognitive failure rather than as a failure of attention. In this sense, the continued study of distractibility as a form of attention may be, as Neisser (1976) implied, superfluous and, therefore, best discarded. Thus, it is relevant to examine alternative explanatory frameworks that promise greater utility in expanding our understanding of the particular behaviors that are frequently interpreted as failures in some aspect of selective attention.

One such alternative can be derived from an examination of cognitive demands inherent in tasks used in the distractibility studies reviewed here. For example, one could argue that proximal and non-color embedded distraction tasks were probably more cognitively demanding than were distal or embedded color distraction tasks. In other words, the former tasks probably required a more sophisticated set of perceptual skills and/or cognitive strategies than did the latter.

Authors (e.g., Gibson & Rader, 1979; Neisser, 1976) have argued that previous knowledge or schema serve to direct perceptions and attention. Learning-handicapped children, by definition, have been identified as possessing limitations in some areas of cognitive function. If one adopts a cognitive perspective, it could be argued that such limitations may lead to relatively impoverished schema and/or an immature knowledge base which may, in turn, result in a more limited repertoire of strategies and perceptual skills (Chi, 1981). As such, it should not be surprising that performance of youngsters with known cognitive limitations would be most vulnerable to disruption on tasks that make greatest cognitive demands.

The pattern of results uncovered in this review could be interpreted to correspond with this expectation. That is, for the most part, learning-handicapped youngsters exhibited poorest performance on the most cognitively demanding tasks (i.e., proximal and non-color embedded distraction). On the other hand, their performance was indistinguishable from their nonhandicapped counterparts on the less cognitively demanding distal and embedded color distraction tasks. The cognitively demanding nature of the former tasks may have exceeded the limited strategic and/or perceptual skills of the learning handicapped youngsters who were studied, whereas the latter (less cognitively demanding) tasks may have been well within their repertoire.

Clearly, future research efforts are needed to systematically assess the limits of this interpretation. The point, however, is that such a view shifts the emphasis from attention per se to processes in the broader cognitive domain.

A number of other conceptualizations were referred to throughout this section which could also serve as alternatives to the notion of distractibility. These are meant to serve as illustrations, and should not be taken as an exhaustive list. Included were references to efforts in the areas of salience (e.g., Odom, 1972; Odom et al., 1977; Odom & Guzman, 1972; Odom & Lemond, 1975), integrality (e.g., Shepp & Swartz, 1976; Smith, 1981; Smith & Kemler, 1977; Strutt et al., 1975), and development of systematic search skills (e.g., Wright and Vliestra, 1975), areas which have their basis in the normal developmental literature.

These conceptualizations are appealing because they provide rich, theoretically based directions for future research. Despite this appeal, however, it is relevant to note that each has been used to guide and interpret research on particular tasks. The suitability of these approaches in interpreting performance on a broader range of tasks may be limited. Also, all require greater examination before their ultimate utility in providing information about cognitive processes in learning handicaps can be assessed. Their rich contribution to the normal developmental literature, however, suggests that their potential in this respect is promising.

SUMMARY AND CONCLUDING COMMENTS

Arguments presented throughout this chapter suggest that few distinctions exist between groups of learning-disabled and hyperactive youngsters on measures thought to reflect attention processes. Rather, with few exceptions, both groups perform more poorly than control groups on vigilance, reaction time, and tasks that employ particular types of embedded distractors. Neither group appears impaired in studies where distal distractors are employed. Thus, both groups appear to exhibit similar performance patterns on measures traditionally thought to reflect attention processes.

Of course, it is possible that both groups are performing similarly but for different reasons. Few data are currently available, however, that could be used to directly assess this possibility. It would appear that future research where carefully defined subgroups are directly compared, perhaps in longitudinal designs, would offer more suitable evidence on this issue. But, until such data are available, it is necessary to conclude that few differences in attention processes exist between hyperactive and learning-disabled groups. As such, the remaining conclusions can be considered as applicable to both these groups as well as to other youngsters identified as having mild learning handicaps.

The second point made in this review has to do with the nature of learning-handicapped youngsters' problems in sustained and selective attention. These areas were selected for review because they frequently are cited as aspects of attention on which learning-handicapped youngsters are often observed to demonstrate impaired performance. With respect to sustained aspects of attention, the evidence is consistent: Children with a variety of learning handicaps are consistently observed to perform more poorly than nonhandicapped peers on both vigilance and reaction-time tasks. They are also reported to exhibit physiological responses while working on reaction-time tasks that reflect lowered levels of attention. Because vigilance and reaction-time tasks are thought to require high levels of sustained attention for good performance, consistently poor performance of learning-handicapped youngsters is most often interpreted as reflecting impaired ability to sustain attention. Thus, it appears reasonable to conclude that many learning-handicapped youngsters have problems in sustaining attention to task, a conclusion reached in other papers (Douglas & Peters, 1979; Krupski, 1980).

In the case of selective attention, however, no such conclusion can be drawn. Although there is widespread belief that learning-handicapped youngsters suffer from impairment in selective attention, a critical review of research in this area suggests this belief is, at best, an oversimplification. The present review provides only equivocal support for the common conception of learning-handicapped youngsters as being distractible. Rather, evidence demonstrated that more pronounced distractibility in learning-handicapped youngsters was task-specific, leading to the conclusion that distractibility was not a very useful explanatory construct and would best be discarded. In its place, it was suggested that task-specific impairments uncovered in distractibility studies could be more parsimoniously considered in the broader context of cognitive processing demands rather than within the poorly defined context of distractibility.

If one discards the notion of distractibility, then a major area of research thought to represent current knowledge of selective attention in learning-handicapped youngsters lacks foundation. The other body of research most often associated with the study of selective attention—incidental learning—has also been described as contributing little to an understanding of selective attention processes (Fleisher, et al., 1984). Thus, if neither incidental learning nor distractibility are appropriate literatures from which to draw conclusions about selective attention, what, one might ask, is? One answer to this question is that, given the difficulties in operationalizing the concept of selective attention, it may best be discarded as well. To continue to consider particular processing impairments as attention problems may serve only to compound the already considerable confusion surrounding the area of attention in learning-handicapped populations.

ACKNOWLEDGMENTS

The author would like to thank Anita Johnson, Barbara Keogh, and Joseph Torgesen for their helpful comments on an earlier draft of this chapter, and Georgia Malcolm for her careful editorial assistance.

REFERENCES

Aman, M. G. (1979). Cognitive, social, and other correlates of specific reading retardation. *Journal of Abnormal Child Psychology, 7,* 153–168.

Anderson, R. P., Halcomb, C. G., & Doyle, R. B. (1973). The measurement of attentional deficits. *Exceptional Children, 39,* 534–539.

Atkinson, B. R., & Seunath, O. H. M. (1973). The effect of stimulus change on attending behavior in normal children and children with learning disorders. *Journal of Learning Disabilities, 6*(9), 569–573.

Blackwell, S. L., McIntyre, C. W., & Murray, M. E. (1983). Information processed from brief visual displays by learning-disabled boys. *Child Development, 54,* 927–940.

Brackup, E. S., & Knopf, I. J. (1978). The effects of extraneous speech on visual vigilance performance of children. *Child Development, 49,* 505–508.

Brown, R. T., & Wynne, M. E. (1984). Attentional characteristics and teacher ratings in hyperactive, reading disabled, and normal boys. *Journal of Clinical Child Psychology, 13,* 38–43.

Browning, R. M., (1967). Effect of irrelevant peripheral visual stimuli on discrimination learning in minimally brain-damaged children. *Journal of Consulting Psychology, 31,* 371–376.

Carter, J. L., & Diaz, A. (1971). Effects of visual and auditory background on reading test performance. *Exceptional Children, 38,* 43–50.

Chi, M. T. H. (1981). Knowledge development and memory performance. In M. P. Friedman, J. P. Das, & N. O'Connor (Eds.). *Intelligence and Learning.* New York: Plenum Press.

Cohen, N. J., & Douglas, V. I. (1972). Characteristics of the orienting response in hyperactive and normal children. *Psychophysiology, 9,* 238–245.

Conners, C. K. (1969). A teacher rating scale for use in drug studies with children. *American Journal of Psychiatry, 126,* 884–888.

Copeland, A. P., & Reiner, E. M. (1984). The selective attention of learning disabled children: Three studies. *Journal of Abnormal Child Psychology, 12,* 455–470.

Copeland, A. P., & Wisniewski, N. M. (1981). Learning disability and hyperactivity: Deficits in selective attention. *Journal of Experimental Child Psychology, 32,* 88–101.

Cruickshank, W. M. (1975). The education of children with specific learning disabilities. In W. M. Cruickshank & G. O. Johnson (Eds.). *Education of Exceptional Children and Youth* (3rd ed.). Englewood Cliffs, NJ: Prentice-Hall, Inc.

Dainer, K. B., Klorman, R., Salzman, L. F., Hess, D. W., Davidson, P. W. & Michael, R. L. (1981). Learning-disordered children's evoked potentials during sustained attention. *Journal of Abnormal Child Psychology, 9,* 79–94.

Delamater, A. M., Lahey, B. B., & Drake, L. (1981). Toward an empirical subclassification of "learning disabilities": A psychophysiological comparison of "hyperactive" and "nonhyperactive" subgroups. *Journal of Abnormal Child Psychology, 9,* 65–77.

Denton, C. L., & McIntyre, C. W., (1978). Span of apprehension in hyperactive boys. *Journal of Abnormal Child Psychology, 6,* 19–24.

Douglas, V. I., & Peters, K. G. (1979). Toward a clearer definition of the attentional deficit of hyperactive children. In G. A. Hale & M. Lewis (Eds.). *Attention and Cognitive Development.* New York: Plenum Press.

Doyle, R. B., Anderson, R. P., & Halcomb, C. G. (1976). Attention deficits and the effects of visual distraction. *Journal of Learning Disabilities, 9*(1), 59–65.

Firestone, P., & Douglas, V. (1975). The effects of reward and punishment on reaction times and autonomic activity in hyperactive and normal children. *Journal of Abnormal and Child Psychology, 3,* 201–216.

Fleisher, L. S., Soodak, L. C., & Jelin, M. A. (1984). Selective attention deficits in learning disabled children: Analysis of the data base. *Exceptional Children, 51,* 136–141.

Gibson, E., & Rader, N. (1979). Attention: The perceiver as performer. In G. A. Hale & M. Lewis (Eds.). *Attention and Cognitive Development.* New York: Plenum Press.

Goldberg, J. O., & Konstantareas, M. M. (1981). Vigilance in hyperactive and normal children on a self-paced operant task. *Journal of Child Psychology and Psychiatry, 22,* 55–63.

Hagen, J. W. (1967). The effect of distraction on selective attention. *Child Development, 38,* 685–694.

Hallahan, D. P., Reeve, R. E. (1980). Selective attention and distractibility, In B. K. Keogh (Ed.). *Advances in Special Education.* Vol. 1 (pp. 141–181). Greenwich, CT: JAI Press.

Hebben, N. A., Whitman, R. D., Milberg, W. P., Andresko, M., & Galpin, R. (1981). Attentional dysfunction in poor readers. *Journal of Learning Disabilities, 14,* 287–290.

Hoy, E., Weiss, G., Minde, K., & Cohen, N. (1978). The hyperactive child at adolescence: Cognitive, emotional, and social functioning. *Journal of Abnormal Child Psychology, 6,* 311–324.

Kahneman, D. (1973). *Attention and effort.* Englewood Cliffs, NJ: Prentice-Hall, Inc.

Keogh, B. K., & MacMillan, D. L. (1983). The logic of sample selection: Who represents what? *Exceptional Education Quarterly, 4,* 84–96.

Keogh, B. K., & Margolis, J. S. (1976). A component analysis of attentional problems of educationally handicapped boys. *Journal of Abnormal Child Psychology, 4,* 349–359.

Keogh, B. K., Major-Kingsley, S. Omori-Gordon, H. P., & Reid, H. (1982). *A system of marker variables for the field of learning disabilities.* New York: Syracuse University Press.

Kirchner, G. L., (1976). Differences in the vigilance performance of highly active and normal second-grade males under four experimental conditions. *Journal of Educational Psychology, 68,* 696–701.

Kirchner, G. L., & Knopf, I. J. (1974). Differences in the vigilance performance of second-grade children as related to sex and achievement. *Child Development, 45,* 490–495.

Klorman, R., Salzman, L. F., Pass, H. L., Borgstedt, A. D., & Dainer, K. B. (1979). Effects of methylphenidate on hyperactive children's evoked responses during passive and active attention. *Psychophysiology, 16,* 23–29.

Krupski, A. (1975). Heart rate changes during a fixed reaction time task in normal and retarded adult males. *Psychophysiology, 12,* 262–267.

Krupski, A. (1980). Attention processes: Research, theory, and implications for special education. In B. K. Keogh (Ed.). *Advances in Special Education.* Vol 1 (pp. 101–140). Greenwich, CT: JAI Press.

Krupski, A. (1984). Display vs. memory search for digits and faces among mentally handicapped and MA-matched nonhandicapped youngsters. *British Journal of Developmental Psychology, 2,* 231–242.

Krupski, A., Raskin, D. C., & Bakan, P. (1971). Physiological and personality correlates of commission errors in an auditory vigilance task. *Psychophysiology, 8,* 304–311.

Kupietz, S. S. (1976). Attentiveness in behaviorally deviant and nondeviant children: I. Auditory vigilance performance. *Perceptual and Motor Skills, 43,* 1095–1101.

Kupietz, S. S., Camp, J. A., & Weissman, A. D. (1976). Reaction time performance of behaviorally deviant children: Effects of prior preparatory interval and reinforcement. *Journal of Child Psychology and Psychiatry, 17,* 123–131.

Lambert, N. M., & Sandoval, J. (1980). The prevalance of learning disabilities in a sample of children considered hyperactive. *Journal of Abnormal Child Psychology, 8,* 33–50.

Lasky, E. Z., & Tobin, H. (1973). Linguistic and nonlinguistic competing message effects. *Journal of Learning Disabilities, 6*(4), 243–250.

Loiselle, D. L., Stamm, J. S., Maitinsky, S., & Whipple, S. C. (1980). Evoked potential and behavioral signs of attentive dysfunctions in hyperactive boys. *Psychophysiology, 17,* 193–201.

Lovie, A. D. (1983). Attention and behaviourism: Fact and fiction. *British Journal of Psychology, 74,* 301–310.

McIntyre, C. W., Murray, M. E., Cronin, C. M., & Blackwell, S. L. (1978). Span of apprehension in learning disabled boys. *Journal of Learning Disabilities, 11*(8), 468–475.

Michael, R. L., Klorman, R., Salzman, L. F., Borgstedt, A. D., & Dainer, K. B. (1981). Normalizing effects of methylphenidate on hyperactive children's vigilance performance and evoked potentials. *Psychophysiology, 18,* 665–677.

Moray, N. (1969). *Attention: Selective processes in vision and hearing.* London: Hutchinson.

Neisser, U. (1976). *Cognition and reality.* San Francisco: W. H. Freeman & Co.

Nober, L. W., & Nober, E. H. (1975). Auditory discrimination of learning-disabled children in quiet and classroom noise. *Journal of Learning Disabilities, 8*(10), 656–659.

Noland, E. C., & Schuldt, W. J. (1971). Sustained attention and reading retardation. *The Journal of Experimental Education, 40,* 73–76.

Nuechterlein, K. H. (1983). Signal detection in vigilance tasks and behavioral attributes among offspring of schizophrenic mothers and among hyperactive children. *Journal of Abnormal Psychology, 92,* 4–28.

Odom, R. D. (1972). Effects of perceptual salience on the recall of relevant and incidental dimensional values: A developmental study. *Journal of Experimental Psychology, 92,* 285–291.

Odom, R. D., Cunningham, J. G., & Astor-Stetson, E. (1977). The role of perceptual salience and type of instruction in children's recall of relevant and incidental dimensional values. *Bulletin of Psychonomic Society, 9,* 77–80.

Odom, R. D., & Guzman, R. D. (1972). Development of hierarchies of dimensional salience. *Developmental Psychology, 6,* 271–287.

Odom, R. D., & Lemond, C. M. (1975). The recall of relevant and incidental dimensional values as a function of perceptual salience, cognitive set, and age. *Journal of Experimental Child Psychology, 19,* 524–535.

Pelham, W. E., (1979). Selective attention deficits in poor readers? Dichotic listening, speeded classification, and auditory and visual central and incidental learning tasks. *Child Development, 50,* 1050–1061.

Radosh, A., & Gittelman, R. (1981). The effect of appealing distractors on the performance of hyperactive children. *Journal of Abnormal Child Psychology, 9,* 179–189.

Rosenthal, R. H., & Allen, T. W. (1978). An examination of attention, arousal, and learning dysfunctions of hyperkinetic children. *Psychological Bulletin, 85,* 689–715.

Rosenthal, R. H., & Allen, T. W. (1980). Intratask distractibility in hyperkinetic and nonhyperkinetic children. *Journal of Abnormal Child Psychology, 8,* 175–187.

Rosvold, H. E., Mirsky, A. F., Sarason, I., Bransome, E. D., & Beck, L. H. (1956). A continuous performance test of brain damage. *Journal of Consulting Psychology, 20,* 343–350.

Rugel, R. P., Cheatam, D., & Mitchell, A. (1978). Body movement and inattention in learning-disabled and normal children. *Journal of Abnormal Child Psychology, 6,* 325–337.

Rugel, R. P., & Rosenthal, R. (1974). Skin conductance, reaction time, and observational ratings in learning-disabled children. *Journal of Abnormal Child Psychology, 2,* 183–192.

Samuels, S. J. (1967). Attentional process in reading: The effect of pictures on the acquisition of reading responses. *Journal of Educational Psychology, 58,* 337–342.

Shepp, B. E., & Swartz, K. B. (1976). Selective attention and the processing of integral and nonintegral dimensions: A developmental study. *Journal of Experimental Child Psychology, 22,* 73–85.

Smith, L. B. (1981). Importance of the overall similarity of objects for adults' and children's classifications. *Journal of Experimental Psychology: Human Perception and Performance, 7,* 811–824.

Smith, L. B., & Kemler, D. G. (1977). Developmental trends in free classification: Evidence for a new conceptualization of perceptual development. *Journal of Experimental Child Psychology, 24,* 279–298.

Sroufe, L. A., Sonies, B. C., West, W. D., & Wright, F. S. (1973). Anticipatory heart rate deceleration and reaction time in children with and without referral for learning disability. *Child Development, 44,* 267–273.

Strauss, A. A., & Lehtinen, L. (1947) *Psychopathology and education of the brain-injured child.* New York: Grune & Stratton.

Strutt, G. F., Anderson, D. R., & Well, A. D. (1975). A developmental study of the effects of irrelevant information on speeded classification. *Journal of Experimental Child Psychology, 20,* 127–135.

Swanson, H. L. (1980). Auditory and visual vigilance in normal and learning disabled readers. *Learning Disability Quarterly, 3,* 71–78.

Swanson, L. (1981). Vigilance deficit in learning disabled children: A signal detection analysis. *Journal of Child Psychology and Psychiatry, 22,* 393–399.

Swanson, H. L. (1983). A developmental study of vigilance in learning-disabled and non-disabled children. *Journal of Abnormal Child Psychology, 11,* 415–429.

Sykes, D. H., Douglas, V. I., & Morgenstern, G. (1973). Sustained attention in hyperactive children. *Journal of Child Psychology and Psychiatry, 14,* 213–220.

Sykes, D. H., Douglas, V. I., Weiss, G., & Minde, K. K. (1971). Attention in hyperactive children and the effect of methylphenidate (Ritalin). *Journal of Child Psychology and Psychiatry, 12,* 129–139.

Torgesen, J. (1975). Problems and prospects in the study of learning disabilities. In M. Hetherington & J. Hagen (Eds.). *Review of Research in Child Development.* Vol. 5. Chicago: University of Chicago Press, 1975).

Torgesen, J. K. (1982). The study of short-term memory in learning-disabled children: Goals, methods, and conclusions. In K. D. Gadow & I. Bialer (Eds.). *Advances in Learning and Behavioral Disabilities.* Vol 1. Greenwich, CT: JAI Press.

Treisman, A. M. (1969). Strategies and models of selective attention. *Psychological Review, 76,* 282–299.

Wright, J. C., & Vliestra, A. G. (1975). The development of selective attention: From perceptual exploration to logical search. In H. W. Reese (Ed.). *Advances in Child Development and Behavior.* Vol 10. New York: Academic Press.

Zahn, T. P., Abate, F., Little, B. C., & Wender, P. H. (1975). Minimal brain dysfunction, stimulant drugs, and autonomic nervous system activity. *Archives of General Psychiatry, 32,* 381–387.

Zahn, T. P., Little, B. C., & Wender, P. H. (1978). Pupillary and heart rate reactivity in children with minimal brain dysfunction. *Journal of Abnormal Child Psychology, 6,* 135–147.

Zentall, S. S., & Shaw, J. H. (1980). Effects of classroom noise on performance and activity of second-grade hyperactive and control children. *Journal of Educational Psychology, 72,* 830–840.

Zentall, S. S., Zentall, T. R., & Barack, R. C. (1978). Distraction as a function of within-task stimulation for hyperactive and normal children. *Journal of Learning Disabilities, 11*(9), 540–548.

Zentall, S. S., Zentall, T. R., & Booth, M. E. (1978). Within-task stimulation: Effects on activity and spelling performance in hyperactive and normal children. *Journal of Educational Research, 71*, 223–230.

7

Social Relationships of Learning-Disabled Children*

RUTH PEARL
MAVIS DONAHUE
TANIS BRYAN

INTRODUCTION

The term "learning disabled" suggests that children with this label face difficulty primarily in the academic domain. However, learning-disabled children's problems are not circumscribed to this one area alone. There is now considerable evidence that learning-disabled children encounter problems not only in their academic endeavors but in their social relationships as well. In fact, there is even some evidence that the factors that first set these children apart from their classmates, thereby triggering the referral and diagnostic process, may be problems in social adjustment rather than academic underachievement (Bryan & Bryan, 1978b). This salience of learning-disabled children's social difficulties is ironic as most definitions of learning disabilities explicitly exclude social or emotional maladjustment as a primary characteristic.

Attention to learning-disabled children's social problems is warranted for a number of reasons. First, children's social experiences can influence such things as their feelings of competence and their perceptions of others' expectations for their behavior, factors which, in turn, can affect

* Preparation of this manuscript was supported by a research contract from the Office of Special Education, Department of Education (US OE 300 800 621) with the Chicago Institute for the Study of Learning Disabilities, College of Education, University of Illinois, Chicago.

193

Psychological and Educational
Perspectives on Learning Disabilities

✕children's academic behavior. Therefore, an examination of learning-disabled children's social interactions may shed some light on the reasons behind the maladaptive behaviors these children often manifest in achievement situations (see Licht & Kistner, Chapter 8, this volume). Second, social adjustment, not just academic achievement, is now considered by many to be an important goal for special education programs. Because difficulties in peer relationships during childhood have been found to be predictive of adjustment problems in later life (e.g., Roff, Sells, & Golden, 1972; Cowen, Pederson, Babigian, Izzo, & Trost, 1973), findings that learning-disabled children have difficulty in their relationships with classmates indicate that this is an area deserving of some concern. Finally, a focus on learning-disabled children's relationships with others is important simply because there is evidence that these children live in a less friendly and accepting world than do their peers. Awareness of the causes of others' negative reactions to learning-disabled children may lead to strategies for improving the social experiences of these children.

This chapter reviews research on elementary school, learning-disabled children's social relationships, with a focus on their interactions with non-disabled peers. The first section deals with the attitudes of others toward these children. The second section describes the behaviors exhibited by learning-disabled students in their classrooms and in other interactions with children. The third part explores some possible causes of learning-disabled children's social difficulties. The final part describes the current status of research on remediation of learning-disabled children's social problems.

ATTITUDES OF OTHERS TOWARD
LEARNING-DISABLED CHILDREN

One of the most telling indications that many learning-disabled children experience troubled interpersonal relationships is found in research on others' attitudes toward these children. Using a variety of methods, a substantial number of studies have examined children's, teachers', and parents' feelings about learning-disabled children. Even strangers' first impressions of these children have been examined. These studies show that reactions of others to these children often tend to be more negative and deprecating than is the case for nondisabled children.

CLASSMATES

Classmates' attitudes toward learning-disabled children have been assessed through the use of sociometric measures, which are of two major types. In the first, children are asked to nominate classmates who fit different favorable or unfavorable descriptions. For example, children might be questioned about who would make a good class president, or whom they would not want to invite to their birthday party. In the second type of sociometric measure, children are asked to rate every child in their class, thereby indicating their feelings regarding all their classmates. For example, children might be asked to indicate the degree to which they would want to work with each of the children in the class. These two sociometric methods appear to assess somewhat different dimensions of peer status. Nominations measure popularity, rejection, and isolation; rating scales measure children's general level of peer acceptance (Gresham, 1981a; Hymel & Asher, 1977).

Both methods have been used with learning-disabled children and their classmates. Although the procedures used have differed considerably over studies and the results have not been entirely consistent, the studies indicate clearly that most learning-disabled children do not attain the same level of sociometric status as do their nondisabled peers.

The first study examining the sociometric status of learning-disabled children was conducted by Bryan (1974a). Third, fourth, and fifth-graders were asked to name classmates who were and were not desired as friends, classroom neighbors, and guests at a party. The children were also asked questions like, "Who is handsome or pretty?" "Who finds it hard to sit still in class?"and "Who is always worried and scared?" Learning-disabled students received fewer positive and more negative nominations than did their nondisabled counterparts. Rejection was especially strong for learning-disabled girls.

Many of the children who participated in Bryan's (1974a) study were readministered the sociometric measures with their classmates a year later (Bryan, 1976). At this point, the children were in classes with new teachers and for the most part, new classmates. Learning-disabled children again received fewer positive and more negative votes than did nondisabled children. Hence, despite the fact that approximately 75% of the learning-disabled children's classmates were different from those in their class the previous year, the learning-disabled children's social status remained low.

Using a variety of sociometric methods, studies that followed similarly found that learning-disabled children were frequently rated less positively than their nondisabled classmates, and were often less popular, more rejected, or more ignored (Bruininks, 1978a, 1978b; Donahue & Prescott, 1983; Garrett & Crump, 1980; Horowitz, 1981; Scranton & Ryckman, 1979; Sheare, 1978; Siperstein, Bopp & Bak, 1978; Siperstein & Goding, 1983). Although future research may further clarify the nature of peers' attitudes to learning-disabled children (or to different types of learning-disabled children), the studies to date clearly indicate that in most classrooms, learning-disabled children are not as well liked or accepted by their fellow students as other children.

TEACHERS

Findings that teachers have lower expectations for the future academic performance of learning-disabled children than of nondisabled children (Boersma & Chapman, 1982) are not especially surprising in light of the fact that learning-disabled children are presumably identified on the basis of their learning problems. However, it appears that the negative view of learning-disabled children held by teachers is not limited to the area of the children's academic performance (Feagans & McKinney, 1981; McKinney, McClure & Feagans, 1982; Siperstein & Goding, 1983).

For example, in one study (Touliatos & Lindholm, 1980), teachers considered learning-disabled children to have more conduct problems, personality problems, immaturity, and psychotic signs than other children. These characteristics were perceived as increasing with age for the learning-disabled children, whereas they were thought to first increase, but then decline for nondisabled students. In another study (Bryan & McGrady, 1972), learning-disabled children were given lower ratings than nondisabled students on cooperation, attention, ability to organize, ability to cope with new situations, social acceptance, acceptance of responsibility, completion of assignments, and tactfulness. The learning-disabled children also were rated lower on such factors as promptness, comprehension of class discussions, and learning directions.

Other studies have shown that teachers make distinctions between the characteristics of learning-disabled children and those of children with other types of special problems. For example, Keogh, Tchir, and Windeguth-Behn (1974) asked teachers to describe the characteristics of children who seemed to them to be at risk for learning disabilities or for retardation. Compared to their descriptions of children who might be retarded, the children at risk for learning disabilities were described by teachers in both a middle-socioeconomic status, suburban Anglo community and a low-socioeconomic status, urban black community in terms that seemed more negative and pejorative. These children more frequently were described as disruptive, hyperactive, and as having short attention spans. Many teachers in the suburban schools also described these children as aggressive, withdrawn, having no sense of responsibility or self-discipline, and having poor interpersonal relationships.

Moore and Fine (1978) gave teachers questionnaires in which they were asked to indicate items descriptive of 10-year-old boys who were either learning disabled, educable mentally handicapped, or normal. The learning-disabled children were perceived by the teachers as "socially distant, somewhat frustrated, and pessimistic."Learning-disabled children were given ratings intermediate between the other two groups of children on such qualities as leadership, self-confidence, and helplessness. Similarly, learning-disabled children were given teacher ratings that indicated problems of a greater quantity or severity than average children, though of lesser quantity or severity than emotionally disturbed children (McCarthy & Paraskevopoulos, 1969).

Apparently, then, many teachers consider learning-disabled children to possess a variety of negative and bothersome characteristics, especially in comparison to nondisabled children. In fact, one study (Garrett & Crump, 1980) directly asked teachers to sort the names of their students on a scale ranging from "most preferred" to "least preferred" and found that teachers indicated a lower preference for learning-disabled children than for nondisabled students. Hence, learning-disabled children appear, to many teachers, to be difficult students to have in one's classroom.

PARENTS

In addition to the evidence that learning-disabled children are not particularly appealing playmates or students, they also do not appear to be easy children to live with. A number of studies have explored the effects of raising a learning-disabled child on parental attitudes toward their child and their home life.

The most extensive investigation of parental attitudes included both mothers and fathers of learning-disabled and nondisabled children (Owen, Adams, Forrest, Stolz & Fisher, 1971). Because every subject in the study had a younger or older, same-sex, nondisabled sibling, comparisons could be made not only between parents of learning-disabled and nondisabled chldren, but also between the attitudes parents held toward each of their children. Parents of learning-disabled children perceived their children more negatively than did parents of nondisabled children on 7 of 13 characteristics, including perseverance in and out of school, anxiety, verbal abilities, motor coordination, impulse control, and ability to structure their environment. Compared to their siblings, learning-disabled children were also considered to have less verbal ability, less impulse control, less ability to structure their environment, and more anxiety. Further, relative to both unrelated, nondisabled children and nondisabled siblings, learning-disabled children were described as having more serious problems and as causing their parents to worry more about them.

Both mothers and fathers reported putting more pressure for academic accomplishment on the learning-disabled children than on their siblings. Furthermore, families with a learning-disabled child were rated as having a less well-organized and a less emotionally stable home environment than other families.

A number of the findings from this investigation have been confirmed, extended, and qualified in smaller studies (Doleys, Cartelli, & Doster, 1976; Gerber, 1976; Goldman & Barclay, 1974; Humphries & Bauman, 1980; Strag, 1972; Wetter, 1972). For example, indications that maternal attitudes and expectations of their learning-disabled sons may be influenced by birth order were found in a study by Epstein, Berg-Cross, and Berg-Cross (1980). Families with a first-born learning-disabled son and second-born nondisabled son were found to be under greater stress than families with only a second-born learning-disabled son, or families with no learning-disabled children; mothers underestimated the first-born learning-disabled child's skills, yet overestimated the normal second-born child's abilities.

Mothers' beliefs about the causes of their children's successes and failures were examined by Pearl and Bryan (1982a). Compared to mothers of nondisabled children, mothers of learning-disabled children attributed their children's successes more to luck and less to ability; their failures were attributed less to bad luck and more to a lack of ability. When asked to make causal attributions about their own successes and failures with the home environment, mothers of learning-disabled children also viewed their own successes less positively and their own failures more negatively than did control mothers.

In a subsequent study (Bryan, Pearl, Zimmerman, & Matthews, 1982), mothers of learning-disabled children were found to characterize their children relative to mothers of nondisabled children as having fewer academic strengths, more academic weaknesses, fewer behaviors likely to facilitate academic achievement, and lower achievement in a number of areas. Further, mothers of learning-disabled children were more pessimistic about their learning-disabled children's future success than were mothers of nondisabled children. When asked to describe what might cause their children to do poorly in the future, mothers of learning-disabled children were more likely than other mothers to attribute future failures to personal characteristics of the child and to outside influences. Other studies also have found that mothers of learning-disabled children expect less future academic success from their children than do mothers of nondisabled students (Boersma & Chapman, 1982; Chapman & Boersma, 1979).

These studies indicate that parents readily seem to recognize their learning-disabled children's personality and social difficulties, as well as their academic problems. It appears that the task of parenting a learning-disabled child poses special challenges, and parental attitudes seem to reflect their efforts to deal with these challenges.

STRANGERS

The evidence is clear that learning-disabled children are not viewed in a particularly favorable light by those people who interact with them almost every day, namely, their classmates, their teachers, and their parents. However, there is also a body of research that suggests that familiarity with the learning-disabled child is not even necessary for an unfavorable attitude to be evoked. In other words, learning-disabled children do not appear to make good first impressions, even on strangers who have had no interpersonal interactions with them and who are unaware of their learning difficulties.

In a series of studies of the immediate impressions that learning-disabled children elicit, J. Bryan and his associates asked various groups of people to watch brief videotaped segments showing a learning-disabled or nondisabled child interacting with another person (Bryan & Sherman, 1980; Perlmutter & Bryan, 1984). The viewers then rated each child on the personality dimensions of adaptablitity and social hostility, using a 20-item scale. In each study, the raters were completely unaware of the academic or social history of the children, or of the purposes of the studies.

In one study (Bryan & Perlmutter, 1979), for example, female college students viewed videotapes of children in fourth and fifth grades teaching a bowling game to same-age and same-sex classmates. Judges were presented only the video information, only the audio information, or both audio and video information. Although these segments were less than 3 minutes long, the viewers rated the learning-disabled girls as less socially desirable than the nondisabled children, particularly when only nonverbal information was available.

Another study suggests that the finding of negative first impressions may not generalize to younger children with learning disabilities (Bryan, Bryan, & Sonnefeld, 1982). College students were asked to rate learning-disabled and nondisabled boys in grades 2 and 4 as they pretended to put on a television talk show. Among children playing the interviewer role, learning-disabled children in the fourth grade were judged less positively than nondisabled classmates; however, surprisingly, learning-disabled second-graders elicited *more* favorable impressions from judges than nondisabled second-graders.

Another purpose of this study was to examine the immediate impressions made by the nonverbal behavior of normally achieving children who were interacting with a learning-disabled child, that is, to determine whether there is a contagion effect of first impressions. Immediate impressions of the children were found to be correlated with the immediate impressions of their partners, even though each judge rated only one of the two partners and could see only the child being rated. Although the nondisabled boys who were interviewed by second-grade, learning-disabled subjects were actually perceived more favorably than those interviewed by second-grade nondisabled subjects, the reverse was true for fourth-grade subjects. In other words, these results suggest that by the fourth grade, interaction with a learning-disabled child may make normally achieving children feel uncomfortable, thereby placing them at a social disadvantage.

In general, then, it appears that learning-disabled children beyond the second grade rapidly elicit negative first impressions from children as well as adults, and in a variety of communicative situations. However, the nature of the apparently subtle behaviors that elicit these attitudes remains a mystery. The previously described research on the attitudes of people who are familiar with the learning-disabled child suggests, however, that learning-disabled children do not easily counteract these initial negative impressions during subsequent interactions.

SUMMARY

Classmates, teachers, and parents seem to find relationships with learning-disabled children to be more difficult than those with nondisabled children, and even the first impressions of strangers are likely to be more negative. The important question, of course, is why these children are viewed so negatively.

Some have suggested that others' attitudes may be a result of assumptions that are made about children who have academic problems, particularly when they have actually been labeled "learning disabled." Although this may play a part, it does not seem to be solely responsible for eliciting the reactions learning-disabled children receive. For example, children who viewed a videotaped boy who had been labeled "learning disabled" did not rate him as lower in peer or social acceptance than children who viewed the same videotape without the boy labeled; hence, the label did not result in the disparagement of the boy (Sutherland, Algozzine, Ysseldyke, & Young, 1979). McMichael (1980) found that although poor readers were less popular regardless of their classroom behavior, they were rejected only if their behavior was more antisocial than that of other children. These studies suggest that the negative perceptions others have of learning-disabled children are not likely to be due only to stereotypes held about children with learning problems.

Consequently, it is important to examine learning-disabled children's behavior to see whether behavior patterns can be identified which may be responsible for the negative reactions these children receive. Because the focus of this chapter is on the relationships of learning-disabled children with their peers, the next section will describe learning-disabled children's behavior in school settings and other interactions with children.

LEARNING-DISABLED CHILDREN'S SOCIAL BEHAVIOR

Although there is a large body of research on the behaviors which are related to peer acceptance among nondisabled children (Asher, Renshaw, & Hymel, 1982), there are few studies which provide direct evidence of the relationship between learning-disabled children's behavior and their sociometric status. Therefore, the search for an explanation for these children's low status must be limited to extrapolating from the findings of research that compares the behavior of learning-disabled and nondisabled children. However, whether learning-disabled children's behavior actually causes their low status is, unfortunately, not clear at this point.

BEHAVIOR IN SCHOOL SETTINGS

Examinations of learning-disabled children's classroom behavior usually have had purposes other than just documenting learning-disabled children's relationships with peers. The observation systems used often were designed to also identify learning-disabled children's behavior in regard to tasks, with teachers, and in different classroom contexts. Because of these diverse goals, and because of the difficulty of doing in vivo behavioral coding, these studies tend not to provide detailed descriptions of learning-disabled children's social interactions. In addition, many of the classroom studies either included only boys or did not analyze for sex differences. Nevertheless, these studies suggest that learning-disabled children typically behave differently in their classrooms than do nondisabled classmates, and it is likely that these different behaviors, even when not directly involving classmates, may play a part in eliciting others' negative reactions.

One of the most consistent findings of classroom studies is that learning-disabled children are more off-task or distractible than nondisabled children. This was found with first- and second-grade boys who were in the process of being evaluated for learning or behavior problems (Forness & Esveldt, 1975), and with learning-disabled children in kindergarten through the sixth grade (Bryan, 1974b; Bryan & Wheeler, 1972; Dorval, McKinney, & Feagans, 1982; Feagans & McKinney, 1981, 1982; Gettinger & Fayne, 1982; McKinney, et al., 1982; Richey & McKinney, 1978).

Interactions with teachers seem to reflect learning-disabled children's difficulty in attending to classroom tasks. For example, a number of studies (Chapman, Larsen & Parker, 1979; Dorval, et al., 1982; Feagans & McKinney, 1981, 1982; McKinney et al., 1982; Siperstein & Goding, 1983) reported that learning-disabled students interacted more with their teachers than did classmates. Dorval et al. (1982) found that this was due to the greater frequency of initiations by the teacher directed at behavior management with learning-disabled children. These initiations were most often in response to inattention or rule violations. However, Siperstein and Goding (1983) found that teachers directed more corrective and less supportive behavior to learning-disabled children despite the fact that, in this study, the learning-disabled children did not differ from nondisabled children in their frequency of negative initiations or inappropriate responses.

Some studies did not find that learning-disabled children spent more time in interaction with the teacher (Bryan, 1974b; Bryan & Wheeler, 1972; Richey & McKinney, 1978). Nonetheless, Bryan (1974b) found that a larger proportion of learning-disabled children's interactions with teachers were those in which the teacher helped them with academic work than was true for other children. In addition, this study found that teachers were considerably less likely to respond to the verbal initiations of learning-disabled children than to those of classmates.

Interactions with the teacher and attentiveness are behaviors that are not specifically directed toward classmates; nevertheless, it is possible that these behaviors contribute to classmates' low regard for learning-disabled children. For instance, it might be that a low level of attentiveness is distracting and annoying to other children. It is also possible that the different type of interaction learning-disabled children experience with the teacher signals to classmates, as well as to the learning-disabled children themselves, that the learning-disabled children somehow differ in terms of ability or effort from the rest of the class (Meyer, 1982; Weinstein, 1982). Since children's desire to be like others is influenced by others' relative levels of ability and effort (Nicholls & Miller, 1984), it is possible that children deemed low in the valued dimensions are disdained by their peers.

Research examining learning-disabled children's peer interactions in regular school classrooms has not found learning-disabled and nondisabled children to differ in terms of the amount of time spent in interaction with their classmates. In fact, when children were observed in their regular classrooms, during either randomly selected periods or when the class was involved largely in academic activities, the only difference reported in peer interaction was that the initiations of third-grade learning-disabled children were more likely to be ignored than were those of other children (Bryan, 1974b). Nevertheless, failure to find more substantial differences between learning-disabled and other children may be because the range of possible interpersonal behaviors is relatively constrained in the types of situations in which the children were observed, or because the observation systems used were insensitive to differences that actually occurred.

Few differences were also found in a study comparing the lunchroom behavior of third-, fourth-, and fifth-grade learning-disabled and non-disabled students (Sainato, Zigmond, & Strain, 1983). However, the frequency with which the learning-disabled children made positive initiations actually was negatively related to their sociometric status.

Studies which more closely examined the verbal content of children's interactions during nonacademic periods, or during summer school classes, have found some significant differences in the affective quality of learning-disabled children's conversations with peers versus those between nondisabled classmates. Bryan and Bryan (1978a) analyzed fourth- and fifth-graders' communications during art and physical education classes. Learning-disabled children made more "very nasty" statements and received more rejection statements than did nondisabled classmates. Bryan, Wheeler, Felcan, and Henek (1976) observed third-, fourth- and fifth-graders as they participated in classes in a variety of subjects during summer school. Compared to the nondisabled children, the learning-disabled students made more competitive statements and received fewer "consideration" statements than other children. These studies indicate, then, that in at least some classroom settings and situations, learning-disabled children experience interactions with peers that are more negative in tone than do nondisabled classmates.

BEHAVIOR IN STRUCTURED SITUATIONS

Observational studies of children's interactions in school are valuable because they delineate the behaviors typical of learning-disabled and nondisabled children in this obviously important setting. However, for several reasons, observations in more structured situations are required for a complete description of children's social behavior. First, within a classroom, there can be considerable heterogeneity at any given time in such factors as the size of instructional groups and the types of activities children are engaged in, factors which themselves can affect the behaviors children exhibit (McKinney *et al.*, 1982). These variations within a classroom make it difficult to be confident that children are really being evaluated in comparable situations. Second, the size of classrooms and the large number of children present often preclude detailed assessments of the children's behavior. Third, the testing of specific hypotheses about the children's social behavior can be more systematic in situations designed to evaluate the behavior of interest. For these and other reasons, a number of investigators have examined learning-disabled children's social behavior within specific, relatively structured situations.

One study (Cosden, Pearl, & Bryan, in press) videotaped the interactions of pairs of classmates in the second through eighth grades as they studied for a test. The pairs consisted of either a learning-disabled child and a nondisabled child or two nondisabled children, matched on sex. Half of the pairs were given instructions and incentives to study individually, and half were given instructions and incentives to study cooperatively. The results indicated that, although both types of pairs interacted more in the cooperative condition than in the individual condition, pairs that included a learning-disabled boy interacted less than did pairs of two nondisabled boys. In contrast to the findings for boys, the nondisabled partners of the learning-disabled girls spent more time in interactive behavior than did the other girls.

Although participation in the cooperative groups had somewhat mixed effects on the children's achievement in this study, the results suggest that cooperative study groups provide a setting in which positive interactions between learning-disabled and nondisabled students are likely to occur, especially with girls. Pairs containing a learning-disabled boy worked together less easily than pairs of two nondisabled boys, but still managed to engage in a considerable amount of cooperative study behavior. Assessments of the children's attributions after completing the task, however, indicated that a longer period of positive interaction may be necessary to affect significantly the children's attitudes toward one another. Nevertheless, some positive feelings resulted from participation in the cooperative study groups. Boys in the cooperative condition felt themselves to have more ability than did those in the individual condition; girls in the cooperative condition were more likely to acknowledge their partner's efforts on the task and to want to work with their partner again. Whether the child's partner was a learning-disabled or a nondisabled student did not, itself, affect either boys' or girls' willingness to work with their partner again.

In this study, as well as in the studies which examined children's classroom behavior, it is possible that learning-disabled children's behavior differed from that of other children, at least in part, as a consequence of the difficulty learning-disabled children face when confronted with academic tasks. To establish the generality of behavioral differences between learning-disabled and nondisabled children, it is important to examine the children's behavior in situations in which neither group is at a clear disadvantage. Several studies have examined learning-disabled children's social behavior on nonacademic tasks; these demonstrate that differences between learning-disabled and nondisabled children's behavior are not limited to intellectual situations.

A number of studies assessed learning-disabled children's use of language in their interactions with other children. Bryan and Pflaum (1978) examined whether learning-disabled children adjusted the content and complexity of their speech to meet the needs of different listeners by asking fourth- and fifth-graders to teach a game to a same-age child and to a kindergartner. Compared to the statements of nondisabled children, those of learning-disabled children consisted of shorter T-units—a measure of syntactic complexity—and learning-disabled boys and girls differed from nondisabled boys and girls in whether they tended to direct their longer T-units to peers or to kindergartners.

Learning-disabled children's communications were also examined in a study in which third- through eighth-graders participated in a problem-solving task with two of their classmates (Bryan, Donahue, & Pearl, 1981a). The triads consisting of two nondisabled children teamed with either a learning-disabled child or a third nondisabled child. The children were asked, first, to rank-order the desirability of a list of potential presents for their class and, then, to come to a group consensus. Analyses of the videotaped session indicated that the learning-disabled children participated in the group's discussion as much as nondisabled children, but that their discourse differed in a number of ways. Learning-disabled children were more likely to agree with the others, less likely to disagree, less likely to argue against others' choices, and more likely to respond to requests for clarification and opinion. Learning-disabled children also were less likely to try to keep the group on task and to attempt to maintain the speaker role. Hence, the learning-disabled children participated actively, but did so in a deferential, unassertive manner. Not surprisingly, their preferred gift choices were selected by the group less often than those of nondisabled children. A further finding was that learning-disabled seventh- and eighth-graders were off-task more than their nondisabled counterparts.

To evaluate whether learning-disabled children would be more likely to be assertive and active in maintaining a conversation if they were placed in a socially dominant role, learning-disabled and nondisabled children were asked, in another study, to play the role of a talk show host (Bryan, Donahue, Pearl, & Sturm, 1981). The children were told to interview a nondisabled classmate about television programs and movies for a 3-minute period. Videotapes of the talk shows were examined to assess the hosts' conversational strategies and the guests' responses. Analyses showed that questions comprised a smaller percentage of learning-disabled hosts' utterances than those of nondisabled hosts. Further, a smaller proportion of learning-disabled hosts' questions were process questions, that is, those which encouraged extended responses. Learning-disabled hosts were also less successful in getting their guests to give elaborated responses. Additional evidence that the learning-disabled children were unable to control the conversation was the finding that, of the nine cases where the guest took over the interviewing role from the host, eight of these were dyads with learning-disabled hosts. Moreover, nonverbal behaviors associated with discomfort occurred more for the guests of learning-disabled girls and learning-disabled second-graders than for other children. The results, therefore, indicate that the learning-disabled children were less skillful than the nondisabled children in sustaining a conversation even though they had been assigned the responsibility for doing so.

A subsequent study (Donahue & Bryan, 1983) used a similar talk show format with second- through eighth-grade boys. However, before the interview, half of the subjects heard an audiotape of a dialogue in which process questions, conversational devices (i.e., phrases which acknowledged the preceding speaker's turn), and contingent questions and comments were modeled. Analyses indicated that the learning-disabled children who had heard the dialogue model were as likely as the nondisabled children to ask process questions and comments. Unfortunately, however, for the older learning-disabled children, the increase in the number of process questions produced in this condition actually was accompanied by a decrease in the use of elaborated responses by their guests to this question type. Further, guests of learning-disabled hosts, and particularly those in the dialogue condition, were more likely to request clarification from their hosts than were guests of nondisabled hosts. Thus, although learning-disabled children may have the ability to produce comments and process questions, the content or phrasing may make them harder for others to understand and answer than those of nondisabled children.

SUMMARY

In these studies, the learning-disabled children did not appear to be withdrawn or isolated; in most instances, they participated in interactions with other children as much as nondisabled students. Nevertheless, their behavior often differed from that typical of others. Even though brief exposure to learning-disabled children's nonverbal behavior alone seems sufficent to elicit negative impressions (e.g., Bryan & Perlmutter, 1979), it appears likely that learning-disabled children's atypical conversational behavior also may be responsible for the low regard in which they are held.

The way in which learning-disabled children's verbal behaviors differed from those of other children cannot be easily characterized. At times, learning-disabled children's communications seemed to be more deferential and at other times, more hostile. Although differences in coding systems and other varying methodological factors make comparisons across studies equivocal, it appears that the learning-disabled children's verbal styles may depend on the type of situation in which they were observed. When involved with highly structured tasks in which the type of verbalizations expected of the participants was fairly evident, the learning-disabled children tended to comply on the surface with the expected behavior; however, they did so in a deferential and unassertive manner, sometimes to the point where they seemed to relinquish their role in the conversation. On the other hand, in situations where the expectations for the children's conversational behavior were more ambiguous, learning-disabled children's communications sometimes appeared more negative or less effective.

EXPLANATIONS OF BEHAVIORAL
DIFFERENCES

The issues of why learning-disabled children's behavior appears less appropriate than that of other children and why the tone of their behavior is seemingly so inconsistent have generated a number of different possible explanations. Lack of motivation, difficulties in social perception and understanding, deficits in requisite behaviors, and the children's perceptions about themselves and others all have been cited as factors which may be involved.

In other words, an inappropriate behavior could result from a number of different factors. First, it may occur simply because the child is not motivated to seek social acceptance. Second, a child may intend to behave appropriately, but may fail to do so because he or she misperceives the situation due to difficulty in detecting or understanding important person and contextual cues. Third, a child may perceive these cues but not have the necessary skills to respond appropriately, or may have the skills but, for some reason, fail to activate them. Finally, the child may not behave in ways typical of other children due to either their attitudes about others or themselves. Each of these possibilities is briefly explored below.

MOTIVATION

One possible explanation of learning-disabled children's inappropriate behaviors is that they simply do not care about social acceptance. This, however, does not seem to be the case. Had they not been interested in their peers, it is unlikely that the learning-disabled children would have interacted with them as frequently as they did; in almost every study, learning-disabled children's involvement in social interaction was equal to that of nondisabled classmates.

Other studies also suggest that learning-disabled children want to win social approval. When learning-disabled and nondisabled children were asked whether different socially desirable behaviors were typical of them (e.g., "I always wash my hands before every meal"), learning-disabled children claimed at least as many of these behaviors as did nondisabled students. In other words, when given an easy opportunity to appear in a good light, learning-disabled children were as interested as other children in doing so (Pearl & Bryan, 1982b). In another study, learning-disabled children were given a chance to donate to the March of Dimes some of the money they earned because of their participation in the experiment. Learning-disabled children gave more to the charity than did nondisabled children (Bryan & Bryan, 1974). Although these studies certainly do not yield conclusive evidence on this point, they suggest that most learning-disabled children seem to be motivated to try to win social acceptance.

PROBLEMS IN SOCIAL PERCEPTION AND UNDERSTANDING

Even though learning-disabled children appear eager to be fully accepted members of their social groups, they may have difficulty behaving in the manner expected by others because of problems in social perception. They may overlook or misinterpret social cues to appropriate behavior, that is, facial expressions or voice inflections which indicate that another child is angry, sad, or joking.

A number of lines of evidence support the possibility that learning-disabled children may frequently "misread" social situations. When asked to explain pictures of social situations, learning-disabled children made fewer correct inferences than did nondisabled children (Bruno, 1981; Gerber & Zinkgraf, 1982). Learning-disabled children were also less successful at identifying emotions expressed by individuals in films or videotapes (Bryan, 1977; Wiig & Harris, 1974). Similar results were found when children were asked to make inferences about soap opera segments in which subtle emotional and social relations between the characters were shown (Pearl & Cosden, 1982). The learning-disabled children consistently made more incorrect responses than did the other children. Nevertheless, other studies indicate that if redundant cues are available, or if the children are highly motivated to pay attention, learning disabled students may not differ from nondisabled children in their performance on social perception tasks (Maheady & Maitland, 1982; Stone & LaGreca, 1984).

Other studies have found that, compared to nondisabled children, learning-disabled children made more errors in guessing how other children would feel in different situations (Bachara, 1976) and were less accurate in their understanding of others' thoughts, feelings, and perceptions when these conflicted with their own (Bruck & Hebert, 1982; Dickstein & Warren, 1980; Horowitz, 1981; Wong & Wong, 1980). Less-developed social cognitive skills also seemed responsible for the finding by Sobol, Earn, Bennet, and Humphries (1983) that learning-disabled children differ from nondisabled children in their attributions for social outcomes. Whereas the nondisabled children were more likely than the learning-disabled students to mention as important such factors as the other's motives or the interaction between the personalities involved, the learning-disabled students were more likely to attribute outcomes simply to luck.

Although one study did not find a relationship between learning-disabled children's role-taking skills and parents' and teachers' ratings of the children's peer interactions (Bruck & Hebert, 1982), two studies indicate how the lack of role-taking might be manifested in the children's behavior. In the first study, learning-disabled and nondisabled children were asked what they would say to a peer in hypothetical stiuations in which they had to communicate bad news, for example, that the other child was not chosen for the starring part in the class play. The results indicated that the learning-disabled children were less tactful than were the nondisabled children in that they were less likely to communicate the news in a way that would allow the listener to save face (Pearl, Donahue, & Bryan, in press). On a similar role-playing task, learning-disabled children made requests of various listeners. Compared to nondisabled boys, learning-disabled boys generated fewer persuasive strategies, and their appeals were less adapted to the interests of the listener (Donahue, 1981). These failures to adopt another's perspective may help explain why learning-disabled children's communications sometimes appear more nasty or less effective.

BEHAVIORAL DEFICITS

Another reason for the discrepancies between learning-disabled and nondisabled children's behavior may be that the former do not have the same level of skill available in their behavioral repertoire as other children or do not spontaneously use the skills which they have acquired. For example, learning-disabled children have been found to have deficits in vocabulary and syntactic structure (Donahue, Pearl, & Bryan, 1983; Wiig & Semel, 1980). These, conceivably, could interfere with the children's ability to communicate clearly (Knight-Arest, 1984; Noel, 1980; Spekman, 1981), thereby making their interactions with others more awkward (Bryan, Donahue, & Pearl, 1981b). Since communication ability influences children's friendship choices (Asher & Renshaw, 1981), this could be part of the reason learning-disabled children are low in popularity with their peers.

Other studies have found learning-disabled children to be less skillful on tests of motor abilities. Bryan and Smiley (1983), for example, found that learning-disabled boys had lower performances on physical fitness tests which measured speed, strength, and agility. This lower level of performance may be a reason learning-disabled children were less congenial when observed in physical education classes (Bryan & Bryan, 1978a). In addition, since athletic skills are highly valued by boys (Schofield, 1981), learning-disabled children's deficits in this area may be, in part, responsible for low peer opinion. Conversely, as Siperstein *et al.* (1978) suggest, outstanding athletic ability might help learning-disabled children attain acceptance from their peers.

A related explanation is that learning-disabled children behave differently not because they lack the requisite behavioral skills but because, for some other reason, they do not activate them at the appropriate time. For example, the children may not be aware that a behavior is considered appropriate in a given situation. However, the few studies that have examined learning-disabled children's understanding of behavioral norms have not detected differences. Bryan and Bryan (1974) found that learning-disabled children's attitudes about altruistic behavior did not differ from those of nondisabled children. Bryan and Sonnefeld (1981) assessed children's beliefs about what tactics would be most desirable for ingratiating peers, parents, or teachers in different situations and found no differences between the learning-disabled and nondisabled subjects' ratings of various tactics. Learning-disabled children also responded appropriately to requests for clarification during a referential communicative task, even when the listener's requests were conveyed merely by a puzzled facial expression (Pearl, Donahue, & Bryan, 1981).

Nevertheless, it appears that learning-disabled children sometimes choose an atypical behavior, despite the fact that they have an appropriate response available and they seem to know, when induced to think about appropriate behavior, what action is considered desirable. For instance, when told to "act naturally" in an interaction with an adult, learning-disabled children's behavior was rated more negatively by observers than that of other children. However, when the children were directly told to act in an ingratiating manner, their behavior was rated as high or higher than that of others (Bryan & Sherman 1980; Perlmutter & Bryan, 1984). Further, although learning-disabled children playing the role of talk show hosts were found to use fewer process questions and contingent comments than nondisabled subjects, listening to a brief model was sufficient to increase learning-disabled children's use of these conversational behaviors to the level of the nondisabled children (Donahue & Bryan, 1983). This failure to activate, spontaneously, existing skills has been found to characterize learning-disabled children's performance on cognitive tasks (Torgesen, 1980); it seems reasonable to hypothesize that this "inactive" style could extend to social interaction as well.

An examination of children's requesting strategies (Donahue, 1981) also found that learning-disabled children may at times, elect to use their skills in ways different from other children. Learning-disabled and nondisabled children were asked to make requests of hypothetical listeners who varied on the dimensions of intimacy and power. Compared to the nondisabled girls, the learning-disabled girls were more polite to all listeners. Learning-disabled boys' persuasive appeals reflected lower levels of listener perspective-taking than those of nondisabled boys. However, the politeness and elaborateness of the persuasive appeals given by the learning-disabled boys showed as much variation as those given by the nondisabled boys, but the learning-disabled and nondisabled boys differed in the target toward whom their most polite and most elaborate requests were directed. Hence, even though the learning-disabled children's repertoire of linguistic forms for conveying politeness was not lacking, they differed from other children in the requesting strategies they chose to use.

PERCEPTIONS OF SELF AND OTHERS

Hence, learning-disabled children may have acquired the social skills which nondisabled children demonstrate, but not yet be proficient in recognizing those situations where the use of these skills would be desirable. Another explanation for this puzzling failure to activate skills which appear to be in children's behavioral repertoire relates to their perceptions of themselves and others. That is, their behavioral style may be a reflection of their reactions to the fact that they are more rejected and, in some ways, less competent than their classmates. This hypothesis is supported by evidence that learning-disabled children are all too aware of their shortcomings. They rate their ability lower than do other children in a variety of academic areas (Chapman & Boersma, 1979; Hiebert, Wong, & Hunter, 1982), recognize their social status (Garrett & Crump, 1980; Horowitz, 1981), expect less social success than other children (Sobol et al., 1983), take little credit for success, and are unlikely to think that failures are due merely to a lack of effort (Pearl, 1982; Pearl, Bryan, & Donahue, 1980).

These feelings could very well influence learning-disabled children's choice of behavioral strategies. Even though they may be aware of the expectations for behavior of the typical child, recognition of their academic and social problems could lead them to conclude that a different interactional style would be more appropriate for them. For example, although no differences were found between learning-disabled and nondisabled children in their ratings of the social desirability of various ingratiation tactics for responding to specific social situations (Bryan &

Sonnefeld, 1981), when asked to select which behaviors *they* would use, learning-disabled children chose less socially desirable tactics (Bryan, Sonnefeld, & Greenberg, 1981). Further, it may have been that the learning-disabled children in the small-group, decision-making task (Bryan *et al.*, 1981a) played a deferential role because they were attempting to interact in a manner that would not antagonize their more popular and skilled partners.

Two studies provide more support for the explanation that learning-disabled children's self-perceptions may be, in part, responsible for their communicative behavior. Donahue, *et al.* (1980) found that learning-disabled children were less likely than nondisabled children to request more information when given inadequate clues during a referential communication task. Since the learning-disabled children later demonstrated that they could distinguish adequate from inadequate clues, it appeared that they failed to ask for more information because they assumed that it was their own fault that the clues seemed inadequate rather than that of the clue-giver (Donahue, 1984). In a study described earlier wherein children enacted a TV talk show (Donahue & Bryan, 1983), learning-disabled and nondisabled children were interviewed after completion of the task about their perceptions of good conversational skills. The learning-disabled children's responses indicated that they recognized their communicative difficulties on the task. These two studies suggest that, in some cases, learning-disabled children's feelings of competence or acceptance may have an impact on their behavior.

SUMMARY

All of the aforementioned factors remain viable explanations for learning-disabled children's behavioral differences. In fact, depending on the nature of the situation, none, several, or all of them may play a role. Learning-disabled children may also differ among themselves in the extent to which each of these factors is involved in their behavior; research on whether there are subgroups of learning-disabled children who experience different types of social difficulties is needed.

SOCIAL REMEDIATION

Given the many studies demonstrating that learning-disabled children experience difficulties in the social domain, it is surprising that there has been little research on interventions aimed at improving these children's relationships with others. One reason for this is that, until recently, most studies using sociometric measures have been concerned primarily with establishing whether learning-disabled children do, in fact, have social problems. One major purpose of these studies was to examine whether learning-disabled students have problems in the social domain despite the exclusive focus in the learning-disability definition on deficits in academic achievement. A second major purpose of these studies was to evaluate whether mainstreaming resulted in a successful integration of learning-disabled children with their peers. Hence, although studies using sociometric measures pointed to the need for attention to learning-disabled children's social relationships, many were generated either by definitional concerns within the field of learning disabilities or by an interest in the impact of mainstreaming, rather than by a concern with remedial issues. The attention currently accorded to the social difficulties of learning-disabled children is of relatively recent origin.

A second reason there have been few studies attempting to improve learning-disabled children's social status is that it is not clear what behaviors or skills these programs should address. Most programs developed for nondisabled children have focused on helping children who are withdrawn or who engage in disruptive, antisocial acts (Gresham, 1981b), problems which do not appear to be characteristic of learning-disabled children. Therefore, remediation programs directed at increasing participation or reducing disruptive behaviors are generally not appropriate, and the methods used to address these behaviors may or may not be effective in training other social skills. Further, it is not clear which of the behaviors or skills that do differentiate learning-disabled children from other children are responsible for eliciting others' low regard, or the degree to which these need to be changed in order to make others' responses more positive. In fact, it is possible that some of the behaviors that differentiate learning-disabled children actually may be adaptive responses by these children to their low sociometric status (Renshaw & Asher, 1982). Changing these behaviors might, therefore, result in exacerbating learning-disabled children's social difficulties.

Although a number of promising programs aimed at improving learning-disabled children's social skills have been proposed, systematic research on the remediation of these children's social problems has proceeded slowly. Nonetheless, there have been a number of recent studies which assessed changes in learning-disabled children's social skills or social status as a function of some type of experimental treatment (Schumaker & Hazel, 1984). These studies have examined the impact both of interventions focused on the learning-disabled child and those focused on the classroom environment and structure. Because there has been so little research in this area with elementary school children, several interventions used with learning-disabled adolescents will also be described below.

INTERVENTIONS FOCUSED ON THE CHILD

Since it has long been recognized that exposure to individuals modeling different behaviors can be a major influence on children's learning and performance, some studies have examined the effect of observing models on learning-disabled children's behavior. However, few of these have focused on models' effects on these children's social behavior. Schwartz and Bryan (1971) showed that learning-disabled children did not differ from nondisabled children in the likelihood that they would imitate charitable or greedy models. Nevertheless, the learning-disabled children made more errors in imitating the models than did the nondisabled children. Donahue and Bryan (1983) found that exposure to an audiotape of a child modeling different conversational behaviors increased the use of these behaviors by learning-disabled children.

Another intervention method used to promote improved social acceptance and behavior is a procedure in which children are given "coaching" about different social skills. In this procedure, the instructor gives low-status children verbal instructions about targeted behaviors, discusses antecedent and consequent events associated with the behaviors, provides the children with an opportunity to practice the behaviors, and then gives them feedback concerning the adequacy of their performance. In studies primarily with nondisabled students, coaching has resulted both in an increased use of the targeted social skills and an improvement in the children's sociometric status (Ladd, 1981; Oden & Asher, 1977).

A training method incorporating elements of both coaching and modeling was used in a study by Hazel, Schumaker, Sherman, & Sheldon (1982) to teach eight social skills to learning disabled, nondisabled and juvenile delinquent high school students. These particular social skills were selected because they had been judged as necessary and important for adolescents by groups of adolescents, parents and professional judges (Schumaker, Hazel, Sherman, & Sheldon, 1982). The skills included accepting and giving negative feedback, making conversation, following instructions, negotiating, giving positive feedback, problem solving, and resisting peer pressure. The training was conducted in small groups, twice weekly for 10 weeks. The adolescents discussed the skills and the situations where they might be applicable, rehearsed the skills by role-playing, and gave one another evaluative feedback. All three groups were found to show improved performance in role-playing the different skills following training, although the learning-disabled students continued to do somewhat more poorly on the cognitive problem-solving scenarios. Unfortunately, however, a generalization study that examined whether three learning-disabled students who were individually taught social skills using a similar training method found little generalization from the role-playing situations to the students' natural environment (Schumaker & Ellis, 1982).

More promising findings were reported in two other studies that used a combination of teaching techniques, including features from modeling, coaching, and reinforcement procedures. In a study teaching such behaviors as smiling and sharing to four learning-disabled children, the behaviors taught did generalize to the classroom, and were still evident 1 month after the intervention (Cooke & Apollini, 1976). LaGreca and Mesibov (1981) concentrated on teaching conversational skills to four learning-disabled boys who had been rated as having peer-interaction problems. After modeling, coaching, and behavioral rehearsal, the boys improved their conversational skills when interacting with unfamiliar peers to a level approximating the control group, that is, four learning-disabled boys who demonstrated no social skill deficits.

INTERVENTIONS FOCUSED ON THE CLASSROOM

Whereas interventions directed at specific children focus on remediating these children's social skill deficits, interventions at the classroom level focus on the potential of the classroom structure to optimize the types of interactions the children experience. The most researched classroom intervention is the use of cooperative group activities, a procedure which sometimes includes the use of rewards based on the group's combined performance.

Encouraging results were found in a variety of studies which used cooperative instructions and reward structures during academic work (Bryan, Cosden, & Pearl, 1982; Cooper, Johnson, Johnson, & Wilderson, 1980; Cosden et al., in press; Madden & Slavin, 1983; Slavin, Madden, & Leavey, 1982). For example, Madden and Slavin (1983) examined the effects of having academically handicapped children work with nonhandicapped children in groups in which they checked each other's answers on math problems and were rewarded for their group's combined performance. Participation in these cooperative groups resulted in a reduction of the number of academically handicapped children who were rejected, although no increase occurred in the number chosen as a friend or workmate. Cooperative instructions and reward structures also have been used during swimming classes, resulting in an increase in the frequency of learning-disabled boys' friendly interactions with nondisabled peers (Martino & Johnson, 1979).

Another intervention approach has focused more broadly on the classroom curriculum and organization. Odom, Jenkins, Speltz, and De-Klyen (1982) designed the Integrated Preschool Curriculum (IPC) to integrate young children at risk for learning disabilities into preschool classes with nondisabled children. The curriculum consists of a number of components, including highly structured play activities, assessment by the teacher, and direct instruction of social skills. The proportions of interactive and proximity play of the children in the IPC were compared to that of children in classrooms without this curriculum. It was found that children in the IPC classes exhibited a greater proportion of interactive and proximity play, whereas those in the comparison classes engaged in a greater proportion of isolated play. Further, in the IPC classes, the nonhandicapped children involved handicapped children in interactive play to a greater extent than in the contrast curriculum.

Meece and Wang (1982) compared the social outcomes of two types of mainstreaming programs. The first was a traditional program in which handicapped children were mainstreamed in the afternoon only; in the morning, these children received instruction in a resource room. In the second, the children were mainstreamed for the entire school day in an "adaptive learning" program that stressed both individualized instruction and student-initiated learning. Participants in the study were first-through-third grade, mildly handicapped students (a group that included mostly learning-disabled children), and nonhandicapped students. A peer nomination measure, administered in the fall of the school year, revealed that overall, fewer handicapped children were named as a desired play or work partner than would have occurred by chance. However, more of the children in the adaptive learning program received cross-group nominations (e.g., nonhandicapped children nominating handicapped children) than in the more traditional program. Classmates' ratings, assessed in the spring, indicated that the handicapped children in the traditional program were rated lower than nonhandicapped classmates, although this was not the case in the adaptive learning classroom. In addition, the handicapped children in the adaptive learning programs gave themselves higher ratings on a scale measuring their self-esteem and evaluations of their social and cognitive competence.

SUMMARY

These two models of social intervention appear to be based on different assumptions about the causes of learning-disabled children's social problems. Child-focused models appear to assume that learning-disabled children lack particular skills which are important for satisfying social interaction, and that these skills will not be acquired without explicit instruction or modeling. Although these few studies suggest that many social skills can be taught, individuals using these procedures need to be concerned with whether the newly acquired skills will be applied to settings other than the training situation. Care must be taken in choosing the particular behaviors targeted for intervention so as to not to interfere with behaviors which, in fact, actually may be helping the children cope with their situation.

In contrast to child-focused approaches, classroom-based interventions seem to reflect the belief that learning-disabled children can easily acquire the prerequisite skills and abilities, or can learn when and where to use their existing skills, if the social ecology is arranged to encourage more frequent and more meaningful interactions with nondisabled peers. Since both assessment and intervention take place in the environment where these skills are most needed, that is, instructional groups or classrooms, the concern for generalizability is minimized. This approach also seems to be less costly than interventions focused on the child in terms of teacher time, and lessens the possibility inherent in the child-focused approach that the intervention itself might draw undesirable attention to the learning-disabled child.

Depending on the nature and causes of the children's social difficulties, then, different remediation approaches seem implicated. For example, teaching particular social behaviors may be ineffective for the child who lacks the social perception to know when to apply them, and unnecessary for the child who has mastered these behaviors but is not motivated to use them. Clearly, more research is needed on methods to identify individual learning-disabled children's social deficits and the interventions best suited for their remediation. However, it is already certainly clear that learning-disabled children's relationships with others, not only their academic problems, require attention.

REFERENCES

Asher, S. R., & Renshaw, P. D, (1981). Children without friends: Social knowledge and social skills training. In S. R. Asher and J. M. Gottman (Eds.). *The Development of Children's Friendships*. (pp. 273–296). Cambridge: Cambridge University Press.

Asher, S., Renshaw, P., & Hymel, S., (1982). Peer relations and the development of social skills. In S. G. Moore and C. R. Cooper (Eds.) *The Young Child: Reviews of Research.* Vol. 3 (pp: 137–158). Washington, D.C.: National Association for the Education of Young Children.

Bachara, G. H. (1976). Empathy in learning disabled children. *Perceptual and Motor skills, 43,* 541–542.

Boersma, F. J. & Chapman, J. W. (1982). Teachers' and mothers' academic achievement expectations for learning disabled children. *Journal of School Psychology, 20,* 216–221.

Bruck, M. & Hebert, M. (1982). Correlates of learning disabled students' peer interaction patterns. *Learning Disability Quarterly, 5,* 353–362.

Bruininks, V. L. (1978a). Actual and perceived peer status of learning disabled students in mainstream programs. *Journal of Special Education, 12,* 51–58.

Bruininks, V. L. (1978b). Peer status and personality of learning disabled and nondisabled students. *Journal of Learning Disabilities, 11,* 29–34.

Bruno, R. M. (1981). Interpretation of pictorially presented social situations by learning disabled and normal children. *Journal of Learning Disabilities, 14,* 350–352.

Bryan, J., H., Bryan, T. & Sonnefeld, J. (1982). Being known by the company one keeps: The contagion of first impressions. *Learning Disability Quarterly. 3,* 19–28.

Bryan, J. H. & Perlmutter, B. (1979). Females adults' immediate impressions of learning disabled children. *Learning Disability Quarterly, 2,* 80–88.

Bryan, J. H., & Sherman, R. (1980). Immediate impressions of nonverbal ingratiation attempts by learning disabled boys. *Learning Disability Quarterly, 3,* 19–28.

Bryan, J. H., & Sonnefeld, L. J. (1981). Children's social desirability ratings of ingratiation tactics. *Learning Disability Quarterly, 4,* 287–293.

Bryan, J. H., Sonnefeld, L. J., & Greenberg, F. Z. (1981). Ingratiation preferences of learning disabled children. *Learning Disability Quarterly, 4,* 170–179.

Bryan, T. H. (1974a). Peer popularity of learning disabled children. *Journal of Learning Disabilities, 7,* 621–625.

Bryan, T. H. (1974b). An observational analysis of classroom behaviors of children with learning disabilities. *Journal of Learning Disabilities, 7,* 26–34.

Bryan, T. H. (1976). Peer popularity of learning disabled children: A replication. *Journal of Learning Disabilities, 9,* 307–311.

Bryan, T. H. (1977). Childrens' comprehension of non-verbal communication. *Journal of Learning Disabilities, 10,* 501-506.

Bryan, T. & Bryan, J. (1974). Learning disabled children's attitudes toward altruism and donation behavior. Unpublished manuscript.

Bryan, T. H., & Bryan, J. H. (1978a). Social interactions of learning disabled children. *Learning Disability Quarterly, 1,* 33–39.

Bryan, T. H. & Bryan, J. H. (1978b). *Understanding Learning Disabilities,* 2nd. Ed. Sherman Oaks, CA: Alfred.

Bryan, T., Cosden, M., & Pearl, R. (1982). The effects of cooperative goal structures and cooperative models on learning disabled and nondisabled students. *Learning Disability Quarterly, 5,* 415–421.

Bryan, T., Donahue, M., & Pearl, R. (1981a). Learning disabled children's peer interactions during a small-group problem solving task. *Learning Disability Quarterly, 4,* 13–22.

Bryan, T., Donahue, M., & Pearl, R., (1981b). Studies of learning disabled children's pragmatic competence. *Topics in Learning and Learning Disabilities, 1,* 29–39.

Bryan, T., Donahue, M., Pearl, R., & Sturm, C. (1981). Learning disabled children's conversational skills: The "TV Talk Show." *Learning Disability Quarterly, 4,* 260–270.

Bryan, T., & McGrady, H. (1972). Use of a teacher rating scale, *Journal of Learning Disabilities, 5,* 199–206.

Bryan, T., Pearl, R., Zimmerman, D., & Matthews, F. (1982). Mothers' evaluations of their learning disabled children. *Journal of Special Education, 16,* 149–160.

Bryan, T., & Pflaum, S. (1978). Social interactions of learning disabled children: A linguistic, social, and cognitive analysis. *Learning Disability Quarterly, 1,* 70–79.

Bryan, T., & Smiley, A. (1983). Learning disabled boys' performance and self-assessments on physical fitness tests. *Perceptual and Motor Skills, 56,* 443–450.

Bryan, T. & Wheeler, R. (1972). Perception of learning disabled children: The eye of the observer. *Journal of Learning Disabilities, 5,* 484–488.

Bryan, T. H., Wheeler, R., Felcan, J., & Henek, T. (1976). "Come on dummy": An observational study of children's communications. *Journal of Learning Disabilities, 9,* 661–669.

Chapman, J. W., & Boersma, F. J. (1979). Learning disabilities, locus of control and mother attitudes. *Journal of Educational Psychology. 71,* 250-258.

Chapman, R. B., Larsen, S. C., & Parker, R. M. (1979). Interactions of first–grade teachers with learning disordered children. *Journal of Learning Disabilities, 12,* 225–230.

Cook, T. P., & Apolloni, T. (1976). Developing positive social-emotional behaviors: A study of training and generalization effects. *Journal of Applied Behavior Analysis, 9,* 65–78.

Cooper, L., Johnson, D. W., Johnson, R., & Wilderson, F. (1980). The effects of cooperative, competitive, and individualistic experiences on interpersonal attraction among heterogeneous peers. *Journal of Social Psychology,111,* 243–252.

Cosden, M., Pearl, R., & Bryan, T. (in press). The effects of cooperative versus individual goal structures on learning disabled and nondisabled students. *Exceptional Children.*

Cowen, E. L., Pederson, A., Babigian, H., Izzo, L. D., & Trost, M. A. (1973). Long-term follow-up of early detected vulnerable children. *Journal of Consulting and Clinical Psychology, 41,* 438–446.

Dickstein, E. B., & Warren, D. R. (1980). Role taking deficits in learning disabled children. *Journal of Learning Disabilities, 13,* 378–382.

Doleys, D., Cartelli, L., & Doster, J. (1976). Comparison of patterns of mother-child interaction. *Journal of Learning Disabilities 9,* 371–375.

Donahue, M. L. (1981). Requesting strategies of learning disabled children. *Applied Psycholinguistics, 2,* 213–234.

Donahue, M. L. (1984). Learning disabled children's conversational competence: An attempt to activate the inactive listener. *Applied Psycholinguistics, 5,* 21–35.

Donahue, M., and Bryan, T. (1983). Conversational skills and modeling in learning disabled boys. *Applied Psycholinguistics, 4,* 251–278.

Donahue, M., Pearl, R., & Bryan, T. (1980). Learning disabled children's conversational competence: Responses to inadequate messages. *Applied Psycholinguistics, 1,* 387–403.

Donahue, M., Pearl, R., & Bryan, T. (1983). Communicative competence in learning disabled children. In I. Bialer and K. Gadow (Eds). *Advances in Learning and Behavioral Disabilities.* Vol.II (pp. 49–84). Greenwich, JAI Press.

Donahue, M., & Prescott, B. (1983). Young learning disabled children's conversational episodes in dispute episodes with peers. Chicago: Chicago Institute for the Study of Learning Disabilities.

Dorval, B., McKinney, J. D., & Feagans, L. (1982). Teachers' interaction with learning disabled children and average achievers. *Journal of Pediatric Psychology, 17,* 317–330.

Epstein, J., Berg-Cross, G., & Berg-Cross, L. (1980). Maternal expectations and birth order in families with learning disabled and normal children. *Journal of Learning Disabilities, 13,* 273–280.

Feagans, L., & McKinney, J. D. (1981). The pattern of exceptionality across domains in learning disabled children. *Journal of Applied Developmental Psychology, 1,* 313–328.

Feagans, L., & McKinney, J. D. (1982). Longitudinal studies of learning disabled children. Paper presented at the Association for Children and Adults with Learning Disabilities, Chicago.

Forness, S. R., & Esveldt, K. C. (1975). Classroom observations of children with learning and behavior problems. *Journal of Learning Disabilities, 8,* 382–385.

Garrett, M. K., & Crump, W. D. (1980). Peer acceptance, teacher references, and self-appraisal of social status among learning disabled students. *Learning Disability Quarterly, 3,* 42–48.

Gerber, G. (1976). Conflicts in values and attitudes between parents of symptomatic and normal children. *Psychological Reports, 38,* 91–98.

Gerber, P. J., & Zinkgraf, S. A. (1982). A comparative study of social-perceptual ability in learning disabled and nonhandicapped students. *Learning Disability Quarterly, 5,* 374–378.

Gettinger, M. & Fayne, H. R. (1982). Classroom behaviors during small group instruction and learning performance in learning disabled and nondisabled children. *Journal of Educational Research, 75,* 182–187.

Goldman, M., & Barclay, A. (1974). Influence of maternal attitudes on children with reading disabilities. *Perceptual and Motor Skills, 38,* 303-307.

Gresham, F. M. (1981a). Validity of social skills measures for assessing social competence in low-status children: A multivariate investigation. *Developmental Psychology, 17,* 390-398.

Gresham, F. M. (1981b). Social skills training with handicapped children: A review. *Review of Educational Research, 51,* 139–176.

Hazel, J. S., Schumaker, J. B., Sherman, J. A., & Sheldon, J. (1982). Application of a group training program in social skills and problem solving to learning disabled and nondisabled youth. *Learning Disability Quarterly, 5,* 398–408.

Hiebert, B., Wong, B., & Hunter, M. (1982). Affective influences on learning disabled adolescents. *Learning Disability Quarterly, 5,* 334–343.

Horowitz, E. C. (1981). Popularity, decentering ability, and roletaking skills in learning disabled and normal children. *Learning Disability Quarterly, 4,* 23–30.

Humphries, T., & Bauman, E. (1980). Maternal child-rearing attitudes associated with learning disabilities. *Journal of Learning Disabilities, 13,* 459-462.

Hymel, S., & Asher, S. R. (1977). Assessment and training of isolated children's social skills. Paper presented at the meetings of the Society for Research in Child Development, New Orleans. (ERIC Document Reproduction Service No. ED 136 930).

Keogh, B. K., Tchir, C., & Windeguth-Behn, A. (1974). Teachers' perceptions of educationally high risk children. *Journal of Learning Disabilities, 7,* 43–50.

Knight-Arest, I. (1984). Communicative effectiveness of learning disabled and normally achieving 10- to 13-year-old boys. *Learning Disability Quarterly, 7,* 237-245.

Ladd, G. W. (1981). Effectiveness of a social learning method for enhancing children's social interaction and peer acceptance. *Child Development, 52,* 171–178.

LaGreca, A., & Mesibov, G. 1981. Facilitating interpersonal functioning with peers in learning disabled children. *Journal of Learning Disabilities, 14,* 197-199.

McCarthy, J. M., & Paraskevopoulos, J. (1969). Behavior patterns of learning disabled, emotionally disturbed, and average children. *Exceptional Children, 36,* 69-74.

McKinney, J. D., & Feagans, L. (1983). Adaptive classroom behavior of learning disabled students. *Journal of Learning Disabilities, 16,* 360–367.

McKinney, J. D., McClure, S., & Feagans, L. (1982). Classroom behavior of learning disabled children *Learning Disability Quarterly, 5,* 45–52.

McMichael, P. (1980). Reading difficulties, behavior, and social status. *Journal of Educational Psychology, 72,* 76–86.

Madden, N. A., & Slavin, (1983). Effects of cooperative learning on the social acceptance of mainstreamed academically handicapped students. *Journal of Special Education, 17,* 171–182.

Maheady, L., & Maitland, G. (1982). Assessing social perception abilities in learning disabled students. *Learning Disability Quarterly, 5,* 363-370.

Martino, L., & Johnson, D. W. (1979). Cooperative and individualistic experiences among disabled and normal children. *The Journal of Social Psychology, 107,* 177–183.

Meece, J. L. & Wang, M. C. (1982). A comparative study of the social attitudes and behaviors of mildly handicapped children in two mainstreaming programs. Paper presented at the Annual Meeting of the American Educational Research Association, New York.

Meyer, W. U. (1982). Indirect communications about perceived ability estimates. *Journal of Educational Psychology, 74,* 888–897.

Moore, J., and Fine, M. J. (1978). Regular and special class teachers' perceptions of normal and exceptional children and their attitudes toward mainstreaming. *Psychology in the Schools, 15,* 253–259.

Nicholls, J. G. & Miller, A. T. (1984). Development and its discontents: The differentiation of the concept of ability. In J. G. Nicholls (Ed.). *The Development of Achievement Motivation* (pp.185–219). Greenwich, JAI Press.

Noel, N. M. (1980). Referential communication abilities of learning disabled children. *Learning Disability Quarterly, 3,* 70–75.

Oden, S. & Asher, S. (1977). Coaching children in social skills for friendship making. *Child Development, 48,* 495–506.

Odom, S. L., Jenkins, J. R., Speltz, M. C., & DeKlyen, M. (1982). Promoting social integration of young children at risk for learning disabilities. *Learning Disability Quarterly, 5,* 379-387.

Owen, R. W., Adams, P. A., Forrest, T., Stolz, L. M. & Fisher, S. (1971). Learning disorders in children: Sibling studies. *Monographs of the Society for Research in Child Development, 36,* No. 144.

Pearl, R. (1982). Learning disabled children's attributions for success and failure: A replication with a labeled learning disabled sample. *Learning Disability Quarterly, 5,* 183–186.

Pearl, R., & Bryan, T. (1982a). Mothers' attributions for their learning disabled child's successes and failures. *Learning Disability Quarterly, 5,* 53–57.

Pearl, R., & Bryan, T. (1982b). Learning disabled children's self-esteem and desire for approval. Paper presented at the Conference of the Association for Children and Adults with Learning Disabilities, Chicago.

Pearl, R., Bryan, T. H., & Donahue, M. (1980). Learning disabled children's attributions for success and failure. *Learning Disability Quarterly, 3,* 3–9.

Pearl, R., & Cosden, M. (1982). Sizing up a situation: Learning disabled children's understanding of social interactions. *Learning Disability Quarterly, 5,* 371–373.

Pearl, R., Donahue, M., & Bryan, T. (in press). The development of tact: Children's strategies for delivering bad news. *Journal of Applied Developmental Psychology.*

Pearl, R., Donahue, M., & Bryan, T. (1981). Children's responses to nonexplicit requests for clarification. *Perceptual and Motor Skills, 53* 919–925.

Perlmutter B., & Bryan, J. H. (1984). First impressions, ingratiation and the learning disabled child. *Journal of Learning Disabilities, 17,* 157–161.

Renshaw, P. D. & Asher, S. R. (1982). Social competence and peer status. In K. H. Rubin and H. S. Ross (Eds.) *Peer Relationships and Social Skills in Childhood.* (pp. 375–395). New York: Springer–Verlag.

Richey, D. D., & McKinney, J. D. (1978). Classroom behavioral styles of learning disabled children. *Journal of Learning Disabilities, 11,* 297–302.

Roff, M., Sells, S. B., & Golden, M. M. (1972). *Social adjustment and personality development in children.* Minneapolis: University of Minnesota Press.

Sainato, D. M., Zigmond, N., & Strain, P. (1983). Social status and initiations of interation by learning disabled students in a regular education setting. *Analysis and Intervention in Developmental Disabilities, 3,* 71-87.

Schofield, J. W. (1981). Complementary and conflicting identities: Images and interactions in an interracial school. In S. R. Asher and J. M. Gottman (Eds.). *The Development of Children's Friendships* (pp. 53–90). Cambridge: Cambridge University Press.

Schumaker, J. B., & Ellis, E. S. (1982). Social skills training of LD adolescents; a generalization study. *Learning Disability Quarterly, 5,* 409–414.

Schumaker, J. B., & Hazel, J. S. (1984). Social skills assessment and training for the learning disabled: Who's on first and what's on second? Part II. *Journal of Learning Disabilities, 17,* 492–499.

Schumaker, J. B., Hazel, J. S., Sherman, J. A., & Sheldon, J. (1982). Social skills performances of learning disabled, non-learning disabled, and delinquent adolescents. *Learning Disability Quarterly, 5,* 388-397.

Schwartz, T., & Bryan, J. (1971). Imitation and judgments of children with learning disabilities. *Exceptional Children, 38,* 157–158.

Scranton, T. & Ryckman, D. (1979). Sociometric status of learning disabled children in an integrative program. *Journal of Learning Disabilities, 12,* 402–407.

Sheare, J. B. (1978). The impact of resource programs upon the self-concept and peer acceptance of learning disabled children. *Psychology in the Schools, 1978, 15,* 406–412.

Siperstein, G. N., Bopp, M. J., & Bak, J. J. (1978). Social status of learning disabled children. *Journal of Learning Disabilities, 11,* 98–102.

Siperstein, G. N., & Goding, M. J. (1983). Social integration of learning disabled children in regular classrooms. Greenwich, CT: JAI Press.

Slavin, R. E., Madden, N. A., & Leavey, M. (1982). Combining cooperative learning and individualized instruction: Effects on the social acceptance, achievement and behavior of mainstreamed students. Paper presented at the Conference of the American Educational Research Association, New York.

Sobol, M. P., Earn, B. M., Bennett, D., & Humphries, T. (1983). A categorical analysis of the social attributions of learning disabled children. *Journal of Abnormal Child Psychology, 11,* 217–228.

Spekman, N. (1981). A study of the dyadic verbal communication abilities of learning disabled and normally achieving fourth-and fifth-grade boys. *Learning Disability Quarterly, 4,* 139–151.

Stone, W. L. & LaGreca, A. M. (1984). Comprehension of nonverbal communication: A reexamination of the social competencies of learning disabled children. *Journal of Abnormal Child Psychology, 12,* 505–518.

Strag, G. A. (1972). Comparative behavioral ratings of parents with severe mentally retarded, special learning disability and normal children. *Journal of Learning Disabilities, 5,* 631–635.

Sutherland, J. H., Algozzine, B., Ysseldyke, J. E., & Young, S. (1979). What can I say after I say LD? Research Report No. 16, Institute for Research on Learning Disabilities, Minneapolis: University of Minnesota.

Torgesen, J. (1980). Conceptual and educational implications of the use of efficient task strategies by learning disabled children. *Journal of Learning Disabilities, 13,* 364–371.

Touliatos, J., & Lindholm, B. W. (1980). Dimensions of problem behavior in learning disabled and normal children. *Perceptual and Motor Skills, 50,* 145–146.

Weinstein, R. S. (1982). Expectations in the classroom: The student perspective. Paper presented at the meetings of the American Educational Research Association, New York.

Wetter, J. (1972). Parent attitudes toward learning disability. *Journal of Special Education, 38,* 490–491.

Wiig, E. H., & Harris, S. P. (1974). Perception and interpretation of nonverbally expressed emotions by adolescents with learning disabilities. *Perceptual and Motor Skills, 38,* 239–245.

Wiig, E., & Semel, E. (1980). *Language assessment and intervention for the learning disabled.* Columbus, Ohio: Charles E. Merrill.

Wong, B. Y., & Wong, R. (1980). Role-taking skills in normal achieving and learning disabled children. *Learning Disability Quarterly, 3,* 11–18.

8

Motivational Problems of Learning-Disabled Children: Individual Differences and Their Implications for Treatment

BARBARA G. LICHT
JANET A. KISTNER

INTRODUCTION

In recent years, there has been considerable interest in understanding the motivational consequences of chronic academic failure in learning-disabled (LD) children. Although there has been a great deal of controversy surrounding the definition of learning disabilities (e.g., Shepard, Smith, & Vojir, 1983; Ysseldyke, Algozzine, Shinn, & McGue, 1979), there is little dispute that the children identified as LD all have experienced repeated academic failures. It has been proposed (e.g., Douglas & Peters, 1979; Thomas, 1979; Torgesen, 1980) that, as a consequence of these failures, LD children learn to doubt their intellectual abilities and come to view their achievement efforts as futile. According to this analysis, these beliefs lead the children to become frustrated and/or to give up very quickly in the face of difficulty. This, in turn, contributes to further failure which reinforces the belief that they do not have the abilities to succeed. As this belief is strengthened, even their successes are likely to be interpreted in its light. Therefore, whatever successes the children do achieve are likely to be seen as indications that they were lucky, the teacher was helpful, or that the task was particularly easy. Experiencing

225

Psychological and Educational
Perspectives on Learning Disabilities

some success, then, is not likely to provide much satisfaction for these children, nor is it likely to raise their level of confidence. Thus, what has been proposed is a vicious cycle which may result in children who exert very little effort, gain little pleasure from academic tasks, and perhaps, even devalue academic achievement altogether.

In the present chapter, we will provide evidence that a large number of LD children enter this vicious cycle. However, we will show that there are also individual differences among LD children in terms of how they interpret and respond to their failures. For example, some LD children believe that continued effort will result in success; and consequently, they tend to persist in the face of difficulty. The existence of these individual differences demonstrates that although entrance into the vicious cycle is very likely for LD children, it is not inevitable. The purpose of this chapter is to examine some of the factors that are likely to contribute to individual differences among LD children in terms of how they are affected by their academic failures. On the basis of this examination, we will suggest some potential strategies for preventing children from entering the vicious cycle. Finally, we will explore some strategies for dealing with children who have already developed the debilitating belief that their achievement efforts are futile.

As suggested, there is considerable evidence that LD children are likely to enter the vicious cycle (see Licht, 1983, for review). First, the achievement-related beliefs of LD children generally conform to the predictions. When they approach new academic tasks, LD children tend to hold lower expectations for success than their peers (Boersma & Chapman, 1981; Butkowsky, 1982; Butkowsky & Willows, 1980); and when they do succeed, LD children are less likely to see this as reflecting on their abilities (Butkowsky & Willows, 1980; Pearl, 1982; Pearl, Bryan, & Herzog, 1983). Instead, they are likely to credit their successes to luck (Pearl, 1982) or to the ease of the task (Butkowsky & Willows, 1980). Their failures, however, are seen as reflections of their abilities. LD children are more likely than their peers to attribute their difficulties to insufficient ability (Butkowsky, 1982; Butkowsky & Willows, 1980; Licht, Kistner, Ozkaragoz, Shapiro, & Clausen, 1985; Palmer, Drummond, Tollison, & Zinkgraff, 1982); and they are less likely to view their difficulties as changeable through their own efforts (Butkowsky & Willows, 1980; Licht et al., 1985; Pearl, 1982; Pearl, Bryan & Donahue, 1980). There is even some evidence that LD children may generalize these beliefs to tasks on which they have not experienced failure (Butkowsky, 1982; Butkowsky & Willows, 1980).

The beliefs of LD children may, in part, reflect reality. That is, many of their difficulties may, indeed, stem from ability deficits. However, as suggested earlier, there is evidence that adoption of these beliefs contributes to further problems. When children believe that their failures are due to insufficient ability, this leads to a deterioration in their performance on difficult tasks. For some, deterioration results from lessening their efforts. Others may continue to try, but are unable to do their best because of anxiety or the distracting things they say to themselves (e.g., "I knew I couldn't learn this") (Diener & Dweck, 1978; Miller, in press; see also Wine, 1982). In either case, this results in a lower level of performance than these children are capable of achieving. In contrast, when children view their failures as an indication that they did not try hard enough or that they did not use the proper strategy, they are more likely to maintain or even improve their performance in the face of difficulty (Andrews & Debus, 1978; Chapin & Dyck, 1976; Diener & Dweck, 1978; Dweck, 1975; Dweck & Reppucci, 1973, Fowler & Peterson, 1981; Licht & Dweck, 1984; Weiner, 1979). These results are compelling as they have been obtained in both correlational and experimental studies. Studies of the latter kind have tended to be treatment studies where children who attributed their failures to insufficient ability were taught to attribute their failures to insufficient effort instead. Comparisons with control groups demonstrated that altering children's causal attributions for failure resulted in increased persistence in the face of difficulty. (These treatment studies are discussed in more detail later in this chapter.) It should be noted here that teaching these children that failure implies they need to try harder not only results in increased persistence, but, generally, it is realistic as well. That is, existence of ability deficits in children does not imply that their efforts are completely useless. Rather, continued effort is even *more* essential for these children.

The data presented thus far strongly suggest that LD children are at risk for developing motivational problems that interfere with their work. However, just as all LD children are not homogeneous with respect to the nature and degree of their intellectual deficits (Shepard, *et al.*, 1983; Torgesen, 1982), LD children are not homogeneous with respect to the way in which they respond to repeated failures. Although a large proportion of LD children do feel incapable of succeeding on even the simplest academic tasks, there are some who appear to have maintained confidence in their abilities by blaming the teacher for their difficulties. Others respond more adaptively by attributing their difficulties on classroom tasks to insufficient effort (Licht, *et al.*, 1985). In line with these different beliefs, not all LD children respond to difficulty by giving up (Licht *et al.*, 1985; Speece, McKinney, & Appelbaum, 1985).

There are several factors that may be contributing to individual differences among LD children in terms of how they interpret and respond to their academic failures. Perhaps, the most straightforward prediction is that the children who experience failure most frequently would be the most likely to doubt their abilities and to show a deterioration of motivation. Some support for this prediction comes from a recent study (Kistner & Licht, 1984), which found that LD children who were performing at or above grade level in at least one academic subject were significantly more likely at attribute their failures to insufficient effort than LD children who were below grade level in all areas. Other relevant data come from studies which differentiated reading deficits from other deficits. It has been suggested that since reading skills are necessary to succeed in most all subjects, those who have difficulty in reading are expected to have the most pervasive academic problems. Butkowsky (1982), for example, found that children who were disabled in reading were more apt to doubt their abilities and show low persistence than children who were disabled in math, even when the experimental task involved math. In a similar vein, Black (1974) examined a group of elementary school children, all of whom had been referred to a clinic for learning problems and were failing one or more subjects. He identified a subgroup of this population that was at or above grade level on standardized reading tests and another subgroup that was reading below grade level. As predicted, the subgroup with documented reading problems had lower self-concept scores than the other subgroup and showed a greater decrease in their self-concept over the years. (The most plausible explanation of these studies is that the more frequent children's failures, the more likely they are to doubt their abilities. However, one can not rule out the possibility that the direction of causality is reversed. That is, perhaps, the belief that they are incapable of succeeding leads to the least amount of effort and, thus, the greatest amount of failure.)

Although the frequency of failure is one of the factors that seems to affect how strongly LD children will doubt their abilities, it is by no means the only factor. Not only do we find that some children who fail frequently are confident that they will eventually succeed, but there are also some highly successful children who seriously lack confidence in their abilities (Licht, Linden, Brown, & Sexton, 1984; see Licht & Dweck, 1983 for review). This underscores the importance of looking for factors other than children's actual abilities which can contribute to their motivational patterns.

Research shows that a number of classroom variables may contribute to individual differences in how children interpret and respond to their failures. For example, even when LD children exhibit similar academic deficits, they may receive different types of feedback from their teacher.

Although some LD children are likely to receive negative feedback for their conduct (e.g., disruptive behavior) in addition to their work, the negative feedback that others receive may refer exclusively to the intellectual quality of their work. Additionally, while some LD children may receive praise for an effortful attempt, others may receive praise only when their answer is completely correct. As discussed later, these and other feedback differences can have important, and sometimes unexpected, consequences for children's beliefs about their abilities. A number of researchers also have suggested that the way in which teachers structure the classroom more generally (e.g., the degree to which the quality of each child's work is judged against the performance of others versus judged against his/her own past performance) may determine the degree to which children view academic failure as reflecting on their abilities as opposed to their efforts.

There is also a growing body of research which finds developmental differences in how children interpret and respond to failure. This is important to our analysis for two reasons. First, two LD children may manifest different levels of confidence and persistence in the face of failure simply because they differ in age, and children of different ages react differently to failure. Second, specific patterns of teacher feedback and specific classroom structures may have different effects, depending on the age of the child.

Family variables may also influence the beliefs and behavior of LD children (e.g., Chapman & Boersma, 1979; Pearl & Bryan, 1982). However, the focus of the present chapter is on the classroom environment—particularly elementary school. Our goal is to clarify how classroom variables, developmental differences, and the interaction of these factors can contribute to individual differences in the confidence and persistence of LD children.

CHILDREN'S PERCEPTIONS OF THEIR ABILITIES: A DEVELOPMENTAL ANALYSIS

As suggested earlier, there are developmental differences in how failure affects children's perceptions of their own abilities. However, before we examine these differences, it is instructive first to examine developmental differences in children's conceptualizations of ability, or intelligence. This will provide a framework for understanding developmental differences in how children respond to failure (see Dweck & Elliott, 1983; Nicholls & Miller, 1984; Stipek, 1984, for discussions).

Although there has been a great deal of controversy over the years surrounding the definition of intelligence (e.g., see Cronbach, 1975; Tuddenham, 1962), most adults tend to think of intelligence as the capacity to learn new things quickly and easily. Thus, someone who acquires new knowledge and skills with very little effort is considered to be more intelligent than someone who has to expend a great deal of effort to learn the same material. Additionally, although knowledge and skills can be increased continuously through one's efforts, one's intellectual abilities are considered to be relatively stable. Social comparisons also play an important role in the adult's view of intelligence. That is, successful completion of a task only can be taken as evidence of high ability if that task is difficult for most of one's peers; failure to master a task only is indicative of low ability if most of one's peers can master that task (Jagacinski & Nicholls, 1984; Nicholls & Miller, 1984).

In contrast to adults, children in the very early school years (i.e., kindergarten and first grade) tend to view intellectual ability as a direct, positive function of how hard you try. In other words, the more you try, the more you will learn, and the more intelligent you will become (Harari & Covington, 1981; Nicholls, 1978; Stipek, 1981; Stipek & Tannatt, 1984; see Nicholls & Miller, 1984, for review). Thus, unlike adults, who tend to view intelligence as a stable capacity or entity, young children consider intelligence to be incrementing continually through their efforts (see Bandura & Dweck, 1983). Consistent with their tendency to see effort and ability as positively related, young children often view successes that have been achieved with a great deal of effort as evidence of higher ability than when the *same* success is achieved with very little effort (Kun, 1977; Nicholls & Miller, 1984). Additionally, social comparisons enter less prominently into the judgments of young children (Boggiano & Ruble, 1979; Feld, Ruhland, & Gold, 1979; Nicholls, 1978; Ruble, Boggiano, Feldman, & Loebl, 1980; Ruble, Parsons, & Ross, 1976; Stipek & Tannatt, 1984). They need not perform better than, or even as well as, their peers to rate their abilities as high. Very young children are likely to feel that they are high in ability simply by virtue of the fact that they have mastered a new task or that they performed better than in the past (Nicholls & Miller, 1984).

Over the school years, children undergo gradual changes in how they view the construct of intelligence. One of the earlier changes concerns the use of social comparison information. Although children as young as kindergartners will, to some degree, use information about the performance of others to infer the difficulty of a task (Shaklee, 1976), it is generally not until they are at least 7 years old that the majority of children understand that they must perform better than their peers to be considered high in ability (Nicholls, 1978, 1980; Ruble *et al.*, 1980; Ruble *et al.*, 1976). However, most 7-year-olds still tend to believe that their abilities are changeable through their efforts. Thus, being low in ability is not necessarily seen as a permanent state of affairs.

There are some conditions (e.g., when the questions asked of children place little demands on their memory and the instructions orient them toward an "entity" view of intelligence) under which 7-year-olds (or even younger children) will acknowledge that someone with low ability will have to work harder than someone with high ability (Karabenick & Heller, 1976; Surber, 1980); and there are a small number of young children who do view ability as stable (Dweck & Bempechat, 1984). However, it is not until age 10 that the majority of children begin to view intelligence as a capacity that limits the utility of their efforts (Nicholls, 1978; Nicholls & Miller, 1984; Rholes, Blackwell, Jordan, & Walters, 1980). Even at age 10, the concept of intelligence as a fixed capacity is not fully developed; it may not become fully developed until age 13 or even later (Harari & Covington, 1981; Nicholls, 1978).

There are two important implications of this developmental analysis for understanding how children at different ages are affected by failure (see Nicholls & Miller, 1984; Stipek, 1984). First, one would predict that prior to age 7, children who were performing more poorly than their peers would not feel that their ability was low as long as they were regularly making progress and learning new things. Second, even after age 7, if these children conclude that they are low in ability, this conclusion should not be seriously debilitating until around age 10, since prior to that time, ability is still seen as changeable through their efforts. Thus, they can still hold onto the possibility that, with continued effort, they can become high in ability. However, by age 10 and beyond, children's growing belief that intelligence is a stable capacity makes the implications of being low in ability more serious. Therefore, they should be more debilitated when faced with information that reflects negatively on their ability.

There is considerable evidence to support the prediction that, with increasing age, comes increasing vulnerability to the debilitating effects of failure. Some researchers have examined the degree to which young children who are performing poorly in school are aware of their low academic standing. The most typical finding is that it is not until age 7 or even 8 that there is a significant relationship between children's actual achievements and their self-ratings of achievement or ability (Eshel & Klein, 1981; Nicholls, 1978, 1979; Stipek, 1981). In the earlier years, children's self-ratings tend to be unrealistically high, with most children rating themselves near the top of the class. These self-ratings show a steady decline over the years (reflecting increased accuracy) (Nicholls,

1978; Rholes *et al.*, 1980; Ruble *et al.*, 1980; Stipek & Tannatt, 1984), with a very noticeable drop occurring between second and third grades (Eshel & Klein, 1981).

There is direct evidence that failure is most likely to have seriously debilitating effects on children's performances after age 10. Rholes et al. (1980) examined the degree to which kindergarten, first-, third-, and fifth-graders were affected by failure on an achievement-type task. Although children in the first, third, and fifth grades all lowered their ratings of their ability to perform the task as a result of experiencing failure, it was only the fifth-graders who also showed a decrease in persistence and performance. Similarly, Miller (in press) found that sixth-graders showed debilitation of performance following failure, but second-graders did not.

On the basis of the developmental data just presented, it seems reasonable to predict that young LD children will be less likely than older ones to conclude that they are low in ability and to decrease their achievement efforts as a result of failure. It is important to note, however, that although the data clearly suggest that young children are less vulnerable to the debilitating effects of failure, the data do not suggest that young children are *immune*. Although children's affective responses to failure become stronger with age, children in the first grade (Ruble *et al.*, 1980), and even earlier (Ruble *et al.*, 1976), rate their mood more negatively after experiencing failure than success. This may be an important finding as it suggests a noncognitive mechanism which may mediate the effects of failure for younger children (see Seligman & Maier, 1967). That is, although young children may not understand the long-term implications of their failure experiences, the fact that being told that your answer is wrong is less pleasant than experiencing success may be enough to cause young LD children to dislike academic tasks (see Torgesen & Licht, 1983, for discussion). After all, children need not believe they are low in ability to prefer being off-task to working. Along these same lines, Harter (1978) reviewed research on effectance motivation, which suggests that when children in early childhood fail in their attempts to master intellectual tasks, mastery of these tasks may lose (or fail to develop) reinforcement value.

Research on the consistency and salience of failure also supports the contention that young children are not completely immune to the debilitating effects of failure. Specifically, this research suggests that there are some conditions under which certain individuals will become aware of their academic standing at an earlier age than is typical. Stipek (1981) hypothesized that when children experience failure on a very consistent basis, they are more likely to become aware of their abilities at an early age. To test this, she examined the relationship between the actual classroom achievements of children in kindergarten through the third grade and the children's evaluations of their own abilities. However, unlike previous researchers who correlated these two variables across all members of the classrooms, Stipek (1981) only employed children who were in the lower and upper thirds of their class. She did this so as to include only children who would have received fairly consistent failure versus success feedback. Her results confirmed the predictions. Whereas previous researchers did not find a significant relationship between children's achievements and their self-ratings before the third or fourth grade, Stipek (1981) found this relationship to be significant as early as the second grade. Perhaps this relationship would have emerged even earlier if more extreme groups of low- versus high-achievers were employed (see also Shaklee, 1976).

Even if children do not experience failure on a consistent basis, there are some classroom variables that may make the failures they do experience very salient to them. For example, it appears that when children's relative performances are highly visible to them (e.g., by the use of public star charts), then even kindergarten and first-grade children may accurately assess their academic standing (Stipek & Tannatt, 1984; see also Stipek, Roberts, & Sanborn, 1983, cited in Stipek, 1984). Thus, although very young children typically do not incorporate the level of their past performances into their self-evaluations, there are some factors that may cause them to do so.

There are also data which suggest that some children under age 10 may show the behavioral consequences of failure. Research on children with arithmetic problems shows that children's past performance and the type of feedback they receive from the teacher can influence their feelings of self-efficacy (Bandura & Schunk, 1981; Schunk, 1982; Schunk, 1983). The research also suggests that low self-efficacy can have a negative impact on their subsequent persistence. Although each of these studies included some 10-year-olds in their sample, the average age of the subjects was between 8–9 (see also Hisama, 1976). A recent study by Hebert and Dweck (1984) found that children's beliefs about their abilities can have behavioral consequences at an even earlier age. Preschool children were made to experience success at one task, but were unable to complete another. When given the option of returning to one of the two tasks, the majority of children demonstrated persistence by returning to the uncompleted (i.e., failure) task; and they maintained a highly positive mood throughout. There were, however, a number of children who chose to return to the task they had successfully completed. What is particularly noteworthy is that the children who chose the success task were more likely to attribute their difficulties to insufficient ability. Perhaps, these results emerged at such an early age because of the highly salient failure and success experiences in this study.

In sum, the research shows that young children are considerably less vulnerable to the debilitating effects of failure than are older children. Those under the age of 7 are likely to maintain a high opinion of their abilities; and even when they do conclude that they are low in ability, this may not lead to persistence problems until late elementary school. Thus, some of the differences among LD children in their motivational patterns may reflect differences in their ages. However, even within a given age, there are important individual differences. Some very young LD children may come to believe that their efforts are fruitless and show low persistence as a result. Likewise, there appear to be some older LD children who have maintained more adaptive achievement orientations. Individual differences in the magnitude of children's learning problems are, in part, responsible. However, there are other important determinants as well. In the sections that follow, we will examine some classroom variables that seem to mediate whether children's learning problems will foster the development of maladaptive beliefs and behaviors in the elementary school years.

PATTERNS OF TEACHER FEEDBACK

As suggested earlier, the specific pattern of teacher feedback that children receive appears to be an important determinant of children's self-evaluations. Thus, LD children who receive different kinds of teacher feedback may develop different beliefs about their abilities and show different levels of persistence when they confront difficulty.

In the late 1960s and early 1970s, it was frequently argued that the majority of children with learning problems received considerably less praise and more criticism than their peers, and that this pattern of feedback communicated to the children that the teacher thought poorly of their abilities (Rosenthal & Jacobson, 1968). Whereas the general proposition that teacher expectancies can influence children's behavior has received some recent support (Raudenbush, 1984; see Brophy, 1983, for review), researchers have challenged the specific proposition that high rates of criticism and low rates of praise necessarily convey low teacher expectancies as well as the proposition that poor achievers regularly receive this particular pattern of feedback.

THE TYPE OF FEEDBACK THAT CHILDREN WITH LEARNING
PROBLEMS ARE LIKELY TO RECEIVE

Although some classroom observations have found that low achievers receive lower rates of praise and higher rates of criticism than do high achievers (e.g., Brophy & Good, 1970; Cooper & Baron, 1977), there appears to be considerable variability among teachers in the degree to which they give this differential treatment to high versus low achievers (Babad, Inbar, & Rosenthal, 1982; Weinstein, Marshall, Brattesani, & Middlestadt, 1982; see Brophy, 1983 for review). In fact, many teachers show the reverse pattern (Alpert, 1974; Haskins, Walden, & Ramey, 1983; Weinstein, 1976). That is, they give *higher* rates of praise and *lower* rates of criticism to low achievers in an apparent attempt to encourage them. At times, when these children fail to produce any work that is praiseworthy, teachers may even give praise after a relatively poor performance (Brophy, 1981).

In addition to individual differences among teachers, there are behavioral differences among children which seem to elicit different patterns of teacher feedback. For example, the children who are most likely to receive more praise and less criticism than their performances would warrant are the ones teachers perceive as low in ability, but high in effort (Brophy & Evertson, 1981; Rest, Nierenberg, Weiner, & Heckhausen, 1973; Weiner & Kukla, 1970). Children who appear consistently to be unhappy are also likely to receive high rates of praise and low rates of criticism. In contrast, children who are defiant and pose classroom management problems are likely to receive high rates of criticism, as are children who are consistently restless and/or careless. Finally, there are some children who seem to elicit both high rates of criticism for their inappropriate behavior as well as high rates of praise and encouragement. These are the children described as immature and those described as low in both persistence and ability (Brophy & Evertson, 1981). In general, then, it seems that teachers respond with more empathy and are more likely to use praise as a means of encouragement when children's failures appear to be due to factors that are beyond their control (Brophy & Rohrkemper, 1981; Cooper & Burger, 1980; Medway, 1979).

Since LD children variously have been described by almost all of the above-mentioned behavioral characteristics, one might predict that, as a group, they would receive both higher rates of praise and of criticism than their peers. In fact, there is some evidence for this hypothesis (Chapman, Larsen, & Parker, 1979; Dorval, McKinney, & Feagans, 1982). However, in view of recent work demonstrating that there are different behavioral subtypes within the LD group (McKinney & Feagans, 1983; Speece *et al.*, 1985), the most reasonable prediction is that different subtypes are likely to receive different patterns of teacher feedback. For example, one might predict that the subset of LD children who are characterized by conduct problems (e.g., disruptiveness) will receive high rates of criticism and low rates of praise. However, teachers might go out of their way to praise those LD children who are viewed as "considerate and hard-working," even though the quality of their work may be no better than the work of the children with conduct problems. Still other subtypes might receive somewhat different patterns of feedback. As described next, these different patterns of teacher feedback can contribute to further variability among LD children in terms of the beliefs they are likely to develop concerning their abilities.

THE CONSEQUENCES OF DIFFERENT PATTERNS OF
TEACHER FEEDBACK

As suggested earlier, it originally was hypothesized that low rates of praise and high rates of criticism lead children to believe that the teacher thinks poorly of their abilities. Although there is evidence that this can occur, more recent work shows that it is not always the case. In fact, for some children, the reverse may actually occur. As discussed in the last section, teachers are likely to praise poor work if they perceive the student to be low in ability and high in effort. It was hypothesized (Meyer, Bachmann, Biermann, Hempelmann, Ploger, & Spiller, 1979; Weinstein, 1976) that recipients of this feedback would accurately infer the teacher's perceptions that led to the feedback. Thus, praise for poor work should lead students to believe the teacher thinks they are low in ability. A systematic series of laboratory studies conducted by Meyer *et al.* (1979) provides convincing evidence that this does occur—at least for most adults and teenagers. Their results for children in late elementary school (fifth grade) suggest that the more cognitively advanced children interpret the feedback in a manner similar to teenagers and adults, whereas the less-advanced ones do not. Instead, the less-advanced children of this age seem more likely to interpret the teacher's feedback at face value. That is, praise is interpreted as a positive reflection on their abilities, and criticism is interpreted as reflecting negatively.

An investigation by Dweck, Davidson, Nelson, and Enna (1978) also demonstrates that some children in the late elementary school years do not take praise and criticism at face value. More specifically, their results suggest that when a large proportion of negative feedback refers to nonintellectual matters such as neatness, instruction following, or bad conduct—factors that reflect more on the children's efforts than their abilities—then children become less likely to interpret bad grades as an indication that they are low in ability. Instead, they are likely to interpret these as indicating that they were not trying hard enough or, perhaps, as a reflection of the teacher's negative attitude toward them. (Although blaming the teacher may be less adaptive than blaming their own efforts, attributing their difficulties to the teacher may not be as debilitating in the long run as attributing their difficulties to insufficient ability [Dweck, Goetz, & Strauss, 1980; Licht et al., 1985].) By contrast, when the teacher rarely criticizes the children for nonintellectual matters (i.e., negative feedback is only given for intellectual matters such as the correctness of the child's answers), then whatever negative feedback the children do receive (even if it occurs infrequently) is more likely to be viewed as reflecting negatively on their abilities. In a similar vein, Dweck et al. (1978) also suggested that when praise is given frequently for nonintellectual matters—such as compliance or neatness—then praise may cease to be seen as reflecting positively on the children's abilities. Further, this may occur even in cases where the teacher actually does think highly of the child's abilities.

In the early elementary school years, it appears that children are more likely to interpret the teacher's feedback at face value, that is, praise implies high ability; criticism implies low ability. For example, in the Meyer et al. (1979) study, the vast majority of the third-graders (83%) responded in this way. Other research (Meid, 1971, cited in Harter, 1978) using first-graders as subjects, indicates that when young children are presented with both subjective evaluations from the teacher and objective performance data, it is the teacher evaluations that have the greatest impact on the children's self-evaluations. This suggests that, when teachers give praise after an objectively poor performance, children in early elementary school will tend to believe they have done well (see also Weiner, Graham, Stern, & Lawson, 1982).

In contrast to the studies just mentioned, some studies of teacher effectiveness suggest that some children in the early and mid-elementary school years may respond in the manner that is more characteristic of older students. For example, it has been shown that in high socioeconomic (SES) schools, the most effective teachers in second, third (Brophy & Evertson, 1976), and fourth grades (Good, Ebmeier, & Beckerman, 1978) gave relatively little praise of any kind, and, at times, used mild criticism to convey high expectancies and encourage improvement. Results for low SES schools showed the reverse. That is, the teachers who were successful with low socioeconomic children often praised effortful attempts, even when the answers were not entirely correct. They also gave relatively little criticism for poor work, although improper conduct (e.g., disruptiveness) was criticized (see Brophy, 1979).

Perhaps this SES difference occurs because the teachers' feedback is interpreted differently by high versus low SES children; or perhaps, the positive feedback given to low SES children serves to make an otherwise negative environment more positive.

In sum, although the data concerning the consequences of different patterns of teacher feedback are complex, some consistencies do emerge. For adults, teenagers, and cognitively advanced elementary school children, praise for effort and work habits may lead students to discount teacher praise as a positive reflection on their abilities. Therefore, giving high rates of praise for nonintellectual matters may inadvertently lead to lower levels of confidence. However, for young students, particularly those of low SES and/or those with learning problems, praising an effortful attempt may be an effective motivational strategy. Thus, this type of feedback may be one of the factors that enables some LD children to maintain their confidence and motivation. In fact, it is the opinion of many teachers that low-achieving students need this kind of encouragement (Haskins *et al.*, 1983). However, it is very important that this conclusion be viewed tentatively until researchers examine the long-term effects of this type of feedback in studies where the teacher's feedback is experimentally manipulated. In other words, the research which showed that the teachers who were most effective with low achievers used this type of feedback was correlational. Thus, it is possible that the effectiveness of these teachers was due to some other aspect(s) of their teaching strategies.

Furthermore, when researchers do test the long-term effectiveness of using praise to encourage poor achievers, they are likely to find that simply praising children for performing very easy tasks that require little effort is not likely to promote persistence in the face of difficulty (Chapin & Dyck, 1976; Dweck, 1975). Undoubtedly, to be effective in the long run, this positive feedback should be contingent on *effortful* attempts and should convey specific information about what would lead to further improvements (see also Brophy, 1981; Dweck, in press). In the next section, we will explore the ways in which teachers structure their feedback more generally—in particular, the goal structure of the classroom.

GOAL STRUCTURE OF THE CLASSROOM

The goal structure of the classroom is another variable that can influence children's beliefs about whether they are incapable of performing the task or whether they should simply try harder. Basically, three types of goal structures have been identified: competitive, individualistic, and cooperative (see Ames and Ames, 1984, for review). Researchers have characterized these three structures in terms of how a child's success is related to the successes of his/her peers. In the competitive structure, the quality of a child's work is judged against the performances of other children. Thus, the likelihood that a particular child will succeed (i.e., receive praise and/or rewards) is *negatively related* to the successes of his/ her peers. In the cooperative structure, several children work together in student-led groups toward a common goal. This goal may be the completion of a single group product or the goal may be to have the combined achievements of the individual members exceed a certain criterion. In either case, the likelihood that a particular child will succeed in a cooperative setting is *positively related* to the successes of his/her fellow group members. Finally, in the individualistic structure, the quality of each child's performance is judged individually. Thus, the likelihood that a given child will succeed is *unrelated* to the successes of other children.

Although there are some important moral, political, and social implications of these different goal structures, it is their motivational and academic consequences that are of relevance to the present discussion. In this respect, it is likely that most LD children will not fare well under highly competitive conditions. Competitive learning conditions heighten the degree to which children focus their attention on how smart they are relative to their peers (Ames, 1984; Ames, Ames, & Felker, 1977; Jagacinski & Nicholls, 1984). In contrast, in the individualistic goal structure, where social comparisons are less relevant, children are more apt to focus on the role that their efforts play in determining their achievements (Ames, 1984; Ames & Ames, 1981) and to focus on the demands of the task (e.g., "I need to make a plan about how to do these next puzzles") (Ames, 1984). This is a particularly appealing aspect of the individualistic structure. When children's low evaluations of their abilities are realistic, perhaps, the most reasonable goal of treatment is to focus their attention away from how smart they are relative to their peers and onto what they must do to master the tasks at hand (see also Dweck, in press; Elliott & Dweck, 1983; Nicholls, 1983). Indeed, this may be a good strategy for children who are high in ability as well (see Ames, 1978; Sexton, Licht, Brown, & Linden, 1984).

When adopting an individualistic goal structure, a number of issues must be considered. First, merely evaluating children individually and encouraging them to work at their own pace is not likely to be adequate. Children will work harder, learn more, and feel more efficacious when working toward goals that are specific and proximal (i.e., goals that specify how much should be accomplished in each work period) than when simply encouraged to work at their own pace and solve as many problems as they can (Bandura & Schunk, 1981). Second, even within an explicitly individualistic structure, children may become highly competitive—particularly when they are all working toward the same criterion and their progress is highly visible to their peers (Crockenberg & Bryant, 1978; Ames & Felker, 1979). For LD children, working toward the same criterion that is set for their classmates may be just as frustrating as an explicitly competitive structure. A potential solution is suggested by research on children's conceptions of intelligence (Dweck, in press; Nicholls, 1983). That is, it is likely that individualistic structures will be most effective when the quality of a child's work is evaluated primarily in terms of how it compares to that child's own past performances, with praise and rewards being contingent upon improvement rather than absolute level of performance (see also Brophy, 1983). Although there has not been a great deal of research on this particular type of individualistic structure, there is some evidence of its effectiveness with both nursery school (Masters, Furman, & Barden, 1977) and middle-school children (Slavin, 1980).

Another issue to consider with repect to individualistic structures is that this approach does *not* imply that teachers should avoid all feedback (e.g., grades) that conveys how children are performing relative to their peers. After all, for people to make realistic decisions (e.g., about career goals), they need to know how well they have mastered the same skills as those mastered by most other people their age. What we mean to imply is that the focus of the teacher's daily feedback should be on the degree to which children are improving their performances. There is one further issue concerning the use of an individualistic goal structure. This approach does *not* imply that teachers must individualize all their instruction or that children must learn and practice what they have learned in complete isolation from their peers. That is, it seems likely that teachers can direct their feedback toward the children's improvements even when instructing in a group setting.

Like the individualistic structure, cooperative structures have been proposed as a way of minimizing attention to individual differences in ability and of increasing children's motivation to learn. A large body of literature has examined the effectiveness of cooperative groups; and on the basis of this literature, several conclusions seem warranted. First, although much of the research has employed college or high-school students, it has been shown that children as young as first-graders can work together cooperatively in ways that can enhance their learning (Nevin, Johnson, & Johnson, 1982; Skon, Johnson, & Johnson, 1981). A second conclusion is that, for cooperative work groups to function well, rewards should be contingent upon the combined achievements of the individual group members rather than contingent upon a single group product (see Slavin, 1983, for discussion). Apparently, the latter contingency allows some children to contribute and learn more than others. A third conclusion is that a cooperative goal structure can be an effective way to decrease the salience of individual differences in ability (Ames & Felker, 1979) and to raise the self-evaluations of poor performers (Ames, 1981).

Although the above conclusions concerning cooperative structures sound promising, there are a number of important qualifications. Laboratory research which manipulated the success and failure of groups suggests that the benefits of working in a cooperative structure may occur only under conditions of group success. More specifically, Ames (1981) found that when the group succeeded in reaching its goal, the self-evaluations of the poor performers within the group were enhanced. That is, they evaluated their ability and deservedness more highly than they did in the competitive condition, even though their actual performance was the same across conditions. However, when the group failed to reach its goal, the self-evaluations of the poor performers were not enhanced, and the good performers seemed to suffer. That is, the good performers evaluated themselves more harshly than their performances warranted (see also Ames & Felker, 1979).

In a related vein, Cosden, Pearl, and Bryan (1982) found that when learning-disabled and nondisabled boys were paired together in cooperative dyads, the performances of the nondisabled boys suffered, and the performances of the LD boys did not seem to benefit. Observations suggested that these dyads were relatively unsuccessful at interacting cooperatively. (Female dyads did not show these problems, although there was no apparent benefit of cooperation.) However, a follow-up study (Bryan, Cosden, & Pearl, 1982) did suggest that with older children (seventh & eighth grade) and prior training in how to work together cooperatively, dyads of learning-disabled and nondisabled boys can work together successfully. The training increased the children's cooperative interactions and the amount that they learned during the cooperative sessions.

Perhaps, the most important qualifications concern the methodology that has been used to evaluate how the effectiveness of cooperative structures compares to that of other structures. As mentioned earlier, the three structures are contrasted conceptually in terms of how the successes of different children are interrelated. However, when the different goal structures are operationally defined, they tend to differ from one another on other dimensions as well. Thus, when the cooperative condition is found to be superior, it is difficult to determine whether this is because of the cooperative goal structure or because of some other aspect of the program that is confounded with the goal structure.

Perhaps the most common, and admittedly most understandable, confound is that the goal structure is confounded with the structure of the learning situation. More specifically, when comparing the cooperative versus individualistic structures, children in the individualistic condition virtually are always instructed to study the material alone, without any peer interaction (e.g., Johnson, Skon, & Johnson, 1980; Nevin et al., 1982; Skon et al., 1981; Slavin & Tanner, 1979). (As indicated earlier, working alone is not an inherent part of the individualistic structure.) Thus, it is not possible to determine whether the cooperative condition was superior because the children were working cooperatively toward the same goal or because children enjoy and benefit from hearing the ideas of their peers.

A less common confound concerns the *specificity* of the goals that are set for children in different goal structures. That is, in some studies (e.g., Nevin et al., 1982; Skon et al., 1981; Slavin, Leavey & Madden, 1984), children in the cooperative structure are presented with a *specific* goal (e.g., for each member to be able to answer *all* the questions or for the collective achievements of the individual members to exceed a predetermined criterion), whereas children in the individualistic structure simply are told to do as many problems as they can. As indicated earlier, the setting of specific, proximal goals facilitates children's performances, and could, therefore, have contributed to the superiority of the cooperative structure.

In sum, it appears that both individualistic and cooperative goal structures can reduce children's attention to individual differences in ability and enhance motivation. However, it is not at all clear, despite a large body of research, whether one goal structure is more effective than the other, or whether there are certain conditions (e.g., types of academic tasks, types of LD children) where one structure is more effective than the other. To address these issues, researchers must take greater care in operationalizing each structure. First, one must ensure that other dimensions are not confounded with the goal structure. Second, each of the goal structures must be tested in their most effective form. Perhaps the only way to insure a "fair" comparison of different goal structures (or any treatments) would be to survey the major proponents of each model to ensure that they approved of the way in which their model was being operationalized (e.g., see Paul & Lentz, 1977).

ATTRIBUTION RETRAINING TREATMENTS

Our discussions of classroom goal structures and patterns of teacher feedback suggest some ways to alter the classroom environment that might promote greater confidence and persistence in LD children. However, in addition to these strategies, a more direct approach should also be considered, particularly when children have already developed a maladaptive motivational pattern. That is, if one's goal is for LD children to develop a more adaptive attributional style, then one should teach them, in a fairly direct fashion, to attribute their difficulties to factors that are under their control, such as insufficient effort. As Dweck (in press) suggests, even if we could create a classroom environment where children with low levels of confidence could make progress without experiencing much failure, it also would be necessary to alter their attributional styles so they could function adaptively when failure does occur. After all, children cannot always be protected from failure. Furthermore, there is, indeed, empirical support for the utility of directly teaching children to alter their attributional styles. When children who attribute their difficulties to factors that are beyond their control are taught to attribute their difficulties to insufficient effort, this is likely to result in increased persistence when confronted with difficulty (Andrews & Debus, 1978; Dweck, 1975; Fowler & Peterson, 1981; Medway & Venino, 1982; Thomas & Pashley, 1982). This approach is referred to as "attribution retraining" (AR).

Although there are several variants of the AR approach, generally, it includes two basic components. First, in the context of performing an academic or academic-like task, the child is confronted with some "failure." This failure is not severe in magnitude, but might consist of some very difficult problems that are interspersed among a series of problems that are within the child's level of ability. Likewise, the child may, on a predetermined number of occasions, be given more work to complete than is possible in the allotted time. The second component involves directly teaching the child to attribute these failures to insufficient effort. For example, after failing to complete the work within the alloted time, the trainer might say, "You didn't finish in time. That means you should have tried harder." Some investigators also have taught children to attribute their successes to effort—for example, "You did well. That means you were trying hard."

As is true with all treatment approaches, some qualifications regarding the effectiveness of AR are in order. The effectiveness of AR may depend on the manner in which the trainer stresses the importance of the child's efforts. There are a number of strategies for communicating to children that they can improve their performances by increasing their efforts, and these strategies may differ greatly in their effectiveness. For example, Schunk (1982) evaluated the effectiveness of two treatments that stressed the importance of the children's efforts and found them to be differentially effective. In both treatments, the children periodically were asked to report on the progress they were making in an instructional packet for subtraction skills. In one treatment, the trainer responded by saying "You've been working hard." In the other, the trainer responded with "You need to work hard." Whereas the former resulted in increased skills acquisition and feelings of self-efficacy, the latter did not. Similarly, Miller, Brickman, & Bolen (1975) found that having the teacher implore students to work harder (e.g., "You should try more on arithmetic") was not an effective motivator; however, having the teacher communicate that she viewed them as hard-working (e.g., "You're working harder in arithmetic") was effective at improving their arithmetic performance and self-esteem (see also Schunk, 1983, for another comparative study).

There are several factors that may explain the differential effectiveness of these (and other) attributional statements. It is likely that the crucial message to convey to children is not simply that they are not trying hard enough, but rather that with increased effort comes increased success. In other words, some optimism for success must be conveyed. As Schunk (1982) suggests, it is possible that the treatment he found to be ineffective (i.e., "You need to work hard") communicated to the children that they were generally doing poorly, and there may have been nothing to indicate that increased effort would substantially change the situation. In contrast, the effective treatment ("You've been working hard") may have conveyed positive feedback about the children's progress in addition to any message it conveyed about the importance of effort.

In addition to the specific wording of the attributional statements, there are other aspects of the treatment that may affect the amount of optimism conveyed. Children's optimism is likely to vary as a function of how much success versus failure they are experiencing. Although experiencing some success (particularly success that is attained with little effort) is not enough to build confidence that subsequent difficulties can be overcome (Chapin & Dyck, 1976; Clifford, 1978; Dweck, 1975), it is undoubtedly the case that at least a *moderate* amount of success is necessary. In the Dweck (1975) study, for example, where AR led to dramatic increases in persistence, children experienced 2 or 3 failure trials per session (each of which was followed by an attributional statement) in the context of 12 or 13 success trials. Perhaps, the message that increased effort will lead to increased success is more believeable when the children already are experiencing some success. Thus, when employing AR, it might be important to ensure that the training task(s) are at a level where a moderate amount of success is possible. Thus, the failure that is experienced might, indeed, seem surmountable with increased effort.

The *scheduling* of the failure that is experienced during treatment is another factor that might affect the degree to which children learn to maintain optimism in the face of difficulty. As predicted by learning theory, children learn to be more persistent in the face of failure when treatment exposes them to failure that continues for varying amounts of time. For example, the training task used by Chapin and Dyck (1976) consisted of a series of sentences to read aloud. Some sentences were well within the children's reading level, and some contained words that were very difficult. These investigators (Chapin & Dyck, 1976) found that when training exposed children to no more than one difficult sentence in succession, they did not learn to be as persistent as they did when training exposed them to failure of varying lengths. Sometimes, there was only one difficult sentence in succession, whereas, at other times, there were two or three difficult sentences in succession. Undoubtedly, in this latter condition, children learned that the presence of two or three difficult sentences was not necessarily an indication that the sentence which followed would be too difficult for them.

In addition to conveying optimism, the training situation should be set up so as to ensure the validity of the children's new attributions (see Dweck, 1977). In other words, AR may motivate children to test the validity of these new attributions. However, unless their increased effort actually does pay off, treatment effects are likely to be short-lived. Perhaps, one way to ensure that increased efforts will result in improved performance is to combine AR with training in general problem-solving skills (see Meichenbaum, 1980; Meichenbaum & Asarnow, 1979) and/or with training in specific task strategies. In other words, when we suggest that insufficient effort is contributing to the poor performances of LD children, we are in no way implying that these children do not also require skills training.

It seems likely that the most effective approach would be to teach task strategies and more adaptive attributions in an *integrated* approach. It is important to note that we are suggesting more than just teaching new task strategies and attributions during the same training sessions. Rather, we are suggesting that increased effort is more likely to pay off if children are told explicitly *how* to try harder. Likewise, there is evidence from the skills-training literature that merely teaching children how to use a new strategy (e.g., Kennedy & Miller, 1976; Paris, Newman, & McVey, 1982) or arranging for them to experience more success when they use the strategy (Fabricius & Hagen, 1984) does not ensure that they will use the strategy when they are not explicitly instructed to do so. To ensure that they will use the strategy again, they need to *believe* that the use of that strategy will contribute to their subsequent success. That is, they need to attribute their success, at least in part, to the use of that strategy (Fabricius & Hagen, 1984; Moynahan, 1978). Thus, it seems that the effects of AR can be enhanced by incorporating some strategy training, and the use of new strategies that have been successfully trained is enhanced when the appropriate attributions for those strategies are taught. However, as research on almost every treatment approach has shown, if one wishes to ensure the long-term maintenance and generalization of the new strategies and new attributions, one undoubtedly will need to train on a variety of tasks, across a variety of settings, over a reasonably long period of time (Kendall & Braswell, 1982; Meichenbaum & Asarnow, 1979).

Implicit in the integrated approach suggested here is that the children's difficulties are, at least in part, due to ineffective task strategies. In fact, some investigators specifically have suggested that children should be taught to attribute their difficulties to ineffective task strategies (Anderson & Jennings, 1980; McNabb, 1984). This suggestion stems from a number of concerns that have been raised against training children to make attributions to effort. Although some of these concerns (e.g., effort is often not enough.) are addressed by having the trainer stress *both* the children's efforts and their strategies, some concerns are not. For example, it may be difficult for some students to attribute their difficulties to insufficient effort because they might see this as an admission of laziness (e.g., Medway & Venino, 1982). As indicated earlier, teachers respond most favorably to those students whom they perceive as consistently trying hard. Not only are students aware of how much their teachers value effort (Nicholls, 1978; Weiner et al., 1982), but many students share this value as well (Covington & Omelich, 1979b; Harari & Covington, 1981; Weiner & Peter, 1973). Thus, although attributing their difficulties to insufficient effort may allow them to maintain optimism about their ability to succeed, it also conveys a negative message about how "good" they are (Covington & Omelich, 1979a).

It has been proposed that attributing failure to ineffective strategies might be a solution to this problem since this attribution seems to imply less blame on the part of the child. As suggested in a study by McNabb (1984), teachers view children as less blameworthy when the children's difficulties appear to stem from ineffective strategies than when they appear to stem from insufficient effort. At present, however, it is not known whether teaching children to attribute their difficulties to ineffective strategies will be as effective as stressing the role of both strategies and effort. It is our prediction that teaching both attributions will be most effective. Our concern is that stressing only the role of ineffective strategies might prompt children to try a variety of strategies in succession, without investing much effort in any one of them. Furthermore, although increased effort is frequently not enough, there are many instances where simply paying attention to the teacher or opening the book and attempting the problems will help greatly.

Another factor that might influence the effectiveness of AR is the age of the child. In light of the developmental differences discussed earlier, one might predict that younger LD children would be less likely to benefit from AR. Since younger children are less likely to believe that they permanently lack the capacity to succeed, there may be less need for a treatment that stresses their ability to overcome their difficulties with increased effort. It is possible that younger LD children might benefit more from positive feedback for small improvements and effortful attempts. On the other hand, it is possible that the best way to teach children an adaptive attributional style is to start when they are very young—before they have come to believe that their efforts are useless. Since very young children are less upset by failure, it may be easier to teach them to use failure as a cue that they need to try harder. These predictions, of course, remain to be tested.

One final qualification is that AR is not expected to cure or prevent all motivational problems. For example, if a child's motivation is low because his/her family devalues academic achievement, then AR is not likely to be effective. AR is most apt to help when children have the desire to learn, but they either believe that they are incapable of doing so or they do not realize the importance of trying harder when they confront difficulty.

In sum, there is considerable support for the utility of the AR approach, and we are beginning to understand some of the variables that mediate its effectiveness. However, the perennial conclusion "more research is needed" is clearly in order. First, whereas it seems that the attributional statements must be worded so as to convey optimism, more comparative studies are needed to determine the best way to do this without conveying inaccurate information (e.g., indicating that the children are performing much better than they really are). Second, although it appears that at least a moderate amount of success is necessary in AR, it would be helpful to know more about the boundaries within which this moderate amount should fall. Third, even though we know that a variable schedule of failure will promote greater persistence than a fixed schedule, it would be useful to know more about the way in which the effectiveness of AR varies as a function of different variable schedules. Fourth, we clearly need to examine the relative effectiveness of teaching children to attribute their failures to insufficient effort versus ineffective strategies versus an integration of these two factors. Fifth, in light of the developmental differences discussed earlier, it is important to examine whether the answers to the above questions vary as a function of the child's age. Finally, since most of the AR research has been conducted in a laboratory, it is important to determine how best to conduct treatment in an actual classroom setting.

CONCLUSIONS

In this chapter, we have presented evidence that LD children are at risk for developing motivational problems. As a consequence of their repeated failures, they are likely to believe that their abilities are low and their achievement efforts are futile. These beliefs, in turn, are likely to lead to low persistence. However, we also have stressed the existence of individual differences across and within ages. By doing so, the point we wish to make is that these motivational problems are not inevitable. There are some LD children who have gotten the important message that the existence of ability deficits does not mean their efforts are useless.

Although it is not entirely clear how teachers can best convey this message to LD children, we know that it is not likely to occur by simply imploring children to work harder, nor by giving easy work that does not require much effort. Teachers need to attend to the subtle (and not so subtle) messages that their feedback may convey to different types of children, and they need to attend to the overall goal structure of the classroom. It is our hope that with continued research in these areas, we will gain further insights into the most beneficial ways to deal with the motivational problems that LD children are likely to develop. The message that hopefully was conveyed in the various sections of this chapter is that we have already made progress toward this end.

ACKNOWLEDGMENTS

The authors gratefully acknowledge the helpful suggestions of Joseph Torgesen, Carol Dweck, and Molly Sexton. Special thanks also are due to Cathy Cronin for her assistance with the library work.

REFERENCES

Alpert, J. L. (1974). Teacher behavior across ability groups: A consideration of the mediation of Pygmalion effects. *Journal of Educational Psychology, 66,* 348–353.

Ames, C. (1978). Children's achievement attributions and self-reinforcement: Effects of self-concept and competitive reward structure. *Journal of Educational Psychology, 70,* 345–355.

Ames, C. (1981). Competitive versus cooperative reward structures: The influence of individual and group performance factors on achievement attributions and affect. *American Educational Research Journal, 18,* 273–287.

Ames, C. (1984). Achievement attributions and self-instructions under competitive and individualistic goal structures. *Journal of Educational Psychology, 76,* 478–487.

Ames, C., & Ames, R. (1981). Competitive versus individualistic goal structures: The salience of past performance information for causal attributions and affect. *Journal of Educational Psychology, 73,* 411–418.

Ames, C., & Ames, R. (1984). Systems of student and teacher motivation: Toward a qualitative definition. *Journal of Educational Psychology, 76,* 535–556.

Ames, C., Ames, R., & Felker, D. W. (1977). Effects of competitive reward structure and valence of outcome on children's achievement attributions. *Journal of Educational Psychology, 69,* 1–8.

Ames, C., & Felker, D. W. (1979). An examination of children's attributions and achievement-related evaluations in competitive, cooperative, and individualistic reward structures. *Journal of Educational Psychology, 71,* 413–420.

Anderson, C. A., & Jennings, D. L. (1980). When experiences of failure promote expectations of success: The impact of attributing failure to ineffective strategies. *Journal of Personality, 48,* 393–407.

Andrews, G. R., & Debus, R. L. (1978). Persistence and the causal perception of failure: Modifying cognitive attributions. *Journal of Educational Psychology, 70,* 154–166.

Babad, E. Y., Inbar, J., & Rosenthal, R. (1982). Pygmalion, Galatea, and the Golem: Investigations of biased and unbiased teachers. *Journal of Educational Psychology, 74,* 459–474.

Bandura, A., & Schunk, D. (1981). Cultivating competence, self-efficacy, and intrinsic interest through proximal self-motivation. *Journal of Personality and Social Psychology, 41,* 586–598.

Bandura, M., & Dweck, C. S. (1983). Children's conceptions of intelligence in relation to achievement goals and patterns of achievement-related cognition, affect, and behavior. Unpublished manuscript, Pennsylvania State University.

Black, W. F. (1974). Self-concept as related to achievement and age in learning-disabled children. *Child Development, 45,* 1137–1140.

Boersma, F. J., & Chapman, J. W. (1981). Academic self-concept, achievement expectations, and locus of control in elementary learning-disabled children. *Canadian Journal of Behavioural Science, 13,* 349–358.

Boggiano, A. K., & Ruble, D. N. (1979). Competence and the overjustification effect: A developmental study. *Journal of Personality and Social Psychology, 37,* 1462–1468.

Brophy, J. E. (1979). Teacher behavior and its effects. *Journal of Educational Psychology, 71,* 733–750.

Brophy, J. E. (1981). Teacher praise: A functional analysis. *Review of Educational Research, 51,* 5–32.

Brophy, J. E. (1983). Research on the self-fulfilling prophecy and teacher expectations. *Journal of Educational Psychology, 75,* 631–661.

Brophy, J. E., & Evertson, C. M. (1976). *Learning from teaching: A developmental perspective.* Boston: Allyn and Bacon, Inc.

Brophy, J. E., & Evertson, C. M. (1981). *Student characteristics and teaching.* New York: Longman, Inc.

Brophy, J. E., & Good, T. L. (1970). Teachers' communication of differential expectations for children's classroom performance: Some behavioral data. *Journal of Educational Psychology, 61,* 365–374.

Brophy, J. E., & Rohrkemper, M. M. (1981). The influence of problem ownership on teachers' perceptions of and strategies for coping with problem students. *Journal of Educational Psychology, 73,* 295–311.

Bryan, T., Cosden, M., & Pearl, R. (1982). The effects of cooperative goal structures and cooperative models on LD and NLD students. *Learning Disability Quarterly, 5,* 415–421.

Butkowsky, I. S. (August 1982). The generality of learned helplessness in children with learning difficulties. Paper presented at the Annual Convention of the American Psychological Association, Washington, DC.

Butkowsky, I. S., & Willows, D. M. (1980). Cognitive-motivational characteristics of children varying in reading ability: Evidence for learned helplessness in poor readers. *Journal of Educational Psychology, 72,* 408–422.

Chapin, M., & Dyck, D. G. (1976). Persistence in children's reading behavior as a function of N length and attribution retraining. *Journal of Abnormal Psychology, 85,* 511–515.

Chapman, J. W., & Boersma, F. J. (1979). Learning disabilities, locus of control and mother attitudes. *Journal of Educational Psychology, 71,* 250–258.

Chapman, R. B., Larsen, S. C., & Parker, R. M. (1979). Interactions of first-grade teachers with learning-disordered children. *Journal of Learning Disabilities, 12,* 225–230.

Clifford, M. M. (1978). Have we underestimated the facilitative effects of failure? *Canad. Journal of Behavioral Science/Rev. Canad. Sci. Comp., 10,* 308–316.

Cooper, H. M., & Baron, R. M. (1977). Academic expectations and attributed responsibility as predictors of professional teachers' reinforcement behavior. *Journal of Educational Psychology, 69,* 409–418.

Cooper, H. M., & Burger, J. M. (1980). How teachers explain students' academic performance: A categorization of free response academic attributions. *American Educational Research Journal, 17,* 95–109.

Cosden, M., Pearl, R., & Bryan, T. (1982). The effects of cooperative versus individual goal structures on learning-disabled students' performance and interactions. Unpublished manuscript, Chicago Institute for the Study of Learning Disabilities. Chicago Circle: University of Illinois.

Covington, M. V., & Omelich, C. L. (1979a). Effort: The double-edged sword in school achievement. *Journal of Educational Psychology, 71,* 169–181.

Covington, M. V., & Omelich, C. L. (1979b). It's best to be able and virtuous too: Student and teacher evaluative responses to successful effort. *Journal of Educational Psychology, 71,* 688–700.

Crockenberg, S., & Bryant, B. (1978). Socialization: The "implicit curriculum" of learning environments. *Journal of Research and Development in Education, 12,* 69–78.

Cronbach, L. J. (1975). Five decades of public controversy over mental testing. *American Psychologist, 30,* 1–14.

Diener, C. I., & Dweck, C. S. (1978). An analysis of learned helplessness: Continuous changes in performance, strategy, and achievement cognitions following failure. *Journal of Personality and Social Psychology, 36,* 451–462.

Dorval, B., McKinney, J. D., & Feagans, L. (1982). Teacher interaction with learning-disabled children and average achievers. *Journal of Pediatric Psychology, 7,* 317–330.

Douglas, V. I., & Peters, K. G. (1979). Toward a clearer definition of the attentional deficit of hyperactive children. In G. Hale & M. Lewis (Eds.). *Attention and Cognitive Development* (pp. 173–247). New York: Plenum Press.

Dweck, C. S. (1975). The role of expectations and attributions in the alleviation of learned helplessness. *Journal of Personality and Social Psychology, 31,* 674–685.

Dweck, C. S. (1977). Learned helplessness and negative evaluation. *The Educator 14,* 44–49.

Dweck, C. S. (in press). Motivation. In R. Glaser and A. Lesgold (Eds.). *The Handbook of Psychology and Education* Vol I. Hillsdale, NJ: Lawrence Erlbaum Associates.

Dweck, C. S., & Bempechat, J. (1984). Entity versus incremental theories: Generality across domains and changes across ages. Unpublished manuscript. Harvard University.

Dweck, C. S., Davidson, W., Nelson, S., & Enna, B. (1978). Sex differences in learned helplessness: II. The contingencies of evaluative feedback in the classroom and III. An experimental analysis. *Developmental Psychology, 14,* 268–276.

Dweck, C. S., & Elliott, E. S. (1983). Achievement motivation. In E. M. Hetherington (volume editor) and P. H. Mussen (editor), *Handbook of Child Psychology* (Vol IV, pp. 643–691). New York: John Wiley & Sons.

Dweck, C. S., Goetz, T. E., & Strauss, N. L. (1980). Sex differences in learned helplessness: IV. An experimental and naturalistic study of failure generalization and its mediators. *Journal of Personality and Social Psychology, 38,* 441–452.

Dweck, C. S., & Reppucci, N. D. (1973). Learned helplessness and reinforcement responsibility in children. *Journal of Personality and Social Psychology, 25,* 109–116.

Elliott, E. S., & Dweck, C. S. (1983). Achievement goals as a determinant of children's achievement. Unpublished manuscript, University of Illinois at Urbana-Champaign.

Eshel, Y., & Klein, Z. (1981). Development of academic self-concept of lower-class and middle-class primary school children. *Journal of Educational Psychology, 73,* 287–293.

Fabricius, W. V., & Hagen, J. W. (1984). Use of causal attributions about recall performance to assess metamemory and predict strategic memory behavior in young children. *Developmental Psychology, 20,* 975–987.

Feld, S., Ruhland, D., & Gold, M. (1979). Developmental changes in achievement motivation. *Merrill-Palmer Quarterly, 25,* 43–60.

Fowler, J. W., & Peterson, P. L. (1981). Increasing reading persistence and altering attributional style of learned helpless children. *Journal of Educational Psychology, 73,* 251–260.

Good, T. L., Ebmeier, H., & Beckerman, T. (1978). Teaching mathematics in high and low SES classrooms: An empirical comparison. *Journal of Teacher Education, 29,* 85–90.

Harari, O., & Covington, M. (1981). Reactions to achievement behavior from a teacher and student perspective: A developmental analysis. *American Educational Research Journal, 18,* 15–28.

Harter, S. (1978). Effectance motivation reconsidered: Toward a developmental model. *Human Development, 21,* 34–64.

Haskins, R., Walden, T., & Ramey, C. T. (1983). Teacher and student behavior in high- and low-ability groups. *Journal of Educational Psychology, 75,* 865–876.

Hebert, C., & Dweck, C. S. (1984). Individual differences in helplessness and mastery-orientation among pre-schoolers. Unpublished manuscript, Harvard University.

Hisama, T. (1976). Achievement motivation and the locus of control of children with learning disabilities and behavior disorders. *Journal of Learning Disabilities, 9,* 387–392.

Jagacinski, C. M., & Nicholls, J. G. (1984). Conceptions of ability and related affects in task involvement and ego involvement. *Journal of Educational Psychology, 76,* 909–919.

Johnson, D. W., Skon, L, & Johnson, R. (1980). Effects of cooperative, competitive, and individualistic conditions on children's problem-solving performance. *American Educational Research Journal, 17,* 83–93.

Karabenick, J. D., & Heller, K. A. (1976). A developmental study of effort and ability attributions. *Developmental Psychology, 12,* 559–560.

Kendall, P. C., & Braswell, L. (1982). Cognitive-behavioral self-control therapy for children: A components analysis. *Journal of Consulting and Clinical Psychology, 50,* 672–689.

Kennedy, B. A., & Miller, O. J. (1976). Persistent use of verbal rehearsal as a function of information about its value. *Child Development, 47,* 566–569.

Kistner, J. A., & Licht, B. G. (February 1984). Cognitive-motivational factors affecting academic persistence of learning disabled children. Paper presented at the Meeting of the Association for Children and Adults with Learning Disabilities, New Orleans, LA.

Kun, A. (1977). Development of the magnitude—covariation and compensation schemata in ability and effort attributions of performance. *Child Development, 48,* 862–873.

Licht, B. G. (1983). Cognitive-motivational factors that contribute to the achievements of learning disabled children. *Journal of Learning Disabilities, 8,* 483–490.

Licht, B. G., & Dweck, C. S. (1983). Sex differences in achievement orientations: Consequences for academic choices and attainments. In M. Marland (Ed.). *Sex Differentiation and Schools* (pp. 72–97). London: Heinemann Educational Books, Ltd.

Licht, B. G., & Dweck, C. S. (1984). Determinants of academic achievement: The interaction of children's achievement orientations and skill area. *Developmental Psychology, 20,* 628–636.

Licht, B., Kistner, J., Ozkaragoz, T., Shapiro, S., & Clausen, L. (1985). Causal attributions of learning disabled children: Individual differences and their implications for persistence. *Journal of Educational Psychology, 77,* 208–216.

Licht, B., Linden, T., Brown, D., & Sexton, M. (1984). Sex differences in achievement orientations: An "A" student phenomenon. Poster presented at the Convention of the American Psychological Association, Toronto, Canada. (ERIC Document Reproduction Service No. ED252783).

McKinney, J. D., & Feagans, L. (1983). Adaptive classroom behavior of learning disabled students. *Journal of Learning Disabilities, 16,* 360–380.

McNabb, T. (1984). A comparison of the affective consequences of ability, effort, and strategy attributions for academic failure. Paper presented at the Annual Convention of the American Psychological Association, Toronto, Canada.

Masters, J. C., Furman, W., & Barden, R. C. (1977). Effects of achievement standards, tangible rewards, and self-dispensed achievement evaluations on children's task mastery. *Child Development, 48,* 217–224.

Medway, F. J. (1979). Causal attributions for school-related problems: Teacher perceptions and teacher feedback. *Journal of Educational Psychology, 71,* 809–818.

Medway, F. J., & Venino, G. R. (1982). The effects of effort feedback and performance patterns on children's attributions and task persistence. *Contemporary Educational Psychology, 7,* 26–34.

Meichenbaum, D. (October 1980). Teaching thinking: A cognitive—behavioural perspective. Paper presented at the NIE–LRDC Conference on Thinking and Learning Skills. Pittsburgh, PA.

Meichenbaum, D., & Asarnow, J. (1979). Cognitive—behavioral modification and metacognitive development: Implications for the classroom. In P. C. Kendall and S. D. Hollon (Eds.). *Cognitive—Behavioral Interventions: Theory, Research, and Procedures* (pp. 11–35). New York: Academic Press.

Meyer, W.-U., Bachmann, M., Biermann, U., Hempelmann, M., Ploger, F.-O., & Spiller,

H. (1979). The informational value of evaluative behavior: Influences of praise and blame on perceptions of ability. *Journal of Educational Psychology, 71*, 259–268.

Miller, A. (in press). A developmental study of the cognitive basis of performance impairment after failure. *Journal of Personality and Social Psychology.*

Miller, R. L., Brickman, P., & Bolen, D. (1975). Attribution versus persuasion as a means for modifying behavior. *Journal of Personality and Social Psychology, 31*, 430–441.

Moynahan, E. D. (1978). Assessment and selection of paired associate strategies: A developmental study. *Journal of Experimental Child Psychology, 26*, 257–266.

Nevin, A., Johnson, D. W., & Johnson, R. (1982). Effects of group and individual contingencies on academic performance and social relations of special need students. *Journal of Social Psychology, 116*, 41–59.

Nicholls, J. G. (1978). The development of the concepts of effort and ability, perception of academic attainment and the understanding that difficult tasks require more ability. *Child Development, 49*, 800–814.

Nicholls, J. G. (1979). Development of perception of own attainment and causal attributions for success and failure in reading. *Journal of Educational Psychology, 71*, 94–99.

Nicholls, J. G. (1980). The development of the concept of difficulty. *Merrill-Palmer Quarterly, 26*, 271–281.

Nicholls, J. G., (1983). Conceptions of ability and achievement motivation: A theory and its implications for education. In S. G. Paris, G. N. Olson, and H. W. Stevenson (Eds.). *Learning and Motivation in the Classroom* (pp. 211–237). Hillsdale, NJ: Lawrence Erlbaum Associates.

Nicholls, J. G., & Miller, A. T. (1984). Development and its discontents: The differentiation of the concept of ability. In J. G. Nicholls (Ed.). *The Development of Achievement Motivation* (pp. 185–218). Greenwich, CT: JAI Press.

Palmer, D. J., Drummond, F., Tollison, P., & Zinkgraff, S. (1982). An attributional investigation of performance outcomes for learning-disabled and normal-achieving pupils. *The Journal of Special Education, 16*, 207–219.

Paris, S. G., Newman, R. S., & McVey, K. A. (1982). Learning the functional significance of mnemonic actions: A microgenetic study of strategy acquisition. *Journal of Experimental Child Psychology, 34*, 490–509.

Paul, G. L., & Lentz, R. J. (1977). *Psychosocial treatment of chronic mental patients. Milieu versus social-learning programs.* Cambridge, MA: Harvard University Press.

Pearl, R. A. (1982). LD children's attributions for success and failure: A replication with a labeled LD sample. *Learning Disability Quarterly, 5*, 173–176.

Pearl, R. A., & Bryan, T. (1982). Mothers' attributions for their learning disabled child's successes and failures. *Learning Disability Quarterly, 5*, 53–57.

Pearl, R. A., Bryan, T., & Donahue, M. (1980). Learning disabled children's attributions for success and failure. *Learning Disability Quarterly, 3*, 3–9.

Pearl, R. A., Bryan, T., & Herzog, A. (1983). Learning disabled and nondisabled children's strategy analyses under high and low success conditions. *Learning Disability Quarterly, 6*, 67–74.

Raudenbush, S. W., (1984). Magnitude of teacher expectancy effects on pupil IQ as a function of the credibility of expectancy induction: A synthesis of findings from 18 experiments. *Journal of Educational Psychology, 76*, 85–97.

Rest, S., Nierenberg, R., Weiner, B., & Heckhausen, H. (1973). Further evidence concerning the effects of perceptions of effort and ability on achievement evaluation. *Journal of Personality and Social Psychology, 28*, 187–191.

Rholes, W. S., Blackwell, J., Jordan, C., & Walters, C. (1980). A developmental study of learned helplessness. *Developmental Psychology, 16*, 616–624.

Rosenthal, R., & Jacobson, L. (1968). *Pygmalion in the classroom: Teacher expectation and pupil's intellectual development.* New York: Holt, Rinehart & Winston.

Ruble, D. N., Boggiano, A. K., Feldman, N. S., & Loebl, J. H. (1980). Developmental analysis of the role of social comparison in self-evaluation. *Developmental Psychology, 16,* 105–115.

Ruble, D. N., Parsons, J., & Ross, J. (1976). Self-evaluative responses of children in an achievement setting. *Child Development, 47,* 990–997.

Schunk, D. H. (1982). Effects of effort attributional feedback on children's perceived self-efficacy and achievement. *Journal of Educational Psychology, 74,* 548–556.

Schunk, D. H. (1983). Ability versus effort attributional feedback: Differential effects on self-efficacy and achievement. *Journal of Educational Psychology, 75,* 848–856.

Seligman, M. E. P., & Maier, S. F. (1967). Failure to escape traumatic shock. *Journal of Experimental Psychology, 74,* 1–9.

Sexton, M., Licht, B., Brown, D., & Linden, T. (August 1984). Predictors of children's responses to difficulty: Their definitions of intelligence. Paper presented at the Annual Convention of the American Psychological Association. Toronto, Canada.

Shaklee, H. (1976). Development in inferences of ability and task difficulty. *Child Development, 47,* 1051–1057.

Shepard, L., Smith, M. L., & Vojir, C. P. (1983). Characteristics of pupils identified as learning disabled. *American Educational Research Journal, 20,* 309–331.

Skon, L., Johnson, D., & Johnson, R. (1981). Cooperative peer interaction versus individual competition and individualistic efforts: Effects on the acquisition of cognitive reasoning strategies. *Journal of Educational Psychology, 73,* 83–92.

Slavin, R. E. (1980). Effects of individual learning expectations on student achievement. *Journal of Educational Psychology, 72,* 520–524.

Slavin, R. E. (1983). When does cooperative learning increase student achievement? *Psychological Bulletin, 94,* 429–445.

Slavin, R. E., Leavey, M. B., & Madden, N. A. (1984). Combining cooperative learning and individualized instruction: Effects on student mathematics achievement, attitudes, and behaviors. *The Elementary School Journal, 84,* 409–422.

Slavin, R. E., & Tanner, A. M. (1979). Effects of cooperative reward structures and individual accountability on productivity and learning. *Journal of Educational Research, 72,* 294–298.

Speece, D., McKinney, J., & Applebaum, M. (1985). Classification and validation of behavioral subtypes of learning disabled children. *Journal of Educational Psychology, 77,* 67–77.

Stipek, D. J. (1981). Children's perceptions of their own and their classmates' ability. *Journal of Educational Psychology, 73,* 404–410.

Stipek, D. J. (1984). The development of achievement motivation. In R. Ames and C. Ames (Eds.). *Research on Motivation in Education.* Vol. 1 (pp. 145–174). Orlando: Academic Press.

Stipek, D. J., & Tannatt, L. M. (1984). Children's judgments of their own and their peers' academic competence. *Journal of Educational Psychology, 76,* 75–84.

Surber, C. F. (1980). The development of reversible operations in judgments of ability, effort, and performance. *Child Development, 51,* 1018–1029.

Thomas, A. (1979). Learned helplessness and expectancy factors: Implications for research in learning disabilities. *Review of Educational Research, 49,* 208–221.

Thomas, A., & Pashley, B. (1982). Effects of classroom training on LD students' task persistence and attributions. *Learning Disability Quarterly, 5,* 133–144.

Torgesen, J. K., (1980). Conceptual and educational implications of the use of efficient task strategies by learning disabled children. *Journal of Learning Disabilities, 13*, 364–371.

Torgesen, J. K. (1982). The use of rationally defined subgroups in research on learning disabilities. In J. P. Das, R. F. Mulcahy, and A. E. Wall (Eds.). *Theory and Research in Learning Disabilities* (pp. 111–131). New York: Plenum Press.

Torgesen, J. K., & Licht, B. G. (1983). The learning disabled child as an inactive learner: Retrospect and prospects. In J. D. McKinney and L. Feagans (Eds.). *Current Topics in Learning Disabilities.* Vol I (pp. 3–31). Norwood, NJ: Ablex Publishing Corp.

Tuddenham, R. D. (1962). The nature and measurement of intelligence. In L. Postman (Ed.). *Psychology in the Making* (pp. 469–525). New York: Alfred A Knopf.

Weiner, B. (1979). A theory of motivation for some classroom experiences. *Journal of Educational Psychology, 71*, 3–25.

Weiner, B., Graham, S., Stern, P., & Lawson, M. E. (1982). Using affective cues to infer causal thoughts. *Developmental Psychology, 18*, 278–286.

Weiner, B., & Kukla, A. (1970). An attributional analysis of achievement motivation. *Journal of Personality and Social Psychology, 15*, 1–20.

Weiner, B., & Peter, N. (1973). A cognitive-developmental analysis of achievement and moral judgments. *Developmental Psychology, 9*, 290–309.

Weinstein, R. S., (1976). Reading group membership in first grade: Teacher behaviors and pupil experience over time. *Journal of Educational Psychology, 68*, 103–116.

Weinstein, R. S., Marshall, H. H., Brattesani, K. A., & Middlestadt, S. E. (1982). Student perceptions of differential teacher treatment in open and traditional classrooms. *Journal of Educational Psychology, 74*, 678–692.

Wine, J. D. (1982). Evaluation anxiety: A cognitive-attentional construct. In H. W. Krohne and L. Laux (Eds.). *Achievement, Stress, and Anxiety* (pp. 207–219). Washington, DC: Hemisphere.

Ysseldyke, J. E., Algozzine, B., Shinn, M., & McGue, M. (1979). Similarities and differences between underachievers and students labeled learning disabled: Identical twins with different mothers (Research Report No. 13). Minneapolis: University of Minnesota Institute for Research on Learning Disabilities.

PART III

Treatment Approaches

In this section, six different approaches, or technologies, for the treatment of learning-disabled children are discussed. These approaches range from one (computer-assisted instruction) that is essentially untested with learning-disabled children to others (drug therapy and applied behavior analysis) for which an extensive research literature is available. Only one of these approaches (applied behavior analysis) is currently being widely used with learning-disabled children, although all of them certainly have the potential for widespread use in the future. With the exception of phonological training, all the approaches considered here have general applicability in helping learning-disabled children to be more successful in a variety of areas.

William Pelham's chapter (Chapter 9) on stimulant therapy with hyperactive and learning-disabled children provides an extensive discussion of drug effects on learning both in the laboratory and in the classroom. One of his most important points is that previous reviews of research in this area may have taken a much too pessimistic view of the potential benefits of drug therapy for learning in the classroom. In contrast to the controversy surrounding use of drugs to enhance learning, there is almost universal agreement that many of the instructional techniques derived from applied behavior analysis are effective in increasing specific skills in learning-disabled children. In the second chapter in this part, Mark Koorland (Chapter 10) provides an update on recent advances in the use of behavioral technology with learning-disabled children and suggests areas that are most in need of attention to increase the effectiveness of this approach.

The chapter by Jean Schumaker, Donald Deshler, and Edwin Ellis (Chapter 11) is similar to the following one by Ellen Bouchard Ryan, Keri Weed, and Elizabeth Short (Chapter 12) in suggesting the need for training learning-disabled children to use more effective strategies in coping with academic and social situations. Whereas the former chapter focuses on the role of strategy training in the context of a complete intervention program for adolescents, the latter chapter provides an extensive and theoretically based exposition of the general value of strategy training, or cognitive behavior modification, with learning-disabled children of all ages.

The final two chapters in this section discuss phonological training and computer-assisted instruction, respectively. Joanna Williams (Chapter 13) provides a concise, but thorough, treatment of the potential value of training in phonological analysis as a part of reading instruction. Her chapter builds on the discussion of learning-disabled children's problems with phonological processing that was presented in the previous section. The final chapter of the book discusses the most recently developed remedial technology for learning-disabled children: classroom computers. The discussion of this topic by Joseph Torgesen (Chapter 14) focuses on evidence for the effectiveness of computer-assisted instruction with other populations of children, how computers may be most effectively used with learning-disabled children, and what must be done before computers can become an important instructional tool in learning-disabilities classrooms.

9

The Effects of Psychostimulant Drugs on Learning and Academic Achievement in Children with Attention-Deficit Disorders and Learning Disabilities

WILLIAM E. PELHAM, JR.

INTRODUCTION

Whether the psychostimulant drugs affect the learning and academic achievement of hyperactive (HA), attention-deficit disordered (ADD), and learning-disabled (LD) children is a widely debated question.[1] There is an apparent consensus that stimulants have either no effect or a very small effect on ADD and LD children's learning and academic achievement (Aman, 1980; Aman & Werry, 1982; Barkley & Cunningham, 1978; Cantwell & Carlson, 1978; Gadow, 1983; O'Leary, 1980; Rie & Rie, 1977; Werry, 1981). This conclusion is somewhat surprising, given that most of the authors noted that studies of stimulant effects on learning have left much to be desired with regard to methodological rigor. In this chapter, I take the position that the methodological problems in the studies that show no beneficial drug effect on learning, especially with regard to long-term, academic achievement, are so numerous and per-

---

[1] The terms *hyperactivity* and *attention deficit disorder* are used interchangeably in this chapter.

259

vasive that no conclusions should be drawn from them. Further, there are reasonably convincing data from short-term studies showing that stimulants both improve learning as measured on laboratory tasks and increase productivity on classroom academic tasks. Therefore, I argue that stimulants are likely to improve academic achievement in those ADD and LD children whose performance is improved on these short-term measures. This review is selective, primarily highlighting those studies that have demonstrated positive drug effects and focusing discussion on problems in the studies that have failed to reveal beneficial effects.

LABORATORY STUDIES

Most of the research directed at the question of stimulant effects on learning has been conducted in the controlled conditions of the laboratory. Stimulant effects on ADD and LD children's performance on a wide variety of cognitive tasks have been studied (for reviews see Barkley, 1976; Cantwell & Carlson, 1978; Conners & Werry, 1979; Swanson & Kinsbourne, 1979). The goal of this line of research has been to determine the effects of stimulants on the children's cognitive deficits. It has been assumed that if these cognitive deficits mediated achievement and if stimulants corrected these deficits, then the children's academic achievement would improve. These tasks can be divided into two broad categories: (1) those that measure components of information processing involved in learning, and (2) those that measure learning itself.

EFFECTS ON COMPONENT PROCESSES

Attention

Stimulants have been shown to have large and consistent effects on sustained attention (vigilance), as measured in several different paradigms. ADD and LD children's performance deficits on vigilance tasks generally take the form of a faster decrease compared to controls in correct response rate over time in lengthy (e.g., 15–30 minutes) and boring tasks (Douglas & Peters, 1979; Pelham, 1981). Stimulants reduce this deviant-control difference in performance deterioration for both LD and ADD children (Aman & Werry, 1982; Dykman, Ackerman, & Mc-Cray, 1980; Michael, Klorman, Salzman, Borgstedt, & Dainier, 1981; Sykes, Douglas, & Morgenstern, 1972).

In contrast to the positive results on vigilance tasks, the findings are mostly negative with regard to selective attention, defined as the degree to which performance deteriorates when irrelevant or distracting information is added to a task. Stimulant effects have been studied on such tasks even though ADD and LD deficits have not been firmly established on them (Douglas & Peters, 1979; Ford, Pelham, & Ross, 1984; Harvey, Weintraub, & Neale, 1984). With few exceptions (e.g., Ackerman, Dykman, Holcomb & McCray, 1982), stimulants do not improve performance on distraction indices on such tasks as the Children's Embedded Figures Test (CEFT), the Fruit Distraction Test, the rod and frame test, and dichotic listening tasks (e.g., Campbell, Douglas & Morgenstern, 1971; Conners & Rothschild, 1968; Hiscock, Kinsbourne, Caplan, & Swanson, 1979; Zahn, Abate, Little, & Wender, 1975). Some visual-scanning tasks that do not involve distraction and nondistraction conditions but that are interpreted by their authors as indexing selective attention have shown stimulant effects (e.g., Dykman *et al.*, 1980; Flintoff, Barron, Swanson, Ledlow, & Kinsbourne, 1982).

Memory

Performance on tasks that tap various aspects of memory sometimes improves with stimulant administration and sometimes does not. Two doses of methylphenidate (MPH) had no effect on accuracy, mean RT, or scanning rate on a span-of-apprehension task (Peeke, Halliday, Callaway, Prael, & Reus, 1984). In two other studies employing dichotic listening tasks in which the subject was to repeat a brief list of words that he had just heard, stimulants had no effect (Conners & Rothschild, 1968; Hiscock *et al.*, 1979). In contrast, in an influential dose-respone study, Sprague and Sleator (1977) found that a low, but not a high, dose of MPH increased HA children's accuracy and reduced their response latency on a short-term memory-scanning task.

Stimulants facilitated performance on a single-trial, free recall task in two other studies (Peeke *et al.*, 1984; Weingartner, Rapoport, Buchsbaum, Bunney, Ebert, Mikkelsen, & Caine, 1980). These studies examined the interaction between depth of memory processing and drug effects in an attempt to identify the aspects of the memory process that were affected by stimulants. Weingartner *et al.* (1980) asked their subjects, both normal and HA boys, to select from a word triplet the word that did not belong to the group on the basis of either meaning or sound. The former distinction was assumed to require semantic processing, whereas the latter was thought to induce acoustic processing of the words. Overall, positive effects of .5 mg/kg dextroamphetamine were observed on both free and cued recall for both the HA and normal boys. There was a trend for drug effects to be greater on acoustically processed words for the HA boys and on the semantically processed words for the normal boys. Weingartner *et al.* speculated that amphetamine enhanced the type of coding operations on which the subjects relied in nondrug states and that stimulants do not enhance academic performance in HA children because the children have an apparent deficit in semantic processing that is not corrected by stimulants.

Peeke *et al.*'s (1984) results are somewhat different. In their study, different levels of processing (structural, acoustic, and semantic) were induced by requiring children to answer different kinds of questions about words that were flashed on a screen. The number of words recognized and recalled was always greatest in the semantic condition, and a low (10 mg), but not a high (21 mg), dose of MPH facilitated performance across depth-of-processing conditions. In this study, HA children processed semantically when that kind of processing was induced, and MPH facilitated semantic and acoustic processing equally.

Event-Related Potentials

Several studies have examined drug effects on event-related, cortical potentials (ERPs). By examining drug effects on different components of the ERP, researchers have sought to identify stages of processing that are affected by stimulants in HA children. The first studies failed to find consistent stimulant effects on early ERP components thought to reflect selective attention and arousal (e.g., Hall, Griffin, Moyer, Hopkins & Rapoport, 1976). The late ERP component, P300, has been studied recently, as it is presumed to reflect higher-order processes such as stimulus evaluation, comparisons among items in memory, and decision making (Hillyard & Kutas, 1983). Results in the small number of studies have been contradictory. For example, one study that measured P300 latency failed to find effects of two doses of MPH and concluded that the drug exerts its effects only after the cognitive processes tapped by P300 have been completed (Halliday, Callaway, & Naylor, 1983). In contrast, Klorman and colleagues reported normalizing MPH effects (increases) on P300 amplitude to target stimuli in a sustained attention task (Klorman, Salzman, Bauer, Coons, Borgstedt, & Halpern, 1983; Klorman, Salzman, & Borgstedt, in press). Unfortunately, Halliday *et al.* did not find MPH effects on P300 amplitude in their study, and Klorman and others did not report latencies in their research. Resolution of these conflicting findings thus awaits further research.

Summary

Stimulants have been shown to have salutary effects on tasks that tap various aspects of attention and memory, notably vigilance and recall tasks. The data are not, however, conclusive regarding the precise stages of information processing that are affected by stimulants. The failure to find stimulant effects on selective attention indices and on early ERP components suggests that stimulants do not affect the perceptual processes that comprise early processing stages. Klorman's work suggests that stimulant effects in vigilance tasks may be mediated through a higher-order stage of processing rather than a simple increase in the length of time that children can sustain attention to the tasks. Further, the results of different memory studies were somewhat contradictory. Drugs failed to interact consistently with most of the variables manipulated, including depth of processing, scanning rate, and distraction. Stimulants apparently do not exert their effects on memory tasks via the processing stages tapped by these manipulations. Finally, stimulant effects do not depend on cognitive deficits, as normal children and adults show performance improvements on many tasks when they receive stimulants (Klorman, Bauer, Coons, Lewis, Peloquin, Perlmutter, Ryan, Salzman, & Strauss, 1984; Rapoport, Buchsbaum, Weingartner, Zahn, Ludlow, & Mikkelsen, 1980; Weiss & Laties, 1962).

Discovery of the cognitive pathway through which stimulants exert their effects is an important goal, although it is primarily of theoretical interest. Such knowledge cannot necessarily be used to draw inferences regarding stimulant effects on learning. In recognition of this dilemma, research directed at stimulant effects on tasks that measure learning itself has proceeded concurrently with the study of drug effects on stages of processing.

EFFECTS ON LEARNING

Numerous studies have shown that stimulants have a beneficial effect on paired-associate learning (PAL) for children with either learning or behavior problems (Conners & Rothschild, 1968; Conners, Rothschild, Eisenberg, Schwartz, & Robinson, 1969; Dalby, Kinsbourne, Swanson, & Sobol, 1977; Gan & Cantwell, 1982; Gittelman-Klein & Klein, 1976; Swanson & Kinsbourne, 1976; Swanson, Kinsbourne, Roberts & Zucker, 1978). Stimulant effects in these studies are substantial, often reaching a 25–40% decrease in errors.

Other types of learning tasks have been used much less frequently, but the results are similar to those found on PAL tasks. For example, one study employed nonsense words that the subjects had to learn to spell (Stephens, Pelham & Skinner, 1984). Figure 1 shows the effects that .3 mg/kg MPH and 1.9 mg/kg pemoline had on learning during acquisition in that task. Another study involved repeated reading of a paragraph until children could correctly answer comprehension questions about its content. Although no drug effect relative to placebo was found on the number of trials to criterion during initial learning, a drug effect was found at 2-hour recall, implying that MPH had improved initial learning (Rie & Rie, 1977). Finally, MPH (.3 and .7 mg/kg) decreased hyperactive children's error rate and increased their correct response rate on a re-peated acquisition task (Walker, 1982). Less substantial but significant stimulant effects were reported in two studies that analyzed learning-acquisition curves in reading and memory tasks (Ackerman & Dykman, 1982; Greenstein, Pelham, Torgesen, Bender, Adams, Atkins, Schell, & White, 1983).

Two single-subject studies employed actual academic tasks to evalu-ate stimulant effects (Pelham & Bender, 1984; Schell, Pelham, Bender, & Andre, in press). The subjects in both studies were multihandicapped children with severe ADD, severe learning problems, and IQs in the mildly retarded range. Both children learned grade-appropriate, sight-vocabulary words in sessions that varied across days, according to whether the child received placebo or .3 mg/kg MPH. In both cases, 40%

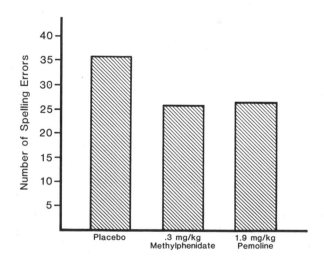

Figure 1. Number of errors made in placebo, .3 mg/kg MPH, and 1.9 mg/kg pemoline conditions during acquisition of nonsense spelling words.

improvements in learning (increase in correct responses or decrease in errors) were obtained in the active drug condition. Pelham and Bender (1984) also examined the subjects' learning of grade-appropriate, spelling words and found a 50% decrease in errors on drug relative to placebo days.

Beyond studies of initial learning, stimulant effects on retention of learned material have been studied. When the retention intervals are relatively brief, for example, 2 hours, and the children are still in drug states, drug effects have been found (Ackerman & Dykman, 1982; Rie & Rie, 1977). In contrast, in three studies when retention was tested over days, stimulant effects were not obtained (Aman & Sprague, 1974; Gan & Cantwell, 1982; Steinhausen & Kreuzer, 1981). Neither Aman and Sprague nor Steinhausen and Kreuzer found drug effects at initial learning, however, which makes it difficult to draw conclusions about their failure to find effects at retention. More positive findings were reported by Stephens et al. (1984), who employed PAL and spelling tasks, and tested learning and 1-week retention for .3 mg/kg MPH and an equivalent dose of pemoline. They reported savings in relearning from 10% to 19%, depending on the task and the drug. Similarly, in one of the single-subject studies reported above, there was a 16% differential in favor of MPH when relearning on placebo at the end of the 4-week protocol was measured for words originally learned under MPH and placebo conditions (Pelham & Bender, 1984).

All five of these retention studies were analyzed for state-dependent learning (SDL), a pattern of drug effects such that material learned in one drug state fails to transfer completely when retention is tested in a different state. In a controversial SDL study, Swanson and Kinsbourne (1976) reported a substantial transfer decrement from PAL learning in a MPH state to retention in a placebo state. In contrast to their results, however, no other studies, which have employed a variety of drugs, dosages, and tasks, have found any evidence for SDL (Gan & Cantwell, 1982; Pelham & Bender, 1984; Stephens et al., 1984).

In summary, salutary stimulant effects have been found in the laboratory across a variety of learning tasks in many different samples of children. This conclusion appears to hold both for initial acquisition and for retention. The only study that assessed drug effects on initial learning and retention in an individual child found beneficial effects at both times. Relatively fewer studies have assessed retention, however, and drug effects often have not been as large as those obtained during initial learning.

By what mechanisms stimulants may affect learning is not well understood. The drugs are thought to improve sustained attention and increase inhibitory control over impulsive responding, thereby increasing children's concentrated task effort and improving learning (Cantwell & Carlson, 1978; Conners & Rothschild, 1968; Dalby et al., 1977; Douglas, 1983). Few studies, however, have manipulated parameters that affect learning, and alternative explanations for stimulant effects remain largely unexplored.

CLASSROOM STUDIES

Laboratory studies are not the only source of information regarding stimulant effects on learning. Although performance on laboratory learning tasks is correlated with academic achievement, the shared variance very rarely reaches 50% and is usually on the order of 25% (Stevenson, Hale, Klein, & Miller, 1968). A logically direct and potentially fruitful approach to addressing stimulant effects on academic achievement is to examine directly the effects of stimulants on classroom measures of academic functioning. Inferences regarding the relationship between laboratory measures of cognitive functions and classroom performance thus are avoided and the data obtained are more directly related to academic achievement.

STANDARDIZED ACHIEVEMENT TESTS

The dependent measures used in most studies of stimulant effects on classroom learning have been standardized academic-achievement tests. Aman (1980) and Barkley and Cunningham (1978) reviewed these studies and concluded that they provide no evidence that stimulants enhance academic achievement. A typical study is the one reported by Rie, Rie, Stewart, and Ambuel (1976a), in which children who were underachieving in reading received MPH and placebo for 12 weeks each in a crossover design. The Iowa Test of Basic Skills (ITBS) was administered at baseline and following each drug period. Although scores for all ITBS subtests were higher for the drug period than for the placebo period, only one of six subtests revealed a significant drug effect.

This study is representative of most of the controlled studies that have used achievement tests to assess stimulant effects. The studies assessed medication effects over periods ranging from 3 to 15 weeks, with 4–6 weeks as the typical length. As did Rie et al. (1976a), a number of studies have reported effects on one or two achievement subtests (Conners et al., 1969; Conners, Taylor, Meo, Kurtz, & Fournier, 1972; Rie, Rie, Stewart, & Ambuel, 1976b). Often, however, no significant drug effects have been obtained (Conners & Taylor, 1980; Finnerty, Soltys, & Cole, 1971; Gittleman-Klein & Klein, 1976; Hoffman, Engelhardt, Margolis, Polizos, Waizer, & Rosenfeld, 1974). In addition to these short-term, controlled studies, several 2–5-year, uncontrolled, follow-up studies have measured achievement. Most have failed to find evidence of beneficial stimulant effects on standardized tests (Charles & Schain, 1981; Loney, Kramer, & Kossier, 1981; Riddle & Rapoport, 1976) or other measures of classroom achievement (Weiss, Kruger, Danielson, & Elman, 1975).

The most striking aspect of these classroom achievement studies is the absence of drug effects relative to the laboratory studies of learning. Whereas the laboratory studies often yielded 25–40% reductions in errors with drug relative to placebo, only rarely have significant effects been obtained in the classroom studies, and the average effect is considerably less than 25% (Kavale, 1982). The failure of these studies to provide evidence for beneficial stimulant effects forms the crux of the argument that stimulants do not affect academic achievement (Aman, 1980; Barkley & Cunningham, 1978). Before that conclusion is drawn, however, an alternative plausible explanation for these studies' collective failure should be addressed: These studies have numerous methodological inadequacies that compromise their findings. In particular, the sensitivity of achievement tests, individual differences, drug dosing, compliance, and time-course effects are factors that warrant examination.

ACHIEVEMENT TEST SENSITIVITY

Although achievement tests are the most appropriate measure for assessing academic gains over an entire school year or longer, their validity is questionable over the shorter time periods characteristic of drug studies, usually 4–12 weeks (Barkley & Cunningham, 1978) and occasionally as long as 18 weeks (e.g., Gittelman, Klein, & Feingold, 1983). Using the Wide Range Achievement Test (WRAT) arithmetic test as an example, Sprague and Berger (1980) argued that standardized achievement tests are insufficiently sensitive to detect achievement gains over such brief time periods. Because of the small number of items on the WRAT and the relatively large, standard error of measurement, the average 8-year-old ADD or LD child "would have to gain at a rate far above the expected average rate" for significant improvement to be revealed after an 8–12 week drug trial (Sprague & Berger, 1980). Although stimulants appear to improve academic performance in some children, they do not work miracles and will not result in academic gains that are far above the normal rate. The most appropriate interpretation of the null results in these studies is that 4–15-week time spans are insufficient for achievement tests to detect the effects of drugs or any other intervention. An educational psychologist would not evaluate the effectiveness of a new instructional program with a study that lasted only 8 weeks and employed a standardized achievement test as the sole dependent measure, and there is no reason to expect such a design to yield useful information regarding the effects of stimulants on learning.

DRUG DOSE

A lack of attention to drug-dose factors may have played an important role in the failure to find stimulant effects on achievement. ADD children's improvement in performance on cognitive tasks appears to be maximized most often at relatively low doses of MPH. In a groundbreaking study, the effects of placebo, .3 mg/kg, and 1.0 mg/kg MPH were compared on short-term-memory task performance in the laboratory and on classroom ratings on the Abbreviated Conners Teacher Rating Scale. The lower dose of medication facilitated performance on the cognitive task for the majority of children but had a lesser effect on teacher ratings, whereas the higher dose had both a major beneficial effect on the teacher ratings and an adverse effect on short-term-memory performance (Sprague & Sleator, 1977). This general pattern of findings has been supported across a variety of samples and tasks in children (Brown & Sleator, 1979; Peeke et al., 1984; Pelham et al., in press-a; Poling & Breuning, 1983; R. L. Sprague, personal communication, February 1983; Swanson et al., 1978; Swanson, Sandman, Deutsch, & Baren, 1983). At the same time, the precise dose above which MPH begins to have an adverse effect on cognition is not yet known. Although .3 mg/kg is the most widely accepted figure, beneficial effects on some cognitive tasks have been reported at doses as high as .6–1.0 mg/kg MPH (Dykman et al., 1980; Klorman et al., 1983; Pelham et al., in press-a; Poling & Breuning, 1983; Solanto & Conners, 1982; Walker, 1982), .5 mg/kg dextroamphetamine (Weingartner et al., 1980), and 112.5 mg pemoline (Pelham et al., 1980).

The reason for the discrepancies between Sprague's initial reports and others showing cognitive improvement at higher doses are unclear. One explanation is that these differences can be explained by the notion of task specificity of drug response (Swanson, Barlow, & Kinsbourne, 1979; Swanson & Kinsbourne, 1979). These researchers argue that drug effects invariably will be obtained on relatively simple cognitive tasks, such as continuous performance tasks, and that high doses on such tasks will not adversely affect performance in the way they harm performance in more complex tasks (see also Robbins & Sahakian, 1979). Solanto and Conners (1982) offered this same explanation for their finding of positive MPH effects with doses up to 1.0 mg/kg on a serial reaction time task. Further, they noted that adverse effects of 1.0 mg/kg were not apparent in the least difficult condition of Sprague's short-term-memory task.

Indeed, studies that failed to reveal adverse effects of high (1.0 mg/kg) doses of MPH usually employed relatively simple tasks. At the same time, doses of MPH as high as .7 mg/kg and 112.5 mg pemoline enhanced performance on several tasks (reading comprehension, paired-associate learning, and repeated acquisition) that involved complex cognitive processing (Pelham et al., in press-a; Pelham et al., 1980-a; Walker, 1982). Further research is needed to provide information regarding the dose levels beyond which stimulants have adverse effects on cognition.

It should be noted that beneficial drug effects could be obtained on a cognitive task, but this effect could be accompanied by adverse side effects. For example, large decreases in social interactions have been reported for some children with low-to-moderate-stimulant levels (Barkley & Cunningham, 1979; Pelham, in press; Pelham & Bender, 1982). Other negative side effects, including weight loss, can accompany stimulant doses (e.g., .6 mg/kg b.i.d.) that have been shown to produce cognitive improvement on simple tasks (Mattes & Gittelman, 1983). There are thus numerous reasons to avoid stimulant doses considerably higher than .3 mg/kg MPH (or equivalent).

One of the major reasons that previous investigations failed to find stimulant effects on learning and achievement may be that dosages considerably higher than .3 mg/kg MPH were administered in the great majority of studies (and in all long-term achievement studies). If the assertion is correct that .3 mg/kg MPH is the optimal dose for cognitive improvement in most children, then positive effects on achievement would not be expected in studies that employed higher doses. In the longest follow-up study reported to date, the mean daily dose of MPH was 30 mg (approximately .6 mg/kg per dose or 1.2 mg/kg/day) with a range from 20 mg to 80 mg (Weiss et al., 1975). In another follow-up study (Charles & Schain, 1981; Charles, Schain, & Guthrie, 1979; Schain & Reynard, 1975), the mean doses of MPH (usually given in a single morning dose) ranged from .6 mg/kg to 1.3 mg/kg over the 5 years of treatment. The corresponding mean single doses of MPH for the two most carefully controlled short-term studies were .42 mg/kg (.84 mg/kg/day; Rie et al., 1976a) and .79 mg/kg (1.58 mg/kg/day; Gittelman-Klein & Klein, 1976). Stimulant dosages in most of the laboratory studies of cognition reviewed earlier also have been similarly high. In these studies, tested dosages were often at a mean of 30 mg MPH or its equivalent—.6 to 1.0 mg/kg per dose—with a range from 5 to 60 mg—.3 to 1.4 mg/kg (e.g., Campbell, Douglas, & Morgenstern, 1971; Charles, Schain, Zelniker, & Guthrie, 1979; Dykman et al., 1980; Sykes, Douglas, Weiss, & Minde, 1971; Weingartner et al., 1980).

With one exception, Weingartner et al., all of these studies employed dosages individually titrated according to physician's global judgment of improvement. Thus, there was substantial variation in dosages received; many of the children in each study were receiving doses higher than the average doses noted above. Individually titrated doses may be so high because the variable on which titration is based directly or indirectly is often teacher report rather than performance on a cognitive task (Gadow, 1981). Because teacher ratings show greatest improvement with high doses of medication, the great majority of children in previous studies may have received mean doses of stimulants that improved social behavior but were 50–400% higher than the dose that may maximize improvement in cognitive abilities.

Because dose has not been systematically manipulated in long-term studies, it is not certain that lowered doses would have produced greater achievement gains. It is noteworthy, however, that two studies with clearest evidence of academic gains employed doses in the .3 mg/kg range (Pelham, Schnedler, Bender, Miller, Nilsson, Budrow, Ronnei, Paluchowski & Marks, in press-b; Satterfield, Cantwell, & Satterfield, 1979). Negative results on learning or achievement that involved doses of psychostimulants higher than .3 mg/kg MPH or its equivalent that were not titrated on cognitive measures should not be interpreted as evidence that stimulants failed to enhance learning or achievement.[2]

COMPLIANCE

In laboratory studies of drug effects, medication usually has been administered by experimenters, and thus, it has been ensured that children actually receive the intended medication. In most studies of achievement, however, parents usually have administered medication,

---

[2] Dextroamphetamine is generally considered to be twice as potent as MPH and, therefore, is prescribed in amounts half that of MPH. However, I am not aware of any studies that have empirically demonstrated this relationship with children on cognitive tasks. Pemoline is considerably less potent than MPH. Between four and six times as much pemoline as MPH is required to produce the same effect on an academic task with an ADD child (Pelham et al., 1980-a; Pelham, in press-a).

and whether actual administration has followed prescribed procedures usually is not known. Noncompliance with drug regimen is considered by some to be the greatest problem in evaluating the results of field studies of stimulant effects. Two recent studies assessed compliance to stimulant-drug regimens. Only 55% of parents who agreed to participate in one 12-month, drug-treatment study were still administering medication after 10 months, and half of the discontinuers did so after only 4 months (Firestone, 1982). Noting that only 10% of the discontinuers discussed it with the project personnel in advance, Firestone (1982) concluded that "less diligent supervision of these families would have led to inflated estimates of compliance rates" (p.453). In another study, even when parents reported that they were giving the drugs, the percentage of days on which urinalysis confirmed parental report averaged only 67% (Kauffman, Smith-Wright, Reese, Simpson, & Jones, 1981).

Most drug-treatment studies report dropout rates or rates of inconsistent administration that are considerably less than these percentages. This suggests that many parents in such studies must fail to report that they have discontinued their child's medication or do not give it regularly. In one 6-month study, 38% of the children in the drug-treatment groups did not receive medication regularly and/or according to the prescribed regimen (Conrad, Dworkin, Shai, & Tobiessen, 1971). Although widely cited as having failed to show beneficial stimulant effects on achievement, none of the reviews that cite the Conrad et al. (1971) study note that many children did not receive the described treatment (e.g., Aman, 1980; Barkley & Cunningham, 1978; Gadow, 1983; O'Leary, 1980).

In contrast, the medication effects shown in Figure 1, which are considerably larger than Conrad et al.'s, were obtained in studies in which the experimenters administered medication, thus ensuring that all subjects actually received it. This contrast suggests that noncompliance is a likely source of the discrepancies that exist between laboratory studies of cognitive performance, in which compliance is ensured and beneficial drug effects are often found, and classroom studies of achievement, where the rate of compliance appears to be low and where drug effects on achievement are rare.

A number of suggestions to improve medication compliance in clinical practice have been made (e.g., Epstein & Cluss, 1982; Peck & King, 1982). In research endeavors, care should be taken to include only data from subjects who are known to have received medication (e.g., through urinalysis checks).

TIME COURSE OF STIMULANT EFFECTS

MPH, the most commonly used stimulant, has a brief time course in which cognitive and physiological effects are detectable 1 hour after ingestion and peak approximately 2 hours after ingestion. The drug's effects then decrease linearly for 2 or 3 additional hours (Gualtieri, Wargin, Kanoy, Patrick, Shen, Youngblood, Mueller, & Breese, 1982; Kupietz, Winsberg & Sverd, 1982; Shaywitz, Hunt, Jatlow, Cohen, Young, Pierce, Anderson, & Shaywitz, 1982; Solanto & Conners, 1982; Swanson et al., 1978). MPH treatment thus does not result in a steady, state-drug effect. Instead, the drug has a 4–6-hour time course, during only 2 or 3 hours of which—60–90 minutes on either side of the peak—is there an optimal drug effect. There are few data that bear directly on this point, but it is not unlikely that, at relatively low dosages, optimal stimulant effects on cognitive tasks will be obtained only during this 2–3 hour period.

In the vast majority of laboratory studies and in the few classroom studies in which stimulant effects are clear, children have been tested during the time when an optimal drug effect is expected (e.g., Pelham et al., 1980; Pelham et al., in press-a; Stephens et al., 1984). In most classroom studies, however, stimulants have been administered without regard to when a child will be performing academic tasks throughout the day. For example, in a study that failed to show stimulant effects on academic measures, the two academic measures were given only 25 minutes and 70 minutes following MPH administration, times that are prior to, or at the beginning of, the optimal period (Wolraich, Drummond, Salomon, O'Brien, & Sivage, 1978).

This brief time course may severely limit stimulant effects on learning in natural classroom settings, as the drugs are typically administered. For example, a typical 7:00 AM (breakfast) dose of MPH exerts an optimal effect on learning primarily from 8:00 AM until 10:00AM. If school beings at 8:45 AM, a child receiving a single morning dose of MPH may be optimally medicated with regard to cognitive skills between 8:45 and 10:00 AM. Another drug dose at noon adds 2 hours of optimal effect during a period of the day when few academic tasks are performed.

The actual time that elementary-school children spend engaged in academic tasks is surprisingly small. For example, one set of findings suggested that children spend less than 70 hours per year acquiring basic reading and math skills (Berliner & Rosenshine, 1977). Based on a 180-day school year, this averages less than 39 minutes per day. Unless these few minutes overlap with the time of optimal drug effect, medicated children may not derive any academic benefit from medication. It is not far-fetched to hypothesize that mismatches between time course and task performance may be a major reason that beneficial effects of stimulants on classroom achievement have not been found.

Unfortunately, the data that would confirm this hypothesis are not yet available. There are very few studies that have described the time course of stimulant effects, and even fewer that have compared the time course across different dependent measures. One question that can be raised is why stimulant effects are so clear in natural classroom settings on measures of social behavior if this time-course variable is as critical as I have suggested (Conners, 1983). Behaviors such as noncompliance and classroom disruption, common types of social behavior measured in drug studies, may have a wider therapeutic "window" than may cognitive skills. Those behaviors may respond to a wider range of doses and may, therefore, be less influenced by peak-effect levels than measures of cognition. At least one recent study has shown, for example, that MPH has different time-action effects on activity level and reaction time (Solanto & Conners, 1982). The authors of that study suggested that attentional and motor inhibition in hyperactive children may correspond to different neurophysiological substrates and thus have different responses to MPH.

The fact that more salient stimulant effects are evident on measures of social behavior than on measures of cognition does not detract necessarily from the argument that time-course variables may be important determinants of stimulant effects on cognitive measures.

A further question is: What can be done to adjust for time-course limitations in stimulant administration in the natural environment? The desirability of maintaining MPH dosages at a low level argues against administering MPH at more frequent intervals (e.g., 2 hours) to maintain a steady state effect (cf., Briant, 1978). Instead, individual dosing regimens could be coordinated with the times that a child engages in classroom academic tasks, a complicated, but perhaps necessary, undertaking. Alternatively, pemoline, timed-release dextroamphetamine, and slow-release MPH all have longer half lives and should have longer periods of peak effect (e.g., Pelham et al., 1980-a).

INDIVIDUAL DIFFERENCES

It has been known for some time that there are large individual differences in ADD children's responses to stimulants (Conners, 1972). For example, on a paired-associate learning (PAL) task, 60–70% of medicated ADD children show improved performance at relatively low doses, with a three- or fourfold range across children in the dose that is most effective. The other 30–40% of ADD children show either no effect of medication or impaired performance at all doses (Swanson & Kinsbourne, 1979; Swanson et al., 1978; Swanson et al., 1983). Further, these differences in drug response vary from task to task (Swanson et al., 1979).

Similarly, there is considerable variability in the degree of academic deficit in the HA children that typically have served as subjects in studies of stimulant effects on achievement. Some of the children have deficits in achievement; some are concurrently diagnosable as LD. However, whether the child has an academic deficit rarely has been considered in evaluating drug effects on achievement. Conners (1983) has noted that this failure is "tantamount to testing the effects of an anticancer drug in a sample for which information is absent regarding whether the patients have the disease or not" (p.49). Further, the subject areas vary in which ADD and LD children exhibit academic deficits, and there is evidence that stimulants may have different effects on different academic areas (Pelham et al., in press-a). Some children might improve in one subject area and other children in another (e.g., Conners, 1972). These effects might or might not be most apparent in subject areas in which children have the greatest deficits, and they may depend on stimulants' effects on the deficient area of functioning (Conners, 1983; Gittelman et al., 1983; Gittelman-Klein & Klein, 1976; Rie et al., 1976a).

Although these individual difference dimensions have been known for years, researchers who have examined drug effects on classroom achievement generally have ignored them and averaged data across individuals, tasks, and dosages. The result is that data that apply only to the average child have been presented, and potentially beneficial, individual, drug effects have been obscured. To gather accurate information about stimulant effects on learning and achievement, experimenters must ensure that group-analysis procedures do not mask individual academic deficits, individual responsiveness to medication, and both beneficial and adverse interactions between the two.

SUMMARY

Even though there is little research that has involved direct manipulations of test sensitivity, drug variables, and individual differences, it should be apparent from this discussion that there is good reason to question the validity of the negative results obtained in many studies of stimulant effects on achievement. A carefully controlled study is needed before the lack of positive findings in previous studies is elevated to the level of fact.

CLASSROOM PREDICTORS OF ACHIEVEMENT

Classroom Measures

The difficulties involved in the use of achievement tests to measure stimulant effects have led to the use of alternative measures. A number of recent studies thus have assessed drug effects on the dependent measures that have been used in applied behavior analysis in classroom settings: objective samples of classroom behavior and performance that are related to achievement (Catania & Brigham, 1978). Stimulant effects typically have been measured on disruptive behavior, on-task behavior, and academic productivity.

Because the amount of children's participation in learning tasks appears to be one of the best predictors of school achievement (Berliner & Rosenshine, 1977), stimulant-effected reductions in any behaviors that are incompatible with academic task performance (e.g., noncompliance with teacher requests, classroom disruption, off-task behavior) would be expected to improve achievement. Two of the most salient and most consistent effects of stimulants in the classroom are a reduction in disruptive behaviors and an increase in on-task behavior (Cantwell & Carlson, 1978; Conners & Werry, 1979). Both of these general stimulant effects *should* increase medicated children's involvement in assigned learning tasks, thus facilitating achievement. That this has not been demonstrated empirically has been labeled a fundamental paradox in the study of stimulant effects (Conners, 1983). However, if changes in classroom disruption and on-task behavior were not accompanied by an increase in academic productivity, then achievement changes would not be expected.

It has been widely thought that stimulant effects on classroom disruption are not accompanied by changes in academic productivity (e.g., Barkley & Cunningham, 1978), but recent data are now available that show this to be a premature conclusion. In addition to improvement in on-task and disruptive behavior, stimulants increase the amount of work that children accomplish while medicated. For example, Figure 2 shows the number of arithmetic problems that ADD children completed correctly in supervised, 15-minute periods under different doses of MPH (Pelham *et al.*, in press-a) and pemoline (Pelham *et al.*, 1980-a). In both studies, the arithmetic problems selected were ones that the children knew how to complete but on which they needed continued prac-

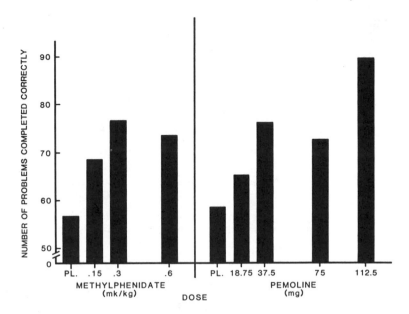

Figure 2.   Number of arithmetic problems completed correctly in 15-minute, supervised, special classroom periods as a function of methylphenidate and pemoline doses.

tice. Compared to placebo conditions, the ADD children in these two studies increased their productivity on arithmetic seatwork assignments by 30–50% while medicated. Similar findings on phonics and arithmetic tasks have been reported in other recent single-subject studies (Rapport, Murphy, & Bailey, 1982; Sprague & Berger, 1980), and comparable results have been found on reading comprehension, sight vocabulary, and nonsense-spelling measures (Pelham, in press; Pelham & Bender, 1984; Pelham et al., in press-a; Schell et al., in press). In each of these studies, the number of correct responses that children made in a given period of time increased in drug relative to placebo conditions. An alternative dependent measure is whether children complete their assigned classwork. In one study, the percentage of days on which children completed all of their assigned classroom tasks increased from 59% on placebo days to 78% on days when they received .3 mg/kg MPH (Pelham, in press). Sixteen of 20 subjects showed this beneficial effect.

Several studies failed to find beneficial stimulant effects on academic productivity (e.g., Ayllon, Layman & Kandel, 1975; Wolraich et al., 1978). In every case, however, results were compromised by at least one of the serious methodological limitations discussed in this essay. It appears that when measures are taken with appropriate methodological control, large increases in academic productivity accompany the well-known stimulant effects on classroom disruption. It is interesting to note that Bradley and Bowen (1940) reported changes in arithmetic productivity in one of the first studies of stimulant effects on disturbed children. These effects were overshadowed by the larger, more salient effects that were obtained on social behavior, providing the initial impetus for the prevalent belief that stimulants improve behavior but not learning.

Additional research clearly is needed, especially regarding reading and spelling skills, which generally show smaller drug facilitation than do arithmetic skills. At the same time, these stimulant-related changes in academic productivity are noteworthy. The importance of these findings is indicated by the role that task engagement and practice are assigned in theories of instruction (e.g., Berliner & Rosenshine, 1977; Cronbach, 1977; Gagne, 1977). It has long been an established fact in the laboratory study of paired-associates learning that overlearning (continued repetition of correct responses past a criterion) results in increased retention in proportion to the degree of overlearning (Krueger, 1929; Postman, 1962; Underwood, 1964). In the classroom, both with regard to reading (LaBerge & Samuels, 1974) and arithmetic (Resnick & Ford, 1981; Yoshida, 1980), practice well beyond the initial acquisition of a skill is necessary for most efficient utilization of the skill. This may be especially true for children who are having academic problems, highlighting the value of any intervention that increases practice of accurate responses in the classroom (Gadow, Torgesen, & Dahlem, in press-a; Torgesen & Young, 1983). Instructional models with a strong emphasis on carefully graded, supervised, and reinforced practice have been shown to be more effective for academically disadvantaged children than models without that emphasis (Becker & Gersten, 1982; Berliner & Rosenshine, 1977; Brophy, 1979; Catania & Brigham, 1978; Gadow et al., in press-a).

Previous studies of stimulant effects on learning and achievement may have been partially misdirected in their focus on laboratory tasks that measured only the acquisition of novel information. These studies essentially ignore the potential benefits to learning of increases in practice on academic tasks in the classroom. Drug effects on practice previously have been dismissed with the observation that stimulants affect only performance and not real learning (e.g., Gittelman et al., 1983; Rie & Rie, 1977). If performance in the form of accurate practice affects achievement, however, then stimulant-facilitated increases in seatwork performance would be expected to lead to increased achievement. For example, the results depicted in Figure 2 lead to the prediction that, all other things being equal, medicated ADD children who show individual responses similar to these group averages will show long-term arithmetic gains relative to appropriate control children.

The importance of these results depends on whether changes in these classroom behaviors predict long-term changes in achievement. This assumption is a common one that underlies much behavioral and educational research. These classroom measures are logically more directly related to achievement than are laboratory measures of information processing, and there is evidence that they predict achievement (Berliner & Rosenshine, 1977). At the same time, whether changes in these variables predict changes in achievement within children is not yet known. This approach to measuring the effects of pharmacological, as well as behavioral and educational, interventions on achievement thus requires validation.

CONCURRENT INTERVENTIONS

A major question that has received attention only very recently is whether drug effects are dependent upon concurrent therapeutic or instructional interventions (e.g., Gadow, 1983; Gadow, Torgesen, Greenstein, & Schell, in press; Pelham, 1983; Pelham, in press; Pelham & Murphy, in press; Schroeder, Lewis, & Lipton, 1983; Sprague, 1983). The intuitive answer to that question is an obvious "yes." No matter how much stimulants affect task productivity or accuracy, if the instructional or motivational conditions necessary for learning are not present, then the potential benefits the drugs offer will not be realized. There is growing empirical evidence that stimulant effects on laboratory learning tasks and in the classroom, indeed, can be facilitated by concurrent interventions. There is also suggestive evidence that stimulant effects can be reduced by certain concurrent variables.

INCENTIVE VARIABLES

Several recent studies have examined the interaction between behavior-modification programs and psychostimulant medication. Suggestive evidence has been found that the effects of relatively low MPH dosages apparently are enhanced by concurrently implemented behavioral programs. In one placebo-controlled study, a dose of .25 mg/kg MPH had an effect on on-task classroom behavior that was half that of a .75 mg/kg dose during a medication probe when no behavioral intervention was in effect. After 13 weeks of behavioral intervention, however, a second medication probe revealed that the two doses had equivalent effects on on-task behavior (Pelham *et al.*, 1980-b). Behavioral treatment thus interacted with MPH dose. increasing the efficacy of the lower dose more than the higher one.

In a study discussed previously, .3 mg/kg MPH, reward, and task structure were manipulated to study a 5-year-old boy's acquisition of sight words (Schell *et al.*, in press). MPH alone resulted in improved performance. Reward and structure together acted similarly. When reward, structure, and MPH were combined, the treatment effects on two dependent measures (percentage of and number of correct responses) were enhanced additively. As shown in Figure 3, the drug had an interactive effect with reward on the number of words learned to criterion, with an MPH effect that was five times greater in the reward-plus-structure condition than in the nonreward conditions. Similar results were obtained on measures of on-task behavior, classroom disruption, or academic achievement in other studies in which behavior modification (and, in some cases, other forms of psychotherapy) and low dosages of MPH were employed (Pelham, in press; Pelham *et al.*, in press-a; Pelham *et al.*, in press-b; Satterfield, Cantwell, & Satterfield, 1979; Schell, Pelham, Adams, Atkins, Greenstein, White, Bender, Bailey, Shapiro, Law, Darling, & Case, 1983). In each study, MPH effects appeared to be larger when behavioral programs were in effect than they otherwise would have been.

Incentive variables may also affect drug response in laboratory studies. Consider, for example, Sprague and colleague's studies, which consistently demonstrate clear effects of .3 mg/kg MPH (e.g., Brown &

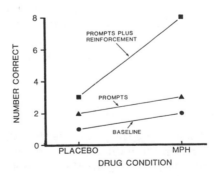

Figure 3.   Number of sight words learned to criterion in baseline, structure, and reward-plus-structure conditions on placebo and .3 mg/kg MPH days.

Sleator, 1979; Sprague & Sleator, 1977; Sprague & Berger, 1980). An oft-overlooked aspect of their standard experimental procedure is that their subjects are rewarded with points that are used to purchase items at a reinforcement "store." If the drug effects obtained in these studies depended to some extent on the presence of concurrent incentives, as in Schell *et al.* (in press), it is possible that other studies' failures to find beneficial effects of the same dose of MPH on similar tasks may result from the absence of incentives during task performance (e.g., Aman & Werry, 1982; Steinhausen & Kreuzer, 1981).

Further, Douglas (1983) argued that ADD children are unusually sensitive to reward and that intermittent reinforcement schedules thus have a detrimental effect on their performance, presumably from the frustrative nonreward involved in nonreinforced trials (Parry & Douglas, 1983). If ADD children perform particularly poorly in partial reinforcement conditions and thus have much room for improvement, one might predict that stimulants would have larger effect when an ADD child is partially reinforced only, compared to a task in which the child receives continuous or no reinforcement. Such a pattern was obtained in one of the case studies discussed earlier (Pelham & Bender, 1984). The child performed much more poorly in conditions when he was rewarded on only part of the trials, compared to a nonreward condition, and the larger MPH effects were apparent in the reward condition.

If stimulant effects depend on a child's level of central nervous system (CNS) arousal, an oft-made but unproven hypothesis (Hastings & Barkley, 1978; Rosenthal & Allen, 1977), then the presence of any other conditions, including reward, that affected arousal could influence stimulant effects. Any combination of incentive condition and stimulant that raised arousal above an optimal level would be predicted to disrupt performance. Further, if the optimal level of arousal for cognitive performance were lower than tha optimal level for behavioral improvement (e.g., Sprague & Sleator, 1977), then combined interventions that improved behavior might impair academic performance. This possible inhibitor reward-drug interaction has not been studied.

INSTRUCTIONAL VARIABLES

The major point of the above discussion is that stimulant effects appear to depend, in part, on the nature of concurrent contingencies and reinforcers. In a similar fashion, instructional variables that are either explicit or implicit in task presentation or task materials may influence drug effects on learning (Gadow, 1983; Werry, 1981). For example, Kupietz, Richardson, Gadow, and Winsberg (1980) studied the effects of 5 mg and 10 mg MPH on acquisition of a beginning-reading vocabulary for nine adult subjects. In addition to varying drug conditions, the authors presented the simulus items both in a standard paired-associates fashion (simultaneous presentation) and in a progressive-presentation mode that was designed to (and did) facilitate rapid learning. Beneficial drug effects were obtained only in the standard paired-associates presentation. Comparable studies with HA/LD children have yet to be conducted, but this study suggests that if instruction is optimized, stimulant effects may not be obtained (indeed, the drugs may not be needed). What if instruction is minimized? Neither MPH nor pemoline significantly facilitated the acquisition of spelling words in two studies in which the spelling words were studied by the children independently in classroom settings (Pelham *et al.*, in press-a; Pelham *et al.*, 1980-a). In contrast, when children learned spelling words in a structured interaction with adult testers who insured task adherence, beneficial effects were found for both MPH and pemoline (Pelham, in press; Stephens *et al.*, 1984). A similar result is obtained when three classroom studies that we have conducted are compared. In one study (Schell *et al.*, 1983), the classroom was relatively less structured and only on-task behavior was rewarded, whereas, in two other studies, the classroom was more highly structured, and both task completion and accuracy, in addition to on-task behavior, were reinforced (Pelham, in press; Pelham *et al.*, in press-a). Although all three studies found MPH-induced improvement in on-task behavior, only the two studies in which academic performance directly was rewarded found substantial drug effects on academic productivity and accuracy.

SUMMARY AND IMPLICATIONS

Although the data are preliminary and conclusions, therefore, drawn judiciously, it appears that an appropriate balance must be struck between instructional variables, concurrent interventions, and stimulant treatment for drug effects on academic performance to be maximized and, in some cases, even obtained. There is considerable evidence that concurrent behavioral interventions enhance stimulant effects on classroom behavior. Most of these studies, however, have focused on classroom behavior rather than academic performance (Pelham & Murphy, in press). This fact should prompt more frequent use of concurrent treatment strategies with a focus on classroom academic performance. Additionally, studies of these putative interactions between reinforcement contingencies and drug effects, especially at the dosages that may maximize cognitive improvement, could clarify discrepancies in previous studies. For example, HA children in laboratory-testing situations are notoriously difficult to control, and most investigators use motivational procedures to get the children to perform the tasks. However, variations in reward or punishment procedures on such tasks rarely have been manipulated and, often, have not even been reported as procedures in drug studies. Their effects on drug conditions have thus gone unnoticed. Fewer studies have addressed the role that instructional variables might play in mediating drug effects, but it appears that instructional variables or classroom structure can influence whether drug effects on learning are found.

These points also have important implications for the interpretation of studies that have examined drug effects over time in the natural classroom environment. For example, much has been made of the fact that none of the long-term (e.g., 3–5 years), follow-up studies have revealed beneficial, stimulant effects on achievement (e.g., Barkley & Cunningham, 1978). However, stimulant therapy has been implemented in addition to whatever form of instruction or intervention the child happens to be receiving in his regular school setting without controlling for possible interactions among medication, instructional programs, and concurrent behavioral interventions. Given the complex relationships among these variables, it is not likely that many children in these studies received medication in contexts that facilitated beneficial stimulant effects.

INTERPRETATIONAL ISSUES

ANTIMEDICATION BIASES: SKILLS OR PILLS?

Different evidential standards appear to have been applied to interpretation of stimulant effects on learning than have been applied to the effects of other inteventions. For example, just as with medication, there are no studies that have shown, compared to appropriate control, beneficial effects of behavior modification alone on HA or LD children's achievement-test performance. Nonetheless, based on several studies showing that behavior modification improved HA children's reading and arithmetic seatwork (e.g., Ayllon et al., 1975; Wolraich et al., 1978), the same reviews that concluded that stimulants have no beneficial effect concluded that behavior modification *does* improve achievement (e.g., Barkley & Cunningham, 1978; O'Leary, 1980). Similarly, behavioral procedures have been shown to have beneficial effects on academic product measures in LD children (Gadow et al., in press-a). These studies most often have measured changes in academic productivity and classroom behavior with the assumption that such changes will predict changes in long-term achievement. If those data are interpreted as evidence of behavior modification's effects on achievement, then the results shown in Figure 2, which are based on comparable dependent measures, comparable underlying assumptions, and a larger N than the behavioral studies, should be similarly interpreted.

The argument being made is not that the available data definitively demonstrate beneficial stimulant effects on achievement. The studies that have been reviewed suggest that that is the case, but they are not yet conclusive. The data regarding behavioral and other treatments, however, are no more conclusive. The point is that the evaluative standards applied to pharmacological treatments should be the same as those applied to nonpharmacological interventions. As has been the case for some time (e.g., Grinspoon & Singer, 1973), there appears to be a general unwillingness to conclude that drugs have any potential benefit for children with academic deficits. Rather than being data-based, these biases against medication appear to be based on personal beliefs about the role of drugs in society, and they should be recognized as such. When presented as scientific fact, such personal biases have the unfortunate effect of detracting from the goal of discovering a maximally effective treatment for the children of concern.

LOGICAL ERRORS

A number of investigators have suggested that stimulant drugs do not and should not be expected to improve learning in HA or LD children because they do not correct the cognitive or physiological deficits that are thought to underlie the disorders (e.g., Aman & Werry, 1982; Barkley & Cunningham, 1978; Gadow, 1983). Because neither the cognitive and physiological substrates of hyperactivity and LD nor the mechanisms of stimulant action are known, it is difficult to respond to this argument empirically. It constitutes a logical fallacy, however, to base a conclusion regarding underlying variables on treatment effects or lack thereof. Even though it is known that A, under certain conditions, causes B, given that B or *not* B obtains, no conclusions can be drawn about A. Although behavioral interventions are, at least, partially effective treatments, is it necessary to conclude that they exert their effect by affecting directly the underlying neurophysiological substrates of these dysfunctions? Neither the presence nor absence of behavioral or stimulant effects on learning can be attributed to effects on underlying substrates of learning deficits, and any argument to the contrary is specious.

Several authors have argued that even though there are methodological problems in many studies of stimulant effects on learning, the remarkable consistency of negative findings overrides the methodological problems. This is clearly an unfounded conclusion, as it assumes that 20 flawed studies that fail to reject the null hypothesis should carry more weight than one such study. If the 20 studies were methodologically sound, then increased confidence in the findings relative to a single study would be justified. The remarkably consistent aspect of this literature is the inadequate methodology, not the negative results.

RISKS AND BENEFITS OF STIMULANT EFFECTS

Meta-analyses have shown that the average magnitude of stimulant effects on academic measures is sufficient to move up a treated child 15 percentile points in a control-group ranking (Kavale, 1982). In the recent studies discussed above, the average effect was even larger, between 25–30%, than in the studies reviewed by Kavale (Pelham et al., 1980-a; Pelham, in press-a; Stephens et al., 1984). Nonetheless, these effects are considerably smaller than stimulant results on measures of classroom social behavior, such as direct observations or teacher ratings (Kavale, 1982; Pelham et al., in press-a). This observation has led to questions regarding the social significance of the effects (e.g., Gadow, 1983). Even though relatively small, however, a mean improvement of 15% is not insignificant. Improvement from 60% to 70% on a test would change a child's grade from failing to passing. Given the high rate of academic failure in HA samples (e.g., Lambert & Sandoval, 1980; Weiss, Hechtman, Perlman, Hopkins, & Wener, 1979) and obviously in LD samples, such a change could have considerable social significance. Further, the relatively small effects reported by Kavale (1982) were averaged over all of the limiting factors discussed above (e.g., dose, measure insensitivity, and individual differences). It is likely that some of the subjects had responses to medication that were considerably greater than these averages. If that were the case, then the rational response would be to identify those children who showed a beneficial effect rather than to dismiss drug effects as small and unimportant.

Of course, the potential benefits of stimulants must be weighed against the risks involved in long-term administration. Stimulant medication would not be useful if beneficial effects were accompanied by adverse treatment-emergent symptoms (TES) or if the beneficial effects were limited by SDL. Many TES that caused concern a decade ago, such as reduction in growth (Safer & Allen, 1973; see also Mattes & Gittelman, 1983), are apparently controllable as long as low dosages of medication are employed and the drugs are administered only during school hours (Satterfield, Cantwell, Schell, & Blaschke, 1979). Similarly, although one early study reported SDL in HA children treated with MPH (Swanson & Kinsbourne, 1976), the bulk of the data suggests that SDL is not apparent with relatively low dosages of stimulants (Gan & Cantwell, 1982; Stephens *et al.*, 1984).

In contrast, other TES, such as social withdrawal (Barkley & Cunningham, 1979; Pelham, in press; Pelham & Bender, 1982), motor tics, and Tourette's syndrome (Denckla, Bemporad, & MacKay, 1976; Lowe, Cohen, Detlor, Kremenitzer, & Shaywitz, 1982), are apparent even at relatively low dosages. These TES are potentially quite serious and deserve intensive monitoring and medication withdrawal if detected. Other than these TES and rare idiosyncratic responses, the best available data suggest that no adverse TES are associated with stimulant therapy. At the same time, there are few studies of very long-term stimulant use, and such studies must be conducted before it can be stated with certainty that no latent TES will develop in medicated children.

CONCLUSIONS

Both laboratory and classroom studies that have been reviewed show there is reason to believe that stimulant drugs may have beneficial effects on learning and academic achievement in, at least, a subset of ADD and LD children. Because no study has been conducted that assessed stimulant effects under optimal conditions and used appropriate measures, previous negative findings should not be interpreted as evidence that stimulants have no beneficial effect on learning or academic achievement in ADD and LD children. Regarding stimulant effects on academic achievement, professionals are faced with two tasks: (1) the identification in clinical settings of individual children whose academic achievement might benefit from stimulant therapy; and (2) the design and implementation of studies that can clarify the conflicting data and address the numerous unanswered questions on this topic.

SUGGESTIONS FOR CLINICAL PRACTICE

The approach taken recently to the task of identifying children who will respond positively to stimulant treatment has been to search for cognitive laboratory measures that can be used to predict drug effects on classroom academic performance (Swanson & Kinsbourne, 1979). However, no variables as yet have been identified that enable accurate prediction of an individual ADD or LD child's response to psychostimulant medication on academic measures (Gadow, 1983; Pelham, 1983). Further, in classroom settings in the natural environment, stimulant effects are almost never assessed even with the most rudimentary procedures, that is, asking a child's teacher whether the medication appears to be helpful (Gadow, 1981). For all practical purposes, stimulants appear to be used with a "prescribe and hope" philosophy.

An alternative to this abysmal lack of monitoring is to use single-subject methodology to gather information directly in the classroom on the academic and behavioral measures discussed above and to do this in the context of a double-blind, placebo-controlled, multiple-dose, multiple-dependent-measure, drug trial (Pelham, 1982; Pelham, in press; Pelham & Murphy, in press, Schell et al., in press). Rather than having to draw inferences about achievement from responses on laboratory cognitive tasks, a child's performance on daily academic tasks can be analyzed under different drug conditions. A child who exhibited a substantial beneficial effect on ecologically valid classroom measures could be given a relatively long-term (e.g., 1 year) trial of stimulant medication. A blind placebo probe should be conducted after 3–6 months to ensure that a medicated child continues to show a positive medication response on daily academic tasks. An achievement test and school grades over the year of treatment should be employed as dependent measures, and the child's gains during his or her premedication year should be used as a baseline for comparison. Only if this comparison yields clear evidence of a beneficial drug effect should a child who has been placed on stimulants for academic reasons be maintained on medication.

The prospect of having to conduct an elaborate assessment on every child who receives a stimulant may be unsettling. It should be noted that what is being recommended is simply a very careful, functional analysis of a child's response to medication. The same degree of complexity is required in a single-subject analysis of the effects of a behavioral treatment with an ADD child (e.g., Atkins, White, Pelham, Adams, & Case, 1985). Given the very poor quality of medication evaluation and follow-up in clinical settings, medication assessment procedures such as these (see also Steinfeld, 1980; Wells, Conners, Imber, & Delameter, 1981) appear necessary, despite their time consumption and expense, to ensure appropriate and effective use of stimulant medication for individual children in clinical practice.

FUTURE RESEARCH

As in other areas of psychopharmacology and psychopathology (Buchsbaum & Haier, 1983), it is likely that the individual differences

discussed earlier in response to stimulants are influenced by the nature
·of the underlying physiological, cognitive, and etiological bases of a
child's disorder (Conners, 1972; Cunningham & Barkley, 1978; Douglas,
1983; Dykman et al., 1980; Hunt, Cohen, Shaywitz, & Shaywitz, 1982;
Solanto & Conners, 1982; Swanson et al., 1983). To date, however, little
research has been conducted, utilizing well-defined, biological markers
and reliable measures of learning. Such research, conducted initially in
controlled laboratory conditions, is needed to shed light on the interplay
between these domains.

In addition to such laboratory studies, which are essential to our understanding of the stimulants, ADD, and LD, more studies of stimulant
effects on achievement in the natural environment are needed. As I have
discussed, direct measurement of classroom performance is a less inferential approach to studying drug effects on academic achievement than
laboratory studies, and it merits increased usage in child psychopharmacology. More widespread use of this approach with a special emphasis
on single-subject methodology may facilitate solution of some of the
methodological problems discussed above.

It is reassuring to note that although the methodological inadequacies
in this literature are ubiquitous, the majority of recent studies have met
most of the minimum requirements for a methodologically adequate
drug study that were described over a decade ago—placebo control,
random assignment of subjects, double-blind, standardized dosages
and evaluations, and appropriate statistical analyses (Sprague & Werry,
1971). Over the past 10 years, considerably progress has been made in
the sense that experimenters (myself included) have been making more
sophisticated mistakes than in the previous decade.

Suggestions regarding further improvements in methods and procedures used to study stimulant effects on achievement, including consideration of dependent measures, drug variables, concurrent interventions and instruction, and individual differences have been offered
throughout this chapter (see also Breuning, Poling, & Matson, in press).
In addition, I have listed (elsewhere) guidelines regarding how not to
conduct an evaluation of stimulant effects on HA/LD academic achievement (Pelham, 1983). If researchers make as much progress over the
next 10 years in dealing with these methodological concerns as has been
made over the past decade, we should see a definitive answer forthcom-
ing to the question of whether stimulant drugs improve achievement in
HA and LD children.

Given the refractory nature and poor long-term prognoses of these
disorders, discovery of an effective treatment is imperative. Well-designed studies that test for beneficial drug effects under optimal conditions must be conducted, and the clinical use of psychostimulants must

be improved dramatically. Only when such efforts fail to find positive effects should we abandon the hypothesis that psychostimulant drugs can facilitate learning and achievement in HA and LD children.

ACKNOWLEDGMENTS

The author wishes to thank the following individuals who made helpful comments on an earlier version of this manuscript: Barb Licht, Ken Gadow, Bob Sprague, Barbara Henker, Jim Swanson, Marcel Kinsbourne, Keith Conners, and Joe Torgesen. Portions of this chapter appeared as an invited review in *Thalamus*, the Journal of the International Academy for Research in Learning Disabilities (Pelham, 1983).

REFERENCES

Ackerman, P. T., & Dykman, R. A. (July 1982). Automatic and effortful information-processing deficits in children with learning and attention disorders. *Topics in Learning and Learning Disabilities, 12–22.*

Ackerman, P. T., Dykman, R. A., Holcomb, P. J., & McCray, D. S. (1982). Methylphenidate effects on cognitive style and reaction time in four groups of children. *Psychiatry Research, 7,* 199–213.

Aman, M. G. (1980). Psychotropic drugs and learning problems: A selective review. *Journal of Learning Disabilities, 13,* 87–97.

Aman, M. G., & Sprague, R. L. (1974). The state-dependent effects of methylphenidate and dextroamphetamine. *Journal of Nervous and Mental Disease, 158,* 268–279.

Aman, M. G., & Werry, J. S. (1982). Methylphenidate and diazepam in severe reading retardation. *Journal of the American Academy of Child Psychiatry, 1,* 31–37.

Atkins, M. S., White, K. J., Pelham, W. E., Adams, P. M., & Case, D. E. *Behavioral and pharmacological treatment of a hyperactive, aggressive child.* Manuscript submitted for publication. 1985.

Ayllon, T., Layman, D., & Kandel, H. J. (1975). A behavioral/educational alternative to drug control of hyperactive children. *Journal of Applied Behavior Analysis, 8,* 137–146.

Barkley, R. (1976). Predicting the response of hyperkinetic children to stimulant drugs: A review. *Journal of Abnormal Child Psychology, 4,* 327–348.

Barkley, R. A., & Cunningham, C. E. (1978). Do stimulant drugs improve the academic performance of hyperactive children? *Clinical Pediatrics, 17,* 85–92.

Barkley, R. A., & Cunningham, C. E. (1979). The effects of Ritalin on the mother–child interactions of hyperactive children. *Archives of General Psychiatry, 36,* 201–208.

Becker, W. C., & Gersten, R. A. (1982). Follow-up of follow-through: The later effects of the Direct Instruction Model on children in fifth and sixth grades. *American Educational Research Journal, 19*(1), 75–92.

Berliner, D. C., & Rosenshine, B. (1977). The acquisition of knowledge in the classroom. In R. C. Anderson, R. J. Spiro, & W. E. Montague (Eds.). *Schooling and the Acquisition of Knowledge* (pp. 375–396). Hillsdale, NJ: Lawrence Erlbaum Associates.

Bradley, C., & Bowen, M. (1940). School performance of children receiving amphetamine (benzedrine) sulfate. *American Journal of Orthopsychiatry, 10,* 782–788.

Breuning, S. E., Poling, A. D., & Matson, J. L. (Eds.) (in press). *Applied psychopharmacology: Methods for assessing medication effects.* New York: Grune & Stratton.

Briant, R. H. (1978). An introduction to clinical pharmacology. In J. S. Werry (Ed.). *Pediatric psychopharmacology: The Use of Behavior Modifying Drugs in Children.* New York: Brunner/Mazel.

Brophy, J. E. (1979). Teacher behavior and its effects. *Journal of Educational Psychology, 71,* 733–750.

Brown, R., & Sleator, E. (1979). Methylphenidate in hyperkinetic children: Differences in dose effects on impulsive behavior. *Pediatrics, 64,* 408–411.

Buchsbaum, M. S., & Haier, R. J. (1983). Psychopathology: Biological approaches. In M. R. Rosenzweig & L. W. Porter (Eds.). *Annual Review of Psychology,* Vol. 34, (pp. 401–430). Palo Alto: Annual Reviews, Inc.

Campbell, S. B., Douglas, V. I., & Morgenstern, G. (1971). Cognitive styles in hyperactive children. *Journal of Child Psychology and Psychiatry, 12,* 55–67.

Cantwell, D. P., & Carlson, G. A. (1978). Stimulants. In J. S. Werry (Ed.). *Pediatric psychopharmacology: The Use of Behavior Modifying Drugs in Children.* New York: Brunner/Mazel.

Catania, A. C., & Brigham, T. A. (1978). *Handbook of applied behavior analysis: Social and instructional processes.* New York: Irvington.

Charles, L., & Schain, R. (1981). A four-year follow-up study of the effects of methylphenidate on the behavior and academic achievement of hyperactive children. *Journal of Abnormal Child Psychology, 9,* 495–505.

Charles, L., Schain, R. J., & Guthrie, D. (1979). Long-term use and discontinuation of methylphenidate with hyperactive children. *Developmental Medicine and Child Neurology, 21,* 758–764.

Charles, C., Schain, R. J., Zelniker, T., & Guthrie, D. (1979). Effects of methylphenidate on hyperactive children's ability to sustain attention. *Pediatrics, 64*(4), 412–418.

Conners, C. K. (1972). Psychological effects of stimulant drugs in children with minimal brain dysfunction. *Pediatrics, 49*(5), 702–708.

Conners, C. K. (1983). The effects of psychostimulants on academic achievement in hyperactive and learning-disabled children: A commentary on the paper by W. E. Pelham. *Thalamus, 3*(1), 49–54.

Conners, C. K., & Rothschild, G. H. (1968). Drugs and learning in children. In J. Hellmuth (Ed.). *Learning Disorders.* Vol. III (pp. 191–217). Seattle, WA: Special Child Publications.

Conners, C. K., Rothschild, G. H., Eisenberg, L. Schwartz, L. S., & Robinson, E. (1969). Dextroamphetamine sulfate in children with learning disorders. *Archives of General Psychiatry, 21,* 182–190.

Conners, C. K., & Taylor, E. (1980). Pemoline, methylphenidate, and placebo in children with minimal brain dysfunction. *Archives of General Psychiatry, 37,* 922–932.

Conners, C. K., Taylor, E., Meo, G., Kurtz, M. A., & Fournier, M. (1972). Magnesium pemoline and dextroamphetamine: A controlled study in children with minimal brain dysfunction. *Psychopharmacologia, 26,* 321–336.

Conners, C. K., & Werry, J. S. (1979). Psychopharmacology. In H. Quay & J. Werry (Eds.). *Psychopathological Disorders of Childhood* (2nd ed.). New York: John Wiley & Son.

Conrad, W. G., Dworkin, E. S., Shai, A., & Tobiessen, J. E. (1971). Effects of amphetamine therapy and prescriptive tutoring on the behavior and achievement of lower class hyperactive children. *Journal of Learning Disabilities, 4,* 45–53.

Cronbach, L. J. (1977). *Educational psychology* (3rd Ed.). Atlanta: Harcourt Brace Jovanovich.

Cunningham, C. E., & Barkley, R. A. (1978). The role of academic failure in hyperactive behavior. *Journal of Learning Disabilities, 11,* 274–280.

Dalby, J. T., Kinsbourne, M., Swanson, J. M., & Sobol, M. P. (1977). Hyperactive children's underuse of learning time: Correction by stimulant treatment. *Child Development, 48,* 1448–1453.

Denckla, M. A., Bemporad, J. R., MacKay, M. C. (1976). Tics following methylphenidate administration. *Journal of the American Medical Association, 235,* 1349–1351.

Douglas, V. I. (1983). Attentional and cognitive problems. In M. Rutter (Ed.). *Behavioral Syndromes of Brain Dysfunction in Childhood* (pp. 280–329). New York: The Guilford Press.

Douglas, V. I., & Peters, K. G. (1979). Toward a clearer definition of the attentional deficit of hyperactive children. In G. A. Hale & M. Lewis (Eds.). *Attention and Cognitive Development* (pp. 173–248). New York: Plenum Press.

Dykman, R. A., Ackerman, P. T., & McCray, D. S. (1980). Effects of methylphenidate on selective and sustained attention in hyperactive, reading-disabled, and presumably attention-disordered boys. *Journal of Nervous and Mental Disease, 168,* 745–752.

Epstein, L. H., & Cluss, P. A. (1982). A behavioral medicine perspective on adherence to long-term medical regimens. *Journal of Consulting and Clinical Psychology, 50,* 950–971.

Finnerty, R., Soltys, J., & Cole, J. (1971). The use of D-amphetamine with hyperkinetic children. *Psychopharmacologia, 21,* 302–308.

Firestone, P. (1982). Factors associated with children's adherence to stimulant medication. *American Journal of Orthopsychiatry, 53*(3), 447–457.

Flintoff, M. A., Barron, R. W., Swanson, J. M., Ledlow, A., & Kinsbourne, I. (1982). Methylphenidate increases selectivity of visual scanning in children referred for hyperactivity. *Journal of Abnormal Child Psychology, 10,* 145–161.

Ford, C. E., Pelham, W. & Ross, A. (1984). The role of selective attention and rehearsal in the auditory short-term memory performance of poor and normal readers. *Journal of Abnormal Child Psychology, 12,* 127–142.

Gadow, K. D. (1981). Drug therapy for hyperactivity: treatment procedures in natural settings. In K. Gadow & J. Loney (Eds.). *Psychosocial aspects of Drug Treatment for Hyperactivity.* Boulder, CO: Westview Press.

Gadow, K. D. (1983). Effects of stimulant drugs on academic performance in hyperactive and learning disabled children. *Journal of Learning Disabilities, 16,* 290–299.

Gadow, K. D., Torgesen, J. K., & Dahlem, W. E. (in press-a). Learning disabilities. In M. Hersen, V. B. Van Hasset & J. L. Matson (Eds.). *Behavior Therapy for the Developmentally and Physically Disabled: A Handbook.* New York: Academic Press.

Gadow, K. D., Torgesen, J., Greenstein, J., & Schell, R. (in press-b). Learning disabilities. In M. Hersen & S. E. Breuning (Eds.). *Pharmacological and Behavioral Treatment: An Integrated Approach.* New York: Wiley & Sons.

Gagne, R. M. (1977). *The conditions of learning* (3rd. ed.). Atlanta: Holt, Rinehart & Winston.

Gan, J., & Cantwell, D. P. (1982). Dosage effects of methylphenidate on paired associate learning: Positive/negative placebo responders. *Journal of the American Academy of Child Psychiatry, 21,* 227–242.

Gaultieri, C. T., Wargin, W., Kanoy, R., Patrick, K., Shen, C. D., Youngblood, W., Mueller, R. A., & Breese, G. R. (1982). Clinical studies of methylphenidate serum levels in children and adults. *Journal of the American Academy of Child Psychiatry, 21,* 19–26.

Gittelman-Klein, R., & Klein, D. F. (1976). Methylphenidate effects in learning disabilities. *Archives of General Psychiatry, 33,* 655–664.

Greenstein, J., Pelham, W. E., Torgesen, J. K., Bender, M., Adams, P., Atkins, M., Schell, R., White, K. (August 1983). Effects of methylphenidate on acquisition of reading sight vocabulary and multiplication facts. Paper presented at the Annual Meeting of the American Psychological Association, Anaheim, CA.

Grinspoon, L., & Singer, S. B. (1973). Amphetamines in the treatment of hyperkinetic children. *Harvard Educational Review, 43*(4), 515–555.

Hall, R. A., Griffin, R. B., Moyer, D. L., Hopkins, K. H., & Rapoport, M. (1976). Evoked potential, stimulus intensity and drug treatment in hyperkinesis. *Psychophysiology, 13,* 405–418.

Halliday, R., Callaway, E., & Naylor, H. (1983). Visual evoked potential changes induced by methylphenidate in hyperactive children: Dose response effects. *Journal of Electroencephalography and Clinical Neurophysiology, 55,* 258–267.

Harvey, P., Weintraub, S., & Neale, J. (1984). Distractibility in learning-disabled children: The role of measurement artifact. *Journal of Learning Disabilities, 17,* 134–137.

Hastings, J. E., & Barkley, R. A. (1978). A review of psychophysiological research with hyperkinetic children. *Journal of Abnormal Child Psychology, 6,* 413–448.

Hillyard, S. A., & Kutas, M. (1983). Electrophysiology of cognitive processing. In M. R. Rosenzweig & L. W. Porter (Eds.). *Annual Review of Psychology.* Vol. 34 (pp. 33–61). Palo Alto, CA: Annual Reviews Inc.

Hiscock, M., Kinsbourne, M., Caplan, B., & Swanson, J. M. (1979). Auditory attention in hyperactive children: Effects of stimulant medication on dichotic listening performance. *Journal of Abnormal Psychology, 88*(1), 27–32.

Hoffman, S., Engelhardt, D., Margolis, R., Polizos, P., Waizer, J., & Rosenfeld, R. (1974). Response to methylphenidate in low socioeconomic hyperactive children. *Archives of General Psychology, 30,* 354–359.

Hunt, R. D., Cohen, D. J., Shaywitz, S. E., & Shaywitz, B. A. (1982). Strategies for study of the neurochemistry of attention deficit disorder in children. *Schizophrenia Bulletin, 8,* 236–252.

Kauffman, R. E., Smith-Wright, D., Reese, C. A., Simpson, R., & Jones, F. (1981). Medication compliance in hyperactive children. *Pediatric Pharmacology, 1,* 231–237.

Kavale, K. (1982). The efficacy of stimulant drug treatment for hyperactivity: A meta-analysis. *Journal of Learning Disabilities, 15,* 280–289.

Klorman, R., Bauer, L. O., Coons, H. W., Lewis, J. L., Peloquin, L. J., Perlmutter, R. A., Ryan, R. M., Salzman, L. F., & Strauss, J. (1984). Enhancing effects of methylphenidate on normal young adults' cognitive processes. *Psychopharmacology Bulletin, 20.*

Klorman, R., Salzman, L. F., Bauer, L. O., Coons, H. W., Borgstedt, A. D., & Halpern, W. I. (1983). Effects of two doses of methylphenidate on cross-situational and borderline hyperactive children's evoked potentials. *Electroencephalography and Clinical Neurophysiology, 56,* 169–185.

Klorman, R., Salzman, L. F., & Borgstedt, A. D. (in press). Brain event/related potentials as a tool for evaluating cognitive deficits in attention-deficit disorder and stimulant therapy. In L. Bloomingdale (Ed.). *Attention Deficits Disorder.* Vol. 3. New York: Spectrum.

Krueger, W. C. F. (1929). The effect of overlearning on retention. *Journal of Experimental Psychology, 12,* 71–78.

Kupietz, S. S., Richardson, E., Gadow, K. D., Winsberg, B. G. (1980). Effects of methylphenidate on learning a "begining reading vocabulary" by normal adults. *Psychopharmacology, 69,* 69–72.

Kupietz, S. S., Winsberg, B. G., Sverd, J. (1982). Learning ability and methylphenidate (Ritalin) plasma concentration in hyperkinetic children: A preliminary investigation. *Journal of the American Academy of Child Psychiatry, 21,* 27–30.

Lambert, N., & Sandoval, J. (1980). The prevalence of learning disabilities in a sample of children considered hyperactive. *Journal of Abnormal Child Psychology, 8,* 35–50.

Loney, J., Kramer, J., & Kosier, T. (1981). Medicated versus unmedicated hyperactive adolescents: Academic, delinquent, and symptomatological outcome. Poster presented at the Annual Meeting of the American Psychological Association, Los Angeles, CA.

Lowe, T. L., Cohen, D. J., Detlor, J., Kremenitzer, M. W., & Shaywitz, B. A. (1982). Stimulant medications precipitate Tourette's syndrome. *Journal of the American Medical Association, 247,* 1729–1731.

Mattes, J. A., & Gittelman, R. (1983). Growth of hyperactive children on maintenance regimen of methylphenidate. *Archives of General Psychiatry, 40*(3), 317–321.

Michael, R. L., Klorman, R., Salzman, L. F., Borgstedt, A. D., & Dainer, K. B. (1981). Normalizing effects of methylphenidate on hyperactive children's vigilance performance and evoked potentials. *Psychophysiology, 18,* 665–677.

O'Leary, K. D. (1980). Pills or skills for hyperactive children. *Journal of Applied Behavior Analysis, 13,* 191–204.

Parry, P. A., & Douglas, V. I. (1983). Effects of reinforcement on concept identification in hyperactive children. *Journal of Abnormal Child Psychology, 11,* 327–340.

Peck, C. L., & King, N. J. (1982). Increasing patient compliance with prescriptions. *Journal of the American Medical Association, 248,* 2874–2877.

Peeke, S., Halliday, R., Callaway, E., Prael, R., & Reus, V. (1984). *Effects of two doses of methylphenidate on verbal information processing in hyperactive children.* Manuscript submitted for publication.

Pelham, W. E., (1981). Attention deficits in hyperactive and learning disabled children. *Exceptional Education Quarterly, 2,* 13–24.

Pelham, W. E. (1982). Childhood hyperactivity: Diagnosis, etiology, nature and treatment. In R. Gatchel, A. Baum, & J. Singer (Eds.), *Behavioral Medicine and Clinical Psychology: Overlapping Disciplines.* Hillsdale, NJ: Lawrence Erlbaum Associates.

Pelham, W. E. (1983). The effects of stimulant drugs on academic achievement in hyperactive and learning disabled children. *Thalamus, 3,* 1–47.

Pelham, W. E. (in press). Behavior therapy, behavioral assessment, and psychostimulant medication in treatment of attention deficit disorders: An interactive approach. In L. Bloomingdale, J. Swanson, & R. Klorman (Eds.). *Attention Deficit Disorders: New Directions.* Vol. IV. New York: Spectrum.

Pelham, W. E., & Bender, M. E. (1982). Peer relationships in hyperactive children: Description and treatment. In K. Gadow & I. Bailer (Eds.). *Advances in Learning and Behavioral Disabilities* Vol. 1. Greenwich, CT: JAI Press.

Pelham, W. E., & Bender, M. E. (1984). *Behavioral assessment of psychoactive drug effects on a child's learning and behavior in an inpatient psychiatric setting.* Unpublished manuscript. Department of Psychology, Florida State University, Tallahassee, FL.

Pelham, W. E., Bender, M. E., Caddell, J. M., Booth, S., & Moorer, S. (in press-a). The dose-response effects of methylphenidate on classroom academic and social behavior in children with attention deficit disorder. *Archives of General Psychiatry.*

Pelham, W. E., & Murphy, H. A. (in press). Behavioral and pharmacological treatment of hyperactivity and attention deficit disorders. In M. Hersen and S. Breuning (Eds.). *Pharmacological and Behavioral Treatment: An Integrative Approach.* New York: Wiley.

Pelham, W. E., Schnedler, R. W., Bender, M. E., Miller, J., Nilsson, D., Budrow, M.,

Ronnei, M., Paluchowski, C., & Marks, D., (in press-b). The combination of behavior therapy and methylphenidate in the treatment of attention deficit disorders: A therapy outcome study. In L. Bloomingdale (Ed.). *Attention Deficit Disorder.* Vol. III. New York: Spectrum.

Pelham, W. E., Schnedler, R. W., Bologna, N., & Contreras, A. (1980-b). Behavioral and stimulant treatment of hyperactive children: A therapy study with methylphenidate probes in a within-subject design. *Journal of Applied Behavior Analysis, 13,* 221–236.

Pelham, W. E., Swanson, J., Bender, M., & Wilson, J. (September, 1980). *Dose-response effects of pemoline on hyperactivity: Laboratory and classroom measures.* Paper presented at the Annual Meeting of the American Psychological Association, Montreal, Canada.

Poling, A., & Breuning, S. E. (1983). Effects of methylphenidate on the fixed-ratio performance of mentally retarded children. *Pharmacology, Biochemistry, & Behavior, 18,* 541–544.

Postman, L. (1962). Retention as a function of degree of overlearning. *Science, 135,* 666–667.

Rapoport, J. L., Buchsbaum, M., Weingartner, H., Zahn, T. P., Ludlow, C., & Mikkelsen, E. J. (1980). Dextroamphetamine: Cognitive and behavioral effects in normal and hyperactive boys and normal men. *Archives of General Psychiatry, 37,* 933–934.

Rapport, M., Murphy, A., & Bailey, J. (1982). Ritalin vs. response cost in the control of hyperactive children: A within-subject comparison. *Journal of Applied Behavior Analysis, 15,* 205–216.

Resnick, L. B., & Ford, W. W. (1981). *The Psychology of mathematics for instruction.* Hillsdale, NJ: Lawrence Erlbaum Associates.

Riddle, D., & Rapoport, J. (1976). A 2-year follow-up of 72 hyperactive boys. *Journal of Nervous and Mental Disease, 162,* 126–134.

Rie, D. R., & Rie, H. E. (1977). Recall, retention and Ritalin. *Journal of Consulting and Clinical Psychology, 45,* 967–972.

Rie, H. E., Rie, E. D., Stewart, S., & Ambuel, J. P. (1976-a). Effects of methylphenidate on underachieving children. *Journal of Consulting and Clinical Psychology, 44,* 250–260.

Rie, H. E., Rie, E. D., Stewart, S., & Ambuel, J. P. (1976-b). Effects of methylphenidate on underachieving children: A replication. *American Journal of Orthopsychiatry, 46,* 313–322.

Robbins, T. W., & Sahakian, B. J. (1979). "Paradoxical" effects of psychomotor stimulant drugs in hyperactive children from the standpoint of behavioral pharmacology. *Neuropharmacology, 18,* 931–950.

Rosenthal, R., & Allen, T. (1977). An examination of the attention arousal and learning dysfunctions of hyperactive children. *Psychological Bulletin, 85,* 689–716.

Safer, D. M., & Allen, R. P. (1973). Factors affecting the suppressant effects of two stimulant drugs on the growth of hyperactive children. *Pediatrics, 51,* 660–667.

Satterfield, J. H., Cantwell, D. P., & Satterfield, B. T. (1979). Multimodality treatment. *Archives of General Psychiatry, 36,* 965–978.

Satterfield, J. H., Cantwell, D. P., Schell, A., & Blaschke, T. (1979). Growth of hyperactive children treated with methylphenidate. *Archives of General Psychiatry, 36,* 212–217.

Schain, R. J., & Reynard, C. L. (1975). Observations on effects of central stimulant drug (methylphenidate) in children with hyperactive behavior. *Pediatrics, 55,* 709–716.

Schell, R. M., Pelham, W. E., Bender, M. E., & Andre, J. (in press). A concurrent assessment of behavioral and psychostimulant interventions on the learning and behavior of a developmentally disabled child with attention deficit disorder. *Behavioral Assessment.*

Schell, R., Pelham, W., Adams, P., Atkins, M., Greenstein, J., White, K., Bender, M., Bailey, J., Shapiro, S., Law, T., Darling, J., & Case, D. (May 1983). *The effects of a response cost program on classroom behavior of hyperactive children.* Paper presented at the Annual Meeting of the Association for Behavior Analysis, Milwaukee, WI.

Schroeder, S. R., Lewis, M. H., & Lipton, M. A. (1983). Interactions of pharmacotherapy and behavior therapy among children with learning and behavioral disorders. In K. Gadow & I. Bialer (Eds.). *Advances in Learning and Behavioral Disabilities.* Vol. 2 (pp. 179–225). Greenwich, CT: JAI Press.

Shaywitz, S. E., Hunt, R. D., Jatlow, P., Cohen, D. J., Young, J. G., Pierce, R. N., Anderson, G. M., & Shaywitz, B. A. (1982). Psychopharmacology of attention deficit disorder: Pharmacokinetic, neuroendocrine, and behavioral measures following acute and chronic treatment with methylphenidate. *Pediatrics, 69,* 688–694.

Solanto, M. V., & Conners, C. K. (1982). A dose-response and time-action analysis of autonomic and behavioral effects of methylphenidate in attention deficit disorder with hyperactivity. *Psychophysiology, 19,* 658–667.

Sprague, R. L. (1983). Use of behavior modification and educational techniques in the treatment of the hyperkinetic syndrome. In M. Rutter (Ed.). *Behavioral Syndromes of Brain Dysfunction in Childhood* (pp. 404–421). New York: Guilford Press.

Sprague, R. L., & Berger, B. D. (1980). Drug effects on learning performance: Relevance of animal research to pediatric psychopharmacology. In R. M. Knights & D. J. Bakker (Eds.). *Treatment of Hyperactive and Learning-Disabled Children* (pp. 167–184). Baltimore: University Park Press.

Sprague, R. L., & Sleator, E. K. (1977). Methylphenidate in hyperkinetic children: Differences in dose effects on learning and social behavior. *Science, 198,* 1274–1276.

Sprague, R. L., & Werry, J. S. (1971). Methodology of psychopharmacological studies with the retarded. In N. R. Ellis (Ed.). *International review of research in mental retardation.* Vol. 5 (pp. 147–212). New York: Academic Press.

Steinfeld, B. I. (November 1980). A multimethod approach to the assessment of the stimulant drug response in a hyperactive child. Paper presented at the Annual Meeting of the Association for the Advancement of Behavior Therapy, New York.

Steinhausen, H., & Kreuzer, E. (1981). Learning in hyperactive children: Are there stimulant-related and state-dependent effects? *Psychopharmacology, 74,* 389–390.

Stephens, R. S., Pelham, W. E., & Skinner, R. (1984). The state-dependent and main effects of methylphenidate and pemoline on paired-associated learning and spelling in hyperactive children. *Journal of Consulting and Clinical Psychology, 523,* 104–113.

Stevenson, H. W., Hale, G. A., Klein, R. E., & Miller, L. K. (1968). Interrelations and correlates in children's learning and problem solving. *Monographs of the Society for Research in Child Development, 33*(7).

Swanson, J. M., Barlow, A., & Kinsbourne, M. (1979). Task specificity of responses to stimulant drugs in laboratory tests. *International Journal of Mental Health, 8,* 67–82.

Swanson, J. M., & Kinsbourne, M. (1976). Stimulant-related state-dependent learning in hyperactive children. *Science, 192,* 1354–1357.

Swanson, J. M., & Kinsbourne, M. (1979). The cognitive effects of stimulant drugs on hyperactive children. In G. A. Hale & M. Lewis (Eds.). *Attention and Cognitive Development* (pp. 249–274). New York: Plenum Press.

Swanson, J., Kinsbourne, M., Roberts, W., & Zucker, K. (1978). Time-response analysis of the effect of stimulant medication on the learning ability of children referred for hyperactivity. *Pediatrics, 61,* 21–29.

Swanson, J. M., Sandman, C., Deutsch, C., & Baren, M. (1983). Methylphenidate (Ritalin) given with or before breakfast: Part I. Behavioral, cognitive and electrophysiological effects. *Pediatrics, 72,* 49–55.

Sykes, D., Douglas, V., & Morgenstern, G. (1972). The effect of methylphenidate (Ritalin) on sustained attention in hyperactive children. *Psychopharmacologia, 25,* 262–274.

Sykes, D. H., Douglas, V. I., Weiss, G., & Minde, K. K. (1971). Attention in hyperactive children and the effect of methylphenidate (Ritalin). *Journal of Child Psychology and Psychiatry, 12,* 129–139.

Torgesen, J. K., & Young, K. A. (1983). Priorities for the use of microcomputers with learning-disabled children. *Journal of Learning Disabilities, 16,* 234–237.

Underwood, B. J. (1964). Degree of learning and the measurement of forgetting. *Journal of Verbal Learning and Verbal Behavior, 3,* 112–129.

Walker, W. M. (1982). Psychostimulants. In S. E. Breuning & A. Poling (Eds.). *Drugs and Mental Retardation* (pp. 235–267). Springfield, IL: Charles C. Thomas.

Weingartner, H., Rapoport, J. L., Buchsbaum, M. S., Bunney, W. E., Ebert, P. M. H., Mikkelsen, E. J., & Caine, E. D. (1980). Cognitive processes in normal and hyperactive children and their response to amphetamine treatment. *Journal of Abnormal Psychology, 89,* 25–37.

Weiss, B., & Laties, V. (1962). Enhancement of human performance by caffeine and the amphetamines. *Pharmacological Review, 14,* 1–36.

Weiss, G., Hechtman, L., Perlman, T., Hopkins, J., Wener, A. (1979). Hyperactives as young adults. *Archives of General Psychiatry, 36,* 675–681.

Weiss, G., Kruger, E., Danielson, U., & Elman, M. (1975). Effects of long-term treatment of hyperactive children with methylphenidate. *Canadian Medical Association Journal, 112,* 159–165.

Wells, K. C., Conners, C. K., Imber, L., & Delameter, A. (1981). Use of single-subject methodology in clinical decision-making with a hyperactive child on the psychiatric inpatient unit. *Behavioral Assessment, 3,* 359–370.

Werry, J. S. (1981). Drugs and learning. *Journal of Child Psychology and Psychiatry, 22(3),* 283–290.

Werry, J. S., & Aman, M. (1975). Methylphenidate and haloperidol in children. Effects on attention, memory and activity. *Archives of General Psychiatry, 32,* 790–795.

Wolraich, M., Drummond, T., Salomon, M. K., O'Brien, M. L., & Sivage, C. (1978). Effects of methylphenidate alone and in combination with behavior modification procedures on the behavior and academic performance of hyperactive children. *Journal of Abnormal Child Psychology, 6,* 149–161.

Yoshida, H. (1980). Effects of drill practice on aptitude in learning of mathematics. *Journal of Educational Psychology, 72,* 706–715.

Zahn, T., Abate, F., Little, B., & Wender, P. (1975). Minimal brain dysfunction, stimulant drugs and autonomic nervous system activity. *Archives of General Psychiatry, 32,* 381–387.

10

Applied Behavior Analysis and the Correction of Learning Disabilities

MARK A. KOORLAND

INTRODUCTION

Educating children with learning disabilities is an endeavor involving numerous professional groups such as psychologists, educators, physicians, and social workers. Behavioral psychology exerts an influence resulting from increased sophistication in classroom applications as well as a clear and compelling demand by practitioners for academic interventions that are effective and efficient. Learning-disabilities (LD) professionals are acutely aware of accountability for actions as well as parental demands for growth or progress in LD children. Indeed, growth of the LD field was often in response to parent pressure for increased services. Now that the establishment of LD services is intact and school systems regularly identify children for placement in special classes (Mercer, Forgone & Wolking, 1976), the particulars of remedial corrective techniques receive more frequent attention than in the past. The myriad of techniques and their diverse proponents are entering a period where empirical validation for instructional models and techniques are valued objectives (Chandler, 1981).

There is a rich history of attempts to individualize instruction for regular and special education (Schwartz & Oseroff, 1975; Stephens, 1970). Attempts to identify individual differences and to teach LD children accordingly can be traced to the efforts of pioneer workers such as Strauss and Werner (Bryan & Bryan, 1978). Individualized or clinical

297

Psychological and Educational
Perspectives on Learning Disabilities

approaches in education embody the idea of careful individual analysis and search for appropriate methods and techniques to generate student learning. The field of learning disabilities exemplifies the concern for the individual. The work of numerous researchers (Frostig, 1967; Kephart, 1960; Kirk & Kirk, 1971) on specialized testing systems designed for individual programming decisions attests to the importance of individualization as an instructional principle in this field.

Applied behavior analysis (ABA), although growing from a stronger research base than traditional clinical teaching activities (Chandler, 1981), embodies principles of individual analysis and programming based on the learner's uniqueness. ABA promotes close inspection and evaluation of environmental variables that influence learning and performance (Baer, Wolf, & Risley, 1968). Basic behavioral research involving systematic attention to the environment has produced not only principles of behavior, but also a technology enabling subtle adjustments in programming needed to influence the performance of each learner (Johnston & Pennypacker, 1980). Learning difficulty is conceived as resulting from insufficient reinforcement or from learned inappropriate responses to instructional stimuli (Dolly, 1980; Throne, 1973). Individual analysis and subsequent direct adjustment of antecedent and consequent events temporally surrounding the learner's response become the primary means by which behaviorally oriented instructors attempt to correct learning disorders.

The utility of applied behavior analysis for special educators is underscored by the increasing frequency of behavioral studies with learning-disabled individuals (Rose, Koorland, & Epstein, 1982; Treiber & Lahey, 1983). It is interesting to note that in the review of studies employing ABA interventions with LD students by Rose, Koorland, and Epstein (1982), 25 studies were found within a 12-year period. A review conducted for this chapter showed 19 in the subsequent 5-year period. Thus, studies closely following behavior-analysis principles with learning disabilities have approximately doubled in frequency over the last 4 years. Additionally, there is growing interest in cognitive behavior modification, based on operant principles and employing repeated-measures research strategies characteristic of ABA.

Behavior modification and the ensuing system of applied behavior analysis offer a conceptual framework and set of practices that relate well to the daily realities of instructional management for children and adolescents with learning disabilities. Practices in applied behavior analysis have had major impact on exceptional student education and are congruent with emphases on individualized instruction in the learning-disabilities field (Hallahan & Kauffman, 1976).

BEHAVIORAL INSTRUCTIONAL PRACTICES

In the classroom, the behavioral model is operationalized, using relatively direct procedures (Stephens, 1970). These procedures consist of the following four steps: (1) pinpoint the behavior targeted for change, (2) measure the behavior directly and repeatedly, (3) institute a change in events antecedent to the behavior and/or change the consequences of the behavior, and (4) evaluate and try again if goals are not attained.

The first procedure, pinpointing, reflects the applied dimension of ABA. Behaviors of concern are directly relevant or closest to the targeted academic response. If reading is taught, it is analyzed and reduced to its component steps and students are taught the task hierarchy that is appropriate, given their entry-level skills. Pinpointing is used to denote the highly specific description of behavior. For example, *"sees written words and says words"* is more refined than the term "reads" and describes an exact response topography. "Reads" has other meanings and would be refined and stated differently, depending on the particular aspect of reading that is targeted. The level of precision at the beginning step sets the stage for accurate measurement and verification of interventions.

The measurement activity following the pinpointing of behavior to be changed can be performed in numerous ways. Faithful quantifications of the actual overt behavior are sought. Measurements are taken frequently in a repeated fashion over time and graphed. Graphing conventions vary widely, but all serve to permit visual analysis of behavior change. The reference point in the visual analysis is baseline data obtained prior to treatment. Changes are judged in light of overall trends or slope of the data following intervention and the difference between ending values of baseline data and beginning values of the treatment data.

Changes in the immediate environment are made to accelerate or decelerate students' responses. Change efforts may be directed at teaching materials or at the way materials are presented. Stimuli that indicate the required response are presented in a fashion enabling control of the responses, for example, teaching dissimilar alphabet letters before similar ones. Change efforts may also be directed at the consequences following responses. The contingent presentation and withdrawal of certain reinforcers can be changed. Consequences to decrease the probability of certain responses may be presented. Or, varying combinations of the above can be designed to alter responding.

During instruction, data are monitored to determine if satisfactory progress is occurring. Formative evaluation is one of the essential differentiating features of a behavioral model of teaching. If change does not occur, reinspection of the sequence of teaching events, stimulus materials, teacher directions, or any event thought influential on the responses is altered and the subsequent data monitored. In the behavioral model, it is difficult to teach from programs demanding rigid adherence to a certain sequence of curricular steps, because the instructor must attend to student data and be responsive to changes contradicting expected learner progress.

ANTECEDENT CONTROL

Antecedent events constitute the majority of what is called "teaching," the imparting of information, skills, facts, and the like. Homme, C'DeBaca, Cottingham, and Homme (1970) discuss behavior in terms of a three-term contingency and refer to changing behavior as a behavioral engineering task.

There is a contingent relationship between the discriminative stimulus and the learner's performance (Figure 1). The discriminative stimulus sets the occasion for responses that will be reinforced (Ferster & Perrott, 1968). Although not a cue or signal in the sense of causing behavior, it is the event that discriminates when behavior will have a contingent relationship with a reinforcing consequence. Getting a desired performance or approximation of the performance to occur in the presence of the "correct" stimulus and then reinforcing the performance is how the behavioral engineer comes to develop stimulus control. Keeping the three-term contingency in mind, learning disabilities may be conceptualized as faulty stimulus control. Learners may say "M" in the presence of "N," "saw" in the presence of "was," and "5" in the presence of "3 + 1 =   ." Teaching activities typically concentrate on establishing stimulus control. Homme *et al.* (1968) point out the rule for correcting faulty

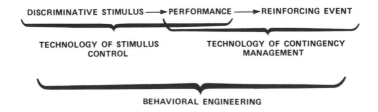

Figure 1.   Relationships between the three-term contingency and behavioral engineering. (From Homme *et al.*, 1968. What behavioral engineering is. *Psychological Record, 18,* 425–434. Reprinted with permission.)

stimulus control is the same as that used to establish it in the first place. Stimulus control is established by reinforcing desired performance in the presence of the stimulus that is appropriate for the response.

A technique used by Knowlton (1980, 1982) with elementary learning-disabled students illustrates how to develop stimulus control. Picture cues were used to establish the correct response in the presence of words on flash cards. After the students began saying correct responses in the presence of the word/picture card, the picture was gradually faded out until written words only controlled verbal responses. Knowlton (1980) used a clever technique to produce the fading prompt. Stimulus materials consisted of cards with words on the lower half and pictures on the upper half. Pieces of tracing paper were stacked and taped over the picture half until it was no longer visible. Subsequently, control of the verbal response was transferred from pictures to written text.

Demonstration, modeling, and feedback are additional antecedent events used to obtain stimulus control. Blankenship and Baumgartner (1982) taught subtraction with borrowing to nine elementary learning-disabled students. The teacher demonstrated how to solve the problems and then told the students to model the teacher on a similar problem. Students were told if their answers were correct or incorrect. If incorrect, they watched and performed again. All students reached 100% accuracy on instructed problems at some point during the 6 days of treatment. Some generalization to more complex problems was noted.

Direct instruction uses a number of antecedent components that enable the production of correct student responses. Gettinger (1982) identified the essential components of direct instruction as involving teacher-pacing of activities, small group instruction, continuous and controlled practice, sufficient time allotted for learning, immediate corrective feedback, and questioning at a level to ensure success. Phonics-based direct instruction such as *DISTAR* (Direct Instruction System for Teaching Arithmetic and Reading) *Reading Program* (Englemann & Bruner, 1968) has been found generally quite effective (Abt Associates, 1977; Stallings & Kaskowitz, 1974). Gettinger (1982) used *DISTAR* with eight elementary-aged, learning-disabled students. Although focusing on management of inappropriate classroom behavior, clear improvement in word recognition was noted. Students' accuracy improved from 45% to 84%.

CONTINGENCY MANAGEMENT

The application of contingency management techniques, particularly in the area of social behavior, is well documented (Raschke, Stainback,

& Stainback, 1982). Investigations of LD children and delivery of reinforcing events have involved a number of strategies. Rose and others
(1982) reported studies that demonstrated token economies, use of peer
tutors as contingency managers, a combination of feedback and tokens
on handwriting, academic grades used as tokens, differential teacher
attention, and monetary reinforcement on reading and comprehension.
They concluded that many complex academic tasks can be controlled by
reinforcement. Myers and Hammill (1982) suggested that often it may be
more that a child *will not* work rather than he or she *cannot* work. Children not performing for motivational reasons benefit from careful contingency management.

A study by Deno and Chiang (1979) provides a good example of
effective contingency management with LD children. They were able
substantially to reduce several errors in LD boys with a median age of 10
years, 6 months. Students received plastic beads for each letter seen and
named correctly. The letters, *p, d, b,* and *q,* were commonly reversed by
these students. In an untimed, letter-presentation condition, baseline
performance for all subjects ranged from 60%-86% correct. After reinforcement, four of the five students named letters with better than 90%
accuracy. In a timed presentation, results were less dramatic for some
students, but nevertheless clear. Most interesting was that the results
were obtained in 1 day during a 10-minute period.

Contingencies that decrease responses are used infrequently in academic modification. Practitioners are cautious in using consequences
that reduce behavior because of concern for undesirable side effects,
although there are strategies to offset these effects (Doty, McInnis, &
Paul, 1974). Response cost, a technique where value is removed contingently, has been used in a few studies with learning-disabled students.
Sindelar, Housaker, and Jenkins (1982) used response cost in combination with differential reinforcement of other behavior (DRO) to reduce a
second-grade, learning-disabled girl's frequency of looking away from
her book. In the DRO condition, the student read from a workbook and
earned a token for each half page read without looking away. In the
response cost condition, she started the sessions with 12 tokens. The
first look-away during a half page segment cost a token. Other look-
aways during that segment were recorded but not fined. Upon introduction of the response cost condition, following the DRO, the mean frequency of looking away dropped by 56% and, upon a second
introduction, the frequency dropped by 57%. It was also noted that
decreases in look-aways during response cost resulted in oral-reading
rate increases above rates obtained during DRO.

An important element of contingency management is delivery schedules of reinforcing consequences. Unpredictable schedules such as those encountered with gambling, for example, create quite durable and persistent responding. Besides creating more persistent behavior, intermittent reinforcement should be less cumbersome for a teacher. Additionally, intermittent reinforcement avoids reinforcer satiation by limiting exposure to the reinforcing event. A systematic effort to investigate variable reinforcement was undertaken by Blankenship and Baumgartner (1982) with six elementary learning-disabled students. Variable reinforcement, combined with demonstration and modeling to improve arithmetic subtraction performance, entailed informing students that, on some days, points toward school supplies would be earned and on other days no points could be earned. This was carried out, cleverly, by having students draw from a container printed slips of paper stating either "points," or "no points." Before intervention, accuracy averaged 18.2%. In the follow-up phase, accuracy averaged 76%. Because this study tested the effects of several components, however, it is difficult to determine the unique effects of the variable reinforcement component.

Numerous variations in contingency management are possible. Speltz, Shimamura, and McReynolds (1982) based rewards with 12 learning-disabled students on group-average performance, on the work of a low-achieving student, or on the work of a randomly selected student. The purpose of the study was to evaluate group social interactions, but correct math performances data of four of the students was also obtained. Two of the students did their best work when contingencies were based on the group's performance and two did best when the group reward was based on an identified, low-performing student. Interestingly, the authors noted that group contingencies did not encourage negative behavior among the children. The potential use of group contingencies for improvement of academic behaviors is yet to be thoroughly investigated. Use of various reinforcement-scheduling methods and group contingencies appears to have merit in reducing the need for consistent one-to-one intervention.

MEASUREMENT

Measures of academic performance within applied behavior analysis are typically expressed using percentage-correct or time-based measures such as frequency (rate) of correct and incorrect responses (Billingsley & Liberty, 1982). Frequency measures are more sensitive and precise than percentage-correct measures (White & Haring, 1976).

Precision teaching is a measurement and evaluation system based on direct, daily, and continuous recording of behavior, using behavior frequency (Pennypacker, Koenig, & Lindsley 1972). Precision teaching is used to assess effects of instructional events designed to modify targeted behaviors. Precision teaching proponents advocate that high-response frequencies be an instructional objective. Bower and Orgel (1981) point out that teachers initially should disregard error frequencies during the acquisition stage of learning and encourage students to produce correct responses at the highest rates possible. Pennypacker (1974) states that traditional concern for accuracy may, in fact, serve to slow down children's performance to the extent that it may be nonfunctional. Daily precision-teaching practices are centered around building a student's fluency in academic skills. Goals for academic responses are set in terms of rate. Daily instructional decisions for each student are made using graphed frequency measures for feedback. The instructional strategy is to increase frequencies over time toward a selected rate, change to a more difficult step in the curriculum, and repeat the process.

The use of charted, direct daily measurement has been suggested for making many kinds of instructional decisions. Koorland (in press) outlined a diagnostic teaching procedure for choosing optimal teaching methods for individual learners. The procedure directs the teacher to assemble a pool of items, currently unknown to the student. If the instructor wishes to evaluate two or more teaching methods, items are randomly divided into sets corresponding to each method. For 3 or 4 days, the teacher, holding instructional time constant, teaches, probes, and charts students' correct and incorrect rate data for each method. Various teaching methods are evaluated by inspecting trends of their respective data, both for correct and error trends. The method producing the most rapid acquisition, determined by the steepest uptrend for correct and/or the steepest downtrend for error rate is chosen for continued use with the student. In a study (Koorland, in press) using this procedure, two methods for teaching sight words were compared. The subject, a first-grade boy referred for learning-disability services, was taught using flash cards showing either a word and picture prompt, or a printed word only. Cards with prompts were explained and the child was asked to look at the word and say the word. On successive days, the prompt was faded by reducing its size and print intensity. The word-only cards were explained initially and missed words were supplied. Both drill and picture prompt cards were shown for 10 minutes each session. Timed probes were given immediately following each method. On the fourth day, the prompts produced the lowest rate of errors. Figure 2 shows the data for each method. The measurements and graphing indicated, for this student, fading picture prompts were superior to

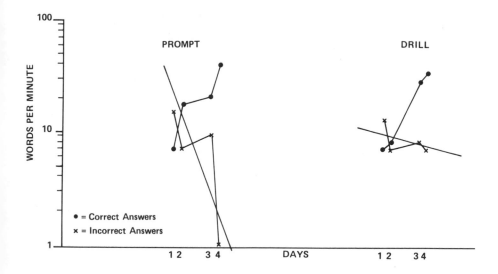

Figure 2.   Words per minute read correctly and incorrectly for a first-grade boy. (From Koorland, in press. The try procedure: A precision diagnostic teaching strategy. *Journal of Special Education Technology*. Reprinted with permission.)

drill in decreasing incorrect answers. The chart permits the teacher to visually interpret the differences and actual measurement of the trends is not always necessary.

The procedure used in the last example employed a strategy very similar to the multielement baseline design appearing in behavioral research. The next section is a discussion of repeated-measures designs characteristic of ABA, and shows applications with learning-disabled subjects.

EXPERIMENTAL LOGIC AND DESIGN CONSIDERATIONS

The experimental designs in ABA are part of the methodological innovations characterizing the field and offer the capability to meet the diverse needs of researchers and clinicians working with disabled students (Guralnick, 1978). To evaluate the persuasive power of various designs, it is instructive to review design logic.

The essential logic used in ABA is affirmation of the consequent (Sidman, 1960). Changes in data after introduction of a treatment lead to the conclusion that the independent variable is responsible for the observed changes. This, of course, is a risky experimental strategy because a number of other events could precipitate data changes at the approximate time a treatment is applied. To rule out happenstance, another affirmation of the consequent is sought. Previously presented treatments may be removed and subsequent reversals in the data noted. The reversal in the data provides a second affirmation of the consequent. Three affirmations would convince most readers that a functional relation between treatment and behavior exists. The following are acceptable, single-subject research designs used to evaluate behavioral treatments with the learning disabled.

REVERSAL DESIGNS

A design involving presentation and removal of a treatment, termed A–B–A, is a reversal design. Numerous variations of this design exist—BAB, ABAB—and if one chooses to evaluate an additional treatment, ABAC denotes the examination of two different treatments, with return to baseline occurring before the introduction of the second treatment (C). Often, treatments are assembled in a package (Hartmann, Shigetomi, & Barrios, 1978), and an A–BC–A design would be used for evaluation. Treatment components could be separated in later stages to note individual contributions to the effect by using an A–BC–A–B–A–C design. Treatments occasionally are ordered consecutively as in an A–B–C–D arrangement. In this latter design, interpretation is difficult because of potential treatment-order-interaction effects (Campbell & Stanley, 1963), a problem prevalent in other research models as well.

Gettinger (1982) used a reversal design to study the effects of a direct instruction program on the off-task behavior of elementary LD children. Achievement gains were of secondary interest in this study, an example of presenting antecedent events as treatment. Gettinger (1982) used three dependent measures, illustrated in Figure 3.

In this data display, the C phase represents a follow-up period of data collection, not a second-treatment presentation. The effect of the treatment most clearly is noted on the nonacademic behavior (not attending to instruction, blackboard, etc.), and the change in the data occurs after introduction ot the treatment. In the nonacademic measure, the change is rapid and pronounced. The other measures change but not to the same extent. The design worked here because the dependent measures were reversible to their original state. When reversibility is a possible problem, the multiple baseline design is employed.

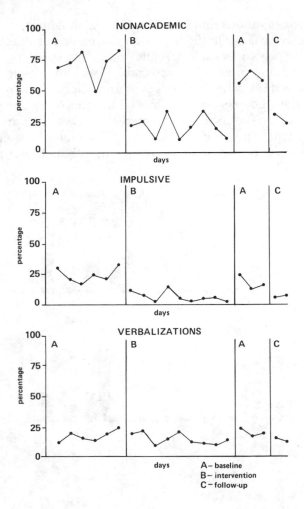

Figure 3.   Mean percentage of occurrence of three target behaviors for eight LD children across baseline and treatment phases. (From Gettinger, 1982. Improving classroom behaviors and achievement of learning-disabled using direct instruction. *School Psychology Review.* 11, 329–336. Reprinted with permission.)

MULTIPLE BASELINE DESIGNS

Certain behaviors are irreversible. The treatment can be withdrawn but, for example, in the case of reading instruction, once students acquire the skill, they might not return to the former behavior nor is it desirable to reverse for ethical reasons (Bailey, 1977). The thorny problem of irreversibility is handled by successive or lagged introductions of the treatment at various times across subjects, situations, or behaviors. Each successive change in the data is an affirmation of the consequent.

Figure 4 displays a multiple baseline design across behaviors used by Knowlton (1980). A prompt fading technique was introduced in a lagged fashion across three behaviors (sets of words). Upon introduction of the treatment, the student's accuracy moved up noticeably and was maintained over time. The focus of the intervention was on varying conditions antecedent to the student's response. The multiple baseline design primarily is used to examine one treatment, although it is possible to

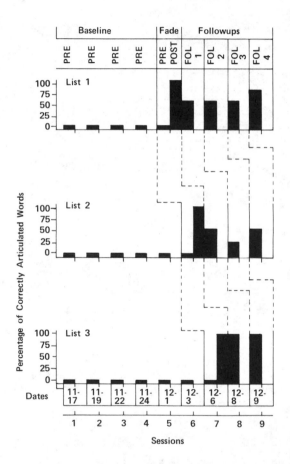

Figure 4.   Effects of fading on a student's acquisition and retention of sight words. PRE = pretest; POST = posttest; FOL = followup. (From Knowlton, 1980. Effects of picture fading on two learning-disabled students' sight-word acquisition. *Learning Disabilities Quarterly, 3,* 88–96. Reprinted with permission.)

examine more than one if the design incorporates features to avoid treatment-order confounding (Bailey, 1977). Additional treatments involve obtaining longer baselines, often difficult to do in the natural environment. The multielement baseline design assists in overcoming some of these difficulties.

MULTIELEMENT BASELINE DESIGNS

A recently emerging design, the multielement baseline design (Sidman, 1960; Ulman & Sulzer-Azaroff, 1975) involves rapid alternation of treatments (Barlow & Hayes, 1979). Because the design permits the investigation of more than one treatment at a time, it lends itself well to examination of different curricula or teaching procedures within the same student. The obvious usefulness of this design for individual, instructional decision making is one of its most important advantages (Koorland, in press). Another feature of the multielement design is that the more effective treatment appears relatively quickly because of the rapid alternation of conditions.

Rose, McEntire, and Dowdy (1982) used the multielement baseline design to compare two error-correction procedures, supplying the correct word or giving prompts to sound words out. Figure 5 displays the results for five elementary LD students. For most, the word-supply procedure provided higher correct rates of reading during probes.

CHANGING CRITERION DESIGNS

This particular design requires that the treatment influence behavior to the extent necessary to change it to a predetermined criteria. Criteria then are changed and, if the treatment again moves behavior to the new criteria, then a functional relationship is shown. An example of this design is found in a study by Schloss, Sedlak, Elliott, and Smothers (1982). A sixth-grade, LD student was required to perform math problems. The number attempted and the number correct necessary for reinforcement were specified, and the student subsequently met the requirements (see Figure 6). Then, progressively, the requirements were increased and those requirements were achieved. The controlling function of reinforcement was demonstrated across five changes in criteria. Five affirmations of the consequent were attained with one student. The desirability of this design for use with academic behavior is easily appreciated, especially when one considers the irreversibility issue.

Hartmann and Hall (1976) offer some guidelines in the use of the

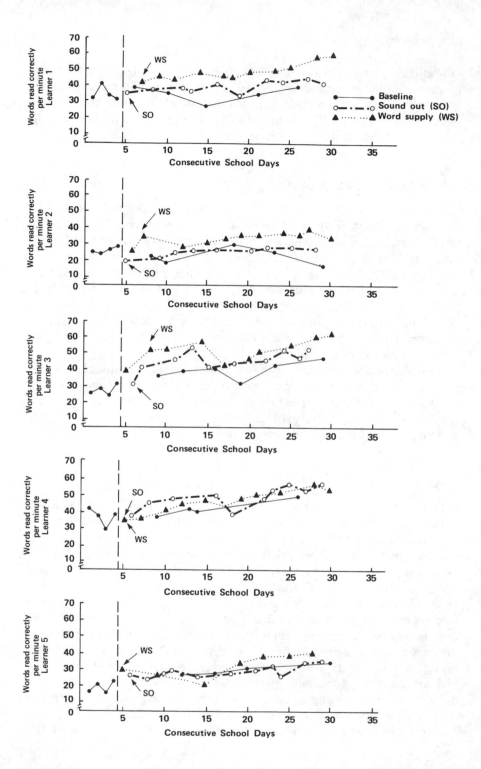

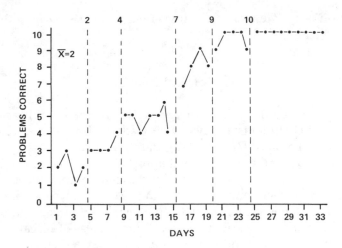

Figure 6.   Changing criterion for problems. (From Schloss, Sedlack, Elliott, & Smothers, M. 1982. Application of the changing criterion design in special education. *The Journal of Special Education, 16,* 359–367. Reprinted with permission.)

changing criterion design. First, phase changes should demonstrate stability to rule out changes in data caused by historical, maturation, or measurement variables. Second, baseline data should be obtained for a length of time longer than ensuing treatment phases to demonstrate that the changes in data that coincide with a criterion shift are not part of a naturally occurring cycle of variability. Additionally, baseline data should be stable or changing in a nondesigned direction to show a clear contrast when the treatment is introduced. Third, criterion shifts should be sizeable to demonstrate clear changes in the dependent measure. Fourth, if highly variable data exist and the study's results are unclear, then as a check against uncontrolled variables, a less stringent change in criterion shift can be made. If the data show a clear declining trend, then the case can be made for a functional relationship between the independent and dependent variable.

Applied behavior analysis has been used to investigate numerous treatments and their relationship to academic dependent measures. The

Figure 5.   Effects of systematic error-correction procedures on the rates of correctly read words. (From Rose, McEntire, & Dowdy, 1982. Effects of two error-correction procedures on oral reading. *Learning Disabilities Quarterly, 5,* 100–105. Reprinted with permission.)

next section is a review of recent investigations with learning-disabled students.

RECENT RESEARCH

A number of recent reviews of behavioral methods with academic responses of LD students are available (Gadow, Torgesen, & Dahlem, 1985; Hobbs & Lahey, 1977; Rose, Koorland, & Epstein, 1982; Treiber & Lahey, 1983). Generally, conclusions about the effectiveness of behavioral procedures have been favorable. Studies have employed behavioral measurement practices and employed individual analysis. On a short-term basis, academic deficits have been alleviated. Problems, however, have been noted with research designs, randomness of research effort, generalization, and concentration on narrowly defined skills.

The review in this section is designed as an extension of work by Rose *et al.* which was current through approximately 1979. Research reports for this review were obtained from 1979 onward and were selected if: (1) subjects were identified as currently having the status of learning disabled: (2) research designs reflecting ABA practices were employed (A–B designs were not included since they are extremely limited experimentally); and (3) an academic response was measured. Table 1 displays pertinent information from the 19 available studies.

SUBJECTS AND SETTINGS

Male participants outnumber females approximately 2:1 and this, probably, reflects identification practices in the public schools. The majority of studies were concerned with elementary-aged children, 7–11 years old. Fewer studies included older students (Roberts & Smith, 1980; Swanson, 1981). The older students appear to receive services primarily in self-contained classes although, in a few studies, the setting was not clearly described. Settings ranged from the least restrictive resource room to highly specialized, university-supported classrooms used for research and teacher training.

ACADEMIC BEHAVIOR

In many studies, more than one type of academic behavior served as the dependent variable (Hallahan, Lloyd, Kosiewicz, Kauffman, & Graves, 1979; Roberts & Smith, 1980; Schimek, 1983; Swanson, 1981). This is a commendable practice because the interrelation of these skills

TABLE 1
Selected ABA Research: Intervention Modifying LD Students' Academic Behavior

Identifying number	Authors (date)	N (CA range)	Setting/ description	Academic behavior (dependent measure)	Treatment	Design	Reliability
1	Blankenship & Baumgartner (1982) A	4F 5M (8–11)	Resource	A (% acc)	D, M, F, TR, Verb	Multi-S AT F	–
2	Blankenship & Baumgartner (1982) B	6	Resource	A (% acc)	D, M, F, TR, Verb, VA	ABA + F	–
3	Deno & Chiang (1979)	5M (9–11)	Severe, full-time, child service demonstration center	Saying prev. reversed letters (% acc)	TR	Multi-S with return to baseline	–
4	Gettinger (1982)	4M 4F (7–8)	Remedial class for LD/BD	WR (% acc)	DI, F	ABAC	+
5	Graham (1983)	1F 2M (10–11)	Resource	H (5-point numerical rating of letters)	M Verb	Multi-S AT + F	+
6	Hallahan et al. (1979)	1M (7)	Self-contained class	H (CR) A (CR)	C/P (to attend to task)	Multi-R with reversals + AT + F	+
7	Knowlton (1980)	1M 1F (8–10)	Resource	WR	Fading C/P	Multi-R + F	–

TABLE 1 (Continued)
Selected ABA Research: Intervention Modifying LD Students' Academic Behavior

Identifying number	Authors (date)	N (CA range)	Setting/description	Academic behavior (dependent measure)	Treatment	Design	Reliability
8	Kosiewicz et al. (1981)	1M (10)	Self-contained	H (teacher numerical rating)	Self instruction (reviewed writing rules), self-correction	ABCBC with multielement features	+
9	Lloyd et al. (1981) A	4M (8–9)	Self-contained	A-Multi (% acc)	M preskills C/P, TR	Multi-S AT	+
10	Lloyd et al. (1981) B	3M (8–9)	Self-contained	A-Division (% acc)	M VA, R	Multi-S +F	–
11	Roberts & Smith (1980)	8M (10–12)	Self-contained	WR (CR & IR) RC (% acc)	TR M verb	Multi-S & crossover	+
12	Rose & Furr (1984)	4M (8–11)	Resource	WR (CR)	C/P	Multi-S and settings	+
13	Rose, McEntire, & Dowdy (1982)	4M 1F (8–11)	Resource	WR (CR)	C/P	Multielement	+
14	Schimek (1983)	1F (8)	Primary learning-disabilities class	Circling digraphs in words (% acc) WR (% acc) Words spelled (% acc)	TR VA C/P	ABCD + F	–
15	Sindelar et al. (1982)	1F (7)	Resource	WR (wpm)	VA, TR response/cost	ABCBC	+

16	Spetz et al. (1984)	4F 8M (7–10)	University-sponsored class	A (CR)	TR VA	A_1 A_2BCDE	+
17	Swanson (1981) A	1F 2M (8–9)	University-sponsored class	RC (% acc) WR (% acc)	TR self-recording	Multi-S + changing criterion	+
18	Swanson (1981) B	2M (9–14)	Self-contained	RC (% acc) WS (wpm)	R self-recording	Multi-S + changing criterion	+
19	Swanson (1981) C	5M 3F (9–14)	Receiving exceptional student services	RC (% acc)	TR self-recording	Multi-S	+

Codes for Table 1:

Treatments
C/P = cues/prompts
D = demonstrations
M = modeling
F = feedback
R = reinforcement
TR = token reinforcement
VA = variable arrangement
  of consequences
Verb = verbal intervention
DI = direct instruction

Academic behaviors
WR = words read
WS = words read silently
A = arithmetic
H = handwriting
RC = reading comprehension
Dependent measures
(% acc) = percentage accuracy
(CR) = correct rate
(IR) = incorrect rate
(wpm) = words per minute

Designs
Multi-S = multiple baseline across subjects
Multi-R = multiple baseline across responses
AT = additional treatments
F = follow-up phase
A = baseline
B = treatment #1
C = treatment #2
D = treatment #3
E = treatment #4

can be assessed as well as the generality of treatments, if applied across different behaviors. Often, studies with oral or silent reading included comprehension measures. For example, Roberts & Smith (1980) used an intervention package to increase correct reading rate, decrease incorrect rates, or increase accuracy on comprehension questions. The relationship among these academic behaviors provided some interesting results. When targeting correct or incorrect reading rates, it was found that improvement occurrred with no effect on comprehension. When comprehension was targeted, it could be improved with no negative effect on reading rates. Swanson (1981) was able to use similar measures, some of the same treatments, and replicated the results of Roberts and Smith (1980).

On a less optimistic note, most studies used percentage accuracy as the dependent measure. Some of the difficulties with this measure, such as lack of precision, were discussed earlier. Most handwriting studies used a rating or scoring system to evaluate handwriting qualitatively (Graham, 1983; Kosiewicz, Hallahan, & Lloyd, 1981). For example, Graham (1983) used a system where each letter printed by a subject was rated on a five-point scale. Judges were told that letter formation was the primary concern. The dependent variable was the sum of five ratings on each letter taught. Kosiewicz and others (1981) used a more complex scoring system and reported percentage of points obtained out of all possible in the session. Other used a direct-rate measure of legibly written words (Hallahan et al., 1979).

A few studies using rate as a measure of academic behavior reported words read or problems completed per minute (Sindelar et al., 1972; Speltz et al., 1982), or only correct responses per minute (Hallahan et al., 1979; Rose, McEntire & Dowdy, 1982; Rose & Furr, 1984). Without reporting incorrect responses per minute, it is extremely difficult to make any judgments about the subject's accuracy. Some investigators employed the practice of subtracting errors from correct responses per minute and reporting the result as correct rate (Rose, McEntire & Dowdy, 1982; Rose & Furr, 1984). This practice has the potential to obscure changes in rate when correct and error responses per minute go up or down at the same rate. Only Roberts and Smith (1980) reported both rate correct and rate incorrect in reading and thus provided a complete measure.

TREATMENTS

The majority of studies used reinforcement, which included simple verbal praise (Lloyd, Saltzman, & Kauffman, 1981), preselected activities available during contingent free time (Swanson, 1981), and token systems. Token systems were employed in one-half the studies. The systems generally used recorded points as the medium of exchange. Deno and Chiang (1979), however, used beads which would later be traded for pennies at a 10 to 1 exchange rate. Swanson (1981) also used tokens backed up by pennies or activities. Sindelar *et al.* (1982) used tangible tokens that were dropped in a box for the student. The backup reinforcers consisted of candy, games, time outside, or other unspecified reinforcers. Most studies used token systems as an adjunct to other treatments. When reinforcement parameters were the focus of the investigation, a tangible exchange medium was always used with money as a backup reinforcer.

Antecendent events were a major part of treatments in 11 studies. Although often a component of a treatment package, including contingencies, a number of antecedent events were examined alone. For example, Gettinger (1982) used direct instruction to modify three inappropriate behaviors, nonacademic, impulsive, and off-task vocalization, in eight learning-disabled children. Academic behavior was recorded and included pre- and post-tests on trained and novel (untrained) words. Treatment was direct instruction in phonic elements for 9 days. The instruction was teacher-directed, step by step, taking place in small groups. Repeated trials were given until mastery was achieved and repeated practice and immediate corrective feedback was provided. Results indicated that nonacademic and impulsive behavior were reduced when direct instruction was employed (see Figure 3). Inappropriate verbalizations were not affected by the intervention. On academic measures, children read an average of 45% of the trained words correctly during baseline and 84% after treatment. In addition, the percentage of novel words read correctly changed from 29% at baseline to 63% after treatment.

In a study on handwriting, Graham (1983) modeled the formation of letters while providing verbal descriptions of the modeled response. A clearly detailed treatment description, including each step, was provided. Briefly, steps involved dicusssion of the target letter's formation, including writing the letter three times. The examiner wrote the letter while describing the process. The student traced the letter with his finger while verbally describing the process of the letter's formation. Then, the student modeled the examiner's verbal prompts while writing the letter. Eventually, the student took over more of the writing and, finally, wrote from memory. The treatment was moderately effective; however, no generalization to untrained letters occurred. The treatment took place over a 5-hour period, and Graham (1983) concluded that it was not cost effective, given the results. The author also concluded that the rather involved number of steps may have been too complex and the self-guiding statements may have interfered with the writing.

In another manipulation of antecedent conditions, Rose and Furr (1984) taught sight words by two different methods. In the first condition, students were exposed to cards containing both a picture and a word, whereas in the other condition, the cards only had printed words on them. Students simply were told the word during the instructional session until they needed no help in reading it. After instruction, students were tested with word-only cards. Three of the four students in the study responded better for words taught without picture cues. The fourth student performed equally under both conditions. Although this finding is the opposite of Knowlton's (1980), there is a difference between the two studies in technique. Knowlton (1980) used a fading procedure and Rose and Furr (1984) never removed the picture cues during training.

The three examples considered here involved teacher control of instruction. In a very different set of studies, the primary focus of intervention was the self-instructional behaviors of students. For example, Swanson (1981) reported three studies involving reading and self-grading. In one experiment, students recorded reading errors, such as omission and substitutions, on individual charts. Tokens were used to reinforce accurate performances of the recording, self-correction during reading, and keeping below preset criteria for errors. Results showed oral reading errors were reduced. The next study emphasized self-recording of work time spent on reading. Silent words read per minute were increased with no changes in comprehension. The third study used self-scoring of comprehension question errors. Results showed improved accuracy on comprehension questions.

DESIGNS

The designs employed represent a greater degree of sophistication than noted in previous academic ABA studies (Rose, Koorland, & Epstein, 1982). The multiple baseline design across subjects was used frequently, which is reasonable since irreversibility is a common problem with academic-dependent variables. Some designs combined the multiple baseline type with additional treatment phases (Blankenship & Baumgartner, 1982; Graham, 1983; Hallahan et al., 1979; Lloyd et al., 1981). Additional treatments, of course, are difficult to evaluate as they immediately follow the original treatment. One of these designs included a return to baseline condition (Deno & Chiang, 1979), an infrequent strategy because the multiple baseline design usually is used on suspected irreversible behaviors and a reverse is considered an unexpected occurrence (Bailey, 1977).

Multielement baseline designs, suited for comparing treatments, were also employed. Rose, McEntire & Dowdy (1982) compared two treatments with this design. Kosiewicz (1981) incorporated multielement features in a reversal design to assess two choice options on two handwriting treatments. Treatments consisted of teacher instruction on handwriting rules or student self-correction of handwriting. After a baseline phase, teachers imposed either treatment on alternating days. In the next phase, the student chose either treatment. There was a reveral to teacher choice followed by a reversal to student choice. The student peformed best under student choice, and in this condition, chose self-correction. Also, performance during self-correction exceeded the teacher-instruction option. Kosiewicz and her associates (1961) handled a potentially confounding problem in an astute manner. Under the first student-choice condition, the student chose self-correction 17 days and teacher instruction 5 days. During second teacher-choice phase, control for unequal opportunities to experience the treatments was obtained by providing the same 3:1 ratio of self-correction to teacher instruction observed during the previous student-choice phase.

In a clever combination of designs, Swanson (1981) combined a multiple baseline design with a changing criterion design, taking advantage of the changing criterion design to demonstrate control over oral-reading errors and silent-reading rate while looking for changes in the subjects' reading comprehension accuracy. This is one of the first uses of the changing criterion design with LD students.

INTEROBSERVER RELIABILITY

Evaluation of the technical adequacy of observational data-collection procedures, in terms of observer reliability, is a standard practice in ABA (Kelly, 1977). Studies were reviewed for their attention to interobserver reliability, and Table 1 indicates the presence or absence of reliability data by a plus or minus. The majority of studies provided reliability information. A number of studies, however, indicated that reliability was satisfactory yet provided no data about reliability values or procedures (Blankenship & Baumgartner, 1982; Knowlton, 1980; Lloyd et al., 1981). Other studies provided no information about reliability at all (Deno & Chiang, 1979; Schimek, 1983). Of the studies reporting reliability data, a number provided the proportion or number of measures that were checked for reliability (Kosiewicz et al., 1981; Lloyd et al., 1981;

Rose, McEntire & Dowdy, 1982; Rose & Furr, 1984; Speltz *et al.*, 1982; Swanson, 1981). For example, Speltz and others (1982) stated that observers were present during all 14 sessions of their study. Kosiewicz *et al.* (1981) stated that 28 scoring-agreement checks took place and that this number was 35% of the days scored. Other indicated whether reliability data had been obtained during various conditions (Roberts & Smith, 1980; Rose, McEntire, & Dowdy, 1982; Rose & Furr, 1984; Sindelar *et al.*, 1982; Swanson, 1981). Information about reliability checks across conditions is valuable, because the reported number of checked sessions, although helpful, is, nevertheless, limited when complete procedural information is sought. Rose, McEntire, & Dowdy (1982) reported that teachers were monitored to verify the correctness of the planned interventions. This is the only study reporting this aspect of procedural detail in connection with reliability.

A number of calculations are employed when determining the reliability of observers. The majority of studies employed time-interval recording. Reliability data gathered on time intervals often are derived by dividing the number of intervals that two observers agreed upon by the total of intervals agreed and disagreed to and multiplying by 100. Concerns have been raised that this calculation inflates the resulting reliability estimate because, usually, there is high agreement on intervals in which no behavior was observed. Hartmann (1977) discussed advantages of effective percentage reliability measures that focus only on intervals in which behavior was present. Effective percentage calculations offer a more sensitive interobserver reliability measure. Speltz *et al.* (1982) performed the only study using effective percentage for reliability computation.

INTERVENTIONS AND ACADEMIC FOCUS

Figure 7 indexes studies, identified by their numbers from Table 1, by interventions and academic behavior. The focus of intervention is shown across the top of the figure. Studies with intervention components applied contingently to increase behavior probability are listed in the accelerating column. Contingent interventions that varied delivery schedules are listed in the varying arrangements column. Contingent interventions designed to reduce behavior are noted under deceleration. Studies using self-involvement as the major treatment mode are listed in that column. Interventions that are primarily antecedent to student behavior are divided into use of systematic prompts or cues, and combined or singular use of demonstration, modeling, or feedback. Although aca-

	Antecedent Events			Consequent Events		
	Demonstration Modeling/Feedback	Prompts or Cues	Student Self Involvement	Decelerating	Accelerating	Varying Arrangements
Reading	4_O, 11_I	7, 13, 14_I, 12	17_I, 18_I	14_O	3, 11_I, 14_I, 17_I, 18_I, 15_O	14_I
Reading Comprehension	11_I		17_I, 18_I, 19		11_I, 17_I, 18_I, 19	
Arithmetic	1_G, $9_{G,I}$, $10_{G,I}$, 2_G	$9_{G,I}$	6_O		$9_{G,I}$, $10_{G,I}$, 16_O, 2_G	2_G, $10_{G,I}$, 16_O
Spelling		14_I		14_I	14_I	14_I
Handwriting	5, 8	6_O	5, 6_O, 8			

Figure 7. Applied behavior analysis studies with LD students, indexed by intervention and academic target behavior. Subscripts indicate primary focus of the research: G = generalization; I = interrelation of academic areas/subskills; O = other behavior.

demic behaviors were evaluated in all studies, other topics were frequently of primary interest to the investigators. These other topics included: 1) relation among academic areas or subskills, 2) other behaviors such as on-task time, and 3) generalization across time, or behaviors. Subscripts in Figure 7 indicate these three areas.

It is interesting to note the concentration of interventions across the academic target behaviors. Reading enjoyed the widest range of interventions with arithmetic next. Spelling appears as the least-examined area in terms of studies and intervention techniques. Arithmetic-word problems is an area that was not addressed by any of the reviewed studies.

Across all academic areas, the use of accelerating consequences, specifically reinforcement, delivered either directly or mediated through a token system, appears as a frequently included behavior-change tactic. This finding coincides with previous findings (Rose, Koorland, & Epstein, 1982). Related, but less frequently used as the focus of intervention, are varied consequence arrangements. Variations in consequence delivery were found most in studies using arithmetic; however, the

MARK A. KOORLAND

primary foci of the studies were generalization, self-instruction (Graham, 1983), and the relationship of subskills to performance of complex tasks (Lloyd et al., 1981).

Antecedent variables were incorporated somewhat less frequently in the reviewed studies. Involvement of researchers with these variables roughly is divided between use of demonstration/modeling/feedback and prompting/cueing strategies. The few handwriting studies focused exclusively on manipulation of antecedent variables. Six studies employing student self-involvement are found in the review. These studies concentrated primarily on reading and handwriting. Hallahan and others (1979) have summarized the four components that workers in this area regard as a basis for self-control. These include self-assessment, self-recording, self-determination of reinforcement, and self-administration of reinforcement. Self-recording was the component found in the majority of these studies.

PRIMARY FOCUS OF STUDIES

Although all studies were relatively successful at modifying academic responses, the investigations often centered on other questions. Numerous studies examined aspects of generalization such as response maintenance over time (Blankenship & Baumgartner, 1982; Lloyd et al., 1981; Roberts & Smith, 1980; Schimek, 1983; Swanson, 1981). The attention to generalization is commendable, since this has become central in questions on the efficacy of behavioral procedures (McLeskey, Rieth, & Polsgrove, 1980; Pawlicki, 1970; Stokes & Baer, 1977).

Other researchers attempted to modify behaviors that could influence, or be influenced by, academic performance. Staying on task (Gettinger; 1982; Hallahan et al., 1979; Sindelar et al., 1982) and social interaction among students (Speltz et al., 1982) were examined most frequently. In the study by Speltz et al. (1982), discussed earlier, students were asked about the contingency arrangement they preferred. The low-functioning students wanted their performance to be the basis for the group's contingent reinforcers, and during this condition, their peers interacted with them in the most helpful manner. The inclusion of student-opinion information is innovative and offers a novel perspective on treatment effect.

Researchers frequently were interested in a subskill's contribution to more complex academic behavior. Two investigations examined the relation between reading rate and comprehension (Roberts & Smith, 1980; Swanson, 1981); little was found. Lloyd et al. (1981) focused on teaching rote-counting sequences for multiplication facts, and a strategy for using this skill. Improved performance and subsequent generalization to novel problems was obtained as a result of the training. In another example of subskill training, Schimek (1983) taught students to identify digraphs in words and noted subsequent improvements in spelling. The investigation of relationships among subskills and more complex behavior is commendable and begins to address concerns raised about inattention to the general area (Gadow et al., in press).

Two of the six self-involvement studies examined the effectiveness of self-involvement itself. Kosiewicz et al. (1981) found student choice of treatment produced positive results on handwriting. Graham (1983) noted moderate results that appeared to be situation-specific, not generalizing to untrained letters. Swanson's (1981) studies used self-involvement, but the relationship of reading to comprehension was the focus. Hallahan et al.'s (1979) study has a self-involvement component although on-task behavior was the primary behavior under investigation.

CONCLUSIONS

Rose, Koorland, and Epstein (1982) noted that systematic replication, replicating previous research with subtle changes in procedure, are important for LD research. It appears as if researchers are slowly moving in this direction. There is compelling evidence that behavioral interventions are effective in the direct modification of academic deficits (Treiber & Lahey, 1983). Investigations of generality over time and responses are taking place more frequently than in the past. Although most studies still employ a variety of reinforcement strategies, they are not focusing on consequent events as the primary behavior change strategy to the same extent as in the past. Rather, effort is being directed at antecedent treatments such as clever techniques for providing and fading prompts and cues (Knowlton, 1980; Knowlton, 1982; Schimek, 1983).

Issues related to cost effectiveness and practicality have been noted (Myers & Hammill, 1982) and researchers are becoming aware of such concerns (Deno & Chiang, 1979; Graham, 1983). Efficiency as a topic is a product of a maturing field of study. It is difficult to discuss cost issues unless there is a system that provides a predictable set of effects.

Previously reviewed studies showed a dissimilarity of investigative focus (Rose, Koorland, & Epstein, 1982). This state of affairs has lessened with the concentration on generalization noted in this particular review. It is, nonetheless, clear that the field continues to look at a wide range of treatment options across many academic responses. As noted in Figure 7, no area, save oral reading, has had consistent research applied to it.

Designs found in recent studies tend to be versatile and innovative. Combined designs useful for examining complex relationships among variables were found. Designs incorporating multielement features, as well as use of the changing criterion design, are examples. Using designs appropriate for the constraints of irreversibility are necessary for continued investigation of academic dependent variables.

Unfortunately, there are questionable technical aspects noted in some studies that need careful consideration. Dependent measures were used that were not as precise as they should be. For example, some investigators reported only correct response rates. Reliability information was absent or described so briefly that serious doubts about technical adequacy could arise. These weak technical aspects are not difficult to correct, however.

FUTURE DIRECTIONS

The efficacy of behavioral procedures with LD children is well established (Treiber & Lahey, 1983). As behavioral applications continue, it is likely that a number of areas will continue to receive attention and new areas of investigation will emerge.

Continued pursuit of generalization issues will, no doubt, predominate. This concern with generalization is critical to the value of an intervention system showing results as predictable as ABA. If they are not the central focus of future studies, questions about generalization will be an important adjunct to investigations of any new intervention with LD children. This adjunct status is evident in the numerous designs, including follow-up components or measurement of responding to untrained tasks. In the future, reinforcement-scheduling effects may be explored further as an avenue to generalization of behavior over time. Use of strategy training may hold promise for generalization across responses, but much more work is needed in this area.

The issue of cost efficiency and effectiveness will be addressed more frequently. As systems continue to come under tighter fiscal constraints, cost considerations will take on a greater sense of urgency. Also, in an attempt to increase cost efficiency, early academic intervention with behavioral methods should be investigated more completely. Of the studies considered for this review, none contained subjects that were under 7 years of age. Yet, educational systems frequently engage in early identification activities at the preschool level. The behavioral model has produced impressive results with other preschool through third grade, high-risk students (Stallings & Kaskowitz, 1974). Application to those identified early as LD would seem to be a logical sequel. Activity with the youngest students could provide the most important cost benefit, reducing the need for comprehensive remedial services later.

There is a noticeable absence of behavioral strategies directed at language behavior in learning-disabled children. The problem has been noted elsewhere (Myers & Hammill, 1982). The technology of ABA lends itself to investigation of verbal behavior as well as other academic concerns. Perhaps investigators are attracted by the behaviors used to identify LD in the schools, primarily reading difficulties. However, difficulties with verbal behavior, couched in terms of language disorders, are also considered an important problem for LD children (Bryan & Bryan, 1978). Future studies should begin to focus on this area, but not until there are careful specifications of what learning-disabled, verbal behavior actually is.

A fascinating area that has had minor attention is prompting and cueing. A handful of studies have explored various techniques for facilitating the transfer of stimulus control from prompts to task-related stimuli with the learning disabled. Recently, Touchette and Howard (1984) investigated schedules of reinforcement and their contribution to the transfer of stimulus control with retarded children. This line of research has obvious implications for future behavior analysis with learning-disabled students.

The areas discussed here represent only a sampling of those in which behavioral researchers can make important contributions. The improvement of learning-disabled children's behavior will proceed as helping professionals are trained in behavioral technology. If the relatively brief history of behavior analysis is predictive of the future, basic behavioral principles will continue to be applied in novel ways to address individual limitations, and the subsequently validated practices will contribute to an improving technology.

REFERENCES

Abt Associates. (1977). *Education as experimentation: A planned variation model (Vol. IV).* Boston: Abt Associates.

Baer, D. M., Wolf, M. M., & Risley, T. R. (1968). Some current dimensions of applied behavior analysis. *Journal of Applied Behavior Analysis, 1,* 91–97.

Bailey, J. S. (1977). *Handbook of research methods in applied behavior analysis.* Tallahassee: Florida State University.

Barlow, D. H., & Hayes, S. C. (1979). Alternating treatments design. One strategy for comparing the effects of two treatments in a single subject. *Journal of Applied Behavior Analysis, 12*, 199–210.

Billingsley, F. F., & Liberty, K. A. (1982). The use of time based data in instructional programs for the severely handicapped. *Journal of the Association for the Severely Handicapped, 7*, 47–55.

Blankenship, C. S., & Baumgartner, M. D. (1982). Programming generalization of computational skills. *Learning Disability Quarterly, 5*, 152–162.

Bower, B., & Orgel, R. (1981). To err is divine. *Journal of Precision Teaching, 2*(1), 3–12.

Bryan, T. H., & Bryan, J. H. (1978). *Understanding learning disabilities*. Sherman Oaks, CA: Alfred Publishing.

Campbell, D. T., & Stanley, J. C. (1963). *Experimental and quasiexperimental designs for research*. Chicago: Rand McNally.

Chandler, H. N. (1981). Research and teachers: The interface remains fractured. *Journal of Learning Disabilities, 14*, 604–607.

Deno, S. L., & Chiang, B. (1979). An experimental analysis of the nature of reversal errors in children with severe learning disabilities. *Learning Disability Quarterly, 2*, 40–45.

Dolly, J. P. (1980). The role of stimulus control in instructional design for learning disabled children. *Journal for Special Education, 16*, 235–242.

Doty, D. W., McInnis, T., & Paul, G. L. (1974). Remediation of negative side effects of an on-going response-cost system with chronic mental patients. *Journal of Applied Behavior Analysis, 7*, 191–198.

Englemann, S., & Bruner, E. (1968). *Distar reading level I*. Chicago: Science Research Associates.

Ferster, C. B., & Perrott, M. C. (1968). *Behavior principles*. New York: Appleton-Century-Crofts.

Frostig, M. (1967). Testing as a basis for educational therapy. *Journal of Special Education, 2*, 12–34.

Gadow, K. D., Torgesen, J. K., & Dahlem, W. E. (1985). Learning disabilities. In M. Hersen, V. B. Hasselt, & J. L. Matson (Eds.). *Behavior Therapy for the Developmentally and Physically Disabled: A Handbook* (pp. 310–351). New York: Academic Press.

Gettinger, M. (1982). Improving classroom behaviors and achievement of learning disabled using direct instruction. *School Psychology Review, 11*, 329–336.

Graham, S. (1983). The effects of self instructional procedures on LD students' handwriting performance. *Learning Disability Quarterly, 6*, 231–234.

Guralnick, M. J. (1978). The application of single-subject research designs to the field of learning disabilities. *Journal of Learning Disabilities, 11*, 415–421.

Hallahan, D. P., & Kauffman, J. M. (1976). *Introduction to learning disabilities: A psychobehavioral approach*. Englewood Cliffs, NJ: Prentice-Hall.

Hallahan, D. P., Lloyd, J., Kosiewicz, M. M., Kauffman, J. M., & Graves, A. W. (1979). Self-monitoring of attention as a treatment for a learning disabled boy's off-task behavior. *Learning Disability Quarterly, 2*(3), 24–32.

Hartmann, D. P. (1977). Consideration in the choice of interobserver reliability estimates. *Journal of Applied Behavior Analysis, 10*, 102–116.

Hartmann, D. P., & Hall, R. V. (1976). The changing criterion design. *Journal of Applied Behavior Analysis, 9*, 527–532.

Hartmann, D. P., Shigetomi, C., & Barrios, B. (May 1978). *Design considerations in applied behavioral research*. Paper presented at the Annual Meeting of the Association of Behavior Analysis, Chicago.

Hobbs, S. A., & Lahey, B. B. (1977). The behavioral approach to "Learning Disabled" children. *Journal of Clinical Child Psychology, 6*, 10–14.

Homme, L., C'DeBaca, P., Cottingham, L., & Homme, A. (1970). What behavioral engineering is. In R. Ulrich, T. Stachnik, & J. Mabry (Eds.). *Control of Human Behavior*. Vol. 2 (pp. 17–23). Glenview, IL: Scott Foresman.

Johnston, J. M., & Pennypacker, H. S. (1980). *Strategies and tactics of human behavioral research*. Hillsdale, NJ: Lawrence Erlbaum Associates.

Kelly, M. B. (1977). A review of the observational data-collection and reliability procedures reported in *The Journal of Applied Behavior Analysis, 10*, 97–101.

Kephart, N. C. (1960). *The slow learner in the classroom*. Columbus, OH: Merrill.

Kirk, S. A., & Kirk, (1971). *Psycholinguistic learning disabilities: Diagnosis and remediation*. Urbana: University of Illinois Press.

Knowlton, H. E. (1980). Effects of picture fading on two learning disabled students' sight word acquisition. *Learning Disability Quarterly, 3*, 88–96.

Knowlton, H. E. (1982). The "QC" approach to teaching basic skills. *The Directive Teacher, 4*,(2), 20–24.

Koorland, M. A. (in press). The try procedure: A precision diagnostic teaching strategy. *Journal of Special Education Technology*.

Kosiewicz, M. M., Hallahan, D. P., & Lloyd, J. (1981). Effects of an LD student's treatment choice on handwriting performance. *Learning Disabilities Quarterly, 4*, 281–286.

Lloyd, J., Saltzman, N. J., & Kauffman, J. M. (1981). Predictable generalization in academic learning as a result of preskills and strategy training. *Learning Disability Quarterly, 4*, 203–216.

McLeskey, J., Rieth, H. J., & Polsgrove, L. (1980). The implications of response generalizations for improving the effectiveness of programs for learning disabled children. *Journal of Learning Disabilities, 13*, 287–290.

Mercer, C. D., Forgnone, C., & Wolking, W. D. (1976). Definitions of learning disabilities used in the United States. *Journal of Learning Disabilities, 9*, 376–386.

Myers, P. I., & Hammill, D. D. (1982). *Learning disabilities: Basic concepts, assessment practices, and instructional strategies*. Austin, TX: Pro-Ed.

Pawlicki, R. (1970). Behavior-therapy research with children: A critical review. *Canadian Journal of Behavioural Science, 1*, 163–173.

Pennypacker, H. S. (1974). Why frequency? The rationale of precise behavior management. Paper presented at First Annual Delaware Symposium on Curriculum, Instruction, and Learning. Newark, Delaware.

Pennypacker, H. S., Koenig, C., & Lindsley, O. R. (1972). *Handbook of the standard behavior chart*. Kansas City, KS: Precision Media.

Raschke, D., Stainback, S., & Stainback, W. (1982). The predictive capabilities of three sources for a promised consequence. *Behavioral Disorders, 7*, 213–218.

Roberts, M., & Smith, D. D. (1980). The relationship among correct and error oral reading rates and comprehension. *Learning Disability Quarterly, 3*, 54–64.

Rose, L. T., & Furr, P. M. (1984). Negative effects of illustrations as word cues. *Journal of Learning Disabilities, 17*, 334–337.

Rose, T. L., Koorland, M. A., & Epstein, M. H. (1982). A review of applied behavior analysis interventions with learning disabled children. *Education and Treatment of Children, 5*, 41–58.

Rose, T. L., McEntire, E., & Dowdy, C. (1982). Effects of two error-correction procedures on oral reading. *Learning Disability Quarterly, 5*, 100–105.

Schimek, N. (1983). Errorless discrimination training of diagraphs with a learning disabled student. *School Psychology Review, 12*, 101–105.

Schloss, P. J., Sedlak, R. A., Elliott, C., & Smothers, M. (1982). Application of the changing criterion design in special education. *Journal of Special Education, 16*, 359–367.

Schwartz, L., & Oseroff, A. (1975). *The clinical teacher for special education.* Tallahassee, FL: Educational Research Institute, The Florida State University.

Sidman, M. (1960). *Tactics of scientific research.* New York: Basic Books.

Sindelar, P. T., Housaker, M. S., & Jenkins, J. R. (1982). Response cost and reinforcement contingencies of managing the behavior of distractible children in tutorial settings. *Learning Disabilities Quarterly, 5,* 3–13.

Speltz, M. L., Shimamura, J. W., & McReynolds, W. T. (1982). Procedural variations in group contingencies: Effects on children's academic and social behaviors. *Journal of Applied Behavior Analysis, 15,* 533–544.

Stallings, J. A., & Kaskowitz, D. H. (1974). *Follow-through classroom observations evaluation.* Menlo Park, CA: Stanford Research Institute.

Stephens, T. M. (1970). *Directive teaching of children with learning and behavioral handicaps.* Columbus, OH: Charles E. Merrill.

Stokes, T. F., & Baer, D. M. (1977). An implicit technology of generalization. *Journal of Applied Behavior Analysis, 10,* 349–367.

Swanson, L. (1981). Modification of comprehension deficits in learning disabled children. *Learning Disability Quarterly, 4,* 189–202.

Throne, J. M. (1973). Learning disabilities: A radical behaviorist point of view. *Journal of Learning Disabilities, 6,* 543–546.

Touchette, P., & Howard, J. S. (1984). Errorless learning: Reinforcement contingencies and stimulus control transfer in delayed prompting. *Journal of Applied Behavior Analysis, 17,* 175–188.

Treiber, F. A., & Lahey, B. B. (1983). Toward a behavioral model of academic remediation with learning disabled children. *Journal of Learning Disabilities, 16,* 111–116.

Ulman, J. D., & Sulzer-Azaroff, B. (1975). Multi-element baseline design in educational research. In E. Ramp & G. Semb (Eds.). *Behavior Analysis: Areas of Research and Application* (pp. 377–391). Englewood Cliffs, NJ: Prentice-Hall.

White, O. R., & Haring, N. G. (1980). *Exceptional teaching* (2nd ed.). Columbus, OH: Charles E. Merrill.

11

Intervention Issues Related to the Education of LD Adolescents

JEAN B. SCHUMAKER
DONALD D. DESHLER
EDWIN S. ELLIS

INTRODUCTION

As learning-disabled children enter the junior and senior high-school environments, they encounter many demands that often serve to underscore the reality of their disabilities. A large gap between academic expectations and student performance often exists. The problems of older LD students are exacerbated further by the broad array of nonacademic expectations that are present in such areas as social and personal development, vocational competence, and successful post-school adjustment. The challenges confronting the LD adolescent and young adult clearly point to the need for interventions that are responsive to the unique characteristics of the individual while being appropriate for the settings within which learning and adjustment must occur.

During the latter part of the 1970s, increased attention was devoted to the educational needs of LD adolescents. Much of the initial attention came in the form of Child Service Demonstration Centers (CSDC) and Handicapped Children Model Projects (HCMP) funded under Title VI–G of PL 91–230 (The Education for All Handicapped Children Act). The purpose of these projects was to design and implement innovative service-delivery models. Significant progress was made with respect to the

Psychological and Educational
Perspectives on Learning Disabilities

articulation of major alternatives for service delivery for LD adolescents. For example, programming alternatives that emphasized curriculum-modification procedures (Hartwell, Wiseman, & Van Ruesen, 1979; Mosby, 1980), intensive basic skill remediation (Meisgeir, n.d.), school-survival skills (Zigmond, 1978), academic-coping skills (Deshler, Alley, & Carlson, 1980), and social skills and personal adjustment (Cox, 1980) were offered. Unfortunately, sufficient data were not generated to document the efficacy of these alternatives nor to indicate a model of choice for LD adolescents. Thus, although the above efforts were successful in delineating some general considerations and directions in intervention practices for LD adolescents, the need for validated interventions was largely unfulfilled when the CSDC and HCMP funding initiatives ended.

Recognizing the need for empirically based research on learning-disabled populations in general, the U.S. Department of Education funded five research institutes to conduct programmatic research in major areas of study within the learning-disability field. One of these institutes, The University of Kansas Institute for Research in Learning Disabilities (KU–IRLD), specified the study of LD adolescents as its main thrust. Since its inception in 1977, the predominant mission of the KU-IRLD has been to develop and validate an intervention model for LD adolescents that meets both effectiveness and feasibility criteria. The plan of action adopted by the KU–IRLD staff is an interactive system of intervention model development (Talley, 1978). This system involves six stages (Figure 1), some of which begin before others, but all of which run parallel and interact in a dynamic way to allow the gradual evolution of a data-based model which is responsive to the needs of LD adolescents and other consumers of the model (e.g., teachers, parents, and administrators).

The research conducted during Stage 1 (Epidemiological Research) provided a descriptive base on which subsequent research could be founded. Through epidemiological research, the specific characteristics of LD adolescents and their environments were determined. This information was, in turn, used to plan interventions that were aimed at alleviating LD adolescents' deficits and which are appropriate for the settings in which the LD adolescent finds him/herself. As interventions have been developed and tested, epidemiological research has been used to determine the characteristics of those students for whom the interventions are most and least effective.

Within Stage 2 research (Model Development and Testing), different *components* of the overall intervention model have been developed and

STAGES   YEARS

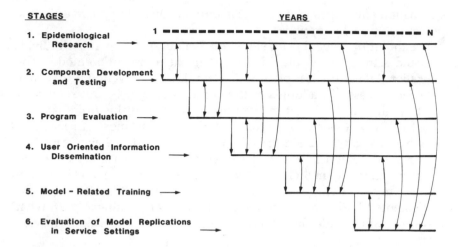

Figure 1.   An interactive system of intervention model development, showing the six stages through which the Strategies Intervention Model has been developed.

tested, using appropriate experimental designs. As either epidemiological data or data from subsequent stages of the system (Stages 2–6) have indicated a need for new intervention components or subcomponents, these new components have been developed. Initially, each component has been tested on a limited number of students and settings to establish its internal validity. Once the relative effectiveness of a component has been established, attention has turned to questions concerning the component's generalizability.

Stage 3 research has addressed the issue central to the validation of any intervention model: Program Evaluation. Once the successful components of the model have been combined within a single setting, program evaluation began. This has entailed the monitoring of a number of measures to determine the overall impact of the model. Consumers of the model have been regularly surveyed to determine their perceptions of the model. In addition, a host of outcome measures, such as student adjustment and success in mainstreamed classes, have been monitored.

Stage 4 of the interactive system deals with the Dissemination of User-oriented Information. During this stage, persons who are interested in using the model *and* who have influence in the policy-making processes of their agencies or institutions have been targeted for dissemination of the model. Precautions have been taken during this stage to focus dissemination efforts primarily on those individuals willing to invest in the process of model adoption.

The intent of Stage 5 (Model-related Training) is to prepare individuals and settings to adopt and implement the intervention model. The educational literature is replete with examples of interventions that have not been successfully adopted by the populace at large because of insufficient training in the target intervention. To prevent this from happening, KU-IRLD research is ongoing to develop the most efficient and effective means of training teachers to use the model. Stage 6 (Evaluation of Model Replications) is designed to address a variety of critical questions related to model replication such as: "Can the model be implemented under different administrative conditions?"; "Can the model be implemented in different types of service delivery settings?"; "In what ways must the model be flexible in order that it be usable in a wide variety of settings?"

As results of evaluations in each stage are obtained, other stages of model development are, in turn, impacted. Thus, if a component of the model is found not to be suitable for certain settings, modifications may be required. Similarly, if certain students do not respond to a given intervention, subsequent epidemiological research may be needed to determine the characteristics and needs of those students. Subsequently, new model components would be developed to meet their needs.

The research system described above has been very productive in facilitating the design and empirical validation of an intervention model for LD adolescents because it has forced KU–IRLD researchers to relate all research studies to a programmatic focus and to base their decisions concerning the model on data. Furthermore, the interactive nature of the system has caused each component of the intervention model to be based on key population and setting attributes.

After 6 years of research, a more complete profile of LD adolescents and their environments is beginning to emerge than has been previously available. The following statements represent those epidemiological findings that have related most directly to KU–IRLD intervention research: (1) academic and cognitive factors are the most powerful in differentiating LD from low-achieving adolescents; (2) given current programming practices, LD adolescents demonstrate a plateauing of basic skills across the high-school grades; (3) LD adolescents demonstrate deficiencies in study skills and learning strategies; (4) many LD adolescents exhibit immature executive functioning; (5) many LD adolescents demonstrate social-skill deficiencies; and (6) secondary-school settings place complex language demands on LD adolescents (Deshler, Schumaker, Alley, Warner, & Clark, 1982; Deshler, Warner, Schumaker, & Alley, 1983; and Warner, Schumaker, Alley, & Deshler, 1980).[1]

Based on the above findings, and as a result of data that have emerged through the development and subsequent testing of different model components, a Strategies Intervention Model has emerged. The major focus of the model is *strategy* interventions in which the emphasis of instruction is on teaching LD adolescents to become autonomously successful in the academic and social realms. A strategy is a technique, principle, or rule which enables a person to function independently and solve problems in ways that will result in positive consequences for the person and others around him/her. Whereas strategy instruction is *by no means* a panacea to the problems encountered by LD adolescents, it is an approach that can increase the degree to which students can successfully cope with their environments.

The major outcome goals associated with the Strategies Intervention Model are to develop students who: (1) can learn and perform tasks independently, (2) can exhibit appropriate social and personal skills, (3) can earn well-deserved, standard high-school diplomas, and (4) can make successful transitions to post-high school settings. A multifaceted and comprehensive intervention model has evolved to enable LD adolescents to attain these goals. The model consists of three major components, and each component is made up of several subcomponents (Figure 2).

The first component of the Strategies Intervention Model is the Curriculum Component. This dimension of the model specifies "what" will be taught to the LD adolescent. There are five subcomponents that have been or are in the process of being validated. First, a set of *task-specific learning strategies* have been designed that enable LD adolescents to cope with specific curriculum requirements. Specific learning-strategy packets in reading, writing, listening, information storage, and test-taking have been developed and validated (Schumaker, Deshler, Alley, & Warner, 1983). A second subcomponent includes *executive strategies* which are taught after students have been taught approximately three–

---

[1] The KU–IRLD staff is carefully following current developments in the LD field related to eligibility criteria for students being placed for LD services. Recent data indicate that many school districts are moving toward more stringent eligibility criteria (Cone & Wilson, 1981; Sheppard, 1983; Mellard & Deshler, 1984). More stringent criteria may result in a change in the predominant characteristics of students placed in LD services. Significant changes in population characteristics most likely would require subsequent changes in the types of interventions offered to the targeted population. The reader is referred to Figure 1 to see the interactive effects of a change in population parameters (an epidemiological variable).

Curriculum Component	Instructional Component	Organizational Component
* Task-Specific Learning Strategies	* Acquisition Procedures	* Communication Procedures
* Executive Strategies	* Generalization Procedures	* Management Procedures
* Social Skill Strategies	* Maintenance Procedures	* Evaluation Procedures
* Motivation Strategies	* Group Instructional Procedures	* Teacher Training and Adoption Procedures
* Transition Strategies	* Material and Instruction Modification Procedures	

Figure 2. The Strategies Intervention Model, showing the three major components and their subcomponents.

five task-specific strategies. These executive strategies enable LD adolescents to independently solve their problems (Ellis, 1983). A set of *social-skill strategies* constitutes the third subcomponent. These strategies have been found to improve the social behavior of LD adolescents in such critical areas as resisting peer pressure, negotiating, and solving problems (Hazel, Schumaker, Sherman, & Sheldon, 1982). The fourth subcomponent, *motivation strategies,* consists of strategies that enable students to set goals and monitor their progress in the attainment of those goals. Specific goal-setting procedures have been developed and validated for LD adolescents to use in Individual Education Plan (IEP) meetings to help ensure that IEP plans will include student-valued objectives (Van Reusen, 1984) and to use in the LD resource room to enhance daily productivity (Seabaugh & Schumaker, 1981). A final subcomponent is a set of *transitional strategies.* These strategies currently are being developed because KU-IRLD research has repeatedly pointed to the difficulties that LD adolescents encounter when they are forced to make the transition to post-school life (Vetter, 1983; White, Schumaker, Warner, Alley, & Deshler, 1980).

The second component of the Strategies Intervention Model is the Instructional Component (see Figure 2). This component of the model specifies "how" specific strategies under the Curriculum Component will be taught to students. The first subcomponent is a set of *Acquisition Procedures* in which are incorporated principles of learning related to direct instruction (such as modeling, learning to mastery, feedback, verbal rehearsal, etc.) to ensure strategy mastery (Deshler, Alley, Warner, & Schumaker, 1981; Deshler et. al., 1982). Specific *Generalization and*

Maintenance Procedures constitute other subcomponents of this dimension of the model. Research has indicated repeatedly that LD adolescents must be taught deliberately to generalize strategies they have learned to ensure their application of the new strategies across different situations and settings (Schmidt, 1983). Furthermore, regular maintenance probes have been found necessary to ensure continued use of strategies over time (Schmidt, 1983). The third subcomponent under the Instructional Component includes *Group Instructional Procedures.* Instructional constraints in most resource-room settings necessitate that students be taught in small groups rather than on a one-on-one basis. Additionally, with the current emphasis on mainstreaming, procedures for teaching strategies in regular classroom settings appeared necessary. Consequently, the instructional model includes procedures for small- and large-group instruction (Beals, 1983; Schumaker & Clark, 1982). These instructional procedures have been found to be as powerful as one-on-one instruction for ensuring strategy acquisition. A fourth subcomponent is a set of procedures for *Material and Instructional Modifications.* The focus of these modifications has been on the regular classroom setting for the purpose of increasing the LD adolescent's comprehension of the curriculum content. Among the procedures developed are advance organizer procedures (Lenz, 1983) and a material modification technique, utilizing a system of marked content textbooks and "paradensed" tape recordings of each textbook chapter (Schumaker, Deshler, & Denton, 1984).

The third major component of the Strategies Intervention Model is the Organizational Component (see Figure 2). This component of the model deals with system accommodation and adoption of the model procedures into ongoing instructional practices and traditions within a given school setting. The first subcomponent is a set of *Communication Procedures.* Foremost among these procedures are specific techniques for ensuring cooperative planning among the school staff on behalf of the LD adolescent (Schmidt, 1983; Schumaker *et al.*, 1983). Also included are procedures for communicating with parents and administrators. A second subcomponent involves a set of *Management Procedures* that specify guidelines for implementing all of the subcomponents in a service-delivery setting. Specification of these management procedures was found central to effective time management in resource-room settings (Schumaker *et al.*, 1983). *Evaluation Procedures* constitute the third subcomponent under the Organizational Component. Implementation of these procedures on a regular basis provides both the teaching staff and researchers with the necessary feedback to modify the instructional program. The *Teacher Training and Adoption Procedures* subcomponent deals with specific procedures for training teachers and administrators in each of the components of the model as well as in the philosophy underscoring the entire model.

The multifaceted Strategies Intervention Model that has evolved during the past 6 years of KU-IRLD research is a comprehensive system that is based on the needs of the LD adolescent population. Significant progress has been made in developing and validating most of the subcomponents discussed above. Nevertheless, the strength of the model appears to rest more in the collective nature of the overall system than in any one subcomponent. The need to conduct research on the entire model under a variety of circumstances is obvious. This research is currently in progress; however, as data have been reviewed and studied in recent months, several issues have surfaced that appear central to the overall development of an intervention model for LD adolescents. The resolution of these issues is seen as central to the validation of an intervention model sufficiently powerful to impact LD adolescents.

In the remainder of this chapter, four issues important for future research on LD adolescent and young adult populations will be addressed. These four issues are: specification of skill instruction, enhancing the intensity of instruction, accommodating curricular expectations, and facilitating independence versus dependence.

SPECIFICATION OF SKILL INSTRUCTION

Unlike remedial services in the elementary grades, instruction for LD students in grades 7–12 has largely been undertaken without a master plan that specifies the scope and sequence of instruction (Hudson & Graham, 1978). The benefits of a specified scope and sequence of instruction are clear. For the teacher, it provides a set of clearly defined end goals and intermediate steps for the teaching process. For the student, a master plan for instruction helps to ensure systematic introduction, practice, and review of skills (in the case of the Strategies Intervention Model, these skills are the strategies in the Curriculum Component) within a given domain and minimizes the omission of large blocks of instruction or the unnecessary repetition of instruction on previously mastered skills. The absence of scope and sequence plans for skill instruction to LD adolescents is detrimental during the secondary grades because of the shortage of instructional time available to overcome a large set of skill deficits and, at the same time, to acquire the required content from the curriculum (Brandis & Halliwell, 1980).

In this section, a set of issues concerning the sequencing of skill instruction for LD adolescents in junior and senior high-school settings is discussed within the context of the Strategies Intervention Model. This discussion is based on the assumption that the primary role of the learning disability teacher is to enhance strategy development and not to deliver curriculum content. The subject-area teacher is seen as the educator with primary responsibility for teaching content to *both* handicapped and nonhandicapped youth.

DIRECT VERSUS INDIRECT INSTRUCTION

An issue related to the sequencing of instruction involves the use of either direct or indirect instruction to teach cognitive strategies (Doyle, 1983). Each approach to instruction has certain strengths as well as limitations. These advantages and disadvantages must be weighed carefully in light of specific learner characteristics and overall instructional goals to structure the learning sequence appropriately.

Direct instruction means that learning strategies are carefully structured for students, and they are explicitly told how to accomplish the specific steps of a sequence to master a given strategy. In short, they are systematically guided through a series of exercises leading to mastery of a cognitive strategy. Furthermore, opportunities for direct practice are frequent, as is the receipt of corrective feedback (Deshler *et al.*, 1981). Although direct instruction has proved effective for some instructional outcomes, Doyle (1983) has specified some potential limitations of direct instruction. First, direct instruction may not be possible in some areas because the strategy is very difficult to communicate in terms that are understandable to the learner. For example, successful bicycle riding requires balancing the bicycle, but telling someone a strategy for accomplishing that particular feat is very difficult, if not impossible. A second limitation is the fact that many of the strategies that effective learners use, especially in the secondary school, have not been identified. For example, the underlying strategies for understanding fiction may not be specified totally, let alone communicated to others. Third, some research suggests that direct instruction that emphasizes the acquisition of specific strategy steps for successfully completing a task may produce immediate results, but the use of the strategy may not generalize to other tasks that are similar in nature (Schumaker *et al.*, 1983) and may not maintain over time (Schmidt, 1983). Brown, Campione, and Day (1981) have argued, based on their work on teaching mildly handicapped students memory strategies, that performance is maintained only if the instructional program continues and is highly structured. Furthermore, they reported an inverse relationship between strategy durability within a given learner and that learner's ability to apply the skill flexibly.

In contrast to direct instruction, proponents of indirect instruction emphasize the central role of discovery learning. The instructional program does only part of the work for students; much of the responsibility is put directly on their shoulders for the design of the most effective strategy to solve the problem at hand (Joyce & Weil, 1980). Given the nature of the secondary curriculum that requires the application of higher-order, executive routines, some researchers and curriculum experts argue for the merits of indirect instruction (Goodlad, 1983; Hoover, 1976). Inherent in this approach to instruction is the underlying assumption that the student has the ability to generate task-appropriate strategies (Meichenbaum, 1977).

Despite the reasonable nature of this approach, limitations to indirect instruction have also been cited in the literature. Cronbach and Snow (1981), for example, found the ability level and background of students to have a direct influence on the effectiveness of indirect instruction. Specifically, their research showed that high-ability students profited from unstructured teaching conditions which allowed them choices in organizing and integrating information; however, low-ability students did not do well under these unstructured or indirect methods.

These findings must be considered carefully as instructional programs are organized for LD adolescents. On the one hand, the instructional goal of developing an independent and responsive learner would call for an emphasis on indirect instructional procedures. On the other hand, the attributes which characterize LD adolescents (Deshler et al., 1982) suggest that they can benefit from a more highly structured teaching methodology. The method of choice may be the delivery of both direct and indirect skill instruction to LD adolescents. In general, instruction initially could be more highly structured and direct in nature. As the LD student acquires facility in dealing with specific curriculum demands *and* in using strategies, the instructional emphasis could shift to a more indirect approach in which the student is encouraged to generate his/her own strategies.

This logic has guided the sequencing of learning-strategies instruction within the Strategies Intervention Model. Currently, a three-step sequence is used to teach learning strategies to LD adolescents. First, a set of task-specific learning strategies is taught that will enable the student to better cope with *specific* curriculum demands (e.g., Schumaker et al., 1982). For example, if students are having difficulty understanding the reading assignments in their classes, they may be taught the Self-questioning Strategy or the Visual Imagery Strategy to improve their comprehension of the material (Clark, Deshler, Schumaker, & Alley, 1984). These strategies often tend to be task- or material-specific (i.e., many materials do not lend themselves to visual image formation) and can be taught effectively, using a teaching methodology emphasizing direct instruction (Deshler et al., 1981). The second phase of instruction for each learning strategy has been the facilitation of student generalization of the task-specific strategy to other contents or situations. Schmidt (1983) utilized an instructional procedure that required LD adolescents to identify different tasks to which the mastered strategy could be applied. In addition, LD students were given the specific assignment to apply the newly acquired strategy in different settings. Positive and corrective feedback were provided for all attempts at generalization. These procedures served to promote generalization of the strategy to tasks similar to the original learning task.

After three–five strategies have been mastered and generalized use of them is apparent, the third phase in the instructional sequence begins. Here, LD adolescents are taught a strategy for generating their own task-specific learning strategies. This third phase is based on the premise that many low-achieving students tend to be production-deficient with respect to strategy generation (Brown et al., 1981). Research has shown that students who progress through this three-step sequence can learn to design their own learning strategies and can use their self-designed strategies to improve their grades in targeted classes (Ellis, 1983). Unfortunately, the long-term effects of this three-step sequence have not been investigated, so that the question of whether the sequence results in the truly independent learner and performer, specified in the goals of the Strategies Intervention Model, remains unanswered. Moreover, the three-phase sequence fails to address many factors that are central to the design of an overall instructional sequence for adolescents.

OTHER FACTORS AFFECTING INSTRUCTIONAL SEQUENCE

Indeed, several additional factors must be considered when making decisions regarding the scope and sequence of strategy instruction for LD adolescents. Four factors on which decisions can be based are immediately apparent. Unfortunately, there are problems and issues associated with basing decisions on each factor.

First, the order of skill instruction can be based on immediate and anticipated curricular demands. KU-IRLD research has identified demands that, in general, are representative of secondary-school settings (Knowlton, 1983; Schumaker & Deshler, 1984). For example, student competence in secondary schools is largely measured through written products (class assignments, written tests, essays, etc.) rather than in-class recitation. What is currently unavailable is a specific breakdown of curriculum demands by subject and grade level. It may be necessary to make these analyses on a school-by-school basis (grades 7–12) because of the strong, building-level effects reported in the literature (Lightfoot, 1983; Miskel, 1982). The availability of these data would provide the necessary cornerstone from which to make decisions regarding the most appropriate strategies to teach students to increase their ability to meet changing curriculum demands.

Second, the order of skill instruction can be based on student motivation. That is, because many LD adolescents drop out of school in the upper grades (Levin, Zigmond, & Birch, 1983; Schumaker, Deshler, Alley, & Warner, 1980), the focus of instruction may be on those skills that produce relatively quick and demonstrable results for the student to demonstrate to the student that his/her time in remedial instruction will be worth the effort. The objective of this approach to instructional design initially is to teach LD students strategies that enable them to achieve immediate gains in an area valued by the students. For example, if a student would like to improve his/her poor performance on classroom tests, he/she might initially be taught a test-taking strategy like SCORER (Carmen & Adams, 1972; Lee & Alley, 1981) or a memorization strategy like the FIRST-letter Mnemonic Strategy (Robbins, 1982). The antithesis of this approach is to teach the student a set of prerequisite skills and gradually to progress to the student-valued strategy. For example, the sequence may require instruction in several reading skills, listening skills, and note-taking skills, all of which might be considered prerequisite to test-taking strategies. This sequence may be desirable for the highly motivated student who is favorably inclined toward school, but the resultant outcomes may be too gradual for the highly discouraged learner (Adelman & Taylor, 1983).

A third consideration in specifying an order to skill instruction for LD adolecents is whether to use a "reverse order" approach (Zigmond, Vallecorsa, & Silverman, 1983). This approach is based on the premise that the limited instructional time available for intervention with LD adolescents should not be wasted in teaching seemingly logical but unnecessary prerequisite skills. Levin et al. (1983), for example, argue that the remediation process should begin by determining how well a student can perform on the most difficult skill. If reasonable progress can be made on this difficult skill, instruction continues. If a high degree of failure is encountered, instruction is to proceed backward until a skill that the student can master is reached. They argue that this approach to the instructional process is efficient from a time standpoint and effective from a learning standpoint. Nevertheless, there are some potential shortcomings associated with this approach. First, a significant amount of instructional time can be wasted before the teacher discovers that a student has been started at too high a level. This approach also runs the risk of putting students into a failure situation as they work from difficult tasks in a reverse order to ones they can eventually handle. Students who have a long history of failure and who experience additional failure have a tendency to resist future encounters with similar tasks (Zeaman & House, 1963).

A fourth consideration relates primarily to the *scope* of instructional skills to be taught to LD adolescents. Up to this point, the *sequence* of strategies within a given domain (i.e., task-specific learning strategies) has been addressed. Given the broad set of deficits that LD students bring to the secondary school, a correspondingly broad set of skills beyond the academic strategy domain appears required for ultimate success in school and post-school life. For example, skill deficits have been documented in career and life-adjustment areas (Vetter, 1983; White *et al.*, 1980), social and personal areas (Deshler & Schumaker, 1983), transition to non-school environments (Clark, 1980), and basic academic skills areas (Goodman & Mann, 1976). The solution as to how much of a student's program should be devoted to different areas of skill instruction only can be made through a careful consideration of such variables as the student's age, the student's previous remedial education history, and the student's long-term educational and career goals. The successful integration of all the desired instructional entities into the limited time available for instruction would appear to require a highly trained teacher. The decision-making technologies used in business and industry (Keeney & Raiffa, 1976) may be applicable to the complex problem of creating the most profitable programming mix for a given student (Alley, 1981).

SUMMARY

In conclusion, the need to turn programming and research attention to the issue of the scope and sequence of strategy instruction for LD adolescents is obvious. It is unlikely that an ideal scope and sequence for instruction will emerge. The learner, curricular, and setting variables that must be considered are too numerous to result in any one solution. Nevertheless, future research on the factors discussed in this section should, hopefully, facilitate the organization of instruction for LD adolescents. One variable that should not be ignored, regardless of the approach taken in determining instructional organization, is student input. Our data have strongly underscored the importance of involving the LD adolescent in all major programming decisions (Seabaugh & Schumaker, 1981; Van Reusen, 1984). To do so should maximize the student's motivation and vested interest in the instructional program.

ENHANCING THE INTENSITY OF INSTRUCTION

The issue of intensity of instruction is especially relevant with regard to secondary LD students. These students have few years left before graduation to learn basic skills and strategies. They are often in a "sink or swim" situation, especially upon entry into high school where they are expected to pass a number of required courses. Since the gap between the demands they must meet in high-school courses and their academic skills is wide (Schumaker & Deshler, 1984), passing those required courses is a difficult task indeed. Probably as a result of this gap, few LD adolescents actually remain in school, with numbers dropping off drastically in the junior and senior years (Levin et al., 1983; Schumaker et al., 1980). To prevent this failure from occurring, powerful interventions are needed that will quickly help these students.

Given the wide gap between LD secondary students' skill levels and the demands they are expected to meet in secondary school, it appears that the intervention model that will help them best will incorporate intensive instruction within its teaching methodology and other instructional practices. Meyen and Lehr (1980a) defined intensive instruction as "a set of circumstances that have an impact on the actual interaction of the learner in the instructional situation" (p. 23). This set of circumstances has been described as including variations in such factors as teacher/pupil ratio, time on task, academic response time, teacher presentation rates, teacher feedback, expectancy climate, and patterns of teacher–pupil interaction. The basic goal with regard to intensity of instruction is to determine the set of circumstances that produces the highest productivity in terms of learning and achievement for a given student.

The task of delineating such a set of circumstances is a tall order in light of the paucity of research in the area. In fact, no research has focused on the identification of comprehensive *combinations* of circumstances to enhance productivity. A few research studies (most of them conducted in fields other than the LD field) have focused on the effects of a single instructional variable on achievement. For example, Glass and Smith (as reported in Cahan & Filby, 1979) conducted a meta-analysis of research studies that were completed in the past 50 years to determine the teacher-pupil ratio that produces the highest achievement rates. They determined that achievement appears to increase as the teacher-pupil ratio is lowered. The best achievement gains resulted when class size was reported to be below 15 pupils (per teacher); however, they noted that there were many instances where small class size was not related to high achievement and concluded that the nature of the instruction being delivered in a class must interact with class size.

Another instructional variable that has been studied in relation to academic productivity is the variable called "time on task." This usually is defined as the proportion of class time that a student spends attending to instructional activities. Although several studies have shown that time on task can be increased through the manipulation of contingencies (e.g., White-Blackburn, Semb, & Semb, 1977), self-control procedures (e.g., Lloyd, Hallahan, Kosiewicz, & Kneedler, 1982), teacher prompts (Knapezyk & Livingston, 1974), and teacher presentation rates (e.g., Carnine, 1976), some studies have shown that increased time on task does not necessarily increase academic productivity (Ferritor, Buckholdt, Hamblin, & Smith, 1972; Lloyd et al., 1982; Marholin & Steinman, 1977).

In response to this latter finding, a series of recent research studies has been conducted to investigate the relationship of a variable called "academic response time" to achievement. Academic response time is defined as the proportion of allocated instructional time that students are *actively* engaged in academic tasks (e.g., reading, writing) (Stanley & Greenwood, 1981); it is only a portion of on-task time. Passive attention to tasks (e.g., listening to a lecture, watching a movie) is not included in this variable. In contrast to on-task time, the variable of academic response time appears to be highly related to achievement (e.g., Greenwood, Delquadri, & Hall, in press; Greenwood, Dinwiddie, Terry, Wade, Stanley, Thibadeau, & Delquadri, 1983). Despite the apparent importance of academic response time, researchers have found that LD elementary students spend an average of only 12% of their day actively responding to academic tasks (Thurlow, Graden, Greener, & Ysseldyke, 1982). This means that only about 45 minutes of each school day are being well-utilized with regard to academic achievement with these students. This pattern seems to continue throughout the school years. Goodlad (1983) reported that about 70% of class time across all grades involves "teacher talk." This means that an average of only 30% of the class hour is available for active academic responding plus other activities (e.g., preparing for and cleaning up after activities).

Another variable closely tied to academic response time is the "opportunity to learn" variable (Delquadri, Greenwood, & Hall, 1979; Reith, Polsgrove, & Semmel, 1980; Rosenshine & Berliner, 1978). This is the time allocated to instruction in an individual's life. Harneschfeger and Wiley (1978), for example, have reported that some school calendars include as many as 69 more days of instruction per year than others. When a number of extra school days is combined with high levels of academic response time, it seems logical that achievement would be enhanced (Greenwood, Delquadri, Stanley, Sasso, Whorton, & Schulte, 1981). Indeed, the National Commission on Excellence in Education in its recent report entitled *A Nation at Risk* (Gardner, 1983), has recommended for all students that "significantly more time be devoted to learning the New Basics. This will require more effective use of the existing school day, a longer school day, or a lengthened school year" (p. 29).

An additional variable that may be related to intensive instruction is the "time required to learn" variable (Bloom, 1974; Carroll, 1963; Gettinger & White, 1979). Since individuals differ widely in the time required to master one unit of material and mastery rates are widely acknowledged to be longer for special education populations, this variable must be taken into account when planning instructional time for LD students. A given student's history of mastering skills should be considered when determining the optimal opportunity to learn requirement of that student. Clearly, given the heterogenity of the LD population, all LD students should not automatically receive the same amount of services.

Expectancy climate is another variable that may be related to the intensity of instruction present in a classroom. Expectancy climate for students can be loosely defined as the set of expectancies a teacher communicates to his/her students about what they are to achieve. Some authors (e.g., Fishbein & Ajzen, 1972) believe that when high-expectancy levels are communicated by teachers, students are more likely to produce. When low-expectancy levels are communicated, students are likely to produce less. Thus, if special-education teachers communicate to their LD students that the classroom is a place for serious learning activity and that they are expected to complete the same kinds of assignments as their nonhandicapped peers, the LD students will be more likely to work hard to meet that goal. If, on the other hand, teachers communicate that LD students cannot complete work on their own, require help with every assignment, and need constant supervision, their students will be less likely to work diligently. Despite the logic inherent in this argument, and although progress has been made in developing methods to measure some aspects of expectancy climate (e.g., Miskel, Bloom, & McDonald, 1982), there have been no studies systematically examining the effects of communicated expectancies on the achievement of LD adolescents. Such research clearly is required.

In addition to communicating appropriate expectancies to students, teachers might enhance the intensity of instruction in their classrooms by utilizing empirically validated instructional methods. One instructional method that may enhance the intensity of instruction is called "Precision Teaching." Teachers using this instructional method define the behaviors to be taught, count or measure the behavior, chart the behavior, establish performance aims or desired outcomes, and evaluate student progress on a regular basis (Lovitt & Fantasia, 1983). In other words, teachers using precision-teaching techniques are in touch, usually on a daily basis, with a student's strengths and weaknesses and with the student's actual progress in relation to a goal. Having such close contact with each student's programming may enable teachers to enhance the intensity of instruction in their classrooms since they can ensure that daily programming is appropriate. It stands to reason that the use of precision-teaching techniques should be related to achievement. Indeed, the findings of a few research studies have supported this idea. For example, Lovitt and Fantasia (1983) found that LD elementary children whose teachers used precision-teaching techniques exhibited significantly higher gains in reading than those whose teachers did not use the techniques; however, no research has been done in this regard with LD adolescents.

Finally, another factor that seems to be related to intensity of instruction is the motivation of a student to learn. It seems reasonable that a student who is highly motivated to learn will come in contact with more learning experiences than one who is not so motivated. Seabaugh and Schumaker (1981), for example, found that LD students who had been taught self-control (self-motivating) procedures completed eight times as many lessons per day than they did when other motivation procedures involving extrinsic contingencies were in effect. Related to this higher level of lesson completion were higher-achievement gains for the students trained in self-control techniques when they were compared to a group of students that were not trained in self-control techniques. Thus, the type of motivation procedures being utilized by a teacher may serve to enhance the intensity of instruction in the special-education classroom.

This review of the factors that may be related to intensity of instruction illuminates the need for research to be undertaken with regard to the intensity of instruction provided within the Strategies Intervention

Model. Current programming policies need to be scrutinized and alternatives need to be evaluated. For instance, current programming for LD adolescents across the country usually entails 1–2 hours of time in a resource-room program, whereas the remainder of the day is spent in mainstream classes (Deshler, Lowrey, & Alley, 1979). Recent research (Schumaker, Warner, Deshler, & Alley, n.d.) has shown that LD students spend an average of 50% of the class hour in resource rooms engaged in instructional activities (on-task time). About 70% of this instructional time is spent actively responding to academic tasks. Based on a 50-minute class period, this translates into approximately 18 minutes of academic remediation per day for the student supposedly receiving special-education services for 1 hour a day. The same research (Schumaker et al., n.d.) has suggested that, within the Strategies Intervention Model, the percentage of instructional time can be increased to as high as 82% of resource-room time and that academic response time can be as high as 90% of instructional time. Such intensity of instruction was achieved by specifying expectancies to the students about how time was to be spent upon entering the classroom and, at the end of class, specifying policies with regard to how class time is to be spent, and utilizing the Learning Strategies Curriculum, which incorporates most of the aspects of precision teaching and requires a high rate of academic responding. These techniques doubled the amount of time students were spending on remedial work to 37 minutes per day.

Unfortunately, such a block of time is inadequate when compared to what must be accomplished by an LD secondary student who is simultaneously floundering in required mainstream classes. Experience with the Strategies Intervention Model indicates that students can learn an average of three to four learning strategies per year if they attend class in the resource room for one class period per day. This is relatively slow, given the demands they are expected to meet in their required courses. Clearly, some innovative alternatives to the present 1-hour-per-day, plod-along programming currently being offered to LD secondary students are needed. Meyen and Lehr (1980b) suggested that highly intense instructional programs be offered to LD students for, perhaps, 2–3 months. They argued that students need to accept the costs of remediation (e.g., postponement of graduation) which are small compared to the costs of "living a life inhibited by marginal performance" (Meyen & Lehr, 1980a, p. 23).

Such an intensive program has been utilized in the Synergistic Education System developed at the University of Houston by Meisgeier (n.d.). LD secondary students in this program take part in a High Intensity Learning Center for a 12- or 18-week period for 3 consecutive hours each day. Thereafter, the student takes part in more regular, resource-room programming. Unfortunately, there are no empirical data available to allow comparisons among this kind of programming and other programs. In addition, it is unclear when a high intensity period would be most helpful for students. Since some LD students in the early junior high-school grades seem to exhibit immature cognitive functioning with regard to complex strategies acquisition, ninth or tenth grade may be a more appropriate time for such intensive instruction than the seventh grade.

Meyen and Lehr (1980b) also recommend continuous instruction involving summer school programs for students at crucial points in their educational programs. This would seem to be a feasible alternative to the high-intensity period during the school year; probably, it also would be a more popular alternative because students would not need to postpone their graduation date.

Regardless of the method chosen to increase LD students' opportunity-to-learn time, care needs to be taken in arranging the instructional practices that take place during that time. The developers of the Strategies Intervention Model have made some progress in determining practices that result in a high proportion of student time being devoted to active academic responding. Additional research is called for that compares the effectiveness of alternative means of increasing instructional time, that shows the relationship of academic response to achievement within the Strategies Intervention Model, and that clearly shows that a variety of service delivery settings can achieve the same levels of academic response time, using the same set of instructional policies and practices. Additional research is needed to determine the best ways to establish a positive expectancy climate in the classroom, to utilize empirically validated instructional methods like precision teaching, and to intrinsically motivate students to work hard and learn quickly. Until such research is complete, there is little hope of providing LD adolescents the intensity of instruction they so sorely need.

ACCOMMODATING CURRICULAR EXPECTATIONS

With a major focus of the Strategies Intervention Model on the facilitation of performance of LD adolescents in mainstreamed settings, it is imperative that any changes and developments in the requirements and expectations of the secondary curriculum be carefully noted and monitored. As the demands of the secondary curriculum change, so must the support services available to LD students if they are to successfully respond to existing mainstream requirements. During recent months, a spate of studies and reports have been published, outlining ways in which public schools, in general, and secondary schools, in particular, should change in order to upgrade the quality of the American educational system (Boyer, 1983; Gardner, 1983; Goodlad, 1983; Shelby & Coleman, 1983). Although each of these documents takes a unique approach to analyzing our educational system, a common thread runs through them; that is, a major part of the proposed solution to upgrading the skills of high-school graduates is in increasing the basic exit requirements and performance expectations for all students. Gardner (1983), for example, proposes that the school day be expanded and graduation requirements be raised.In an effort to upgrade the mathematics and science competencies of students, Shelby and Coleman (1983) recommended that significantly more hours be spent by all students in mathematics and science instruction. Boyer (1983) argues for the establishment of a core curriculum, in part to do away with tracking. It is yet to be determined exactly how many of these recommendations will actually be put into practice, and it is quite likely that a general movement to raise standards and expectations in secondary schools will result. Such a trend will have a direct impact on LD adolescents and will affect how the Strategies Intervention Model must be implemented to help students succeed under altered curricular expectations. Some of the anticipated impacts are discussed in the remainder of this section.

First, altered requirements in the general curriculum may affect *what* is taught during special education instruction. Perhaps, the most dramatic example of this has been the impact of the minimum competency testing (MCT) movement in affecting the instructional emphasis in special education. Minimum competency examinations have been instituted in many districts to assure accountability and to restore credibility for the high school diploma (Pullin, 1980). Because of the value placed on good performance on these examinations, a large majority of special-education instructional time with LD students is often spent preparing them to successfully meet the test standards. One study, conducted in Kansas, reported that parents of LD adolescents, secondary LD teachers, and secondary-content teachers indicated that the mastery of the test objectives should be required for LD adolescents as well as nonhandicapped students (Meyen, Alley, Scannell, Harnden, & Miller, 1982). Such endorsements have the potential of influencing the amount of instructional time allotted to prepare LD students to pass such examinations.

On the assumption that LD students will be required to pass MCTs to receive high school diplomas, research is needed to determine the best ways of helping LD students meet minumum competency objectives. Instead of researching ways to alter the format of the MCT administration for LD adolescents, which does not seem to improve their scores (Meyen *et al.*, 1982), it might be prudent to explore ways of teaching LD students strategies for approaching MCTs. Additionally, when MCT practices are adopted by a school which utilizes the Strategies Intervention Model, researchers might explore the relationship between MCT test performance and experience with previous learning-strategy instruction. On the one hand, students with histories of strategy instruction may perform significantly better than students who have not received the instruction. On the other hand, the instruction may have little effect because the strategies are designed for traditional academic tasks, and MCTs may include a testing format which is relatively alien to the student. Other research might address the degree to which students can generalize their use of strategies to the MCT task.

Second, as the demands of the secondary curriculum increase, so must the number of skills mastered by LD adolescents increase to enable them to cope with these raised expectations. Epidemiological data collected by KU–IRLD staff members show that LD students exhibit a broad array of skill deficits by the time they reach the secondary grades (Deshler *et al.*, 1982). It is likely that the number and severity of these deficits may be magnified as curricular expectations are raised. An initial instructional response may be to "push even harder" to aid the LD student to master these additional skills. In a sense, this instructional approach is one designed to address the *breadth* of skills students are lacking. That is, the instructional goal for the LD adolescent becomes one of teaching skills to ameliorate as many skill deficiencies as possible in the limited time available.

This course of action is complicated by the findings of Schmidt's (1983) research on skill mastery and generalization by LD adolescents. In essence, Schmidt (1983) was trying to determine how much and what type of instruction must be provided to LD adolescents in resource-room settings to ensure their mastery *and* generalization of written-language learning strategies to regular class settings. He found that, for many students, a significant number of instructional activities (i.e., some combination of an eight-step acquisition procedure described by Deshler *et al.*, 1981; a three-phase transfer sequence; a self-control procedure developed by Seabaugh & Schumaker, 1981; and cooperative planning procedures based on the work of Laurie, Buchwach, Silverman, & Zigmond, 1978), as well as a significant time investment was required to ensure generalization of the strategies by LD students to the regular classroom.

Perhaps, the most revealing aspect of this study was the limited effect that acquisition procedures (Deshler *et al.*, 1981) alone had on generalization. In spite of reaching skill mastery in the resource room through the acquisition procedures, little generalization was noted until the additional instructional procedures (i.e., transfer, self-control, or cooperative planning) were used. These data indicate that instructional procedures for LD adolescents may require a more thorough, or *in-depth*, coverage than traditionally has been offered in resource-room instruction. One potential consequence of providing such in-depth instruction on a given skill is to limit the time available to address a large number of skill deficits exhibited by the student. In short, these findings have focused KU-IRLD attention on a critical instructional issue; that is, resolving the seemingly conflicting requirements for both breadth and depth of instruction for the LD adolescent.

Among the options to be considered in pursuing a solution to this issue are the following. First, although preliminary data exist on the demands of secondary settings (Schumaker & Deshler, 1984), there remains a major need to design procedures to accurately and quickly assess the demands of secondary settings so as to determine the exact nature of the curricular and life-adjustment demands that an LD adolescent must meet. By more accurately understanding the curricular expectations, the broad number of skills required for success may be reduced or, at least, weighted according to importance. This, in turn, may allow teachers additional time to provide in-depth instruction in high-priority skill areas. Second, research studies addressing questions similar to the one studied by Schmidt (1983) need to be conducted. For example, what is the effect of altering the order of the instructional procedures used by Schmidt (1983)? Or, how would the incorporation of some intensity of instruction variables (Meyen & Lehr, 1980a, 1980b) affect the generalization of skills across settings and time? In short, much is yet to be understood about the exact nature of factors facilitating or impeding strategy generalization and the requirements for depth of instruction. Also, a major challenge in resolving this instructional issue is the design of instructional procedures that are sufficiently powerful to ensure *both* strategy generalization and sufficient attention to the broad array of skills that LD adolescents must possess for success in secondary schools.

A third impact of the heavy content requirements of secondary schools on the learning-disabled student is the inability of resource-room instruction alone to provide LD students with sufficient support to ensure their success in each of their classes as well as to provide them with the necessary skills/strategies to make them more efficient learners. In short, if the instruction provided in the resource room is viewed as the primary source of intervention, it is unlikely that the LD adolescent will receive sufficient support to succeed in most secondary school environments. As the Strategies Intervention Model has evolved, it has become apparent that material and instructional interventions in settings other than the resource room (e.g., the regular classroom) by instructors other than special educators (e.g., subject-area teachers) are required.

Several interventions that have taken place outside the resource-room setting recently have been reported in the literature. Mosby (1980) has advocated the use of procedures that match each student's strongest learning modality with the method of instruction or testing. Hartwell and others (1979) have developed methods for producing a Parallel Alternative Curriculum that is designed to maintain the same content objectives as the regular curriculum but varies the delivery mode and format. Schumaker, Deshler, and Denton (1984) have designed a procedure whereby paraprofessionals can highlight classroom texts used in core subjects with a specified marking system and can make paradensed tape recordings of key information to be learned. Lenz (1983) has developed a procedure for use by content teachers in which they begin each class session with an advance organizer for the purpose of facilitating the students' comprehension of the information delivered. Common to all of the above systems are the following characteristics: they go beyond the resource-room setting, they involve nonspecial educators, and they alter the existing system of content delivery. Significant gains and benefits for the LD student have been reported for some of these intervention efforts (e.g., Schumaker *et al.*, 1984).

Although there is considerable appeal in the major goal associated with these approaches (i.e., altering the mode and format of content delivery to allow the LD student to comprehend the content), there are also some potential difficulties. First, each of these approaches necessitates the cooperation and, in many cases, changes in the activities of several teachers within a school building. Bringing about such changes can be very difficult, especially if administrative support is not strong. Second, calls for teacher change and commitment to the educational needs of LD and other low-achieving students are coming at a time when there are mounting pressures on these same teachers to ensure that the talented students excel and that the performance of the normal achievers in their classes is raised. The need for increased support and training for the content teacher in making accommodations and modifications for all learners is obvious.

In spite of the potential problems involved in instituting these interventions, the challenge is worthwhile because the mounting pressures to improve our schools' efforts may create learning situations that will be counterproductive for the learning disabled. One example of a movement that could impact negatively the success of LD students is an effort to have the publishers of elementary and secondary school texts change their texts to meet the calls for stiffer requirements (Bridgman, 1983). Such a move to modify instructional materials for capable students must be coupled with comparable efforts to appropriately modify instructional materials for students who lack the skills to benefit from content instruction. Intensified efforts need to be undertaken not only to design material and instructional modification procedures that are effective in allowing LD adolescents to comprehend the secondary curriculum but that can be readily adopted and used by the majority of secondary-content teachers without compromising their role as content experts.

A fourth factor that relates to the emphasis on increased curricular requirements for secondary students is the glaring fact that most LD adolescents come to the secondary school already markedly deficient in basic content knowledge (Schumaker & Deshler, 1984). LD adolescents have not mastered comparable amounts of content when compared to their successfully achieving peers. This is due, in part, to the following factors. First, because of their learning inefficiencies, they lack the necessary skills to master content at the same rate and with the same degree of effectiveness as their nonhandicapped peers. Second, because of prolonged placement in resource-room programs that usually emphasize skill acquisition (versus content acquisition), LD students are denied exposure to a large amount of content information. These factors may inhibit the LD student's ability to benefit from experiences in the secondary curriculum.

By definition, a major instructional goal of secondary schools is the delivery of content information. A student's ability to successfully benefit from a curriculum is, in part, contingent upon the existing knowledge base or pool of prior knowledge the student possesses. A prior knowledge base allows the student to better understand the significance of material, to select main points, and to disregard trivia. Cognitive psychologists have recently underscored the power of prior knowledge (Brown *et al.*, 1981), scripts (Shank, 1983; den Uyl & van Oostendorp, 1980), and schema (Spiro, 1980) in facilitating comprehension by the learner. Marshall and Glock (1978), in studying the relationship between prior knowledge and reading comprehension, have suggested that prior knowledge more profoundly may affect comprehension than manipulations in text structures, and Kintsch, Kozminsky, Streby, McKoon, and Keena (1975) have argued that text difficulty actually may be a function of prior knowledge. In essence, then, a major demand of the secondary setting is that students must bring a general storehouse of information with them to the learning situation. LD individuals find themselves in a very perilous situation in this regard, and in light of expected and stiffer content expectations, their situation may be exacerbated (Schumaker & Deshler, 1984).

Addressing the problem of a deficiency in prior knowledge is extremely complex, but, clearly, the answers to this problem are ones that might come from sources beyond special-education services and, quite possibly, from sources external to the school itself. The provision of general enrichment experiences has been a problem plaguing educators who work with culturally different populations for years. Some of the courses of action that may be worth pursuing would include the following: home instructional programs, enrichment instruction during the summer months, creative use of educational television and microcomputers, and specification of key background knowledge required to master any textbook chapter with accompanying instruction in key concepts and knowledge. It seems logical that efforts to enrich the experiential and knowledge backgrounds of LD students must be implemented through a master plan beginning in the lower grades. Although special educators do not have the license or expertise to deliver content, they may have to assume a major role in ensuring that adequate content instruction is provided through related services.

To summarize, in light of the recent movement to upgrade the quality of secondary education, a number of impacts are expected in the area of educating the secondary LD student. Altered requirements are likely to impact what is taught by secondary educators, the breadth versus depth of what is taught, the number of educators who will, of necessity, become involved in providing effective content instruction for these students, the kinds of instructional procedures that will be used to teach that content, and the methods for providing these students with sufficient background knowledge to make use of new content. Research is called for in each of these areas to ensure that interventions for LD adolescents sufficiently allow them to address the increased demands expected at the secondary level of education.

FACILITATING INDEPENDENCE VERSUS DEPENDENCE

With all the emphasis on *providing* secondary LD students with appropriate and effective instruction such that they can successfully meet the demands of the secondary-school setting, often it is easy to lose sight of one of the special needs of the adolescent population in general. Adolescents are proceeding from a stage in which they are totally dependent on the direction and protection of adults to a stage in which, hopefully, they will be independent and responsible for themselves. It seems logical that the job of secondary teachers is to aid adolescents in this process as much as possible. Adolescents must be prepared to face life on their own, make their own decisions, express their own thoughts and wishes, set and accomplish their own goals, be independent learners, and accept responsibility for their own mistakes. Unfortunately, the majority of today's secondary, special-education programs do not focus on the important goal of facilitating independence. Instead, dependence is reinforced by programs in which secondary students spend as much as 65% of class time being tutored on their assignments (Schumaker et al., 1983). In many cases, this tutoring consists of teachers telling students the answers to questions for them to copy down, and quizzing students on facts that have not been related to each other. Such teaching tactics only foster dependence and the feeling that one cannot succeed on his/her own.

In some ways, the popularity of this tutorial approach is not surprising, given the psychology of those who are attracted to the special-education teaching profession. As Dyer (1978) noted, giving help can be a seductive process which leads one to offer assistance or to control another's environment more to meet one's own needs than to satisfy those of the other person. This can be a dangerous pitfall, for, as Green and Zigler (1962) observed, mildly handicapped students tend not to fall back on cognitive resources to promote successful problem solving because of their restricted cognitive abilities. Instead, they tend toward "outer directedness," an excessive reliance on external cues for feedback. Zigler (1966) and Turnure (1975) argue that some mildly handicapped students learn to distrust their own abilities and resort to external cues for successful problem solving and as sources of feedback.

From a pedagogical perspective, instructors may, inadvertently, encourage outer-directed behaviors when providing instruction. Although addressing personal needs to help others by acting as the controlling agent and frequently offering help, they may be training their charges to be more dependent on others for problem solving, guidance, and feedback. Sizer (1984) expressed a concern that "students are rarely expected to educate themselves. They are 'delivered a service' and are expected to carry few burdens in their schools" (p. 681). Surely, the atmosphere of dependency that seems to pervade secondary special education has far-reaching implications. For one thing, it can lead LD individuals to avoid academic pursuits altogether (Adelman, 1978). It stands to reason that most LD students who have been taught that they cannot succeed in academic activities on their own will avoid those activities as much as possible.

Clearly, if LD adolescents are to become self-confident and independent, educators will have to resist the temptation to be their all-knowing protectors. In addition, techniques of fostering independence will need to be adopted for use in special education programs. One way is through the use of the Learning Strategies Curriculum. Studies have shown that LD students who have mastered certain learning strategies can achieve *A* and *B* grades on regular classroom tests independently (Schumaker *et al.*, 1984) and independently can write themes that compare favorably with themes written by normal students (Schmidt, 1983). Thus, the Learning Strategies Curriculum is a well-validated tool for promoting independence. It stands to reason, however, that other tools for facilitating independence can also be adopted by special educators. In the remainder of this section, three such techniques/tools will be explored, including student participation in Individualized Education Plan (IEP) formulation, student direction of daily and weekly progress, and loose structuring.

IEP FORMULATION

One reasonable way to promote independence in LD adolescents is to give them a major voice in formulating their IEPs. Public Law 94–142 states that the student is to participate in the planning of his/her IEP *when appropriate*. Surely, the age of LD adolescents dictates an appropriate situation for participation. Nevertheless, as recent research has shown (Van Reusen, 1984), even when LD adolescents are present at IEP meetings, they participate at minimal levels (e.g., contribute an average of 30 bits of positive, relevant information even when prompted 10 times). They rarely contribute information regarding test results, personal goals, or their own needs, nor do they seek clarification about what is being discussed or planned. As a result of these findings, Van Reusen (1984) developed a program for training LD adolescents to be their own advocates in IEP meetings. Students who received training in self-advocacy emitted large numbers of relevant verbalizations (containing an average of 95 bits of positive relevant information per meeting), and their comments were reflected in the written goals and objectives in their IEPs. Future research in this area needs to build on these positive results to determine the impact of this kind of self-advocacy and participation in long-term planning on students' perceptions of locus of control, on students' achievement while in the program, and on students' eventual success as independent adults.

SHORT-TERM GOAL SETTING

Besides active participation at the IEP meeting level, it may also be inferred that the lawmakers intended handicapped students to partici- pate in decision making throughout the implementation of the plan. One method of facilitating this participation is to teach LD adolescents self-control techniques whereby self-structuring and learning rates can be optimized. Studies conducted by Seabaugh and Schumaker (1981) and Tollefson, Tracy, Johnsen, and Chatman (1983) have demonstrated that LD adolescents can be taught to use self-control skills and that their use of the skills results in an increase in academic productivity. Seabaugh and Schumaker (1981) found that students attending an alter- native high school could be taught self-control skills and that the use of the skills could be maintained, using a series of weekly teacher-student conferences. The conferences were oriented toward evaluation of pro- gress and self-goal-setting by the student. Results of the study indicated that the number of lessons completed by LD students increased by 700%. In addition, students who participated in the self-goal-setting conferences demonstrated greater gains in achievement test scores than a comparison group of LD adolescents who were not taught the self- control skills.

In another study, Tollefson and others (1983) found that LD students could be taught self-control skills in a public-school resource room through a game format and later by having students write contracts during individual conferences with an adult. Following completion of the self-control training, both assignments for the resource room, which were targeted in written contracts, and assignments for regular class- rooms, which were not targeted in the contracts, were completed at higher rates than prior to the training.

Drawing from these research studies, it is evident that a self-control training program can facilitate lesson/assignment completion. What re- mains unclear is the impact this kind of training has on a student's self- confidence and feelings of self-worth and whether independence in other respects is facilitated. Since most handicapped students are accus- tomed to being dependent on their teachers and sometimes become bewildered when they are suddenly given "control," it may be neces- sary to develop a training program that is designed to move the student gradually from the traditional dependency role to a role of indepen- dence. Within this program, students could progress through several stages, gradually assuming more responsibility for decisions regarding their weekly educational program and earning more and more indepen- dence. At the first level, skills would be targeted for the student and daily assignments would be made by the teacher in much the same fashion as the students are accustomed from previous special-educational experiences. Gradually, self-control procedures would be taught to each student. As the students become increasingly more skilled using self-control, they would be allowed to choose strategies and skills they want to learn, set weekly goals for what they want to accomplish and, in general, become active in making decisions regarding their educational programs. Empirical research validating the usefulness of such a tiered system for fostering independence is sorely needed.

LOOSE STRUCTURING

A third way that independence might be facilitated is through progressively looser structuring of the learning environment for each individual learner. In some ways, the use of such a technique contradicts the current emphasis in the special-education field on highly structuring the learning environment to affect optimal performance and learning. This emphasis on structure appears to be well founded. A number of studies have demonstrated that structuring the environment is positively correlated with academic gains (e.g., Stevens & Rosenshine, 1981; Cullinan, Lloyd, & Epstein, 1981); however, one undesirable outcome of this practice is that students may become dependent on the teacher or parent for organizing tasks, decision making, monitoring errors and progress, and evaluating the effectiveness of decisions. In other words, because opportunities for learning by doing are limited in a structured setting, external locus of control and learned helplessness may be reinforced by the very behaviors frequently characterized as effective teaching. Classroom structures which provide little daily and weekly opportunity for student input in or selection of instructional goals, time management, activity monitoring, and rule-setting may, over time, reinforce external locus of control. Efforts of some teachers to be effective by running a highly organized and tightly structured classroom may impede student opportunities for self-structuring. Without these opportunities, students cannot be expected to learn the skills required for autonomous action.

Despite the face validity of this reasoning, there are problems inherent in making *all* special education instruction loosely structured. As suggested by social-learning theory (e.g., Bandura, 1977; Cromwell, 1963), teaching methodologies that are designed to affect independence of action or promote internal locus of control may conflict with instructional goals. That is, academic goals might need to be sacrificed while students learn to be independent learners. Although, in the long run, such an approach might work, the academic sacrifices may be too costly, given the short time available to LD adolescents for special education. An additional problem with loosely structuring all instruction is that it is unclear when, in the learning process, students are ready to have loosely structured instruction. Some students may be ready sooner than others. There may be some prerequisite "independence" skills that must be mastered before a student can be considered to be ready.

One alternative to environments that are either tightly or loosely structured is an environment that provides instruction in independence and allows looser structuring on an individual basis when students are ready for it. Looser structuring may be tied to the learning of individual skills or to the learning process in general. For example, Haring and Eaton (1978) view the learning of a skill as proceeding through several stages: acquisition, proficiency, generalization, and adaptation. Perhaps, at the acquisition phase of learning, instruction in each new skill should be tightly structured, for, at this point, it is highly desirable to control extraneous factors to the maximum extent possible so that the student can focus on the task at hand. The remaining phases perhaps should be progressively less tightly structured; here, students should plan their own time and work toward their own goals. Thus, through the latter stages, a teacher systematically would relinquish control so that the student learns to perform the skill under more natural conditions, and generalization and adaptation of the skill will be enhanced.

Although this alternative appears viable, there has been no research to date that focuses on the relationship of the structure of the learning environment to the independence/dependence of students. Research is needed that identifies objective ways of loosely structuring the learning environment without sacrificing academic gains. In addition, skills that enable students to be successful in less-structured environments need to be identified and means of teaching these skills to LD adolescents need to be developed.

SUMMARY

In conclusion, the concept of teaching LD students to make decisions regarding their educational programs and to self-structure their educational learning experiences flies in the face of traditional practices and beliefs about the need to impose structure upon the lives of these people. It implies changes in traditional roles of special-education teachers. In short, what is being suggested here is that secondary, special-education teachers need to shift their role from professional organizers and help-givers to facilitators of independence. As the student moves into the secondary, special-education setting, he/she should be gradually taught to take an active role in designing the IEP, to make daily and weekly decisions about instruction, and to learn independently. Continued research is needed in the area of developing self-control, self-advocacy, and self-structuring skills in LD adolescents. Self-control techniques need to be refined and correlated with appropriate age and maturity levels. An important research area which needs to be addressed is determining the interface between the instructional sequence and self-structuring of learning activities. Finally, research is needed to investigate techniques for influencing teachers' perspectives concerning special-educational programming for the learning disabled. The nature of teachers' roles in the lives of learning-disabled adolescents requires careful thought and study.

CONCLUSION

The issues presented in this chapter are by no means meant to be exhaustive; rather, they are representative of ones that have surfaced repeatedly in a variety of ways during the research and model-development work that has been done on an intervention model for LD adolescents. The issues discussed have underscored the following about educating and researching LD adolescents. First, a comprehensive intervention model with multiple dimensions is required to sufficiently impact the academic success and life adjustment of these students. Second, the needs of older LD individuals go beyond the academic skill deficits that have traditionally defined this group. A critical need of LD adolescents relates to their goal of independent functioning. Their progress toward this goal must be facilitated by educators. Third, in many instances, the most appropriate solutions to the problems of LD adolescents are ones that extend beyond the resource room and the special educator. Thus, all educators who work with the learning disabled need to be trained to work with these students and to provide special kinds of interventions within the framework of their ongoing instruction. Fourth, to enhance the probability that interventions will be successful with LD adolescents, factors such as the specification of instruction and intensity of instruction need to be addressed. Fifth, because of changing setting demands and changing learner characteristics (through modifications in placement regulations), it is important to collect and interpret data in the context of a research model that forces researchers to systematically accommodate for system and population change.

Beyond the scope of this paper are other issues related to the education of older populations and the successful implementation of validated practices. Specifically, since secondary LD students are members of the adolescent population and have a number of adolescent needs (including the need to make a successful transition to adult life), these needs must be addressed in any comprehensive intervention model. Methods of preparing LD youths for the transition from high school to post-secondary education or work settings, and for supporting them in these settings during their initial adjustment, need to be empirically validated. Finally, to make the interventions that have been shown, through empirical research, to be effective with LD adolescents widely available to this population, major efforts will need to be focused on developing the most efficient means for instituting change in educational programs. This final issue deserves the rapt and devoted attention of educators, for, if our research findings are never put into practice, the promise of positive results with regard to helping a majority of this population will never be realized.

REFERENCES

Adelman, H. S. (1978). The concept of intrinsic motivation: Implications for practice and research with learning disabled. *Learning Disability Quarterly, 1*(2), 43–54.

Adelman, H. S., & Taylor, L. (1983). *Learning disabilities in perspective.* Glenview, Illinois: Scott Foresman and Co.

Alley, G. R. (1981). *Decision analysis of a secondary learning-disabilities intervention problem.* Unpublished research study. Lawrence: University of Kansas Institute for Research in Learning Disabilities.

Bandura, A. (1977). *Social learning theory.* Englewood Cliffs, NJ: Prentice-Hall, Inc.

Beals, V. L. (1983). *The effectiveness of large group instructional procedures on the acquisition of learning strategies by LD adolescents.* Unpublished doctoral dissertation. Lawrence: The University of Kansas.

Bloom, B. S. (1974). Time and learning. *American Psychologist, 29,* 682–688.

Boyer, E. L. (1983). *High school: A report on secondary education in America.* New York: Harper & Row.

Brandis, M., & Halliwell, R. (1980). *Verification of procedures to serve handicapped students: Final report-secondary component.* (Contract No. 300–79–0702). Silver Springs, MD: Applied Management Sciences.

Bridgman, A. (November 23, 1983). Publishers asked to join effort to improve schooling. *Education Week,* pp. 8, 18.

Brown, A. L., Campione, J. C., & Day, J. D. (1981). Learning to learn: On training students to learn from texts. *Educational Researcher, 10*(2), 14–21.

Cahan, L. S., & Filby, N. N. (1979). The class size/achievement issue: New evidence and a research plan. *Phi Delta Kappan, 60,* 492–495.

Carmen, R. A., & Adams, W. R., Jr. (1972). *Study skills: A student's guide for survival.* New York: John Wiley & Sons.

Carnine, D. W. (1976). Effects of two teacher-presentation rates on off-task behavior, answering correctly, and participation. *Journal of Applied Behavior Analysis, 9,* 199–206.

Carroll, J. B. (1963). A model of school learning. *Teachers College Record, 29,* 682–688.

Clark, G. M. (1980). Career preparation for handicapped adolescents: A matter of appropriate education. *Exceptional Education Quarterly, 1,* 11–18.

Clark, F. L., Deshler, D. D., Schumaker, J. B., & Alley, G. R. (1984). Visual imagery and self-questioning: Strategies to improve comprehension of written materials. *Journal of Learning Disabilities, 17*(3), 145–149.

Cone, T. E., & Wilson, L. R. (1981). Quantifying a severe discrepency: A critical analysis. *Learning Disability Quarterly, 4,* 359–371.

Cox, J. (1980). Operation Divert: A model program for learning-disabled juvenile offenders. In R. H. Riegel and J. P. Mathey (Eds.). *Mainstreaming at the Secondary Level: Seven Models That Work,* (pp. 8–11). Plymouth, MI: Wayne County Intermediate School District.

Cromwell, R. L. (1963). A social learning approach to mental retardation. In N. R. Ellis (Ed.). *Handbook of Mental Deficiency,* (pp. 41–91). New York: McGraw-Hill Book Co.

Cronbach, L. J., & Snow, R. (1981). *Aptitudes and instructional methods* (2nd ed.). New York: Irvington.

Cullinan, D., Lloyd, J., & Epstein, M. H. (1981). Strategy training: A structured approach to arithmetic instruction. *Exceptional Education Quarterly, 2,* 41–50.

Delquadri, J., Greenwood, C. R., & Hall, R. V. (June 1979). *Opportunity to respond: An update.* Invited address at the 5th Annual Meeting of the Association for Behavior Analysis, Dearborn, MI.

Den Uyl, M., & van Oostendorp, H. (1980). The use of scripts in text comprehension. *Poetics, 9,* 275–294.

Deshler, D. D., Alley, G. R., & Carlson, S. A. (1980). Learning strategies: An approach to mainstreaming secondary students with learning disabilities. *Education Unlimited, 2*(4), 6–11.

Deshler, D. D., Alley, G. R., Warner, M. M., & Schumaker, J. B. (1981). Instructional practices for promoting skill acquisition and generalization in severely learning disabled adolescents. *Learning Disability Quarterly, 4,* 415–421.

Deshler, D. D., Lowrey, N., & Alley, G. R. (1979). Programming alternatives for learning-disabled adolescents: A nationwide survey. *Academic Therapy, 14,* 389–397.

Deshler, D. D., & Schumaker, J. B. (1983). Social skills of learning-disabled adolescents: Characteristics and intervention. *Topics in Learning and Learning Disabilities, 3,* 15–23.

Deshler, D. D., Schumaker, J. B., Alley, G. R., Warner, M. M., & Clark, F. L. (1982). Learning disabilities in adolescent and young adult populations: Research implications. *Focus on Exceptional Children, 15*(1), 1–12.

Deshler, D. D., Warner, M. M., Schumaker, J. B., & Alley, G. R. (1983). Learning strategies intervention model: Key components and current status. In J. McKinney & L. Feagans (Eds.). *Current Topics in Learning Disabilities.* Vol. 1 (pp. 245–283). Norwood, NJ: Ablex Publishing Corp.

Doyle, W. (1983). Academic work. *Review of Educational Research, 53*(2), 159–199.

Dyer, W. G. (1978). Implications of the helping relationship between learning disabled students and their teachers. *Learning Disability Quarterly, 1,* 55–61.

Ellis, E. S. (1983). *The effects of teaching learning-disabled adolescents an executive strategy to facilitate self-generation of task specific strategies.* Unpublished doctoral dissertation. Lawrence: University of Kansas.

Ferritor, D., Buckholdt, D., Hamblin, R. L., & Smith, L. (1972). The non-effects of contingent reinforcement for attending behavior on work accomplished. *Journal of Applied Behavior Analysis, 5,* 299–306.

Fishbein, M., & Ajzen, I. (1972). Attitudes and opinions. In P. H. Mussen & M. R. Rosenzweig (Eds.). *Annual Review of Psychology,* (Vol. 23, pp. 487–544). Palo Alto, CA: Annual Reviews Inc.

Gardner, D. P. (1983). *A nation at risk: The imperative for educational reform.* Washington, DC: The National Commission on Excellence in Education.

Gettinger, M., & White, M. A. (1979). Which is the stronger correlate of school learning? Time to learn or measured intelligence. *Journal of Educational Psychology, 71,* 405–412.

Goodlad, J. (1983). *A place called school.* New York: McGraw-Hill Book Co.

Goodman, L., & Mann, L. (1976). *Learning disabilities in the secondary schools: Issues and practices.* New York: Grune & Stratton.

Green, C., & Zigler, E. (1962). Social deprivation and the performance of retarded and normal children on a satiation task. *Child Development, 33,* 499–508.

Greenwood, C. R., Delquadri, J. C., & Hall, R. V. (1984). Opportunity to respond and student academic performance. In W. L. Heward, T. E. Heron, J. Trap-Porter, & D. S. Hill (Eds.), *Focus on behavior analysis in education,* (pp. 55–88). Columbus, OH: Charles E. Merrill.

Greenwood, C. R., Delquadri, J. C., Stanley, S., Sasso, G., Whorton, D., & Schulte, D. (1981). Allocating opportunity to learn as a basis for academic remediation. *Monograph in Behavior Disorders,* 22–33.

Greenwood, C. R., Dinwiddie, G., Terry, B., Wade, L., Stanley, S., Thibadeau, S., & Delquadri, J. (1983). *Experimental analysis of the achievement effects produced by low versus high opportunity to respond instruction.* Unpublished manuscript. Lawrence: University of Kansas.

Haring, N. G., & Eaton, M. D. (1978). Systematic instructional procedures: An instructional hierarchy. In N. G. Haring, T. C. Lovitt, M. D. Eaton, & C. L. Hansen (Eds.). *The Fourth R: Research in the Classroom,* (pp. 23–48). Columbus, OH: Charles E. Merrill.

Harneschfeger, A., & Wiley, D. E. (1978). Classroom control: Room and time for improvement. *Educational Technology, 13,* 27–29.

Hartwell, L. K., Wiseman, D. E., & Van Reusen, A. K. (1979). Modifying course content for mildly handicapped students at the secondary level. *Teaching Exceptional Children, 12*(1), 28–32.

Hazel, J. S., Schumaker, J. B., Sherman, J. A., & Sheldon, J. (1982). Application of a group training program in social skills and problem solving to learning disabled and non-learning disabled youth. *Learning Disability Quarterly, 5,* 398–408.

Hoover, K. H. (1976). *The professional teacher's handbook: A guide for improving instruction in today's middle and secondary schools* (2nd ed.). Boston: Allyn & Bacon.

Hudson, F. G., & Graham, S. (1978). An approach to operationalizing the IEP. *Learning Disability Quarterly, 1,* 13–32.

Joyce, B., & Weil, M. (1980). *Models of teaching.* Englewood Cliffs, NJ: Prentice-Hall, Inc.

Keeney, R. L., & Raiffa, H. (1976). *Decisions with multiple objectives: Preferences and value tradeoffs.* New York: John Wiley and Sons.

Kintsch, W., Kozminsky, E., Streby, J., McKoon, G., & Keena, J. M. (1975). Comprehension and recall as a function of content variables. *Journal of Verbal Behavior, 14,* 190–214.

Knapczyk, D. R., & Livingston, G. (1974). The effects of prompting question-asking upon on-task behavior and reading comprehension. *Journal of Applied Behavior Analysis, 7,* 115–121.

Knowlton, H. E. (1983). *Secondary regular-classroom teachers' expectations of learning disabled students* (Research Report No. 75). Lawrence: The University of Kansas Institute for Research in Learning Disabilities.

Laurie, T. E., Buchwach, L., Silverman, R., & Zigmond, N. (1978). Teaching secondary learning-disabled students in the mainstream. *Learning Disability Quarterly, 1,* 62–72.

Lee, P., & Alley, G. R. (1981). *Training junior high school LD students to use a test-taking strategy* (Research Report No. 38). Lawrence: The University of Kansas Institute for Research in Learning Disabilities.

Lenz, B. K. (1983). *The effect of advance organizers on the learning and retention of learning disabled adolescents within the context of a cooperative planning model.* Unpublished doctoral disseration. Lawrence: The University of Kansas.

Levin, E. K., Zigmond, N., & Birch, J. W. (April 1983). *A follow-up study of 52 learning-disabled adolescents.* Paper presented at AERA, Montreal.

Lightfoot, S. L. (1983). *The good high school.* New York: Basic Books, Inc.

Lloyd, J. W., Hallahan, D. P., Kosiewicz, M. M., & Kneedler, R. D. (1982). Reactive effects of self-assessment and self-recording on attention to task and academic productivity. *Learning Disability Quarterly, 5,* 216–227.

Lovitt, T. C., & Fantasia, K. (1983). A precision teaching project with learning disabled children. *Journal of Precision Teaching, 3,* 85–91.

Marholin, D., & Steinman, W. M. (1977). Stimulus control in the classroom as a function of the behavior reinforced. *Journal of Applied Behavior Analysis, 10,* 465–478.

Marshall, N., & Glock, M. (1978). Comprehension of connected discourse: A study into the relationship between structure of text and information recalled. *Reading Research Quarterly, 14,* 10–56.

Meichenbaum, D. (1977). *Cognitive behavior modification: An integrated approach.* New York: Plenum Press.

Meisgeier, C. (n. d.). *Synergistic education.* Houston, TX: University of Houston Office of Publications.

Mellard, D. & Deshler, D. (1984). Modeling the condition of learning disabilities on post-secondary populations. *Educational Psychologist, 19*(3), 188–197.

Meyen, E. L., Alley, G. R., Scannell, D. P., Harnden, G. M., & Miller, K. F. (1982). *A mandated minimum competency testing program and its impact on learning disabled students: Curricular validity and comparative performances* (Research Report No. 63). Lawrence: University of Kansas Institute for Research in Learning Disabilities.

Meyen, E. L., & Lehr, D. H. (1980a). Evolving practices in assessment and intervention for mildly handicapped adolescents: The case for intensive instruction. *Exceptional Education Quarterly, 1,* 19–26.

Meyen, E. L., & Lehr, D. H. (1980b). Perspectives on instructionally least restrictive environments: Instructional implications. *Focus on Exceptional Children, 12,* 1–8.

Miskel, C. (1982). *Structural linkages, expectancy climate, and school effectiveness* (Research Report No. 58). Lawrence: The University of Kansas Institute for Research in Learning Disabilities.

Miskel, C., Bloom, S., & McDonald, D. (1982). *Effects of structural coupling and expectancy climate on the effectiveness of learning strategies intervention: A pilot study to establish reliability and validity estimates* (Research Report No. 57). Lawrence: The University of Kansas Institute for Research in Learning Disabilities.

Mosby, R. (1980). The application of the developmental by-pass procedure to LD adolescents. *Journal of Learning Disabilities, 13*(1), 21–27.

Pullin, D. (1980). Mandated minimum competency testing: Its impact on handicapped adolescents. *Exceptional Education Quarterly, 1*(2), 107–116.

Reith, H. J., Polsgrove, L., & Semmel, M. I. (1979). Relationship between instructional time and academic achievement: Implications for research and practice. *Education Unlimited*, 1(6), 53–56.

Robbins, D. A. (1982). *FIRST-letter mnemonic strategy: A memorization technique for learning disabled high school students*. Unpublished Master's Thesis. Lawrence: University of Kansas.

Rosenshine, B. V., & Berliner, D. C. (1978). Academic engaged time. *British Journal of Teacher Education*, 4, 3–16.

Schmidt, J. (1983). *The effects of four generalization conditions on learning disabled adolescents' written language performance in the regular classroom*. Unpublished doctoral dissertation. Lawrence: University of Kansas.

Schumaker, J. B., & Clark, F. L. (1982). *An approach to learning strategies training for groups of secondary students* (Research Monograph No. 11). Lawrence: The University of Kansas Institute for Research in Learning Disabilities.

Schumaker, J. B., & Deshler, D. D. (1984). Setting demand variables: A major factor in program planning for the LD adolescent. *Topics in Language Disorders Journal*, 4, 22–40.

Schumaker, J. B., Deshler, D. D., Alley, G. R., & Warner, M. M. (1980). *An epidemiological study of learning disabled adolescents in secondary schools: Details of the methodology*. (Research Report No. 12). Lawrence: The University of Kansas Institute for Research in Learning Disabilities.

Schumaker, J. B., Deshler, D. D., Alley, G. R., & Warner, M. M. (1983). Toward the development of an intervention model for LD adolescents. *Exceptional Education Quarterly*, 4(1), 45–74.

Schumaker, J. B., Deshler, D. D., Denton, P. H. (1984). An integrated system for providing content to LD adolescents using an audio-taped format. In W. M. Cruickshank and J. M. Kliebhan (Eds.). *Early Adolescence to Early Adulthood*, (Vol. 5, (pp. 79–107). Syracuse, NY: Syracuse University Press.

Schumaker, J. B., Deshler, D. D., Denton, P. H., Alley, G. R., Clark, F. L., & Warner, M. M. (1982). Multipass: A learning strategy for improving reading comprehension. *Learning Disability Quarterly*, 5, 295–304.

Schumaker, J. B., Warner, M. M., Deshler, D. D., & Alley, G. R. (n. d.). *The evaluation of a learning strategies intervention model for LD adolescents* (Research Report No. 67). Lawrence: The University of Kansas Institute for Research in Learning Disabilities.

Seabaugh, G. O., & Schumaker, J. B. (1981). *The effects of self-regulation training on the academic productivity of LD and NLD adolescents* (Research Report No. 37). Lawrence: The University of Kansas Institute for Research in Learning Disabilities.

Shank, R. (1983). A conversation with Roger Shank. *Psychology Today*, 17(4), 28–36.

Shelby, C. C., & Coleman, W. T. (1983). *Educating Americans for the 21st century*. Washington, DC: National Science Board Commission on Precollege Education in Mathematics, Science, and Technology.

Sheppard, L. (1983). The role of measurement in educational policy: Lessons from the identification of learning disabilities. *Educational Measurement: Issues and Practice*, 2(3), 4–8.

Sizer, T. R. (1984). *Horace's compromise: The dilemma of the American high school*. Boston: Houghton-Mifflin Co.

Spiro, R. J. (1980). Prior knowledge and story processing: Integration, selection, and variation. *Poetics*, 9, 313–327.

Stanley, S. O., & Greenwood, C. R. (1981). *CISSAR: Code for instructional structure and student academic response: Observer's manual*. Kansas City, KS: Juniper Gardens Children's Project, Bureau of Child Research, University of Kansas.

Stevens, R., & Rosenshine, B. (1981). Advances in research on teaching. *Exceptional Education Quarterly, 2*(1), 1–10.

Talley, T. L. (November 1978). *Teaching family problems in a national perspective.* Keynote address presented at the National Teaching Family Association, Boys Town, Nebraska.

Thurlow, M. L., Graden, J., Greener, J. W., & Ysseldyke, J. E. (1982). *Academic responding time for LD and non-LD students* (Report #72). Minneapolis, MN: Institute for Research on Learning Disabilities.

Tollefson, N., Tracy, D., Johnsen, E., & Chatman, J. (1983). *Teaching learning disabled students goal implementation skills* (Research Report No. 69). Lawrence: The University of Kansas Institute for Research in Learning Disabilities.

Turnure, C. (1975). Cognitive development and role-taking ability in boys and girls from 7 to 12. *Developmental Psychology, 11,* 202–209.

Van Reusen, A. K. (1984). *A study on the effects of training learning disabled adolescents in self-advocacy procedures for use in the IEP conference.* Unpublished doctoral dissertation, Lawrence: University of Kansas.

Vetter, A. (1983). *A comparison of the characteristics of learning disabled and non-learning-disabled young adults.* Unpublished doctoral dissertation. Lawrence: University of Kansas.

Warner, M. M., Schumaker, J. B., Alley, G. R., & Deshler, D. D. (1980). Learning disabled adolescents in the public schools: Are they different from other low-achievers? *Exceptional Education Quarterly, 1*(2), 27–56.

White, W. J., Schumaker, J. B., Warner, M. M., Alley, G. R., & Deshler, D. D. (1980). *The current status of young adults classified as learning disabled during their school career* (Research Report No. 21). Lawrence: University of Kansas Institute for Research in Learning Disabilities.

White-Blackburn, G., Semb, S., & Semb, G. (1977). The effects of a good-behavior contract on the classroom behaviors of sixth-grade students. *Journal of Applied Behavior Analysis, 10,* 312.

Zeaman, D. & House, B. J. (1963). The role of attention in retardate discrimination learning. In N. R. Ellis (Ed.). *Handbook of mental deficiency,* (pp. 159–223). New York: McGraw-Hill Book Co.

Zigler, E. (1966). Research on personality structure in the retardate. In N. R. Ellis (Ed.), *International review of research in mental retardation* (Vol. 1, pp. 77–108). New York: Academic Press.

Zigmond, N. (1978). A prototype of comprehensive services for secondary students with learning disabilities. *Learning Disability Quarterly, 1*(1), 39–49.

Zigmond, N., Vallecorsa, A., & Silverman, R. (1983). *Assessment for instructional planning in special education.* Englewood Cliffs, NJ: Prentice-Hall Inc.

12

Cognitive Behavior Modification: Promoting Active, Self-Regulatory Learning Styles*

ELLEN BOUCHARD RYAN
KERI A. WEED
ELIZABETH J. SHORT

LEARNING-DISABLED CHILDREN AS PASSIVE LEARNERS

Learning-disabled children exhibit a variety of maladaptive behaviors. Equally diverse are the causal agents precipitating and sustaining their underachievement. Meichenbaum (1976) advocates a cognitive functional approach to the investigation of learning disabilities. This approach does not trivialize the importance of physiological and neurological deficits, but it does recognize that the most effective remediation may be far removed from the original precipitating cause (see Henker, Whalen, & Hinshaw, 1980). Within the cognitive functional paradigm, deficits in cognitive processes are assessed and improvements in cognitive processing are related to improvements in appropriate behavior. Some specific characteristics of learning-disabled children which have been targeted for intervention include: a passive approach to academic and problem-solving tasks (Torgesen, 1977), motivational/attributional defi-

---

* Preparation of this chapter was supported by a grant from the Natural Sciences and Engineering Research Council of Canada.

cits (Butkowski & Willows, 1980; Pearl, Bryan & Donahue, 1980), lack of metacognitive awareness (Douglas, 1981; Hallahan & Kneedler, 1979; Paris & Myers, 1981; Wiens, 1983), impulsivity (Lloyd, Hallahan, & Kauffman, 1980), and hyperactivity (Blackman & Goldstein, 1982).

The purpose of this chapter is to examine the relevance of cognitive behavior modification (broadly conceived) for remediating the learning difficulties of LD children. First, we present evidence that the differences between potential and performance are particularly striking for these children. Two major causes for these discrepancies are discussed: lack of metacognitive awareness and cognitive/motivational problems. Second, the basic principles of cognitive behavior modification as an intervention approach are described. Third, application of this technique to learning, in particular academic domains, is reviewed in detail. Fourth, conclusions are drawn concerning future directions in realizing the promise of this type of intervention and in evaluating its success.

DISCREPANCIES BETWEEN POTENTIAL AND PERFORMANCE

Learning-disabled children have been characterized as passive or inactive learners in light of their failure to attend selectively, to organize material to be learned, to use mnemonic and comprehension strategies, or to maintain on-task behavior. Nevertheless, the evidence suggests that learning-disabled children can behave strategically if instructed to do so (Torgesen, 1977; Wong & Jones, 1982; Wozniak, 1975). The presence of specific information-processing deficits among learning-disabled children (Torgesen, 1982; Vellutino, 1979) does not negate the importance of strategic processing behaviors. On the contrary, the use of active strategies may permit learning-disabled children to compensate for basic deficiencies.

Soviet researchers refer to the discrepancy between what children are capable of achieving and their actual developmental level as the zone of "proximal development" (Day, 1983; Vygotsky, 1978). Basically, the zone is the difference between what children are capable of doing without assistance and what they can accomplish with the help of another person or with modified materials. Brown and French (1979) have suggested that the width of the zone is indicative of intelligence, with more intelligent children demonstrating the ability to learn readily when interacting with a teacher, thereby exhibiting a wider zone. Two measures of zone width have been employed in American studies (Brown & Ferrara, in press; Hall & Day, 1982). The first measure consists of the number of hints or prompts required by the child to attain a criterion level of task mastery; the second involves assessment of the child's ability to transfer recent learning to similar, but novel, tasks.

It has been suggested that learning-disabled children have zone widths equivalent to those of normally achieving children and significantly wider than mentally retarded children (Brown & Ferrara, in press; Day, 1983; Hall & Day, 1982; Wozniak, 1975). Hall and Day (1982) compared these three groups of children with respect to the two measures of zone width described above. The pattern of results generally supported this hypothesis, although the data only approached significance. LD children needed more prompts to learn the criterion rule than normally achieving children, but were equally proficient on a near-transfer task. Further research is needed to elaborate and substantiate these findings.

If learning-disabled children are similar to normally achieving peers in terms of zone width, then why are they not achieving according to their potential? Some possible reasons involve metacognitive deficits with the associated lack of strategic behavior, response style problems, and lack of motivation. Since Licht and Kistner have discussed the motivational deficits of learning-disabled children elsewhere in this volume (Chapter 8), we briefly will focus on their difficulties with metacognition and response style.

Metacognitive Deficits

Metacognition refers to awareness of the person, task, and strategy variables affecting cognitive performance, along with the use of that knowledge to plan, monitor, and regulate performance (Brown, Bransford, Ferrara, & Campione, 1983; Flavell, 1981). Recently, researchers have used the concept of metacognition to account for the failure to apply known skills in novel situations appropriately (Borkowski & Cavanaugh, 1979; Schneider, 1985).

Metacognitive deficits have been found among learning-disabled children and with other subpopulations of slow learners who have characteristics in common with learning-disabled children (e.g., poor readers and impulsive children). Douglas (1981) compared memory-strategy use of 9–10-year-old normal and learning-disabled children. Although no differences were found between the two groups of children with respect to external storage strategies, learning-disabled children were deficient in internal storage strategies such as verbal rehearsal. LD children have also been found to be lacking in task-approach skills, including the ability to focus on the relevant task information (Hallahan & Kneedler, 1979).

Borkowski, Peck, Reid, and Kurtz (1983) investigated children's meta-memory knowledge as a mediator of strategy transfer for reflective and impulsive children. Approximately equal numbers of impulsive and reflective children were assigned to either an experimental group who received instructions on rehearsal and search strategies or a no-strategy control group. Metamemory not only correlated with strategic behaviors on tests of strategy transfer, but this correlation remained significant when the measure of impulsivity was removed statistically. These findings support the hypothesis that metamemory, rather than cognitive tempo, mediates the effectiveness of a trained strategy in terms of its durability and generalizability.

Although most metacognitive research has focused upon the memory domain, some relevant work has also been conducted in the reading domain. Metareading comparisons of good and poor readers have addressed three main areas: awareness of the features and functions of reading, the ability to monitor comprehension, and knowledge and application of strategies (Brown, 1981; Downing, 1979; Ryan, 1981). In comparison to their skilled peers, poor readers manifest less awareness of the communicative/informational functions of reading, an overemphasis on decoding, less knowledge concerning appropriate processing strategies, and less sensitivity to their own level of comprehension (Canney & Winograd, 1979; Paris & Myers, 1981; Short & Ryan, 1984). Thus, metacognitive investigations provide a substantial basis for the notion that inactive or impulsive learning styles may be the consequences of inadequate understanding of the relationships among tasks, strategies, and outcomes.

Response Style

Two other common characteristics of learning disabled children are relevant to the cognitive functional approach: hyperactivity (inappropriate attentional behaviors, especially off-task behavior) and impulsivity (fast, inaccurate responding on the Matching Familiar Figures Test— MFFT). In their review of studies investigating learning disabilities, Blackman and Goldstein (1982) concluded that a significantly higher incidence of both hyperactivity and impulsivity exists among learning-disabled children than in the normal population. Although there is little empirical evidence that decreasing hyperactivity and impulsivity leads directly to achievement gains, it is commonly accepted that impulsive behaviors and inappropriate attentional behaviors need to be controlled before academic behavior can be changed (Bryant & Budd, 1982; Burgio, Whitman, & Johnson, 1980; Friedling & O'Leary, 1979).

COGNITIVE BEHAVIOR MODIFICATION AS AN APPROACH TO INTERVENTION

Cognitive behavior modification has recently emerged as a technique for realizing the learning potential of learning-disabled children (Harter, 1982; Meichenbaum, 1976). We believe it to be especially promising because the approach addresses two of the key difficulties of learning-disabled children—self-regulation of strategy use and motivation. Five characteristics common to these procedures (Lloyd, 1980) are: (1) students are involved as active participants in the learning process, (2) overt verbalization usually is required at some point, (3) the desired response is identified by a series of discrete steps, (4) modeling of the target strategy is employed during training, and (5) the goal of training is a planful, reflective response style. Besides general or executive strategy training, task-specific strategies are sometimes involved. Implementation of these five techniques should emphasize to the students the relationships between their actions and task outcome.

Cognitive strategy training, problem solving, self-control procedures, and self-instructions all are included under the general category of cognitive behavior modification (Whitman, Burgio, & Johnston, 1983). Developmental psychologists have long been aware of the striking improvements in memory, problem solving, and comprehension following strategy training or instruction (see Brown et al., 1983). The rationale for cognitive strategy training is based on the distinction between process and performance. The goal is to explain and alter behavior by reference to the underlying cognitive processes. Much of the improvement in memory, for example, with increasing age has been shown to be attributable to the development of mnemonic strategies, rather than an increase in capacity (Pressley, 1982). Such findings for memory and other cognitive domains highlight the importance of cognitive strategy training for children experiencing learning difficulties.

Due to the limited success of specific strategy training in producing continued and generalized improvements in academic behavior, researchers have become aware of the need to incorporate more generalized metacognitive instruction into training procedures (Borkowski & Cavanaugh, 1979; Brown et al., 1983). Brown, Campione, and Day (1981) contrast "blind" training with "informed" strategy training, which includes explanations regarding the function and use of the strategy or feedback linking performance changes to strategy use. Positive effects on strategy use and transfer generally have been found following feedback regarding the value of the strategy (Kennedy & Miller, 1976; Ringel & Springer, 1980).

According to Brown *et al.* (1981), self-control (self-monitoring) training goes beyond informed training by providing specific, metacognitive training in planning, checking, and monitoring. The metacognitive components are not necessarily specific to the target task, but rather constitute a general strategy for approaching any problem-solving situation. Several strategy training studies have shown that strategies incorporating self-control features actually maintain and generalize to slightly different tasks (Brown, Campione, & Barclay, 1979; Lodico, Ghatala, Levin, Pressley, & Bell, 1983).

Self-instructions provide a framework to unify the developmental psychologists' appeal for self-control training (Brown *et al.*, 1981; Pressley, 1982) with behavioral methodology (Meichenbaum & Goodman, 1971; Whitman *et al.*, 1983). This chapter focuses particularly on self-instructional training.

Self-instructional procedures have been based on two key notions of Soviet theory—the internalization of speech into thought and the zone of proximal development (Vygotsky, 1978). As in the natural sequence of development, the learner moves from other-regulation to internalized self-regulation of problem-solving behaviors. As outlined by Meichenbaum and Goodman (1971), the five sequential steps for self-instructional training are: (1) task performance by instructor while self-verbalizing, (2) performance by student while the instructor verbalizes, (3) active performance by student while self-instructing aloud, (4) active performance by student while whispering, and (5) task performance while self-instructing covertly. What the learner could only achieve previously in interaction with another (i.e., level of proximal development) now becomes the goal for the child instructing himself.

Self-instruction is thought to promote the maintenance of learned skills and strategies by providing a general framework for problem solving, by providing feedback, and by inducing self-control over the entire process. Self-instructional content, as proposed by Meichenbaum and Goodman (1971), includes five motivational/metacognitive components: planning, general and specific strategy instructions, monitoring/feedback mechanisms, error correction, and self-reinforcement. Many of these components may be especially valuable for LD children because of their deficiencies in precisely these areas. To concretize our discussion of these aspects of self-instructions, an illustration of self-instructional steps is taken from Johnston's (1983) arithmetic study (see Table 1).

Steps 1 and 2 facilitate planful, reflective responding. Many learning-disabled children do not stop to consider the task requirements or the best way to approach a task (Hallahan & Kneedler, 1979). Instead, they adopt an impulsive response style, which may be the result of inade-

TABLE 1
Illustration of Self-Instructions[a]

Step	Statement
1	How do I begin? I think about what I have to do. I have to remember to talk to myself. I need to work slowly and carefully and to check my work.
2	What kind of math problem is this? It's an add problem. I can tell by the sign. I know how to solve add problems. So I can begin.
3	What do I add? I start with the top number in the one's column.
4	What do I do next? It has two numbers, so I have to carry.
5	Now what do I add? I go to the ten's column.
6	Is the answer right? I need to check it.
7	I got it right I'm doing very well.

[a] From Johnston (1983).

quate metacognitive understanding (Borkowski *et al.*, 1983). By responding impulsively, for example, many children overlook the plus or minus sign of a computation. Self-instructions provide concrete strategies for how to proceed (e.g., think about what has already been learned, go more slowly, and monitor). In addition, Step 2 specifically focuses attention on the relevant aspects of the task.

Of course, encouraging children to proceed in a slow, systematic manner is useful only if children have the prerequisite knowledge necessary to answer the self-oriented questions correctly. Steps 3, 4, and 5 provide instructions for how to solve the problem. Depending on the goal of the intervention, these steps may be very general, or in the case of addition, quite specific. Several investigators have examined the effects on training and transfer of varying the content of self-instructions. Kendall and Wilcox (1980) found that a conceptual approach was superior to concrete self-instructions at follow-up in terms of teacher ratings of self-control and hyperactivity. In a comparison of specific and more general self-instructions, Schleser, Meyers, and Cohen (1981) found that specific instructions improved performance on the training task (MFFT), but that children who had learned the more general instructions were more proficient on the transfer task (a perceptual, perspective-taking task). If continued and generalized use of self-instructions governing well-learned skills is the goal of training, it appears helpful to include more generalized problem-solving statements. On the other hand, instructions for new skills should be sufficiently specific to ensure learning. It might well be that the content of self-instructions should be faded gradually from the more specific to the more general.

Step 6 fulfills an accuracy monitoring/feedback function. Although not included here, process monitoring can also be included. For example, students periodically may question whether they are proceeding systematically through all of the problem-solving steps. By monitoring both process and outcome, students should come to understand the causal connection between them. In other words, they should learn that the task outcome is dependent upon their own actions. For example, Lodico *et al.* (1983) demonstrated that self-monitoring of strategy utility helped children to select the most appropriate strategy subsequently and to explain why it was best.

A basic assumption is that the self-instructional approach places the targeted behavior under the learners' own controlling influence. Rather than the experimenter or teacher giving directions to be followed, the children themselves verbalize the instructions and carry them out. It follows logically that learned-helpless children will become more motivated to try to achieve once they realize, through using self-instructions, that they can actually have some control over outcomes (Henker, *et al.*, 1980). A few studies have attempted to assess the attributional consequences of self-instructional training; however, the results are inconclusive (Johnston, 1983; Short, 1981).

Strategies for coping with failure also may be included in Step 6. For example, if the answer is not correct, the student may respond, "I must have done something wrong. But that's O.K. I can erase and try again." Rather than giving up and adopting a passive style of response, the child persists until the answer is correct. Again, the belief that the failure is controllable is reinforced.

The last step in most self-instructional routines is self-reinforcement. Recent literature has suggested that external reinforcement tends to decrease the intrinsic value of the activity, thereby decreasing students' motivation to engage in it in the future (Harter, 1982; Lepper, 1981). Having children provide their own reinforcement should circumvent this problem, and at the same time, give them a feeling of pride and accomplishment.

The motivational and metacognitive components of self-instructional routines may be applied in a variety of instructional domains. With specific skills training included, self-instruction should allow learning-disabled children to achieve at a level closer to their full potential.

PROMOTING ACTIVE SELF-REGULATORY LEARNING STYLES

In this section, we review the use of cognitive behavioral techniques in domains relevant to the LD child: impulsivity; on-task behavior; and the specific academic areas of arithmetic, reading, and writing. When possible, the metacognitive and motivational components of the cognitive behavior modification techniques involved in the treatment effect will be delineated. It is important to keep in mind that substantial variability in the selection and implementation of the above components exists across studies.

REDUCING IMPULSIVITY

Accurate evaluation of the effectiveness of cognitive behavior modification for reducing impulsive responding is difficult. Instead of providing a detailed explanation of the training procedure, many reports merely indicate they followed Meichenbaum and Goodman's (1971) training procedures (see Arnold & Forehand, 1978; Egeland, 1974; Nelson & Birkimer, 1978). Although it is assumed that this means the five-step training program, beginning with modeled self-verbalizations and ending with the student covertly instructing, the content of the self-instructions is more variable. In many studies, the information provided is not sufficient to determine if both general and specific problem-solving strategies were included, if both accuracy and strategy use were monitored explicitly, and if coping with failure and self-reinforcement statements were included.

Meichenbaum and Goodman's (1971) study with impulsive children generated much excitement and subsequent research. Their focus on the MFFT, the defining task for impulsivity, as the target task for intervention has been maintained by most other investigators. Although the consistent use of a common task permits outcome comparisons among the studies, more attention to academically relevant activities would be beneficial.

In their first study, Meichenbaum and Goodman (1971) evaluated a self-instructional package which included planning statements, general strategy instructions, self-monitoring/feedback, error correction, and self-reinforcement and social praise for improving performance of second-grade hyperactive, low-intelligence children. At the end of four 30-minute sessions, the five children in the self-instructional condition and the five in an attentional control condition (who received an equivalent amount of practice on the target task) all significantly improved their performance on the picture arrangement subtest of the WISC, Porteus Maze, and MFFT latency. One month later, both groups remained significantly better on these measures than the pre-post control group. However, no generalization to classroom behavior was found, nor were decreases in MFFT errors obtained. In a second study with kindergarten and first-grade impulsive children, Meichenbaum and Goodman (1971) evaluated the effectiveness of modeling plus self-instructions as compared to modeling alone and an attention control group. More specific task strategies were included in the training this time. With only one training session, children in both the modeling and modeling plus self-instruction conditions increased their latency on the MFFT, as compared to the attention control. Only the modeling plus self-instruction group showed fewer MFFT errors. Generalization and maintenance were not assessed.

Differences in the students involved in the two studies and the type of training used may help to explain the discrepant results. The attention-control condition led to significant improvements only in the first study, whereas self-instructions yielded changes in MFFT errors only in the second study. These discrepancies might be accounted for by the age of the students, their disorder (i.e., hyperactive versus impulsive), or length/specificity of training. The differential findings here and across subsequent studies suggest that self-instructions might be relatively more effective for some children than for others.

Cullinan, Epstein, and Silver's (1977) study with learning-disabled children supports this hypothesis. Cullinan et al. (1977) assessed the effects of modeling and modeling plus self-instruction with 9–12-year-old, impulsive children who were also diagnosed as learning disabled. Although the training was similar to that of Meichenbaum and Goodman (1971), the results were not. Whereas the former had found increases in latency for both training groups and a decrease in errors for only the self-instructional group, Cullinan et al. (1977) found significant decreases in errors for both training groups and no significant change in latency. The authors suggest learning-disabled, impulsive children may be more resistant to programs aimed at increasing response latency than normally achieving, impulsive children. Another study with 6–13-year-old, learning-disabled children confirmed the efficacy of self-instructions relative to an attention and pre-post control group for improving

MFFT accuracy (Steele & Barling, 1982). Further, the results suggested that children with an internal locus of control were more likely to use self-verbalizations during training. This last finding highlights the importance of individual differences among students in research on the relative efficacy of interventions.

The content of the training package is also relevant for the results produced. Arnold and Forehand (1978) compared the value of self-instructional training to a response cost procedure for modifying the impulsive responding of 4–5-year-old, low-income children in a two-by-two factorial design. Accuracy on the KRISP (a preschool version of the MFFT) and on classroom match-to-sample tasks was assessed immediately following five training sessions and again 2 weeks later. Although no significant effects were obtained on the KRISP, the two groups who received self-instructional training did make significantly fewer errors on classroom tasks. Addition of the response cost procedure had no effect. The outcome is especially significant since the match-to-sample post-test tasks were quite different from the mazes and copying tasks used during the training.

Egeland (1974) specifically evaluated the outcome of training a task-specific scanning strategy as compared to a more general delay condition (i.e., pause before responding) and a pre-post control group on MFFT errors and latency scores as well as generalization to reading comprehension and vocabulary with second-grade impulsive children. After eight training sessions, the 26 children in the scanning strategy condition made fewer errors, took longer to respond, and improved their reading comprehension relative to the pre-post control group. Children in the delay condition also made significantly fewer errors than the control group and showed a trend toward longer latencies, but did not improve on reading comprehension. At the 6-month follow-up, only children in the strategy condition continued to show significantly fewer errors and longer latencies on the MFFT.

The effects of specific strategy training and self-versus-tutor verbalizations were examined with first-grade impulsive children by Bender (1976). Training and post-test materials consisted of several match-to-sample tasks including letters, cards, and drawings. Following four training sessions, the 24 children who received strategy training took significantly longer to respond on the post-tests than did non-strategy-trained children. Further, the 12 children in the self-instruction-plus-strategy group showed a trend toward fewer errors. No significant generalization to the MFFT was found, although the strategy-plus-self-instructions groups did show a trend toward better accuracy and longer latency.

The effects for verbalization were clearer in the study by Schleser, Meyers, and Cohen (1981) with 60 6–8-year-old children. They compared MFFT performance for children given self-instructional training with the performance for children in a content-only control group. Self-instructions facilitated performance in terms of accuracy, reflectivity, and efficiency of information processing. Simply listening to the monitoring, evaluation, and analysis statements was not sufficient for improvement. The active participation of the child promoted by the overt-to-covert rehearsal of self-instructions was a necessary ingredient.

The importance of the self-reinforcement component of self-instructional routines for second- and third-grade impulsive children was investigated by Nelson and Birkimer (1978). Only children receiving self-instructions which included self-reinforcement inproved in accuracy and latency, as compared to a self-instructional group without self-reinforcement, an attentional control, and an assessment-control group. However, maintenance and generalization were not assessed, and specific training instructions were not delineated.

In summary, evidence for the effectiveness of self-instructional procedures in modifying impulsivity is gradually accumulating, especially for the MFFT. Researchers have begun to address the role of specific components of the full treatment. Generally, studies involving more sessions and employing more specific task strategies show greater changes on target tasks (see also Douglas, Parry, Marton, & Garson, 1976).

ON-TASK BEHAVIOR

Hyperactivity (or developmental attentional disorder) is another common characteristic of learning-disabled children. As compared with the research on impulsivity, cognitive behavior modification research in this area has tended to employ more varied and ecologically valid tasks. For example, behavioral observations as well as teachers' ratings have been employed as indices of hyperactivity. On-task behaviors, including paying attention and sitting still, have been targeted for intervention. Often math or handwriting worksheets are employed to train on-task behaviors. Consequently, changes following training often are assessed in these academic tasks.

Bornstein and Quevillon's (1976) highly cited study has been the impetus for further investigations of cognitive behavior modification of off-task behavior. In this study, self-instructions were employed in a multiple baseline design to increase the on-task behavior of three disruptive boys in preschool. Significant changes in classroom behavior were reported immediately following the 2-hour training session, and these improvements were maintained in a 3-month follow-up.

Friedling and O'Leary (1979) attempted unsuccessfully to replicate this study with slightly older hyperactive children (second- and third-graders). Accuracy and rate of on-task behavior were evaluated on math and reading tasks of low- and high-difficulty levels. No differences were found for on-task behavior or accuracy, except on the easy math tasks. The only apparent differences in training between these two studies concerned reinforcement. Friedling and O'Leary (1979) controlled for teacher attention, whereas Bornstein and Quevillon (1976) did not. In addition, Bornstein and Quevillon (1976) used external reinforcement in the initial training tasks. It may well be that some self-instructional situations require external reinforcement, at least initially.

In contrast to the single session used by Bornstein and Quevillon (1976), most successful modifications of on-task behavior involve many sessions. In a multiple baseline design, Burgio et al. (1980) used self-instructions to increase the on-task behavior of two educably mentally retarded children. Besides the usual cognitive and metacognitive aspects of the self-instructional routine, Burgio et al. (1980) employed a distraction innoculation procedure to facilitate classroom generalization. That is, the children were systematically and sequentially exposed to slides of distracting situations, to audio distractors, and to "live" distractors in multiple sessions in the training setting. Training tasks consisted of math and printing worksheets, and generalization to phonics worksheets was assessed. Substantial decreases in off-task behavior occurred, with some generalization to the classroom. Some improvements in both accuracy and rate of math performance were found, but no changes in printing or phonics occurred.

All three of the above studies employed similar training routines following Meichenbaum and Goodman's (1971) five-step procedure. Also included in the three studies were: focusing of attention on the problem, specific task strategies, coping with failure statements, and self-reinforcement. Although the positive aspects of these studies suggest potential attentional and academic benefits of self-instructions for disruptive, hyperactive children, the lack of stable findings underscores the need for research delineating the subject, task, and situational parameters under which training is likely to be successful.

Focusing on one subject variable, Bugental, Whalen, and Henker (1977) proposed that self-instructions should be differentially effective depending on whether children believed they had control over events in their lives. Self-control training (including task strategies, monitoring, and self-reinforcement) was compared to a social reinforcement condition (including task strategies and external reinforcement) for hyperactive children. Children with a high degree of personal control benefited from the self-control training whereas those children with a low degree of personal control benefited from the social reinforcement condition. Likewise, children not on medication benefited more from the self-control training than those on medication for hyperactivity. For both conditions, training consisted of 12 individual sessions employing academic worksheets. Post-training assessments found improvements on the Porteus/Maze, but not on the Conners Hyperactivity Scale. Academic performance was not assessed.

Locus of control and level of medication are only two of the many subject variables that could influence the effects of cognitive behavior modification. Systematic assessments also are needed of the effects of student age, diagnosis, cognitive level, and background knowledge.

The type of reinforcement given is one aspect of on-task training that has been widely studied. In a multiple baseline design, Edgar and Clement (1980) compared self versus teacher reinforcement for four, underachieving fourth-grade boys. Following 3 months of instructions on reading, writing, and math tasks, the children who self-reinforced made relatively greater improvement on reading, writing, and attending behavior than children who received reinforcement from the teacher. Yet, Varni and Henker (1979) found external reinforcement to be valuable. In a multiple baseline design across behaviors, they evaluated the effectiveness of self-instructions (including task strategies and coping with failure) before and after the addition of self-monitoring and to reinforcement procedures. During the monitoring phase, three hyperactive boys monitored their performance, and, in the final phase, external rewards were given if they met a preset criterion. Self-instructions alone produced no change in reading or math performance, on-task behavior, or hyperactivity. When self-monitoring was implemented as well, performance on all these dependent measures improved somewhat; with external reinforcement, clear changes were seen.

Hallahan and his colleagues are involved in continuing investigations of the effectiveness of cognitive behavior modification techniques with learning-disabled children (see the excellent review by Hallahan, Kneedler, & Lloyd, 1983). In their self-monitoring paradigm, each child carries with him a cassette recorder with earphones. At selected intervals, a tone sounds and the students record whether they were on-task at the time. Back-up reinforcers occasionally are employed to reward the students for meeting a criterion for paying attention. The authors conclude that self-monitoring leads to increases in attending behavior and, to a certain extent, to improvements in academic productivity (i.e., rate of problems solved) which have been maintained up to 10 weeks. Changes in task accuracy have not been systematically examined. In terms of procedures responsible for the improvements in on-task behavior, Hallahan *et al.* (1983) have shown that the cue to record attending behavior and the actual recording were necessary elements during training, but that both of these could be faded successfully. They further demonstrated that these changes could be produced without reliance upon external reinforcers.

In summary, even though the numbers of subjects tend to be small, substantial progress has been made in modifying attentional behaviors with self-instructions. Moreover, subject variables such as locus of control and level of medication have been examined. Componential analysis, essentially, has been restricted to the comparison of internal and external reinforcements. The self-monitoring component can be expected to be especially valuable for LD children since the relationship between actions and outcomes thereby are highlighted.

ARITHMETIC

The groundwork for studies employing self-instructions to teach math skills was laid by research containing certain components of Meichenbaum and Goodman's (1971) cognitive behavior modification approach (Grimm, Bijou, & Parsons, 1973; Lovitt & Curtis, 1968; Smith & Lovitt, 1975), including verbalizations and modeling. Lovitt and Curtis (1968) demonstrated substantial improvements in the rate and accuracy of solving math problems for an 11-year-old boy who was required simply to read the problem aloud before writing a response. Grimm *et al.* (1973) utilized students' verbalizations to reinforce correct problem-solving strategies on number-concept problems. This procedure increased the accuracy of the two retarded, emotionally disturbed boys dramatically.

In a study with learning-disabled boys, Smith and Lovitt (1975) analyzed the effects of modeling on math performance. Teacher verbalization and written models of the procedures necessary to solve a math problem enhanced the learning process. When the demonstration and written model components were analyzed separately, the demonstration was found to be successful for improving the performance of most of the seven boys, whereas the written model was only effective for one. When learning occurred in the set of problems taught, it generalized to new problems with the same operation (e.g., learning to subtract with two-digit numbers generalized to subtraction with three-digit numbers).

One classroom study investigating the effects of self-instruction on the acquisition of math skills was conducted by Leon and Pepe (1983). Learning-disabled and mentally retarded children were taught by their teachers, using one of two procedures. The first procedure involved the traditional methods of modeling, instruction, and positive practice; the second procedure included those techniques as well as self-instructional procedures. Both procedures appeared to be effective; however, greater generalization to math operations not directly taught was observed for the self-instruction group.

Attempting to isolate effective treatment components, Barling (1980) examined the relative effectiveness of task-oriented self-instruction only, self-reinforcement, self-monitoring, and external feedback on both math and verbal tasks for third- through sixth-grade-school children. Whereas no differences following training were found with regard to accuracy or persistence on the verbal task (PPVT), significant differences were found on the math task. The 28 children who received both self-monitoring and self-reinforcement were superior, in terms of both persistence and accuracy, to any of the other groups. Children in the self-monitoring condition were next, followed by self-instructions alone (i.e., general task strategy, overview, problem definition). Hence, it appears that the self-reinforcement and self-monitoring components typically included with self-instruction are essential.

In a series of three studies, Johnston and her colleagues have examined the effectiveness of self-instructions for teaching addition and subtraction with regrouping (i.e., carrying and borrowing). Following Meichenbaum and Goodman's (1971) procedures, the three educably mentally retarded children taught to self-instruct showed significant increases in accuracy during training conditions (Johnston, Whitman, & Johnson, 1980). To make the self-instructional training techniques relevant to the classroom, Whitman and Johnston (1983) replicated their first study, using a multiple baseline across groups of children. Nine mildly retarded children were taught in groups of three to use self-instructions. The earlier results were replicated, thereby indicating the viability of self-instructions for the classroom situation.

The third study (Johnston, 1983) utilized a two-by-two factorial design to assess the effects of self- versus didactic instructions and the specificity of instructions for normal first-graders differing in their math knowledge. Specific instructions consisted of attention focusing and questions/answers on how to do the math problems. The condition with general-plus-task-specific instructions included the above as well as planning, checking, and self-reinforcement (see Table 1). Self- and didactic procedures were the same, except that children in the didactic condition did not verbalize the statements. Self-instruction produced more accurate problem solving than didactic instructions. Acquisition took longer, probably due to the added chore of coordinating the verbalizations along with the computational procedures; and fewer problems were solved. However, no difference remained in the number of problems solved after the 1-month maintenance period. Frequency of self-verbalizations related to more accurate problem solving. The content of self-instructions determined the effectiveness; the general-plus-task-specific instructions were more effective, especially for the less competent children. Finally, evidence for maintenance and for generalization to the classroom was obtained.

In summary, self-instructional procedures have been applied successfully to improve math accuracy in a small number of studies. Some evidence of maintenance and generalization of math performance has been obtained, and initial demonstrations of the importance of self-instructing, self-monitoring, and self-reinforcement have been conducted.

READING

Poor readers, including many learning-disabled children, fail to attend systematically to sentence and prose structures, tend not to monitor meaning while reading, fail to attend selectively to the most important information, and do not discriminate effectively between useful and harmful reading strategies (Paris & Myers, 1981; Ryan, 1981). The extent of remediation possible through strategy training is limited by basic deficits in decoding accuracy, automaticity, and memory (Perfetti & Lesgold, 1977). Yet, the likelihood that poor comprehenders can be assisted by strategy training is underscored by a variety of studies showing substantial, often striking, improvements when comprehension strategies are imposed.

Thus, unsuccessful readers have exhibited better comprehension when instructed to use mental imagery (Levin, 1973; Pressley, 1976), to paraphrase sections of text while reading (Doctorow, Wittrock, & Marks, 1978), to rate the importance of idea units before recall (Worden & Nakamura, 1982), and to use supplied cue questions before reading each section (Wong, 1979). Hence, it appears that much of poor readers' comprehension difficulty is due to an inactive, non-strategic approach to text.

In the tradition of blind-strategy training, several studies have shown that poor readers can acquire strategies which promote comprehension. Weaver (1979) showed that training in a systematic strategy for sentence construction in an anagram task could improve the reading comprehension of third-grade children. Subsequently, White, Pascarella, and Pflaum (1981) taught young learning-disabled children the same strategy. Significant transfer to a cloze test of reading comprehension was obtained for those children with adequate, initial reading ability. Fourth-grade poor readers in a study by Hansen and Pearson (1983) made significant advances relative to controls in drawing inferences from their reading when taught to make inferences about story characters before reading a story and given experience in answering inferential questions. Academically less successful fifth-graders improved their ability to recall information from a difficult passage after training in the generation of precise elaborations of implicit text (Franks, Vye, Auble, Mezynski, Perfetto, Bransford, Stein, & Littlefield, 1982).

Informed strategy-training studies have incorporated persuasive messages for the learners concerning the importance of the procedures taught for enhancing reading comprehension. Our own sensitivity to the value of such persuasion is illustrated by the increasing emphasis placed on feedback concerning the payoffs of the target strategy across a series of experiments on semantic integration (Ledger & Ryan, 1982; Ledger & Ryan, 1982, 1985; Ryan, Ledger, & Robine, 1984; Ryan, Ledger, & Weed, 1983). Recall for pictograph sentences by prereaders and beginning readers was facilitated by brief instruction in sentence orientation, motoric enaction and imagery strategies. In the early studies, we ended each training session with the statement that the target strategy would help children remember the pictograph sequences better. In the third study, children also were asked to repeat what they were supposed to do and to state why the strategy was useful. Finally, children in the fourth study graphed their progress during the training days and the link between their strategic activity and that progress specifically was emphasized. Within and across these studies, it seems clear that children perform better the more aware they are of the nature of the trained strategy and its usefulness.

Arguing that many cognitive interventions are too brief, are too removed from the classroom, and provide too little metacognitive instruction to support continued use of the target strategies, Paris and Cross (1983) report an important training study. It was conducted in eight intact classrooms (grades 3 and 5) over a 4-month period. Conditional knowledge about when and why to use reading-comprehension strategies was emphasized whereas a variety of reading skills involving evaluation, planning, and regulation were taught during weekly lessons. Approximately 90 children participated at each grade level, half of whom received the experimental treatment; the other participated in control sessions. Metacognitive instruction significantly increased both children's awareness about reading strategies and their reading comprehension. Furthermore, before and after instruction, reading awareness and comprehension were significantly correlated, highlighting again the role of metacognitive awareness in cognitive performance.

Self-monitoring is a key ingredient of the self-instructional procedure. Striking findings of generalization of a self-checking strategy were obtained for EMR children by Brown *et al.* (1979). Two groups of EMR children (MA=6 and MA=8 years) were taught to study for a relatively difficult, serial recall test until self-testing convinced them they would succeed. Self-testing is a complex executive function as it involves self-evaluation, identification of unlearned items, directed study of these, and assessment of readiness. Compared to controls, the trained children in the older age group were able to demonstrate better performance 2 weeks after training on an unprompted post-test, whereas the younger group only showed the benefits in prompted post-tests. One year later, the older trained children had not only maintained their strategic behavior but they exhibited significant advantages over controls on a generalization test of prose recall. Not only was the overall level of recall higher, but their sensitivity to the differential importance of idea units was also better.

Using self-instructional procedures, Short and Ryan (1984) taught fourth-grade poor readers to study a story for subsequent recall by asking themselves questions derived from a story grammar. We were interested in the relationship between the learned-helpless attributions and passive learning style of poor readers. Thus, one half of the strategy-trained poor readers also were given attribution retraining which focused upon the relationship between their effort with the strategy and outcomes and upon the general role of effort in the successes and failures of good as well as poor readers. The other half received no direct information regarding the link between effort and outcome. Control groups consisted of an attribution-retaining group not taught any strategy and untrained skilled readers. After three sessions, both strategy-trained groups recalled the story grammar components in an unprompted maintenance test as well as the skilled readers, thereby exihibiting a dramatic increase over the control group and over their own pretest performance. The trained groups were able to generalize the strategy, taught for a single episode, to a more complex double-episode flashback story. These trained readers also exhibited significantly greater metareading awareness than the control children. Analyses of underlining data showed significantly more activity by trained children. Even though the readers given both the self-instructional strategy training and the attributional self-statements showed consistently better performance than the other strategy group, the differences were not significant.

In an attempt to approximate better the regular classroom setting, Short, Yeates, Feagans, and McKinney (1983) extended the previous findings of Short and Ryan (1984) with poor readers to a wider range of readers (both average and skilled) and to a group setting. Skill acquisition was clearly demonstrated not only in the recall and note-taking data, but also in the quality of summaries written. Evidence for far generalization also was obtained in their superior free recall of a lengthy expository passage as compared to that of untrained readers. Taken together, both studies suggest that the provision of metacognitive skills through self-instructions appears to direct the children's attention to critical aspects of the text and appears to promote comprehension monitoring skills.

Brown and Palincsar (1982) discussed ways to induce learning from texts by means of informed, self-control training. Of particular interest here, they reported a study in which they evaluated a training package which can be considered a response-guidance form of self-instruction. Many sessions were provided for four poor comprehenders in a multiple baseline approach. Two training interventions were employed: corrective feedback in which the children read, asked for help, answered questions, and then learned why answers were wrong; and strategy training in which the experimenter and children played an interactive learning game paraphrasing main ideas of sections of text, organizing pieces of information, predicting questions, hypothesizing the content of the remainder of the passage, and commenting on any confusions in the text. Two students received corrective feedback first, and the two others received strategy training first. Asking for help and rereading were measured as concurrent indices of monitoring. The more successful intervention was the one in which students first received corrective feedback concerning answers to questions and then received strategy training. Perhaps, the use of corrective feedback prior to strategy training is a critical feature of training packages with children lacking preexisting knowledge and skills for successful completion of the task. Moreover, the corrective feedback may have evoked LD children's background knowledge about the structure of stories. Generalization to the classroom and the regular classroom teacher was assessed via spontaneous probes. Improved performance in terms of reading comprehension was observed for three of the four children. Also, long-term maintenance was obtained at a moderate level, and a further boost occurred with reintroduction of strategy training. Besides quantitative measures of strategy maintenance and generalization, qualitative measures of comprehension monitoring via question-asking behavior indicated the children made active strategic attempts to process the texts.

In their study of metacomprehension, Wong and Jones (1982) taught 60 learning-disabled students from grades 8 and 9, and 60 normally achieving Grade 6 students a 5-step, self-questioning training program in which they learned to monitor their understanding of important textual units. The five steps taught were: (1) what are you studying this passage for, (2) find the main ideas in the passage and underline them, (3) think of a question about the main idea you underlined, (4) learn the answers to your questions, and (5) always look back at your questions and answers to see how each successive question and answer provides you with more information. Training substantially increased subjects' awareness of important units of text and their reading comprehension, as well as their ability to formulate questions about target units. As the authors conclude, the fact that training did not enhance the performance of the achieving students highlights the inactive nature of the learning-disabled students' reading.

Comparing the effects of modeling with self-instructions, Malamuth (1979) trained fifth-grade poor readers to internalize a set of task-approach behaviors (i.e., task clarification, cognitive rehearsal, self-reinforcement, and coping with errors) in one systematic scanning task and two tasks involving answering comprehension questions about cartoons. Despite the small samples (16 versus 17 children), the responses to comprehension items after reading a story were significantly better for the experimental group than the modeling control group, who were provided with models of the same target components but without the explicit instruction to employ these self-management behaviors via internal speech.

Also examining the importance of experimenter-guided internalization, Fowler and Peterson (1981) focused on the coping component of the self-instructional approach. Twenty-eight children, 9–13 years of age, were identified as poor readers and as learned helpless in the sense that they did not relate failure outcomes to lack of effort. Children were assigned to one of four conditions. Children in the direct attribution-training condition experienced modeling of appropriate effort attributions for both success and failure outcomes. After rehearsing these attribution self-statements both overtly and covertly in the first session, children were prompted for their effort attributions during oral reading on scheduled success and failure trials in the next two sessions. In contrast, indirect attribution training differed in that the experimenter provided the effort attributions. Both indirect and direct forms of attribution training increased children's task persistence as compared to children in control groups. However, only the direct attribution training altered children's attributions to effort for success and failure on the Intellectual Achievement Responsibility Scale (Crandall, Katkowsky, & Crandall, 1965). The effect on persistence may have been due to the tendency to internalize spontaneously the experimenter's interpretive statements. In contrasting this study with Malamuth (1979), we are inclined to speculate that some self-instructional components are easier to internalize than others.

In summary, strategy-training studies for poor readers have been numerous, although self-instructional training has been included only in a minority. An inactive approach to reading can be readily modified by self-instructional procedures, although evidence for maintenance and generalization is still slight. Componential analysis, thus far, has focused on self-verbalization versus modeling.

WRITING

In contrast to reading comprehension, fewer strategy-training studies intended to improve the composing of text have been conducted. Bereiter and Scardamalia (1982) describe their extensive examination of the strategies and knowledge involved in composition writing. Arguing that children often fail to display their knowledge about writing, they have demonstrated important improvements in children's writing when various forms of procedural facilitation to reduce task overload are provided. Since some of their studies evaluate the effects in unprompted posttests, these can be interpreted as part of the blind-strategy-training tradition.

Bereiter and Scardamalia (1982) list several types of procedural facilitation which have proved useful in enhancing children's writing. First, procedures that mimic the executive processes of mature writers can be provided through simplified routines, which minimize the need for attention at the executive, supervisory level. For example, children taught to prepare for a composition on a particular topic—by listing all the words that might be used—showed much more varied and elaborated content in their subsequent writing. Likewise, children's writing improved when they used a deck of directive cards cueing them on what to do for each sentence. Providing children with a limited set of options from which to select can structure the open-ended writing exercise and also can obligate children to focus on matters above the level of the individual sentence. Providing labels to make tacit knowledge more accessible (e.g., for discourse structures and goals) is important so they can be worked into executive routines without cognitive overload. In another project, Scardamalia and Paris (1983) showed that intermediate-grade students taught about specific discourse structures (e.g., statement of belief, counterargument, elaboration, example, and repetition) used these structures more frequently in their compositions, but the overall quality did not improve. Hence, the training assisted them with local, but not with whole-text, planning. Although Bereiter and Scardamalia (1982) have not assessed self-instructional procedures, it is clear that their work provides a rich foundation of task analyses, identified strategies, and writing-related subtasks for researchers interested in developing such procedures. For example, the findings of the last study suggest the importance of incorporating the specific skills taught within a self-instructional package focusing on monitoring the whole text.

According to Rubin (1980), three characteristics of school-designed writing activities make learning to write a painstaking process. These include the solitary nature of the task, the primary emphasis on low-level details (i.e., spelling and punctuation) rather than the process of communication, and the presentation of writing tasks independent of reading tasks. Rubin (1980) proposes an educational device called the "story maker" based on a tree-diagramming notion which requires children to select from possible story segments those components which can best apply to a particular story theme (e.g., suspense, humor). The story maker procedure reunites the reading and writing process and makes the act of writing public. The first phase of the story maker procedure requires no writing, but rather sensitizes children to critical organizational features of stories—children select the order of events/story segments designed to match a particular theme. A second stage, the "prefab story maker" requires some writing and greater sensitivity to structural differences in texts (e.g., flashbacks). The final phase, the "story-maker maker" procedure requires children to construct their own stories, thereby relying totally on their knowledge of story structure and creativity, Children are encouraged to work in groups to enhance their sensitivity to issues of story sense and their motivation for story revision. This story maker procedure is a promising tool for focusing children's attention on communication as the purpose of writing. This procedure could be adapted readily as a self-instructional strategy.

The writing of good summaries was the target task for our only illustration of self-instructional training of writing (Day, 1981). Brown and Day (1983) had earlier identified five summarization rules used in expert summaries and described the developmental patterns for students of varying ages. Use of two rules (delete redundancy and delete trivia) was fairly universal, but use of the other three rules increased regularly with age (superordination, selection of topic sentences, and invention of topic sentences). Since the performance of junior college students on the latter rules was unexpectedly poor, this population was selected for a training study. Four types of training were provided in two sessions to both average and poor readers (enrolled in a remedial English course): general self-management, specific rule instruction, general self-management with specific rules, and rules integrated with specific self-management. It should be noted that the steps in all conditions were presented and modeled by the experimenter and that internalization by the students was not specifically trained. Analyses indicated that improvement in the use of summarization rules occurred only for students taught the specific rules, that average students improved more than the poor students, and that the rules-plus-conditions excelled only for the most difficult rule. The primary implication of this study concerns the critical importance of specific knowledge or strategies within self-management schemes.

In summary, writing is a highly active process, requiring the orchestration of a variety of subskills and goals. Moreover, it is precisely lack of self-management executive skills that appears to be the major obstacle to better writing of compositions, essays, and stories. Hence, it is remarkable that self-instructional strategy training has been assessed only once in this domain.

METHODOLOGICAL ISSUES AND FUTURE DIRECTIONS

We have argued that self-instructional procedures can be very valuable for learning-disabled children. From a theoretical viewpoint, these procedures offer the support and experiences necessary for LD children to overcome two critical problems, metacognitive deficiencies and lack of motivation. From an empirical perspective, the foregoing review of strategy training demonstrates that self-instructional procedures can be effective in modifying impulsive and inattentive behaviors and in improving academic performance in reading, writing, and arithmetic. We, therefore, propose that future research with LD children focus more heavily on evaluations of self-instructional training. Furthermore, given the relative lack of self-instructional studies in reading and especially in writing, we would recommend particular emphasis upon these two domains.

Such future studies should take into account some of the methodological issues which have arisen in earlier work. First, the efficacy of self-instructional training has not been overwhelming despite the strong theoretical arguments on its behalf. Although maintenance of training benefits has been good, generalization to slightly different tasks or to the classroom typically has been weak. Thus, additional effort needs to be devoted to enriching the training to yield strong generalization effects. Some suggestions which have been made include use of conceptual strategies rather than concrete strategies, explicit integration of specific and general strategies, specific mention of generalization as a goal, instruction on how to generalize, and specific generalization experiences within the training (Borkowski & Cavanaugh, 1979; Brown *et al.*, 1983; Brown & Palincsar, 1982; Kendall & Wilcox, 1977; Ryan, 1981; Stokes & Baer, 1977). The practical impact of training improvements must be strengthened by enhancing both maintenance and generalization.

Second, the necessity of particular components of self-instructional training must continually be assessed. Our review of empirical studies provided illustrations of componential analysis (e.g., self-instructing versus modeling, self versus external reinforcement, self versus external monitoring). However, the findings have been inconsistent and the analysis non-systematic.

The inconsistency of findings is disconcerting. Some lack of replication undoubtedly is due to small sample sizes and to the wide variation in sample characteristics. Thus, a sample may be selected to be impulsive, but the children may or may not also be learning disabled or hyperactive. However, some of the inconsistency may be related to particular variations in subjects, tasks, or situations. Thus, age and locus of control have appeared as critical determinants of training impact. The necessity of deliberate instruction in internalization may well differ across the components (i.e., content versus monitoring versus reinforcement). Task difficulty or relatedness of test to training task also affects relative component effectiveness. For example, inclusion of very specific concrete strategies enhances performance on the target task whereas inclusion of generalized strategies enhances performance on transfer tasks.

Our recommendation to invest in self-instructional training for LD children may seem to conflict with the findings that children with an external locus of control benefit less from this self-oriented training. The fact that LD children typically show inappropriate motivational cognitions does pose difficulties for planning suitable training. However, it is precisely this pervasive, dysfunctional orientation which needs to be altered in the typical LD child. Combining external reinforcement and external monitoring with self-regulation in initial stages of training is one effective way of taking into account an external orientation. Furthermore, it should be recognized that training will have to be more extensive and prolonged than for more internally oriented students.

A final methodological issue is the necessity to measure actual use of self-instructions (Ryan, 1981; Whitman *et al.*, 1983). Direct measurement of use of strategic behaviors allows one to establish the link between those behaviors and resulting performance. Self-instructional training may not show improvements at immediate post-test, maintenance, or generalization because the trained behaviors are not being used. For example, poor generalization could result from abandonment of strategy, from poor application of the strategy, or despite good application of the strategy. Training effects are diluted when some students use the trained strategy and others do not (Borkowski & Cavanaugh, 1979). It is important to know whether training leads to slight improvements for everyone or to great improvements for a minority who actually use it.

In conclusion, we believe that the cognitive behavior modification approach, especially self-instructional training, provides an excellent base upon which to develop techniques for leading LD children to behave actively and strategically in academic settings. The research challenge for the next decade is to identify the components which promote optimal maintenance and generalization for these students.

REFERENCES

Arnold, S. C., & Forehand, R. (1978). A comparison of cognitive training and response cost procedures in modifying cognitive styles of impulsive children. *Cognitive Therapy and Research, 2,* 183–187.

Barling, J. (1980). A multistage multidependent variable assessment of children's self-regulation of academic performance. *Cognitive Behavior Therapy, 2,* 43–54.

Bender, N. (1976). Self-verbalization versus tutor verbalization in modifying impulsivity. *Journal of Educational Psychology, 68,* 347–354.

Bereiter, C., & Scardamalia, M. (1982). From conversation to composition: The role of instruction in a developmental process. In R. Glaser (Ed.), *Advances in Instructional Psychology.* Vol. 2. Hillsdale, NJ: Lawrence Erlbaum Associates.

Blackman, S., & Goldstein, K. M. (1982). Cognitive styles and learning disabilities. *Journal of Learning Disabilities, 15,* 106–115.

Borkowski, J. G., & Cavanaugh, J. C. (1979). Maintenance and generalization of skills and strategies by the retarded. In N. R. Ellis (Ed.), *Handbook of Mental Deficiency: Psychological Theory and Research.* Hillsdale, NJ: Lawrence Erlbaum Associates.

Borkowski, J. G., Peck, V. A., Reid M., & Kurtz, B. E. (1983). Impulsivity and strategy transfer: Metamemory as mediator. *Child Development, 54,* 459–473.

Bornstein, P. H., & Quevillon, R. P. (1976). The effects of a self-instructional package on overactive preschool boys. *Journal of Applied Behavior Analysis, 9,* 179–188.

Brown, A. L. (1981). Metacognitive development and reading. In R. J. Spiro, B. Bruce, & W. F. Brewer (Eds.), *Theoretical issues in reading comprehension* (pp. 453–482). Hillsdale, NJ: Lawrence Erlbaum Associates.

Brown, A. L., Bransford, J., Ferrara, R. A., & Campione, J. C. (1983). Learning, remembering, and understanding. In J. Flavell & E. M. Markman (Eds.), *Carmichael's Manual of Child Psychology*. Vol. 1 (pp. 77–166). New York: John Wiley & Sons.

Brown, A. L., Campione, J., & Barclay, C. R. (1979). Training self-checking routines for estimating test readiness: Generalization from list learning to prose recall. *Child Development, 50,* 501–512.

Brown, A. L., Campione, J., & Day, J. D. (1981). Learning to learn: On training students to learn from texts. *Educational Researcher, 10*(2), 14–21.

Brown, A. L., & Day, J. D. (1983). Macrorules for summarizing texts: The development of expertise. *Journal of Verbal Learning and Verbal Behavior, 22*(1), 1–14.

Brown, A. L., & Ferrara, R. A. (in press). Diagnosing zones of proximal development: An alternative to standardized testing? In J. Wertsch (Ed.), *Culture, Communication, and Cognition: Vygotskian Perspectives*. New York: Academic Press.

Brown, A. L., & French, L. A. (1979). The zone of potential development: Implications for intelligence testing in the year 2000. *Intelligence, 3,* 253–271.

Brown, A. L., & Palincsar, A. S. (1982). Inducing strategic learning from texts by means of informed, self-control training. *Topics in Learning and Learning Disabilities, 2*(1), 1–17.

Bryant, L. E., & Budd, K. S. (1982). Self-instructional training to increase work performance in preschoolers. *Journal of Applied Behavior Analysis, 15,* 259–271.

Bugental, D. B., Whalen, C. K., & Henker, B. (1977). Causal attributions of hyperactive children and motivational assumptions of two behavior-change approaches: Evidence for an interactionist position. *Child Development, 48,* 874–884.

Burgio, L., Whitman, T., & Johnson, M. (1980). A self-instructional package for increasing attending behavior in educable mentally retarded children. *Journal of Applied Behavior Analysis, 13,* 443–459.

Butkowski, I. S., & Willows, D. M. (1980). Cognitive-motivational characteristics of children varying in reading ability: Evidence for learned helplessness in poor readers. *Journal of Educational Psychology, 72,* 408–422.

Canney, G., & Winograd, P. (1979). Schemata for reading and reading comprehension performance. Urbana: University of Illinois Center for the Study of Reading, Technical Report #120.

Crandall, V. C., Katkowsky, W., & Crandall, V. J. (1965). Children's beliefs in their own control of reinforcements in intellectual achievement situations. *Child Development, 36,* 91–109.

Cullinan, D., Epstein, M. H., & Silver, L. (1977). Modification of impulsive tempo in learning disabled pupils. *Journal of Abnormal Child Psychology, 5,* 437–444.

Day, J. D. (1981). Training summarization skills: A comparison of training methods. Paper presented at the Biennial Meeting of the Society for Research on Child Development, Boston.

Day, J. D. (1983). The zone of proximal development. In M. Pressley & J. Levin (Eds.), *Cognitive Strategy Research: Psychological Foundations*. New York: Springer-Verlag.

Doctorow, M., Wittrock, M. C. & Marks, C. (1978). Generative processes in reading comprehension. *Journal of Educational Psychology, 70,* 109–118.

Douglas, L. C. (1981). Metamemory in learning-disabled children: A clue to memory deficiencies. Paper presented to the Society for Research on Child Development, Boston.

Douglas, V., Parry, P., Marton, P., & Garson, C. (1976). Assessment of a cognitive training program for hyperactive children. *Journal of Abnormal Psychology, 4,* 389–410.

Downing, J. (1979). *Reading and reasoning*. New York: Springer-Verlag.

Edgar, R., & Clement, P. (1980). Teacher-controlled and self-controlled reinforcement with underachieving Black children. *Cognitive Behavior Therapy, 2,* 33–56.

Egeland, B. (1974). Training impulsive children in the use of more efficient scanning strategies. *Child Development, 45,* 165–171.

Flavell, J. H. (1981). Cognitive monitoring. In W. P. Dickson (Ed.). *Children's Oral Communication Skills.* New York: Academic Press.

Fowler, J. W., & Peterson, P. L. (1981). Increasing reading persistence and altering attributional style of learned helpless students. *Journal of Educational Psychology, 73,* 251–260.

Franks, J. J., Vye, N. J., Auble, P. M., Mezynski, K. J., Perfetto, G. A., Bransford, J. D., Stein, B. S., & Littlefield, J. (1982). Learning from explicit versus implicit texts. *Journal of Experimental Psychology: General, 111,* 414–422.

Friedling, C., & O'Leary, S. G. (1979). Effects of self-instructional training on second- and third-grade hyperactive children: A failure to replicate. *Journal of Applied Behavior Analysis, 12,* 211–219.

Grimm, J., Bijou, S., & Parson, J. (1973). A problem-solving model for teaching remedial arithmetic to handicapped young children. *Journal of Abnormal Child Psychology, 7,* 26–39.

Hall, L. K., & Day, J. D. (1982). The zone of proximal development as a method of differentiating mentally retarded, learning-disabled and normally achieving children. Paper presented at the Annual Meeting of the American Educational Research Association, New York.

Hallahan, D. P., & Kneedler, R. D. (1979). Strategy deficits in the information processing of learning-disabled children. Charlottesville, VA: University of Virginia Learning Disabilities Research Institute, Technical Report, #6.

Hallahan, D. P., Kneedler, R. D., & Lloyd, J. W. (1983). Cognitive behavior modification techniques for learning-disabled children: In J. D. McKinney & L. Feagans (Eds.). *Current topics in learning disabilities* Vol. 1. New York: Ablex Publishing.

Hansen, J., & Pearson, P. D. (1983). An instructional study: Improving the inferential comprehension of good and poor fourth-grade readers. *Journal of Educational Psychology, 75,* 821–829.

Harter, S. (1982). A developmental perspective on some parameters of self-regulation in children. In P. Karoly & F. H. Kanfer (Eds.). *Self-Management and behavior change: From theory to practice.* New York: Pergamon Press.

Henker, B., Whalen, C. K., & Hinshaw, S. P. (1980). The attributional contexts of cognitive intervention strategies. *Exceptional Education Quarterly, 1,* 17–30.

Johnston, M. B. (1983). *Self-instruction and children's math problem solving: A study of training, maintenance, and generalization.* Unpublished doctoral dissertation. Notre Dame, IN: University of Notre Dame.

Johnston, M. B., Whitman, T. L., & Johnson, M. (1980). Teaching addition and subtraction to mentally retarded children: A self-instructional program. *Applied Research in Mental Retardation, 1,* 141–160.

Kendall, P. C., & Wilcox, L. E. (1980). Cognitive behavioral treatment for impulsivity: Concrete versus conceptual training in non-self-controlled problem children. *Journal of Consulting & Clinical Psychology, 48,* 80–91.

Kennedy, B. A., & Miller, D. J. (1976). Persistent use of verbal rehearsal as a function of information about its value. *Child Development, 47,* 566–569.

Ledger, G. W., & Ryan, E. B. (1982). The effects of semantic integration training on recall for pictograph sentences. *Journal of Experimental Child Psychology, 33,* 39–54.

Ledger, G. W., & Ryan, E. B. (1985). Effects of enaction, imagery, and sentence training on recall for pictograph sentences. *Journal of Experimental Child Psychology, 39,* 531–545.

Leon, J. A., & Pepe, H. J. (1983). Self-instructional training: Cognitive behavior modification for remediating arithmetic deficits. *Exceptional Children, 50*(1), 54–61.

Lepper, M. R. (1981). Intrinsic and extrinsic motivation in children: Detrimental effects of superfluous social controls. In W. A. Collins (Ed.), *Aspects of the development of competence. Minnesota symposium on child psychology.* Vol. 14. Hillsdale, NJ: Lawrence Erlbaum Associates.

Levin, J. R. (1973). Inducing comprehension in poor readers: A test of a recent model. *Journal of Educational Psychology, 65,* 10–24.

Lloyd, J. (1980). Academic instruction and cognitive behavior modification: The need for attack strategy training. *Exceptional Education Quarterly, 1,* 53–64.

Lloyd, J., Hallahan, D. P., & Kauffman, J. M. (1980). Learning disabilities: Selected topics. In L. Mann & D. Sabatino (Eds.), *The Fourth Review of Special Education.* New York: Grune & Stratton.

Lodico, M. G., Ghatala, E. S., Levin, J. R., Pressley, M., & Bell, J. A. (1983). The effects of strategy-monitoring training on children's selection of effective memory strategies. *Journal of Experimental Child Psychology, 35,* 263–277.

Lovitt, T. C., & Curtis, K. A. (1968). Effects of manipulating antecedent events on math response rate. *Journal of Applied Behavior Analysis, 1,* 329–333.

Malamuth, Z. N. (1979). Self-management training for children with reading problems: Effects on reading performance and sustained attention. *Cognitive Therapy and Research, 3,* 279–289.

Meichenbaum, D. (1976). Cognitive factors as determinants of learning disabilities: A cognitive functional approach. In R. Knights & D. Bakker (Eds.), *The neuropsychology of learning disorders: Theoretical approaches* (pp. 423–442). Baltimore: University Park Press.

Meichenbaum, D., & Goodman, J. (1971). Training impulsive children to talk to themselves: A means of developing self-control. *Journal of Abnormal Psychology, 77,* 115–126.

Nelson, W. J., Jr., & Birkimer, J. C. (1978). Role of self-instructions and self-reinforcement in the modification of impulsivity. *Journal of Consulting & Clinical Psychology, 46,* 183.

Paris, S. G., & Cross, D. R. (1983). Ordinary learning: Pragmatic connections among children's beliefs, motives, and actions. In J. Bisanz, G. Bisanz, & R. Kail (Eds.). *Learning in Children* (pp. 137–169). New York: Springer-Verlag.

Paris, S. G., & Myers, M. (1981). Comprehension monitoring, memory, and study strategies of good and poor readers. *Journal of Reading Behavior, 13,* 5–22.

Pearl, R., Bryan, T., & Donahue, M. (1980). Learning disabled children's attributions for success and failure. *Learning Disabilities Quarterly, 3,* 3–9.

Perfetti, C. A., & Lesgold, A. M. (1977). Discourse comprehension and sources of individual differences. In M. A. Just & P. A. Carpenter (Eds.). *Cognitive Processes in Comprehension.* Hillsdale, NJ: Lawrence Erlbaum Associates.

Pressley, G. M. (1976) Mental imagery helps 8-year-olds remember what they read. *Journal of Educational Psychology, 68,* 355–359.

Pressley, M. (1982). Elaboration and memory development. *Child Development, 53,* 296–309.

Ringel, B. A., & Springer, C. J. (1980). On knowing how well one is remembering: The persistence of strategy use during transfer. *Journal of Experimental Child Psychology, 29,* 322–333.

Rubin, A. (1980). Making stories, making sense. Reading Education Report #14. Urbana: University of Illinois Center for the Study of Reading.

Ryan, E. B. (1981). Identifying and remediating failures in reading comprehension: Toward an instructional approach for poor comprehenders. In G. E. MacKinnon & T. G. Waller (Eds.). *Advances in Reading Research.* Vol. 3 (pp. 224–262.) New York: Academic Press.

Ryan, E. B., Ledger, G. W., & Robine, D. M. (1984). Effects of semantic integration training on the recall for pictograph sentences by kindergarten and first grade children. *Journal of Educational Psychology, 76,* 371–382.

Ryan, E. B., Ledger, G. W., & Weed, K. A. (1983). Semantic integration of pictograph sentences through imagery. Paper presented to the American Educational Research Association, Montreal.

Scardamalia, M., & Paris, P. (1983). The development of explicit discourse knowledge and its function in text representation and planning. Unpublished manuscript. Toronto: York University.

Schleser, R. S., Meyers, A. W., & Cohen, R. (1981). Generalization of self-instructions: Effects of general versus specific content, active rehearsal, and cognitive level. *Child Development, 52,* 335–340.

Schneider, W. (1985). Developmental trends in the metamemory-memory behavior relationship: An integrative review. In D. Forrest-Pressley, G. E. MacKinnon, & T. G. Waller (Eds.). *Metacognition, cognition, and human performance.* New York: Academic Press.

Short, E. J. (1981). *A self-instructional approach to remediating the use of schematic knowledge, causal attributions, and task persistence of less-skilled readers.* Unpublished doctoral dissertation. Notre Dame, IN: University of Notre Dame.

Short, E. J., & Ryan, E. B. (1984). Metacognitive differences between skilled and less skilled readers: Remediating deficits through story grammar and attribution training. *Journal of Educational Psychology, 76,* 225–235.

Short, E. J., Yeates, K. O., Feagans, L., & McKinney, J. D. (1983). The effects of story grammar strategy training on comprehension monitoring. Unpublished manuscript. Chapel Hill, NC: University of North Carolina.

Steele, K., & Barling, J. (1982). Self-instructions and learning disabilities: Maintenance, generalization, and subject characteristics. *Journal of General Psychology, 106,* 141–154.

Stokes, T. F., & Baer, D. M. (1977). An implicit technology of generalization. *Journal of Applied Behavior Analysis, 10,* 349–367.

Torgesen, J. K. (1977). Memorization processes in reading-disabled children. *Journal of Educational Psychology, 69,* 571–578.

Torgesen, J. K. (1982). The learning-disabled child as an inactive learner: Educational implications. *Topics in Learning and Learning Disabilities, 2*(1), 45–52.

Varni, J. W., & Henker, B. (1979). A self-regulation approach to the treatment of three hyperactive boys. *Child Behavior Therapy, 1,* 171–192.

Vellutino, F. R. (1979). *Dyslexia: Theory and research.* Cambridge: MA: MIT Press.

Vygotsky, L. S. (1978). *Mind in society: The development of higher psychological processes.* Cambridge, MA: Harvard University Press.

Weaver, P. A. (1979). Improving reading comprehension: Effects of sentence organization instruction. *Reading Research Quarterly, 15,* 129–146.

White, C. V., Pascarella, E. T., & Pflaum, S. W. (1981). Effects of training in sentence construction on the comprehension of learning-disabled children. *Journal of Educational Psychology, 73,* 697–704.

Whitman, T. L., Burgio, L., & Johnston, M. B. (1983). Cognitive behavioral interventions with mentally retarded children. In A. Meyers & W. E. Craighead (Eds.). *Cognitive Behavior Therapy for Children.* New York: Plenum Press.

Whitman, T. L., & Johnston, M. B. (1983). Teaching addition and subtraction with regrouping to educable mentally retarded children: A group self-instructional training program. *Behavior Therapy, 14,* 127–143.

Wiens, J. W. (1983). Metacognition and the adolescent passive learner. *Journal of Learning Disabilities, 16,* 144–149.

Wong, B. Y. L. (1979). Increasing retention of main ideas through questioning strategies. *Learning Disabilities Quarterly, 2,* 42–47.

Wong, B. Y. L., & Jones, W. (1982). Increasing metacomprehension in learning-disabled and normally achieving students through self-questioning training. *Learning Disabilities Quarterly, 5,* 228–240.

Worden, P. E., & Nakamura, G. V. (1982). Story comprehension and recall in learning-disabled versus normal college students. *Journal of Educational Psychology, 74,* 633–641.

Wozniak, R. (1975). Psychology and education of the learning disabled child in the Soviet Union. In W. M. Cruikshank & D. P. Hallahan (Eds.). *Perceptual and learning disabilities in children.* Syracuse: Syracuse University Press.

13

The Role of Phonemic Analysis in Reading

JOANNA P. WILLIAMS

INTRODUCTION

It has been 20 years since the appearance of the English translation of the initial Russian studies on phonemic analysis training (Elkonin, 1963; Zhurova, 1963). These straightforward investigations, reported in sparse detail, proposed that such training precede reading instruction. This work has led to 2 decades of intense research activity, which continues to this day.

Many studies, both correlational and experimental, have been done. In addition, several instructional programs that include phonemic analysis tasks have been developed. As a result of this work, new and interesting questions are now being addressed, and this research should lead to a better understanding of phoneme analysis and of useful techniques for instruction. The purpose of this essay is to review the research to date and to examine the issue as it is seen now.

It should be noted that phonemic analysis and phonemic blending have been called skills of "linguistic awareness" (Mattingly, 1972), "phonemic awareness" (Golinkoff, 1978), and "linguistic insight" (Ehri, 1979), on the grounds that they involve an awareness of the abstract units of which speech is composed. More recently, the term "phonemic knowledge" has begun to appear (e.g., Perfetti, Beck, & Hughes, 1981). Many of these terms are used in this paper. The terms *awareness, insight, knowledge,* and *skills* do not imply any differences in the actual phonemic

399

Psychological and Educational
Perspectives on Learning Disabilities

tasks administered; where possible, I have tried to be specific in describing the experimental tasks.

Why should these skills be taught? The orthography of the English language is based on the alphabetic principle. That is, there is a correspondence between letters and sounds. English orthography is very complex, so that the sounds—phonemes—are not represented in any simple one-to-one way by letters. Rather, the 26 letters of the English alphabet, singly and in combination, map on to the language's 40-odd phonemes with considerable complexity. Some letters and letter combinations represent more than one phoneme, and some individual phonemes correspond to more than one letter or letter cluster.

The rationale for recommending that children learn how to segment words into phonemes is quite understandable from the perspective of a decoding approach to instruction. If the central task of the beginning reader is seen as learning to identify and use the correspondences between letter and sound, then phonemic analysis and blending are two fundamental component skills. To identify the correspondences, it is necessary to be able to isolate the units, both in orthography and in the sound stream, such that the appropriate mappings between orthography and sound can be made. Perhaps, from the perspective of a whole-word approach to instruction, these phonemic skills matter less. Yet most children who have been taught to read by a nondecoding method do pick up information about correspondences inductively, on their own. Presumably, these children have been able without direct instruction to isolate orthography and sound units and to note their correspondences.

THE BEGINNINGS OF INTEREST IN
AUDITORY SKILLS

In the 1950s, phonemic analysis, if it had been mentioned at all, would probably have been dubbed an "auditory skill," and as such, would have been of little interest. Although it is obvious that the reading task contains both visual and auditory components, for many years, there was little interest in its auditory aspects. Although Vernon (1957) in her classic work, *Backwardness in Reading,* pointed out the need for both visual and auditory skills in reading, most citations of this work mention only the visual modality.

During the 1950s and 1960s, difficulties inherent in the visual differentiation and identification of letters were emphasized in analyses of children's problems in beginning reading. Much research was done to demonstrate the relationship between visual skills and reading achievement (e.g., Goins, 1958), and instructional materials and techniques were developed that focused heavily on fostering children's visual/perceptual abilities (e.g., Frostig & Horne, 1964). However, it has been acknowledged in the last few years (Bateman, 1979; Williams, 1977) that such instructional programs do not do the job that they were intended to do; that is, they do not lead to better reading.

Faced with disillusionment about the benefits of visual training, those interested in reading instruction turned their interest to the auditory modality. This coincided with the resurgence of interest in the study of language that followed Chomsky's revolutionary work (1957) in linguisitics. A view of reading as a "language skill" came to predominate (Vellutino, 1977). This focus on language may be the reason why work on the auditory aspects of reading seems, at least so far, not to have gone off on a useless tangent as did the older work on visual aspects.

Early studies led to the general conclusion that auditory skills were indeed important to reading, but, as Routh and Fox (1984) point out, this work did not focus specifically on phoneme analysis. Relationships between a variety of auditory tasks and either reading readiness or first- and second-grade reading achievement were demonstrated (e.g., Dykstra, 1966; Harrington & Durrell, 1955; Monroe, 1932). Some studies focused specifically on blending. Chall, Roswell, and Blumenthal (1963), for example, found that blending ability as assessed in the first grade was highly related to reading achievement. Balmuth (1972) found that blending ability on a task involving nonsense syllables was related to silent-reading achievement.

The opinion held by most experts today is that the problem of the poor reader is not a general auditory one, but rather one of language perception. One recent study that supports this position was done by Brady, Shakweiler, and Mann (in press). They compared poor and good readers on two auditory perception tasks, one involving words, the other nonspeech environmental sounds. Each task was presented under both favorable and unfavorable signal-to-noise ratios. They found that poor readers made more errors when listening to speech in noise, but there were no differences in the other three conditions.

A FOCUS ON PHONEMIC ANALYSIS

Two 1963 publications by Russian psychologists represent the earliest work on the topic of phonemic analysis. Zhurova (1963) found that many children between the ages of 3 and 6 could not isolate the first phoneme of simple words, and, moreover, that attempts to teach this skill often were not successful. She concluded that such children would have difficulty in learning to read.

Elkonin (1963) developed a method to train children to isolate and identify individual phonemes within words. This method included a visual model to make the task of phoneme analysis more concrete. The model involved diagrams, in which a series of connected squares represented a word, each square represented a phoneme, and discs were used to count off the phonemes. The discs were gradually replaced during the course of instruction with the appropriate letters. Elkonin (1973) reported that prereaders who were taught with this method mastered phonemic analysis quickly, and that they also showed improvement "in various aspects of learning literacy" (p. 219).

Starting about 1970, there was a rash of work on phonemic analysis. It was established early that proficiency in the analysis of spoken language shows a clear developmental progression and that it is related to reading. Calfee, Lindamood, & Lindamood (1973) developed a test that required the manipulation of phonemes and found that performance improved with age and that the test was a good predictor of reading achievement. Liberman, Shankweiler, Fischer, and Carter (1974) designed a task that involved tapping out the number of speech segments contained in one- to three-syllable words. Young children did not show great proficiency on this task, but they improved from preschool to kindergarten and from kindergarten to first grade. Performance was better on syllable segmentation tasks than on phoneme segmentation tasks. The first-graders' scores on the segmentation task were related to their reading achievement in the second grade. Helfgott (1976) found a significant correlation between kindergarteners' scores on a similar segmentation task and their reading achievement 1 year later, in first grade.

Using a different task, which involved the deletion of sound segments, both syllables and phonemes (e.g., "say *mat* without the *m*"), Rosner and Simon (1971) found significant correlations between segmentation ability and performance on the language arts subtests of the Stanford Achievement Test at all grade levels from kindergarten to the sixth grade. The correlations remained significant when IQ was controlled, except at the sixth-grade level.

Whereas most studies have shown that young children are quite poor at phoneme analysis, Fox and Routh (1975) demonstrated that even 3-year-olds were able to do some phoneme analysis if the task was presented very simply and if appropriate guidance was given. Performance on both word and syllable segmenting reached a ceiling level at age 4 years; performance on phonemic segmenting did not reach ceiling until age 6. These investigators also found a significant correlation between phonemic segmenting ability and word recognition as measured by the Peabody Individual Achievement Test.

An explanation for the fact that children find phoneme analysis difficult is offered by research conducted by Liberman, Cooper, Shankweiler, and Studdert-Kennedy (1967). These investigators showed that the acoustic characteristics of a phoneme are modified by the other phonemes in a word or syllable and that the cues for recognizing the phonemes in a word occur simultaneously as well as sequentially. Thus, the component sounds of a word as we sound it out (e.g., "c-a-t") are not actually segments of the spoken word; blending is an abstraction.

Phoneme skills also have been shown to be correlated with responsiveness to instruction. Fox and Routh (1976) found that 4-year-olds who were proficient at phoneme analysis were better than their nonproficient peers at a laboratory simulation of reading training (a paired-associates task, with letterlike forms as stimulus materials and phonemes as responses). Only the proficient subjects profited from phonic-blend-training. These findings are difficult to interpret, however, because IQ was not controlled. Goldstein (1976) administered a test of both phoneme analysis and phoneme synthesis to 4-year-olds who then were given several weeks of reading instruction. With IQ controlled, scores on this test predicted performance after instruction on tests of reading single words and of reading words in a story context. Other studies that have demonstrated correlations between segmenting skill and reading achievement, often assessed by standardized reading tests (Firth, 1972; Jusczyk, 1977; Zifcak, 1976).

It is important to note that children may not demonstrate phonemic segmentation skills even though they do demonstrate other related skills. Liberman (1973) found that some of her reading-disabled subjects who could not segment were able to discriminate between phonemes and to provide the correct phonemes for individual letters. Wallach, Wallach, Dozier, and Kaplan (1977) also showed that many nonreading kindergartners could discriminate between phonemes but that few of these children could segment.

PHONEMIC ANALYSIS TRAINING

Given that there is substantial correlation between phonemic skill and success in reading, what is the evidence that training in these skills will lead to improvement in reading? The Russian work by Elkonin (1963,

1973), mentioned above, provided some preliminary data that suggested that such training would indeed help reading.

As would be expected, the extensive research activity of the 1970s was accompanied by attempts to develop instructional programs that incorporated training on phonemic skills. Five instructional programs have appeared to date. The first was that of Lindamood and Lindamood (1969). A distinctive feature of this program was its emphasis on the labeling of articulatory movements of the mouth (e.g., *p* is a lip-popper). A second program, developed by Rosner (1971; Rosner & Simon, 1971), focused on the skills of adding, omitting, substituting, and rearranging phonemes. Four- and 5-year-olds who were trained with this program over the course of several months improved in their ability to handle initial phonemes in words. In another study, Rosner (1974) instructed nonreading first-graders for 14 weeks; control children received no instruction. The trained group significantly outperformed the untrained group. Moreover, there was some evidence of transfer: The experimental group was able to read a significantly greater number of words that had not been used in training as well as words from the training sequence.

Although the above-mentioned programs focused rather specifically on phonemic skills, the following three are more comprehensive programs into which phonemic training has been incorporated. Venezky's Pre-Reading Skills program (1976) was designed for low-ability kindergarten children. The program consisted of five units, three of which taught visual readiness skills and two, auditory. The first auditory unit taught phoneme matching: individual phonemes were presented, outside of any word context. The children were trained to associate each sound with a picture of an object that produces that sound. The second auditory unit taught phoneme blending. Kindergartners were successful at both learning and retaining the picture-sound associations and at blending phonemes after going through the program.

Wallach and Wallach (1976) designed a beginning reading program that focused heavily on phonemic-analysis training, to be administered in a one-to-one tutorial setting. Low-readiness first-graders who received this program performed significantly better than control subjects on several reading measures, including standardized tests and report-card grades.

Williams (1979) developed a decoding program, "The ABD's of Reading," specifically for learning-disabled children, to be used as a supplement to their regular classroom instruction. This program taught explicitly both phoneme analysis and phoneme blending. Children between the ages of 7 and 12 in special classrooms for the learning-disabled in

New York City improved in phoneme skills and in decoding skill after using the program.

In connection with an extensive evaluation of this program, Williams (1980) sought to determine whether the instruction produced transfer to unlearned material as well as improvement in performance on content that had been used in training. Even though this experiment was based on actual classroom instruction, it was possible to monitor the training in such a way as to ensure that there was no direct training on the content to be used in assessing transfer. The results of this experiment indicated that the children were able to decode novel trigrams, both familiar words and nonsense combinations, after instruction.

Whenever a particular group of children who were being trained with the instructional materials reached a particular point in the program, a short test was administered. At the same time that each of these groups was tested, a control (nontrained) group was randomly chosen, and the children in it were given the same test. There were two such testing points in the program, one when the children had completed phoneme analysis, blending, and decoding training on trigrams composed of a total of 9 letters, and the other after the children had completed such training on trigrams composed of 15 letters.

On both tests, there was a similar pattern of results. The experimental group performed substantially better than the control group did on unfamiliar trigrams (made up of letters that had been used in training but which had never been presented in that combination) as well as on familiar trigrams (which *had* been used in training). In addition, the experimental group performed almost as well on nonsense trigrams as on real-word trigrams, whereas the control group performed much better on real words. This latter finding suggested that the control subjects' performance was more likely to be based on their ability to read sight words than on their decoding skills.

The fact that instructional programs that incorporate phonemic training have been demonstrated to be effective suggests strongly that phonemic training makes reading instruction more effective. But this fact does not constitute proof, of course, for it is impossible to evaluate the effects of the phonemic training components apart from the effects of all of the other components of the program. Thus, this work, although promising, remains inconclusive; more focused research is necessary.

Moreover, the phonemic training tasks used in these programs were very different from one another. Indeed, this is also true for the tasks used in the research studies on the topic. Lewkowicz (1980) did an intensive analysis of phonemic tasks used in both research and instructional development. She argued that until the similarities and differences among tasks are known, and until it is understood specifically which tasks are related to reading and in what way, it will not be possible to determine which of them are, in fact, useful in instruction. Moreover, it may be that certain tasks are useful only in the early stages of instruction and other tasks only in the later stages.

Lewkowicz (1980) listed ten tasks that have been used to teach or to test phonemic skills: (1) sound-to-word matching, (2) word-to-word matching, (3) recognition of rhyme, (4) pronunciation of an isolated phoneme in a word, (5) phonemic segmentation (articulating separately all sounds in a word, in the correct order), (6) counting phonemes, (7) blending, (8) deletion of a phoneme from a word, (9) specifying which phoneme has been deleted, and (1) phoneme substitution. Some of these tasks would seem to be more related to reading than others (or to each other); however, the evidence that has appeared is difficult to evaluate in this regard because of the differences in age of subjects, type of reading test, and statistical method.

Lewkowicz's (1980) logical analyses of these tasks led her to conclude that blending and segmentation are the basic phonemic tasks, and that it is these two tasks that belong in an instructional program. One additional task, isolation of the initial phoneme of a word, should also be useful in that it is a helpful preliminary activity in segmentation. In contrast, most of the other tasks on the list are more complicated and probably more difficult than segmentation, and thus, she concluded, will probably not be helpful in a training program.

THE RELATIONSHIP BETWEEN PHONEMIC ANALYSIS AND INSTRUCTIONAL METHODS

Most of the work discussed so far has, explicitly or implicitly, implicated a decoding approach to reading instruction. Goldstein (1976), for example, used the Fuller (1974) ball-stick-bird method, which can be considered a kind of decoding approach; and Williams's (1979) program was clearly a decoding approach. Are phonemic skills related in the same way to different types of reading instruction? It would seem, on the face of it, that phonemic ability would not be as good a predictor of success in nondecoding-oriented instruction and that the value of phonemic training would depend on the general characteristics of the reading instruction into which it was incorporated.

Baron and Treiman (1980; see also Treiman and Baron, 1981) have addressed this question in a laboratory setting. These investigators classified children according to Baron's (1979) distinction between "Phoenician-style" readers, that is, children who can use the rules that relate spellings to sounds, and "Chinese-style" readers, children who cannot do so and who, therefore, use word-specific associations (memorized associations between individual, whole printed words and their pronunciations). Baron and Treiman (1980) found that phonemic analysis ability was correlated more highly with the ability to use sound-spelling rules than with the ability to use word-specific associations. This study suggested that the value of phonemic training would be greater when the reading instruction was decoding-oriented.

A further study (Treiman and Baron, 1983) attempted to demonstrate experimentally that phonemic analysis training helps children take advantage of spelling-sound rules in learning to read. Treiman and Baron (1983) showed that children are more likely to transfer spelling-sound rules when reading words whose spoken forms they had been trained to analyze than when reading words whose spoken forms thay had not been trained to analyze. In this study, the experimental manipulations were carried out within subjects. The first part of training consisted of extensive segmentation and blending training on certain spoken syllables, plus repetition of but no analysis of other spoken syllables. Then there was a reading task: Children were taught to read four items that corresponded to the spoken syllables used in the first part of training. For example, the items read would be H, EM, HEM, and LIG. HEM is related to the two smaller items on the list (H and EM), so that if the child has been given phonemic analysis training, the pronunciation of HEM can be deduced from the two small items. This is not true of LIG. (Similar control items, related and unrelated, were also used in the reading task.) It was predicted that transfer of spelling-sound correspondences learned from the two small items would speed the learning of the related item but would be of no help with the unrelated item.

Kindergartners did make fewer errors on the related item than on the unrelated item in the analysis condition; this was not true in the control condition. Treiman and Baron (1983) interpreted their data as indicating a causal link between phoneme analysis training and the learning of spelling-sound rules; they concluded that phonemic analysis training can, in fact, promote reading skill, because children who can explicitly analyze spoken words into their phonemic components are able to learn the correspondences between phoneme units and letter units.

This conclusion must remain tentative, however, because the children were not given an equivalent amount of additional training in segmenting and blending parts of LIG to match the additional training that occurred on H and EM during the reading task. That is, the better performance on HEM might have been due to the extra oral segmentation and blending practice that the child received (on H and EM) and not to the fact that there was sound-symbol training on H and EM.

DOES READING IMPROVE PHONEMIC SKILL?

Our focus up to this point has been on the hypothesis that phonemic ability leads to success in reading. The findings to date, in fact, are persuasive in indicating that phonemic skills do enhance the acquisition of reading skill. A strong hypothesis based on such findings would be that the ability to analyze phonemes is a prerequisite of reading; that is, that a child must have that ability in order to learn to read. Mattingly (1972), for example, proposes that structural knowledge of speech is a prerequisite of reading readiness and that this structural knowledge matures between the ages of 5 and 7. An alternative interpretation is simply that phonemic analysis ability facilitates reading; that is, it is not necessary to have this ability in order to learn to read but this ability does allow children to make faster and easier progress in learning to read.

But there may also be other relationships between these two variables. The causality may also go the other way: It may be that linguistic segmentation is a consequent, as well as an antecedent, of learning to read. (See Backman, 1983; Ehri, 1979, for discussions of these alternatives.)

Ehri (1983) is a major proponent of the idea that phonemic ability is a consequent of reading instruction. She claims (e.g., Ehri, 1983) that learning to read aids in the development of awareness of the nature of spoken language. When a child learns to read and spell, she argues, a visual representational system for speech (i.e., print) is acquired. The acquisition of this system, since it is built onto the child's knowledge of spoken language, may lead to modifications in his/her competencies in speech. Moreover, although print maps speech systematically at both the lexical and the phonetic levels, the effects of print probably are helpful especially at the phonetic level because of the problems inherent in segmenting the speech stream (see the discussion of the Liberman *et al.*, 1967, findings above).

Ehri (1975) concluded that readers (first-graders) had a better understanding of the constituents of speech than did pre-readers (kindergartners) on the basis of findings showing that the readers had a more sophisticated understanding of the concept of "word," were more proficient at picking out a word that differentiated two similar sentences, and were also more proficient at certain phonemic tasks, for example, dividing sentences into words and words into syllables. This correlational evidence is similar to that reported by other investigators but interpreted in a different way.

Backman (1983) compared the performance on a phoneme deletion task of a group of early readers, that is, kindergartners who surpassed a 1.5 grade-level criterion on the word-identification subtest of the Woodcock Reading Mastery Test (Woodcock, 1973), with that of a group of nonreading kindergartners: The early readers scored significantly higher. In fact, they scored as well as did a group of second-graders who had similar Woodcock (1973) scores. (It should be noted that there were no differences among the three groups of subjects in the ability to tap out the number of phonemes in a word. This fact corroborates the suggestion of Lewkowicz [1980] that there be an intensive analysis and comparison of the several phonemic tasks that have been used in research.)

Ehri and Wilce (1979) have provided a different type of evidence. In this study, children were asked to identify the number of phonemes in words and nonsense syllables. Some of them used their knowledge of spelling to help them in the task. But this strategy sometimes led to incorrect answers. For example, children might claim that "boat" had four phonemes, because they counted the silent *a*; nonsense syllables containing a long vowel (which might be spelled with a silent *e*) were also sources of this kind of error. Thus, the authors argued, knowledge of the written language affects the way spoken language is perceived.

A study by Morais, Cary, Alegria, and Bertelson (1979) provided additional evidence in support of this point of view. Illiterate adults were found not to be able to delete and add phonemes to nonsense words, a task that is extremely simple for literate adults. This finding suggested that the awareness of the phoneme as a linguistic unit is not a necessary concomitant of cognitive development; rather, probably, it is a function of learning to read.

If phonemic ability does emerge during reading acquisition, how does it happen? Would the specific nature of the method of instruction help determine the development of this ability? Alegria, Pignot and Morais (1982) administered a segmentation test to first-graders who had 4 months of either phonics instruction or whole-word instruction. The task required the child to reverse two syllables (say *dira* when you hear *radis*—the subjects were French-speaking) or two phonemes (say *so* when you hear *os*) in an utterance. Whereas there were no differences between the two groups on syllable reversal, the phonics-taught group was better on phoneme reversal. Also, performance on phonemic reversal was correlated with the teacher's evaluation of the child's reading level only in the phonics-trained group (although, for syllable reversal, this correlation was significant for both instructional groups). These results thus support Ehri's (1983) notion that experience with print leads to awareness of phonemic relationships in speech; they also indicate that the development of phonemic skill does depend on the particular way in which one is taught to read.

The hypothesis that phonemic skills are a consequence of reading instruction is certainly not incompatible with the hypothesis that phonemic skills help in the acquisition of reading skill. Indeed, the evidence suggests that both hypotheses are correct and that there is a reciprocal relation between phonemic ability and reading instruction. Both Ehri (1979) and Liberman, Liberman, Mattingly, and Shankweiler (1980) have discussed this as a reasonable conclusion based on the data to date.

Perfetti, Beck and Hughes (1981) agree, but they claim that the phonemic knowledge that leads to reading acquisition is not exactly the same phonemic knowledge that learning to read produces. On the basis of a longitudinal study over the course of an entire first-grade year, which they analyzed in terms of time-lag correlations, Perfetti *et al.* concluded that phoneme synthesis (blending) is necessary for reading. (See also Scherzer and Goldstein, 1982.) On the other hand, other phonemic tasks, such as identifying the number of phonemes in a word or deleting a phoneme from a word, have different information-processing characteristics, and performance on such analytic tasks is enhanced by reading instruction. Thus, speech knowledge and print knowledge interact as they emerge, and each enhances the development of the other.

SHOULD LETTERS BE USED IN PHONEMIC TRAINING?

If, in fact, possession of a visual representational system does enhance knowledge of spoken language, then, presumably, the use of letters of the alphabet should aid in the acquisition of phonemic analysis skill. It seems reasonable that *some* form of visual representation, certainly, would be of help in instruction. Elkonin's (1963) original training procedure, described above, used discs as visual representations of phonemes; in the initial part of training, the discs were unmarked. This instructional technique has been borrowed by others (e.g., Williams, 1979).

Lewkowicz and Low (1979) found that learning to do phoneme analysis is easier if such visual markers—in the form of blank counters—are provided than if no visual markers are provided. But Ehri's (1983) work suggests that letters would be more effective as phoneme representations than unmarked tokens. In an attempt to answer this question, Hohn and Ehri (1983) trained kindergarten children to segment two- and three-phoneme blends. Training with letters and training with tokens were comparable in terms of trials to criterion, but an error analysis indicated that children who had been given letters were better able to break blends apart into single phonemes. On the post-test, both training groups analyzed transfer (untrained) blends equally well, better than did a no-training control. However, the letter-training group was better on the blends on which they had been trained. The authors interpreted their data as supporting the idea that training incorporating letters is more advantageous. Haddock (1976) also found that it was more effective to train children to blend using an auditory-visual approach (with letters as well as sounds), than with an auditory-only approach.

Consensus has not been reached on this point, however. Other data, in some ways very similar to Hohn and Ehri's (1983), have been used to support just the opposite conclusion. For example, Marsh and Mineo (1977) trained preschool children to recognize isolated phonemes presented in word contexts. When there was a redundant visual cue (an uppercase grapheme), performance was better in training but was no better in transfer. On the basis of these findings, Marsh and Mineo (1977) recommended taking a completely auditory approach in the beginning stages of word analysis.

It is possible, of course, that the decision to provide some initial phonemic training without letters (but with unmarked tokens) will depend on the learner: Learning-disabled children, who often suffer from information overload, might well benefit from such training, whereas other children might do just as well, or better, if phonemic training involved letters from the very beginning.

Lewkowicz (1980) has suggested that if, as the evidence seems to indicate, reading instruction improves phonemic awareness as well as vice versa, then an optimal instructional program will be a "staggered" one. That is, an effective program would alternate (1) segmentation and blending training (with or without letters) on a few word types and (2) decoding practice on the words just segmented and blended, rather than providing extensive phonemic training on many word types before beginning any decoding. Williams' program (1980) did this; phoneme analysis and blending were first taught using nine phonemes and then decoding instruction was given using those letter/sound correspondences. Following this, six more phonemes were introduced, first for phonemic training and then for decoding.

RELATED READING PROBLEMS IN OLDER CHILDREN

Phonemic analysis ability is correlated with reading ability beyond the period of beginning instruction. Research by Fox and Routh (1980, 1983) is relevant here. Fox and Routh (1980) looked at the phonemic segmentation performance of a group of children who were completing first grade. They found that children with severe reading disability performed significantly more poorly than did normally achieving children and children only mildly disabled. (The latter group was slightly but not significantly poorer than the normal group.)

Fox and Routh (1983) published a follow-up on some of their original severely disabled and normal subjects. These follow-up groups were matched on IQ on the Peabody Picture Vocabulary Test. At the time of the follow-up, the children were about 9 years old, and the disabled group scored at the ceiling of the phonemic segmentation test on which they had done so badly 3 year before. However, their scores were significantly poorer than those of the normal readers in other ways. On the basis of scores on the Camp–Dolcourt adaptation of the Boder test, it was found that the disabled group was more than two grades below the normal group in reading. Moreover, the two groups differed significantly in the types of spelling errors they made. The disabled readers were very deficient in phonetic spelling ability, and they showed a tendency to make bizarre errors. Many of them could be characterized as "disphonetic" spellers (Boder, 1973).

Fox and Routh (1983) suggest, following Boder (1973), that these disabled readers will continue to have reading and spelling problems into adulthood. The basic problem for these youngsters, according to Fox and Routh (1983), involves the analysis and use of phonemic information. The first manifestation of such a problem may be difficulty in segmenting syllables into phonemes. At the first-grade level, the problem may show up as a reading difficulty; later, it may show up as a lack of phonetic spelling ability.

SUMMARY

Phonemic analysis represents an aspect of the task of beginning reading that has been ignored for much too long. Research has indicated its genuine importance, and the value of providing effective instruction to children who have difficulties in this area seems clear (Kochnower, Richardson, & DiBenedetto, 1983). The recent instructional programs that have incorporated phonemic tasks as program components have shown promise, although much work remains to be done in terms of determining the design of an optimal program. Much of the information necessary for the specification of an optimal program will come from further research on some of the fundamental issues addressed in the studies reported here as well as on issues not yet identified. The payoff for continued work in this area appears to be substantial.

REFERENCES

Alegria, J., Pignot, E., and Morais, J. (1982). Phonetic analysis of speech and memory codes in beginning readers, *Memory and Cognition, 10,* 451–456.

Backman, J. (1983). The role of psycholinguistic skills in reading acquisition: a look at early readers. *Reading Research Quarterly, 18,* 466–479.

Blamuth, M. (1972). Phoneme blending and silent reading achievement. In R. C. Aukerman (Ed.). *Some Persistent Questions on Beginning Reading* (pp. 106–111). Newark, DE: International Reading Association.

Baron, J. (1979). Orthographic and word-specific mechanisms in children's reading of words. *Child Development, 50,* 60–72.

Baron, J., & Treiman, R. (1980). Use of orthography in reading and learning to read. In J. F. Kavanagh & R. L. Venezky (Eds.). *Orthography, Reading and Dyslexia* (pp. 171–189). Baltimore: University Park Press.

Bateman, B. (1979). Teaching reading to learning-disabled children. In L. B. Resnick and P. A. Weaver (Eds.). *Theory and Practice of Early Reading,* Vol. I (pp. 227–260). Hillsdale, NJ: Lawrence Erlbaum Associates.

Boder, E. (1973). Developmental dyslexia: A diagnostic approach based on three atypical reading-spelling patterns. *Developmental Medicine and Child Neurology, 15,* 663–687.

Brady, S., Shankweiler, D. & Mann, V. (in press). Speech perception and memory coding in relation to reading ability. *Journal of Experimental Child Psychology.*

Calfee, R. C., Lindamood, P., & Lindamood, C. (1973). Acoustic/phonetic skills and reading: Kindergarten through twelfth grade. *Journal of Educational Psychology, 64,* 293–298.

Chall, J. S., Roswell, F. G., & Blumenthal, S. H. (1963). Auditory blending ability: A factor in success in beginning reading. *Reading Teacher, 17,* 113–118.

Chomsky, N. *Syntactic structures.* (1957). The Hague: Mouton Publishers.

Dykstra, R. (1966). Auditory discrimination abilities and beginning reading achievement. *Reading Research Quarterly, 1,* 5–34.

Ehri, L. C. (1975). Word consciousness in readers and prereaders. *Journal of Educational Psychology, 67,* 204–212.

Ehri, L. C. (1976). Word learning in beginning readers and prereaders: Effects of form class and defining contexts. *Journal of Educational Psychology, 68,* 832–842.

Ehri, L. C. (1979). Linguistic insight: Threshold of reading acquisition. In T. G. Waller & G. E. MacKinnon (Eds.). *Reading Research: Advances in Theory and Practice.* Vol. 1. New York: Academic Press.

Ehri, L. C. (1983). How orthography alters spoken language. In J. Downing & R. Valtin (Eds.). *Language Awareness and Learning to Read.* New York: Springer Verlag.

Ehri, L. C., & Wilce, L. S. (1979). The mnemonic value of orthography among beginning readers. *Journal of Educational Psychology, 71,* 26–40.

Elkonin, D. B. (1963). The psychology of mastering the elements of reading. In B. Simon & J. Simon (Eds.). *Educational Psychology in the U.S.S.R.* London: Routledge & Kegan Paul.

Elkonin, D. B. (1973). U.S.S.R. In J. Downing (Ed.). *Comparative Reading* (pp. 551–579). New York: Macmillan.

Firth, I. *Components of reading disability.* (1972). Unpublished doctoral dissertation. Canberra, Australia: University of New South Wales.

Fox, B., & Routh, D. K. (1975). Analyzing spoken language into words, syllables, and phonemes: A developmental study. *Journal of Psycholinguistic Research, 4,* 331–342.

Fox, B., & Routh, D. K. (1976). Phonemic analysis and synthesis as word-attack skills. *Journal of Educational Psychology, 68,* 70–74.

Fox, B., & Routh, D. K. (1980). Phonemic analysis and severe reading disability in children. *Journal of Psycholinguistic Research, 9,* 115–119.

Fox, B., & Routh, D. K. (1983). Reading disability, phonemic analysis, and dysphonetic spelling: A follow-up study. *Journal of Clinical Child Psychology, 12,* 28–32.

Frostig, M., & Horne, D. (1964). *The Frostig program for the development of visual perception.* Chicago: Follett.

Fuller, R. (1974). Breaking down the IQ walls: Severely retarded people can learn to read. *Psychology Today, 8,* 97–102.

Goins, J. T. (1958). Visual perceptual abilities and early reading progress. *University of Chicago Supplemental Educational Monographs,* No. 87. Chicago, IL.

Goldstein, D. M. (1976). Cognitive-linguistic functioning and learning to read in preschoolers. *Journal of Educational Psychology, 68,* 680–688.

Golinkoff, R. M. (1978). Critique: Phonemic awareness skills and reading achievement. In F. B. Murray & J. J. Pikulski (Eds.). *The Acquisition of Reading: Cognitive, Linguistic, and Perceptual Prerequisites* (pp. 23–41). Baltimore, MD: University Park Press.

Haddock, M. (1976). Effects of an auditory and an auditory-visual method of blending on the ability of prereaders to decode synthetic words. *Journal of Educational Psychology, 68,* 825–831.

Harrington, S. M. J., & Durrell, D. (1955). Mental maturity versus perception abilities in primary reading. *Journal of Educational Psychology, 46,* 375–380.

Helfgott, J. A. (1976). Phonemic segmentation and blending skills of kindergarten children: Implications for beginning reading acquisition. *Contemporary Educational Psychology, 1,* 157–169.

Hohn, W. E. & Ehri, L. C. (1983). Do alphabet letters help prereaders acquire phonemic segmentation skill? *Journal of Educational Psychology, 75,* 752–762.

Jusczyk, P. W. (1977). Rhymes and reasons: Some aspects of the child's appreciation of poetic form. *Developmental Psychology, 13,* 599–607.

Kochnower, J., Richardson, E., & DiBenedetto, B. (1983). A comparison of the phonic blending ability of normal and LD children. *Journal of Learning Disabilities, 16,* 348–351.

Lewkowicz, N. K. (1980). Phonemic awareness training: What to teach and how to teach it. *Journal of Educational Psychology, 72,* 686–700.

Lewkowicz, N. K., Low, L. Y. (1979). Effects of visual aids and word structure on phonemic segmentation. *Contemporary Educational Psychology, 4,* 238–252.

Liberman, I. Y. (1973). Segmentation of the spoken word and reading acquisition. *Bulletin of the Orton Society, 23,* 65–77.

Liberman, A. M., Cooper, F. S., Shankweiler, D., & Studdert-Kennedy, M. (1967). Perception of the speech code. *Psychological Review, 74,* 431–461.

Liberman, I. Y., Liberman, A. M., Mattingly, I. G., and Shankweiler, D. (1980). Orthography and the beginning reader. In J. F. Kavanaugh and R. L. Venezky (Eds.). *Orthography, Reading and Dyslexia*. Baltimore, MD: University Park Press.

Liberman, I. Y., Shankweiler, D., Fischer, F. W., & Carter, B. (1974). Explicit syllable and phoneme segmentation in the young child. *Journal of Experimental Child Psychology, 18,* 201–212.

Lindamood, C. H., & Lindamood, P. C. (1969). *Auditory discrimination in depth.* Boston, MA: Teaching Resources.

Marsh, G., & Mineo, R. J. (1977). Training preschool children to recognize phonemes in words. *Journal of Educational Psychology, 69,* 748–753.

Mattingly, I. G. (1972). Reading, the linguistic process and linguistic awareness. In J. F. Kavanaugh & I. G. Mattingly (Eds.). *Language by Ear and by Eye.* Cambridge, MA: MIT Press.

Monroe, M. (1932). *Children who cannot read.* Chicago: University of Chicago Press.

Morais, J., Cary, L., Alegria, J., & Bertelson, P. (1979). Does awareness of speech as a sequence of phones arise spontaneously? *Cognition, 7,* 323–331.

Perfetti, C. A., Beck, I. L., & Hughes, C. (April 1981). *Phonemic knowledge and learning to read: A longitudinal study of first graders.* Paper presented at the Biennial Meeting of the Society for Research in Child Development, Boston.

Rosner, J. (1971). *Phonic analysis training and beginning reading skills* (Publication Series No. 19). Pittsburgh, PA: University of Pittsburgh, Learning Research and Development Center.

Rosner, J. (1974). Auditory analysis training with prereaders. *The Reading Teacher, 27,* 379–381.

Rosner, J., & Simon, D. P. (1971). The Auditory Analysis Test: An intial resport. *Journal of Learning Disabilities, 4,* 384–392.

Routh, D. K., & Fox, B. (1984). *Mm . . . is a little bit of May: Phonemes, reading and spelling.* In K. D. Gadow & I. Bialer (Eds.). *Advances in Learning and Behavioral Disabilities,* Vol. 3. Greenwich, CT: JAI Press.

Scherzer, C. E. and Goldstein, D. M. (1982). Children's first reading lesson: variables influencing within-lesson emotional behavior and post-lesson achievement. *Journal of Educational Psychology, 74,* 382–392.

Treiman, R., & Baron, J. (1981). Segmental analysis ability: Development and relation to reading ability. In G. E. MacKinnon & T. G. Waller (Eds.). *Reading Research: Advances in Theory and Practice.* Vol. 3. New York: Academic Press.

Treiman, R. & Baron, J. (1983). Phonemic analysis training helps children benefit from spelling-sound rules. *Memory and Cognition, 11,* 382–389.

Vellutino, F. R. (1977). Alternative conceptualizations of dyslexia: Evidence in support of a verbal deficit hypothesis. *Harvard Educational Review, 47,* 334–354.

Venezky, R. L. (1976). Prerequisities for learning to read. In J. R. Levin & V. L. Allen (Eds.). *Cognitive Learning in Children: Theories and Strategies* (pp. 163–185). New York: Academic Press.

Vernon, M. D. (1957). *Backwardness in reading.* Cambridge, England: Cambridge University Press.

Wallach, L., Wallach, M. A., Dozier, M. G., & Kaplan, N. E. (1977). Poor children learning to read do not have trouble with auditory discrimination but do have trouble with phoneme recognition. *Journal of Educational Psychology, 69,* 36–39.

Wallach, M. A., & Wallach, L. (1976). *Teaching all children to read.* Chicago: University of Chicago Press.

Williams, J. P. (1977). Building perceptual and cognitive strategies into a reading curriculum. In A. S. Reber & D. L. Scarborough (Eds.). *Toward a Psychology of Reading* (pp. 257–288). Hillsdale, NJ: Lawrence Erlbaum Associates.

Williams, J. P. (1979). The ABD's of reading: A program for the learning-disabled. In L. B. Resnick & P. A. Weaver (Eds.). *Theory and Practice of Early Reading.* Vol. 3 (pp. 179–195). Hillsdale, NJ: Lawrence Erlbaum Associates.

Williams, J. P. (1980). Teaching decoding with an emphasis on phoneme analysis and phoneme blending. *Journal of Educational Psychology, 72,* 1–15.

Woodcock, R. (1973). *Woodcock Reading Mastery Tests.* Circle Pines, NM: American Guidance Service.

Zhurova, L. E. (1963). The development of analysis of words into their sounds by preschool children. *Soviet Psychology and Psychiatry, 2,* 17–27.

Zifcak, J. (1976). Phonological awareness and reading acquisition in first grade children. Doctoral dissertation. *Dissertation Abstracts International, 1977, 38,* 6655A-6656A. (University Microfilms No. 78-06, 156). Storrs, CT: University of Connecticut.

14

Computer-Assisted Instruction with Learning-Disabled Children

JOSEPH K. TORGESEN

INTRODUCTION

Of all the intervention techniques for learning-disabled children described in this volume, computer-assisted instruction (CAI) has generated the most excitement and publicity over the last several years. National conferences are being held to explore the uses of computers in educating children, new journals are being started to report research and opinion, and organizations like the Association for Children and Adults with Learning Disabilities are devoting major portions of their meetings to computer-related topics. In addition, schools are spending millions of dollars to acquire computer hardware and software to use in the classroom.

The most important impetus for the current enthusiasm and activity in the area of computer-assisted instruction has been the development of microcomputer technology, which makes computers widely available for reasonable cost. Objective evidence for the effectiveness of computer-assisted instruction has played little role in creating the optimistic spirit of educators about the potential role for computers in helping children learn. Rather, it is the computer's intuitive appeal as an instructional device that is exciting to educators. After all, the computer can be programmed to deliver timely reinforcement and feedback, it can individualize instruction, and it can present information in many interesting and dynamic formats. In theory at least, computer-assisted instruction

417

Psychological and Educational
Perspectives on Learning Disabilities

can be designed in accordance with a number of proven educational principles that are often hard for teachers themselves to implement.

This chapter will focus on the use of computers to assist in the instruction of learning-disabled children. Since there are very little data available on this subject, the chapter cannot concentrate simply on an evaluation of empirical work. Rather, three general topics will be discussed. First, the evaluation data that are available will be presented along with brief comments about the evaluation task itself. Second, potential uses for computers with LD children will be considered. Here, I will discuss which uses of computers appear to be most promising at present. The focus of this discussion will be on instruction with elementary-aged learning-disabled children, as the use of computers with older (high-school aged) children may be quite different. Finally, the steps that must be taken before computers can assume an important role in the education of LD children will be outlined.

EVALUATION OF COMPUTER-ASSISTED INSTRUCTION

There can be no single, or simple, answer to questions about the effectiveness of computer-assisted instruction. Asking if CAI is effective is like asking if teachers are effective. The answer to the question depends critically on the specific instructional transactions delivered by the teacher or computer. The effectiveness of CAI depends completely on the specific configuration of hardware and software that is being evaluated. Thus, it is not appropriate to ask such questions as "Is CAI effective with learning-disabled children?" Instead, we can ask more focused questions about whether it is possible, at the present time, to program computers to deliver effective instruction to these children.

EVALUATION OF CAI WITH NON-LEARNING-DISABLED CHILDREN

Attempts to answer questions about the effectiveness of CAI have, at least, a 20-year history. Most of the early work on computer-assisted instruction in reading and mathematics took place at Stanford University under the direction of Patrick Suppes (Suppes, Jerman, & Brian, 1968). This work led to the development of comprehensive instructional programs that were implemented on mainframe computers, using remote response terminals. These programs were carefully and repeatedly evaluated, and they produced impressive results for both reading

(Fletcher & Atkinson, 1972) and math (Suppes & Morningstar, 1969) instruction. Programs that were subsequently developed for wider use, but which retained many of the features of the early programs, were also evaluated positively. In one of the largest educational experiments ever conducted (Holland, 1980), CAI in math, reading, and language arts was evaluated in Los Angeles County with thousands of students over a 4-year period. Although children receiving CAI in math showed impressive and consistent achievement advantages over control children not exposed to CAI, the results for reading were mixed (both positive and negative) and, overall, were not as impressive as those for math.

In contrast to the failure to find impressive instructional effects of CAI in reading in the Los Angeles study, Roblyer and King (1983) recently have reported the results of a meta-analysis of 12 studies that does suggest computers can deliver effective instruction in this area. These investigators found that subjects who were exposed to CAI achieved, on the average, approximately two-thirds of a standard deviation above control groups on a variety of reading measures.

Although they represent interesting demonstrations that computers can deliver effective instruction in reading and math, the studies just cited do not really answer questions about the potential effectiveness of CAI with learning-disabled children. Both the computer hardware and software evaluated in these studies is markedly different than that which is currently available for use in resource rooms with LD children. For example, one of the most impressive reading programs (Fletcher & Atkinson, 1972) provided an integrated series of drill activities on a variety of reading skills, employed a digitized audio system that allowed rapid access (32 msec) to over 6000 messages, and allowed elaborate computations to be made so that the drill and practice it provided to each student could be individualized, based on each child's response history. Furthermore, it was administered in computer labs by specially trained teachers. Thus, both the software and the instructional conditions under which it was administered are very different from those currently being used with microcomputers. A final problem with these early studies, in terms of their relevance to concerns about use of computers with LD children, is that the children studied were not learning disabled. However, many of the children were from cultural minority groups that traditionally have problems mastering basic skills in reading and math similar to those shown by LD children. Thus, there is substantial evidence that computers can be programmed to deliver effective instruction to children who experience special problems acquiring academic skills in regular classroom settings.

Even though the results from these early studies do not help us answer questions about the effectiveness of currently available computer programs with LD children, they do provide some information that may help to guide our use of computers with these children. For example, after considering the information derived from the Los Angeles County study, Ragosta (1982) concluded that CAI was effective primarily because it followed sound educational principles rather than because it was delivered by a computer. That is, it was not so much the unique aspects of computer technology that made it effective, but effectiveness resulted from using the technology in a way that conformed with established educational principles. In her words:

> The success of CAI in this study may be related to the successful practices identified in other effectiveness studies: mastery learning, high academic learning time, direct instruction, adaptability and consistency of instruction, an orderly atmosphere with expectation of success in basic skills, the use of drill, and equal opportunity for responses from all students with a high probability of success in responding (Ragosta, 1982, pp. 32–33).

All of these procedures have been shown to lead to higher achievement in the regular classroom; they are also part of most modern recommendations for the education of children with learning disabilities (Hallahan & Kauffman, 1976; Hammill & Bartel, 1975; Maxwell, 1980). The most significant conclusion here is that, if computers become important learning tools for LD children, it will be because they are managed effectively to implement sound educational practice rather than because of special features of computer technology such as high-resolution graphics, animation, or sound effects (Hofmeister, 1984).

STUDIES OF CAI WITH LEARNING-DISABLED CHILDREN

The need for careful management practices in CAI with LD children is underlined by the contrast between two studies that evaluated CAI in math with samples of learning disabled subjects. The more impressive of these two studies (Trifiletti, Frith, & Armstrong, 1984) found that 40 minutes of CAI in math per day was more than twice as effective as equivalent amounts of instruction delivered by regular, resource-room procedures. The effectiveness of this particular program was demonstrated not only by differences in the number of new math skills mastered by each group (experimental versus control), but also by differences in improvement on standardized math tests over the course of 9 months of instruction.

In contrast to this study, McDermott & Watkins (1983) compared regular and computer-delivered instruction in math over a similar time period, but found no difference in the effects of the two programs on math achievement. The major difference between the CAI in these two studies appeared to involve the extent to which each program represented an integrated, carefully managed sequence of instruction. For example, Trifelletti *et al.* (1984) attributed the success of their program to: (1) its use of a data-based management system involving a specific decision algorithm applied to daily reports on speed and accuracy of responding, (2) emphasis on mastery learning, and (3) the use of contingency management techniques that produced a high volume of completed homework.

As impressive as the study by Trifeletti *et al.* (1984) is, it still leaves a number of questions unanswered. For example, the average achievement gains of the control group (3 months, expressed in grade-equivalent units on a standardized test) are significantly less than those that have been reported elsewhere for 9 months of resource-room instruction (McKinney & Feagans, 1981). Thus, the large differences between the CAI and control groups in this study may be due to particularly ineffective instruction in the control condition rather than particularly effective instruction by the computer program. In fact, the yearly achievement gains in this study for the CAI condition (8-months' gain) are very similar to those reported elsewhere (McKinney & Feagans, 1981) as standard achievement expectations for LD children receiving special instruction. Of course, Trifeletti *et al.* (1984) may have selected subjects with particularly severe disabilities, but that is not immediately obvious from their report of subject characteristics.

The interpretive problems remaining from this otherwise excellent study suggest at least two important considerations for evaluation studies that contrast CAI with traditional forms of instruction. First, we must be careful not to pit CAI against "straw man" instructional programs that are not representative of the best alternatives available. Associated with this point is the necessity to report carefully the elements of "control" instructional conditions so that consumers of research can evaluate the program against which CAI is being compared. Second, as in all research with learning-disabled children, the characteristics of the sample should be very carefully and fully reported. Trifeletti *et al.* (1984) for example, reported neither the average IQ of their sample nor the socioeconomic status of their subjects. Both of these variables can be considered basic "marker" variables for samples used in LD research (Keogh, Major-Kingsley, Omori-Gordon, & Reid, 1982).

As sparse as the data are on evaluation of CAI in math with LD children, it is even less available for reading instruction. Thus far, two studies have been reported that indicate CAI can be used to increase specific reading skills in LD children. Rashotte and Torgesen (1985) demonstrated that a computer-administered, repeated reading program could increase word-recognition speed, while Spring and Perry (in press) showed useful applications of computer technology to instruction in simple word analysis skills. I expect that the next few years will produce increasing numbers of studies that illustrate successful computer applications for specific aspects of reading skill in LD children. As useful as such studies are, they are no substitute for extensive evaluations of more broadly based reading skills. We will not have convincing research evidence to support CAI with learning-disabled children in the area of reading until we can show a socially significant impact on their overall reading skills in both short-term and long-term evaluations.

In sum, there is ample evidence available right now that computers can be programmed to deliver effective instruction in reading and math. However, since most of this evidence comes from studies of large, integrated software packages delivered on mainframe computers, it does not directly address questions about the effectiveness of the more fragmented programs currently available for microcomputers. However, both the evaluation data that are available, as well as common sense, suggest that computers can be used effectively to accomplish specific educational goals if they are managed efficiently. What we do not know is whether computers will actually prove to be more effective in delivering certain kinds of instruction than procedures that are both less expensive and already available. As Fletcher and Suppes (1972) have suggested, "In designing computer assisted instruction, the issue is not what teachers can do and what computers can do. The problem is to allocate to teachers and computers, those tasks that each does best" (p. 45). We turn now to a consideration of ways that the unique capabilities of computers might most effectively be utilized in the instruction of LD children.

POTENTIAL USES OF COMPUTERS WITH LD CHILDREN

One of the unique advantages of computers over other educational tools is their enormous flexibility. They can be programmed to do many different things. Because of this flexibility, it will be difficult for teachers to decide how to allocate relatively scarce computer resources in educating their students. For example, it has been suggested that computers can be used to improve complex skills such as those involved in writing, problem solving, or reading comprehension (Shiffman, Tobin, & Buchanan, 1982). They are suitable also for use in helping to improve such relatively simple skills as rapid reading of individual words or fluent solution of single-digit math problems. Although focus on the more complex skills may be more exciting and intellectually challenging for teachers and program developers, a number of authors (Lesgold, 1983; Torgesen & Young, 1983; Wilkenson, 1983) have suggested that the most profound and immediate impact of computers on the education of LD children will occur by using them to foster the mastery of simple academic skills. They argue that using computers to provide a special kind of practice on skills that are first introduced by the teacher is one of the best ways to utilize the unique capabilities of computers while focusing on the most severe educational problems of LD children.

USING COMPUTERS TO BUILD BASIC SKILLS

The argument in favor of using computers to help LD children practice basic academic skills has three elements. First, there is now good evidence that ability to successfully accomplish complex tasks requires fluency in the execution of subskills that must be coordinated during task solution. For example, Resnick (1981) suggests that, "at least certain basic computational skills—number facts and simple algorithms—need to be developed to the point of automaticity so they can avoid competing with higher-level problem-solving processes for limited space in working memory" (pp. 32–33). The key point is: Subskills need to be overlearned so that they can be executed both accurately and fast, not simply accurately.

In the area of reading, Perfetti and Lesgold's (1977) "verbal efficiency" hypothesis suggests that reading comprehension depends critically on the fluent execution of subskills such as word decoding and identification of the meaning of individual words. More recently, Lesgold and Resnick (1982), have produced convincing empirical evidence that the development of fluent decoding skills for individual words precedes increases in reading comprehension, rather than the other way around. They interpret their findings to indicate the dependency of more complex processes (comprehension) on the fluent execution of relatively simple ones (word decoding).

The second element of the argument that computers should be used to help build fluency in basic academic skills in LD children comes from data indicating that these children experience particular difficulties mastering the subskills required for more complex tasks in reading and math. The evidence here is particularly strong in the area of reading. As Stanovich (1982a, 1982b) has pointed out, the primary locus of difficulty for most poor readers is at the individual word rather than discourse level of processing. Children with severe reading disabilities have problems both applying phonetically based, word-analysis procedures to new words and with rapidly recognizing words that they can pronounce accurately if given sufficient time. Research has shown that LD children do not have special problems using context to help them decode words; rather, their primary problem involves acquisition of skill in fluently recognizing words on the basis of their graphemic representation (Stanovich, 1980). As Perfetti (1983) indicates, "context-independent word coding is that which distinguishes skilled from less-skilled readers, rather than use of context" (p. 146).

The evidence for differences between LD and other children in fluency on math subskills is less strong than in the area of reading. LD children generally are less impaired in math than they are in reading (Frauenheim, 1978). However, learning-disabled children generally score below normal learners on simple tests of mathematics calculation, even when there is no time constraint (Kaufman, 1981). Thus, many of the problems that these children experience on more complex problems such as becoming confused, or losing their place, or making "careless" errors, may be due to difficulty in coordinating insufficiently learned subskills rather than a lack of attention or effort.

As Resnick (1981) has suggested, the best way to overlearn component skills is to practice them to a level of mastery that involves both a speed and accuracy criterion. The third element of the present argument for the use of computers to deliver supplementary practice to LD children revolves around the fact that these children probably are not receiving enough practice on academic skills in most regular classroom, or even resource-room settings. For example, one recent observational study found that LD children spent only 12% of their total time in school involved in direct response to academic tasks (Thurlow, Graden, Greever, & Ysseldyke, 1982). Other research (Berliner & Rosenshine, 1977) has shown that the amount of practice children actually receive on basic reading tasks is variable from class to class, and overall is very low.

Problems which limit effective practice time for LD children are related to scarcity of both technological and human resources. For example, it is difficult in most classrooms for teachers to keep sensitive records of the response rates of children on various tasks. Practice generally is administered as seatwork in workbooks, a method which does not facilitate an assessment of fluency of responding. In many beginning reading programs that teach important subskills, children often move through the program based on the accuracy of their responses, with little consideration for the ease or speed of their responses (Lesgold & Resnick, 1982). In most resource rooms, teachers are occupied with introducing new concepts or material and correcting misconceptions, rather than providing carefully monitored practice to their students. There is not enough teacher time available to provide the kind of individualized practice that many LD children may need in order to overlearn subskills to the extent that they easily can be applied on complex tasks.

The ability to deliver large amounts of effective practice is one of the most well-established strengths of CAI. In almost all of the positive evaluations of CAI outlined earlier, computers were used to provide supplemental practice on skills that had previously been taught by teachers. As Ragosta (1982) suggests, "The advantage of the computer for drill-and-practice activities lies in the computer's efficient use of time. For only 10–20 minutes daily, truly individualized drill-and-practice can be used to instruct students at their own ability levels, to provide immediate feedback to each response, to move students ahead on the basis of their mastery of subject matter, to keep records of each student's placement in each strand of each curriculum, and to do this with demonstrable effectiveness over a period of years" (p. 32).

In sum, the argument in favor of utilizing computer resources to increase the academic responding time of LD children on mastery-oriented practice activities focuses on the particular educational needs of these children and matches these needs to special, and proven, strengths of computer-based instruction. However, since the positive evaluations of computer practice activities have almost all been done with complex software packages implemented on mainframe computers, we need to determine the extent to which currently available software for microcomputers follows effective practice procedures.

CHARACTERISTICS OF EFFECTIVE PRACTICE

In a recent discussion of this topic, Salisbury (1984) suggests that we know a great deal more about the characteristics of effective practice than currently is being implemented in microcomputer software. For example, effective practice should be designed to avoid interference effects, and should contain provisions for appropriately spaced review. Interference effects are avoided by carefully limiting the size of the initial practice set and gradually increasing its size as material is mastered. Spaced review requires the reintroduction of material at specified intervals after it is initially learned.

In her consideration of the characteristics of effective practice, Resnick (1981) reviewed research indicating that, at certain stages of learning, "mixed practice" was more effective than "isolated" practice. Mixed drill involves practicing several different skills during the same block of time. In this form of practice, relatively small numbers of trials are given for each skill, and practice on all skills is spread over time. In contrast, isolated drill involves intensively practicing one skill and then moving on to practice a different skill. Although mixed is more effective than isolated drill at later stages of learning, Resnick (1981) also made the point that isolated drill is more effective when material is first being learned, or when chronic errors are being corrected. This is consistent with Salisbury's (1984) conclusion that concentrated practice on small amounts of information is helpful to avoid interference effects when material is practiced for the first time.

Three other important characteristics of effective practice for LD children are appropriate spacing, individualization, and an emphasis on speed as well as accuracy of response. Spaced practice is accomplished by having children practice for relatively brief periods spread over different days, rather than practicing for the same total period of time in one or two sessions. Emphasizing speed as well as accuracy requires either a program structure allowing the teacher to require increasingly rapid responses from the student to receive credit for correct answers, or it involves careful measurement of response times so that the teacher (or program) can determine when responses have become sufficiently over-learned to move to another skill.

Attaining truly individualized practice is much more difficult than assuring either proper spacing or measurement of speed. Senf (1983) has suggested that computers can be programmed to provide individualization in at least two different ways. These methods involve either quantitative or qualitative individualization. The former involves varying the amount of practice in a given area based on student performance, whereas the latter involves different kinds of instruction based on student needs. Traditionally, computers (particularly mainframe computers with large, complex software packages) have excelled at providing quantitative individualization. It has proven very difficult to program for qualitative individualization because it requires a well-developed theory specifying the important ways that children differ from one another in their instructional needs. These types of theories are very rare indeed.

IMPLEMENTATION OF EFFECTIVE PROCEDURES

How well does software currently available for microcomputers follow these guidelines for effective practice on basic skills? In general, most software now available does not provide practice that consistently utilizes the majority of these procedures. Although individual software packages have strengths in one or two of these areas, none that I know of currently provides for computer-directed implementation of all effective procedures. For example, many programs allow the teacher to focus on small sets of information during initial stages of practice (avoidance of interference effects); a few provide speed-oriented practice; and all allow the teacher to determine whether practice will be spaced or intensive. Some programs also provide a type of individualization by requiring that children meet a specific response criterion (usually in terms of accuracy) before moving to a new skill. However, few programs provide automatically for appropriately spaced review, and few also are capable of providing the kind of mixed practice that may be helpful at later stages of learning a set of skills.

Many programs provide reports of student responses that allow the teacher to individualize the child's practice sessions. Teachers, if they are careful, may be able to manage the CAI in their classrooms in accord with many of the principles of effective practice. However, because of limitations in the complexity of most programs, none of them is capable of directing practice sessions effectively without continual adjustments from the teacher. This contrasts with many programs implemented on mainframe or minicomputers that collect extensive response data, evaluate it in preprogrammed decision algorithms, and adjust practice items in accordance with the child's response history and instructional needs.

An example of currently available software in reading that has many of the characteristics of an effective practice program is the new Hint and Hunt series from DLM/Teaching Resources. This program was designed by researchers at the Learning Research and Development Center of the University of Pittsburgh to provide practice decoding words containing different medial vowels and vowel combinations. The programs are organized in two separate phases. In the first phase, the vowel sounds are introduced and the child practices reading various words and nonsense syllables in which the vowels from the practice set are imbedded. High-quality, digitized speech is used to present the sounds associated with the different vowels. In the second phase, the child receives speed-oriented practice in reading words with medial vowels (or vowel combinations) from the practice set. The instruction in both phases is organized to allow intense practice on a small set of items, with new items being introduced as previously practiced items are mastered. The program also provides a form of spaced review by reintroducing previously practiced items as the child moves through the different practice sets. In the first, or nontimed phase, individualization of practice is accomplished by requiring the child to meet a given accuracy requirement before moving to the speed-oriented practice game. Finally, the teacher is able to alter the speed requirements in the practice game so that the child can be induced to increase his/her response speed with continual practice. The only difficulty with this program is that it does not keep permanent records of student responses, so that the teacher must be available to note what the child has accomplished, or must depend on the child to keep track of response data. This is a good example of a program that allows the teacher to manage efficient practice for the child, but does not aid as much as it might in the management process.

In the area of math instruction, the Spark 80 program from Precision People provides a good example of software incorporating many of the features of effective practice. As noted earlier (Trifiletti et al., 1984), this program has been evaluated positively in comparison to "normal resource room instructional procedures." It provides a comprehensive sequence of instructional, drill, and assessment activities for 112 basic math skills ranging from math readiness to fractions. The program continuously measures speed and accuracy of response and issues automatic reports to aid in the management of instruction. For example, in their evaluation study, Trifiletti et al. (1984) used the following algorithm to guide their instruction: "1) if accuracy was less than 60% tutorial instruction was applied; 2) if accuracy was 60% to 89% with a speed of less than 40 digits per minute, drill instruction was applied; 3) if accuracy was at least 90% with a speed of 40 digits per minute or more, word problems were introduced; and, 4) when word problem performance was 80% or above, the skill was considered mastered" (p. 72). Using this algorithm, children were moved successively through the program as they mastered individual skills. Since the program provided instruction on many different skills, the authors also were able to use mixed, rather than isolated, practice. That is, they required students to work on 3–5 deficient skills during each 40-minute practice session.

These comments on the use of computers to provide supplemental practice on component skills in reading and math may be summarized as follows: (1) there is a clear need for LD children to have better and more intensive practice experiences on component skills; (2) we know a great deal about the characteristics of effective practice for these types of skills; (3) computers can be programmed to provide effective practice; and (4) most currently available software for microcomputers does not adequately implement many effective practice procedures. Although some software provides response data that will allow the teacher to use it in an effective manner, the essential management tasks are left to the teacher. Thus, the present effectiveness of even the best microcomputer drill programs depends upon the teacher's ability (and time) to carefully monitor student progress and make a variety of educational decisions. Hopefully, as programming sophistication and hardware capabilities increase, the computer will be able to take over more and more of the crucial management role.

OTHER INSTRUCTIONAL USES FOR COMPUTERS

Although one of the main points of this chapter is that computers may have their most important impact on the education of elementary-aged LD children by helping them to master the components of reading and math, there are certainly other potential uses for computers with these children. Word-processing programs have the potential to make writing tasks easier, and such activities as within-school mail systems and information networks can help to make writing a more meaningful activity for many children. Programs that simulate the operation of natural systems (in science and social studies, for example) can help students learn the dynamic properties of such systems easier than more static textbook materials.

One of the most ambitious, far-reaching, and complex uses of computers is to modify the way children think and approach problems. The most widely publicized way of doing this is through the use of interactive computer-programming experiences such as that provided by the Logo language. In the words of Logo's principal architect, Seymour Papert (1980): "learning to communicate with a computer may change the way other learning takes place" (p. 6). In essence, the claim is that experience in the Logo environment can make children better thinkers, more logical, and better able to break problems down into their parts so they can be solved effectively. After observing a number of LD children working with Logo, Weir & Watt (1981) also noted the potential of the Logo programming experience to: (1) improve their fine motor skills, (2) increase short-term memory, (3) help them learn to use feedback more effectively; and (4) move them from concrete to more abstract levels of thinking. In addition to these cognitive effects, these authors also suggested that the success experienced by many LD children when programming the computer can help to change their attitudes toward school and build self-confidence.

These initial reports of LD children's success in using Logo are exciting because they suggest a way to use the computer to help children become more effective problem solvers. This is clearly an area in which many LD children need special help (Torgesen & Licht, 1983). It is also very appealing to think that the Logo experience may help to get LD children more actively involved in their learning so they will become more responsible and excited about school. However, all the evidence we have thus far about the use of Logo with LD children is anecdotal, and even evaluations of Logo with normal children are ambiguous (Watt, 1982). We simply do not have good evidence that the Logo programming experience is as powerful, particularly for LD children, as its developers claim.

It is possible, for example, that the Logo experience may be beneficial for some rather unique LD children with strong conceptual or visual/spatial skills, but much less effective with less able LD children. The history of learning disabilities is replete with examples of the failure of indirect remedial techniques to have positive effects on the academic attainments of LD children (Arter and Jenkins, 1979; Torgesen, 1979). In evaluating the use of Logo with these children, it will be important to address many of the same questions as with any other indirect remedial technique. Researchers must determine, for example, whether problem-solving skills learned in the Logo environment are manifest on other, more traditional academic tasks. We must also learn whether the excitement and attitude changes that LD children show when working with the computer can be harnessed to improve their performance in other areas. Unless we can document that programming experiences with Logo have these general kinds of effects, it will be difficult to justify the use of these methods with LD children, particularly if they divert the teacher's attention from the fundamental academic problems of their students.

NEEDS FOR THE FUTURE

Although computers have made a powerful impression on education, no one would contend that they are currently fulfilling their promise in the education of either normal or children with special needs. Thus far in this chapter, we have seen that computers can play an effective role in helping children to acquire important academic skills, and we have also considered how they might be particularly helpful to learning-disabled children. In addition, we have become acquainted with some of the limitations of software that is currently available for microcomputers. In this section, we will consider briefly several developments whose occurrence seems necessary to support the growth of CAI as an effective remedial tool with learning-disabled children. Developments in four areas will be considered: (1) research, (2) teacher training, (3) service delivery, and (4) changes in hardware and software.

RESEARCH

It would be naive to assume that positive research evaluations of CAI will have much of an impact on its assimilation into resource rooms over the short-term. Decisions to purchase computers and to experiment with CAI are not being made right now on the basis of solid evidence for the effectiveness of current microcomputer systems. Rather, teachers are experimenting with CAI because it is an exciting new technology with enormous intuitive appeal as an instructional tool. Furthermore, whether computers continue to be used over the long term probably will depend more on the personal experiences of thousands of teachers than it will on the results of formal evaluations.

However, careful empirical research on CAI is important for two reasons. First, evaluation projects can identify particularly effective software systems, and they can also help us to understand the most effective ways to implement CAI in resource rooms. Much of this evaluation research will focus on software packages that are available commercially, and it should be helpful to teachers and administrators in deciding which systems to purchase. Some of this type of research will compare CAI with other, noncomputer-based instruction. However, a good share of it should be focused on comparing the relative effectiveness of alternative software systems. Although positive research evaluations of CAI will not be the most important factor in determining its continued use in the classroom, it is hard to imagine that CAI will find its most effective uses in the classroom without the support of creative evaluation research.

A second type of research that will support the development of CAI as an instructional tool involves the careful analysis of specific procedures that may be incorporated within computer-based instructional systems. This type of research is different from evaluation projects in that it attempts to establish general principles for effective computer-based instruction. It is more analytical, in that individual instructional variables will be more carefully controlled than in most evaluation projects. For example, Wilkenson (1983) has identified several characteristics of computer-presented text that may be helpful in reading instruction. These characteristics are unique to computer-guided reading experiences, so their usefulness in increasing reading skills is presently unknown. Basic research programs investigating instructional procedures that are uniquely available on computers will be of immense help to educators who are trying to engineer more effective instructional software.

TEACHER TRAINING

The second development that must occur before computers can be used effectively with LD children involves teacher training. Although they do not have to be programmers, teachers must be trained so that they understand both the capabilities and limitations of computer technology. Teachers have generally insisted that programs be written that can be integrated with other classroom activities to support traditional instructional goals. However, as educators become more familiar with computer capabilities, they may find it desirable to alter some of the ways they teach to take advantage of unique computer capabilities. For example, the timing and measurement capabilities of computers may support the wider adoption of goals involving new criteria for mastery of component skills in reading and math. Knowledge of computer limitations may help teachers avoid unnecessary fears that computers soon will replace them as the primary instructional agent in the classroom.

SERVICE DELIVERY

Even with adequate support for the development of CAI through research and teacher training, computer applications in the resource room will continue to be limited until adequate numbers of computers are available. Just as there needs to be a higher teacher-student ratio for LD than normal children, there probably needs to be a higher computer-student ratio. This is true particularly if computers are to be used to support the development of basic academic skills rather than simply to promote computer literacy or enrichment activities. As we have seen, computers have unique capabilities in the delivery of high-quality practice in basic skills, and LD children almost certainly have a much greater need for this type of practice than children who learn normally. We have recently completed a $1\frac{1}{2}$ year project to study the use of computers in a learning-disabilities resource room (Young, Torgesen, Rashotte, & Jones, 1983). We estimate that LD children require a basic minimum of $\frac{1}{2}$ hour per day on the computer if CAI is to have a significant, and broad, impact on their academic skills. If the average resource room serves 30 children, this means that each resource room must have three computers. Although schools have been purchasing computers in record numbers, we are a long way from having enough of them to allow CAI to be an integral part of instruction for LD children.

DEVELOPMENTS IN HARDWARE AND SOFTWARE

Finally, improvements in both hardware and software are required to support more effective utilization of CAI with LD children. With respect to hardware, the main limitation is one of memory. Memory limitations in currently available (and affordable) microcomputers make it very difficult to construct good tutorial programs, and they limit the effectiveness of many practice programs. Within current memory limitations, it is impossible to write programs with complex branching activities that also operate rapidly. There is simply not enough room in core storage to load large programs. If a program must retrieve information or program steps from peripheral storage (disk or cassette) to branch effectively, it will be too slow to operate efficiently (Yeager, 1977). As was indicated in an earlier section, the effectiveness of many practice programs is limited because they do not contain procedures to automatically individualize practice based on student-response history. At least part of the failure to provide this feature in current programs is related to the limited processing capacity of currently available microcomputers.

There are two major ways that software for microcomputers must be improved. The first, and most easily accomplished change, is simply to improve the instructional design, relevance, and management systems for the type of software that is currently available. Software for microcomputers is generally quite fragmented. That is, a given piece of software deals with only a limited range of skills that are taught or practiced only over a limited range of development. Assuming that it is well-written and follows sound educational procedures, this type of software can be helpful in improving specific skill deficiencies in LD children. However, computers will not realize their full potential as instructional tools until complete sets of integrated software are available. This second type of change requires two types of integration. First, it involves development of complete software systems that provide instruction and/or practice on a broad range of skills across several developmental levels. Second, it requires that curriculum developers provide an integrated package of computer and noncomputer instructional materials that complement one another. The development of such complete systems is the best way to ensure that teacher-led and computer-directed instructional activities work in a complementary fashion to support the learning of LD children.

REFERENCES

Arter, J. A., & Jenkins, J. R. (1979). Differential diagnosis-prescriptive teaching: A critical appraisal. *Review of Educational Research, 49,* 517–555.

Berliner, D. C., & Roseshine B. (1977). The acquisition of knowledge in the classroom. In R. J. Spiro, R. C. Anderson, & W. E. Montague. (Eds.). *Schooling and the Acquisition of Knowledge* (pp. 375–396). Hillsdale, NJ; Lawrence Erlbaum Associates.

Fletcher, J. D., & Atkinson, R. C. (1972). Evaluation of the Standard CAI program in initial reading. *Journal of Educational Psychology, 63*(6), 597–602.

Fletcher, J. D. & Suppes, P. (August 1972). Computer-assisted instruction in reading: Grades 4–6. *Educational Technology,* 45–49.

Frauenheim, J. G. (1978). Academic achievement characteristics of adult males who were diagnosed as dyslexic in childhood. *Journal of Learning Disabilities, 11,* 476–483.

Hallahan, D. P., & Kauffman, J. M. (1976). *Introduction to learning disabilities: A psychobehavioral approach.* Englewood Cliffs, NJ: Prentice-Hall.

Hamill, D. D. & Bartel, M. R. (1975). *Teaching Children with Learning and Behavior Problems.* Boston: Allyn & Bacon.

Hofmeister, A. (1984). *The learning disabled in the information age.* Presented at Annual Meeting of ACLD, New Orleans.

Holland, P. W. (April 1980). *Computer-assisted instruction: A longitudinal study.* Panel presentation at the AERA Annual Conference, Los Angeles, CA.

Kaufman, A. S. (1981). The WISC–R and learning-disabilities assessment: State of the art. *Journal of Learning Disabilities, 14,* 520–526.

Keogh, B. K., Major-Kingsley, S., Omori-Gordon, H., & Reid, H. P. (1982). *A system of marker variables for the field of learning disabilities.* Alexander R. Luria Research Monograph Series. Syracuse: Syracuse University Press.

Lesgold, A. M. (1983). A rational for computer-based reading instruction. In A. C. Wilkenson (Ed.). *Classroom Computers and Cognitive Science* (pp. 85–105). New York: Academic Press.

Lesgold, A. M., & Resnick, L. B. (1982). How reading difficulties develop: Perspectives from a longitudinal study. In J. P. Das, R. F. Mulcahy, & A. E. Wall (Eds.). *Theory and Research in Learning Disabilities* (pp. 155–188). New York: Plenum Press.

Maxwell, M. (1980). *Improving student learning skills.* San Francisco: Jossey-Bass Publishers.

McDermott, P. A., & Watkins, M. W. (1983). Computerized versus conventional remedial instruction for learning-disabled pupils. *The Journal of Special Education, 17,* 81–88.

McKinney, J. D., & Feagans, L. (1981). Learning disabilities in the classroom. (Grant No. GOO–76–0522–4). Final report to Bureau of Education for the Handicapped. Washington, DC: United States Office of Education.

Papert, S. (1980). *Mindstorms: Children, computers, and powerful ideas.* New York: Basic Books.

Perfetti, C. A. (1983). Reading, vocabulary, and writing: Implication for computer-based instruction. In A. C. Wilkensen (Ed.). *Classroom Computers and Cognitive Science* (pp. 70–84). New York: Academic Press.

Perfetti, C. A., & Lesgold, A. M. (1977). Discourse comprehension and sources of individual differences. In M. Just & P. Carpenter (Eds.). *Cognitive Processes in Comprension* (pp. 215–237). Hillsdale, NJ: Lawrence Erlbaum Associates.

Ragosta, M. (April 1982). Computer-assisted instruction and compensatory education: The ETS/LAUSD study-overview of the final report. Washington, DC: U.S. National Institute of Education.

Rashotte, C. A., & Torgesen, J. K. (1985). Repeated reading and reading fluency in learning-disabled children. *Reading Research Quarterly, 20,* 180–188.

Resnick, L. B. (1981). The psychology of drill and practice. In L. B. Resnick & W. W. Ford, (Eds.). *The psychology of Mathematics for Instruction* (pp. 11–37). Hillsdale, NJ: Lawrence Erlbaum Associates.

Roblyer, M. D., & King, F. J. (January 1983). *Reasonable expectations for computer-based instruction in basic reading skills.* Paper presented at the Meetings of the Association for Educational Communications and Technology, New Orleans.

Salisbury, D. F. (April 1984). *Cognitive Psychology and its implications for designing drill and practice programs for computers.* Paper presented at Annual Meetings of the American Educational Research Association, New Orleans.

Schiffman, G., Tobin, D., & Buchanan, B. (1982). Microcomputer instruction for the learning disabled. *Journal of Learning Disabilities, 15,* 557–559.

Senf, G. M. (1983). Learning disabilities challenge courseware. *The Computing Teacher, 10,* 18–20.

Spring, C., & Perry, L. (in press). Computer-assisted instruction in word decoding for educationally handicapped children. *Journal of Educational Technology Systems.*

Stanovich, K. E. (1980). Toward an interactive-compensatory model of individual differences in the development of reading fluency. *Reading Research Quarterly, 16,* 32–71.

Stanovich, K. E. (1982a). Individual differences in the cognitive processes of reading I: Word decoding. *Journal of Learning Disabilities, 15,* 485–493.

Stanovich, K. E. (1982b). Individual differences in the cognitive processes of Reading II: Text-level processes. *Journal of Learning Disabilities, 15,* 549–554.

Suppes, P., Jerman, M., & Brian, D. (1968). *Computer-assisted Instruction: Stanford's 1965–1966 arithmetic program.* New York & London: Academic Press.

Suppes, P., & Morningstar, M. (1969). Computer-assisted instruction. *Science. 166,* 343–350.

Thurlow, M. L., Graden, T., Greever, T. W., & Ysseldyke, J. E. (1982). *Academic responding time for learning disabled and non-learning disabled students* (Technical Report #72). Minneapolis, Minnesota: Institute for Research on Learning Disabilities.

Torgesen, J. K. (1979). What shall we do with psychological processes? *Journal of Learning Disabilities, 12,* 514–521.

Torgesen, J. K., & Licht, B. (1983). The learning-disabled child as an inactive learner: Retrospect and prospects. In J. D. McKinney, & L. Feagans (Eds.). *Topics in Learning Disabilities.* Vol. 1. (pp. 3–32). Rockville, MD: Aspen Press.

Torgesen, J. K., & Young, K. (1983). Priorities for the use of microcomputers with learning-disabled children. *Journal of Learning Disabilities, 16,* 234–237.

Trifiletti, J. J., Frith, G. H., & Armstrong, S. (1984). Microcomputers versus resource rooms for L. D. students: A preliminary investigation of the effects on math skills. *Learning Disability Quarterly, 7,* 69–76.

Watt, Daniel (August 1982). Logo in the schools. *Byte Publications, Inc.,* 116–123.

Weir, S., & Watt, D. (1981). Logo: A computer environment for learning-disabled children. *The Computing Teacher, 8,* 11–19.

Wilkenson, A. C. (1983). Learning to read in real time. In A. C. Wilkenson (Ed.). *Classroom Computers and Cognitive Science* (pp. 127–142). New York: Academic Press.

Yeager, R. F. (1977). Lessons learned in the PLATO Elementary Reading Curriculum Project. ED 139 966. Arlington, VA: ERIC Document Reproduction Service.

Young, K., Torgesen, J. K., Rashotte, C. A., & Jones, K. M. (1983). *Microcomputers in the Resource Room: A handbook for Teachers.* Tallahassee, FL: Leon County Public Schools.

Author Index

Numbers in italics refer to pages on which complete references are found.

A

Abate, F., 169, 170, *191*, 261, *295*
Ackerman, B., 98, *127*
Ackerman, P. T., 260, 261, 264, 265, 268, 270, 287, *288, 290*
Adams, A., 91, *118*
Adams, Jr., W. R., *360*
Adams, M. J., 10, *53*
Adams, P. A., 149, *158*, 197, 222, 264, 279, 281, 286, *288, 291, 293*
Adelman, H. S., 60, *79*, 340, 354, *360*
Adler, S., 98, 99, *126*
Airasian, P., 76, *79*
Ajzen, I., 344, *362*
Alegria, J., 140, 152, *154, 158*, 409, *413, 415*
Alford, J., 100, *121*
Algozzine, B., 59, 64, 67, 72, *79, 84*, 107, 108, 109, *116, 131*, 201, 223, 225, *255*
Allen, R. P., 284, *293*
Allen, T. W., 173, 179, 180, 181, 183, 184, *190*, 280, *293*
Alley, G. R., 330, 332, 333, 334, 338, 339, 340, 341, 342, 346, 348, 349, *360, 361, 363, 364, 365*
Allington, R., 98, 99, *116*
Alpert, J. L., 235, *249*
Aman, M. G., 89, 90, 91, *116*, 165, *188*, 259, 260, 265, 266, 269, 271, 280, 283, *288, 295*
Ambuel, J. P., 266, 269, 274, *293*
Ames, C., 239, 240, 241, *249*
Ames, L., 105, *116*
Ames, R., 239, *249*

Anderberg, M. R., 45, *84*
Anderson, C. A., 246, *249*
Anderson, D. R., 177, 185, *191*
Anderson, G. M, 272, *294*
Anderson, J. R., 11, *53*
Anderson, M., 105, *116*
Anderson, R. P., 165, 167, 168, *118*
Andre, J., 264, 276, 279, 286, *293*
Andresko, M., 183, *189*
Andrews, G. R., 227, 243, *249*
Apolloni, T., 216, *220*
Applebaum, M., 227, 235, *254*
Arkell, C., 60, 62, 66, 68, *81*
Armstrong, S., 420, 421, 428, *435*
Arnett, M., 89, *116*
Arnold, S. C., 375, 377, *392*
Arter, J. A., *53*, 61, 66, *79*, 107, *116*, 430, *433*
Asarnow, J., 245, 246, *252*
Ashcroft, S. C., 60, 62, 66, 68, *81*
Asher, S. R., 195, 201, 210, 214, 215, *218, 219, 221, 222*
Atkins, M. S., 264, 279, 281, 286, *288, 291, 293*
Atkinson, B. R., 181, 182, 183, *188*
Atkinson, R. C., 419, *434*
Auble, P. M., 384, *394*
Ayllon, T., 276, 282, *288*

B

Babad, E. Y., 235, *249*
Babigian, H., 194, *220*

437

C

Subject Index